A HISTORY OF THE AFRICAN
AMERICAN NOVEL

A History of the African American Novel offers an in-depth overview of the development of the novel and its major genres. In the first part of this book, Valerie Babb examines the evolution of the novel from the 1850s to the present, showing how the concept of black identity has transformed along with the art form. The second part of this book explores the prominent genres of African American novels, such as neo-slave narratives, detective fiction, and speculative fiction, and considers how each one reflects changing understandings of blackness. This book builds on other literary histories by including early black print culture, African American graphic novels, pulp fiction, and the history of adaptation of black novels to film. By placing novels in conversation with other documents – early black newspapers and magazines, film, and authorial correspondence – *A History of the African American Novel* brings many voices to the table to broaden interpretations of the novel's development.

VALERIE BABB is Franklin Professor of English and Director of the Institute for African American Studies at the University of Georgia. Among her publications are *Whiteness Visible: The Meaning of Whiteness in American Literature and Culture* (1998), *Black Georgetown Remembered* (1991) and *Ernest Gaines* (1991). She edited *The Langston Hughes Review* from 2000 to 2010. She has lectured extensively in the United States and abroad, and has presented a Distinguished W. E. B. Du Bois Lecture at Humboldt University, Berlin, Germany.

A HISTORY OF
THE AFRICAN
AMERICAN NOVEL

VALERIE BABB

University of Georgia

CAMBRIDGE
UNIVERSITY PRESS

University Printing House, Cambridge CB2 8BS, United Kingdom

One Liberty Plaza, 20th Floor, New York, NY 10006, USA

477 Williamstown Road, Port Melbourne, VIC 3207, Australia

4843/24, 2nd Floor, Ansari Road, Daryaganj, Delhi – 110002, India

79 Anson Road, #06-04/06, Singapore 079906

Cambridge University Press is part of the University of Cambridge.

It furthers the University's mission by disseminating knowledge in the pursuit of education, learning, and research at the highest international levels of excellence.

www.cambridge.org
Information on this title: www.cambridge.org/9781107061729
DOI: 10.1017/9781107448773

First published 2017

Printed in the United States of America by Sheridan Books, Inc.

A catalogue record for this publication is available from the British Library.

Library of Congress Cataloging-in-Publication Data
Names: Babb, Valerie Melissa, author.
Title: A history of the African American novel / Valerie Babb.
Description: Cambridge; New York, NY: Cambridge University Press, 2017. |
Includes bibliographical references and index.
Identifiers: LCCN 2017003112 | ISBN 9781107061729 (hardback : alk. paper)
Subjects: LCSH: American fiction – African American authors – History and criticism. | African Americans in literature.
Classification: LCC PS374.N4 B24 2017 | DDC 813.009/896073–dc23
LC record available at https://lccn.loc.gov/2017003112

ISBN 978-1-107-06172-9 Hardback

For M. D. B., D. L. B., H. M. B., and J. M. D. C.,
Always.
Love, Peace.

The novel, even more than sculpture or painting, is the flower of culture.

Charles Chesnutt

Contents

vii

Illustrations

Acknowledgments

Many have helped me along the road to this history. It began with a Schomburg Center for Research in Black Culture Scholars in Residency Fellowship, and I would like to thank Colin Palmer, along with my fellow scholars, for invaluable readings. The curators at the Schomburg Center, particularly Diana Lachatenere, Emerita Assistant Director for Collections and Services, and Steven Fullwood, Assistant Curator, generously gave of their time and knowledge and were invariably gracious. Louise E. Wyche, Head of Reference Services at the Asa H. Gordon Library of Savannah State University, and the archivists at Howard University Morgan Spingarn Research Center provided guidance and encouragement in equal doses. Special thanks to Dawud Anyabwile, Guy A. Sims, and Brian McGee who opened up my conception of what a graphic novel could be, and to Nathan Copeland for facilitating. Additional thanks are extended to the University of Georgia Willson Center for Humanities and Arts for aid in subvention and for the many forms of intellectual support they provide to faculty researching and teaching in the humanities.

I am particularly grateful for the forbearance of my colleagues and friends as I complained about everything from unreadable manuscripts, to spotty research access, to never having enough time. Special thanks to Kendra Freeman whose spirit kept me sane. My gifted graduate students continue to inspire me. Tareva Leselle Johnson, without whom this work would not have been possible, gives me faith in the next generation of scholars, as does Colette Rodgers. My undergraduates and the many discussions we have had about novels were always in my mind as I wrote.

As always, I thank my son, Jaren, for his continued love, patience, and support as I droned on about topics that could not possibly be of interest to him. Many thanks also to the folks at Sheats Barber and Beauty: Mr. Sheats and Mrs. Sheats; Barbara, aka "Babs"; Ashleith; Kim; Linda; Tess; Chris; LeRoy, and, of course, Mr. B. You all have shown me that having "A Room of One's Own" is possible anywhere.

PART I

History

Introduction: The Problem with
the Title of this Volume

The title of this study was selected by the publisher. As I began writing, however, I found the term *African American* resonated differently with each novelist discussed in this volume. For some, it was not common usage in their time; for others, it was too restrictive because it connoted a vexed racial category or it did not take into account the variety of ethnicities to which people with African antecedents belong; still others felt it aptly described who they were. The varying responses to the nomenclature showed cultural identity to be less a fixed entity and more a process of coming to terms with the legacies of African encounters with Europe, the Caribbean, and the Americas. The many events, considerations, and reconsiderations that went into creating an identity variously called black, colored, negro, Negro, African American, Afro-American, African American again, and black again, over the course of the seventeenth to the twenty-first centuries, reveal much about how different nations and ethnicities were coalesced into a race.

In the United States, the region at the core of this study, much history underlies these changes in terms. For those raced as white, "black" solidified the dominant identity of whiteness that art, politics, and popular culture made synonymous with American. "Colored" and "negro," used as segregationist terms, vivified for many whites on the social margins what freedom and privilege meant. For those raced as black, the advocacy implied in changing designations recorded responses to the end of enslavement, the demand for civil rights, and the reshaping of larger American culture. This advocacy further suggested metaphors and strategies for other marginalized groups, from the nineteenth-century women's movement to twentieth and twenty-first century LGBTQ activism, as each mounted their efforts for social recognition and enfranchisement. Throughout these cultural metamorphoses, novels produced by writers raced as black made clear that once the significances of these terms were understood, so too was much of human political, social, economic, and historical dynamics.

As this study developed, the term "black" rang truer for me than African American because the former seemed more consistent with social history in conveying a cultural amalgam of social identities and resulting products. That said, both terms – black and African American – appear here used interchangeably, to refer to a racial group, but with black having the greater preponderance because it embraces links to geographies beyond the United States. I use both terms to characterize the novels produced by writers of varying degrees and configurations of Africanness, as they manifest their understandings of enslavement, constructions of race in the United States, and a composite, complex culture. The novels discussed here solidified a group, while reverberating with tensions of caste, ethnicity, geographic origins, and negotiations across these lines of difference. Coming out of this body of work is a record of self-articulation characterized by valences within collective identity.

This study seeks to do more than record the publication of African American novels; it endeavors to consider the ideas contributing to their development. Underlying discussions of particular novels are the questions, What makes a novel African American or black? How do we handle the relationship between writer and novel when a writer's race is unknown? When a writer chooses to identify as other than black? Or when a writer once thought to be black is somehow identified as other?

A History of the African American Novel is divided into two parts: the first, a consideration of the development of the novel and the second a consideration of its major genres. Chapter 1 begins by examining what sources beyond the slave narrative contributed to forming the novel, among them legends, prenational black writings, and black periodicals. It then moves to novels of the pre-emancipation moment and how these expanded received traditions as they shaped a genre that would cement group identity. The writings of Hannah Crafts, Harriet Wilson, William Wells Brown, and Martin Delany reveal that what it meant to be black in America was very much in flux, but the engagement and reengagement of their subject matter by readers and other writers went far to solidifying early notions of African American community.

Chapter 2 considers the challenges faced by turn-of-the-twentieth-century novelists such as Paul Laurence Dunbar, Sutton E. Griggs, and Charles Chesnutt as they attempted to break into the world of mainstream publishing. Post-emancipation novels built a foundation of characters, themes, and plots unique to the culture they wished to preserve, but because they created a space where African American writers could imagine a different reality, and because in some cases such imagining resulted in transgressive content, bringing a black novel to print was not an easy endeavor. Charles Chesnutt experienced repeated rejection of his novels and had to rewrite his work to fit the demands of Houghton Mifflin. In 1901 Sutton E. Griggs found the Orion Publishing Company to make his books available for a black readership. African American periodicals continued to serialize novels and were joined by publishing houses such as T. Hamilton, formed by the publisher of *The Anglo-African Magazine*; the Colored Co-operative Publishing Company; and Du Bois and Dill Publishers. Their efforts facilitated the popular embrace of novels at an early time in their evolution.

As publishing outlets opened to Rudolph Fisher, Zora Neale Hurston, Langston Hughes, and Jessie Fauset, novels explored the differences between race and culture, and Chapter 3 examines the ways novelists assessed what elements identified blackness and how this identity should be portrayed. The varying opinions that resulted manifested themselves in growing experimentation with literary forms. Vernacular elements indigenous to black culture found an increasing presence in novels, and writers adapted popular forms to portraits of black life. The popularity enjoyed by black novelists during the 1930s is frequently said to have reached a nadir with the economic privation of the Depression, but as Chapter 4 observes, the success of Richard Wright, William Attaway, and Ann Petry suggests otherwise. Ann Petry's *The Street* was the first novel by an African American to sell more than a million copies. Richard Wright's *Native Son* became a Book-of-the-Month-Club selection, and Frank Yerby saw two of his historical novels adapted as films. During the post–World War II period, black novels' critiques of class and expression of malaise resonated with a variety of audiences wearied by war and insecure in their own economic footing.

Throughout its history, the African American novel has found itself in an art-politics dyad. The rhetoric of the debate as to whether the genre was protest or art became strident during the 1960s and 1970s. As so many reviews written during this period indicate, most works were perceived as social protest. Chapter 5 will consider the limitations of this duality and the breadth of aesthetics in novels by Clarence Major, William Melvin Kelley, Colleen Polite, John Oliver Killens, Rosa Guy, and John A. Williams. While novel writing was often theorized as intricately intertwined with community building, the artistry of these works is clearly visible in their use of montage, fantasy, and stream-of-consciousness.

Dexter Fisher and Robert B. Stepto's edited volume *Afro-American Literature: the Reconstruction of Instruction* (1979), Houston Baker's

Blues, Ideology, and Afro-American Literature: A Vernacular Theory (1984), Henry Louis Gates's *The Signifyin(g) Monkey: A Theory of African-American Literary Criticism* (1988), and Barbara Christian's *Black Women Novelists: The Development of a Tradition, 1892–1976* (1980) are just some of the critical studies contributing to recognition of an African American canon. Chapter 6 considers the confluence of literature and criticism that gave the novel an increased presence in the academy and increased cultural esteem. The 1970s–1990s was a watershed moment when black novels received national and international accolades. A record number made frequent appearances on *The New York Times* best-seller list, and many won prestigious awards including the Pulitzer Prize, the PEN/Faulkner Award, and the Nobel Prize. Amid the canon wars that engulfed the academy, a body of critical theory identified the structures that constituted African American literary tradition.

Chapter 7 considers the group of writers who would fall under Greg Tate's term "Bohemian Cult Nats," among them Trey Ellis, Mat Johnson, and Danzy Senna. At the turn of the twenty-first century, their novels question much of the received understandings of African American literature and its relation to racial identity. In the nineteenth century, slavery and black disenfranchisement necessitated consensus on the existence of black community. Fissures in this consensus became apparent and gained overt expression from the 1920s to the 1980s. Where contention was problematic for earlier eras, in the epoch many term postmodern, creative inspiration seems to thrive without a clear consensus as to what blackness is, and a generation of novels converses about essentialism, post-blackness, and hybridity. Freed from the constraints of their progenitors who had to argue first for the existence of black humanity, then for the existence of black art, their postmodernist practices produce novels that are heterogeneous, multivalent, and indeterminate, terms that reflect the nature of black existence since its beginnings in the United States, but are now less problematically acknowledged.

The deeper investigation of form is the concern of the second part of the history as its chapters look at the prominent genres of African American novels: neoslave narratives, detective fiction, speculative fiction, graphic novels, pulp fiction, and the adaptation of novels from page to screen. Unique to African American fiction, the neoslave narrative engages contemporary concerns while illuminating how tied slavery was not only to American historical development, but also to conceptions of national identity. Like the reconceptualization of form accomplished in the neoslave narrative, the African American detective novel takes the popular forms of crime novels, police procedural, and American noir, and constructs detective figures illuminating race, racism, and the dynamics of authority. Reconstruction is again evident when writers make the legacies of a forced transatlantic crossing and social domination into black speculative novels. Science fiction, futurism, and fantasy embrace futuristic ideas to challenge traditional ways of seeing. In "ghetto novels," "black pulp fiction," "black romance," "urban fiction," or "street fiction," all terms for popular black novels, the increasing class divide within black communities is apparent. The controversy surrounding the forms and representations employed by popular genres provide a fertile site for contemplating self-conception, composition, canon formation, and audience, at a time when these categories are increasingly complex. Racial complexity is literally seen in black graphic novels. Mixing text and image underscores how cultures diagram race. The nuances of representation are also discoverable in looking at the many African American novels adapted to the screen. From Oscar Micheaux's *The Homesteader* (1917), to Alice Walker's *The Color Purple* (1982), to Walter Mosley's *Devil in a Blue Dress* (1990), filmic treatment of black novels reflects the nation's moods as it engages race, gender, class, and sexuality. Part II closes with considering the influence of African American novels on black diasporan writers not born in the United States. Transnational inquiry reveals the impact African American novels have had on literature acknowledging a shared history. Considering the implications of diaspora sheds light on the mutations within a racial consciousness of kind.

Richard Wright once defined a novel as "a way of enlarging and increasing our sense of life" (Wright, *Conversations* 214). This is particularly true of the African American novel. It gave a people a means of understanding their racial and cultural selves, and later gave them arenas to contest these understandings. The genre helped a culture cohere itself. As definitions of authorship, genres, and periods are always changing, as new information and archives are discovered, no literary history can or should be definitive. This work contributes to the discoveries of those before it, and hopes to be a bridge to those that will come after. The critical framework within this history derives primarily from examining cultural moments of the novels and their authors' ideas on writing. There is copious scholarly work on African American literature, and some of these are referenced in endnotes and the appendix accompanying this volume. Within the text, I have chosen to foreground writers' voices.

Any history of the African American novel is, in essence, a history of African American intellectual thought. The more we understand the production and reading of these novels and the discussions they generate, the more we can augment an understanding of black cultural history in the Americas.

CHAPTER I

Out of Many One: The Beginnings of a Novelistic Tradition, 1850s–1900s

1.1 Writing and the Making of "African Americans"

When Michael Gomez observes that the "development of an initial capture account that points the finger exclusively at the European and excludes any mention of his African counterpart ... marks an important stage in the emergence of the African American aggregate identity" (207), he might well be characterizing the basis of the written saga that would lay the groundwork for the African American novel. The repetition of a particular history – a taking of Africans by Europeans, the exactitude of servitude in America on plantations owned by whites, and the often self-engineered redemption from this servitude – would, in large part, cement many peoples of different African origins into a race. This narrative of shared enslavement became the foundational element of a consciousness of kind that would produce a body of literature engaging this history throughout its development. One of the earliest forms within this body was the slave narrative, and scholars have convincingly demonstrated its influence on traditions of black writing.[1] Indeed, early African American novels mirror the arc of an enslaved black subject undergoing religious and liberatory redemption. But other influences might also have been at work in shaping their content. Though we may never know the many worldviews, rituals, and expressive forms that eventually found expression in the novel, as Frances Smith Foster suggests in her essay on the origins of African American print culture, it is time to ask what other elements informed African American literature.

Ayuba Suleiman Diallo (1701–1773) was an African Muslim who, in his memoir, recalled an odyssey from old world to new. Might the memory of his prominence in Senegambia before he was enslaved have influenced nineteenth-century imaginings of an African past? How well known were the ethnographically detailed letters of Philip Quaque, the first African ordained as a minister of the Church of England, describing what it was

9

like to live as a free missionary within British slavery in eighteenth-century Cape Coast? To what extent did the exegesis in *The Diary of Ben Ali* written by Bilali Mohammed, a slave from Sapelo Island, Georgia, inform the growing interest in Islamic culture, evident in early black print culture?[2] Poet, essayist, and writer of local Rhode Island histories, Esther Bernon Carpenter, records Senegambia, nicknamed "Gambia," from Narrangansett Island recounting his history and his father:

> [He] Lived in a great palace, oh, ever so big; and you go in at the silver door, up to the gold-iron *teppitones* [stepping stone, author's addition], and over the door was a pretty little gold iron dog … [B]etter than iron, and handsomer than gold, gold iron was … And then you go through long, *long* entries, till last you come to the gold-iron throne … and the king sitting on it, beautifully dressed in white man's clothes, British captains have made his father, oh, such fine presents; Gambia don't know *how* many! (Carpenter 63)

How many other such descriptions circulated orally and inspired the imaginations of early writers?

In addition to narratives and memories of Africa, the more transgressive criminal narratives of early African Americans might also have been sources. Joseph Mountain's 1790 confession was dictated to an amanuensis on the occasion of his execution. Accused and executed for rape, Mountain, in his own words within the narrative, denies his part in the sexual assault even while the frame asserts his guilt and lays the foundation for future representations of the overly sexualized black male.[3] The details of his life that Mountain recalls include his piracy, his life as a servant, sailor, highway robber, voyages from the colonial United States to London, Jamaica, and Lisbon, and his marriage to Nancy Allingame, "a white girl of about 18 years of age … possessed of about 500£ in personal property," a detail which leads his amanuensis to add in an asterisked note, "The reader will please to recollect, that Negroes are considered in a different, point of light in England, from what they are in America. The blacks have far greater connection with the whites, owing to the idea which prevails in that country, that there are no slaves" (13). Mountain's story is delivered with his trademark phrases "Deliver or death" (5) and "Deliver, or I'll cool your porridge" (9), and a rebel voice, outside American slavery and defying boundaries of race and social authority, emerges. This voice is contained and silenced by the frame. Narratives such as his and *The Life, and Dying Speech of Arthur, A Negro Man* (1768), where Arthur confesses to the crime of rape, warns slaves and indentured servants against deserting their master, but also gives details of sailing adventures, cross-dressing as a Squaw and hiding among Indians to avoid recapture into indentured servitude, were part of jeremiads at executions and later were published in broadsides such as *The American Bloody Register*. With audiences of thousands gathering to view the executions, and many reading of the deaths, they rapidly became part of public lore. Part of this public was black. Might this written tradition be a possible source for early novels with black outsiders not afraid to use a gun as they fought alongside their messianic fugitive slave counterparts? Though we can't know how much of this content influenced the action and imagery of early novels, we should be cognizant of the myriad potential sources and content available to early creators. While enslavement and abolition as recounted in the tales of fugitives were certainly catalysts for themes and subject matter of fiction, and while books were brought into being with the assistance of the abolitionist press, black would-be novelists were part of a multifaceted discourse that included works written by authors working in Arabic; works from the western European canon; and oral stories passed from generation to generation, region to region. What we see by the time the novel emerges in the nineteenth century are the effects of all of these forms.

Reconstructing the novelistic history of a marginalized and devalued group is always a challenge. Literary archivists rarely thought the work of racial and cultural outsiders important, and even the writers themselves did not always create works with an eye to future posterity. One archive that does assist in documenting the influences on the novel is black periodicals. The content within *The Anglo-African Magazine*, *Freedom's Journal*, *Frederick Douglass's Paper*, *The Colored American Magazine*, *The Christian Recorder*, and others shows the many imaginative forms that shaped the nascent genre: early black poetry of Phyllis Wheatley, Jupiter Hammon, and George Moses Horton; essays on global blackness; excerpts of western literary classics; and the ephemera of jokes, sayings, and parables. In their role as information clearing-houses for a formative racial community, black periodicals are a very good source for viewing the many strands that went into weaving the literary texture of early novels. Because of increasing black literacy rates and access to print culture, the rise of black newspapers coincided with the novel's beginnings. In fact, many early novels were first serialized in black periodicals. Both forms reveal black belief in the printed word as a means of speaking for the race and sustaining its improvement.

The Anglo-African Magazine owned and published by Thomas Hamilton serialized Martin R. Delany's *Blake* from 1859 to 1861 and William Wells Brown's *Miralda; or, The Beautiful Quadroon: A Romance of Slavery Founded on Fact*, in 1860. Its motto was a line from Virgil's Aeneid – "Et nigri

Memnonis arma" ("the black arms of Memnon"). The motto exemplifies the way publishers perceived themselves as word warriors.[4] Content in the paper makes clear that its mission was tripartite: to uplift those still in or newly emerging from slavery in the South; to better the race by urging economic self-sufficiency; and to instruct the race in the reward of temperance and religious observation. The prospectus for the periodical might also have served as a prospectus for the early African American novel:

> To chronicle the population and movements of the colored people.
>
> To present reliable statements of their religious, as well as their moral and economic standing.
>
> To present statements of their educational condition and movements, and of their legal status in the several states . . .
>
> To give an elaborate account of the various books, pamphlets, and newspapers, written or edited by colored men . . . (Penn 119)

Many editors and publishers were themselves former slaves or born to enslaved parents. The establishment of these papers was their intellectual liberation, and through the post-emancipation period the periodicals became sites of advocacy for full social and political enfranchisement for all Americans.

The geographical breadth of the newspapers' publication locales created and extended a readership, of which novels would subsequently take advantage. *Howard's Negro American*, for instance, was published in Harrisburg, Pennsylvania by James H. W. Howard, who in 1886 would write the novel *Bond and Free*; *The Afro-American Budget* was published in Evanston, Illinois by the Reverend J. S. Woods; *The Pacific Appeal*, whose stated object was to be "the organ and representative of the Colored population of the Pacific Coast" (*Appeal* 2), was established in San Francisco in 1862 by Peter Anderson and edited by Phillip A. Bell who earlier had established *The Colored American* in New York. *The Pacific Appeal* ran a back and forth between William H. Yates, writing as "Amigo" and William Wells Brown over Brown's *The Black Man, His Antecedents, His Genius, and His Achievements* (1863), and illustrated the way newspapers provided forums for literary debates.[5] That so many novels were serialized in the black press facilitated greater sharing than the solitary act of reading alone. Readers with greater literacy skills imparted content to those with lesser skills. Those in one region shared with those of another. These interactions created a populace through writing and reading.

Although they are most often analyzed as organs of civil advocacy and racial uplift, black periodicals of the early to mid-nineteenth century exhibit the variety of imaginative reservoirs writers would later draw upon. In their pages are poetry, argumentative essays, and all manner of excerpted and serialized fiction. They provided black readers the opportunity to see a world beyond the United States. One good example is *Freedom's Journal*, the first black-owned and operated newspaper published in the United States.[6] Even when discussing enslavement, for instance, it expanded the context to situate slavery diasporically:

> France during the past year has improved her legislation on this subject, having subjected to banishment, and a fine equal to the value of ship and cargo ... The Netherlands have indeed acceded to a mutual right of search; but their colonial functionaries place themselves in opposition to the government ... Spain evinces one unvarying course of evasion in the colonial functionaries, and, indifference, if not faithlessness, in the government ... Portugal for a long time refused to abandon this trade on the score of the necessity of her transatlantic possessions. But though Brazil is now independent, the trade continues, and Portugal has recently advanced a claim to carry it on for the supply of her African islands, the Cape de Verds, &c. whence it is easy to take slaves to Brazil or Cuba." (*Freedom's Journal* 1.27 [September 14, 1827], 105)

Through reprints of Islamic sermons, the paper familiarized readers with other religious traditions, and displayed Islam's continued influence in black America, even though the nineteenth century would see a rise of Protestant evangelism that later will impress the content and style of novels.

By far the key focus of *Freedom's Journal* was racial uplift, and all issues are replete with announcements of the establishment of schools and mutual aid societies; but the *Journal*, like many of its counterparts, also gives a sense of the ordinary details that will enrich setting and plot in a fiction that is too often read as, to paraphrase J. Saunders Redding, a literature of necessity (xxix). Advertisements for an Indian doctor/botanist, ads for the sale of sperm oil, and an advertisement for a boarding house are joined by humorous anecdotes drawn from an assortment of local and international regions. "Varieties" columns ran jokes featuring attempts at ethnic dialect. The paper lifts liberally from domestic periodicals catering to many races and ethnicities such as *The Provincial Freeman* and *The National Era*, and borrows from papers across the Atlantic such as *John Bull* and *The London Weekly Review*. Original and reprinted poetry on a variety of subjects were the intermezzos between pieces on the natural sciences and prosaic summary of news events. Even corny jokes had their place: "Conundrum. Why is a Tragedy a more natural performance in a Theatre than a Comedy? – Because the boxes are always in Tiers" (*Freedom's*

Journal, 2.4, April 18, 1828, 25). In the first half of the nineteenth century, many papers wrote for two audiences – the freed and the still enslaved – and reflected the necessity and difficulty of racial bonding that would be elaborated upon in fiction. "We would not be unmindful of our brethren who are still in the iron fetters of bondage," wrote the editors of *Freedom's Journal*. "They are our kindred by all the ties of nature; and though but little can be effected by us, still let our sympathies be poured forth, and our prayers in their behalf, ascend to Him who is able to succour [sic] them," (1.1, March 16, 1827, 2). Many postbellum novels absorbed this duality, as writers were as varied as their readers.

One of the most influential papers on the formation of black fiction was *Frederick Douglass's Paper*. Frequently it included excerpts of novels, among them Charles Dickens's *Bleak House*, and literature reviews. These served as models for early writers. Through them authors were shown which traditions early black taste arbiters deemed acceptable. Douglass's paper also reprinted content from the popular magazines of the day such as *Godey's Lady's Book*, *Harpers*, London's *Daily News*, and *The Atlantic Monthly*. As Douglass's paper matures, the amount of borrowed content is greatly reduced, and in its stead is subject matter highlighting black political, social, and economic power. Douglass also included a call for African American letters:

> It is a fact that cannot be too deeply regretted, that while **American** litera-
> ture is rapidly growing into universal appreciation, the name of no **colored
> American** has as yet been blazoned upon its rolls of heraldry. – Our Prescotts,
> and Bancrofts, our Coopers and Hawthorns, our Bryants and Whittiers, all
> belong, by birth and complexion, to that race which so arrogantly claims for
> itself an intellectual superiority, and assigns to its darker hued compatriots a
> lower rank in the scale of mental being. It is true indeed, that upon happier
> shores, the achievements of our brethren in the department of letters have
> fully demonstrated the fact that the descendants of Africa are not want-
> ing in poetic power, not in the brilliant imagination which characterizes
> the novelist. The lyre sounded sweetly beneath the gifted touch of Putchin
> [sic]; and the lively and prolific pen of the author of Monte Christo [sic]
> has caused the readers of two worlds to thrill with admiration. Yet alas! ...
> A Wheatley, indeed, may have sung in brief, yet admirable snatches, while
> in her chains; a Horton may have caused the dark wall of his prison house
> to echo to notes so sublime as almost to persuade surrounding lordlings to
> grant him freedom ... Still, **colored American** literature exists only, to too
> great an extent, in the vast realm of probability. (September 23, 1853, 3)

For Douglass, the literary canonical legacy for black writers was constituted by Pushkin, Dumas, Wheatley, and Horton, but he hoped for more, a tra-dition recognizable as free, American, and deriving from black antecedents.

The turn of the twentieth century saw an even greater cross-fertilization between the black press and the emerging black novel. *The Colored American Magazine* described itself as "an illustrated monthly" periodical "devoted to... the development of Afro-American art and literature." Under the editorship of Pauline Hopkins who was also a major contributor, it emphasized the building of a black tradition seeking to draw upon a "vast and almost unexplored treasury of biography, history, adventure, tradition and folk lore poetry and song" (May 1900, 60). Seeking to expand the world of its readers, it served multiple needs. Its content included a great deal of commentary on international events.[7] Its mission combined moral uplift and mass appeal. It retold biblical stories, while including quirky profiles, for example, Louis Yett – "A Negro Sampson" able to lift with his teeth a dining room table with a man sitting on it yet bossed by his 90-pound wife (November 1900, 47). Its etchings and later photos could be purchased as prints to decorate a home. One very popular one was a photograph of a visibly black baby (reminiscent of the new year portrayed as an infant) seated upon a draped American flag titled, "The Young Colored American" (see Figure 1.1). Sold as "Artwork that should be in Every Home," it announced black Americans as *American*. The paper's travel narrative pieces delivered escapism, while the recording of local goings-on – the organization of mutual aid societies, schools, practical medical health advice – addressed immediate needs. Readers were kept abreast of major race events such as The Exhibit of American Negroes at the 1900 Paris Exposition that it covered through detailed illustrated reportage.

With front covers that frequently placed photographs of prominent black citizens in a floral frieze border incorporating Phillis Wheatley on one side and Frederick Douglass on the other next, *The Colored American Magazine* visually staked the claim for a literary tradition (Figure 1.2), while its commentary voiced it:

> Doubtless there are many thousands of intelligent white men and women, and possibly some of our own race, who have spent many hours reading "The Three Musketeers," "Monte Cristo," and other works of the older and younger Dumas. Many of these readers probably did not know that they were reading the work of mulattoes, of men with a great deal of pure African blood in their veins. Our race is apparently the under dog in the battle of nations just at present. However, we once led the fight, as anyone can learn by studying the Negro nose and Negro lips of the old Sphinx rising above the desert sands. Our day will come again. (*CAM* 2.1 [November 1900], 76)

Taking ownership of the French, Dumas situates this formative canon in established tradition and argues for the intellectual and artistic capabilities

From photo by Purdy, Boston.

Figure 1.1 "The Young Colored American."
Beinecke Rare Book and Manuscript Library, Yale University.

Figure 1.2 *Colored American Magazine* cover.
Beinecke Rare Book and Manuscript Library, Yale University.

of black peoples; linking it to the Sphinx is in keeping with wider attempts in black American cultural discourse to imagine Egypt (and elsewhere Ethiopia) as the cradle of black civilization. The duality of the tradition, both western and African, is early on established.[8]

With its reviews of works by writers from a variety of races and ethnic backgrounds, its short stories and novellas, and even its listing of the book premiums offered to subscribers who sent full payment (choices included *Uncle Tom's Cabin* [1852], *The Three Guardsmen* [1902], and *The Scarlet Letter* [1850]), *The Colored American Magazine* reflected the growing print culture surrounding African American novels. The paper created a venue for black thought, black literary talent, and developed a readership. Agents in Illinois, Massachusetts, Maine, Tennessee, Rhode Island, Indiana, Iowa, North Carolina, and Pennsylvania helped form a national literary economy among black Americans, something that would be crucial to the dissemination of novels. Serial publication of many of novels nurtured a genre, a readership, and invited public participation through editorial commentary between installments.

Like *The Colored American Magazine*, *The Christian Recorder*, the organ of the African Methodist Episcopal Church, offered its readership access to a wide variety of literature while upholding its commitment to keeping them abreast of missionary activities. It serialized Frances Ellen Watkins Harper's novellas *Minnie's Sacrifice* (1869), *Sowing and Reaping* (1876–1877), and the *Trial and Triumph* (1888–1889), as well as William Steward's *John Blye* (1878), the story of young John, born free, ensconced in the security and domesticity of his family only to face subsequent battles with racism and mob violence, as he becomes an engineer at a local mill. Through hard work, education (particularly learning a variety of European languages from the local immigrants), and military service, he rises socially and gains diplomatic appointments. *The Recorder* offered articles on religious philosophy, domestic values, reprints of the pillars of western European poetry, and early literary criticism through essays introducing and analyzing the work of John Dryden, Thomas Parnell, and Alexander Pope. It aimed to provide readers with what was perceived as the necessary materials for attaining cultural refinement. As early as 1861, it created a book depository, and as Elizabeth McHenry reminds us in *Forgotten Readers: Recovering the Lost History of African American Literary Societies* (2002), black reading societies and depositories responded to a growing desire to assert race pride through the act of the literary arts.

Periodicals of this period reflect the myriad aims and content that would manifest in novels, the audiences to whom these novels would be addressed, and the problems that they would face in securing and retaining readership. The papers further provide examples of the variety of black communities and problems with asserting positive self-images. In periodicals publishing serialized novels of pride and uplift, it was not unusual to see advertisements for "Black Skin Remover. A Wonderful Face Bleach" and ads for hair straighteners such as "Scott's Magic Hair Straightener and Grower," which promises "to make kinky, harsh and stubborn hair grow long, straight, soft, pliable and glossy" (*CAM*, November 25, 1899, n. pag.).⁹ These advertisements were in conversation with serialized works that had near-white heroes and heroines as symbols of liberty and desirability. They give a sense of the psychological impact of internalizing American cultural devaluations of blackness. Class fissures are visible in the distinctions made between those who are educated, free, financially able, and those who were not. The many discussions and debates reflected in these periodicals duplicated what was occurring in guilds, salons, and literary societies. Like their more ephemeral predecessors, the novels would embrace this content while challenging American society to alter its view of black Americans.

The foregoing discussion of Islamic sources, orality, criminal narratives, and periodicals is meant to extend conceptions of African American novelistic sources. Reading early novels with slaves and fugitives as main characters, with flights to liberation as plots, and with religious redemption as a main theme, it is easy to see where narratives of the enslaved made their mark. What is less easy to see are the other veins writers mined.

1.2   Novel Firsts

For a good portion of known African American literary history, William Wells Brown, author of *Clotel; Or, the President's Daughter* (1853), was the first African American to write a novel. For a brief moment it seemed as if Julia C. Collins author of the unfinished *Curse of Caste; or The Slave Bride*, which appeared serially in *The Christian Recorder* in 1865, would be the first African American woman to write a novel.¹⁰ History now suggests that the title of first African American novel by a man or woman belongs to Hannah Crafts's *The Bondwoman's Narrative*, though the dates of her novel's publication, 1853–1861, cannot definitively be said to predate Brown, and some, with the exception of Gregg Hecimovich, have debated her racial background.¹¹ Why are firsts so important? First is a concept imposed in hindsight. As a canon is shaped, a first creates a path for others to follow. Firsts mark history, and they set up signposts for later critical investigations. For a people marginalized and stereotyped as having no history, firsts create origins and argue against inferiority while offering proof to justify social acceptance.

Some firsts are especially suited to inaugurate an African American novel tradition. William Wells Brown's *Clotel*, for instance, serves well with themes that will be repeated in later novels: a critique of the concept of race and a critique of enslavement in the "land of liberty." It even had a degree of salacious value. Brown's novel could easily be headlined in the following manner: "FORMER MULATTO SLAVE WRITES FIRST BLACK NOVEL. USES DAUGHTER OF FOUNDING FATHER TO DECRY SLAVERY. OTHER RACE VOICES SURE TO FOLLOW." Hannah Crafts's novel would headline less neatly and sit less comfortably as the progenitor of black novels: "WRITER OF UNKNOWN RACE (soon to be resolved in new upcoming scholarly book) WRITES NOVEL (MAYBE AUTOBIOGRAPHY?) AGAINST SLAVERY. RECALLS HAPPY MOMENTS WITH KIND MASTERS. CONDEMNS SLOTH OF OTHER SLAVES." *Clotel* is a novel laden with political critique and clearly written with a public in mind. *The Bondwoman's Narrative* records the ambiguities of identity formation within enslavement and is more individualistic. Together they exemplify the diversity that characterized black novels from their beginning. While different in tone and emphasis, the commonalities of *Clotel* and *The Bondwoman's Narrative* point to the elements of early black novels: plots involving attempts to secure freedom, mulatto heroes and heroines with darker blacks as good and bad foils, and hypocrisies of Christian and democratic ideals.

Examining Brown as a novelist is aided by an extensive body of preserved writing. In addition to his novels, in addition to his contributions to the antislavery periodicals *The Liberator, Frederick Douglass's Paper*, and the *National Anti-Slavery Standard*, in addition to the versions of his autobiographical narrative, a play and a travel narrative, there is also his history, *The Black Man: His Antecedents, His Genius, and His Achievements* (1863). Brown not only writes fiction, he posits himself as a representative voice for a people. Born in Kentucky in 1816, he was the son of a slave and a white relative of his master. He escaped in 1834, and worked on a steamboat ferrying fugitives across Lake Erie to Canada. His career as an abolitionist began in the Western New York Anti-Slavery Society, and he and his wife became active advocates, often opening their home to traveling antislavery lecturers. Upon meeting Charles Lenox Remond and Frederick Douglass, Brown was introduced into a network of ideas that would influence not only his abolitionist work, but also the themes of his novels. He used the genre of sentiment to effect moral suasion and to voice the growing disaffection with political abolitionism. His subsequent travel to Cuba, Haiti, and Europe evolved into themes questioning the role of emigration in a black future.

Clotel; or, The President's Daughter first appeared in London and would have three reincarnations, *Clotelle: a Tale of the Southern States* (1864) published by James Redpath as part of his *Redpath's Books for the Camp Fire*, a series designed for union soldiers to combat the tedium of camp life;[12] *Clotelle; or, The Colored Heroine: A Tale of the Southern States* (1867), published in Boston; and *Miralda; or, The Beautiful Quadroon: A Romance of Slavery Founded on Fact* (1860), a serialized version published in *The Weekly Anglo-African*, then published in book form by the black publisher Thomas Hamilton.[13] Just as reading all the editions of Frederick Douglass's autobiography (*Narrative of the Life of Frederick Douglass* [1845], *My Bondage and My Freedom* [1855], and *Life and Times of Frederick Douglass* [1892]) reveals the development of a psyche in response to changing times, values and concerns, so too does considering Brown's novels in toto.

In a review, William Lloyd Garrison captures the political lightning that distinguished the 1853 novel from subsequent versions:

> While the Declaration of Independence is preserved, the memory of Thomas Jefferson, its author, will be cherished, for the clear recognition it makes of the natural equality of mankind, and the inalienable right of every human being to freedom and the pursuit of happiness. But it will also be to his eternal disgrace that he lived and died a slaveholder, emancipating none of his slaves at his death, and, it is well understood leaving one of his own children to be sold to the slave speculators, and thus to drag out a miserable life of servitude. (3)

It is perhaps the inclusion of the Jefferson detail that canonized Brown's 1853 *Clotel*, making it the edition most every reader of the work is familiar with, the one included often in entirety in African American literary anthologies. The novel details the sale of Currer, Clotel, and Althesa, the mistress and daughters, respectively, of Thomas Jefferson; their separate experiences within the system of slavery: Currer as a house servant; Althesa as a woman who lives as a freewoman married to a white man only to be re-enslaved upon his death; and Clotel who becomes the concubine of her owner only to see their daughter, Mary, taken away to become his slave. While attempting to retrieve her daughter, Clotel is trapped on a bridge by slave catchers encroaching from both sides and to escape jumps to her death in full view of the Capitol building.

Clotel is a sentimental work, where white readers are asked to gaze upon the title character, a quadroon, and other tragic mulattos and see themselves. Brown furthers his "see yourself here" theme by depicting the enslavement of the white character Salome (147) and the corruption of familial lineage caused by the licentiousness sanctioned by slavery. The novel is not just sentimental, however; it is also a highly rhetorical work whose advocacy is rendered through reproductions of contrasting documents: the Declaration of Independence and slave sales advertisements; descriptions of the escape attempt of William and Ellen Craft and epigraphs from *Notes on the State of Virginia* theorizing enslavement as a natural state for blacks.[14] The novel demands that readers take action not only to end slavery, but also to preserve the ideals of their nation. *Clotel* includes a variety of discourses, perversions of Christian doctrine to serve the masters' interests (110–115), political speeches (161), poetry (142), and vernacular song (154), all in attempt to show the sham of slavery and to replicate the many voices engaged in debating its ethicalness. Brown essentially constructs a montage, where discrete elements are made part of a whole, but their individual meanings are still evident. His style has often being characterized as chaotic and episodic, but it was in keeping with the style of African American writers who felt no pressure to separate the genres of fiction, poetry, and rhetoric.[15] Brown was postmodern before the term was coined.

When Brown rewrote *Clotel*, the explicit parallel to Jefferson was softened. In the 1853 edition after the title character's jump off Long Bridge he writes: "Thus died Clotel, the daughter of Thomas Jefferson, a president of the United States; a man distinguished as the author of the Declaration of American Independence, and one of the first statesmen of that country" (207). In both the 1864 *Clotelle: A Tale of the Southern States*) and 1867 *Clotelle: The Colored Heroine*, the renamed character's jump is followed by a description of her virtues. It might be argued that the shift to underscore the traits of the heroine reflects the growing emphasis on the qualities necessary for black uplift. Brown's later versions look to life after emancipation rather than life within enslavement. In the 1867 version, Clotelle returned South to set up a school for newly freed slaves. The absence of the rhetorical pastiche of the original gives these versions a relatively straight narrative arc, as Brown moves into the terrain of more conventional novelistic telling.

Representation of slavery was important to Brown in the most literal of terms, and in addition to print, he conveyed his ideas through visual media. The 1853 *Clotel* brings to light his fascination with visual culture. It is in many ways a graphic novel. Its inclusion of visual images, reproduction of newspaper texts, and typographical changes to highlight perspective suggests a rethinking of novelistic form and presages the blending of text and images of later works. As an antislavery advocate, Brown made many tours throughout Europe and on occasion used illustrations to emphasize his point. One poster advertising a speech to be held at Central Hall in South Sheilds, England promised that Brown's discussion of American slavery would be "accompanied by new and splendid Dissolving Views painted expressly for the purpose."[16]

Brown's desire to represent slavery accurately is shared by Hannah Crafts. In the preface to her novel, she claims it to be made up of "unvarnished facts," but the most elusive fact about the work is who was Hannah Crafts. Uncertainty still surrounds the publication date of *The Bondwoman's Narrative*, and debate still continues as to whether she should be included in a canon of black writers. Regardless of the lack of details into Crafts's life, what the novel provides is so detailed an interior portrait of mid-nineteenth-century slave/servant life that Henry Louis Gates, Jr. cites its exactness as evidence of her blackness (*Bondwoman's* xix). What few facts are known of her comes from the novel itself and investigations into census records. Most likely her name was Hannah Bond, she wrote under the name Hannah Crafts, and she escaped slavery in North Carolina subsequently settling in New Jersey where she married.

The Bondwoman's Narrative begins with an apologia in the form of soliloquy that boldly situates a former servant and slave as a writer: "I ask myself for the hundredth time How will such a literary venture, coming from a sphere so humble be received? Have I succeeded in portraying any of the peculiar features of that institution whose curse rests over the fairest land the sun shines upon? Have I succeeded in showing how it blights the happiness of the white as well as the black race?" (Preface 3). The series of reflections reveal a writer contemplating how to construct a novel (and whether or not she succeeded).

Gates's characterization of her work as an autobiographical novel published by a fugitive slave (*Bondwoman's* xx) is fitting, but the work could equally be described as a sentimental, gothic, or picaresque novel. We meet the central character Hannah as a child house servant on the Lindendale plantation. Taught to read and given spiritual guidance by an elderly benefactress, the white Aunt Hetty, discovery of Hannah's skills leads to Hetty and her husband's eviction from their cottage neighboring Hannah's plantation. This abandonment of a female heroine places the novel in the tradition of nineteenth-century sentimental fiction, and begins a theme of contrast between secure domesticity and the lot of slaves. Strains of gothic convention fill the novel through the curse a slave places on the plantation as she and her dog die, hanged from a linden tree; through the impenetrable gloom that sets in on stormy nights; through a series of eerie ancestral portraits lining a hall; and through the many suspicions of spectral presences. In a picaresque retelling of Hannah's life, the novel traverses many regions, from the rural Carolinas to urban Washington, DC, and shows not just the wrongs of slavery, but also class and color stratification within the slave population. Comic elements have a presence as well. At one point an exotic Italian face powder turns Hannah's mistress Mrs. Wheeler's white face black, and she becomes the laughing stock of the city. This farcical treatment highlighting the constructed nature of race based on phenotype is quickly balanced by more serious notes, such as Hannah's description of a slave auction in the nation's capital. The description rings less with the overtones of political outrage found in Brown's *Clotel*, however, and more with lament. The scene and others like it fill Hannah with discontent. As much as feeling the wrongness of selling humans she also feels an antipathy toward blackness for making her a member of an oppressed race. Throughout the novel, color and caste prejudice is honestly revealed. Hannah's descriptions read like those of an outsider, and were her race not "known," one would think one was reading the writings of a white abolitionist. Her account of those in attendance at the quadroon Charlotte's wedding is filled with voyeuristic exoticism. Her reproduction of dialect in contrast to Hannah's own standard English narrative accentuates caste stratification, and throughout there is a tendency to mock the interior beliefs of the slaves as "superstitious." Hannah's desire for a marriage of choice, one that is legitimate in the eyes of God, as well as her utter repulsion to those slavery has turned into beasts, combine to form her resolve to escape.

If the publication date of the *Bondwoman's Narrative* were more definitively known, the extent of black writing influences on Crafts work might be better identified, but many literary allusions suggests she read widely within this tradition. Perhaps taking inspiration from the well-known 1848 escape of Ellen Craft, her character Hannah dresses as a man when she flees. Hannah's experience parallels newspaper accounts of Jane Johnson, the slave who achieved liberty for herself and children with the aid of the Underground Railroad network. References to the senator from Ohio who appeared almost black echo Thomas Corwin in *Clotel*. The garret where Hannah hides clothes in preparation for her escape recalls Harriet Jacobs's *Incidents in the Life of a Slave Girl* (1861). However ambivalent the novel's black portraiture, the work is clearly part of black book culture.

As "firsts," both Brown and Crafts concern themselves with antislavery advocacy, one through the rhetoric of political discourse and the other through a more individualistic vision. Both also reveal a moment where race solidarity is still forming, and it is precisely their writings that contribute to making collective identity. To see in print articulations of shared experience, shared outrage, and shared demands for justice solidifies ideas of community. Cries for an end to slavery play an outsized role in unifying a race, but so too does the recording of cultural elements, and even early novels document vernacular forms. The storytelling or lies, dialect, music, and dance both Brown and Crafts describe comprise the material future writers will delve into in attempts to define a specifically black ethos.

There is, perhaps, another "first" who should be addressed here and that is Emma Dunham Kelley, also writing under the pseudonym "Forget-Me-Not." Kelley is the first writer to be included and then excluded from the canon of African American literature because she was, on subsequent discovery, not black. This unique first-ness reveals the visual power of race, and the importance of constructing antecedents in a culture that uses literary tradition as an estimate of racial worth. Kelley became a black writer through presumption, first by Maxwell Whiteman in a 1955 bibliographical entry *A Century of Fiction by American Negroes* (1955), and later by Henry Louis Gates who included her image on the frontispiece of the Schomburg *Nineteenth-Century Black Women Writers* series (1988). Her hair and facial features were thought to signify black, and once she was catalogued in an "authoritative" print tome published by Oxford University Press, this presumption was fixed. Her placement is an indication of the cultural power of visual and print records to denote race.[17] The desire to have her belong reflects an acknowledgement of canon formation as influential in conferring social acceptance. Recuperating texts and authors as black was key to asserting the validity of black placement in American cultural history.

Kelley's history questions whether we read for racial subtexts if aware of an author's race. For this reader, such subtexts make Kelley's novels *Megda* (1891) and *Four Girls at Cottage City* (1898) far more interesting. They fill novels written for Christian training with racial and religious subversions, for whatever her background, it is evident Kelley enjoys playing with racial markers. *Megda* (1891) follows the conversion of Megda "Meg" Randal, Meg, from a high-spirited, talented young girl, to a properly sober Christian matriarch. She is part of a group of girls attending Madame de Crando's school, a sheltered space in which to teach girls the values of Christian domesticity. In the best of sentimental imagery, they form "a beautiful picture" sitting together in the idealized sphere of a senior lounge dappled in firelight. As her friends, one by one, come to Christianity, Meg struggles because she enjoys worldly ways – performing on stage and dancing – yet in a manner foreshadowing her salvation, she is unsatisfied by the praise and fleeting pleasure she receives from these endeavors. Many sentimental subplots illustrate the pitfalls of false society and the correct religious path to social service and a meaningful life. *Megda* is very much a woman's novel with its long disquisitions on the equality of women and its extolling the sanctity of domestic life. Often it makes its points through literary allusions where novels and discussion of novels give women characters the opportunity to set moral compasses.

The novel appears race-ambiguous, but if we presume Kelley is black, the descriptions of characters become more complicated. Dell is "the beauty of the town" whose has "skin ... dazzling white without one tinge of pink in it" (36). Ethel, the possessor of exemplary moral character, "inherits her fair skin" from "people on her mother's side" who "have very white skin" (108). Maude who falls prey to the desire of material comfort and prestige forms a "strong contrast" to Ethel with "her dark, richly-colored face; large, black eyes and raven hair" (171), and the impoverished Ruth is a small, slight, dark-faced girl" (75). Kelley may be making no reference to race at all, but racing her poses the question: are these descriptions the standard pairings of light with goodness and beauty and dark with evil and lack or something more? Her second novel *Four Girls at Cottage City* (1898) contains Kelley's (now Kelley-Hawkins) most explicit racial reference. In discussing the propriety or impropriety of going to the theater, the following conversation occurs:

> "Well, we go to the theatre on an average of once a month," ...
>
> "Yes, you bet we do," said Jessie, "if we do have to get seats in 'nigger heaven.'"
>
> Garnet looked most indignant. "The idea!" she exclaimed, "I wouldn't say such a thing even in joke, if I were you, Jessie."
>
> "An' sure, I'm *not* saying it in joke. I'm deadly airnest, be jabbers." (81 italics in original)

The possibility of Kelley's blackness might lead to a questioning of what makes Garnet indignant, the idea of being mistaken as one who should sit in "nigger heaven" (the theatre balcony reserved for blacks) or the idea of using the derogatory term. More likely than not, Kelley would not have been remembered were she not identified as one of the "first" African American women novelists. In an interesting reversal, lifting the obscurity imposed on early black writers might have saved an obscure early white author.

The claiming of authors as black "firsts" in spite of their remote African antecedents was a necessity in the nineteenth century as black cultural workers sought to prove racial worth. As the century developed, however, writers who clearly identified themselves as black wrote novels valorizing blackness. The central heroes/heroines offset the colorist hierarchy frequently present in early African American novels. Both Frederick Douglass and Martin Delany created dark representative heroes in their novels.

Written at a time when Douglass was separating himself from the abolitionist politics of William Lloyd Garrison, and published serially in March 1853 in *Frederick Douglass's Paper*, the novella *The Heroic Slave* was based on an actual 1841 revolt on the slave ship *Creole*. As it sailed from Hampton, Virginia, to New Orleans with 134 enslaved, captives seized control, and the boat was turned toward Nassau where Britain gave the enslaved asylum and subsequently freedom.[18] From its setting in Virginia, to the naming of its protagonist Madison Washington to evoke two of the founding fathers, the novella parallels slave revolt with American Revolutionary agitation for freedom.

Madison Washington is as heroic a figure as any character could be. He has saved a boy from drowning, kept a raging bull at bay with a pitchfork, and piloted a ship through a storm. Not only is Madison "of manly form. Tall, symmetrical, round and strong," his face in Othello-esque allusion is "black, but comely," and "there was nothing savage or forbidding in his aspect" (28). His characterization subverts popular notions of blackness, and sets a new standard of physical beauty in early novels. Personifying black masculinity and exceptionalism, Madison is a continuation of the persona Douglass creates for himself in his own narratives. In the Virginia woods evoked through naturalistic imagery that contrasts to the confinement of enslavement, Madison vows to seek his freedom. He reflects on his fate, and airs his uncertainties in a soliloquy overheard by Mr. Listwell who is taken with Madison's physical appearance as well as his articulateness and passion. Listwell vows to end his indifference to slavery and be an active abolitionist. Through twists of fate five years later, Listwell acts on his promise and aids Madison in escaping. Madison cannot enjoy his individual liberty, and returns South from freedom in Canada to seek his wife. In trying to escape she is killed, and he is placed on a ship to be taken further south for resale. While aboard he takes control and leads a rebellion. Many annals exist recounting America's quest for liberty, but Madison's story lives only in "the chattel records of his native State" (*Heroic Slave* 25). The novella corrects recorded history and fills silences in documenting black life. At the end of the novel it is revealed that Listwell tells the story to the narrator. Information on the shipboard insurrection is told from one sailor to another. The emphasis on telling implies that existing written traditions are fallible, incomplete, and in need of new recorders.

The desire to use fiction to write new histories is also evident in Martin R. Delany's *Blake, or the Huts of America* (1859–1862). A social scientist, naturalist, and novelist, the polymath Delany published his own paper *The Mystery* from 1843 to 1847 before becoming coeditor with Frederick Douglass of the *North Star*. Chapters 28–30 of *Blake* appeared in the first issue of *The Anglo-African Magazine* in 1859. Edited by Thomas Hamilton, the paper published many descriptions of resistance to enslavement, including a transcript from the trial and execution of John Brown, as well as the confession of Nat Turner and a description of his execution (*AAM* 1.12, December 1859, 369–399). Leading thinkers such as Edward Blyden, William McCune Smith, and Frances E. W. Harper who advocated blacks taking charge of their own destinies were frequent contributors. *Blake* was a good fit for the paper, and the subject of Delany's first excerpt was the escape of the main character, his family, and his confederates.

The novel was literally front-page news, receiving prominent placement on the first page. Of it the editors observe, "This work differs essentially from all others heretofore published. It not only shows the combined political and commercial interests that unite the North and South, but gives in the most familiar manner the formidable understanding among slaves through the United States and Cuba" (January 1859, 20).[19] The paper's statement shows an increasing emphasis on black vision, agency, and diaspora. All sixteen chapters were run in weekly installments from 1861 to 1862, but current printings of the novel are missing at least six final chapters. Many of the its elements are inspired by Delany's own experiences in recruiting Civil War soldiers, working in the Freedman's Bureau, involvement in Reconstruction politics, and most importantly his efforts to organize a black exodus from the United States. In opposition to the American Colonization Society, which he saw as serving the interests of the whites who had organized it, he disdained the selection of Liberia as a home for black Americans, instead advocating the Caribbean and Central America. In 1854 he organized the National Emigration Convention of Colored People, and in 1858 he led an expedition to the Niger Valley, where he began treaty negotiations as a first step to fulfilling his dream of black migration. His hero reveals a similar desire for self-determination.

Blake is drawn as "black – a pure Negro – handsome, manly and intelligent" (16), and he speaks standard English. Upon returning to his plantation from working elsewhere to find his wife sold and his own sale imminent, he vows never to be subjected to slavery again. He escapes, and the novel follows the fugitive through various regions of the United States, the nations of the Chickasaw and Choctaw, Canada, Cuba, life at sea, and on the Gold Coast as he formulates a plan for international insurrection and the end of slavery. Scenes reveal the complex network that facilitates human enslavement, and the psychological and social practices put in place to ensure slavery's continuation are made evident in his analysis of mulatto slaveholders that act as safety valves and buffers. In Blake's search for his wife Maggie, the novel explores a geographical diaspora among the various segments of Cuban black society. Verisimilitude is strengthened by blending real personages and events into fiction. Gabriel de la Concepción Valdéz (Placido), a 1840s Cuban poet whose lays include antislavery advocacy, serves as the model for Blake's cousin Plácido. The conspiracy of slaveholders to ship slaves in spite of the ban on trans-Atlantic trade that opens the novel echoes the histories of illegal slavers such as the *Echo* or the *Wanderer*.

Blake follows in the tradition of other early novels in its use of multiple discourses: prose, poetry, representations of song, and footnotes to interject commentary on the veracity of a described practice. Also present are the conventions of naturalistic description, an emphasis on secure domesticity, and an indictment of Christian hypocrisy within slavery. Delany deepens his peers' engagement of black vernacular content, however. Hoodoo and rootwork have a prominent place in the novel, though Delany is cautious in their presentation, exhibiting the ambivalence fostered by ideas of Christian uplift. Blake refers to the impotency of conjure in freeing slaves: "Now you see … how much conjuration and such foolishness and stupidity is worth to the slaves in the South" (136), yet there is also an extraordinarily detailed description of the Dismal Swamp, North Carolina as a site of resistance and refuge for black revolutionaries. The varying views of conjure's foolishness and conjurers as revolutionary patriots constitute a double-voiced narrative, one in keeping with then middleclass, Protestant, upwardly mobile sensibilities that conjure is something to reject, and one desirous of retaining vernacular links to an honorable past. Other dualities indicate a novel adhering to existing literary convention yet aware of the significances of alternative forms of expression. Dialect, for instance, is spoken by characters who are most obsequious, most under the grasp of slavery, Blake's in-laws Mammy Judy and Old Joe, while those less acquiescent to slavery's regime tend to speak standard English. Native Americans, too, are given stereotypical dialect (86–87) as a means not only to symbolize their othering in American culture, but also of critiquing their slaveholding traditions; however, dialect is also used to render the deeper tones and meanings within songs and interjections of motherwit. Even at a time when novelists are very much concerned with proving themselves as writers and thinkers, Delany includes elements ridiculed in educated circles, sensing their intrinsic cultural worth.

Most early African American novels concentrate on the fugitive slave and use this figure to examine questions of humanity and citizenship. One, however, extends this convention to examine nominally free blacks living in the North. Frank J. Webb's *The Garies and Their Friends* (1857) opens on the Southern plantation of the white Clarence Garie, the wealthy owner, and Emily, his common-law wife whom he purchased out of slavery. They live with their two children in luxuriance that whispers of a decadence that allows a man to own his wife. Realizing neither she nor their children have any protection within slavery, Emily, pregnant with another child and wanting it to be born free persuades her husband to move the family North, though Garie warns her that the North has its own prejudice.

Once they move, Emily seeks the company of "coloured" people with status and education.[20] The black and prosperous Mr. Walters surprises Clarence with his wealth and refinement and helps the Garies secure a home. The black Ellis family prepares it for their arrival. Through the Ellises, Webb provides readers a glimpse into the world of black libraries, reading circles, debating clubs, and even chemical labs. The spoilers of this northern haven are the Garies' neighbors, the white Stevenses. Mrs. Stevens initially ingratiates herself, attracted to their status as her husband is to their money, but once she discovers Emily's race, she socially isolates them and forces the removal of the Garie children from the school they love by threatening a white exodus. Her husband for his part, in plot twists befitting nineteenth-century melodrama, discovers that he is a descendant of an exiled Garie sister and concocts a plot to have Garie killed so that he can inherit the entire family fortune. He manipulates economic and race fears of Philadelphia working class whites, and a white mob descends on several black homes. Mr. Garie is shot, and his wife who has just given birth dies with the infant in her arms while hiding from the mob. The remaining two Garie children are orphaned and with their father's death and Stevens's machinations they are disinherited. They are separated with the boy, Clarence, growing up passing for white, and the girl Emily remaining in the black community. Separating the siblings introduces a passing plot. Emily stays happily in the black community and will eventually marry Charlie Ellis, but Clarence's passing and engagement to a white woman who does not know his race leads to tragedy. Clarence and Emily represent two themes that gain traction in novels of the late nineteenth century: the error of passing and the expression of black pride.

First published in London, *The Garies* contained an "authentication" provided by Harriet Beecher Stowe. Stowe was a great supporter of both Frank Webb and his wife Mary, facilitating an 1857 reading Mary gave of *The Christian Slave, A Drama Founded on a Portion of Uncle Tom's Cabin* (1855) at Stafford House in London, and the publication of *The Garies*. Stowe recommended the novel to English buyers:

> The author takes pleasure in recommending this simple and truthfully-told story to the attention and interest of the friends of progress and humanity in England.
>
> The representations of their position as to wealth and education are reliable, the incidents related are mostly true ones, woven together by a slight web of fiction (vi).

For a black writer to gain access to a wide readership, it was advantageous to have a white personage, particularly a prominent one, testify to the veracity and capability of the writer; however, the authentication convention begun with the slave narrative made it difficult to see novels as forms beyond historical testimony. A second "authentication" accompanies Webb's work, because the editor had feared that Stowe's preface would not reach the publishing house in time for release. It is "From Lord Brougham," and he quotes from a letter Stowe wrote to her friend where verisimilitude of character and the novel as argument for black capability are the main attraction for her: "The style is simple and unambitious – the characters, most of them faithfully drawn from real life, are quite fresh, and the incident, which is also much of it fact, is often deeply interesting … It shows what I long have wanted to show; what the free people of colour do attain, and what they can do in spite of all social obstacles" (vii).

Stowe's support as a patron can be credited with bringing Webb's novel greater renown, and her influence is also evident in the novel's aesthetics. The lushness of the Garie plantation as a fool's paradise is reminiscent of St. Claire's Louisiana manse; Caddie Ellis's sometimes love of sterile cleanliness without proper humanistic motivation evokes Miss Ophelia's. But Webb tailors scenes of domestic idyll to the realities of black life. For his black characters, in particular, secure domesticity is tenuous. For all the happy homes and unions in the work, Webb provides moving illustrations of idylls that never were because they were sacrificed to racial prejudice. Unlike Stowe, Webb does not use the domestic sphere as a backdrop for black messianism. In his hands, it is a site of black resistance to oppression. The white mob is fought literally on the home front as blacks defend the houses, families, and neighborhoods they have struggled so hard to build. The impact of Harriet Beecher Stowe and *Uncle Tom's Cabin* is evident in other works. Chapters within *Blake* are prefaced with epigraphs from Stowe's poems, and in the plot and characterization of James H. W. Howard's *Bond and Free; A True Tale of Slave Times* (1886) among others.[21] Stowe adapted the facts of black slave life but not its interiority into a blend of sentiment and advocacy. The popularization of her images so framed black experience that writers of all advocacies were influenced by her convention and sensibility.

1.3   Post-Emancipation Novels

For all its employment of sentimental and domestic conventions, *The Garies* provides the first novelistic treatment of characters beyond the plantation. It is as if Webb were writing for an imagined future. Post-emancipation novels followed his vision generally taking enslavement as their beginning but writing of free black futures. The title of James H. W Howard's *Bond and Free; A True Tale of Slave Times* (1886) exemplifies this contrast of past and future. In *Bond and Free*, Purcey, the daughter of the slave Elva and her master, Maxwell, is to be married to a slave from another plantation, William McCullar. Though a marriage for profit the couple falls deeply in love, and "wed," a meaningless act under the system of slavery. Mr. Maxwell soon incurs gambling debts and plans to use William as repayment. Through Purcey and William's attempts to retain their family unit, the novel demonstrates the challenges faced by black families reconstituting after slavery. Its preface directly addresses a readership many of whose members in the early years after emancipation are trying to reunite: "Many of the events of this tale will recall to the minds of not a few some of their own experiences, or the experience of relatives or friends as often rehearsed to them" (3).

Post-emancipation novels build on antebellum themes of enslavement and develop these into postbellum themes of lives lived as free persons. Novels are increasingly concerned with conveying the obstacles to African Americans becoming full citizens. Emancipation was a first step; enfranchisement is the next. Written by Walter H. Stowers and William H. Anderson under the pseudonym Sanda, *Appointed, An American Novel* (1894) focuses on Northern racism limiting educated blacks to menial jobs. Born in Sandusky, Ohio, on August 13, 1857, William H. Anderson moved to Detroit at age sixteen. He was one of the few black correspondents for *The Detroit Free Press* and submitted pieces to *The New York Globe*, as well. He joined forces with Walter H. Stowers, Robert A. Pelham, Jr., Benjamin B. Pelham, and Byron G. Redmond to publish *The Plaindealer*, Detroit's first African American newspaper. In addition to cowriting the novel, Stowers was the author of a series of articles entitled "Our Relation to Labor" that ran in *The Plaindealer*. He attended Mayhews Business University, and graduated with a degree from Detroit Law College in 1895. He was an advocate for black couples fighting restrictive covenants when purchasing homes in predominantly white neighborhoods, and went on to become active in Michigan Republican politics. Both writers had considerable training and acute business sense, though they were frequently denied professional opportunities because of their race. Their black characters are similar.

Appointed is a dense text that embeds philosophical disquisitions in its plot and characterization. Set in 1880s, it centers around the maturation of a group of young white men who, as the novel opens, are about to go sailing on a pleasure yacht. As they watch ferryboats on the water, they opine on the nature of beauty, virtue, and purity; the power of a simple faith versus formal knowledge; and the natural world around them. Its detailed descriptions of Detroit, its waterways, its Native American history, point to an emerging regionalism in black writing. *Appointed* extends the geographical range of early black novels beyond the North and the South, and westward migration becomes a symbol of racial self-actualization.

Among the young men in the circle is the wealthy Seth Stanley, one of two main protagonists whose resources have allowed him a somewhat profligate life. His co-protagonist is John Saunders, a classmate of Seth who is trained as an engineer but cannot obtain work because he is black; instead, he works at the Stanley business as bookkeeper and doubles as valet and steward. Seth admires John and thinks he would have him as a friend were he not black, and through their relationship, *Appointed*, like *The Garies*, explores the hypocrisy of a North blind to its own racism. Getting to know John on a deeper level, Seth is determined to learn more about the roots of his own benign racism. He decides on a trip south to further his awareness. John will be his traveling partner, and through this buddy narrative Stowers and Anderson show the education and conversion of a northern white man. Seth is completely oblivious to the dangers going south will pose for John, thinking that his own whiteness and privilege will protect them. John, in the pattern of a black messianic figure, feels a joint destiny with Seth to lead him to the right ways of thinking.

Their tour of the South is an ethnographic lesson. John lectures Seth extensively on the black unpaid laborers who are responsible for the economic growth of a region, on the establishment of schools for blacks, and on the inadequate financial support for them that results from institutionalized racism. This portion of the novel contains many footnotes quoting statistics, including a table to support John's observations. One footnote explains cultural history of the term "Afro-American":

> This race name has been recently adopted by large numbers of colored people in the United States to show, 1st their origin, and 2d, their present race standing. So far as long residence, a century or more of living, by one's ancestor, and an active participation in a country's affairs can change a race, they claim to have changed and that no other class of people in the country have a better right to be called American. The term Negro, while it may have been aptly applied to their ancestors, they hold, as to themselves, it is, 1st, a misnomer, and 2d, is un-American and alien. (35).

The insertion reflects growing intraracial re-evaluation in the post-Emancipation period. Stowers and Anderson use their footnotes as complementary narratives echoing the novel's theorizing of the significances of race, community, and citizenship.

Appointed can be viewed as an instruction manual for white Americans, one changing conceptions of "the race problem" as being solely about blacks, portraying it instead as a dynamic also involving those raced as white. Pairing Seth and John creates a dialectic of racial difference, but John is not drawn as exceptional to show his parity with Seth. When Seth says to him, "'I do not mean any insult to you, ... for you are different from other colored men,'" John replies, "'Not one bit different from hundreds of others whom I know'" (176–177). His comments democratize black ability. The conception of a small minority of talented exemplars presumes a handicapped majority and allows for rationalizing inequitable access. John becomes an everyman of black potential; however, for all the forward looking represented through his character, his fate embodies ongoing challenges. The graphic portrayal of the performative elements in lynching remind of the wide gap between emancipation and enfranchisement.

Appointed echoes the call for writers to make use of the rich reservoir of black life and experience to create literature. At one point the narrator makes an aside:

> Before we resume the thread of our story we will digress a little to look into John Saunder's surroundings. In so doing we dig into a field of which the average American reader knows less about than he does of Russian life – its incidents, pleasures and perils. This field is rich in romance, and in the story

of the lives of many are incidents, perils, obstacles, despair and triumphs, success and failures, joys, sorrows and pathos, that might command the pens of the most gifted minds to depict in glowing colors. (210)

The many characters who refer to the bestselling novel *Ben Hur,* to Lord Byron, Victor Hugo, Charles Dickens, James Fenimore Cooper, Alexandre Dumas, and George Washington Cable are testament to broad patterns in black reading, and Stowers and Anderson reflect the belief that this audience should see itself in fiction. A good number of writers rose to this challenge.

Written in high Victorian prose, J. Mchenry Jones's *Hearts of Gold, A Novel* (1896) offers a very romantic vision of black life that includes parading masons, a villain who seeks to make a plaything of a woman, and paired couples united happily at the end. It posits black racial identity as a shared set of attitudes that bind people of various physical colorings together, while outlining the class behavior and moral ideals to which blacks should aspire. For a writer so concerned with racial typing, the presence of a "heathen Chinee" stereotype is disturbing, but a reminder of the power of racial caricature, though the figure offers an outsider's take on the senselessness of United States prejudice. Charles H. W. Fowler's *Historical Romance of the American Negro* (1902) is another instance of post-emancipation optimism. In his preface, Fowler makes clear that his intent is to provide a history of black Americans (particularly black military history) from slavery to freedom in the guise of fiction. It is barely a guise, however, as the novel is actually a long, historical essay. Thomas and Beulah, slaves who engineer their freedom, head North, marry and settle in Buffalo, New York. They eventually re-christen themselves Thomas and Beulah Lincoln and become lecturers in an abolitionist circuit. Through a mix of genres – essay, narrative, letters, portraiture, photographs, and travelogues – it introduces readers to in a world beyond bondage as the Lincolns tour the United States and cross the Atlantic on a European holiday.[22]

Though its characters are white, Thomas Detter, author of *Nellie Brown, or The Jealous Wife*, advertises the West as a site of black potential. Only a parenthetical insertion "(Colored)" on the title page following Detter's naming as author indicates his race. It is to Frances Smith Foster's credit that the book was republished in 1996. Trained as a barber, Detter worked as an orator, writer, and businessman, and subsequently lived somewhat nomadically setting up barbershops in among other mining areas Lewiston, Idaho; Sacramento, California; and Elko, Nevada, where he was residing at the time of *Nellie Brown*'s publication. He became active in the western movement for black equality, and was among the first African Americans to serve on a Nevada jury. A writer for the black periodicals, *The Pacific Appeal* and the *San Francisco Elevator*, he was the voice of the black community in eastern Nevada.

Nellie Brown is part of the tradition of failed-marriage plot or divorce novels that began to appear as the mid-nineteenth century saw legal challenges to notions of divorce. It aims to teach a lesson: how jealousy and manipulations by others can ruin moral happiness and family. Mr. Brown is a defendant in a divorce trial because a gossip, Mrs. H., sees him conversing with a woman, referred to as the Widow. Mrs. H. sets in motion a plan to destroy the Brown's marriage while netting her own financial gain. The subject matter is critical of an emerging women's rights movement in its stereotypic caricature of flighty and conniving of women, some several times divorced themselves, who use arguments for women's rights to justify self-serving meddling. Black characters are depicted in an equally stereotypic fashion as mischievous slaves/servants like Nan, a Topsy-like character who when asked the time replies, "Missus, de big hand of de clock is up, and the little one am crossways" (8); or the dialect speaking Bill and Sue. Its overall effect is one of a writer appealing to reactionary nineteenth-century responses to women's rights and desire for racial caricature. The more interesting content of the work are the sketches that accompany the novel. With the exception of the short story, "Octoroon Slave of Cuba," the pieces read as mini western travelogues: "Central Pacific Railroad" details the significance of the railroad and the potential for growth of Elko, Nevada. "Idaho City: Its Customs and Future Prospects" describes the city and the racism that otherwise mars its potential. "Progress of America" is Detter's ode to Revolutionary spirit as he portrays the beauty, industry, and ideals of America and says that blacks are part of this. In his extratextual materials, Detter illustrates a range, from the essay, to the sketch, to the travel narrative, and sells the idea that blacks should "look well to the West."[23]

Whether Lorenzo D. Blackson's *The Rise and Progress of the Kingdoms of Light and Darkness. Or, The Reign of Kings Alpha and Abadon* (1867) is a novel is open to debate. It is listed as such in one of the major databases of black writing, The University of Kansas, The Project on the History of Black Writing, but it is really a combination of essay and morality play evoking both John Bunyan's *Pilgrim's Progress* (1678) and Milton's *Paradise Lost* (1667). Its illustrations are reminiscent of William Blake's illuminated manuscripts. It is placed in this history because it provides background into what will be one of the most profound influences on African American novel writing, the emergence of black Protestantism. In the work's preface,

Blackson makes clear his intent in publishing is to spread the word: "by publishing I can reach many more persons, and consequently might be able to do the larger amount of good" (210).

Biographical information on Blackson is scant, and primarily derives from the "Sketch of the Life of the Author" (3) that begins his work. Born in 1817 to former slaves, Blackson grew up in Christiana, Delaware. He learned to read and write in Baltimore where he was segregated from and often beaten by white students. His parents let him out for service, and he subsequently became a laborer in Pennsylvania. He takes great pride in detailing his African antecedents and is illustrative of black Americans who still have connections to these roots, however tenuous. He notes that his mother's father "was an African prince named Palice Abrutas Darram, who, with a son and a daughter, were stolen away from that country and made slaves." He gives a sense of the diasporic nature of black family life when he notes that his aunt, Yambo, was taken west "and is said to have married an Indian" and his uncle Munch "being a slave, ran away from Delaware many years ago, and very probably changed his name, making it hard for his relatives to find him." He also gives his reason for going into such detail, so that "that this may come under the notice of those spoken of, if alive, and if dead, that some of the surviving friends or relatives might see it, and be able to give us some information regarding our relatives" (3). Publishing is not solely a means of entering literary tradition; it is also a utilitarian act seeking to reconstruct community.

Blackson was raised in the Methodist Episcopal church, but is disillusioned by its racism, and was subsequently baptized into the African Union Church, founded by black minister Peter Spencer, and his religiosity, accounts for the structure of *Rise and Fall*. It employs allegorical naming – Mr. Truth, Mr. Untruth, Mr. Unbelief (54–56) – to trace the march/mark of protestant Christianity (Kingdom of Light) throughout the "four grand divisions of all the terrestrial land, viz: Asia, Africa Europe and America, to which four there is more lately added as a fifth, Oceanica, which comprises all the islands of the sea" (118). Its glorification of religion reveals the emergence of black evangelicalism that will become prominent in subsequent novels.

Over the course of the revivals that moved through the colonies beginning in the 1740s, many of the enslaved and free were converted to Christianity. Historians Albert J. Raboteau, Cedric May, and Michael Gomez are among those who credit evangelicalism with providing blacks the opportunity to preach and interact socially with a variety of races and classes at prayer meetings and revival services.[24] The bedrock tenet of conversion, that all were flawed and needed transformation to be holy, suited a people seeking explanation for the evil of slavery and redemption from it. The institutional power of slavery would, of course, limit black evangelical participation in the South, but many black preachers who had converted would go on to minister to their people as itinerants or as the heads of emerging black churches. Black churches helped articulate and shape black self-understanding, and because of the connections between early novelists and the church, many nineteenth-century novels became key proponents of protestant ideals. The need to let go of African derived religious atavisms, the organizational structure and political voice black churches gave to black communities, and portraits of conversion, would all manifest in themes and plots, as would discussions of the role of women in black churches.[25] One genre clearly displaying this blending is the writings of first-wave womanists who excoriated the legal subordination of women, but made sure that race was front and center in their analysis.

1.4   First-Wave Womanism

Hawthorne's quip about a damned mob of scribbling writers should have included, but most likely did not, African American women authors of the nineteenth century.[26] While many of their works would fall from the public eye, the larger percentage of black novels produced from 1850 to 1901 were written by women. This period of first-wave womanism saw novels expressing a wide array of social issues: the role of race, the role of gender, the roles of domesticity and temperance. Harriet Wilson is one of the earliest examples of nineteenth-century black women activists writing to consider the whiteness implicit in the term women. In an 1859 work that reads like autobiography as much as fiction, she tells the story of Frado, a biracial indentured servant abandoned by her parents and employed by the Bellmont family. While detailing Frado's childhood, her development into womanhood, her subsequent marriage, and the character's impetus for writing, Wilson explores the role of capitalistic patriarchy in constructions of womanhood.

In his article "This Attempt of Their Sister: Harriet Wilson's *Our Nig* from Printer to Readers," Eric Gardner's research shows that most of Wilson's audience was local to the Milford, New Hampshire area, and were mostly white (233–238). Writing where she lived, Wilson was keenly aware of who would support her efforts at authorship. It is interesting, then, that she risks alienating her audience by critiquing both northern white racism and the role of northern white New England women in the oppression

of black women. Wilson's most telling comment on relations within gender comes through her characterizations. Most of the men in the novel
are marginal, and none prevent the cruelty inflicted on Frado by women
characters. Ineffectuality stymies Mr. Bellmont, and illness the son James.
The other sons Lewis and Jack leave home. Frado's abuse happens at the
hands of the "she-devil" Mrs. Bellmont and her daughter Mary. The novel
interweaves traditions of the slave narrative – Frado in virtual enslavement, her religious conversion, her subsequent liberation – with traditions
of sentimental fiction – imagery of house and home, the female heroine abandoned, her attempts to return to secure domesticity. Its aesthetics
symbolize a black woman making use of a tradition most frequently associated with race and one most frequently associated with gender to indicate
the inextricability of the two in her existence.

As much as showing the cruelty of women, through images of commerce
Wilson also shows its cause, a system that treats humans of all classes, races,
and genders as objects meriting different social value. Frado's mother Mag's
social decline comes about because she "surrendered ... a priceless *gem*" (6)
to an undeserving suitor; Jim, the black man who marries her, is "proud of
his *treasure*, – a white wife" (14); and their children are referred to as "an
additional *charge*" "*levied*" by time (14 emphasis added). Mrs. Bellmont is
a calculating woman who encourages her daughter's feelings for a suitor
because "She had counted the acres which were to be transmitted to an only
son" (56). Of her son's marriage to a woman without property, she advises,
"You'd better stay here, at home, and let your wife go. Why couldn't you
try to do better"? (112). Her cruelty stems as much from nature as from fear
that the young girl will occupy equal status with her own daughter. Frado's
being "not many shades darker than Mary" places them in competition, and
Mrs. Bellmont sends her out to the sun to darken her (39). The discourse
of exchange symbolizes the ways in which a patriarchal capitalism makes
humans into things and assigns value based on gender and skin color.

In a novel so full of sentimental conventions, Wilson is at heart a realist
examining how economies of race and gender undercut ideals. She critiques turning human traits into commodities, and in selling her novel
to support herself and her son, she replaces a commodified female with
a book. Wilson writes to ensure her survival and her son's. Subsequent
black women writers enlarged this individualist impetus by creating fiction designed to instruct a race on survival and prosperity in the aftermath
of slavery. Katherine Davis Chapman Tillman, Frances Ellen Watkins
Harper, and Pauline Hopkins, were among those contributing to a tradition of black women's writing in a new black social order.

Born in 1870 in Mound City, Illinois, Tillman attended State University of Louisville in Kentucky and Wilberforce University in Ohio. She published poems in *The Christian Recorder* along with short stories, poems, and critical essays such as "The Negro among Anglo-Saxon Poets," which traced representations of blacks in western European literature. In her writing, she entered into conversations with critic Edward Knight as to whether Shakespeare intended Othello to be black (*Works* 103), and offered analysis of Elizabeth Barret Browning's "The Runaway Slave at Pilgrim's Point" (*Works* 104). Her first novel *Beryl Weston's Ambition: The Story of an Afro-American Girl's Life* (1893) was published serially in *The A. M. E. Church Review*. Like Harriet Wilson, she adopted the tradition and language of nineteenth-century sentimentality and modified these to suit her purpose: providing a blueprint for black economic and spiritual uplift while showing the centrality of black women to this mission.

In an essay "Afro-American Women and Their Work," Tillman outlines what she thought should be the aspirations of black womanhood: "Let us as Afro-American women pledge ourselves to the elevation of our homes. Let us war against intemperance, against infidelity, against gambling in saloons or parlors, against bad literature and immorality of all kind, for these are the demons that destroy our homes" (*Works* 92). Her call to arms was made against a backdrop of cultural representations of black female licentiousness. For instance, in her Civil War diaries, Mary Boykin Chesnut frequently portrays black women as seductresses rather than victims of white male lust. In his specious *The American Negro* (1901), African American William Hannibal Thomas wrote that "Innate modesty is not a characteristic of the American negro women." He continued, "Women unresistingly betray their wifely honor to satisfy a bestial instinct, ... every notion of marital duty and fidelity is cast to the winds when the next moment of passion arrives." A notorious letter by James W. Jack to Florence Belgarnie of England in which he referred to black women as "prostitutes and ... natural thieves and liars" would be the catalyst for Josephine St. Pierre to launch the National Association of Colored Women's Clubs.[27] Tillman's characterization responds to these cultural notions through images of idealized, chaste black womanhood.

The eponymous protagonist in *Beryl Weston* is a prodigy sent to school where she finds both education and religion. While enrolled at "one of the leading Afro-American Colleges in the United States" she receives a telegram informing her that her mother is dead and she must return home. Education must be sacrificed to save the family. Beryl returns to become the woman of the house. She ultimately unites with Norman Warren, a physician described as a "splendid type of Afro-American manhood." He was born into slavery and separated from his mother whom he seeks to rediscover (210–211). Many subplots and twists allow Tillman to stress religious commitment and hard work as the path to black progress. Her other novel *Clancy Street* (1898–1899) is an urban novel limning a black community after slavery. The opening chapter is equally descriptive and analytical as it characterizes denizens of Louisville Kentucky's Clancy Street as so new to freedom they cannot appreciate its seriousness: "Just now they were intoxicated with their new possession, and too often acted like so many children in the face of grave responsibilities that confronted them" (251). Through Anne who is one of the standouts in Clancy street, literate and a minister's daughter, through her family's tribulations as they lose income and subsequently their daughter to typhoid fever, the work posits self-help, not wastefulness and pity, as solutions and foreshadows future black conservatism.

Not all novels meant to instruct a black populace did so with black characters. A certain set of first-wave womanist novels use unraced characters, even though the writers acknowledge their own blackness. Even the illustrations, black and white plates of scenes in the novels offer no visual details countering this race indeterminacy. Amelia E. Johnson contextualizes herself as wife and activist when she includes the title "Mrs." as part of her authorial signature. Married to the black nationalist Reverend Harvey Johnson, she was a proponent of periodicals that provided appropriate literary content for young people. She began *The Joy*, a monthly paper of primarily poems, inspirational writings, and stories.

In all her novels, Johnson uses weak female characters to demonstrate the consequences of women not living up to their responsibility as the bedrock of family and community. In her first novel *Clarence and Corinne; or, God's Way* (1890) her protagonists Clarence and Corinne grow up on the "outskirts of the pretty town of N_____, among neat vine-covered homes" in a "weather-beaten, tumble-down cottage" that is "a blot upon a beautiful picture" (5). What should be the salvation of this desperate situation, a strong, nurturing mother, isn't. After many beatings by her husband, she has given up because she does not have Christian faith to sustain her. The mother dies, and the father abandons his children. Only through the services of a benefactress, their former teacher Miss Gray, do the children survive. In *The Hazely Family* (1894) Mrs. Hazely is lethargic as a wife and mother. Her neglect leads to her daughter Flora being taken in by the kind Aunt Bertha and the cold Aunt Sarah. Both teach her the domestic skills she needs to be a good woman, but upon Bertha's death, Sarah ships Flora back to her mother. At first appalled by the state of the home, Flora, with instruction and inspiration from her friend/neighbor Ruth takes over the household and becomes the proper domestic influence a woman should be. Johnson's final novel, *Martina Meriden, or What Is My Motive?* (1901), is a repetitive and less readable continuation of her theme of the necessity of both a strong female presence and a proper Christian philosophy to life success.

Perhaps no writer made greater use of the written word to both educate a populace and push for gender and racial change than Frances E. W. Harper. Harper worked tirelessly for racial equality, women's enfranchisement, and for temperance, all of which were concerns in her novels. Born free in Maryland in 1825, orphaned at age three, Harper was raised solidly in the black middle-class, but the loss of family would influence her work and writing. Her abolitionist efforts gave her an intimate knowledge of slavery, but the focus of her novels was black life reconstructed. A poet whose published collections included *Moses: A Story of the Nile* (1869) and *Poems on Miscellaneous Subjects* (1854), she authored four novels in all, beginning with *Minnie's Sacrifice* (1869), *Sowing and Reaping* (1876–1877), and *Trial and Triumph* (1888–1889), and ending with *Iola Leroy, or Shadows Uplifted* (1892).[28]

Sowing and Reaping, A Temperance Story and *Trial and Triumph* are Harper's social reform novels. *Sowing* charts the impact of alcohol on domestic life. Interspersed through its critique is commentary on economics, gender, and morality, and women's debates over suffrage.[29] In *Trial and Triumph*, Harper turns her attention to women's education (or lack thereof). The main character Annette is the daughter of a morally dissolute salon keeper. She is perpetually an outsider because of an inherent wit and sagacity that have no outlet until she receives an education. To the traditionalists around her, intellectualism and a rather ordinary outward appearance make her a less than desirable prospective mate. Compounding her marginalization, she is a poet whose talent is not recognized because of the color of her skin. Though selected to give the commencement speech at her graduation, a small racial triumph, she has no money and social graces, and cannot break into the black middle classes.

In *Minnie's Sacrifice*, Miriam, a black slave, and Camilla, the white daughter of her plantation owner, engineer it so that Miriam's grandson, Louis, Camilla's half brother, is sent North to be reared as white with no knowledge of his racial past. As he grows he becomes a true Southerner even in his support of slavery. Minnie, the daughter of her master and his slave mistress, is also sent North away from her mother because her appearance is so white and so much like her father's she has been mistaken as the sister of the mistress's daughter by visiting local society. How these two characters come to terms with their identity, and what paths they subsequently choose introduce one of Harper's main themes, portraying the interiority of the enslaved. The motives of those who fled and those who stayed on the plantation are explored, as are the reasons why some fought for the confederacy and others for the union. Slaves' sentiments of their plantations as being their known world explain apparent allegiances to masters. Harper offers this interiority from both sides of the racial divide through emotional descriptions of white fathers faced with selling their children or the women they love but who are still their slaves. She places human faces on what is frequently described in institutional terms.

A scene in *Minnie's Sacrifice* recurs in Harper's fourth and most famous novel *Iola Leroy, or Shadows Uplifted* (1892), suggesting that the earlier work might have been a testing ground for later ideas. In both a slave woman beaten so badly, she decides to run away hears the voice of the divine telling her to stay and see what miracles faith can bring about; subsequently, because she has stayed her son can locate her, buy her, and they reunite as a family (82–83). *Iola Leroy* tells not only of the eponymous character's abrupt enslavement, but also of the multiple attempts of many characters to reconnect to family lost through sales within slavery. The work went through five editions, suggesting its portrayals of reunification resonated with the realities of her readers. Harper provides many scenes of enslaved communities reconstructing through the sharing of information and in, particular, through the vital role played by religious institutions, revivals, and religious conferences.

Iola Leroy is brought up to believe she is white, the daughter of Eugene and Marie Leroy, a wealthy planter and the slave he manumits and educates. Her father has entreated her mother never to tell the children of their mixed heritage. The death of Eugene Leroy and the machinations of a cousin covetous of Leroy's wealth lead to the re-enslavement of Marie and the enslavement of Iola and her siblings. On the surface, Iola reprises many familiar uses of the tragic mulatto figure. She is chaste, beautiful, and Harper uses the character to highlight the social construction of race and to encourage white readers to see themselves in Iola. Wary that the figure might second beliefs that black merit comes through white bloodlines, Harper includes darker representations of black achievement. Iola's brother Harry will eventually marry one such character, Miss Delany (perhaps an allusive female version of Delany's Blake?) "with dark, expressive eyes, full of thought and feeling," of whom he says, "Neither hair nor complexion show the least hint of blood admixture." To this his sister replies," I am glad of it ... Every person of unmixed blood who succeeds in any department of literature, art, or science is a living argument for the capability which is in the race" (199).

The novel celebrates black agency. Some scenes portray the various methods of coding the enslaved used to pass information about the goings-on of the Civil War and plans for their flights to freedom, among them talking under "pots" so that the patrols would not hear their voices when they met at night. While Harper shows that every slave seeks to be free, her depiction of the conflicts posed by age or leaving loved ones when contemplating flight create complex psychological portraits. She anticipates representations of the transatlantic black world through Africans who are being made into slaves and their attempts at holding on to their traditions. Her dialect is appropriate for characters whose sphere takes them no further than the plantation, and her inclusion of folk wisdom communicates the survival of a culture as much as the survival of a race. The overall effect is a wide vista of black community. Harper constructs *Iola Leroy* to be, finally, a novel of inspiration. She informs readers of black accomplishment mentioning the greats, Ira Aldridge, Alexander Dumas, and Alexander Pushkin, but also mentions the less-familiar salons held both in quarters of Victorian elegance and cottages of former slaves. Toward the end of the novel, a character suggests to Iola that she write a book because "there is an amount of dormant talent among us, and a large field from which to gather materials" (262). In the note that follows the novel, Harper explicitly states that "There are scattered among us materials for mournful tragedies and mirth-provoking comedies" (282) and describes a race that is moving from slave pen to wielding the pen on their own behalf. This doubled assertion is Harper's challenge to writers to begin to capture in fiction black heritage as it is developing in the United States.

In a *Crisis* editorial, W. E. B. Du Bois characterized Harper as a writer more of agency than of art (a charge he would later be subject to himself, ironically). Observing that "she was not a great writer, but she wrote much worth reading," he articulates the way many black nineteenth-century novels came to be read and understood by more contemporary audiences. Du Bois lamented the absence of black writers who could creatively make the most of black experiences. He wrote, "Here is a nation whose soul is still dumb, yet big with feeling, song and story. What are we doing to develop writers to express this wealth of emotion fitly? Very little. We have among ten millions to-day one poet, one novelist and two or three recognized writers of articles and essays" ("Writers" 21). One writer who

Du Bois ignored in his somewhat sweeping yet narrow dismissal, who took up both his and Harper's challenges and created works that went beyond novels of urgency, is Pauline E. Hopkins.

The Congregational Publishing Society had an eye for talent. With the financial support of William Wells Brown, in 1874 they awarded Pauline E. Hopkins ten dollars, gold, for her essay "Evils of Intemperance and Their Remedy." Her short story "The Mystery Within Us" appeared in the first edition of *The Colored American Magazine*, and later the paper's founders formed the Colored Co-operative Publishing Company, which would issue Hopkins's novel *Contending Forces* (1900). While at *The Colored American Magazine* Hopkins, who also published under the name Sarah A. Allen, was editor in charge of a "department devoted exclusively to the interest of women and the home," and her work there was envisioned as "uplifting the colored people of America, and through them, the world" (*CAM* 1.2 May 1900, 62). It was a syncretic view that integrated gender and race and saw women as powerful social agents.

Hopkins was part of the coterie of black women intellectuals that included Anna Julia Cooper, Mary Church Terrell, and Mary Jane Patterson. Along with Walter Wallace, she later established a press and founded the short-lived *New Era Magazine*, which she edited and which began serialization of another Hopkins's work *Topsy Templeton*. The work was advertised as the story of a "modern Topsy," designed to depict "the annoyances and discouragements that a negro endures in the north" and its "keynote" was "the weight of individual effort in the solution of the race question" (*New Era Magazine* 1.1, February 1916, p. 2).[30] What is extant of the work is sentimental in genre: its emphasis on domesticity, the sanctity of motherhood, and its design to prove the worth of the race and the virtue of black women.

Hopkins foreshadows the increasing concern of black writers with form. "Fiction," she writes, "is of great value to any people as a preserver of manners and customs ... It is a record of growth and development from generation to generation. *No one will do this for us; we must ourselves develop the men and women who will faithfully portray the inmost thoughts and feelings of the Negro with all the fire and romance which lie dormant in our history*, and, as yet, unrecognized by writers of the Anglo-Saxon race" (preface *Contending Forces*, 13–14). The reference to the Anglo-Saxon race suggests the desire for recognition, but what Hopkins emphasizes is the need for fiction, created by blacks, to preserve and express black culture. She writes at a time when African American novels are beginning to be evaluated as more than testament to black potential, and her novels meet the standards modern readers increasingly demand of fiction: more fully realized characters and sleeker narrative form. She bridges postbellum writing and the advent of the New Negro Renaissance, and anticipates the growing use of black forms to represent black culture. *Contending Forces* is peppered with humorous anecdotes told in black literary dialect: a minister wooing a woman twice his age for security, the competition between clubwomen at a fair held for the church. Plots incorporate black worksongs, tales of hoodoo trickery, and dances that are part of black tradition including the pigeon wing (also called the buck and wing), juba, and walk 'round. The variety of language and the inclusion of vernacular signify more a concern for cultural accuracy than a concern for audience approbation.

Set in the 1830s, *Contending Forces* tells of Charles Monfort and his family who have moved from Bermuda to the United States once the British outlawed slavery. He pays the price for the monetary greed that makes him want to hold on to his slaves, as lies about his wife Grace having black blood are spread by poor whites envious of his position and by a business associate desirous of Grace. Monfort is assassinated, and his children are enslaved. The novel challenges readers to suss out how this early history relates to the stories of the Smiths, a respectable black middle class family now residing in turn-of-the-century Boston.

Hopkins's next three novels *Hagar's Daughter, A Story of Southern Caste Prejudice* (written under the name of Sarah A. Allen and discussed in more detail in the chapter on detective novels); *Winona, A Tale of Negro Life in the South and Southwest*; and *Of One Blood, Or, the Hidden Self* (a novel of speculative fiction which will be discussed in that chapter) were serialized in *The Colored American Magazine* between March 1901 and November 1903.[31] Hopkins had once hoped to be a dramatist and had written a play *Escaped from Slavery; or the Underground Railroad* (cir. 1879) presented by her troupe, The Colored Troubadours. Her dramatic flair is clearly evident in the pacing of her series. The use of shifts in time builds suspense and this quality of intrigue remains even when the novels are unified in book form.

From its narrator's initial assertion that "Many strange tales of romantic happenings in this mixed community of Anglo-Saxons, Indians and Negroes might be told similar to the one I am about to relate, and the world stand aghast and try in vain to find the dividing line supposed to be a natural barrier between the whites and the dark-skinned races" (287), *Winona* is a deeply multicultural novel.[32] It evokes James Fenimore Cooper's Leatherstocking series with its lush naturalistic descriptions of western New York state landscapes, a region "not polluted by the foul breath of slavery" (288), and its imagining of native American traditions. Unlike Cooper, however, its emphasis is not on discrete racial bloodlines but on the blendings of culture and race that were the fact of the United States. White Eagle is a British man, who, having to leave England, has re-created a life for himself among the Seneca. He is father to Winona, his issue with a "mulattress," and the adopted Judah, a free black. What happens to Winona and Judah once two white strangers land on their island is easily anticipated by readers familiar with novels of this period. The book is a rollicking adventure tale taking readers from north to south, through a murder, incidents of cross-dressing, and vividly interweaving events of John Brown's resistance.

Some have questioned Hopkins's consistent use of near white characters and cross-racial romance. In a letter to the editor of *The Colored American Magazine*, Cornelia A. Condict queries,

> May I make a comment on the stories, especially those that have been serial. Without exception they have been of love between the colored and whites. Does that mean that your novelists can imagine no love beautiful and sublime within the range of the colored race, for each other? I have seen beautiful home life and love in families of altogether Negro blood.
>
> The stories of these tragic mixed loves will not commend themselves to your white readers and will not elevate the colored readers. I believe your novelists could do with a consecrated imagination and pen, more for the elevation of home life and love, than perhaps any other one class of writers. (398–399)

In addition to mentioning the displeasure racial mixing causes to a white readership, Condict, in iterating the power of the novel to uplift, questions why Hopkins seems unable to use examples of fully black characters, happy in their own race. Hopkins, in her response, points out that Condict missed the condemnation of hypocritical race strictures at the heart of these stories:

> My stories are definitely planned to show the obstacles persistently placed in our paths by a dominant race to subjugate us spiritually. Marriage is made illegal between races and yet the mulattoes increase. Thus the shadow of corruption falls on the blacks and on the whites, without whose aid the mulattoes would not exist. And then the hue and cry goes abroad of the immorality of the Negro and the disgrace that the mulattoes are to this nation....
>
> The home life of Negroes is beautiful in many instances; warm affection is there between husband and wife, and filial and paternal tenderness in them is not surpassed by any other race of the human family ... I am glad to receive this criticism for it shows more clearly than ever that white people don't understand *what pleases Negroes*. You are between Scylla and Charybadis [*sic*]: If you please the author of this letter and your white clientele, you will

lose your Negro patronage. If you cater to the *demands* of the Negro trade, away goes Mrs.–. (*CAM* 6.6, March 1903, 399–400)

Hopkins makes many points in this response. She argues that her cross-racial stories reveal the hypocrisy of American sexual politics as they engage race. Her response also highlights the pressure of writing for more than one racial audience; however, it is her comment that Mrs. Condict does not know what "pleases Negroes" that is most revealing of black audience expectations. It can be read in at least two ways: one, that Condict does not understand that black readers appreciate the critique of a false sexual morality; or two, that stories of racial mixing and passing are popular subject matter. There is no way to know which of these intents motivated Hopkins, but it is difficult to ignore the frequency of light-colored protagonists and passing plots in stories designed to reach a black readership.

In addition to offering writers the ability to critique the sexual hypocrisy that produced a range of mixed-raced people, as well as the arbitrariness of what is constructed as "white" and "black," such storylines offer readers the ability to imagine lives lived outside racial confines, and to imagine the subversive power of crossing racial lines. Hopkins was certainly not alone in her fascination with passing characters and racial mixing. Both have been constant literary presences in American literature of the nineteenth and early twentieth centuries (and beyond), not just in the works of black writers, as novels from Mark Twain's *Pudd'nhead Wilson* (1890) to Fannie Hurst's *Imitation of Life* (1934) illustrate. As she stated, Hopkins is a writer seeking to reach the broadest readership possible, and plots of racial crossings and of undiscovered blackness were very popular avenues to this end.

The wide genre ranges, imaginative themes, and trenchant social critique of Hopkins's novels reflect the multivalent interests of black writers and thinkers. In addition to questions of racial constructions and arguments for social justice, her novels presented tear-jerking romance, cliff-hanging adventures, and imaginative forays into fantastic otherworldly experiences. She is exemplary of the nascent literary emancipation the postbellum period brings.[33]

Many early black novels fell out of favor over time, their language seemed distant, their themes Victorian. Their literary quality is uneven, and acknowledged as such even by their contemporary readers. Journalist, author, lecturer, social worker, and clubwoman, Victoria Earle Matthews who founded the White Rose Home in Harlem to provide classes in cooking, sewing, and general education, cautioned that there has been "too much that is crude, rude, pompous, and literary nothings, which ought to have been strangled before they were written much less printed" (182). Almost one hundred years later, Hortense Spillers would observe "even the very act of writing itself, is far more important than any particular aesthetic outcome" (Introduction, Amelia Johnson's *Clarence and Corinne*, xxix). The divergent views in these assessments signal the distance this literature has traveled in its development and interpretation. Matthews desperate for a literature that proved racial mastery of the arts did not enjoy the benefit of historical hindsight that Spillers does. The urgency that demanded excellence often overlooked that novels' contrived, shifting, and improbable plots mirrored the upheavals experienced by people frequently in transit and trying to sustain or reestablish family and community. During their moment, these novels were appreciated because in them readers for the first time saw themselves. Even weaker novels such as *Nellie Brown, The Hazely Family,* and *Sowing and Reaping,* offer insights into cultural and historical interpretations of blackness still necessary to understanding identity and national belonging.

The 1830s–1890s period that inaugurated the African American novel was one of huge social transformation including the end of slavery and movements toward black enfranchisement. What seems overwrought suited an antebellum and postbellum setting where the novel was a form of advocacy. Readers were meant to feel the power of sentiment and through their feelings enact social change, especially at a time when the United States government was reluctant to do so and, with the Fugitive Slave Law and the Dred Scott case, seemed intent on sustaining inequity.

In just over fifty years, African American novels nurtured emerging race consciousness, but such consciousness was by no means homogenous; instead, a far more interesting plurality becomes apparent as plots, characters, settings, dialogue, and vernacular materials were all enlisted to square self-generated definitions of blackness with those of American hegemony.

CHAPTER 2

Publish or Perish: African American Novels, 1900s–1920s

The desire for a recognized tradition of letters articulated by so many late-nineteenth-century black writers began to manifest at the turn of the twentieth century. Ironically at a time when blacks faced increasing reactionary violence in post-Reconstruction America, African American novels gained greater access to the literary marketplace. Handsomely bound editions signified approval at a time termed a nadir by historians such as Rayford Logan. The elections of Hiram Revels and Blanche K. Bruce to the senate and John Mercer Langston to Congress, the passage of the Fourteenth and Fifteenth Amendments (the first guaranteeing formerly enslaved peoples the rights of citizens; the second, guaranteeing the franchise to African American men) seemed distant memories. In their stead was the rise of Southern Democrats determined to do away with black progress through laws instituting segregationist practices or through terror. Turn-of-the-century black novels countered this racial enmity by voicing progressive philosophies and pointing out that the victims of such hatred were not only African Americans, but also American democratic ideals. At a time when black life was increasingly penned in, black novels ventured out into mainstream publishing outlets, thus increasing their effectiveness as organs arguing for black equal opportunity. In some cases, their content made this argument; in others, the race of their writers did.

If one reads any assessment of the state of black American letters at the turn of the twentieth century, the name Paul Laurence Dunbar is ubiquitous. Not so ubiquitous is the name of the United Brethren Publishing Company where he subsidized the publication of his poetry collection *Oak and Ivy* (1893). Hadley & Hadley, Printers and Binders, where he and his friends, attorney Charles A. Thatcher and psychiatrist Henry A. Tobey, subsidized his second collection *Majors and Minors* (1896) was hardly better known. But the dialect poems (the "minors" in the title as contrasted to the standard English "majors") caught the attention of William Dean Howells, as did the poet's portrait in the work's frontispiece. In describing his habit of encouraging unknown authors, Howells notes that when he saw the image that accompanied Dunbar's self-published edition he "felt a heightened pathos ... from the fact that the face ... was the face of a young negro, with the race traits strongly accented." He expanded his description of Dunbar (in a passage that his daughter Mildred Howells omits from her edition of her father's letters) to include the features that struck him: "the black skin, the woolly hair, the thick, out-rolling lips, and the mild soft eyes of the pure African type" ("Life and Letters" 630). Howells is as fascinated by the minimal appearance of other than black antecedents in Dunbar as he is by his talent. For him, the poet is a novel conundrum, a visibly dark black who can write.

Howells's interest in Dunbar and his favorable review encouraged Dodd Mead and Company to take a chance on *Lyrics of Lowly Life* (1896), and the firm would publish all of Dunbar's novels. Dodd Mead built its reputation on fine editions of English literature and scholarly volumes on the fine arts, and each of their Dunbar editions had handsome cover art. His first *The Uncalled* (1898) sports a gold embossed square with the title surrounded by *fleur de lis* (Figure 2.1).[1] The author's initials appear below the square in a black monogram design. To date, the majority of black novels were often self-published or serialized, so Dodd Mead's attention to the presentation of Dunbar's work was notable.

Dunbar, appropriately for a first-time author, expresses gratitude for Howells's interest, and on July 13, 1896 writes a letter of thanks:

> I have seen your article in *Harper's* and felt its effect. That I have not written you sooner is neither the result of willful neglect nor lack of gratitude. It has taken time for me to recover from the shock of delightful surprise. My emotions have been too much for me. I could not thank you without "gushing" and I did not want to "gush." ...
>
> The kindly praise you have accorded me will be an incentive to more careful work. My greatest fear is that you may have been more kind to me than just. (*Life in Letters* 2, 67–68)

Just one year later, March 15, 1897, Dunbar wrote to an unnamed friend and offered a slightly different assessment of Howells's overall impact. In the letter, he critiques the "hollowness" of American book criticism, and notes the "irrevocable harm" done to him by William Dean Howells "in the dictum he laid down regarding my dialect verse." He continues, "I am afraid that it will even influence English criticism." He complains of the pressure of trying to sell books, along with being treated as a novelty: "I am not tired of writing, but I am tired of trying to sell, and running about acting as a curiosity" ("Unpublished Letters" 73). Dunbar was no doubt

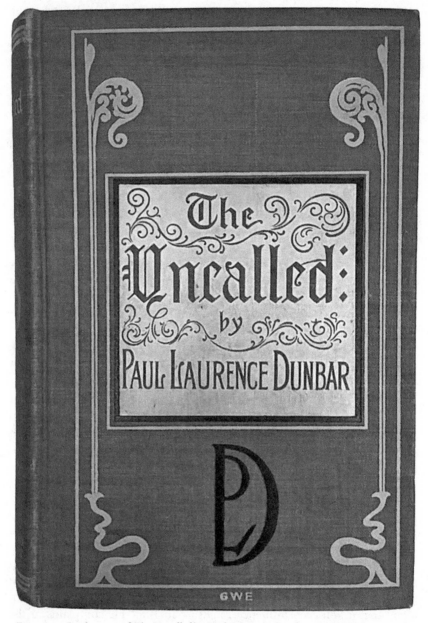

Figure 2.1 Book cover of *The Uncalled* by Paul Laurence Dunbar. Author's photograph.

grateful that Howells brought him to public attention, but reading the first letter in light of the second, one wonders what degree of masking Dunbar performed when he wrote to Howells. Might the "more kind than just" be an indictment of Howells's patronizing? The two letters provide an informative lens through which to read Dunbar's novels. His frustration with being thought of as a dialect poet and racial novelty is clear and is further vented in his novels.[2] While many novels of the period directly take on race, Dunbar's do not. His characters are racially ambiguous, leading some to presume a default whiteness; however, this racial indeterminacy *is* Dunbar's engagement of race, reflecting his uneasy positioning between racial and artistic identities. He liberates his primary protagonists from what he views as the constrictions of being raced, leaving marginalization to his minor black characters who are almost in caricature. The impact of racial limiting is delineated through the frequent appearances of figures silenced by feelings of alienation and, like Dunbar himself, wanting to express themselves on their own terms.

Dunbar's first novel *The Uncalled* (1898) is set in Dexter, Ohio. Frederick Brent is the son of a wife-beating alcoholic brick mason who deserts his family. Reared in poverty and squalor, after his mother dies, Fred is adopted by the stern spinster Hester Prime. A strong disciplinarian, Hester takes care of his material needs, but shows him little affection or nurturing. These he receives from his exchanges with the local reverend's assistant Eliphalet Hodges. Miss Prime decides she will make a preacher out of Fred. The town's assessment that he cannot outrun his destiny torments Fred who begins to manifest outward propriety while harboring inward rage. Fred struggles between what he feels and what is expected of him, between his more progressive ideas and the townsfolk's reactionary conservatism. He is a hard worker, does well at school, and is eventually ordained as a minister. When the town's minister forces him to use the experiences of Sophie, his coworker and the daughter of the truly kind woman who first took him after his mother's death as an example of a woman's fall into sin (it is implied that she is pregnant out of wedlock), he refuses and leaves the ministry and town. Thus begins a journey that takes him through the urbanity of Cincinnati where he is struck by its largeness and repelled by what he views as its moral laxness. An encounter with his father who is now a temperance worker leads to Fred's having to decide whether to make his future in Cincinnati or return to Dexter. Like other Dunbar novels, *The Uncalled* pits the individual against convention, and one wonders if Dunbar is addressing his own feelings toward the mainstream of literary expectations. By making his characters of indeterminate race, he removes authorial identity from his fictional world. He can thus disengage himself from expectations placed on him as a black writer.

The reviews of the work were lukewarm, and *The Uncalled* saw less than moderate sales. *Lyrics of the Hearthside* (1899), which included dialect poems, mitigated some of the financial and reputational loss. Dunbar's next novel *The Love of Landry* (1900), a love story exploring class stratification, did not fare much better in terms of reception. The heroine Mildred is ailing, and her doctor recommends relocation to the dry air of Colorado, a place Dunbar briefly visited himself. While at a ranch, she meets and eventually falls in love with Landry whom she believes to be a mere hand, so she denies her feelings for him. Again Dunbar contrasts individual freedom and societal constraint through Mildred and Landry. Its characters are white, so marked by Mildred's comments on the working conditions of a black train porter. This distancing continues to his next novel, where it assumes sharpened dimensions.

The Fanatics (1901) is a Romeo and Juliet story of the Civil War, and in it Dunbar engages themes preoccupying the post-Reconstruction era: the place of blacks in society and the dangers of anarchic violence. Romeo here is Robert Van Doren, whose father is a transplanted southern gentleman now residing in the fictional Dorbury, Ohio, and Juliet is Mary Waters, whose father is a staunch Unionist and Republican. In a town on the border between north and south they fall in love during the antebellum period, and their parents being friends initially welcome the marriage of their children. The Civil War soon intervenes in the nuptials. Mary's father demands that she stop seeing her beloved and that she declare full allegiance to the Union cause. When he discovers her sewing a keepsake for Bob to take into war, he disowns her. Like Mary and Bob, the town is torn apart by war, and extensive portrayal of the interior thoughts of characters exhibit varying perspectives on the conflict. Transplanted white southerners feel northern aggression must be avenged. White northerners feel saving the union is the patriotic duty of all who call themselves Americans. Southern blacks displaced by the war migrate North in search of new communities but find no solace even among their own in Dorbury. Only when whites threaten violence against all blacks is a tenuous race unity realized. The novel represents the difficulty of forming a black community out of disparate class and regional elements.

Dunbar's technique in framing his black characters would be deemed racist in a novel by a white author. He draws newly arriving slaves as "great, helpless, irresponsible children" (155–156). Another character, "Nigger Ed," the town crier, local joke, and sometimes drunk, is rendered in typically stereotypic terms, afraid of ghosts and needing to have concepts such as "in effigy" explained to him when he thinks a real local politician has been killed. He comes under harsh treatment and mockery by the town, but gradually Dunbar redeems this portrait. Ed is redressed and earns the town's respect (and his own self-respect) after tending to the dead, dying, and maimed of war. This transformation is relatively isolated, however, and it is hard to find black heroism in Dunbar's works. Though he was often cited as a shining representation of black aptitude, he drew black characters who were just the opposite, almost as if to protest subversively the pressure of being the exemplar of his race.[3] He often engages naturalistic themes with helpless characters trapped by environmental circumstances. Often his male characters are young brutes with limited awareness of their motivations, or older men too facile to understand the intricacies of a complex world. His novels are frequently dark, foreshadowing realism and deterministic alienation of 1940s novels.

Dunbar felt that *The Fanatics* might have been his most important work. He had hopes that others would share his valuation, but was disappointed. In a letter, he thanks Dr. F: "I am glad to have you say nice things about 'The Fanatics'. You do not know how my hopes were planted in that book and it has utterly disappointed me. Like that right wrist of your, which I hope is better now, it went very lame upon me and, knowing it as the best thing I have done, discouragement has taken hold upon me" ("Unpublished Letters" 74).

While Dunbar felt *The Fanatics* was his best novel, critics since have given this honor to *The Sport of the Gods* (1901).[4] The novel's setting shifts from Dunbar's familiar Midwest and West, east to New York. As in many works of this period, its villain is the South, drawn not as a region, but as an idea embodying ignorance, hatred, and above all danger. The Hamiltons are a hardworking, proper living family who occupy a neat cottage behind the home of their former master, Maurice Oakley. Flowers, a vegetable garden, and money in the bank show their industry. They have two children, a daughter Kit and a son Joe. Their home life is destroyed when a lie told by Maurice's dilettante brother sends Berry Hamilton to jail as a thief, and the South that will be pictured in so many novels of the post-Reconstruction period manifests. Berry's jailing, disgrace, and lack of support from an envious black community force the Hamiltons to resettle in New York City. The move north proves their undoing. The son, Joe, weak of character and insight spirals into drunkenness and criminal tragedy; the daughter becomes dazzled by the theatre that steals her youth, beauty, and talent; and the mother stymied by her children's indifference and dissolution unknowingly becomes a bigamist when she believes Berry dead. By the book's end, the elderly Hamiltons, after an arduous odyssey, return to their cottage saddened by the course of events that have effectively stolen their children from them.

Like Dunbar, Charles Chesnutt gained rare early access to the American mainstream publishing industry. Facilitating his entry was Walter Hines Page, a transplanted Southerner who championed him and brought him to the attention of Houghton Mifflin. Thanks to Chesnutt's letters, a record exists providing insight into what literature meant to him as a means to economic security, to renown, and to effecting social change while proving the merit of a devalued race. In a letter to George Washington Cable where he cites Albion Tourgé's warning that race might hamper his success, Chesnutt observes optimistically, "I hardly think so, for I am under the impression that a colored writer of literature is something that editors and the public would be glad to recognize and encourage ... I am not afraid to make a frank avowal of my position, and to give the benefit of any possible success or reputation that I may by hard work win, to those who need it most" (McElrath Letters 29). Chesnutt, able to pass as white, goes on to acknowledge that the content of his work associates him with blackness, and that he is content to have his efforts credited to both his talent and a race in need of positive assessment. His own racial identification would always be complicated, and often he spoke of himself as a black man more by allegiance than appearance, or as someone "affiliated" with the black race. He is at once outside and inside, "neither 'nigger', poor white, nor 'buckrah.' Too 'stuck up' for the colored folks, and, of course, not recognized by the whites" (Brodhead 157–158), and from this position he offered unique interrogations of the social constructions of race.[5] Writing novels actually cemented Chesnutt's blackness as his reputation and stature grew, and he would come to envision himself as starting the black literary tradition.[6]

Chesnutt's first novel began as "Rena Walden" but became *The House Behind the Cedars* (1900). It was important to Chesnutt that the book not just be published, but be published in a well-known and respected venue. "I want, of course, the best terms you can offer," he wrote to Houghton Mifflin. "I would prefer that your house bring out the book; the author having been first recognized by you (so far as any high class publication is concerned), and the imprint of your house having the value that it has ... I would want the volume bound in cloth" (McElrath, *Letters* 75–76). He called this work his "favorite child" because the heroine came from a class and color background similar to his own (Crisler 257). In 1921 the *Chicago Defender* asked to publish it serially, and Oscar Micheaux later entered into protracted negotiations with Chesnutt to bring a filmed version to light. The main character John has left his home in Patesville, North Carolina, to pass as the white John Warwick of Clarence, South Carolina, where he can legally be classed as white because of his appearance and less stringent blood laws. Now widowed, he seeks a relative to care for his son Albert by a white woman who did not know his racial secret, but more importantly, he seeks relief from the isolation imposed upon him by abandoning his family and passing. He has returned home to persuade his mother to let his sister Rena join him and pass as well. Molly Walden is of African, white, and Native American descent, but the strains don't matter under the one-drop rule in place in this part of North Carolina. She is, however, born of two free parents, and is thus, nominally free. Rena and John are the issue of Molly Walden and a white gentleman who provides her with the eponymous house behind the cedars, but dies before he can leave his children their proper financial legacy. The Waldens occupy a space between black and white, where they cannot fully enjoy white privilege but are not ready to join ranks with, nor are they fully accepted by, other visibly black residents. The novel displays the fusion of traditions contained in African American novels. On the one hand, it is full of vernacular elements such as dialect and folk philosophies, and, on the other, it frequently makes allusions to chivalric traditions of Walter Scott, *Tristram Shandy* (1759), *Robinson Crusoe* (1719), and *Don Quixote* (1605).

Chesnutt's novels increasingly set forth themes of mob violence. He hoped his second novel *The Marrow of Tradition* (1901), which he thought his best, would do for post-Reconstruction black politics what *Uncle Tom's Cabin* had done for abolitionism. William Dean Howells, who had assisted Chesnutt in gaining a wider audience, characterized it as a "bitter, bitter" novel, even while acceding that it had every right to be ("Psychological Counter-Current" 882–883).[7] Its plot vivifying lynching, disfranchisement, and segregation put in fiction the concerns of nonfiction advocacy. *Marrow* imagines the causes behind the November 10, 1898, race riot in the predominantly black Wilimington, North Carolina. The riot arose in response to Reconstruction-era changes that extended the franchise, increased the number of black public officials, and saw growing black business and educational success. Ultimately, the novel asks what comes after emancipation?

The tragedy in *Marrow* is set in motion by the history recalled by Mammy Jane, the trusted servant of Olivia Merkell Carteret's grandmother. Olivia's father, Sam Merkel, has another daughter by Julia, his black mistress. After the death of Olivia's mother, Julia stays to "keep house," and later it is learned that Sam and she have legally married in secret. Not knowing of the marriage, Olivia's maternal aunt Polly demands to be Julia's replacement. Sam says no, and Polly leaves and takes Olivia. Upon Sam's death, Polly returns to the house and exiles Julia and her daughter Janet. Janet, Olivia's half-sister, grows up and marries the black Dr. Miller, the grandson of a successful former slave who bought his own freedom, and the son of a businessman who became a successful stevedore and then opened his own contracting business for loading and unloading vessels. Miller has been educated in the hospitals of Paris and Vienna, but still faces racism when he tries to practice in his hometown. Olivia marries and has a son with Major Carteret, the editor of the town's newspaper, and a gentleman white supremacist. He is in league with Captain George McBane, a social outcast because he is not an aristocrat, to foment a revolution because both feel blacks no longer know their place. The intricacies of the plot mirror the intricacies of histories and bloodlines that lead to the riot that climaxes the work. Subplots show the fragile existence of black freedom in an era of arbitrary lynching and random brutality. The town has been left without doctors because violence has forced one to flee, has injured another, and occupies all the time of the only one tending to the battered. When Cateret's son takes ill with croup, he must seek out Dr. Miller whose own son has died via a stray bullet in the riot. Miller refuses to help him, and Carteret sees the justice in his refusal. In desperation, Olivia runs to the Millers' home to try and persuade the doctor. He tells her no, but leaves the decision to her half-sister Janet.

The final novel appearing in Chesnutt's lifetime was *The Colonel's Dream* (1905), published by another distinguished house, Doubleday, Page & Company. It describes a failed utopian vision revealing the intransigence of racist relations in the South. Colonel Henry French who moved New York and made his wealth after fighting for the South in the Civil War, returns to his hometown of Clarendon, North Carolina. Immersed in nostalgia for the landscape, architecture, and his memories of the old South, his temporary visit turns permanent. He encounters his former slave, Peter French, whose ability to survive economically is made impossible because of racism and segregation. Seeing Peter replaces nostalgia with the reality of segregated Clarendon. As antebellum and postbellum collide, the Colonel becomes aware of the continued inequity of black life in the post–Civil War South. The difficulties of Reconstruction and white fear of black supremacy are intertwined in many subplots. The novel's pessimism and stark portrayal of violence and racism led to poor sales, and Chesnutt cited an unsympathetic audience as a cause. He became increasingly disillusioned with a public he felt was not ready for books whose central characters are black and treated with complexity and sympathy.

Chesnutt's other extant novels are reprints of unpublished manuscripts. *Paul Marchand, FMC* [Free Man of Color] whose eponymous protagonist is reared as a man of mixed blood and subsequently discovers he is white, was submitted to Houghton Mifflin, Harcourt, Brace, and Alfred A. Knopf, but none published it. *Mandy Oxendine*, another story of the color line, was rejected for publication in 1897, and was never published in Chesnutt's lifetime. *The Quarry*, which recast the theme of passing with a white character who passes for black, came at the height of the Harlem Renaissance in 1928, and Chesnutt hoped a renewed interest in things black would lead to his own literary renaissance. Knopf and, two years later, Houghton Mifflin, both rejected the work. The failure of these novels in Chesnutt's time drove him to write to Walter Hines Page of his decision "to foreswear the race problem stories" (June 29, 1904, McElrath, *Letters* 214), and his subsequent novels, all attempts to appeal to a white audience, include the unfinished *The Rainbow Chasers* in which many suitors pursue widow Julia Gray; *A Business Career*, which traces the fate of Stella Merwin who seeks revenge against the partner she believes caused her father's ruin; and *Evelyn's Husband*, set in the United States, the Caribbean, and Brazil and telling the story of two men, one mature, one young, in love with the same woman.

Chesnutt tirelessly promoted his works, giving readings to audiences, creating independent distribution networks, and coordinating with editors and publishers to have his books placed in prominent spots in bookstores. He requested that Houghton Mifflin send copies of *Marrow* to well-known black activists including Ida Wells Barnett and J. E. Bruce. He suggested W. E. B. Du Bois and Booker T. Washington as readers and endorsers for his works, but to small avail. His activities to engender a black readership for novels showed how difficult a proposition this was, as the populace that could regularly afford to buy books was small.

For a brief period, Chesnutt achieved the publishing success most of his black contemporaries could only wish for. Other writers of this time did not enjoy even the qualified admittance to major publishing houses that he and Dunbar did. In 1899, for instance, Sutton E. Griggs privately published one of the most important works of the period *Iperium in Imperio* under the imprint of The Editor Publishing Company, Cincinnati. Later, in 1901 he established the Orion Publishing Company in Nashville to produce works during the difficult last quarter of the nineteenth century. The rest of his novels appeared under this imprint, with *Overshadowed* being the first in 1901. Orion faced financial difficulties, however, and Griggs hoped the National Baptist Convention would provide a network to urge the purchase of his works, particularly since it was at their request that he wrote *The Hindered Hand* (1905) as a response to Thomas Dixon's *The Leopard's Spots* (1902), but major support was not forthcoming. Besides providing opportunities to publish his own works, Griggs's ventures provided employment to African Americans and a venue for ideas that could not find expression elsewhere.

The post-Reconstruction south is a major character in Griggs's novels, and each work cautions how unchecked racist practices will destroy a people, a region, and a nation. He views the South as a native son, however, not disavowing it but seeking its transformation. While his novels vary in quality, *Imperium in Imperio* (1899) deserved to be brought out by a major press, but its content, which will be explored in the chapter on speculative fiction, virtually guaranteed it would not find a place in an established house at the time. It advocates annexing Texas and the Gulf port access to found a black nation. In addition to being a progenitor for black speculative fiction, it is frequently read as an instance of black nationalist writing.[8] Griggs's other novels do not rise to the quality of *Imperio*, though there are good moments in all. They are all devoted to illuminating brutality against blacks in the South, and offering social and economic foundations for a national future.

The Hindered Hand: or, The Reign of the Repressionist has four main characters: Ensal Ellwood, Earl Bluefield, the newly named (by Ensal) Tiara Merlow (who rejects her surname Douglass because Frederick Douglass has married a white woman), and the passing Eunice Seabright who we later find out is Tiara's sister.[9] Their brother Percy G. Marshall, beloved minister of the town, is passing as well. In Ensal and Earl, Griggs employs one of his favorite conceits, light skinned–dark skinned character pairing with each espousing a different philosophy of achieving race equality. The lighter Earl, initially more radical, opts for race war; the darker Ensal for persuasion and political power. Situating reason and wisdom in darker-skinned characters upends the traditional intraracial color line privileging African Americans who appeared white and situates rational black power in "undiluted" form. Griggs thus reverses the negative impacts of intraracial internalization of color prejudice on black psyche.

Unlike earlier novels with their representations of fugitive slaves, Griggs's works squarely eye the present and future. They critique the many social and financial practices designed to hinder the advance of newly emancipated blacks including loan companies that charge exorbitant interest and use homes purchased by the dint of hard work as collateral. Sharecropping is shown for what it is, a system that continues a de facto enslavement. Many of his novels contain exposés of a racist justice system that fuels an outsize black presence on chain gangs and in reformatories. Griggs frequently includes narrative treatises written by characters and excerpts from newspapers to drive home the distinction between ending enslavement and securing black American citizenship.

It is evident that Griggs was influenced by early womanism. His central female characters hold family and society together in difficult situations. In *Overshadowed* (1901), the main character Erma warns of the dangers economic deprivation poses to blacks, and particularly to black women with no options for self-sufficiency. The strong female protagonist in *Unfettered*, Morlene, works with the male hero Dorlan Warthell, an "ebony-like Apollo" (71) to further black political interests beyond the Republican party, a theme that reflects increasing black disillusionment with the party's failure to create patronage positions for blacks and its compromising with Southern democrats. In his final novel *Pointing the Way* (1908), Clotille Strange and the racially indeterminate Eina Rapona through their tangled misalliances provide a panorama of black social history, relations, and political activism. His female characters represent his belief that the race will succeed only as far as its women do.

Griggs's novels contain many ideas and many contradictions because they speak to two audiences at once. They offer visions of progressive blacks to white readers as arguments for social inclusion, but they also offer detailed analysis of the problems within the race and proposals to move it forward. He decries the practices of the South, yet casts the region as the true home of African Americans. He is not ashamed of African antecedents, yet schemes of migration are not part of his visions. For him, the descendants of the enslaved have been Christianized, exposed to western influences, and are fully part of the American fabric, and even the potential saviors of American democracy. His writing style evidences contrast as well. He blends the formality of nineteenth-century expression with a modernity that emerges in renderings of characters' consciousness and analyses of social situations. The variances are in keeping with a writer straddling a black past and a black future.

Though published independently, the packaging of Griggs's books approximates the finish of the major publishing houses. All the novels have handsome engraved covers with gilt lettering. They bespeak tradition and permanence, the sense of a book to be passed on to posterity. The message they impart is summed up on the cover illustration of *Hindered*

Hand. On the first edition, a rectangular reflecting pool sits at the center surrounded by buildings, the edifice directly at its end evocative of the United States Capitol. Angels, a bird, and the rays of the sun occupy the sky. A black hand is drawn in the lower-left corner reaching forward to this majestic vision, but a white hand checks its reach restraining it by the wrist (Figure 2.2). The cover at once incorporates the promise of partaking and the reality of exclusion, a theme addressed in many post-Reconstruction novels including those of John Edward Bruce.

Most know Bruce for *The Black Sleuth* (1907–1909), which will be discussed as detective fiction, but it was not his only novel. Bruce followed it with *The Awakening of Hezekiah Jones* (1916). The novel's subtitle, *A Story Dealing with Some of the Problems Affecting the Political Rewards Due the Negro* encapsulates its focus. The publisher was Phil H. Brown of Hopkinsville, Kentucky, an organizer active in the Republican National Committee during the presidential elections of 1908–1920. An inexpensive publication, the cover's far right bears an elongated illustration box with an image of a butler or servant in profile, visually representing that despite involvement with the Republican party, blacks had progressed little. The novel's African American hero Hezekiah has political ambitions. He styles himself as power broker, and influential white residents of his town count on him to deliver the black vote to the Republican party. He is seduced by invitations to "front porch tête-à têtes" (59), Cuban cigars, fine wines, scotch, and monetary remuneration. The book details his growth into realizing that no matter how well-intentioned whites are, they ultimately look out for their own interests. The action in the novel is minimal, mainly depicting contrasts between meetings of white political groups and black and showing Hezekiah becoming a true leader of the community, but Bruce engages early twentieth-century black concerns: increasing white ethnic immigration and the cheapening of black labor; blind loyalty to the Republican party; white fear of full black political power; and the need to make social space for educated and professional blacks. The awakening in the title has a dual reference – to Hezekiah who shifts from being a leader in name to a leader in fact, and to whites who need to awaken to blacks as part of American democracy.

Griggs and Bruce both use the South as setting because of its symbolic import to black Americans at the time. They were not alone in identifying the centrality of the south to African American experience. The man who sat with Shakespeare, moved arm in arm with Balzac, and summoned Artistotle and Aurelius also realized that the South was a major symbol in black self-conception.[10] W. E. B. Du Bois was aware that for the

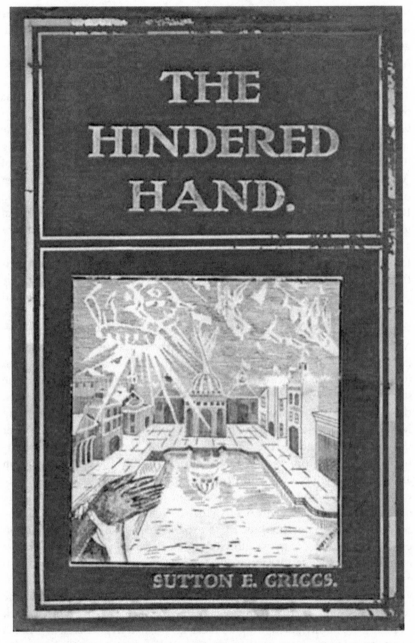

Figure 2.2 Book cover of *The Hindered Hand* by Sutton E. Griggs. Charles L. Blockson Afro-American Collection, Temple University Libraries. Sutton Griggs website.

majority of African Americans, the region was home, however untenable white supremacy sought to make it. For those not of the region, it was ground zero vivifying the fight for racial equality. In his first novel, the Massachusetts-born Du Bois pictured a South of romance, mysticism, and exoticism, and hardship.

The Quest of the Silver Fleece (1911) takes place in a small rural Alabama town, within the heart of the Black Belt. Blessed "Bles" Alwyn, a fifteen-year-old from Georgia runs through the woods where he encounters the sprite-like Zora described as a "warm, ... velvet bronze" (15), dancing in the woods. The exoticism of Zora is paired with atavistic images of Africanist roots. Zora's mother, Elspeth, is a conjure woman, the daughter of an African king. An almost magical bond develops between Zora and Blessed, representing Du Bois's vision of the twin strands of black racial identity. She is exotic, wild, connected to past traditions that give the race a unique quality; he is serious, civilized, the future of the race as it prepares for full membership in American society. In this romanticized vision, neither should be sacrificed for the other.

Bles enrolls in a Negro school headed by an aging white New England woman named Sarah Smith and convinces Zora to enroll as well. Zora struggles to fit in and struggles with the hypocritical attitude of her teacher Mary Taylor who mouths sympathetic race platitudes but believes in inherent black inferiority. To support her schooling, Zora and Bles devise a plan to grow cotton on a tract of land within the swamp where Zora lives. The school is on land owned by the white Cresswells whose wealth is based on the plantation system with cotton its cash crop. They despise everything Ms. Smith and the Negro school stand for because they believe it will alter the racial and economic hierarchy of the South, and because it is siphoning hands away from the field. The storyline takes Bles to Washington and through the political world of black society while Zora enters service to a Southern white lady who travels and provides her with knowledge of the larger world. Plot lines crisscross to give a detailed portrait of the South during Reconstruction. Bles's experiences evoke the manipulation of the black vote; Zora's the difficulty of blacks entering a racist capitalist economy. The Cresswells's interactions with the cotton exchange to sustain an empire sheds light on the simultaneous exploitation of black and poor white laborers. When Mary's baby is born worse than dead, i.e., black, the senior Cresswells's sexual licentiousness across the color line comes back to haunt the family and spotlights racial and sexual hypocrisies. Du Bois's central symbol is cotton, a commodity vital to constructing the wealth of the nineteenth-century United States. He employs it as a vehicle for examining economies of race, gender, sex, and class, and the centrality of blacks to cotton production and by extension to American economic wealth. At the end of the novel, Zora and Bles represent a reconstructed democracy. The society they create symbolizes black cooperative power as an alternative, more humanistic economic model to exploitative capitalism and foreshadows Du Bois's affiliation with Communism later in his life.[11]

The Quest of the Silver Fleece was followed by *Dark Princess, A Romance* (1928), its subtitle explicitly defining its genre, and the novel will be treated in greater detail later, as speculative fiction. It was issued by Harcourt Brace, which had previously published *Darkwater*, his collection of autobiography, essays, spirituals, and poems in 1920. While blacks are gaining increased access to traditional houses, a letter from Du Bois to Harcourt indicates the industry's treatment of black culture was not always informed. He complains of the portrait of his "princess" selected for the cover art. He reproaches the editors for not checking with him before its creation, for he would have reminded them that no white American artist can paint a black person without devolving into caricature. The "magnificent" bronze bust of a "full-blooded Negro" sitting on his desk was done by a French artist, he adds. He sends images of black women as examples (even though his princess is not black) in the hopes that the artist will see that "negro" and ugly are not synonymous.[12] As it turned out, the cover would be the least of Du Bois's problems.

In "The Negro as Writer," an essay for *The Bookman*, John Chamberlain wrote that the novel "bogs the reader before he gets well into it. Characterization eludes Du Bois, probably because he is more interested in the future of the Negro races as a whole than in the Negro as novelist" (607). Similar sentiments were expressed by a reviewer in the *Springfield Republican*: "The truth is, of course, that Du Bois is not a novelist at all, and that the book judged as a novel has only the slightest merit. As a document, as a program, as an exhortation, it has its interest and value" (May 28, 1928). The same criticism could be leveled in the late 1950s when W. E. B. Du Bois's career as a novelist enjoyed a resurgence with *The Black Flame* trilogy: *The Ordeal of Mansart* (1957), *Mansart Builds a School* (1959), and *Worlds of Color* (1961). Feeling more like essays than novels, the trilogy covered multiple epochs and geographies of black history, tracing the Mansart family from the end of the Civil War to the end of World War II, and locating their stories in the American South, North, Africa, and Europe. The trilogy brings all of Du Bois's knowledge of economics, education, religion, sociology, and philosophy to bear in answering the question why white supremacy? Unlike the hopeful author of *Quest*, the Du

Bois of these novels is preparing to renounce his American citizenship and settle in Ghana. He is removed from the moderate politics he championed with the National Association for the Advancement of Colored People (NAACP) and is increasingly questioning the evils of American capitalism and imperialism.

The reviews of *Dark Princess* indicate the increasing scrutiny placed on the art of black novels. Du Bois's reputation garnered widespread critical attention for *Quest* as well as *Dark Princess*, and intensified discussion as to whether black novels were literature or protest. A novel that seemed apart from these debates was James Weldon Johnson's *The Autobiography of an Ex-Coloured Man* (1912). *Autobiography* first appeared as an anonymous edition published by the small firm Sherman, French, and Company. Perhaps encouraged by the title, reviewers in the *New York Times Review of Books* and *Booklist* thought the work nonfiction.[13] If the work was seen as autobiography, the thorny narrative of a black man successfully passing into white society, marrying and having children with a white woman, might have contributed to its muted reception in 1912. By the time Alfred Knopf adopted the work in 1927, however, the reading climate craved voyeuristic forays in to black life, and a well-connected Johnson acknowledged the work amid brisk sales. In "Resurgence of the Negro in Literature," an editorial written for the *New York Age* (April 22, 1922), he notes, "The last twelve months have seen the great publishing houses of New York turn out a half dozen important books by or about the Negroes. This marks a great change when we consider that only a few years ago none of the leading publishers in New York were in the least interested in anything touching upon the Negro. Publishers of books have changed because they have sensed and realized the fact that there is a reading and purchasing public for the kind of book about the Negro now being published" (*Selected Writings* 277). If Johnson had listened to his brother Rosamond, *Autobiography* might be called "The Chameleon." The character's passing gives Johnson latitude to question the social construction of race and the devaluing of blackness.

The novel opens with an unnamed narrator describing his childhood domestic happiness. He lives comfortably, terms himself a "perfect little aristocrat" (7), and criticizes the "niggers" who hit a student with a slate (15). Race soon encroaches on this happiness when he is identified by a schoolteacher as black, upending every conception of himself. He looks at his mother, a woman he thought the most beautiful in the world, and searches for defects once the term "Negro" is applied to the two of them. The work is a bildungsroman describing the narrator's learning to be black, and the book that proves most instructive to him is *Uncle Tom's Cabin*, an allusion nodding to the power exerted by Stowe's imagining of black types, as well as illustrating the absence of black-generated models in American culture. Later, inspired by a speech given by his very-black friend Shiny, the narrator decides to become a "race man," and bring glory to his people. He heads south to enroll in Atlanta University, and when a mishap leaves him penniless he changes his plans of receiving a formal education and instead receives an education that serves as an "entrance into the race" (74). Johnson imbeds an ethnographic travel narrative within his novel. Details of classes of black people – the "desperate," the "servants," the "independent workmen and tradesmen," and the "well-to-do and educated" – as well as their attitudes and relations to whites portray black stratification. Various plot devices explicate one of the work's major themes, the blackness of Americanness.

In Europe, attending the opera *Faust*, the narrator realizes he sits next to his other "family," his white father and half-sister, and this recognition is part of the impetus for his returning South and "resurrecting" black culture to make it classic. The act is cast as a double desire for personal and racial legitimacy. By making black music classical, the forms will achieve "elevation" above the ghettoized areas of St. Louis where they derive, and narrator will achieve recognition that offsets his denied birthright. Johnson distinguishes between high and low culture, indicating his unease with the complete embrace of the very vernacular elements the narrator celebrates.[14] The narrator's determination signifies Johnson's sense of the untapped potential of black material as sources for black artistry, but also signals his sense that these sources need finessing. Nonetheless, what nineteenth-century novels had only hinted at through minimal inclusions of conjure and dialect, Johnson's novel more fully embraces through its form. Among the material it recreates is an archetypal call and response between a black minister and congregation. The narrator attends a local church and describes the "heavenly march," reproducing in literature the drama, rhythms, and back and forth as the minister paints for his congregation a vision of the world yet to come. This passage is followed by one capturing hymn lining, a practice adopted by blacks in the Americas particularly in areas of enforced anti-literacy laws. In spotlighting these elements Johnson foreshadows the growing vernacular usage in novels of the next decade.

The narrator's plan to imbibe inspiration in the heart of the South turns tragic, and in keeping with other post-Reconstruction novels, the dangers of random violence are detailed. He witnesses a lynching, and it humiliates him to be a member of a race that could be treated this way. It further jars him to see human beings – white men, women, and children – being transformed into beasts salivating at the chance to destroy a black life. It is at this point he decides to take advantage of the safety and access whiteness provides.

Ten years after the publication of Johnson's novel, Zara Wright's passing characters faced the same decision. Born in Cincinnati, Wright lived and worked in Chicago. Her two novels, *Black and White and Tangled Threads* (1920) and *Kenneth* (1920) bridged the turn-of-the-century treatments of race and the modern ones that emerge in the 1920s and beyond. Wright received praise in *The Chicago Defender*, but little notice elsewhere, suggesting that her reach was more regional. The passing plots of the novels have unconventional touches. Zoleta Andrews, the heroine of *Black and White*, is the daughter of Harold Andrews and Mildred Yates, the son of a slaveholder and daughter of a slave, respectively. They have left the plantation, to move to England to marry. Subsequently they travel to India, where both die when Zoleta is a child. She is adopted by her white Uncle Paul, and brought back to the plantation to be raised as a member of the former slaveholder's family but suffers at the hands of a resentful aunt and cousin. She marries an English nobleman aware of her heritage, but cannot enjoy the life of the landed gentry while her people suffer. She returns south, passes as white and uses her social position to agitate for equality for the newly freed blacks. The story of her cousin Katherine forms the sequel novel, *Kenneth*, named after Katherine's son by a painter, Guy Randolph who she only later discovers is black. She abandons both husband and son and returns to the United States. Kenneth becomes a prominent lawyer in Louisville, and colorism and sexual politics are considered when his life is paralleled to the difficulties faced by his friend, the dark-skinned Philip Grayson. Wright employs the theme of passing to reveal the artificiality of race, but her treatment of passing, similar to Johnson's, underscores the cultural loss caused by the decision to abandon one's roots.

The importance of roots will occupy novels of the 1920s onward as they tease out whether there really are practices and philosophies that made a unique black culture. While their answers to this question are as varied as their authors, what does emerge is a widening distinction between race and culture. At the end of *Autobiography of an Ex-Coloured Man*, the narrator wonders what he has lost in bartering culture for social ease. Because Johnson so adroitly delineates the richness of black cultural life, the narrator's disavowal is poignant. The narrator has fled blackness as race, a "dwarfing, warping, distorting influence," but he loses blackness as "culture," an "originality and artistic conception, and, what is more, the power of creating that which can influence and appeal universally" (87). Interestingly, by the time the twentieth century comes to an end, the commodification and marketing of black cultural content allows many outside of the race to enjoy identifications the narrator abandons.

George Hutchinson articulates the important link between publishing and cultural awareness when he notes, "Institutions grow up to nourish, transform, exploit, control, and disseminate literary forms. The most important of these institutions in the early twentieth century – when universities had not yet come to dominate our literary culture – were magazines and publishers" (125). Whether through the major publishing houses, independent black publishers, or through serialization in black periodicals, the publishing process contributed to an increased awareness of black self-expression. Entrance into publishing afforded a venue for black novelists to re-appropriate black experience from white writers who frequently skewed it to their own ends. The ability to fictionalize black life provided a new imaginative landscape and yielded new literary content.

By 1930, John Chamberlain could write a retrospective of black writing beginning with Charles Chesnutt and moving on to writers of the 1920s such as Eric Waldron and Claude McKay. A black canon was forming. As its writers shared the publishers who had brought out Hawthorne, Thoreau, Emerson, and Longfellow, inroads into the larger American canon were made. Receiving the same gilt embossing and cover illustrations, little by little acknowledged the cultural worth of their products, and as their books were accepted, the hope grew that their race would be as well. Expansion into modern publishing was fitting for novels portraying the move from post-slavery plantation life to black modernity.

CHAPTER 3

Aesthetics of Race and Culture: African American Novels, 1920s–1940s

"The time has not yet come for the great development of American Negro Literature," wrote W. E. B. Du Bois in 1913. "The economic stress is too great and the racial persecution too bitter to allow the leisure and the poise for which literature calls" ("Negro in Literature" 301–302). By all accounts the time did come by the 1920s and 1930s, and many of the authors who would become staples of the African American canon emerged at this time. Most literary histories credit migration as one major factor in this literary efflorescence as African Americans from the southern United States settled in northern centers – Chicago, Detroit, St. Louis, and New York – to improve their prospects through an expanding work force during the World War I effort. Migrants from the Caribbean and Africa also made homes in the United States. National and transatlantic migrations – whether by agricultural laborers moving to cities, black soldiers in the theatre of war, or by writers and artists – widened interrogations of what constituted blackness. Autobiographies, essays, novels, criticism, and letters captured the ideas of an era that would encompass the New Negro Renaissance.[1] All shared a querying as to whether there were practices that identified black expression, or whether black art was merely "lamp-blacked" American art to paraphrase George Schuyler ("Hokum" 1222). Novels employed themes and aesthetics to hypothesize the distinction between race and culture, where the former describes a commonality formed in contestation and the latter the commonality of indigenous experience.

Manning Marable makes a distinction between race and blackness:

> Race is essentially a group identity imposed upon individuals by others ... Blackness, or African-American identity, is much more than race. It is also the traditions, rituals, values, and belief systems of African American people. It is our culture, history, music, art, and literature. Blackness is our sense of ethnic consciousness and pride in our heritage of resistance against racism ... It is a cultural and ethnic awareness we have collectively

constructed for ourselves over hundred of years. This identity is a cultural umbilical cord connecting us with Africa. (295–296)

Marable's distinction is useful, but to imply a hard separation between culture and race, particularly in the United States, constructs an artificial divide; however, considering the valences between the two assists in discovering the ways many African American novelists of the 1920s to 1940s sought to portray black identity as shaped by something other than contestation with whiteness.

Many creators of the time pondered what makes blackness black. In reflecting on his own *The Souls of Black Folk*, Du Bois describes the style of black writing as "tropical – African" and adds, "This needs no apology. The blood of my fathers spoke through me and cast off the English restraint of my training and surroundings" (Aptheker 9). The romanticism and exoticism found in *Quest of the Silver Fleece* and *Dark Princess* certainly evidence this philosophy. Muralist and illustrator Aaron Douglas specifies the cultural essence that separates black from white in a 1925 handwritten undated manifesto on the journal *Fire!!* letterhead when he describes its contributors, at the time Langston Hughes, Zora Neale Hurston, Gwendolyn Bennett, Bruce Nugent, Wallace Thurman, and John Davis:

> We are group conscious . . .
>
> We believe that the Negro is fundamentally, essentially different from their Nordic neighbors.
>
> We are proud of that difference.
>
> We believe these differences to be greater spiritual endowment, greater sensitivity,
>
> greater power for artistic expression and appreciation. (ADP 1, 9)

Even a writer whose works for the most part portrayed this difference in terms of contestation felt the power of culture. Richard Wright notes that there is a distinct "culture of the Negro which is his and has been addressed to him; a culture which has, for good or ill, helped to clarify his consciousness and create emotional attitudes which are conducive to action. This culture has stemmed mainly from two sources: 1) the Negro church; 2) and the folklore of the Negro people" ("Blueprint" 269–270). What Du Bois and Douglas in an essentialist fashion seek to tie to blood, and what Wright ties to institutions and orality, Toni Morrison will later tie to something more evanescent. In describing her desire to "develop a way of writing that was irrevocably black," that produces a literature that is black, not because of its author's race or its content, but because of "something intrinsic, indigenous, something in the way it was put together – the sentences, the structure, texture and tone" (Gilroy, *Small Acts* 181), she envisions a strategy of writing that might be said to stem from a cultural tradition as much as a racial one. The desire for this indigenous way of being and writing or its rejection shapes novels of the 1920s through 1940s. Some use dialect, jazz, blues, folklore, and the folk in their composition to accomplish it; others use satire to debunk the idea that it exists.

One of the earliest works to attempt a portrait of distinct blackness might not belong in this study. Custom more so than aesthetics have defined Jean Toomer's *Cane* (1923) as a novel. The work does not conform to the sustained narrative generally associated with novelistic structure. Just as its creator actively resisted racial classification, stating that he is of no race but the human, of no class but the human (*Essentials* 24), so too does his work defy generic classification through combining communal narrative, poetry, prose, drama, work songs, and spirituals. Toomer submitted some of the pieces independently to *Dial, Little Review, The Crisis,* and *Secession,* before they appeared collectively as *Cane,* suggesting that he did not consider it a novelistic whole. That said, *Cane* beautifully represents one writer's perception of distinctly African-derived culture.

Cane's circular composition, indicated by the drawn linear arcs separating its sections, reconstructs the black migratory pattern, from rural South to urban North, and in some cases back to rural South. Inspired by his sojourn in Sparta, Georgia, it is an elegy creating a call and response between black past and present, lamenting a "sun [. . .] setting/on a song-lit race of slaves" (12)." In a letter to Waldo Frank, Toomer notes that it is in Georgia that he first saw "the Negro, not as a pseudo-urbanized and vulgarized, a semi-Americanized product, but the Negro peasant, strong with the tang of fields and soil." For Toomer, Southern blackness was uncorrupted: "It was there that I first heard the folk-songs rolling up the valley at twilight, heard them as spontaneous and native utterances" (*Letters* 36). Authentic black culture is grounded in rural folk elements because these are closest to their primitive antecedents. The poem "Conversion," for example, expresses atavistic loss when recalling "African Guardian of Souls/ Drunk with rum,/ [. . .] Yielding to new words and a weak palabra/Of a white-faced sardonic god–." Black culture is warped the further it moves from rural manifestations. The poems "Song of the Sun" and "Georgia Dusk" are redolent with an acknowledgment of the beauty of rural black life, while the urban landscape of "Seventh Street" offers stark contrast to a lost rural beauty. "Kabnis" combines prose and dramatic form to convey the consequences of cultural memory and loss. Black culture came from pain and defeat in Toomer's estimation. He writes of West Virginia, "Life here has not the vividness and distinction of that of middle Georgia. Racial attitudes, on both sides, are ever so much more tolerant, even friendly. Oppression and ugly emotions seem nowhere in evidence. And there are no folk-songs. A more stringent grip, I guess, is necessary to force them through (*Letters* 43).

For all his moving portrayals of rural black Southern culture, *Cane* is written in the voice of an outsider, an observer who sees only the bittersweet shortfalls of blackness. Du Bois in his review of the work notes, "Toomer does not impress me as one who knows his Georgia but he does know human beings; and, from the background which he has seen slightly and heard of all his life through the lips of others, he paints things that are true, not with Dutch exactness, but rather with an impressionist's sweep of color" (Aptheker 69). *Cane*'s impressionism is its innovation. It crosses genres and imbues written tradition with orality to create a portrait of race and region. This portrait was not of a living culture, but one Toomer saw as being of the past. Writing to Waldo Frank he observes, "Don't let us fool ourselves, brother: the Negro of the folk-song has all but passed away: the Negro of the emotional church is fading. A hundred years from now these Negroes, if they exist at all will live in art" (*Letters* 115). That Toomer seems unaware of the fact that such culture is still vibrant and alive indicates the distance between him and his subject, but it is this distance that informs the nostalgia giving *Cane* its unique tone.

Though he attempted to live life as an American with no racial label or identification, Toomer acknowledged that the United States made this impossible. Critics have noted that he abandoned his black identity in favor of an unattainable racelessness and that his work suffered for it. He never wrote anything that approximated the art of *Cane*.[2] Earlier in life, Toomer acknowledged the connection between his black antecedents and creative inspiration when he wrote, "my growing need for artistic expression has pulled me deeper and deeper into the Negro group. And as my powers of receptivity increased, I found myself loving it in a way that I could never love the other. It has stimulated and fertilized whatever creative talent I may contain within me" (*Letters* 70). Though he chafed at the limiting confines of race, he left an inspired cultural representation.

Like Toomer, Waters Turpin and George Wylie Henderson found in Southern culture a reservoir of literary material. Turpin's works are epic in scope, following multiple generations. Reading them today, it is hard to account for his popularity at the time he wrote, with the exception of their glimpses of realistic regional detail. In *These Low Grounds* (1937), the saga of the enslaved Martha and her offspring, Turpin's dialect is clichéd, as are the descriptive images. Of his main character Martha's smile, he writes, "her teeth a white streak in the brown of her face" (4); when she discovers her husband Joe's gambling den, she stands "poised on the threshold, like an angry brown goddess about to scatter destruction on her sinful subjects" (24); in comparing two women, "Gladys was like froth one sipped from sodas. Ellen was more like the potatoes one ate with steak – substantial and a source of nourishment" (317). The plot of the novel piles incident on top of incident, and leaves the reader wondering at their purpose. He includes snatches of the blues as a refrain throughout the work, to simulate a rural environment, but they do not help the rambling novel to cohere. Turpin's second novel *O Canaan!* (1939) has some vivid descriptions of the life along the Maryland shore to its credit, but it struggles to develop its characters in multidimensional ways. Joe Benson is driven north to Chicago by boll weevils and lynching. He is married to Christine Lawson, an octoroon whose family felt she has debased herself by marrying a field "nigger." Initially Joe thrives as a shopkeeper and becomes a leader of his people until his involvement with bootlegging. *O Canaan* attempts an interior perspective fleshing out the Great Black Migration, but the novel's superficiality works against its aims.[3]

George Wylie Henderson, however, anticipates the detailed southern portraits of Zora Neale Hurston. Born in Alabama, he worked in printing before writing fiction upon his graduation from Tuskegee Institute. He was part of the Great Migration, as he and his wife relocated to Harlem in the 1920s, and his works bridge the rural and urban worlds of black America. He enjoyed a large following for his periodical fiction, and contributed to *Redbook* magazine and the *New York Daily News*. *Ollie Miss* (1935), his first novel, opens along a swamp's edge at dusk in Little Texas, Alabama. The central character Ollie is an enigma, slim with smooth dark skin; "simple" inside, governed mostly by her impulses (13), and neither the women nor the men of her community understand her living by her own desires. She is an independent woman foreshadowing Hurston's Janie Crawford. No one knows her origins, but she has settled and now lives with Alex, Caroline, and a constellation of characters that portray the necessity for community in rural farm life. In love with Jule, a hand on a neighboring plantation, Ollie finds herself in a triangle. The subsequent series of events leaves her stabbed and pregnant, and determined to change the course of her life.

White characters in *Ollie Miss* are tangential, and when they do appear they are part of a community of Southerners both good and bad. Racism is present and condemned in the novel, but it is not a central concern. It is used more to delineate individual morality than larger social themes. When Henderson describes ordinariness of field hands who go bed late and get up early, who were people who breathed and had longings and poetry locked inside their souls (105), his ability to evoke the feel and culture of a region is evident. Descriptions of plowing, picking cotton, and growing corn add to the depth of his setting, as does vivid description of a camp meeting where he recasts the call and response between hymn liner and listeners (166). Through alternating between standard narrative and realistically rendered dialect, the novel's language is redolent with the cadences and rhythms of speech. *Jule* (1946) is the sequel to *Ollie Miss*. It provides more characters' backstories for its prequel while telling of Little Jule, Ollie's son, a precocious boy who can read and write. Southern racism and the fear of retaliation when he bests a young white man in a fight force him north, which, because of other migrated southern blacks feels very familiar to him. Less familiar, because it is less explicit, is the northern racism that will constrict him until he learns how to navigate it. It might be said that what separated the lesser-known Henderson from the well-known Hurston was Alice Walker. Sadly, Henderson had no famous author to rescue his good works from obscurity. His portrayals of the south, however, are as deft as any, and it might be argued that his vision of women's agency is even more progressive.

Hurston's ability to imbricate orality into written form transformed her most famous novel *Their Eyes Were Watching God* (1937) from a relatively typical Cinderella tale of a woman seeking her Prince Charming to an argument for the validity of black vernacular culture as a medium for novelistic form. While many feminists embraced *Their Eyes* as the story of a woman coming into her own, Hurston herself saw it as a story of a woman trapped by her beauty, not necessarily her gender (Kaplan 367). Throughout much of the novel, Janie is a somewhat passive character. She resents but accepts her grandmother's marrying her to Logan Killicks, and it is the arrival of Jody Starks promising a new life that lights the fire under her to leave Logan. She resents Jody, and tells him as much, but it is only the arrival of Tea Cake that sets her on the greatest adventure of her life. Hurston frames Tea Cake's beating Janie and the marks it leaves as tokens of his love. These elements complicate a feminist reading of the text, and are by no means new in fiction. What is new is the language and metaphors of orality that convey them. All Hurston's characters affirm their worth through the power of spoken word. Speech allows them to transform themselves from "tongueless, earless, eyeless conveniences" to "lords of sound and lesser things" (9–10). Listeners can feel a switch in Jody's hand when he talks to them (78); Janie's grandmother's greatest dream is to "preach a great sermon about colored women sittin' on high" (31–32). Language is power, a theme Hurston will repeat in *Seraph on the Suwanee* (1948), with the white character Arvay Meserve who must overcome insecurity and reticence to find her voice and save her marriage. White characters in *Seraph* emphasize that culture binds a group as much as race does. A multicultural set of characters share, with little racial tension, the traditions, values, and practices of a region. *Seraph* moves beyond phenotypic definitions of a people and considers the relationship of shared ritual and memory.

The power of language as medium and metaphor is evident throughout all Hurston's novels. Her first, the semi-autobiographical *Jonah's Gourd Vine* (1934) introduces the space which would symbolize the free-flowing power of orality, Joe Clarke's store. Within that symbolic space the primacy of standard English is called into question. *Moses Man of the Mountain* (1939) uses vernacular voice to retell the biblical legend of the Exodus. Southern African American cadences create a subtext, allowing the story of Moses to reverberate with the history of black life during and after slavery. Through this voice, *Moses* is able to give a palpable rendering of the psychological impact of enslavement and the complexities of freedom for a formerly enslaved people. It acts as a counternarrative to the literature of abolition that looked at slavery but not the lives of the enslaved, and it fills the silences left by black narratives that could not elaborate upon individual concerns within abolitionist works designed to advocate for slavery's end. *Moses* anticipates the form of the neo-slave narrative by giving imagined voice to those who could not tell their own story. With call and response, sermons, "lies," pitch-perfect reproduction of regional dialects, and the liberal use of free indirect discourse, Hurston produced a narrative voice, proving the vernacular could create a Great American Novel. Her aesthetics are formed from intrinsic cultural elements that go a long way to signifying the qualities Du Bois, Douglas, and Morrison seek.

Hurston was a complex and, for some of her contemporaries, problematic figure. Carl Van Vechten described her as "picturesque, witty, electric, indiscreet, and unreliable" (Kellner 148). She is author as trickster figure, acutely aware of language and performance. Her writing was criticized for not being in keeping with New Negro Renaissance ideals. Alain Locke, who admired her artistry with folklore and dialect, craved deeper psychological portraits in her fiction; yet, when she offered these insights in nonfiction, he felt that she gave away too many internal racial secrets. On June 2, 1928, Locke wrote to Hurston "I read your <u>How It Feels to Be Colored Me</u> with great pride and interest until I realized that maybe you had opened up too soon. I had that feeling because I had myself several times made the same mistake. The only hope is in the absolute blindness of the Caucasian mind. To the things that are really revolutionary in Negro thought and feeling they are blind" (ALP 164-38, 28). Locke and others felt the gaze of a white audience more keenly than Hurston. Sterling Brown thought her vision too narrow to be potent. By setting *Their Eyes* an all-black town he felt she missed the opportunity to give insights into the impact of race and caste. Ellison criticized her "calculated burlesque" as the trait that prevented her fiction from rising to greater ideals, and he lumped her into the category of earlier writers among them Countee Cullen, Rudolph Fisher, Wallace Thurman, and Jessie Fauset, as writers who seemed unaware of the "experimentation" in American letters inspired by James Joyce, Gertrude Stein, Sherwood Anderson, and Ernest Hemingway.[4] Ellison's idea of technical experimentation was African American-infused modernism, but because Hurston used the vernacular and the rural South as the building blocks to her version of this aesthetic, he disregarded it; nonetheless her fearless employment of folk forms broke new ground because she used them not as quaint local color elements, or as elegy, but to express black life via the creations of black culture.

Toomer, Henderson, and Hurston found what they felt to be the culture of blackness in the southern United States. Jamaican Claude McKay discovered it in a broader, more diasporic geography. After completing *Home to Harlem* (1928), which will be discussed in a later chapter, McKay was living what he called the life of an ascetic in Antibes. In 1927 he went to Marseilles, France, and there encountered "a great gang of black and brown humanity" (*Long Way* 277). Mingling with shopkeepers, bar owners, and even dance great Isadora Duncan stirred him to create a book capturing the kaleidoscopic life there. The resulting novel, *Banjo* (1929), vivifies the global nature of black culture.

Set in Marseilles, *Banjo* embodies transnational blackness, and from this vantage point offers McKay's views on what constitutes essential blackness through the character Ray (who also appears in *Home to Harlem*). Ray frequently contrasts what he sees as the different behaviors and standards of African versus European-derived civilizations, and bemoans the inhumanity of those he terms Anglo-Saxon. The eponymous protagonist personifies the African traits Ray describes abstractly. Banjo is named after his instrument (one adapted from African instruments by blacks in the Americas), and plays with a skill that frequently garners him a monetary reward to which he is indifferent. When another character, Goosey, accuses him of minstrelsy because he will not leave the old accoutrements of slavery behind, Banjo refuses to have himself or his instrument valued by the self-hate that is the genesis of Gosey's statement. Banjo lives by his senses, moving amid a broad cross-section of "Senegalese, Sudanese, Somalese, Nigerians, West Indians, Americans, blacks from everywhere, crowded together, talking strange dialects" (36). His voice, presence, and "Aframericanisms" even find favor with immigration officials. He identifies many of the cultural commonalities among these peoples, for example defining the beguin as "a Martinique variant of the 'jelly roll' or the Jamaican 'burru' or the Senegalese 'bombe'" (89). As the novel's subtitle *A Story Without a Plot* suggests the book is more concerned with evocation than telling.

McKay's use of vernacular elements to typify black culture did not suit all readers. In reviewing *Home to Harlem*, W. E. B. Du Bois wrote, "[I]t looks as though ... McKay has set out to cater for that prurient demand on the part of white folk.... He has used every art and emphasis to paint drunkenness, fighting, lascivious sexual promiscuity and utter absence of restraint in as bold and as bright colors as he can" (785). But Charlotte Mason, patron to McKay and Hughes as well as Hurston, loved what she called its primitiveness, a term that caused Langston Hughes to bristle.[5] In an undated letter to McKay, she wrote that his work was an antidote to the "deadening influence" of Van Vechten's *Nigger Heaven*. It justified her faith that "life and laughter is ready to burst into such brilliant sunshine ... and all the peoples of the world will be freed to recognize the powers of recreation. This is the thing heartfelt too in reading Langston Hughes poems" (ALP 164-99, 16). For Mason, the draw of the primitive lay in its redemptive power, particularly the power it might exercise over whites within an overly industrialized world. For McKay, however, his content was not meant as redemption, but as a means of capturing the essence of black culture. Writing in 1934, he thought that literature might produce "an esthetic interpretation of Negro life, exploiting the Negro's racial background and his racial gifts and accomplishments. We want to encourage Negroes to create artistically as an ethnological group irrespective of class and creed" (Gates and Jarrett 251). The forms McKay thought uniquely black were often the products of those lower on the socioeconomic ladder. Because he included so much of this content in his novels, Langston Hughes in a March 1 letter to Alain Locke rightly predicted that *Home to Harlem* would cause consternation among more conservative segments of black society: "Just finished Claude's *Home to Harlem* and am wild about. It ought to be named *Nigger Hell*, but I guess the colored papers will have even greater spasms than before anyhow. It's the best low-life novel I've ever read ... Up till now, it strikes me, that *Home to Harlem* must be the flower of the Negro Renaissance, – even if it is no lovely lily" (ALP 164-38, 4). This assessment indicates McKay's success in creating an "ethnological" aesthetic, a quality that also manifests in McKay's second novel.

Set in turn-of-the-century Jamaica, *Banana Bottom* (1933) is a postcolonial novel considering the aftermath of race and an imperialist system. The heroine, Bita Plant, is informally adopted by the Craigs, white missionaries who send her to England for education. When she returns to Jamaica, she is an oddity to her people and an experiment to the Craigs. Bita finds herself trying to reconcile a yearning to be part of her home while living up to the Criags's expectations, including marrying the partner they have selected. Bita's position between two worlds contrasts cultural forms and lauds folk forms devalued under colonialism. Through scenes of cultural homecoming, the novel offers an alternative way of representing the world, one that stems from black practices and worldviews.[6]

The literary historian Benjamin Brawley found fault with the influence of vernacular elements on the African American novel. In his mind, not only did they present the sordid, they also allowed authors to abandon the very foundations of grammar and to develop an inherent laziness in the name of art (Gates and Jarrett 233–234). Writers who shared similar unease with employing black vernacular relied on traditional literary forms but still infused these with histories and perspectives they felt particular to black life.

Jessie Fauset resisted the use of folk elements in favor of bending traditional novel forms to critique the perversion of normalcy by societal racism, classism, and colorism. *There is Confusion* (1924) employs the novel of manners as the Marshall, Bye, and Ellersley families come to terms with individual values while navigating race, class mobility, and personal aspirations. *Plum Bun* (1929) uses conventions of the bildungsroman as Angela Murray crosses the color line to become artist Angele Mory but then must reconcile social gains with personal loss. In *Comedy American Style* (1933), the elements of traditional comedy – the presence of lovers, the restoration of an outsider figure to the social structure, and a character with ludicrous shortcomings – are given tragic dimensions by a mother's desire to eradicate all evidence of her black heritage. *The Chinaberry Tree* (1931) upends the conventions of domestic fiction when the home of Sara Strange and her daughter Laurentine is menaced by Sarah's previous existence as the beloved slave mistress of the town's most prominent slaveholder and Laurentine being his daughter. Fauset balances the tensions within her novels with the prosaic lives of her characters to give an interior vision of African American life not always obsessed with oppression.

Fauset's aesthetics left her open to charges of being derivative. Claude McKay viewed her as prim (D. Lewis 124); Addison Gayle later called her style accommodationist (*Reader* 160). Fauset was far from being an accomodationist, however. In a scathing letter to Alain Locke, she reveals the distance she places between herself and others she felt were white appeasers. Accusing Locke of being in the "whatever is white is right" camp, her letter concludes, "your malice, your lack of true discrimination and above all your tendency to play safe with the grand white folks renders you anything but a reliable critic" (ALP 164-28, 41).[7] In his autobiography *The Big Sea* (1940), a work whose descriptions of Harlem party life did much to cement poplar notions of the Harlem Renaissance, Langston Hughes might be said to characterize Fauset's black aesthetic when he describes her salons as containing much poetry, little drink, and few whites to avoid voyeurism, and serious conversation, perhaps in French (189, 191). Her novels are very much like her salons, not voyeuristic, not embodying the folk, but concerned with creating a multicultural black space for the serious exchange of ideas.

The novels of Nella Larsen examine a consciousness of kind as stemming from a psychological space of liminality between places and cultures. In *Quicksand* (1928), Helga Crane, a child of mixed parentage, is a modernist heroine of the post–World War I lost generation, seeking yet unsure of what she seeks. An educated schoolteacher, she is rejected by her white family and feels like an outsider in her own race. Sexual and intellectual stagnation lead her to commence a self-destructive odyssey. She gains employment in the service of a race woman, but the inspiration she initially experiences is fleeting. Her odyssey from south to north, the United States, to Europe refigures African American journeys in search of self-created meanings. Larsen questions the relevance of content that heretofore typified the characteristics of a race to black modernity. The idea of uplift so much a presence in black discourse is undermined as Helga comes to feel she is not educating students, but creating unquestioning cogs to fit within a white system of dominance. Race work leads her to realize the malevolence of black prejudice and the intractability of class prejudice. The fascination with black atavisms quickly devolves into a fascination with primitivism, leading not to Helga's to racial pride but to her being exoticized as an object by her Danish relatives, shamed by public performances of juba dancing while in Denmark, and searching for "Ties that were of the spirit ... not only superficially entangled with mere outline of features or color of skin" (213–214) upon her return to the United States. In the end being a wife and mother of three children born within twenty months of one another and fourth on the way leaves no time for seeking beauty, culture, or uplift.

Larsen's second novel *Passing* (1929) registers liminality through the spectrum of gender and race. Her two contrasting characters, Clare Kendry and Irene Redfield, again exist between spaces, Clare passing as white and not conforming to the strict definitions of appropriate woman-hood and Irene living between certainty and delusion concerning her role as wife and mother. Clare's decision to pass has made her, to borrow Toni Morrison's phrase, "dangerously free" (*Bluest Eye* 159), to break not only rules of racial confinement, but also rules of friendship and marital fidelity. Themes of alienation and rootlessness, along with the questioning of received values, emerge as Larsen portrays modern blackness as a series of negotiations.

For another set of writers, what made a group beyond a shared physical appearance was its shared history. The novels of Walter White show a collective identity forming amid the struggle to survive white violence. *The Fire in the Flint* (1924) gives fictive form to the forty-one lynchings he witnessed passing as white while traveling as assistant field secretary for the NAACP. His second novel, *Flight* (1926), uses the history of Louisiana *gens de couleur libre* as a backdrop exploring passing and regret. There is little of the vernacular or folk in White's work; in fact, he felt that the mores of the middle and upper classes of blacks were as interesting as the lower and provided as much fictional material.

While White incorporated history, other writers reimagined it to diagram intraracial commonality. Arna Bontemps found himself making history as an African American writer forced to burn books. Living in Huntsville, Alabama, during the era of Scottsboro Boys trial, he taught at the Seventh Day Adventist junior college, Oakwood School. His friendship with Langston Hughes and his association with people who came to Alabama to write about and support the defendants caused his ouster for subversion. The school demanded he burn his books on African American life and culture. The incident was one of the motivating factors behind his move to Chicago's South side with his wife and two children. Bontemps began his novel writing career using folk culture to evoke black commonality. Plot and characterization in *God Sends Sunday* (1931) are undergirded by beliefs such as a baby being born with a caul on its face is destined to be lucky. The baby in question is Little Augie, a shy, small boy who feels like an outsider until he grows up to become a successful jockey in

1890s Louisiana. Once he travels to New Orleans, he is transformed into a drinking, cigar-smoking man, full of braggadocio. Characters speaking in the language of their world, locales in St. Louis, the blues motif, and Bontemps's writing being as much poetry as prose fit is squarely within the tradition of *Jule*, *Their Eyes Were Watching God*, and *Home to Harlem*.[8] For his later novels, however, he relied more on history than vernacular to imagine shared culture.

   Black Thunder (1936) was a carefully researched historical fiction. The novel received good critical acclaim across racial lines, though its sales were weak. It begins with the mundane in Richmond, Virginia, a profile of various lives including traveling abolitionists, French printers, politicians, among them James Madison, plantation owners and their slaves, and from this builds to the drama of a slave revolt. The enslaved comprise a community that in 1800 still remembers Africa. When one is killed, the protagonist Gabriel plans an insurrection, but on the night it is to take place a heavy rain destroys the bridge that will take the slaves to Richmond to achieve their ends. The story is told from multiple perspectives. Each slave's response to revolt, even Gabriel's own internal vacillations, show multiple understandings of the ideas of freedom, enslavement, and community. Within their narratives, black philosophies of the world are contrasted. Gabriel's admiration of white technology, the typesetter in a printer's office, for instance, and of "rational" thought, are contrasted with those who believe in conjure and other folk practices. He dismisses the deluge as just weather, rather than see it as an omen, and at his trial concludes, "Maybe we should paid attention to the signs. Maybe we should done that" (214). Bontemps accentuates different forms of literacies from reading the omen of weather, to the freed slave Mingo's liberatory reading of the Bible. There are many forms of language and many passages of indirect discourse fusing multiple voices into a metalanguage able to give simultaneous interior and exterior viewpoints to acts of violence and notions of freedom. *Drums at Dusk* (1939) extends the work of *Black Thunder* to call attention to the diasporic nature of black history in the Haitian revolution.

   Bontemps's lasting friendships with Charles S. Johnson, Langston Hughes, Countee Cullen, Claude McKay, and Rudolph Fisher placed him at the center of the black literary world of the 1920s and 1930s. He was a lifelong friend and frequent collaborator with Langston Hughes. They coauthored the children's book *Popo and Fifina* (1932), and the two also collaborated on the critically acclaimed *The Book of Negro Folklore* (1958). It was Bontemps who suggested to "Lang" that Hughes's "Simple Minded Friend," be a character showing "the application of theoretical questions to his life" (Nichols 30). Not only would this influence the creation of Hughes's Jesse B. Semple, it would in many ways define the nature of Hughes's opus where large issues are rendered through small, personal details.

Perhaps no writer better extracts the qualities of black life that define a group beyond color than Langston Hughes. His *Not Without Laughter* (1930) is a tribute to African Americanness. From church to bordello, the novel integrates black culture within its textual voice. Descriptions of a dance hall filled with the strains of "Easy Rider," representations of "lies," the "dozens," and "sayings," create a distinctive bildungsroman based loosely on Hughes's own experiences in his hometown, Lawrence, Kansas. He blends vernacular creativity with history, through embedding major events – World War I, migration, discrimination – in character experiences and reflections. Larger philosophical discussions on passing and race appear not as treatises but as dialogues. Within the novel, African American identity is a complex of interior lives and creative expression, and not solely a racial principle. Hughes's focus is on blacks who did not transform anger at racial devaluation into murder, rape, obsequiousness or self-destruction, but rather on those characters who drew upon cultural roots and community to transcend devaluation. *Not Without Laughter* is as much title as mandate.

Hughes's "from the ground up" technique would shape all his novels. His second, *Tambourines to Glory*, published much later in 1958, evokes the cultural history of charismatic leaders such as Bishop Ida Bell Robinson who began their own houses of worship to satisfy needs not met by orthodox churches ministering to black Americans.[9] The protagonists Essie and Laura live on welfare in kitchenette apartments until Laura jokingly hits on the idea of their becoming street ministers. Their story brings to light the religious and spiritual elements cohering African American life, and satirizes the way these become corrupted. Essie's calling is self-serving; Laura's more spiritual. Religion and spirituality were areas where black cultural autonomy often could be maintained. From the earliest black presence in what would be the United States, descendants of Africans held on to their own rituals and transformed the ones they were given. The religious syncretism that Essie and Laura finally discover is rooted in the history of blacks cementing a community by creating traditions that spoke to their needs.

Hughes showcased the cultural life that developed from an imposed race classification. He created an aesthetics rooted in this culture and inspired many across the black diaspora including Cuban poet, essayist, and activist journalist, Nicolás Cristóbal Guillén Batista, and the Négritude poets and thinkers Senegalese Léopold Sédar Senghor and Martiniquais Aimé Césaire. For Hughes, blackness was not a limiting category, but rather an identity offering a vast array of aesthetic possibilities. Other writers were not as comfortable with this array. Hughes's "The Negro Artist and the Racial Mountain," famously references a poet, most likely Countee Cullen, who desires to be thought of as a poet and not a black poet. Their divergent views personify the valences of race and culture. In reviewing *The Weary Blues*, Cullen urged Hughes not to be a "racial artist" and suggested he omit jazz rhythms from his poems ("Poet on Poet" 73–74). The heritages of English and American poetry were those of a black poet writing in English, he asserts in the foreword to his anthology *Caroling Dusk* (1927), and throughout the foreword he argues for the insertion of black poets into American tradition as opposed to the creation of a separate category for them (*Caroling* xii). He eschews dialect, characterizing it as an archaic, artificial, limiting form incapable of creating great poetry. For Cullen, folk elements did nothing more than reinforce whites' disapprobation of blacks.

Cullen dedicated his only novel *One Way to Heaven* (1932) to Harold Jackman, with whom it is rumored he had a relationship. In the novel, the one-armed Sam Lucas arrives in Harlem from the south. He enters Mount Hebron African Methodist Episcopal Church and sees Reverend Clarence Johnson giving a classic performance as a black preacher. In the scene, the stylistically conservative Cullen illustrates his discontent with vernacular elements defining black culture. The passage is reminiscent of James Weldon Johnson's "Heavenly March" in *Autobiography of an Ex-Coloured Man* creating a back and forth between description and oration, but rather than a character celebrating the scene Sam sees only the opportunity to fleece a naïve congregation. Among them is Mattie Johnson who he later marries. Religion proves inadequate in meeting the spiritual needs of either. To Sam it is hollow, providing no psychic sustenance, only rules; for Mattie, it fails to achieve the full conversion she seeks to change her womanizing husband. The novel questions the centrality of religion to black communal self-definition, suggesting a revision in orthodoxy is needed to create a meaningful tradition.

The working-class world of Sam and Mattie is contrasted to the milieu of Constancia Brandon, described as an ivory-colored Harlem socialite who hosts notorious salons in her Strivers' Row home. The satirical portrait of Harlem's economic and intellectual elite exposes the ideas of a black "vogue" and a "renaissance" as factitious. Blacks of the talented tenth and white "slummers" discuss missionary work in Africa and spirituals; a white writer tells the black attendees he seeks to write a novel about "your people"; a black poet when asked what his poem means said "it means that niggers have a hell of a time in this God-damned country. That's all Negro poets write about" (162). The salons are exercises concerned with image rather than ideas and have little impact on the day-to-day lives of black laborers. Cullen's parody indicates a trend that will flower fully in the novels of Rudolph Fisher, George Schuyler, and Wallace Thurman. Sometimes comical, sometimes tragic, these works encourage reassessments of black cultural attitudes.[10]

The section headings of Rudolph Fisher's *The Walls of Jericho* (1928) – "Uplift," "Jive," "Walls," "Battle" – are signifiers indicating the way a group has integrated ideas into its self-conception. The novel comes with a glossary, "An Introduction to Contemporary Harlemese," offering definitions and etymologies to school the uninitiated into the histories that gave rise to black systems of signification. Both combine to suggest that Fisher acknowledged a distinctly black epistemology. "Jericho," introduces "The Rats," his term for the working class. Shine, Bubber, and Jinx are movers who take up much of the novel's opening joking about the riot that might break out because a black man has moved into a white neighborhood. He characterizes their joking about so serious an event as "a markedly racial tendency to make light of what actually was grave" (29), and posits the strategy of laughing to keep from crying as a philosophy, explaining how dark people cope with dark days. The "rats" are contrasted to the members of the Litter Rats' Club (a pun on the term niggeratti employed by Hurston, Hughes, and others to characterize the black intelligentsia too fully ensconced in the Dark Tower salon and distanced from life on the street). In a meeting to discuss "The Negro's Contribution to Art and the Lost Sciences of Ethiopia," members of the "Litter Rat's Club" are shocked at lawyer Ralph Merrit's intention to move into a white neighborhood come what may. Their responses represent the gamut of black attitudes toward race relations, from those who feel there must be gradual integration to those who question why the move must be racially significant at all. A rabid hater of whites, Merritt is fair enough to pass, and only his hair texture gives him away. The running joke that he should try "Stay-Straight for those kinks" (36–37) is one instance of cultural take back where the pain that comes from measuring oneself against white standards of beauty is transformed into humor without tragic consequences.

The "Uplift" section engages cross-racial interactions in a comic form through its description of the General Improvement Association (GIA)

ball. A subtle jab at the NAACP the GIA is characterized as an organization that collects a dollar each year, and when there is a lynching down
south sends someone to look at it to make sure it really happened (66).
Caricature of the organization's white partners recall criticism of the
NAACP's integrationist stance. Some white characters attend the gala
because they are determined to contribute to uplift; others because they
like the cachet of being invited guests of the GIA's executive board. One,
Miss Cramp, personifies the Miss Anne figure (a white woman who is
condescending, even if she is sympathetic). She believes in uplift for those
abroad – Poles, Turks, Russians – and only because she has recently hired
a black woman as her maid does it now occur to her that her mission
should have a domestic component. Still other whites present have varying
motives: some come for release, some for voyeurism, others to gather black
material and make a profit by selling it to the white world. The description
of the event reflects the diversity of black community. It is the one event in
Harlem where everyone comes together irrespective of class to contribute
to black advancement, but distinctions still persist. Tiers in the ballroom
show the stratification: lower classes are on the floor dancing; upper classes
in the boxes. Still, the novel affirms that while these groups are a race
by need, they are a culture in their response to music and socialization.
The Walls of Jericho is essentially a love story told amid a vibrant Harlem
that reveals cultural and class clashes as well as the tenuous ties of commonality that make a race.

Polymath George Samuel Schuyler exemplifies the argument that
searching for what makes a culture black is futile. A journalist, essayist, and
novelist, Schuyler was one of the foremost black satirists of the twentieth
century. His wit graced the pages of A. Philip Randolph's and Chandler
Owen's socialist newspaper *The Messenger* (from 1923 to 1928, Schuyler
was assistant and managing editor there), as well as H. L. Mencken's *The
American Mercury*. He joined the editorial staff of the *Pittsburgh Courier*,
an African American paper, and there many of his fictional works were
serialized. His best-known novel *Black No More: Being an Account of the
Strange and Wonderful Workings of Science in the Land of the Free A.D. 1933–
1940* (1931) pokes fun at the idea of distinct racial characteristics through
depicting the search for "chromatic perfection" (preface). As early as 1927,
Schuyler's interest in the color line as material for fiction was evident in
memobooks filled with copious summary notes he made on racial incidents such as a *New York Amsterdam News* piece describing a professor
Griffith Taylor who lectured that all races are mixed, even whites, and an
Arkansas senator's submission of an anti-intermarriage bill for the District

of Columbia in 1926 (Schuyler himself was part of an interracial marriage). He made notations on stories of the consequences of passing and on the request of 3,000 white Mississippi women for their legislature to pass more stringent laws against lynching (SFP 17, 8). *Black No More* uses these and other contradictory discourses to underscore the fallacies of racism.

The novel is dedicated to whites that are sure they have no black blood, an indication of Schuyler's contempt for ideas of racial purity. Its main characters Max Disher and Bunny Brown have weaknesses for white and "yellow women" (3) and enter the Honky Tonk club on New Year's Eve. Max falls for a white female, a slumming Southerner from Atlanta and asks her for a dance. When she responds that she doesn't dance with niggers, he resolves to try Dr. Junius Crookman's medical discovery that promises to turn blacks white in three days; infants in one. Crookman's process is so successful that the entire nation becomes alarmed as "real" whites cannot be told from "fake" ones. In the postscript, Crookman publishes an article stating that his process yields whites who are too white. A new system of discrimination begins, as those who are too white suffer inequity in wages, and people try to darken themselves.

Schuyler shies from incorporations of the folk or vernacular forms as cultural unifiers, and even goes so far to mock the blues as an expressive form by creating comic lyrics to the "The Black Man Blues" as a musical accompaniment chronicling the novel's plot: "I wonder where my big, black man has gone/Oh, I wonder where my big, black man has gone./ Has he done got faded an' left me all alone?" (112). Race is posited as a social construction, and *Black No More* shows how much social order is built upon it. Once "blacks" are "white," Harlem, Mecca of the New Negro, disintegrates as its rental market implodes when residents move because they no longer have to pay black belt rents. Fraternities, churches, anti-lynching, and other social campaigns lose funding. Satirized again is conventional black leadership, represented through the dissolution of the National Social Equality League, an organization that is "never so happy as when someone is barred from a theater or burned to a crisp." Its head Dr. Shakespeare Agamemnon Beard is a parody of Du Bois, and he too turns to Crookman's process once donations dry up and political power wanes (66–68).[11] *Black No More* shows what *doesn't* make blackness. In its pages are statements that there is no such thing as "Negro dialect, except in literature and drama" (14); there is no "wide difference in Caucasian and Afro-American facial characteristics" (15). Yet, even amid these assertions, Schuyler pays homage to some communal traditions such as the "Elks' excursion every summer to Bear Mountain,... pleasant evenings at the Dahomey Casino doing the latest dances with the brown belles of Harlem, [and] the prancing choruses at the Lafayette Theater" (16). In a later scene, Max experiences a sense of loss once he crosses the racial divide. He observes that he misses the "gentle cynicism" (44) of his people. Though Schuyler mocks racial essentialism, at points he seems to suggest that cultural practices generated from within a group make a group.

Schuyler did not always write satire. His second novel, *Slaves Today: A Story of Liberia* (1931), was drawn from a series of articles for the *New York Evening Post*, following his trip to Liberia to investigate its slavery "controversy." In the articles, he sought to expose the irony of slavery by another name existing in a land founded by freed black slaves from the United States. Sidney Cooper Johnson, whose ancestors were Philadelphia freedmen, is president of Liberia. He is famous for papers and proclamations that say nothing elegantly. He faces problems that seem contemporary: a foreign debt that is strangling his economy, citizens leaving the mainstay of the country, agriculture, to come to the cities for political patronage jobs, and his not having enough patronage jobs to secure his power. Rather than work to amend these situations, he exploits the indigenous sovereignties beyond Monrovia. He tasks the brutal David Jackson with exploiting local villages for food and taxes in support of Monrovia. One such village Takama has just enjoyed the marriage of their chief's daughter Pameta to Zo. Romanticized description of the wedding ceremony sets up the world that the dictates of Monrovia will destroy. Jackson arrives in Takama, is outraged he is not feted with food and wine, and beats the chief in front of his people. When the shamed chief retaliates, he and his subjects are killed by Jackson's men. Subsequent scenes reflect slavery. Jackson and his men steal women, levy heavy fines, and control with violence. Young men are conscripted as "laborers" and transported to unknown areas to work plantations. Sexual exploitation is institutionalized through a concubinage system. Religious authorities are ineffectual, and the law and press offer rhetoric but little else.

After the initial publication of his two novels, Schuyler went on to write serials for the *Pittsburgh Courier*, published pseudonymously under the name Samuel I. Brooks. Later the paper serialized *The Black Internationale* and its sequel *Black Empire: An Imaginative Story of a Great New Civilization in Modern Africa*; both will be discussed later in the section on speculative fiction. Schuyler pseudonymously published smaller serial novellas in the *Courier*, many fitting the African action/adventure genre popular in 1930s movies: "Devil Town: An Enthralling Story of Tropical Africa" (June–July 1933); "Golden Gods: A Story of Love, Intrigue and Adventure in

African Jungles" (December 1933–February 1934); "The Beast of Bradhurst Avenue: A Gripping Tale of Adventure in the Heart of Harlem" (novella; published March–May 1934); "Strange Valley" (August–November 1934); and "Ethiopian Stories" (1935). Schuyler makes fantasy, good and bad, out of Africa; in his mind, there is no reality there for black Americans. As he aged his conservatism solidified, as did his anti-communist stance. In the draft of an essay "King No Help to Peace," he even questioned whether Martin Luther King, Jr. in lieu of receiving a Nobel Peace Prize in 1964 should have received a Lenin Prize, since his greatest claim to achieving world peace was roaming the country "like some sable Typhoid Mary," infecting the susceptible with communist ideas similar to those of W. E. B. Du Bois, Paul Robeson, and Eleanor Roosevelt (SFP 17, 7).

The satire of editor, playwright, reporter and essayist, Wallace Thurman, took a more somber intraracial turn. *The Blacker the Berry, A Novel of Negro Life* (1929) examines what Thurman refers to in the novel as "the haunting chimera of intra-racial color prejudice" (72). Dark-skinned, himself, his work opens a curtain on values the standard bearers of the New Negro preferred not to have in public view, but the novel shows that in tragic ways intraracial color obsession is a significant marker of collectivity. *Blacker* follows the awakening of Emma Lou Morgan. She grows up a dark child within a color-conscious family who marry to lighten their skin tones. Her own mother wishes she were a boy because being dark ruins a girl's social chances. Emma is left with a deep color complex that follows her through graduation from high school, attendance at college in Los Angeles, and settlement in Harlem. Everything, her interaction with college peers, her work opportunities, her love relationships, are negatively influenced by perceptions of her color, and she internalizes the assessments that devalue her. She rejects one lover because he is too dark, then moves from one unsatisfactory relationship to the next, allowing herself to be used by men with lighter appearances. The hope that she has at last found in Harlem a locale where her color will be accepted dims, as Emma sees the same attitudes reappear in this cultural metropolis. Only her own self-acceptance will save her. As Thurman writes of Emma, "What she needed to do now was to accept her black skin as being real and unchangeable" (257).

In *Negro Life in New York's Harlem*, Thurman observed that there "is no typical American Negro. There are too many different types and classes. White, yellow, brown and black and all the intervening shades. North American, South American, African and Asian; Northerner and Southerner; high and low; seer and fool – Harlem holds them all, and strives to become a homogenous community despite its motley hodge-podge of incompatible elements" (64). In spite of this diversity, in the novel Harlem holds a unified intraracial response to color gradations. In spite of all the pride of race generated by New Negro awareness, old attitudes to skin color still remain. Rather than demotic expression, music, or perform-ance, *Blacker* makes the somewhat cynical argument that internalizations of the vexed color line cement collective identity. Thurman's second novel *Infants of the Spring* (1932) goes even further in questioning the "deep feel-ing of race" that was "the mainspring of Negro life" (Locke, "Enter the New Negro" 4) by taking aim at the oft-cited means of its coherence, artis-tic expression. *Infants* critiques the impact of a "faddistic American public" (*Blacker* 218–219) desiring black primitivism on the creativity of emerging artists.

An array of characters moves through *Infants*. Some evoke personalities of the Renaissance era, including Dr. Parkes, a steward of younger negro artists and professor at a Negro college (Alain Locke), Sweetie May Carr who entertains whites by launching into stories of her all-black Mississippi town (Zora Neale Hurston), David Holloway, the handsomest man in Harlem whom whites always wanted to paint (Hugh Jackman), and Dr. Manfred Trout who taught medicine and wrote exceptionally good short stories (Rudolph Fisher). In this setting, the protagonist, the writer Ray, questions if the New Negro vogue is inhibiting the "foundation for something truly epochal" (34). He is the novel's conscience. He lives in a building nicknamed Niggeratti Manor in an apartment leased to him by black patroness Euphoria Blake who believes that only with money and art can blacks ever "purchase" freedom (53). The commodification of creative expression implied in the term "purchase" suggests an economy of race and art that is diminishing black talent. Ray's fellow tenants who aspire to being artists include Eustace Savoy who sings Schubert and decries singing spirituals because " 'I have no relationship with the people who originated them' " (65), Pelham Gaylord aka George Jones, a black, short, rotund, obsequious, and untalented poet whose court trial shows that writing bad poetry literally is a crime; and Paul Arabian who manipulates expectations and stereotypes to create a self of his own devising. Modeled after Richard Bruce Nugent, Arabian adopts primitivism when it suits him and crosses lines of gender and geography by inhabiting Harlem and Greenwich Village, two areas in 1920s New York City where a queer presence was emerging.[12]

Paul makes visible an aspect of communal creation that is only recently receiving critical attention, sexuality. Scholarship is engaging publicly what was often only intimated in the unpublished writings of Countee Cullen,

Alain Locke, Bruce Nugent, Langston Hughes, and Wallace Thurman who was himself arrested for having sex with a white hairdresser.[13] Living during an era when homosexuality was criminalized, many feared outright identification and often referenced their sexual sphere through allusion. Repeated descriptors such as "sympathetic" (Hughes to Locke, ALP 164-38, 5) or "belongs to the order" (Cullen to Locke April 1, 1924, ALP 164-90, 37); Hughes's queries to Locke "When are you going to see the leaves with me?" "Came by to get you to go see the leaves" (Hughes to Locke n.d., ALP 164-38, 3, 4); became code for identifying other gays and making future assignations. Their letters reveal that sexuality was a co-constituent in their creative process. In an August 12 letter to Locke from Desengano, Italy, Hughes comments intertwine eroticism with creative expression: "Do let me see you for a time anyway. I like you immensely and certainly we are good 'pals', aren't we? And we shall work together well and produce beautiful things" (ALP 164-38, 4). Bruce Nugent explicitly makes a link between his sexuality and his art when he describes a bout with depression: "A perfectly stupid way to feel and so easily explained psychologically as to appear childish, either from the angle of a homo or duosexual's juxtaposition to life or an artist's. Doubly hard and fascinating when regarded from the angle of both rolled into one." Nugent goes on to remark that he knows three geniuses, the black sculptor James Richmond Barthé, Langston Hughes, and Jean Toomer, adding "Am glad I never knew Gene [sic] for a length of time. Would have fallen in love am afraid and it is not safe to love celestial bodies" (January 24, 1929, ALP 164-75, 18).

The pain of being closeted is evidenced in letters that voice Countee Cullen's contemplation of what will be a disastrous marriage to Yolande Du Bois as the solution to his "problem" (Cullen to Locke August 26, 1923, ALP 164-22, 36), and in his describing the fear that is always at his heels (Cullen to Locke September 30, 1923, ALP 164-22, 36). He expresses relief from feeling othered in a letter of thanks to Locke for sending him a copy of Edward Carpenter's *Ioläus: An Anthology of Friendship* (1908): "I steeped myself in its charming and comprehending atmosphere," he writes, continuing, "It opened up for me soul windows which had been closed; it threw a noble and evident light on what I had begun to believe, because of what the world believes, ignoble and unnatural. I loved myself in it, and thanked you a thousand times as as many delightful examples appeared, for recommending it to me." He closes, "But I suppose some of us erotic lads, vide myself, were placed here just to eat our hearts out with longing for unattainable things, especially for that friendship beyond understanding" (March 23, no year, ALP 164-22, 36). Locke's own self-censure reveals the fusion of same-sex desire and literary imagination: "Yes – I will plead guilty when the bitter time comes 'to corrupting the youth' – but there they are – as Socrates would have said – my spiritual children – Jean Toomer, Langston Hughes, Countee Cullen, [poet] Lewis Alexander, Richard Bruce [Nugent] – [author] Donald Hayes – [scholar] Albert Dunham, – there they are – can a bad tree bring forth good fruit?" (undated note, ALP 164-22, 36). These writers among others constituted one of the most influential critical bodies shaping ideas of black literature and through it, ideas of blackness. Considering their queerness expands understanding of an important writing movement. Many of their works contain ambiguous networks of friendship, lovers, and artistic exchange, probing the intricacies of race, sexuality, and art.[14]

Infants of the Spring ends with Paul committing an exotically and erotically staged suicide, dressing himself in a red silk robe and a batik turban, laying out the sheets of his novel on the floor, then killing himself in his bathtub. The suicide is to be publicity for his novel, but the pages are lost when the bathtub holding him overflows onto them. All that is left is a title page that shows a picture of a skyscraper modeled on Niggeratti manor, drenched in white beams of light, its foundation crumbling (175). It is a scene questioning the lasting significance of the Harlem or New Negro Renaissance. Many writers and artists of the moment are unknown now, their works fleeting. All that remains of their attempts in Thurman's vision was the memory of a flash of bright lights.

Writers of the 1920s and 1930s built upon the hard-won entry into publishing made by writers such as Paul Laurence Dunbar, Charles Chesnutt, and James Weldon Johnson. They enjoyed an unprecedented access to publishers and literary magazines, and closer approximation to one another. Figures such as Carl Van Vechten and Blanche Knopf fostered connections to publishers, independent magazines, and journals;[15] the literary competitions sponsored by *The Crisis* and *Opportunity* magazines and the salons of Alelia Walker offered encouragement; and literary soirees hosted by the likes of Jessie Fauset and Georgia Douglas Johnson provided community.[16] In his introduction to *The Portable Harlem Renaissance Reader*, David Levering Lewis views this cultural moment as a forced phenomenon born of the economic boon of World War I and nurtured by an unexpected confluence of writers in a space into an act of "cultural nationalism" that civil rights activists used to represent an argument for racial equality (xv). In a sense Lewis is right, but the phenomenon went beyond an argument for improved race relations and began theorizing the cultural aspects of blackness. Orality, material rooted in black folk rituals, and musical vernaculars, were embraced as viable means of formulating a collective identity beyond the imposition of race. Where earlier novels contributed to forming the idea of solidarity, literature of the 1920s–1930s began to tease out what might be the traits of that solidarity.

Writing styles announced that African American novels had entered the modern era, leaving much of their nineteenth-century antecedents behind. Realism outstepped sentimentalism; leanness of prose replaced floweriness; and relativism replaced protestant morality. They continued a focus on interracial negotiations but also accentuated intraracial ones. Novels of the 1920s to 1940s represent a move from sharing a common social condition to sharing a common cultural awareness. The collective essence they tried to capture was elusive, but the effort of doing so identified repeated strains within an expressive tradition.

CHAPTER 4

Home of the Brave: African American Novels, 1940s–1960s

Writing from Barcelona, in a letter to Charlotte Osgood Mason, Claude McKay foretold the death of the New Negro Renaissance: "The Negro renaissance movement in America seems a hopeless mess to me. – I cannot help being frank. – If I were in touch with any of the young aspiring Negro artists I'd rather advise them to get as far away as possible from it." In speaking of the "so-called leaders" of the movement he observes, "They have no real idea of what they want to do – what they can get in an artistic form from this life of the Negro. They were much more interested in the opinions of a few white persons of authority – even though these were lacking in the fine aesthetic spirit of appreciation." Langston Hughes was the only writer who escaped criticism, because McKay felt he had "big stuff" in him (February 1930, ALP 164-99, 16). In "Recent Negro Fiction," Ralph Ellison characterized the New Negro fiction of the 1920s and 1930s as "timid of theme" and "technically backward." For him, the 1940s showed a stronger grasp of *American* reality, avoiding the precious exoticism of earlier work (my italics, Ellison's term). Ellison reflects a consensus that the 1940s was a repudiation of New Negro ideologies grounded in an over-reliance on white patronage and the preciousness of uniquely primitive black art. His use of the term *American* is instructive, because though many viewed the 1940s–1960s as ushering in traditions of protest, the period also produced a championing of American sociopolitical structures broadly, while criticizing the denial of blacks a place within these.

Many changes occurred that affected the shaping and emphasis of the novel. For one, coalitions such as the National Negro Congress that brought together civil rights and labor organizations became preferred forums eclipsing salons like the Dark Tower. Organized by John P. Davis, a professor at Howard and presided over by A. Philip Randolph, organizer of the Brotherhood of Sleeping Car Porters, the congress created networking opportunities for writers and thinkers of the 1940s. Richard Wright chaired the panel, "Negro Artists and Writers in the Changing Social Order," and in attendance were Langston Hughes and Margaret Walker. The panel's title indicates yet another philosophical shift, one that sought to extend literature beyond what many saw as the confines of aesthetic rejuvenation championed by New Negro thought.

While Harlem remained a cultural center, a second development was Chicago's emergence as a literary center. One of the major sociological studies of black America, *Black Metropolis* (1945) by Horace Cayton and St. Clair Drake analyzed public housing, poverty, and challenges facing Chicago's black belt, and influenced black sociological inquiry for decades. On the cultural arts front, the 1940 Diamond Jubilee Authority's *American Negro Exposition, Celebrating 75 Years of Negro Achievement* followed in the tradition of the Paris Exposition, London's Crystal Palace, and Chicago's Own Columbia Exposition, becoming the first exhibition of this size to celebrate black history.[1] One of its products was Arna Bontemp's edited Illinois Writers' Project, Works Projects Administration (WPA) *Cavalcade of the American Negro* (1940), a broad history of black contributions to American life from 1865 to 1940, illustrated by Adrian Troy, of the Illinois Art Project. The black population of Chicago grew from approximately 44,000 in 1910 to over 200,000 by 1930, and the George Cleveland Hall branch of the Chicago public library under the leadership of Vivian G. Harsh built a collection that made it a Midwest black cultural research center. A constellation of writers including Gwendolyn Brooks, Margaret Walker, Frank Yerby, and Willard Motley, all helped to usher in the era of Chicago's prominence in the black literary world.

Popular assessment characterizes this period as producing novels of protest, but not all were what Arthur P. Davis in a review of Ann Petry's *The Street* (1946) characterized, not affectionately, as "hard-boiled Negro fiction" (648). Not all rendered black life through the violent, the sensational, or what some might consider the tawdry. Dorothy West, who counted among her friends Zora Neale Hurston (in whose apartment she lived and with whom she shared a lifelong correspondence), Countee Cullen (who proposed to her), and Langston Hughes (who nicknamed her "the Kid" and with whom she traveled to Russia in 1932),[2] centered her works in the black upper-middle classes. She founded *Challenge* magazine in 1934 to spotlight younger writers of the post-Depression Harlem Renaissance circle. Richard Wright worked with her, not always harmoniously, as she transformed *Challenge* into *New Challenge*, in an effort to revitalize what she saw as the artistry of the New Negro period now lost in 1940s. Wright's "Blueprint for Negro Writing" appeared in *New Challenge*, but disagreements over vision and content contributed to the short life of this second venture.

Writing from the historic Oak Bluff section of Martha's Vineyard, West composed *The Living Is Easy* (1948), a critique of capitalistic patriarchy using two families of the black middle and upper middle classes, The Judsons, and the Binneys. Bart Judson, a former slave, has made a successful business importing bananas and has become known as the Black Banana King. Cleo, his color conscious, class conscious wife, looks down on those who are darker and not as economically privileged as she is. She cannot accept the appearance of her own daughter who in her eyes is too dark and doesn't have straight enough hair. She goes so far as to clothespin the daughter's nose to create an aquiline shape. In her relentless drive for prestige and economic security, she manipulates her family, trading meaningful relationships for economic prestige and bringing about deprivation as a result. But Cleo also breaks gender stereotypes, and the novel equally sources the subsequent family tragedy to the lack of opportunities for women beyond wife and mother as much as to Cleo's unchecked ambition.

Living seemed out of place in the radicalizing 1940s. Its emphasis on the dissolution of an upper middle class marriage was in marked contrast to the social realism drawn in other works; yet, its very prosaicness shed light on a good portion of black experience ignored by social realist portraits of lower and working class life. Many years later, West's second novel *The Wedding* (1995) continued her delineation of the black privileged class, and provided a historical context for their attitudinal origins. Set on Martha's Vineyard it chronicles wedding preparations for Shelby Coles, the light-skinned daughter of an upper middle class family part of the exclusive black vacation enclave, the Oval. Her fiancé is Meade Howell, a white jazz musician, disapproved of by the caste-conscious community not only because he is white, but also because his not among the sanctioned professions of doctor or lawyer. Even though it is set amid *Brown v. Board of Education* advocacy, arguments for racial justice have no influence on intraracial values. Characters continue to be concerned with color. Corinne, Shelby's mother, is grateful that she has had two light-skinned daughters: one, Shelby, who can almost pass for white. Corinne does not accede to her darker husband's wishes that they try to have a son because she is afraid of pushing her color "luck." On the eve of her wedding, Shelby is attracted to Lute McNeil, a new-money black married to his white third wife. He is not part of the Oval society and sees Shelby as a symbol of the world denying him entry. He seduces and psychologically abuses her, hypocritically chiding her for leaving her race and not being satisfied with who she is. With settings going back to the Civil War, the novel makes plain how the ancestral histories of former slaves and masters set in motion the prejudices manifesting in modern times.

West examines the tenuous position of a black upper middleclass that has placed total faith in materialism at the expense of personal happiness. Passionless marriages and complicated family dynamics underscore the sacrifice money demands. In the 1940s, her novels did not garner a large popular following in spite of good reviews. The time period was not keyed to novels examining the mores of upper-middle-class blacks. While her fiction appealed to audiences reading magazines such as *Ladies Home Journal* and *Collier's* with whom she tried to publish, it was out of step with the radicalism that larger publishers expected from black writers. By 1995, however, after the feminist and womanist movements, after an editorial partnership with Jacqueline Kennedy Onassis, and after the media ascendency of Oprah Winfrey as a television producer, *The Wedding* enjoyed great success. Its televised version led to a renewed interest in West in the 1990s when American readers became curious about the experiences of the black upper class as evident in the rise of publications such as Lawrence Otis Graham's *Our Kind of People: Inside America's Black Upper Class* (1999) and Adelaide M. Cromwell's *Other Brahmins: Boston's Black Upper Class, 1750–1950* (1994). Fame came to West in the late 1980s, and a boulevard on Martha's Vineyard was renamed in her honor, leading to the reissue of *The Living Is Easy* and the publication of a collection of stories and sketches, *The Richer, the Poorer* (1995).

West's novels were evaluated in a period when popular perception fixed authentic black experiences as being urban and mired in struggle. In postwar black novels, the city took center stage, but it was not the city as envisioned when Harlem was touted as the Mecca of the New Negro. The image of Harlem in Alain Locke's landmark 1925 *Survey Graphic* essay "Enter the New Negro" could not have been more different than that appearing in his 1936, "Harlem: Dark Weather-Vane" in the same journal. In 1925 his Harlem was where "the pulse of the Negro world had begun to beat" (5), but in 1936 it was "prostrate in the grip of the depression and throes of social unrest."[3] Shifting economic conditions were matched by a shifting literary mood. The 1920s celebration of culture and art now seemed quaint to many writers. Assimilationist and exclusively aesthetic philosophies were ousted by ideas that novels needed to offer realistic portrayals condemning inappreciable African American political and economic gains. Writers were influenced by their interactions with the political left. George Schuyler (before his rightward move), Langston Hughes, and Claude McKay, among others, found outlets for their work in

Left Front and *New Masses*. The Communist Party–sponsored John Reed Club brought writers and intellectuals together across racial lines, and in 1933 Richard Wright joined the John Reed Club after his move to Chicago.[4] Hughes and Dorothy West were among the writers who travelled with Louise Thompson to the Soviet Union to make the movie *Black and White*, a failed film envisioned by soviet screenwriter G. E. Grebner as a critique of US race relations.[5] Though many of these writers would become disillusioned with the Party, the philosophies they absorbed are clearly evident in the tone of their novels.[6] Fiction portrayed characters encased in the failures of New Deal policies, and descriptions of union activism and communist rhetoric were increasingly common elements in left-leaning novels.[7]

One factor majorly responsible for the flowering of African American writing in the 1940s was the WPA's Federal Writers' Project (FWP).[8] Designed to employ writers and artists left unemployed during the Great Depression, duties ranged from preparing vocational textbooks, to writing regional writers' biographies, to reportage on local events, to the creation of the American Guide Series designed to introduce readers to each state's history, artistic creations, local lore, and geography. By the late 1930s, ethnic offshoots of these series appeared including *The Italians of New York* (1938), *The Swedes and Finns of New Jersey* (1938), and *Jewish Landsmanschaften of New York* (1938).[9] The FWP captured the voices of former American slaves, recorded black folklore, and created guides to black life in cities, states, and regions of the United States that had heretofore gone unnoticed. Many black writers were enlisted to gather information from the ground up, and the modest funding they received supported their own imaginative pieces.

Under the FWP, Richard Wright participated in the Illinois Writers' Project. His "Ethics of Living Jim Crow" appeared in the Writers' Project–sponsored publication *American Stuff*, a compendium of poems, short stories, and other ephemera issued by Viking Press in 1937. The WPA assisted him in bringing his first work *Uncle Tom's Children* (1938) to print. The Illinois project helped Arna Bontemps produce not only *Cavalcade*, but also *Drums at Dusk* (1939). Ralph Ellison joined the FWP in New York in 1938, and five years later, Roi Ottley who supervised the New York Writers' Project produced the Peabody Award–winning *New World A-Coming* (1943). While participating in the Florida project, Zora Neale Hurston wrote *Their Eyes Were Watching God* and *Moses Man of the Mountain*, and Sterling Brown coordinated a project that would culminate in the influential *The Negro of Virginia* (1940), a collection of African American folklore and history. Frank Yerby, Chester Himes, and Willard Motley were all participants in Writers' Project initiatives. The FWP brought established writers together with younger writers while warding off unemployment during the Depression, and fostered camaraderie, conversation, and inspiration. Not only did the projects provide support for writing, they also provided the opportunity to observe other WPA projects in the Radio Art and Agriculture divisions. As much as materially aiding writers, and creating an ideas exchange, the cross-disciplinary WPA emphasis on American reportage colored novelistic form to produce an emphasis on representing lower and working-class experiences and utilizing realism in portraiture.

Novels predisposed to leftist political theories saw communism and socialism as antidotes to the continued racism and class inequality caused by capitalistic values. Their sometimes strident dissent, interestingly, was embraced by a broad readership. After much redacting, Richard Wright's *Native Son* (1940) became a Book-of-the-Month Club selection; Chester Himes was scheduled for signings at the book departments of New York's Macy's and Bloomingdales; and Ann Petry's *The Street* would sell over one million copies. Many of these works, including Himes's *If He Hollers Let Him Go* (1945) and Willard Motley's *Knock on Any Door* (1949), were later made into films. Perhaps a voyeuristic fascination with "sordidness" and the genre of "social degeneracy" (Davis 648) contributed to their popularity, but another reason for their favor might be that a wide cross-section of the reading public was adjusting to a nation undergoing major transformations after the Depression and two world wars. The protagonists in these works articulated postwar alienation, and their engagement of privation voiced the insecurity of many across racial lines who had lost economic footing. As much as reading about black experience, the American mainstream was reading about itself. The novel that would define the standard of what a black novel should be for years to come was such a success, in part, because it unfolded against a background of Americana.

In "Ten Years of the Book Clubs," publisher John Farrar noted "if a book club distributes a book to forty, fifty, or sixty thousand people through the country, most of them will read it, most of them will talk about it. The news will spread, and rapidly, and the publisher will sell thousands more of the book – providing always that it is liked" (354–355). This was certainly true for Richard Wright's *Native Son* (1940). Many black writers commented on its phenomenal sales and popularity and the pressure its precedent placed on their own endeavors.[10] What made the story of a black teen's transforming the accidental suffocation of his white employer's daughter into a willful self-defining murder so appealing? While *Native Son* may have reinforced white perceptions of black male deviance, it paired this rendering with images of American popular culture. What makes *Native Son* so compelling is its blend of the horrific and the proverbial.

The opening scenes of the novel wed American pastimes with the main character Bigger's exclusion from them. He regards a skywriter creating an airborne advertisement, and when he wishes he, too, could fly a plane his friend Gus reminds him through a series of "ifs" – if he were white, if he had money, and if he were allowed to go to aviation school – of the distance between him and that possibility. Bigger and Gus frequent the movie theatre to see the Depression-era fantasy *Trader Horn* (1931), a film one *New York Times* reviewer described as "[t]hrilling realism … spliced cleverly with rugged fiction," and Wright inserts a newsreel of Mary Dalton and other debutantes enjoying the Florida season.[11] For Bigger, both films are equally fantastic flights of the imagination. The degree to which Bigger has internalized these images is indicated through the reveries he shares with his friends. They "play white," imagining themselves to be in command of military regiments; to be J. P. Morgan selling stock shares; or to be the president convening a cabinet meeting. Bigger's fantasies, like those of Wright's readers, are both powered by 1930s and 1940s Hollywood, and Wright conjures American escapism on multiple levels. On one, white readers become voyeurs in escapist black wretchedness, but on another more subtle level, because of their own economic uncertainty, many share Bigger's desire to escape to an imagined white idyll. In his dreams, they see their own.

The Americanness of *Native Son* is conveyed at the start through its title, but also through plot arcs familiar to American literature. "Fear" is essentially a rags-to-riches storyline but the limits race places on possibility are clearly evident. It opens in the Thomases' kitchenette apartment with the hope that a job with the Daltons will lift Bigger and the family out of impoverishment. Peggy, the Daltons's stereotypically Irish maid found in movies from *The Women* (dir. George Cukor, 1939) to *Another Thin Man* (dir. W. S. Van Dyke, 1939), describes the heights to which Bigger can aspire: not wealth but like his predecessor the black chauffeur Mr. Greene, perhaps he too might go to night school and become a postal worker. The plot of the chase scenes in "Flight" conjures 1930s gangster movies such as *Little Caesar* (dir. Mervyn LeRoy, 1931) and *The Public Enemy* (dir. William A. Wellman, 1931) where antiheros resort to violent crime because social mobility is not an option. The trial scenes of "Fate" evoke courtroom dramas treating prejudice such as *They Won't Forget* (dir. Mervyn LeRoy, 1937) where a Jewish businessman goes on trial for killing a small-town Southern girl. *Native Son* provides a picture of American myths even as it shows the destructive power they exert on individual psyche. It may fall within the tradition of indignant protest, but still employs empathy.[12] The allusions to American popular culture invite readers to see themselves and their part in Bigger's world. In "How Bigger Was Born," Richard Wright notes that Bigger Thomas was not black all the time, he was also white, and modern experiences of alienation, and capitalistic exploitation, had created millions of him (860). *Native Son's* mainstream popularity echoed the nonracial lines along which readers might situate their own understandings of their rapidly changing world.

Wright's next two novels, *The Outsider* (1953) and *Savage Holiday* (1954), did not enjoy the success of *Native Son* perhaps because they were philosophical excursions through dilemmas of alienation.[13] In *The Outsider*, Cross Damon, an intellectual by nature and an outsider even among his friends, takes advantage of a subway accident to fake his death and divest himself of problems of debt, charges of having sex with a minor, and an unhappy relationship. His renaissance comes to naught, however, as four murders and complicity in the suicide of his lover dog him. Published during the communist scare and cold war era, *The Outsider* offers a critique of the uselessness of ideologies, particularly communism, in constructing an improved society.[14] Some felt that the novel signaled Wright's increasing removal from his racial roots in order to break free from the hold of his first novel.[15] *Native Son* so defined what the theme, characterization, and content of a black novel should be that even its creator could not move beyond its formula.

Savage Holiday (1954) was as far away from *Native Son* as a novel could be in characterization, if not in ultimate theme. Wright's protagonist here is a white, well-to-do insurance executive Erskine Fowler, and race is rendered through rare tangential descriptions of black workers. When unmoored from the safety of his professional identity and forced to face his repressed sexuality, Fowler sets a series of bizarre events in motion, and senseless tragedy is the result. Wright wanted the novel to be an exploration of the price of freedom, especially when it comes in contact with societal proscriptions, and he felt that only a white character gave him the means of engaging such a broad theme (Wright, *Conversations* 225). His choice might reflect his own inability to envision a black character that did not pose limits when representing other than racial themes.

With the last novel published in his lifetime, *The Long Dream* (1958), Wright returns to the familiar ground of the segregated South. Rex "Fishbelly" Tucker, the son of a prosperous undertaker, experiences a series of coming-of-age moments each time he crosses the boundary between the

"black belt" of Clintonville, Mississippi, and the white world surrounding it. His lessons in segregationist ideology foster not his submission,
but rather his falling "fatally in love with that white world ... in a way
that could never be cured" (158). Some might argue that Wright articulates
his own response to subjugation here, and similar to Wright, Rex ultimately seeks solace in Paris. Wright composed two additional novels. To
date unpublished, *Island of Hallucination*, is a sequel to *The Long Dream*
and envisioned as a part of a trilogy. It returns to Rex who now lives in
Europe amidst expatriates modeled after James Baldwin, William Gardner
Smith, and artist Ollie Harrington, among others, and imagines Smith and
Baldwin, along with writer and journalist Richard Gibson, as spies for the
Central Intelligence Agency.[16] Wright's other manuscript *A Father's Law*,
drafted in the second half of 1960, involves the black Chief of Police of an
affluent Chicago suburb attempting to solve serial murders while becoming uncomfortable with his university-educated son's extensive knowledge
of the killings. Harper Perennial reissued the unfinished novel in 2008.

   Native Son in varying ways influenced a generation of writers including James Baldwin, Ralph Ellison, and Gwendolyn Brooks. Some compared their efforts to Wright's feat. Chester Himes noted that even though
his novel *If He Hollers* (1945) was well received, compared to Wright who
had become an American writer, he was still marginalized as a black
writer. According to Himes, Wright's precedence placed particular pressure on Baldwin. In the aftermath of his scathing assessment of Wright in
"Everybody's Protest Novel," Baldwin explained his views by saying that
Wright had left nothing else for any other black writers to compose. Himes
recalled him crying while saying that the sons must slay the father (Himes,
Conversations 128, 66). Wright's influence is also evident in the styles of
Frank London Brown and Curtis Lucas.

   Brown in *Trumbull Park* (1959) wrote of African American families
attempting to integrate a Chicago housing development and later, in the
posthumous *The Myth Maker* (1969), a powerful and bleak Dostoevskyian
investigation, of the degeneration of Ernest Day, a man drowned by the
circumstances of race and poverty. Lucas moved from rural Georgia to
Newark's Third Ward in 1946. First predominantly occupied by German
and white ethnic Catholics, then Jews, by the time of Lucas's arrival, it
was primarily black. His writing career began in 1943 with the crime mystery *Flour Is Dusty*. As much as telling a murder story, the novel critiques
how drugs ravage the black community. His most critically acclaimed
work took a more serious turn. In *Third Ward Newark* (1947), the black
teenaged Wonnie Brown is a raped by white men and left for dead in

the Meadowlands after witnessing her friend's murder. Lucas would turn to writing pulp, but his early works recall Richard Wright through their blend of social realism and existentialism. Ann Petry's *The Street* (1946) is often likened to *Native Son*. Petry trained as a social worker and a pharmacist in Connecticut. She would leave that state for New York where she would work for the *Amsterdam News* and as an editor for Adam Clayton Powell's newspaper the *People's Voice*. Her first novel gave fictive form to the need for advocacy she saw while working with the Harlem Riverside Defense Council and The National Association of Colored Graduate Nurses. It exhibits a Wrightian determinism, as an ever-shrinking box encases its main character to tragic end, and like *Native Son*, the novel is as much about white America as it is about black.

The main character Lutie Johnson must find a home for herself and her son Bub in Harlem. As she searches for a place, Benjamin Franklin walks the streets with her, but her reveries of his self-reliance only highlight the gulf between her actuality and anything that might be termed American fulfillment. Lutie experiences not Franklinian individualism but loneliness and isolation. Energy and persistence cannot conquer the snares set for her by the predatory Mrs. Hedges, the madam of a downscale brothel; a shady club and real estate owner, Junto; Boots Smith, a bandleader who desires to use her sexually; and a building superintendent Jones, who fantasizes about her and entraps her son in his plot for revenge. *The Street* intertwines scenes of Lutie's environs and values with representations of the American dream. Her employers are a wealthy white family in Connecticut with a large house, elegant furnishings, and views of the Connecticut River. This domestic scene is far from ideal, filled with material comfort but little meaningful happiness. The failure of materialistic American conformity is at the root of the dissatisfaction of two women at opposite ends of the race and class continuum. Both live in segregated ghettos, and the privilege that sustains one causes the privation of the other.

That *The Street* moved into the sphere of American popular culture is evident in the evolution of its marketing. Initially Houghton Mifflin publicized it through black journals and presses, and they arranged signings at black bookstores, Lewis Michaux's National Memorial Bookstore and the Frederick Douglass Bookstore, among them. Subsequent paperback editions were designed to broaden its popular appeal, treating the novel as if it were pulp fiction. Cover images of 1940s and 1950s editions show an increasingly sexualized Lutie. The first edition's frontal face portrait of a sad-eyed woman changes in the Signet editions of 1949 and 1954 to full body images conveying Lutie more as femme fatale and street walker than mother. Red is the predominant color in Lutie's attire on these later covers. In two she is in a figure hugging dress, and in one a tight off the shoulder red top and a flaring yellow skirt. None of these images captures Petry's Lutie, who is very careful of her appearance and body because she is sensitive to being sexualized and objectified as a black woman. The marketing worked, however, and Petry's novel sold well as late as the 1960s.

Indicating a desire to write multiple types of novels, Petry wrote in a March 6, 1946, letter to Alain Locke that though she planned to keep on writing novels, not "all of them will be about Negroes – though I think we, as a people, offer the richest most fertile field for creative writers" (ALP 164-77, 17). In making whites central characters in her next novels *Country Place* (1947) and *The Narrows* (1953), she follows the tradition of Dunbar's *The Uncalled* and Hurston's *Seraph on the Suwanee*. Laura Dubek describes *Country Place* as belonging to the "white life" genre (58–59), novels published by black writers in the years following World War II that subvert the sentimentality and focus on the white family of postwar movies such as William Wyler's *The Best Years of Our Lives* (1946). *Country Place* (1947) uses the widespread postwar theme of returning veterans unable to readjust to small town America. In a similar vein, *The Narrows* (1953) appears to be in the tradition of "raceless" writing; yet, as Emily Bernard points out in "White Family Values in Ann Petry's, *Country Place*," race is very much a part of the novel. *The Narrows* uses Dumble Street as its setting and has as protagonist African American Link Williams who rescues a woman he discovers is white from the unwanted attention of a disabled veteran. Link and Camilla begin an affair, and once he realizes the she is Camilla Treadwell Sheffield, a married heiress, he questions whether she is using him to fulfill a sexual fantasy. When he breaks off the affair, she tears her clothes and falsely accuses him of rape. He is arrested, but insufficient evidence leads the Treadwell Sheffield clan to take extreme actions to assure Camilla's victory in court. The subsequent sequence of events causes a child's death and eventually Link's. *Country Place* and *The Narrows* interrogate the myth of white normativity and question its impact on those it marginalizes.

Petry was certainly not alone in resisting a publishing world limiting the choices of black writers. Frank Yerby, after failing to place his first book, resolved to minimize race in his work. The unpublished *This Is My Own*, whose central character was a black PhD, gained little traction with publishers in an era when for many *Native Son* and *The Street* dictated the aesthetics of black novels. Yerby wrote for *Challenge, Common Ground, Phylon*, and other left-leaning journals, and he, too, was part of the Illinois

Works Projects Administration. He made his mark not with politics, however, but with nostalgia. Not long after the mania created by *Gone With the Wind*, novel and movie, he wrote *The Foxes of Harrow* (1946). By the end of the year, the book had become a national best seller.

A period piece set in the antebellum south, the novel tells two plantation tales. The central white character of the work is Stephen Fox, who while he can envision a future of black equality and stands for the rights of working whites, is still bound by the feudal system that gives him his privilege. Fox marries Odalie, a haughty and cold woman, but one who gives him the class status he desires. They have a son, Etienne, who grows from being a spoiled child into a malicious man. A parallel story follows the Foxes's footman Achille. The son of a slave who rebelled against French rule, he weds an African princess who later dies attempting to throw herself and child into the levee rather than see her child live as a slave. The child is rescued and grows to be Inch, the second hero of the novel. As much as is possible for a black man in the nineteenth century, Inch lives a Horatio Alger story. He gains literacy, escapes slavery, studies law in France, and meets Frederick Douglass. The Dred Scott decision forces his return to his master Etienne, but by novel's end, Inch, participating in the Reconstruction politics in New Orleans, is part of a new south.

Even though his books incorporated black history, when published Yerby's editors at Dial Press invariably deracinated much of this content before publication. In the editors' introduction to his essay "How and Why I Write the Costume Novel," *Harper's* characterized Yerby as "One of the few successful Negro authors who are not preoccupied specifically with Negro problems" (145). Yerby ultimately assisted in efforts to downplay race, and in the same essay describes in a just barely tongue-in-cheek manner, the formula securing his commercial success. He endeavored never to give readers more than they wanted, and in the late 1940s and 1950s, too much of a commentary on race was more than they wanted. According to Yerby, protagonists should be charming scoundrels, preferably with dark secrets, dominant males because even female readers prefer this (though they will deny it). Female protagonists must be lovely and more immature than the males, and have sexual appeal. Conflict and ennobling themes – the problem of evil, humans' inhumanity to humans, humans' relationship to God, the battle of the sexes – should form the plot's core.

In spite of Yerby's protestations, all his works engage issues of social justice. *The Dahomean* (1971, Heineman brought out a London edition as *The Man from Dahomey* in 1971), viewed as one of his best, centers around the heroic Nyasanu, an African chief's son, betrayed and sold into slavery by his own people, and transported to the United States. In a prefatory note, Yerby states that he made use of Melville J. Herskovits's *Dahomey: An Ancient West African Kingdom* (1938) to create a dispassionate portrayal of slavery, one that did not play to the ideology of racists or black nationalists, but showed the corrupting effect of the enterprise on indigenous culture. His research is evident in the detailed, prosaic scenes of Dahomean life that constitute Nyasanu's life before enslavement and deep psychological interiority once he is renamed Wesley Sparks and transitions from human to chattel. *Goat Song* (1967) focuses on Ariston, a Spartiate hero with unrivaled beauty. Amid scenes of decadent sexuality and sensual abandon, Yerby expresses the sadness of history repeating itself through enslavement and war. The many footnotes in *Judas, My Brother* (1968) expose his concern with how written sources shape institutional power and religious belief.

Yerby appears not to engage social protest, yet his major themes involve inclusion, exclusion, and critiques of unquestioned hegemony. Because none of these explicitly centered on black characters, his novels became part of Doubleday's Dollar Book Club as well as the Literary Guild. By 1954 he had made approximately one million dollars from his writing, exclusive of movie rights. "Few of the Southern housewives who buy Yerby's slick melodramas of sex, sadism and violence know that their favorite author is a Negro," observes a *Time* magazine profile. "Nothing in his stories of strutting white aristocrats, swooning heiresses and yassuhing darkies would declare it, and jacket blurbs, noting that the Georgia-born author formerly taught at Florida A. & M. and Louisiana's Southern University, leave it to the reader to know that these are Negro colleges" ("Golden Corn" 99). Yerby is, in effect, an example of authorial passing, a technique that would also be adopted by the Chicagoan Willard Motely.

Motley, nephew to the artist Archibald Motley, grew up in middle-class surroundings in Chicago's Englewood section, in the home of his grandparents, the only black family in the neighborhood. Published by the *Chicago Defender* at age thirteen, Motley knew early on he wanted to write. While living in Chicago, Hull House, founded by Jane Addams in 1889, became a place for Motley to meet other writers. He was part of the group that launched *Hull House Magazine*, a small literary journal, which became the testing ground for his work. Mentored by Arna Bontemps and friends with Jack Conroy, in 1940 he also worked on the FWP's intiative to create a portrait of "Little Sicily," one of Chicago's Italian neighborhoods. This work, along with his research visits to reform schools and prisons, and his multiracial, multiethnic, impoverished Maxwell Street neighborhood found form in *Knock on Any Door* (1947).

In his initial novel, Motley wrote from the perspective of a white immigrant, Italian American Nick Romano, a Denver native. After Nick's father loses his grocery store and the family's circumstances are reduced, Nick falls in with petty thugs. He is falsely accused of stealing a bike and ends up in reform school where he is abused by both inmates and guards. Upon his release the family moves to Chicago where Nick repeats the lessons he learned in the Denver slums, ultimately escalating to killing a white police officer. Through the perspectives of the black character Sunshine, who first appears as a comic stereotype with a shiny face, pouting lips, and very white eyes; Nick's long-suffering wife Emma; and his lawyer, the social and naturalistic explanations for Nick's actions are presented. Constrictions of class and sexuality are placed on trail along with Nick as Motley censures a society that allows poverty to provide more lessons than any academy, and that sends Nick to the electric chair at age twenty-one.

The rest of Motley's novels also center on white characters. Through flashbacks, *We Fished All Night* (1951) depicts the World War II homecoming of three young Chicago men. One, Don Lockwood is a Polish immigrant who has changed his name from Chet Kosinksi in an effort to something he is not, a war hero. The second, Jim Norris, upholding the image of upright citizen, caring husband and father, considerate employer, devolves into child molestation. The third Aaron Levin, a poet psychologically unhinged by war and haunted by memories of his Jewish father and his erring mother, is committed to a military psychiatric ward. *We Fished All Night* left little space for readers seeking a hopeful vision and was not well received by critics or the public, but its major problem was that it was too broad a story. Motley had envisioned it being part of a two-volume set, but his publishers persuaded him to condense it, and the cohesion of the work suffers. In spite of its unwieldiness, it is a powerful antiwar novel detailing the physical and mental disjunctures soldiers suffer. Two more novels followed. The first, *Let No Man Write My Epitaph* (1958), a sequel about Nick Romano's son (a movie version appeared in 1960); and the second, *Let Noon Be Fair* published posthumously in 1966 set in a fishing village in Mexico, which became Willard's expatriate home. This final novel dramatizes the exploitative overdevelopment of an indigenous space, Las Casas, a fictionalized Puerto Vallarta. Its recreation of a complex gay life and his incorporation of gay characters led to Motley's increased prominence in queer literary studies.[17]

Motley "passed" in many ways and upended the expectations placed on black writers. He was black but created white characters; he was middle-class, yet wrote of the streets. Quiet about his own sexuality, his works are explicitly sexual. *When Knock on Any Door* was issued, he declined to have his photograph accompany the book, and his publisher Appleton-Century made no mention of his race. It sold briskly because it was perceived as a naturalistic study rather than a race novel. When it was later made into a movie starring Humphrey Bogart, Nick's motto in the novel, "live fast, die young, have a good-looking corpse," became part of American popular idiom.

Black novelists of the 1940s frequently provided an aerial view of white American society. The praise accorded to some for writing beyond the supposedly narrow confines of race illuminated the ways whiteness remained a raceless "universal," human condition, and masked their tackling of the marginalization of white laborers and the white underclass. William Attaway's first novel *Let Me Breathe Thunder* (1939) is in effect a road narrative of the American Southwest during the Depression years. Because it had no central black characters, it was cited as proof that blacks could write about whites, but Attaway's depiction of the vicissitudes caused by the collision of undemocratic class and racial practices were largely unnoticed.[18]

From Greenville, Mississippi Attaway was the son of a physician and schoolteacher. His family moved to Chicago to avoid southern impoverishment. He gained popular recognition for composing "Day-O," known better as the "Banana Boat Song," for singer Harry Belafonte. In the 1950s, he was among the earliest African Americans to write scripts for film and television programs such as *Wide Wide World* (1955–1958), a highly rated show sponsored by General Motors and designed to carry live travel segments from across the United States and some international locations into the living rooms of American television viewers.[19] So much of his work made its way into mainstream American culture, but because it existed as guides to America, television shows, popular songs, and a novel with white characters, race never became a central issue. Attaway, too, was a product of the FWP, and while in Chicago he came into contact with Frank Yerby, Arna Bontemps, and Margaret Walker, as he gathered scenes of American life to be incorporated in the guide to Illinois. His FWP experience served him well in writing novels that pulled back the curtain to display aspects of ignored America.

Let Me Breathe Thunder recalls the travels of two white vagrants, Step and Ed, and the young Mexican runaway Hi Boy who rides the rails with them. Along the way, they are subject to the brutalities authorities heap on migrant workers. At one point, all three work on the farm of a white populist Sampson whose idealist class practices are not replicated in his racial attitudes. He insists on working side by side with his hires, while refusing to let his daughter associate with them. The farm workers find recreation at a roadhouse owned by a black woman, Mag. Racial politics come into play when the white Step rapes Sampson's daughter Anna, and Cooper, a black man and former friend of Step and Ed, is unjustly accused. Race trumps friendship as Step and Ed join the lynch mob seeking Cooper. When they themselves seek to escape subsequent violence, they must choose between leaving Hi Boy on the Sampson farm or giving into their affection for him and taking him with them. Their decision has dire consequences for Hi Boy. The characters and settings of the work extend the discussion of race beyond the black–white binary to include prejudice against Latinos and Asians. Mag's comment that "they always hating somebody somewhere" (58) posits race as a broad problem, exacerbated by capitalistic exploitation. Only in the liminal spaces of the railway boxcars can equality potentially exist, even if it is through shared disenfranchisement. While the book captured the ways the Depression fostered the construction of community across class, racial, and ethnic lines, the desperation of its characters shows the fragility of this coalition and the deficiencies in leftist ideals. The content of novels by Richard Wright, Ralph Ellison, and Chester Himes show that the attraction the Communist movement held for blacks during the early 1920s and 1930s was fading, and Attaway's novel resonates with similar sentiments.[20]

Attaway is now most remembered for his novel treating black migration, *Blood on the Forge* (1941). In it, the migration from South to North turns disastrous for the brothers Mat, Melody, and Chinatown. Big Mat seeks to take his brothers out of the racism of Southern sharecropping, but their arrival at the Pittsburgh area steel mills trades one form of racism for another. Attaway shows the breadth of racial hate by juxtaposing the slower tempo of an agrarian Southern life with the jarring rapidity of a mechanized Northern metropolis; yet, in both the characters' economic survival is jeopardized. Southern bigotry is matched by native and immigrant white ethnic workers whose racism stems from fears of unemployment and competition from an influx of blacks. The brothers leave a South destroyed by poor farming methods only to become the exploited laborers of a racist industrial complex destroying the surrounding land and rivers.

Increasingly, black novelists found publisher and audience expectations constricting. Works with black characters that addressed race were dismissed as protest, and with a few exceptions, works that did not engage this content risked being ignored. Chester Bomar Himes, William Gardner Smith, and William Demby all expressed degrees of exasperation with the narrowly construed aesthetic possibilities open to black writers.

Chester Himes's early family background in no way presaged the turns his life would take. The son of a father who was an educator at what were then termed agricultural and mechanical colleges (A and M) and a mother ambitious for her children, the uplift ethos of Booker T. Washington, one of his father's heroes, permeated early home life. His father's unemployment and the move to Cleveland it necessitated threw the family into straightened circumstances, and a disillusioned Himes left Ohio State University and compensated for his growing feelings of anger and alienation through a career in crime. Over time, his record of criminal charges included check forgery, breaking and entering, and grand theft auto. The Ohio State penitentiary was his institution of higher learning, and with his 1934 short story "Crazy in the Stir," inmate 59623, became the first incarcerated writer to appear in *Esquire* magazine. Released from prison in 1936, Himes became a member of the FWP at the Cleveland Public Library. Contributing to the Cleveland Guide in the project series provided him the germs of characterization for the foreign laborers in his novels. After working for American Steel and Wire and other industries in the Cuyahoga Valley of Ohio, Himes moved to Los Angeles, and working in the industrial sector on the West Coast introduced him to a segregation not confined to blacks or to the South.

His first novel, *If He Hollers Let Him Go* (1945), completed with the help of a Rosenwald Foundation fellowship, covered four days in the life of Bob Jones, the lone black foreman in a California shipyard. Bob wants to believe that his job and college education allow him social advantage, but a series of episodes underscore the illusory nature of his hoped-for racial parity. Subsequently, Madge, a white worker who taunts him by saying she will not work with a "nigger," hating and desiring him, accosts him for sex. When he refuses, she falsely accuses him of rape. He is jailed, and even though charges are not forthcoming due to the falsity of her claims, the case is pushed forward by a social system that must not discredit the word of a white woman. *If He Hollers* blends fictional portraits of intraracial black biases with histories of the violence against Mexicans in the Zoot Suit Riots and Japanese internment to show the endemic nature of racism and classism.

Himes enjoyed modest success with *If He Hollers*, but not so with his next novel. *Lonely Crusade* (1947) sold poorly and was often characterized as sacrificing the art of fiction for gratuitous violence.[21] Himes's westward travels, first to Hollywood to unsuccessfully write for the movies and then to San Francisco, provide the backdrop for the story of Lee Gordon who was hired by a labor union to organize African American workers at an aircraft plant in California. Gordon is manipulated by both the owners and union organizers, and is subsequently arrested as the perpetrator of a murder he only witnessed. He becomes more martyr than man, and ultimately takes a stand glorifying the promise of a unified labor movement. Both Himes and his publisher Knopf had high hopes for *Lonely Crusade*, but the bookstores at Bloomingdale's and Macy's pulled the work and canceled book signings. When radio interviews were scrapped as well, Himes blamed the Communist Party for launching a negative campaign against him because of the novel's harsh criticism of Jews and the party. Humiliated, he left the United States as soon as he was able. The reviews actually ran the spectrum from good, calling the novel bold and probing, to bad, likening it to men's room graffiti. Some accused him of anti-Semitism, and indeed even while creating a sympathetic portrait in the character Abe, the novel voices black resentment to Jewish economic power, particularly in black neighborhoods.[22] The poor reviews left an indelible mark on Himes convincing him that a life as an artist offering frank reality was impossible in the United States. He departed for Paris, and joined a growing group of writers, many of whom never returned to live permanently in the United States.

Himes's next three novels were heavily autobiographical. *Cast the First Stone* (1952), a novel of prison life, was extensively edited to appeal to 1950s sensibilities, with much of the sex between men deleted. In 1998 fourteen years after his death, W.W. Norton published the full text as *Yesterday Will Make You Cry*. It is part of Norton's Old School Books, a series of twentieth-century African American pulp novels. *The Third Generation* follows the family of William Taylor, a metallurgist who works as a professor of industrial education. The family's misfortunes and moving through Missouri, Mississippi, and Arkansas mirrors the migrations and challenges of Himes's own family, and within the work he offers a critique of black higher education as an education for second-class status. *The End of the Primitive* (1956) about the affair between black writer Jesse Robinson and a white Kriss Cummings signaled a shift in Himes's work and was heavily based on his relationship with Vandi Haygood, one of two white woman he would live with while in Europe. The protagonist struggles to rebuild his life after his latest book is rejected and he is pilloried in public. Portions of the novel explore gender dynamics through Kriss's relationship with an alcoholic father, a closeted homosexual husband, a former boyfriend who has forced her to have abortions that have left her infertile, and through her attempts to convince Jesse of the parallel between white male exploitation of blacks and white women. In a style that would characterize Himes's future writing, the realistically rendered absurd occurs: Jesse, in a drunken rage, stabs Kriss, and awakes the next morning with no recollection of the incident. Himes characterized it as his favorite work, in spite of its brutality, because he felt the nuance of each word he wrote (Himes, *Conversations* 67). The misogyny in *End of the Primitive* is marked and foreshadows the conventions of hard-boiled dark fantasy that will be part of Himes's later fiction. Kriss's murder represents the destruction of the social power of white womanhood that has been used in American culture to both arouse and damn black masculinity.

Himes reinvented himself as a writer in the late 1950s, and from then until the 1970s created some of the most popular African American detective novels in the genre's history. From *For the Love of Imabelle*, his first, to the reconstructed and posthumously published *Plan B*, he used hustlers, junkies, hoodoo priests, and priestesses to write crime fiction accusing American social violence of ruining humanity. The blend or surrealism and social realism in his detective fiction (discussed later in this work) would throw into haut relief ongoing practices of injustice. Before he died, Himes garnered the acknowledgment he sought for most of his life when he received the Grand Prix de la Littérature Policière, one of France's most prestigious crime fiction awards.

Though he would repudiate the United States and eventually live abroad, Himes expressed a deep Americanness and appeared as much a federalist as Frederick Douglass. As late as a 1974 essay, "Negro Martyrs Are Needed," he urged black revolutionaries to right American injustice and restore the nation to its original vision: "There can be only one (I repeat: *Only one*) aim of a revolution by Negro Americans: That is *the enforcement of the Constitution of the United States*. At this writing no one has yet devised a better way of existence than contained in the Constitution" (159). As document, the Constitution contained all the possibility of American democracy, and could serve as a blueprint for a progressive defense against right-wing fascisms. Its vision for a multiethnic and multiracial democracy was not realized, however, and Himes was a member of a growing expatriate community of black writers in Paris meeting at Café Turnon to discuss black American involvement in the World War II effort and Popular Front politics. William Gardner Smith was among this circle.

Smith's *Last of the Conquerors* (1948) centers on the interracial relationship of the black GI Hayes Dawkins and the white Ilse who is jailed and intimidated by white American military and German civilian police because of her relationship with Hayes. To set the novel against the backdrop of post-Nazi Germany, in a nation that had in the 1930s prohibited interracial and interethnic marriage and reproduction, forces the comparison to American race values that are similarly fascistic. The novel replicates Double V agitation, by querying how a nation with Jim Crow segregation can be a democratizing force. Smith's next novel *Anger at Innocence* (1950) examines the environment's power to shape the individual through the story of love between the middle-aged Ted, a security guard and a young pickpocket. The novel was criticized for having no black characters, but more (and rightly so) for being "synthetic" and weakly written, having characters who were ventriloquist dummies for Smith's propaganda rather than fully imagined creations.[23] It represented a failure after the relative success of *Last of the Conquerors*, and Smith followed with *South Street* (1954), a work presaging 1960s novels concerned with life in deteriorating urban communities. The novel uses now stock urban characters – the numbers runner, an almost prostitute, and a blues singer – but these were innovative in black dramatic fiction at the time, making it Smith's greatest popular success.

Writing in the 1950s, Smith viewed black writers as existing along a continuum of bitterness that ranged from George Schuyler to Richard Wright to Chester Himes. Such bitterness resulted in a stifled form of fiction with two-dimensional ravers, Bigger Thomas being the archetype (W. G. Smith, 298). But Smith also saw black writers as antidotes to the superficiality of American literature: "Emotional depth, perception of real problems and real conflicts is extremely rare in American literature – as it is in American society generally. Instead of issues of significance our fiction (our serious fiction) is overladen with such trite themes as that of Tennessee Williams's *The Roman Spring of Mrs. Stone*. America's is a superficial civilization: it is soda-pop land, the civilization of television sets and silk stockings and murder mysteries and contempt for art and poetry" (W. G. Smith 300–301). Smith never produced an opus with the depth to serve as convincing counter to the blandness he critiques, but his novels record the comprehension and ambivalence distance gave writers looking across the Atlantic at the United States. *The Stone Face* (1963), his last, put into words expatriate qualms over living elsewhere while the civil rights and black power movements were in their ascendency. The stone face of the title is a specter, a conglomeration of whites that have brutalized the main character, Simeon, and he signifies the black expatriate attempting to master an understanding of race while in an elsewhere community.[24]

Emphasis on social critique did not mean the 1940s to 1960s were any less aesthetically experimental than the black Renaissance period. Expatriate William Demby wrote of the United States from Italy, and did so in a highly inventive manner. Born in Pittsburgh, Pennsylvania, he attended West Virginia State University until his conscription into a World War II African American unit sent him to North Africa and Italy. Fluent in Italian, he worked for among others Federico Fellini and Roberto Rossellini, and the Italian New Wave can be seen influencing later works that were avant-garde in form. Critics found Demby's first novel *Beetlecreek* (1950) promising particularly for its reversal of racial victimization. It describes the relationship between a reclusive white man Bill Trapp and a black teenage boy he befriends, and the way the local black community misconstrues their relationship and exacts revenge on Trapp. *The Catacombs* followed 15 years later, and in postmodern fashion fused reflective digressions, newspaper clippings, stream-of-consciousness, nonfiction and fiction, to create a meta-narrative in which a main character named Bill Demby writes about writing about connections between the Cold War, Hollywood ideals, the John F. Kennedy assassination, blackness in European history, and Birmingham violence during the Civil Rights era. His work defied easy placement by a culture wanting to confine black writers in a protest camp.

Demby published two additional novels. *Love Story Black* (1978) features a middle-aged black writer and professor who confounds easy binaries by teaching both medieval and African American literatures. He is assigned to write a magazine article about the nonagenarian Mona Pariss, a once-famous black singer now living on welfare in a tenement. Her life spans black history and reflects black artistic aspirations. As he writes about her, and as their relationship in the end becomes sexual, he enters her historical space. Living in two times at once, he gains illumination, not only about his subject, but also about history, gender, race, and sex. The title for Demby's fourth novel, *Blueboy* (1980), comes from a term describing a very dark and naïve young black. It is the story of an unlikely friendship between two very dissimilar teenagers.[25] His final novel, *King Comus*, treating the relations between blacks and Jews back to the nineteenth century, remains unpublished. Demby's substitution of layered, metaphysical narratives for linear telling accentuates the inter-connectedness of elements social history seeks to keep discrete.

Demby, too, felt pressure to create novels of protest, and he thought the tradition a form of caricature in itself. "At one point, I had wanted to be like the black writers of the earlier times," he said in an interview, "But if I did that, I told myself, I would be a minstrel man" (Kemme n. pag.).

Finding a space that fit individual conceptions of being a writer was difficult for black artists of the late 1940s and 1950s. Chicago writer Gwendolyn Brooks whose chosen genre was poetry was pressured by her publisher to write prose for better sales.[26] Her novel *Maud Martha* (1953) had its genesis in an early prose effort "The American Family Brown" completed in 1946 but never published; instead, portions made their way into Brooks's only novel. Using an urban naturalism to evoke the lives of "kitchenette folks" trying to navigate a city of de facto if not de jure separation, through 34 prose vignettes that imbricate poetry, she delineates women's awareness, while showing the costs of internalizing European standards of beauty. Beauty is far more than physical appearance in the novel. Self-worth, societal acceptance, and economic security depend upon what is conceived of as beautiful. While not wanting to speak for a people, Brooks develops a social voice in *Maude Martha* where the beauty and profundity of everyday black existences are contained in a lyricism designed to be meaningful to that world.

Novels written to be culturally meaningful to the marginalized are radical in that they ignore the approval of the social center. Even more radical are novels that argue that the culture on the margins is integral to definitions of the center. "The history of the American Negro is a most intimate part of American history," suggests Ralph Ellison. "Through the very process of slavery came the building of the United States ... His experience is that of America and the West, and is as rich a body of experience as one would find anywhere. We can view it narrowly as something exotic, folksy, or 'low-down,' or we may identify ourselves with it and recognize it as an important segment of the larger American experience – not lying at the bottom of it, but intertwined, diffused in its very texture."[27] Expounding on the centrality of black culture to the very texture of what is American is a key aspect of Ellison's *Invisible Man* (1952). As *Invisible Man* at its end queries, "Who knows but that, on the lower frequencies I speak for you?" (581).

Often hailed as a classic representation of black experience, Ellison's novel is also hailed as a classic American novel. It garnered a National Book Award in 1953, a Medal of Freedom, the highest civilian honor of the United States, and earned him membership in the Chevalier de l'Ordre des Arts et des Lettres in France. At a time when the terms "black" and "American" were mutually exclusive for many, at a time when many felt the universal mode of black literature was protest, being hailed as a classic often implied deracination. George Mayberry is an instance of many who saw Ellison as a writer able to rise above complaint, a term rapidly becoming synonymous with African American: "*Invisible Man* is a book shorn of the racial and political clichés that have encumbered the 'Negro novel.'[I]t can be said of Ralph Ellison that he is not a Negro writer, but a writer who happens to be a Negro ... The bane of the problem novel, in particular the 'Negro novel,' in America is that the cart of the subject has preceded the horse of artistic sensibility. Having given ample proof of the latter, it can be earnestly hoped that from the underground to which history and human frailty has driven him, Ellison can emerge to write of other places" (n. pag.). In eliding author and character, Mayberry undoes his praise of Ellison's craft, almost reading the work as autobiography. Irving Howe, however, is more nuanced and notes that it would have been impossible for the novel to exist without its connection to black existence: "Some reviewers, from the best of intentions, have assured their readers that this is a good novel and not merely a good Negro novel. But, of course, *Invisible Man* is a Negro novel – what white man could ever have written it? It is drenched in Negro life, talk, music: it tells us how distant even the best of the whites are from the black men that pass them on the streets; and it is written from a particular compound of emotions that no white man could possibly simulate. To deny that this is a Negro novel is to deprive the Negroes of their one basic right: the right to cry out their difference" (n. pag.). Howe's comments walk a fine line as they illustrate the vacillation between cultural difference and commonality, essentially the twoness of black Americanness understood in Du Bosian terms. Ellison so seamlessly integrates two elements much of American discourse sought to keep distinct, that his novel was frequently characterized as "universal," a term encoding "not black." As Howe points out, however, the novel is specifically black in its engagement of black history and black artistic forms, particularly jazz and the blues.

The materiality of black life and expressive forms has long been a concern of Ellison. Upon his arrival in New York, Langston Hughes introduced him to Richard Wright, and Wright helped Ellison gain a position in the New York Writers' Project. As part of his duties, Ellison documented the songs, street tales, and language of New York.[28] *Invisible Man* is a skillful alchemy of black myth, vernacular, ritual, and modern prose. One of the most clever feats is the way it involves the reader in constructing blackness. It provides cues American culture primes us to read as racial, and allows shared knowing to take the place of outright exposition. Descriptors such as "ginger-colored nigger" (21) "biochemical accident to my epidermis," or "spook like those who haunted Edgar Allan Poe" (3) connote race without explicitly denoting it. In the Battle Royal scene, the woman who dances at the event is described as the sum of her parts – hair "yellow like that of a circus kewpie doll," "eyes hollow and smeared a cool blue, the color of a baboon's butt" (19). Culture encourages associating these traits, yellow or blonde hair and blue eyes, with whiteness, even though many of mixed race might have the same traits. The narrator never has to state that she is a white woman. Ellison cleverly shows how the continual repetition of certain imagery and references collude to construct race.

After *Invisible Man*, Ellison spent most of his life writing a second novel, *Three Days Before the Shooting ...* published by Modern Library in 2010. Issued posthumously first as *Juneteenth* in 1999, *Three Days* is an expanded 1,000-page collection of unpublished drafts.[29] The story of the work's provenance, a draft ostensibly lost to fire in Ellison's Massachusetts vacation home in 1967 and its subsequent reconstitution by editors John F. Callahan and Adam Bradley, could make a book in itself.[30] Ellison began composing the work almost immediately after *Invisible Man* and muses to Albert Murray that perhaps some of what was leftover from *Invisible Man* might make it into the next novel (*Trading Twelves*, 16). Told in flashback, *Three Days* is the story of the minister Alonzo Hickman, an elderly black man who attends Senator Adam Sunraider at his death after Sunraider is the victim of an assassination attempt on the senate floor. During his ministrations, Hickman, a jazz musician turned preacher, recalls his adopting a child named Bliss, who accompanied him on his revival tours and rose from a white coffin to provide dramatic effect to Hickman's sermon. At a Juneteenth celebration, a white woman whose accusation of rape was responsible for the lynching of Hickman's brother appears and claims Bliss as her long-lost son. Hickman had hoped to raise Bliss to make right the senselessness of a death caused by racial hatred; instead, Bliss embraces the freedom that comes from passing as white, even though he has spent his life steeped in the black traditions of Hickman's community. The novel's style mirrors Bliss's existence between two worlds. Passages recreating black preaching traditions are contrasted with those recreating segregationist rants. Passages in reportorial style contrast with dense, jazz-like stream-of-consciousness prose. The sweep of the novel embraces slavery's legacy and again highlights the ways cultural commonality binds much more than difference separates.

That *Three Days* was not published in Ellison's life makes it difficult to assess since he never gave his imprimatur to the final version. In an interview discussing the author's transition from typewriter to electric typewriter to laptop, one of the editors of *Three Days*, Adam Bradley, notes, "For Ellison, one of the effects was that it allowed him to pile draft upon draft of the same scene over and over again without solving some of the basic questions of plot and transition that bedeviled the book" (M. Martin n. pag.). Would *Three Days* have been the linear narrative we have in the reconstructed editions, or might Ellison have used more of a Faulkneresque communal narrative as in *The Sound and the Fury* (1929)?

For many critics, Ellison occupies spaces between – between art and protest, between blackness and raceless "universality." The concept of space between is increasingly theorized in the 1950s. It becomes a central motif for James Baldwin, who in life and fiction defied categorization. "Our passion for categorization, life neatly fitted into pegs," he wrote, "has led to an unforeseen, paradoxical distress; confusion, a breakdown of meaning." He continues, "Those categories which were meant to define and control the world for us have boomeranged us into chaos; in which limbo we whirl, clutching the straws of our definitions" (*Notes* 19). All Baldwin's novels reveal intense introspection and the attempt to find place amid dogmas that demand adherence without examination.

Born in Harlem in 1924, Baldwin spent much of his early life trying to conform to the value system of his strictly religious stepfather, David Baldwin, who because of his own unfulfilled aspirations was a severe disciplinarian. Questioning where he fit in the parameters outlined by his stepfather gave form to his first novel *Go Tell It on the Mountain* (1953), and influenced Baldwin's novelistic portraits of liminality. It was the gay African American artist Beauford Delaney who provided Baldwin with a means of reassessing his Harlem upbringing. Baldwin frequented Delaney's Greenwich Village studio, and later credited him with teaching him literally how to see differently. Baldwin describes the instance: "I remember standing on a street corner ... down in the Village, waiting for the light to change, and he pointed down and said, 'Look.' I looked and all I saw was water. And he said, 'Look again,' which I did, and I saw oil on the water and the city reflected in the puddle. It was a great revelation to me. I can't explain it. He taught me how to see, and how to trust what I saw" ("Art of Fiction" n. pag.). In his early twenties, Baldwin relocated to Greenwich Village and moved in a circle of artists/ activists including Lionel Trilling, Henry Miller, and Randall Jarrell. At one point, his roommate was Marlon Brando. Baldwin gained access to the publishing world writing pieces for *Commentary*, *The Nation*, *Partisan Review*, and *The New Leader*. In the late 1940s, he was part of the second generation of rising black stars following in the legacy of Wright, now an established writer. Wright was instrumental in helping Baldwin secure the funds to travel to France and gave Baldwin a literary lodestone against which to launch his own critical philosophy, the result of which would be his critique of Wright's *Native Son* and the beginning of the end of their friendship Wright.[31]

Using the remains of a Rosenwald Fellowship, Baldwin left New York for Paris in 1948 after the suicide of his friend Eugene Worth who jumped off the George Washington Bridge, an event that makes its way into the novel *Another Country* (1962). From here on, much of Baldwin's life and work took take place abroad. *Go Tell It on the Mountain* was begun in Paris and finished in in Loèche-les-Bains, Switzerland; *Another Country* was written in Istanbul, Turkey; *If Beale Street Could Talk* (1974) and *Just Above My Head* (1979) from his home in Saint-Paul-de-Vence in the south of France. One of the most skilled writers of trenchant critiques of race in the United States needed the space of oceans for clarity. Baldwin might have made sojourns back to his home nation – in the late 1950s he travelled through the American South, Birmingham, Tuskegee, Nashville, Montgomery, and Little Rock, covering the Civil Rights movement – but his reflections on being black in America were framed through the lens of being an international subject.[32] At points this positioning makes it difficult to reconcile his relationship to race. Writing to Alain Locke from Paris in 1949 to ask for money, and describing himself as "not a good investment," he confesses, "I'm trying to break out of a kind of literary typecasting – I'm sick, in a way, of being continually expected to write about Negroes and am afraid of the easy success such a road can possibly offer" (February 4, 1949, ALP 164-12,17); yet Baldwin will spend his life writing about being black, continually complicating what this signifies.

Go Tell It on the Mountain was written with the soundtrack of Bessie Smith songs in the background and with Henry James as an advisory presence. James helps him through fundamentals of fiction writing – character, plot, point of view – but Bessie reminds him of his native culture that he left in the United States. Her inspiration is particularly seen in "Part Two: The Prayers of the Saints," where the southern origins of the protagonist, John Grimes are presented. The novel is about the reconstruction of self. It provides in-depth portrait of John's spiritual growth as he seeks to balance an inner and outer self. He resists the religious stringencies of his stepfather Gabriel and resents the fact that Gabriel's preaching has done little to remove the family from the poverty and decay surrounding them in Harlem. He is torn between the sexual and sensual desires he increasingly feels and wanting to live up to his stepfather's strict (if ultimately hypocritical) abhorrence of the flesh. John's conflicts are rendered though a series of displacements. As the Grimes family migrates, the South is displaced by the North; as John grows, the confines of Harlem are displaced by places of artistic openness and refuge, the New York Public Library, the Museum of Natural History, the Metropolitan Museum of Art. Institutions that were once the means employed by a white hegemony to solidify its values through the arts and intellectual pursuit are now the places where John finds his authentic black self.

The quest for an outer space appropriate for an inner self concerns *Giovanni's Room* (1956) as well. David, a character inspired by Lucien Carr's murder of David Kammerer, struggles to come to terms with his love of the pseudonymous Giovanni and with his own sexuality.[33] David knows early on from an experience with a childhood neighborhood friend that he is attracted to men and is terrified because everything in his world tells him this is deviant. Marriage, parenthood, and heterosexuality are safety. He uses women to find "salvation," convinced that marriage will save him from dark desires. For most of the novel, David struggles to "will" himself straight, but the "beast" that Giovanni stirs in him will not quiet (81). His love for Giovanni fills him in turns with elation and terror, love, and hate. When his tortured self forces him to deny his feelings for Giovanni, and when Giovanni spirals downward desperately as a consequence and faces execution by guillotine, David's guilt overwhelms him.

Baldwin has said that *Giovanni's Room* had its genesis in America ("Art of Fiction" n. pag.), and throughout he intimates that the sexual binaries of a puritanical United States are at the root of David's quandary. David can find no space where two men can live as lovers, as partners. He and Giovanni spend much time in the claustrophobic room of the title that Giovanni works tirelessly to renovate, to make pretty. In describing it as "hard work," "insane work" (109), Baldwin equates the effort with the futility of trying to make space for homosexual love in an intolerant society. Baldwin's same sex storyline met with controversy. Knopf, a relatively liberal firm of the 1920s and 1930s, wanted Baldwin to change the characters to black and heterosexual, and rather than do this Baldwin published the work with Dial. Eldridge Cleaver wrote a homophobic critique of both Baldwin's fiction and sexuality.[34]

Because the characters in *Giovanni's Room* are white, many have said that race plays a small role in the novel. Leslie Fiedler sees the novel as Baldwin emerging as "simply a writer," moving past an "obsession" with being black in a white culture (204). Race, however, is central to this novel, but remains invisible because the race in question is white. David Describes himself: "My face is like a face you have seen many times. My ancestors conquered a continent, pushing across death-laden plains, until they came to an ocean which faced away from Europe into a darker past" (9). Here he articulates the foundational myth of American whiteness that from the seventeenth to nineteenth centuries justified Native American removals, the enslavement of Africans, and continued class inequity among white ethnics. Baldwin, in fact, is one of the sharpest critics of whiteness. It is white normativity, implicitly heterosexual, that makes David's sexual love of Giovanni impossible.

Baldwin's third novel *Another Country* was banned by many states because it too used race and sexuality to question American norms. Rufus Scott, no longer able to abide his feelings of societal impotence and his economic impoverishment becomes the abuser of his white partner Leona. Loathing what he has become, he jumps off the George Washington Bridge. The rest of the novel provides multiple perspectives on his suicide and life and how both make his coterie of friends and family reassess their relationship to race and sexuality. Baldwin has said he models himself more on jazz musicians than other writers (*Cross of Redemption*, 40), and indeed *Another Country* intertwines the stories of his characters in a series of riffs. The novel integrates jazz and the blues into textual passages, epigraphs, modes of dialogue, and as thematic elements that deepen characterization.

Tell Me How Long the Train's Been Gone (1968) and *If Beale Street Could Talk* (1974) continue Baldwin's exploration of American social constriction. *Tell Me* does so through Leo Proudhammer, a Harlem-bred African American actor who is part of Greenwich Village bohemia. He has struggled against racial stereotypes and paucity of roles to become a successful actor, but his success leads to other constrictions. He will never be cast in Shakespearean roles, and his wealth has moved him away from his black community. He is involved with the white actress Barbara King and later the Black Nationalist "Black Christopher," a character who combines nationalism and gay pride. The work can be read as Baldwin's response to younger critics such as Amiri Baraka who fault him for being too enthralled by western culture to truly value black culture, and as his assertion that that homosexuality and racial pride are not exclusive.[35] *If Beale Street Could Talk* (1974) conveys from the point of view of a girl what was generally conveyed from the point of view of a boy, the very personal pain of growing up impoverished and marginalized.[36] It has been noted that Baldwin was one of the few black writers of his era to consistently create fully developed women characters (Hernton 139). Through a female voice that blends maturity and innocence, Baldwin explores the deleterious effects of intraracial prejudice as well as the origins of the racism leading to the novel's chain of events.

Just Above My Head (1979), Baldwin's most expansive novel, is an epic encompassing the themes of his other works. "The Soul Emperor" Arthur Montana has died from a heart attack in a London pub. His brother and manager Hall Montana recalls, through montage, his sibling's life, as a tribute and as an aid in coming to terms with his loss. He intertwines their story, along with that of their close friend Julia and her brother Jimmy, into a sweeping narrative of black life that includes migration, the civil rights movement, and growing black internationalization. The novel recalls the breadth of Baldwin's own life spanning the post–Harlem Renaissance, the Depression, the Cold War, the Civil Rights and Black Arts Movement, Viet Nam, the emerging gay rights movement, and black transnationalism.

Much of Baldwin's work after *Another Country* came under criticism. *Tell Me How Long the Train's Been Gone* and *If Beale Street Could Talk* never received the widespread praise of his earlier novels. Some characterized the writing as "trite," holding little that was new.[37] Others deemed it as not political enough, more concerned with inner demons than the demon of racism; and still others felt he had become more an essayist than novelist.[38] While it can be argued that the quality of the novels is uneven, all evince Baldwin's ability to transgress philosophical and genre rules. At their best, they wed the intensely personal, the culturally observant, and the artistic-ally beautiful, with ease. Baldwin has always been a difficult read for some-one. A look at the American Library Association archives shows many of his books banned at different times in different states because of his themes of interracial and same-sex relationships.[39] What makes Baldwin's works difficult for some is precisely what speaks to others, his ability to render humanity's ambiguities.

By the late 1960s Baldwin, constantly on the lecture circuit and viewed by many as a spokesperson of the race, is weary of the pressure of being a great writer. While working on a screenplay for a movie about Malcolm X that was never produced, he writes to his brother David. Otis Redding's song "Sitting on the Dock of the Bay" is playing. Aretha Franklin's "I Wonder" follows, and of the Queen of Soul he writes, "The way she sounds is the way I want to write. You know, there is something fantastically pure and sad, heart-breaking, and yet peaceful in all this horror. What a triumph – to be able to sing about it – to give it back to the world – to save the world, or simply another person (which is the world) by making the person look at the person" (JBP 1, 1). The ranges he describes in Franklin's singing are also quintessentially Baldwin, the pure yet sad, the heart-breaking yet peaceful, and above all his desire to use writing to redeem. What made

Baldwin difficult for his contemporaries to assess now accounts for his resurgence in scholarly and popular attention. His interest in movement within fixed places speaks to the 2000s, a more mobile era amenable to accepting flux rather than fixity. As a person and a writer, Baldwin existed in multiple religious, racial, sexual, national, and transnational spaces at once, all while asserting his Americanness.

The post–World War II period of the African American novel is frequently viewed as a time repudiating the idealism of the New Negro Renaissance. Rather than a disavowal, however, novels of this moment constitute a broadening of the forms and practices of the 1920s and 1930s. The desire for credible representation, the importance of place to imagination, the experimentation with literary form that began in the earlier part of the century still obtain, but are colored by the Depression, two world wars, and continued de facto if not de jure segregation. Social realism and urban naturalism may have been the vehicles for reflections on race and culture, but novels still philosophized on the nuances of African American experiences. The popularity of African American novels at this time suggests that their explorations resonated with many populations in the United States. An era that ostensibly introduced the protest tradition in black writing also made clear how closely tied black cultural history was to traditions of American advocacy.

For all their musings on the state of America, it is remarkable how many novels of this period were written abroad or informed by transnational viewpoints. A constellation of black expatriate writers combined critique and nostalgia into novels, and became noted midcentury social commentators. Their own liminality gave their works perspectives that would resonate with consequent investigations of fluidity between racial, national, and sexual identities.

CHAPTER 5

Black Arts and Beyond: African American Novels, 1960s–1970s

James Baldwin, who had once critiqued Richard Wright for sacrificing humanity to protest, dedicated his 1964 play *Blues for Mr. Charlie* to the memory of Medgar Evers, his widow, and his children. One reviewer characterized *Blues* as having "fires of fury in its belly, tears of anguish in its eyes and a roar of protest in its throat."[1] Baldwin's shift in tone was one instance of the increasing radicalization that would emerge in much black expression of the 1960s–1970s. Similar sentiment could be found in the journals *Liberator, Soulbook,* and *Umbra,* as well as television shows such as *Soul!* and *Like It Is.*[2] Nonfiction works such as Eldridge Cleaver's *Soul on Ice* (1968), Malcolm X's *Malcom X Speaks* (1965), Bobby Seale's *Seize the Time* (1968), and Kwame Touré's (Stokely Carmichael) and Charles Hamilton's *Black Power: The Politics of Liberation* (1967) were circulated through independent book stores, word of mouth, and cemented a philosophy that called for an immediate end to second-class black citizenship. Even the middle-of-the-road *Ebony* magazine in August 1969 produced a special issue "The Black Revolution." Accompanying the cover, a black and white Van Gogh style portrait of a serious-faced, dark black man, was the following caption: "The Black Revolution, which is currently redefining deeply rooted values in a society built largely on the assumptions of black inferiority, and which is the subject of this special issue, is typified by the Afro-wearing young man on the cover. Fiercely proud of all that is entailed in being black, he and his peers – both male and female – have found their black identity and with it an inner strength which rules out forever a return to that traditional brand of race relations that characterized lives of their elders" (4). One cannot help but hear overtones of the New Negro movement in Ebony's description of the time and thinking, as did Henry Louis Gates that this constituted another black renaissance:

> The third renaissance was the Black Arts Movement, which extended from the mid-'60s to the early '70s. Defining itself against the Harlem Renaissance and deeply rooted in black cultural nationalism, the Black Arts writers

imagined themselves as the artistic wing of the Black Power movement. Amiri Baraka, Larry Neal and Sonia Sanchez viewed black art as a matter less of aesthetics than of protest; its function was to serve the political liberation of black people from white racism. Erected on a shifting foundation of revolutionary politics, this "renaissance" was the most short-lived of all. By 1975, with the Black Arts Movement dead, black culture seemed to be undergoing a profound identity crisis. ("Black Creativity" 74)

Writers of the period might well be called the newest of the New Negroes, but Gates sells short the artistry and influence of their works. While many exhibited a stridency of tone and mission, the attention paid to their political content often eclipsed consideration of their craft.[3] Certainly phrases such as "whitey," "the man," or "ofay," conveyed outrage, but this body of writing was more than the angry literature of an angry time. Painting the novels with the broad stroke "black nationalist" elided their many inventive distinctions. Not always receiving their due are the rigor of craft, the invention of language, the juxtaposing of imagery, the aesthetic reimagining of history, and the resituating of the art–politics debate. What might be termed an *ars poetica* for black creators of the time would include the criteria that literature not be separate from struggle and that it come from a black idiom. Novels at this time exhibit both and critique the framing of political speech as artistic weakness as an arbitrary, racialized practice undermining a mode of expression.

Larry Neal, often seen as articulating the aims of the Black Arts Movement in much the same way that Alain Locke articulated the New Negro Renaissance, disdained the idea of protest because it implied pleading with whites for rights that should be inalienable. Rather than protest, he felt that an "aesthetic concerns the shape of one's being in the world" ("A Nation of Flowers" 9, LNP 7, 3). Neal, who coined the term "Black Arts Movement" after seeing Amiri Baraka's poem "Black Art," never intended the term to connote a "fixed ideological position in art." In an unpublished essay titled "Origin of Black Arts Movement," he asserted that there were never any real "tenets" (LNP 7, 10). Considering a black aesthetic meant revisiting questions that black creators had raised before: Was there something within American culture that was distinctly African in origin that made African American expression different from other forms? Does considering this possible uniqueness lead to isolation that stifles creative expression? For Neal, as for others, the starting point for considering these questions was within the community of creation.

Novels of the 1960s and 1970s embraced much of the Black Arts philosophy, particularly its desire to no longer explain blackness to white America, but to portray blackness to black America. In describing the philosophy of the art co-op AFRI-COBRA (African Commune of Bad Relevant Artists) artist, Napoleon Jones-Henderson describes the aims of many creators to treat blackness not through struggle but through positive affirmation: "We began to agitate for the concept of a new aesthetic, a new sense of purpose, a new reason for making … positive images of Black pride, Black self-determination, weapon images in/for the struggle to heal the minds and Souls of Black Folk throughout the Diaspora … Aesthetics, as a functional instrument in the struggle, demanded that we look into our culture for the finest and most cherished elements of 'beauty,' 'good,' 'love,' 'family,' 'music,' and 'spirituality'" (102). Jones-Henderson's language is instructive. "Weapons," clearly places art in the midst of "war," the struggle for developing black worth within a dominant culture, and "functional" stresses that art must be of value to the community.

The many artist-led organizations that arose during this period, personified the philosophy that the artist should not be alienated from his or her community. Among them were Baraka's Black Arts Repertory Theatre-School in Harlem; the Organization of Black American Culture in Chicago that listed among its organizers Hoyt Fuller, Haki Madhubuti (Don L. Lee), and Angela Jackson; and the Umbra Workshop in New York that included Ishmael Reed, Askia Touré, and Calvin Herton.[4] "For us, by us, near us," the popular rallying cry for art during this time had multiple resonances. On one level, it meant that art should be geographically accessible to black communities; on another level, it suggested art should be rooted in the aesthetics and philosophies of black traditions. Dramatic and dance performances in community theatres, poetry readings in artspaces or at protests, and organizing workshops were all means of making art part of daily black life. Murals vivified this philosophy. Most famously, in 1967, at the creation of the 30 × 60 foot *Wall of Respect* in Chicago, poets, musicians, artists, dancers, and rhetoricians all gave performances as OBAC (Organization of Black American Culture) artists painted what would become a symbol of collaboration. Black photographers Bob Crawford and Beuford Smith provided a visual record of the period.

This era also saw the continued development of black presses to address the unmet needs of a readership. Poet Dudley Randall founded Broadside Press in Detroit, while Haki Madhubuti created Third World Press in Chicago. These were joined by The Third Press in New York, Naomi Long Madgett's Lotus Press in Detroit, and Drum and Spear Publishing in Washington, DC. Dudley Randall observed, "My strongest motivations have been to get good black poets published, to produce beautiful books, help create and define the soul of black folk, and to know the joy of discovering new poets. I guess you could call it production for use instead of for profit" (Parks 89–90). While major white firms still published the bulk of black novels the establishment of these outlets became linked to aesthetic mission. These houses hoped to offer a different lens through which black America could look at itself and the world of which it was a part.

At first read, the optimism of Black Arts discourse, the Wall of Respect, and the newly established black presses seem absent from novels in which sex, drugs, and debasement are the crucible through which characters must pass to emerge to a better black self. Cries for unity do not seem reflected in contrasting novelistic visions: where some exhibit explicitly nationalist content, others question nationalism and separatism; where some suggest that art must be a useful political tool, others suggest that the vision of the artist is paramount; and where some writers viewed the separation of art and politics as facilitating racist and bourgeoisie values, others viewed the period as a time when literary rigor gave way to protest. Philosophies vary as naturally they would since the writers themselves are a diverse group, and it is precisely this diversity that is not acknowledged in terms such as "black nationalist protest."

For many, Amiri Baraka personifies the politics of the moment, but his novel also personifies the period's engagement of form. *The System of Dante's Hell* (1965) appropriates the structure of Dante's *Inferno* to explore the relationship between the black artist and western, white civilization. It employs the quest of a black "innocent," and avers that the alienation and confusion of being black and a black artist make Dante's hell enviable. Where Dante explores the state of the soul in death, for Baraka's character LeRoi (also called Roi and Dante), the soul is in a living inferno. Using the urban landscape of Newark as a background, Baraka's circles of hell are reserved for, among others, neutrals who are in a purgatorial vestibule because they have done nothing to advance the black situation, heretics who deny responsibility and enlightenment, and the incontinent who cannot think beyond self-sensuous desire. The influence of the experimental early 1960s Greenwich Village art scene is also evident in the novel, though Baraka has said the he wanted the work to move away from the formulaic avant-garde of poets such as Allan Ginsberg and Charles Olson (Benston 304–306). Its language reads like a faceted prose poem deeply entrenched in jazz rhythms. It bends linear plot into segments representing LeRoi's states of mind/hell and defies any desire for resolution. The nod to Dante is not one of inspiration, but rather one of critique, questioning the appropriateness of traditional, western artistic forms to the African American artist.

Similarly to Baraka, William Melvin Kelley signifies on western traditions in literature. With a title taken from Thoreau's statement and a character named after Shakespeare's Caliban, the artistic influences on *A Different Drummer* (1962) are evident. Kelly began his literary career writing with a hope to go beyond the divide of black and white and to focus on black individuality. His engagement of Thoreau's concern with the individual and the ways society forces him or her into conformity appears throughout his canon and is given a racial dimension. Tucker Caliban, the descendant of an African chieftain who has led many successful slave revolts and even attempted to kill his own baby son rather than see him sold into slavery, hears his African ancestors, and knows they would have resisted the world of exploitative sharecropping in which he finds himself. Like Caliban he repudiates an authority demanding gratefulness for small, condescending kindness, and he makes a personal choice that sets in motion a chain of events, inspiring other black sharecroppers to mount their own rebellions. Kelley uses flashbacks and multiple voices to create layered narratives, in which no character knows more than his or her circumstances would allow. The result is a mosaic of perspectives throwing light on the singularity of Tucker's decisions.

Kelley's second novel *A Drop of Patience* (1965) contrasts individual freedom with multiple forms of institutional constraint. Ludlow Washington, a blind black boy, is abandoned in an institution designed to warehouse rather than care for the disabled. His blindness, on the one hand, provides a degree of liberation because he cannot see color and does not handicap himself by perceived slights; on the other hand, it deprives him of being able to see the color code so important in a southern society. Only his music keeps him from the insanity his situation threatens to impose. Because of his musical talent, he is released to a black bandleader to play with his group, but seeming liberation turns into a different sort of trap in his new surroundings as Ludlow's understanding of his own music making is discordant with the style the band contract demands. Kelley's dexterity in writing passages of syncopated repetition almost onomatopoetically represents Ludlow's gift and desire for freedom for both his music and himself.

Kelley's next novel *dem* (1967) employs satire and is dedicated to "The Black people in (not of) America." The othering in the lowercase title reverses the us/them dichotomy that white American culture imposes to alienate blacks. A series of episodes whose actions seem unrelated are linked by their analysis of American moral bankruptcy. In one, a Korean war veteran and young executive kills his wife and children during a domestic argument, then proceeds to mow the lawn. In another the central character, the white, upper middleclass Mitchell accuses his housekeeper of stealing, more to exercise his white male privilege by devaluing another than to seek justice. The episode that most tellingly reveals Kelley's critique of racial and class legacies occurs when Mitchell's white wife Tam has conceived by superfecundation, the twinning that results from sex with different males. Bored with her upper-middle-class marriage, she is reminiscent of Betty Freidan's "the problem that has no name."[5] In addition to her husband, Tam has a black lover, as is clearly evident in the appearance of one of her twins. Her husband Mitchell begins a search for the father of the black twin and ends up in Harlem, a world alien to him, unable to comprehend the multiple literacies of its residents. Eventually he encounters Calvin Coolidge Johnson, who, unbeknownst to Mitchell, is the man he seeks. Coolidge inverts the history of white slave-holders, forcing black men to accept as their own, children fathered by the masters. As Mitchell comes face-to-face with shouldering the responsibility of raising another man's black child he queries, why me? Cooley's response is why my great-grandfather? (205). The novel *dem* portrays a dominant culture in the dystopia of its own creation.

Kelley's depiction of America's endemic violence and racism reflects a growing militancy in his works. Like many writers, living as an expatriate allowed him to see the United States in a clearer fashion. His time in Paris amid blacks from all over the world and his travel to Jamaica led to an appreciation of diaspora, a desire to learn more about Africa, and to his most experimental work yet, *Dunsfords Travels Everywheres* (1970). Kelly was taken with African oralities, and thought that these could serve as a base for a new novelistic language. Inspired by *Finnegans Wake* (1939) and his sense that James Joyce's experience of being an Irish writer in an English culture was akin to being a black writer in white America, Kelley forms a language blending Harlem vernacular, pidgin English, and Bantu to signify a common diasporic tongue. He uses it in the dream sequences of his dual protagonists Chig Dunford, a Harvard-educated black who relates more easily to whites than blacks, and Carlyle Bedlow, a Harlem resident comfortable only in the circles of the underworld. A Janus-faced duo, they travel through worlds of secret societies, covert operations, and the lower deck of an ocean liner that has a slave hold. Chig and Carlyle seek answers to who they are and what connection they share. The episodes of their odyssey provide the knowledge they seek, yet the information comes through the language of their dreams, one that they cannot interpret once awake when they return to a world of standard English. Artificially imposed modes of expression must be disavowed, the novel suggests, if one is ever to find the voice to tell one's own story.

Kelley exemplifies a cadre of writers within the Black Arts period seeking newer ways to frame black agency, even when drawing the direst circumstances. They privilege instrumentality, however fragile, over determinism. John Oliver Killens is another example, and his regionalism counters perceptions of Black Arts era novels as being urban-centered. All are set in the rural South, and his "nationalists" are for the most part Southern heroes. His novels reclaim the image of the South, making the world below the Mason Dixon Line not a place to disown, but rather a space with histories instructive to present-day black activism.

Both *Youngblood* (1954), Killen's first novel, and his third, *'Sippi* (1967), made use of cadences of orality, and a crucial element in *'Sippi* would be the power of a folktale. Both are rooted in a black rural Southern world he knew well growing up in Macon, Georgia and listening to the stories of his grandmother, Georgia Killens. Using this cultural history as a base, he demonstrates the power of family and community in finding agency. From depicting Joe Youngblood who teaches by example when he refuses to allow his employer to cheat him of his wages, to the more communal act of a young teacher Richard Myles who at great personal cost celebrates Jubilee Day, *Youngblood* radicalizes images of Southern family and community and frames both as necessary to the survival of a healthy black psyche. *'Sippi* extends *Youngblood's* focus on individuals exercising social power to the struggle for voting rights after the *Brown v. Board of Education* decision. Killens makes use of several folk stories. The legend recalling how a black breaks segregationist custom by walking through the front door acts as a Greek chorus throughout the work. The power of the spiritual to cohere community is shown. The refrain, "no more Mister Charlie, just Charlie, no more Miss Ann, just Ann, and no more Mississippi, just 'Sippi," taken from a story popular in the 1960s echoes through the experiences of various characters.[6] Folk commentary in Killens reminds that the past is the foundation of even the most militant future action.

In *And Then We Heard the Thunder* (1963) and *The Cotillion; or One Good Bull Is Half the Herd* (1971), both nominated for the Pulitzer Prize, Killens engages questions of class and community. In *And Then*, a war novel, law student Solly Saunders believes in American ideals and expects rewards for his hard work. He is transformed in World War II by fighting both a German enemy and racists in his own army. His future development hinges on his choosing between materialistic self-advancement or promoting community solidarity. *The Cotillion* (1971) satirizes a northern black middle class who amid the turmoil of the 1960s seeks to hold onto meaningless assimilative traditions. Killens weaves the urban vernacular he heard while living in Harlem and Brooklyn into his prose. His belief in the 'each one teach one' philosophy that influenced many 1960s activists produced two young adult books, *Great Gittin' Up Morning: A Biography of Denmark Vesey* (1971) and *A Man Ain't Nothing but a Man: The Adventures of John Henry* (1975). His last novel *The Great Black Russian: A Novel on the Life and Times of Alexander Pushkin* (1989) uses the Russian black aristocrat and revolutionary as a representation of 1960s black revolutionary spirit. Killens has said that being black in a racist society forms the core of any black person, and that this was the locale from which he wrote. He sought to place what he termed the "idiomatic" essence of black life in all his novels ("Rappin," 103).

Killens interpreted community in a literary sense, and was dedicated to supporting other black writers. Along with Rosa Guy, journalist Walter Christmas, Willard Moore, Jean Carey Bond, and Sarah Wright, he started the Harlem Writers Guild. Its goal was to develop and lead to publication works by writers of the black diaspora.[7] Many were served by the inter-disciplinary space of the Guild including Audrey Lorde, Paule Marshall, Julian Mayfield, Terry McMillan, Sidney Poitier, Ossie Davis, Ruby Dee, Lorraine Hansberry, and Wright, herself, who authored *This Child's Gonna Live* (1969), a stream-of-consciousness relation about a Depression-era family and their battles with out-of-wedlock pregnancy, religious hypoc-risy, and white vigilantism.

How place shapes human understanding was a central concern of Killens as well his Guild cofounder Rosa Guy. Where he examined how segrega-tion encroached on blacks in rural locales, she and peers Alice Childress and Nathan C. Heard, showed that northern urban spaces were equally confined by segregation. Areas too easily written off as ghettos had been drawn in earlier novels as immutable, primarily to explain black pathology to a white readership; in these 1960s novels, however, the ghetto is a cau-tionary space where a black community can see its faults and the practices necessary for transformation.

Rosa Guy draws on her experience of migration from Trinidad to the United States, and her work in factories to support herself and her son while writing, to examine the challenges of the dispossessed. Her first novel *Bird at My Window* (1966) uses montage to involve readers in piecing together the reasons why the main character Wade Williams is straitjacketed and in the prison ward of a New York City hospital. From the outset, it is clear that he is constricted by more than the jacket. A fight between him and his brother Willie Earl has resulted in his sister Faith's near death, and his mother blaming him as the cause of the trouble places him in virtual exile from the family unit. Willie's search for maternal acceptance and fraternal vindication is told through memory and dreamscapes that are interjected into the linear flow of the narrative. The social issues prominent in black discourse of the 1960s are the subject of the flashbacks: the importance of family, education, and community. Wade and his family deteriorate because their urban community deteriorates. In its decay, they see themselves, and the novel not only sheds lights on failing conditions, but also suggests actions to remedy them. Guy's later novels include *A Measure of Time* (1983), about a self-made woman's rise amid the Harlem Renaissance and *The Sun, the Sea, a Touch of the Wind* (1995), the story of artist Jonnie Dash who goes to Haiti to recapture her spirit, but instead falls in with a group of decadent expatriates. The larger part of Guy's work after *Bird at My Window* consists of young reader and children's books, some of which won a Parents' Choice Award, an American Literary Association's (ALA) Best Book for Young Adults award, and The Coretta Scott King Book Award.[8]

To term Guy's novels "young adult" is a misnomer, for their realism is hard-hitting, and their aim to present a model for constructing a healthy racial psyche within a devaluing dominant culture is evident. In a trilogy that includes *The Friends* (1973), *Ruby* (1976), and *Edith Jackson* (1978), she tackles female growth and questions of sexuality. *The Friends* juxtaposes two families, the Caribbean Cathys and the African American Jacksons, and examines black ethnicities and their cultural divergences. The second book in the trilogy takes on a subject few black novels and even fewer young adult novels at the time addressed, lesbianism. Phyllisia's older sister, Ruby, the more compliant daughter, becomes involved with the beautiful and revolutionary-minded Daphne. The sensuousness and naturalness that surrounds Guy's treatment of the relationship, as well as Daphne's decision to sacrifice sexuality for social aspiration, mark new territory. The third novel in the trilogy returns to Edith. She and her three sisters are living in a foster home after the abandonment of her father. To facilitate moving them out of foster care, social workers split them up among different families. The novel details the varying impacts of the girls' environments on their outlooks and outcomes.

Alice Childress, another Harlem Writers Guild member, was very much part of leftist activism in New York, writing for Paul Robeson's *Freedom* and the Marxist journal *Masses and Mainstream*. Her involvement earned her an FBI file, and for much of the 1950s publishers would not print her work. Childress, also a dramatist, winning an Obie for her play *Trouble in Mind* (1955), carries the techniques of drama over to her fiction. *Like One of the Family* (1956) is actually a series of witty monologues in which

Mildred Johnson, a domestic, recalls her life and thoughts to her best friend, Marge. The collection of segments do not have the plot sequence of a novel; rather they cohere through a voice that sheds light on history, culture, and character while giving insight into the meaning of a friendship that restores the humanity that domestic work takes away. Childress also wrote realistic fiction for young adults. *Rainbow Jordan* appeared in 1981, and *Those Other People* (1989) powerfully renders young reactions to homosexuality, child molestation, and mental illness. Other Childress novels include *A Short Walk* (1979), a work encompassing black female cultural history from 1900 to the end of World War II in the life of a single woman, protagonist Cora James.[9]

The Childress work that most shows her concern with the state of the black community in the 1960s–1970s is *A Hero Ain't Nothin' but a Sandwich* (1973). The novel employs multiple narratives to portray the bleakness of the principal character Benjie Johnson's community. Set after the Civil Rights movement, it is evident that little has changed materially in the lives of young men like Benjie. Once a bright student, he sates feelings of inadequacy by gang associations and drugs. Angry and desiring approval, he spirals into heavier drug use and theft; however, the work offers Nigeria Greene, a black nationalist teacher dedicated to his students, and Butler, an honorable maintenance man dating Benjie's mother, as life buoys. The nationalist concern for black men is evident in Childress making these characters vital to communal transformation. It is Butler who holds out the saving hand. The novel ends with him waiting to accompany Benjie to a counseling session, and stressing the role of choice, Childress leaves open the question of whether Benjie arrives.

The life confined by ghettoized space that Guy and Childress paint fictionally was very much Nathan C. Heard's actuality. He learned to write in the New Jersey State Penitentiary. Prior to incarceration, baseball biographies of Lou Gehrig and Babe Ruth, along with soft-core pornography, was the extent of his exposure to "literature"; but while incarcerated he began to read and to study the techniques and thoughts of Jean Genet, Norman Mailer, Samuel Beckett, Chester Himes, and James Baldwin. Literature literally and figuratively saved Heard. When his mother showed the draft of what would become his first novel to his lawyer, the latter passed it to a publisher. *Howard Street* (1968) appeared a month before Heard left prison. Its tense realism contributed to sales of over one half million copies. He went on to teach creative writing at Fresno State College, then at Livingston College at Rutgers University, and later he would be a speechwriter for Newark mayor Kenneth Gibson. *Howard Street* might be termed a progenitor of 1960s urban writing. Other works within the tradition include Claude Brown's *Manchild in the Promised Land* (1965), a semi-autobiographical coming-of-age story detailing a young man's escape from the drug use and the violence that mired Harlem, and Piri Thomas's *Down These Mean Streets* (1967), the memoir of a Puerto Rican-Cuban man whose experiences with street gangs and heroin addiction lead to prison and ultimately his transformation. Heard details the stagnation within Howard Street in Newark, New Jersey, an area that could be representative of many impoverished black city communities. From its opening scene of sex between a prostitute and her john, thorough the descriptions of fights and shoot-outs with police, the novel calls to mind pulp fiction; yet, its deep psychological investigation of characters makes it a novel Nikki Giovanni would characterize as a classic for the sheer power of its technique and perception (71).

The only chance characters on *Howard Street* have of escape is to not believe that the street defines them. Though it recalls the determinism of *Native Son*, its exposition is intended for the world it depicts, not the white world around it. In a bar scene where the local wino, Jackie, a former basketball star with a college scholarship and a former head of the local Boys club, has a debate with a young, crusading white civil rights worker there to assuage his guilt, Jackie observes that only the people within a community can make the changes necessary for its betterment. Howard Street itself is major character, an area whose namesake bar's clock has stood at 1 o'clock for over twenty years. Time changes nothing, and with little variety, residents, known as "the streeters," do the same thing, drink, have sex, and hustle. Intraracial struggles occur amid a populace that includes a black middle class contemptuous of its less fortunate peers. Power struggles erupt between pimps, gangs, and corrupt black police officers, all compensating for their essential powerlessness. Gay queens whom the novel derisively refers to as "fags" suffer abuse and in turn sometimes become abusers. What might be sensationalist voyeurism is turned into poignant portraits through back-stories explaining the cycles trapping the characters. The work is a call to action to change the conditions of too many like communities.

Heard went on to write *To Reach a Dream* (1972), the story of Bart Enos, a pimp living off his girlfriend while dreaming of a bigger move up; *A Cold Fire Burning* (1974), the story of interracial love between a working-class black man, Shadow, and a liberal white woman social worker, Terri, against the backdrop of 1970s politics of race and gender; and *When Shadows Fall* (1977), a sensationalized tale of drug-dealing. His last novel was *House of Slammers* (1983), an exposé of prison life that H. Bruce Franklin, in his book *Prison Writing in 20th-Century America* (1998), would characterize as the most important novel yet published about the American prison (280). All Heard's novels portray harsh realities but all have a fine-tuned attention to character and narrative voice.

The setting that Nathan Heard used in *Howard Street*, what is now called the Central Ward, would be the site of the Newark rebellion of 1967.[10] The violence influenced another writer, who dealt with it through satiric treatment. At the time an editor at the Newark weekly *Advance*, the riots a river away from his Greenwich Village home inspired Ishmael Reed's *The Freelance Pall Bearers* (1967). The naïf Bukka Doopeyduk lives in HARRY SAM and works as an orderly in a psychiatric hospital. HARRY SAM is named after Harry Sam who presides over the corruption of his world while living in Sam's motel on Sam's Island that sits in the Black Bay, a body of water polluted by Sam's own excrement, the result of a gastrointestinal disease that keeps him on the toilet spewing out his waste through large statues of Rutherford B. Hayes. The allusion to a president whose election was only effected by the Compromise of 1877 is one of many ways the novel questions the nation's moral ethics. The egocentric naming is indicative of the one-way thinking that fuels totalitarian corruption. Reed's style of blending African American forms with traditional literary conventions, of referencing vernacular culture such as hoodoo, of sly allusions to multiple literary works and traditions, of mixing typographical style in the print of his novels begins here. He molds the coming-of-age form to show that within the ecosystem of HARRY SAM only perpetuation of power not transformation of injustice is possible. Everything is fair game for Reed's satire. Conjure and the post-riot Newark social initiatives are both skewered through mail order hoodoo lessons offered via the Mojo Retraining Act (4). The meaninglessness of political speech is represented through nonsense words, "Blimp Blank Palooka Dookey" (27). Lyndon Johnson's penchant for bathroom interviews inspires the portrait of SAM on the toilet and enhances the novel's condemnation of the US role in Vietnam symbolized by SAM's pedo-canabalism. Reed's narrative voice is a composite of the fantastic and deeply historical.

Freedom of expression is the subject of Reed's second novel, *Yellow Back Radio Broke-Down* (1969), a western told in ballad form beginning with the incantatory, "Folks. This here is the story of the Loop Garoo Kid" (9). Each paragraph is a verse within the ballad of Loop, a conjurer helped by Chief Showcase, a tech-savvy Native American flying a helicopter. Showcase is not on horseback and is a figure designed to undo the romanticizing of

Native Americans as a people of the past. Together they battle the neo-socialist realist gang who call Loop a "Crazy dada nigger" (35) and resent his forays into the abstract. For them novels must liberate the masses; for Loop novels can be whatever they want to be. In this tension, Reed engages the art versus politics debate. Loop's other nemesis is political corruption in the figure of Drag Gibson, a mascara-wearing cattle baron sought out by the citizens of Yellow Back Radio to subdue their defiant children, a plot line that recalls the stifling of student dissent in the 1960s. The novel's title implies an analysis reducing something into comprehensible units and a reformulation. Yellow Back Radio is scrutinized to see what has led to its deconstruction. The title also indicates Reed's debt to popular culture, as Yellow Back refers to the yellowed pulp that was the material of western magazines and paperbacks. Reed makes use of the myth of the west to critique it and what it has been used to facilitate: the ethos of manifest destiny, Native American removals, and making the terms "white" and "American" synonyms.

Mumbo Jumbo (1972) continues Reed's attention to novel form. That he sets it in the 1920s cannot help but suggest the Harlem Renaissance, as well as suggest the ways in which that period became an artistic marker for black expression. Conventions of the detective novel – a murder, clues, final resolution – drawing and photographic images, time travel, typographical markings in the text, lyrics, clippings from actual newspapers, footnotes that imitate scholarly research, all reveal how the battle between western and non-western world views have characterized human history and art, how one group's knowledge and cultural products are another's mumbo jumbo. PaPa LaBas is a hoodoo detective whose name and being incorporate west African atavisms in the Americas. Jes Grew, an Africanist spirit that causes people to break out in song, dance, and have visions, is a liturgy in search of a text, and Papa LaBas seeks to reunite both. Attempting to counter him and destroy Jes Grew to retain its own cultural supremacy is the Wallflower Order of the Knights Templar. In the novel, the traditions of hoodoo, the blues, and early jazz are enlisted to counter a hegemony that asserts its superiority even while appropriating the creations of its presumed inferiors. The many anachronisms rupture the idea of linear time to show the parallels of repeated histories.

All of Reed's novels focus on form. The Last Days of Louisiana Red (1974) uses the detective story to consider the self-defeating divides within black community; Flight to Canada uses the slave narrative form to examine the freedom of the writer and the difficulty in asserting one's voice to tell one's story; The Terrible Twos (1982) again uses the detective figure to satirize the

Ronald Regan administration's vision of America; and *Reckless Eyeballing* (1986) uses a frame story as Ian Ball, a black playwright who has been "sexlisted," attempts to construct a work that will satisfy Jews and New York women who he feels control the publishing world. Mythology, in this case the Danish creations Black Peter and St. Nicholas, shape *The Terrible Threes* (1989), a sequel to *The Terrible Twos*, into a critique of capitalistic systems. In postmodern fashion, *Japanese by Spring* (1993) blends fiction and nonfiction to satirize academic tyranny. Reed himself is a character within the work *Juice!* (2011), a compendium of television transcripts, courtroom documents, and Reed's own cartoons that eschews chronology to tell how the career of a struggling African American cartoonist is upended by the O. J. Simpson trial.

Reed bucks convention in both writing and publishing. He found fault with the way black writers were historically treated by publishers: the 1920s, he felt, decided that only one writer among many could be a star at a time; in the 1940s the Communist Party placed its imprimatur on writers it felt were appropriately political; in the 1960s black nationalist writers demanded that all blacks be portrayed in a positive way; and in his time feminism influenced who would appear in print (J. D. Mitchell, n. pag.). Resenting not only strictures on what a book should be, but also those dictating what will be published, he founded several small presses, among them I Reed books and Ishmael Reed Publishing Company, to support writers who might not find a home elsewhere.

One literary influence Ishmael Reed cites is Charles Wright (J. D. Mitchell, n. pag.). In the 1950s, Wright worked as a messenger in New York and wrote a weekly column for *The Village Voice*. His experiences served as a base for his first novel *The Messenger* (1963). The work is picaresque, as Wright uses the figure of a messenger to render moving stories of the fringes of New York City, its prostitutes, drag queens, stock traders, lonely wealthy, drug addicts, as well as its famous, Tallulah Bankhead, Julie Harris, and Eli Wallach. Charles, a good-looking wellbuilt black man who is often mistaken for Puerto Rican, describes himself as a "minority within a minority" (88) because of his ambiguous appearance. He sells himself to men in order to subsidize his meager income as a messenger. An avid reader and an appreciator of the art of Chagall and Picasso, Charles wants to be a writer but having to live in New York as a squatter is sapping his talent. His redemption, he feels, can only come through leaving New York, and he purchases a ticket to Mexico, but the novel is intentionally ambiguous as to whether Charles departs or not. *The Messenger* is dedicated to Billie Holiday and Richard Wright, figures popularized as symbols of artistic suffering and intellectual anger. Both elements run throughout the work as Charles searches for something he cannot define. The novel's voice swings between romanticized descriptions of city sounds, sights, and smells, and pulp reportage of the city's ugliness. Its vignettes are told in an episodic manner, taking place in New York, Los Angeles, and Charlie's small hometown of Sedalia, Missouri. It is an impressionistic work, and when the reader stands back from the "dots" the picture of his despair at never having enough money, his alienation, loneliness, and frustration with racial politics of the United States become clear.[11]

Wright's *The Wig* (1966) is more in keeping with novels reflecting the growing black anger of the 1960s. The protagonist Lester Jefferson uses "Silky Smooth," a hair straightener he hopes will not only give him hair the color of burnished gold, called a "wig" in the slang of the times, but will also confer the privileges of whiteness. The traditions of mock heroic epic are employed to highlight the stupidity of Lester's odyssey: he is not noble, but seeks heroism through the cowardly act of trying to be what he is not; he does not attempt a heroic quest for the greater good, but rather seeks only his own material furtherance. Ultimately, he loses both self-love and the love of another. His castration at the end of the novel signals the interest many 1960s novels written by black men will take in black masculinity. Explorations of black anger and art are intimately intertwined with sex and the white female figure. Masculinities in these works are frequently hypersexual, but just as often are struggling, constricted, and ineffectual. Men seek to fulfill the masculinist ideal surrounding them in their society yet are prevented from doing so by the very society manufacturing that ideal. Black masculinities, which include the marginalizing of queerness to assert manliness, are used to question ideas of race, nation, and people. Hal Bennett, Cecil Brown, and Clarence Major all intensely and sometimes graphically explore social potency through sexual potency.

George Harold Bennett settled in Newark upon leaving the south, and at sixteen became a writer for the African American newspaper *Newark Herald News*. His short fiction won him a Pen Faulkner award in 1973, and notice from *Playboy* magazine as one of the most promising new writers of the 1970s. His novelistic techniques have overtures of Faulkner, a writer he cites as an influence. Most are set in the same locale of Burnside, Virginia (modeled after Buckingham, Virginia), and characters appear in multiple novels. His first, *A Wilderness of Vines* (1966) holds up a satirical mirror to intraracial race prejudice. At the close of the Civil War, lighter-skinned blacks own the area's tobacco plantations and darker skinned blacks work in the fields. Lighter skinned orphaned girls are protected in a home run by Miss Whittle, who displays them to prospective marriage suitors, while the darker skinned ones are subject to sexual abuse in the homes of black ministers. Representations of the extremes to which characters filled with self-hate will go lead to a blend of futuristic fantasy and realistic satire that is uneven and often awkward, but foreshadows two major themes of Bennett's novels, self-hate and the representation of black sex in American culture.

In *The Black Wine* (1968), David Hunter uses sex to compensate for self-loathing fueled by comparison to his biracial sister, Clair. The connection between sex and identity is even more explicit in Bennett's best-known novel, *Lord of Dark Places* (1970). Indirect discourse fuses multiple voices into a third-person narrative that tells the story of Joe Market. His father Titus makes him into a false idol for the sake of Titus's invented religion, the Church of the Naked Disciple, a belief system he claims is designed to give blacks a nonwhite-based religion that envisions them as something other than a human evil. Titus encourages followers, male and female, to worship the handsome Joe's body, and to partake visually and sexually of his penis, for a price. By blending religious references with explicit and slangy sexual descriptions, Bennett creates a dissonance that gives the novel a satiric surreality. When Titus is raped and murdered by southern police, Joe is witness and narrowly avoids becoming a victim. He escapes by plunging into a river, and when he emerges from this baptism, he goes North. Racial circumstances are uncomfortably similar there, and Joe enters a picaresque odyssey in which the Nixon administration, the polices of the war in Vietnam, and black nationalism all come under Bennett's satirical swipe. Joe is still the black male sex object engaging in multiple sexual performances with males and females, often as a transaction.

The focus on Joe's sexual organ reflects Bennett's concern with the ways in which the United States has traditionally used representations of black sexuality to sustain white dominance. Many scenes portray black males and females as mired in their own sexual perversion: Titus is the issue of an aunt and her nephew; Titus regularly performs oral sex on Joe; father and son share prostitutes; a father prostitutes his son. In an era stressing the beauty of black people, the love between them, and their unique spirituality, Bennett's portraits contrast markedly showing instead a people who have accepted the negative imagery projected onto them by white society, and who find recourse only through sexual prowess. His novels exhibit the sexism that made advocacy for sexual equality subordinate to advocacy for racial equality. The black male is figured as an emotional child in need of black women to give him back self-regard. Bennett's engagement of phallic myths continues through his later works *Wait Until the Evening* (1974) and *Seventh Heaven* (1976) because he sees part of a black writer's mission as assisting the race in rising above the internalization of imposed definitions of black as filthy, a task he felt most black writers Baldwin and Wright included, were unable to solve within their novels (Newman 362). Bennett would go on to write additional novels penned under the name of Harriet Janeway, and a popular series under the name of John D. Revere.

Bennett was not unique in his intense focus on black male sexuality. Amid frank and sometimes amusing scenes of sexual acts, Cecil Brown in *The Life and Loves of Mr. Jiveass Nigger* (1969) weaves a novel in which the development of the fictitious character (whose life details are very similar to Brown's) satirizes racial perceptions and hierarchies. Unlike his namesake, the nation's first president, the protagonist George Washington is disconnected from his national origins. Born in a southern society the son of a "cussing" father who ends up in prison, George has the status of rebel outsider from birth. Now in Copenhagen he is part of a circle of black expatriates seeking to move beyond the "tired" categories of black and white (58). In their own ghetto abroad, they are distanced from the growing racial unrest in the United States, allowed to stay by a "homesick" American embassy that relishes having a replication of the ghettos they have created at home. The expatriates get information on events in the United States only through reports in Danish newspapers, and their main concern is having sex with white women, an act they vaguely conceive of as protest. George is a work of self-invention, rarely using his given name, making up handles appropriate to the circumstances in which he finds himself. For him, nothing is phony if it is functional. The contempt white America has shown him gives him license to live by his own rules. In need of money, George goes to the US embassy to run a scam on the officials. There he meets an embassy official, a mature woman who supports him as her lover. The novel graphically details his sexual exploits and pairs this with his cultural insights into the hypocrisy of a world that devalues black culture yet appropriates it. A series of extremes (the white daughter of a diplomat having incestuous sex with her father and fearing her own desire for the act to happen again, an episode of sadomasochism, the suicide of his lover), culminating with news of the killing of Malcolm X, force a reconsideration of his role as a gigolo, and triggers his desire to return home. In circular fashion the novel ends as it begins with George contacting the embassy, this time to seek passage home, but whether he transits and changes or finds himself in a perpetuating cycle is unresolved.

Race and sex play prominent roles in Brown's characterization. White females are vehicles through which black males trapped in absurdist racial dynamics seek humanity. The one black female in the work is the beautiful Pat, who terms herself a bad whore because she rarely gets financial reward for her sexual acts. She is more of a token than a meaningful addition to the work. She is there to remind black men that black women, too, can be beautiful, to provide a black nationalist reproductive counterbalance to the interracial relationships. She also is there to remind George that while hiding from overt American racism in Copenhagen, there is a cultural essence he misses. Ultimately George feels that to love a white woman is a weakness, just as for a man to love another man is. His homophobic stance and the stance he begins to express about interracial relationships represent his desire for grounding, to know the border between black and white, to know the border between male and female. At the end of the novel, unlike characters who seek freedom from labels, he expresses the desire for a fixed identity.

Brown's work, like Ishmael Reed's, foreshadows traditions of black post-modernism: it encompasses multiple conventions, among them, narrative, play scripts, and manipulation of typography. His work is one of reference, and asides to other writers are plentiful. His character development, for instance, depends on readers being familiar with Bigger Thomas who is framed as the antithesis to his character George Washington. They are two different kinds of native sons, and their contrast condemns the way Bigger is made to live in fear and masochism.[12] Brown's George is more akin to the other heroes the novel alludes to, Tom Jones and Julien Sorel.[13] Brown employs sharp satire, literary analysis, and folklore. His love of and respect for black oral traditions is evident in all his works including *I, Stagolee* (2006) set in the 1890s, and fictionalizing the story of St. Louis pimp Lee "Stagolee" Shelton's murder of political gang member Billy Lyons. *Days Without Weather* (1982) uses the traditions of black comedy to tell of an African American comedian's struggles in white Hollywood.

Known more for his music than his novels, Gil Scott-Heron also uses sex to explore black masculinity. Written when he was only nineteen, the four main characters in *The Vulture* (1970) manifest different ideas of the black masculine in a novelized morality play set against the backdrop of a deteriorating Harlem of the late 1960s and early 1970s. Spade, a dealer by desperation, Junior, a virtual innocent, Afro, the activist who seeks to empower the community by any means necessary, and IQ who straddles two worlds, each in his own way navigates a wasteland decimating black males. Heron broadens his perspective to contrast nationalist violence and accomodationist ideas in his second novel *The Nigger Factory* (1972). Making use of much of his own experience while attending Lincoln College, the novel tells the story of Earl Thomas, the elected student body president of the historically black Sutton University who faces off against the militant members of Members of Justice United for Meaningful Black Education. The group's acronym, MJUMBE, is Swahili for messenger. Heron's novels capture the various philosophical ideas of late 1960s black culture and depicts black male adjustments to changing cultural times.

Clarence Major's use of sex to represent racial politics is at once explicit and nuanced. With the first page of his first novel *All-Night Visitors* (1969), the reader is confronted with the frank sexual description that will run throughout his works. The protagonist Eli Bolton has no idea of his origins. Is he the son of a white mother who was raped by a black man, as the warden of his orphanage tells him, or is he the son of a white mother traveling through Italy and becoming pregnant? The nebulousness that surrounds his antecedents matches the nebulousness surrounding his self-conception and poses the question of how to establish a healthy black male psyche in a society that consistently perverts black maleness. The segments of the novel move back and forth in time, each offering a small insight into Eli.

Explicit almost pornographic descriptions are the only ways that Eli is able to express his perceptions, at least initially, and these passages are rendered with a tone of desperation rather than eroticism. His sexual organ, the spelling of which mutates phonetically depending on his state of mind, is who he is. Sexual metaphors are how he filters his place in the world. Eating a salad is orgiastic. Fellatio characterizes the materialism of one love interest. The racism of white soldiers appears through savage descriptions of their raping and then killing Vietnamese girls during the war. As Eli grows, as he comes out of his isolation and realizes his responsibility and connection to others, the sexual explicitness disappears. The descriptive language becomes less harsh and more sensuous, focusing less on organs or physical acts and more on their psychological effects. The novel closes with the humane act of Eli inviting a woman and her children thrown out of their apartment by her husband on a stormy night to stay in his apartment while he is at work. What emerges in *All-Night Visitors* is not a vision of black masculinity, but of multiple forms of black masculinities.

In the spirit of the sexual revolution of the 1960s, Major's use of explicit language challenges conventional moralities that have been used to stigmatize and marginalize black men in particular. The result is a degree of freedom from the valuations of a hostile gaze.[14] His language

does not mediate between reader and character; rather, through addressing the reader as a fellow viewer, it places him or her in the scene with
Eli. References, especially to Bronisław Malinowski's *Magic, Science and
Religion* (1948) while Eli observes the residents of the hotel where he is a
desk clerk, emphasize the reader's role in making and interpreting a novel's
meaning.[15] The manipulation of print typography that Major will develop
fully in his other novels engages the eye in constructing import through
visual cues and foregrounds the connection between the visual and literary
arts. Major, also a poet and artist, characterized this novel as an "epic collage poem" and a "drawing done with words" (*Dark and Feeling* 16), and
this characterization exemplifies his aesthetic sensibility, his feeling that all
forms are necessary to eloquent written expression. In *No* (1973), Major
structures his paragraphing to highlight the fragmented nature of the self
and question whether the self can be whole. The narrator who at points
observes the idea of a self to be ridiculous is called by different names.
Increased or decreased indentation indicates whether the central character
Moses Westby is acting as narrator or protagonist as the story of his growth
in a segregated South emerges. The narrator of *Reflex and Bone Structure*
(1975) similarly highlights the role of perception in constructing meaning.
Admitting to being a creation of his own novel-writing imagination, he
warns the reader not to trust his perspective. Gaps might exist in what one
perceives of as truth.

Employing a technique similar to *All-Night Visitors*, *My Amputations*
(1986) eschews longer narrative for episodic vignettes blending recollection and fantasy to reveal the development of Mason Willis from child to
air force soldier to hoodlum, thief, and lecturer. *Painted Turtle: Woman
with Guitar* (1988) uses fables to comment on the role of women and
totem in Mary Etawa's traditional Zuni upbringing. The genres of dream,
mysticism, and the secondary narrative of her lover Baldy mirror her self-
definition. It is a novel about translation, again stressing that meaning is
mediated through the forms in which it is conveyed. Even a narrative that
appears to be a straightforward telling of a return to Atlanta is not. *Such
Was the Season* (1987) juxtaposes language forms, vernacular and standard,
to indicate tensions of perspective and subjectivity as Annie Eliza retro-
spectively tells about the many events coincidental with the homecoming
of her estranged nephew Juneboy.

Major began his career as a visual artist rather than a writer, and the
visual is evident in all his novels' aesthetics, particularly in *Emergency Exit*
(1979), which pairs text and image. For him, painting provides accessible
materials, but writing, the rendering of the speech we take for granted, is

harder to use as a form. He describes himself as a visual thinker envisioning colors, smells, sounds (Rowell and Major 668, 670), and his work breaks down the barriers between poetry, fiction, visual art, and text. It also refuses to construct an artificial wall between art and politics. When he became a contributing editor of the *Journal of Black Poetry*, a publication that also provided a national network for black writers and artists during the Black Arts Movement, he broke with his colleagues over publishing what he saw as a cheap aesthetic of "bull shit and propaganda" (Byerman 46); yet, he did not overlook the oppression that was part of human experience. In an essay "The Black Criteria," he stated that a black poet should use art to cause the downfall of a decadent western civilization (15–16).

Major developed an artistic philosophy of individualism, where the creator must make his or her own choices. As such, critics such as Bernard Bell define Major in the context of modernism or postmodernism, but not the Black Arts Movement, and others mention his eschewing of political message.[16] But he defies any easy either/or categorization. He points out that over the course of black literary development there have been many black aesthetics, many black arts, and they all shared the desire to express race and culture independent of perceptions imposed by the dominant culture (McCaffery 123). To make a space for work such as his, Major cofounded the publishing house Fiction Collective to provide authors freedom from censoring editors. His statements on artistic freedom and his founding of the publishing house are activist endeavors challenging the cultural and political status quo.

Many novelists of the 1960s–1970s were forced to situate themselves along an arts/politics continuum generated by a cultural discourse unconcerned with the nuances of black writing, and many of their works engage and sometimes resist this pressure. John A. Williams began his novel writing career just as the Civil Rights movement was entering its most active period, and the frustration and demands of that time are evident in the themes of his works; however, Williams's treatment of race via exploring the psychological impact of it on the individual often led to his novels being viewed as more concerned with the artistic and personal rather than the political. His first, *The Angry Ones* (1960), has been reissued by W. W. Norton's subsidiary Old School Books, and publisher Marc Gerald's description of the label as one for writers too "street" to be artistic and too artistic to be "street" (Carpenter n. pag.) might characterize Williams's writing as well. His works are rooted in frank frustration and desperation, yet are told lyrically.

The Angry Ones was completed in 1956, but did not appear until 1960. It had difficulty securing a publisher because some houses worried how the material would be received by white readers, especially those from the South. When it did appear, it had been through complete rewrites. The cover of the Ace Books edition in 1960, drawn without Williams's approval, showed a New York skyscraper on the left side, with two head shots on the right – a black man with an angry visage and a white blonde with pouting red lips.[17] In 1975 Chatham House reissued his original version. The work inaugurated ideas he explores over the course of all his novels: the tensions between interracial love and allegiance to one's race, the hypocrisy of American democracy frequently drawn through the figure of the returning black veteran, the importance of black music as an expressive form, and the reconsideration of received history. The protagonist of *The Angry Ones* Stephen Hill is a black World War II veteran working for a New York publishing house. One of his closest associates, Linton Mason, a white former college roommate and editor for McGraw Hill is the foil through which Williams contrasts Stephen's inability to rise in the business with the race privilege that greases Linton's ascendency. The politics of sex is part of their dyad, as well, when jealousy develops once Stephen becomes involved with a white woman, a relationship that is fraught for Stephen as he considers whether it signals betrayal to his own people. Stephen grows increasingly frustrated at his inability to get ahead within the company and, his anger comes to a head with the suicide of his friend Obie Roberts, another black man whose professional opportunities are curtailed.

Williams's next novel *Nightsong* (1961) takes an artist figure as its main character, in this case a musician, and equates artistic expression with personal expression. Creative production explores public and private spheres simultaneously, as it does elsewhere in Williams's novels, *Sissie* (1963), where black music is a metaphor for black memory and in *The Man Who Cried I Am* (1967), where writing becomes a symbolic act of personal and nationalistic freedom. His representation of the artist and creative process is also present in *!Click Song* (1982) and *Clifford's Blues* (1999). Titled after the distinctive sound in the Xosha language *!Click Song* through its paralleling of two writers careers, one black and one white and Jewish, compares the dire effects race places on the black creator as opposed to the white. His last novel *Clifford's Blues* focuses on the rarely addressed World War II history of blacks in Nazi concentration camps. Its framed narrative opens with a letter from Gerald Sanderson to Jayson Jones, asking the latter to read the diary of Clifford Pepperidge, a gay black jazz pianist living a decadent life in Weimar Germany until caught with an American diplomat and forced to spend twelve years in Dachau. To survive the worst of the concentration camp, he strikes a mutually beneficial bargain with a closeted SS officer to "serve" him. The work is a keen examination of the dialectic of power between victims and victimizers. The diary forms the meat of the novel, but the closing frame comments on the ongoing difficulties of publishing black subject matter, as Jones's letter notes the unlikelihood of the work finding a publisher. The scene was prophetic, for Williams had difficulty placing the novel.

Williams's work speaks to the binary of culturally imposed pressure to craft public art for a community or to occupy private expressive space. Defying an artificially imposed opposition his artists often do both, and he frequently invokes black creative history and personages to illustrate the challenges of doing so. When reading *Nightsong* it is hard to avoid thinking of Charlie Parker, an avatar of musical innovation caught in a net of racism, addiction, and the need to create. Williams's protagonist, instead of being nicknamed "Yardbird" or "Bird," is Richie "Eagle" Stokes. Like Parker, he changes the landscape of jazz through the invention of what the novel terms rebop, and like Parker he battles drug and alcohol addiction, dying in his mid-thirties. The novel captures Eagle at the decline of his career. Exploited by the machinery of a white-dominated music industry, in his small way he enacts his own exploitation by manipulating guilty and greedy white liberals for handouts. He rescues from death on the streets the white David Hillary, a former college teacher, who after the death of his wife in a car accident from which he walked away, has descended into alcoholism. They both take solace in the backroom of an east Greenwich Village coffee shop owned by Keel Robinson, who in a label-defying act describes himself as "black white man" (95). He is a Harvard Doctor of Divinity and former minister disillusioned with a religion more concerned with ritual and politics than human salvation, so he makes his coffee shop into a "church" of refuge for musicians. Keel is in love with a white woman, Della a savvy social worker very aware of the impact of American race history even on personal relationships. Heel's similar awareness places him in a double bind loving her yet hating histories of white supremacy.

Williams's evocations of New York's East Village bohemia, kosher butcher shops, laundries owned by Chinese proprietors, and Russian and Polish travel agencies portray a world of artistry and poverty within a society increasingly bankrupt of humanism and concerned only with money and race. Eagle's life embraces black musical history from New York's famed 52nd street jazz corridor, an area he recalls Billie Holiday terming a plantation because the owners made the money while the musicians slaved (47), to the black musical migration from New Orleans to St. Louis to Chicago in an era when bebop was challenging established forms of jazz. His music is transgressive, and he is contemptuous of the authority that does not allow him to benefit from the creativity he generates. Eagle signifies on the appropriations of the language, posture, food, and other elements of black culture that have become core elements of larger American culture without their sources and importance being fully acknowledged.

The Man Who Cried I Am (1967), perhaps Williams's best-known novel, again makes use of the artist as rebel. Told in flashback, Max Reddick recalls his life as he faces death from colon cancer. In many ways, the novel is a *roman à clef.* Though Williams had yet to meet Richard Wright and James Baldwin when writing it, knowledge of their lives suffuse the work.[18] As in *Nightsong* with Charlie Parker, here one cannot help but read and see the histories of Baldwin and Wright intertwined with Williams's own. He gives to his Wright-esque character Harry Ames his own experience of being awarded the Prix-de-Rome by the American Academy of Arts and Letters for *Nightsong,* only to have the honor revoked when it was discovered he was black (and possibly that he was going to marry a white woman). Ames's marriage to a white woman, Charlotte, recalls Richard and Ellen Wright while revealing the impact of racial politics on the personal. The up and coming writer Marion Dawes who is portrayed as always having his hand out evokes James Baldwin, while showing the uneasy place that homosexuality (also implied in the case of Harry Ames) has in Williams's novelistic world where the term "faggot" is used to designate gay men (137). There is a scene where Dawes says to Ames that the son must slay the father, a statement credited to Baldwin (217).[19] Other real-life personages weave in and out of the work, a character suggesting Martin Luther King, Jr. who is criticized for being a race leader chosen for, not by black people, and a patron who facilitates Max's career, Granville Bryant, described as the "Great White Father" (39) very reminiscent of Carl Van Vechten.[20] Max works as speechwriter for a president strongly modeled on John F. Kennedy who sacrifices equal rights for blacks to gain southern support. The novel also examines changing black American perceptions of Africa through its treatment of African leaders who rode to power promising to break European colonial control only to internalize the same capitalistic and race values of their former oppressors.

The Man Who Cried I Am is organized by place, its chapters titled after the cities that spark Max's memories as he recalls his life as first a poorly paid writer, then a novelist seeking to do in literature what Charlie Parker is doing in jazz, then a talented but token journalist, and ultimately the head of a news magazine bureau office. The in-between points of his life are designated as "en route to." Narrative form replicates jazz's recapitulation by taking central motifs and "replaying" them at different points in different forms. Williams has said that the traditional novel form is akin to a house with four corners, not suited to the multidimensional narrative he sought to create. He envisioned himself as part of a generation of black writers – Clarence Major and William Melvin Kelley – who were breaking the form and experimenting with new modes of storytelling ("Novelist" 64).

Both Ames and Reddick become revolutionary figures as they expose the King Alfred plan, a government-sponsored international plot designed to contain and eliminate black people. The plot line is in keeping with the growing black mistrust and anger contemporaneous to Williams's composition, and these elements gain a presence in the retributive imagery in his later works. *Sons of Darkness, Sons of Light* (1969) is written against the history of black churches being bombed and black youth killed by white police. The protagonist Gene Browning, mild-mannered and holding a PhD, contemplates the ineffectiveness of black gradualism and commissions a hit on a policeman who has recently killed a black youth. He approaches an ex-Don from the Italian mafia and through him hires an assassin. Browning's act is the start of a civil war, one the novel implies is the only means of achieving black equality. It incorporates the revenge fantasy Williams sees as a trait in much of black writing: "Revenge, racial redemption, and release from white oppression in all its forms seem to be almost mythic urges for several black writers ... I like to think that my own novels *Sons of Darkness, Sons of Light* (1969) and, to a lesser extent, *Jacob's Ladder* (1987) are within this tradition" (foreword, *Black Empire*, xv). *Jacob's Ladder* through its protagonist, an African American military attaché, warns about the prospect of racial revenge through the consequences of an African nation attaining nuclear capabilities. Though not a supporter of separatist or nationalist views, Williams more and more uses extremism for cautionary effect, and nowhere is this more evident than in *Captain Blackman* (1972). Here time travel traces the experience of black soldiers from the Revolutionary to Vietnam Wars, and hallucinatory dreamscapes consider injustice. When the novel opens, Blackman is in the midst of the Vietnam War, attempting to school Afro-sporting dashiki-wearing soldiers under his charge about black military history. Once he is wounded and trapped by the Viet Cong, his imaginings mix historical fact and place to convey African Americans at war with both the enemies and the racism of the United States.

Williams was not alone in expressing growing black American disaffection through radical characters and plots in fiction. Sam Greenlee's *The*

Spook Who Sat by the Door (1969) draws upon its author's own experiences as a United States Information Agency (USIA) officer for the State Department and alludes to the popular Ian Flemming James Bond series, replacing the potent figure of a white British spy with an African American man who fights to nullify forced societal impotency. Its main character Dan Freeman is one of twenty-three black men selected to integrate the US Central Intelligence Agency (CIA). Rather than being a move toward greater equality, the move is actually the brainchild of a desperate politician who devises it only to secure the black vote he needs to win reelection. Freeman, however, succeeds and goes on to subvert the very institution that has provided his training. When he resigns from the CIA, he takes these skills to his old South Side Chicago neighborhood where he observes a gang called the Cobras who he feels has revolutionary potential. He mentors them, and they set in motion the revolution Freeman envisions but does not live to see.

Written while Greenlee resided in Greece in 1966, *Spook* is fantasy and wish fulfillment, written at a time when black revolutionary fervor is at its height. Having difficulty finding an American publisher, it first appeared in England. Its title at once refers to the pejorative for a black person, tokenism, a spy, and is a synonym of the verb fear. Filled with guides to robbing banks, armories, and building a Molotov cocktail, the novel was criticized as a manual for revolutionaries. The movie that came out of its adaptation was pulled from the theatre after a brief box office run. For its author it represented the desire of young black men to turn the tables on the society that devalued them.[21] Not many have a biography that reads writer, film producer, and diplomat, and while these all describe Greenlee's life, they also describe the sources of his novels' aesthetics. *Spook* and his second work, the eerily prescient *Baghdad Blues* (1976), the story of Chicagoan Dave Burrell, a special agent fluent in Arabic yet still refused service at a Virginia drugstore when entering with his white colleagues, seamlessly blend satire and the popular spy thriller. Both novels shed light on the hypocrisy of a Cold War America desiring to stem the tide of pro-communist feelings while mired in its own racism.

The masculine worldviews of the foregoing novels are evident. As has been frequently noted, the worldviews of the Black Arts and Power movements stressed manhood, and not all proponents of this emphasis were men.[22] At the time, Sonia Sanchez penned a poem "Queens of the Universe," that asserts that the job of black women is to "deal with" a country that "crackerized" and "colonized us" but they must do so "under the direction of blk/men" (29). The desire to end inequality did not always include the inequality between black men and women. Abbey Lincoln would query "Who Will Revere the Black Woman?" and Louise Moore, Vice President of the Domestic Personal Services Workers, in "Black Men vs. Black Women" would call for black women to use "guerilla warfare" to undermine the exclusionary tactics of black nationalist vision. Some characterized the writing style of Carlene Hatcher Polite as tantamount to guerilla warfare, particularly in its head-on engagement of black sexism and its effect on female psyche.

In *The Flagellants* (1966), Jimson and Ideal are the allegorically named main characters: he, after a potentially toxic weed also called the Devil's Snare that is used both to heal and to create hallucinations; she, after something intangible, always sought, rarely attained. Living in Greenwich Village in a city completely indifferent to them, they engage in Socratic dialogues in which the reader learns more about them than they do about themselves. At times accusatory, at times analytical, at times violent, their conversations are written in stream of consciousness revelation that entraps the reader in the flagellant dynamic that is Ideal and Jimson. The language combines the academy and the street. Polite's sentences are looping, containing dissonant metaphors that perfectly capture the self-defeating cycle in which the couple places themselves. The plot is simple; it begins with Ideal, through flashbacks, reflecting on her life in the Bottom. She recalls her great-grandmother's admonition (as well as the old woman's wonderment that anyone could be expected to live up to an ideal) to always stand tall. Most of the novel shows her inability to do so in her present, as she is locked in a self-degrading spiral with her lover. Each attempts to achieve their higher self; each blames the other as being what hinders them from doing so. The drunken back and forth as they quarrel about his lack of employment, her emasculation, their mutual infidelities, perversely makes each feel alive, vindicated, human.

The accusations between Ideal and Jimson comment upon the larger issues of black interpersonal relationships gaining traction in 1960s–1970s discourse. They discuss the figure of the black matriarch, made a household image by the Moynihan Report, and how, as a black woman, Ideal recapitulates the stereotype. The impact of black male phallic power and the idealized white female on black female self-image surrounds every argument. *The Flagellants* does not offer a direct critique of race history, but rather a vivid illustration of the personal costs of this history. Through Jimson and Ideal every debate of the Black Power era is personalized, and in particular the place of the black woman in relationship to black men. While showing the difficulty of the couple finding a healthy way of loving, the novel suggests that black people face the same challenge in finding a healthy way to love themselves and counter the societal myths engendering self-hate. Some felt Polite's focus only on a black woman trying to understand her own complicity in a self-destructive relationship was self-indulgent, lacking conventional character development and interplays of incident; but such assessments inadvertently highlight Polite's innovation. She creates a modernistic novel that through its own form replicates the confusion of her characters.[23]

The Flagellants was composed while Polite was in Paris, a place she migrated to seeking not greater racial freedom but less distraction. Her second novel *Sister X and the Victims of Foul Play* took Paris as its setting in portraying the inquiry into the death of a black nightclub dancer. The novel attempts, not always successfully, to show the tension between being an artist and being an entertainer, and questions whether spectacle is killing black art. Written ten years after *The Flagellants*, though not as widely recognized, the narrative style recalls rapid-fire spoken word poetry. Polite's novels foreshadow the ways forthcoming black women writers will break the binary of black sexism and white feminism that marginalizes black women.

Black novels written through the 1960s and 1970s were composed against increasing black engagement with international politics. The 1955 conference of African and Asian nations held in Bandung, Indonesia, gave voice to a broad condemnation of colonialist and imperialist practices, and this condemnation resonated with blacks in the United States. Then named Cassius Clay, Muhammad Ali's conscientious objection to army induction vivified ethical questions as to whether black soldiers should fight other people of color in a "white man's" war. *The Crisis, Freedomways,* and even the more broadly circulated *Ebony* covered liberation movements in Africa and the Caribbean. When in 1959 a visiting Fidel Castro, mistreated by more than one hotel in downtown Manhattan, moved his delegation to the Teresa Hotel in Harlem, the global reach of activism for social equality manifested itself in very concrete ways. His presence there brought home to many black Americans that their struggle for freedom was part of a broader international one.[24] In less than ten years, Egyptian president Gamel Abdel Nasser (who visited Castro while the latter was in Harlem) ended British control of the Suez Canal; the Congo achieved liberty from France; and Jomo Kenyatta and the Mau Mau struggled against the British for Kenyan independence. The ongoing Algerian war for independence and continued anti-apartheid activism influenced black ideas, and discourses of black American liberation referenced the speeches of Patrice Lumumba,

Mao Zedong, Che Guevara, and Fidel Castro. Martin Luther King, Jr., the embodiment of the Civil Rights Movement's established guard, observed that "violence is as wrong in Hanoi as it is in Harlem" (King n. pag.). Black activist philosophies had gone abroad. In addition to expatriates in Europe, a repatriate community of writers and artists formed in Accra, Ghana. Their vision for a new United States was decidedly Pan African, and their rallying cry was "A Mali in Mississippi; a Ghana in Georgia."

When Ghana gained its independence under Kwame Nkrumah in 1957, and when he offered citizenship to W. E. B. DuBois in 1961, the lure of Ghana proved irresistible to a generation for whom repatriation replaced freedom rides and participation in building the infrastructure of a recently liberated African nation replaced sit-ins. An overview of this community shows it to be a mix of activists agitating for international justice. They were artists, sociologists, and, of course novelists. Much like Harlem during the New Negro Renaissance, post-colonial Gold Coast, renamed Ghana after an ancient empire that included today's Senegal and Mauritania, was a place to be "theorized," to be "thought" of as a site for rebirth. "We, the Revolutionist Returnees,… would sit together over Club beer discussing how we could better serve Ghana, its revolution, and President Nkrumah," writes Maya Angelou, one of the repatriates. "Time was a clock being wound too tight, and we were furiously trying to be present in each giddy moment" (78).

This community of Afros as they were called hosted Malcolm X, Louis Armstrong, and Che Guevara as visiting guests. The unofficial president of the community was novelist Julian Mayfield. After 1954 Mayfield spent much of his time writing while living in Puerto Rico, the homeland of his wife, Ana Livia Cordero who would later establish a women's clinic in Accra and be Du Bois's personal physician. In 1958 he returned to the United States and became part of a coterie of writers having a tremendous impact on 1960s African American literature. One of the central participants in the Harlem Writers Guild, he worked with James Baldwin, John Oliver Killens, Paule Marshall, and Maya Angelou, among others, and published two novels, *The Hit* (1957) and *The Long Night* (1958). An activist and an actor, Mayfield appeared in the Broadway productions of *Lost in the Stars* (1949) and was a member of the Committee for The Negro in Arts which fought discrimination in the theatre. Mayfield became involved in the armed defense movement started by Robert Williams, and along with Amiri Baraka and John Henrik Clarke he arranged for the smuggling of weapons to Williams in Monroe, North Carolina.[25] Wanted by officials for his involvement, Mayfield left the United States and ultimately settled in Ghana where Nkrumah appointed him press secretariat and editor of *The African Economist.*

Much of the writing produced in Ghana was autobiographical – Ed Smith's *Where To Black Man* (1967), Leslie Alexander Lacy's *Rise and Fall of a Proper Negro* (1970), Maya Angelou's *All God's Children Need Traveling Shoes* (1991), and Pauli Murray's *Song in a Weary Throat: An American Pilgrimage* (1987) – and were written in hindsight. Though its duration was short, 1961–1966 when Nkrumah was ousted, and its output modest, it did for novelists of a new generation what Paris had done for an earlier one: gave them the knowledge that United States was not the global center. It provided a powerful draw for modern discontents seeking a model for the new black world they sought to build, and it personified the philosophical change in black American perspectives moving beyond the traditional civil rights paradigms. Ghana embodied a black agency that fit perfectly with the budding "black is beautiful" moment of the 1960s that freed many black Americans from internalizations of inferiority.

Clarence Major recalls telling Ralph Ellison, "I'm doing a piece on the black novel and you're in it." Ellison's response was, "but I'm a Negro" (*Dark and Feeling* 22). The humorous exchange illuminates a shift in conceptions of identity over the score beginning in the 1960s. For many, riots in cities as geographically varied as Newark, New Jersey; Buffalo, New York; Detroit, Michigan, and Tampa, Florida, fostered dissatisfaction with what the term Negro signified. A growing awareness of international anti-racist, anti-colonial, and anti-imperialist initiatives influenced people to call themselves Afro-American or black. Novels of the 1960s–1970s captured the turmoil of this era and its major shifts in domestic and international affairs. While they heavily engaged politics, they did so through far more artistic means than has generally been acknowledged. Their dissonant forms were perfectly in keeping with social expressions of desperation, anger, and futility and signaled that black writing no longer had to carry what Toni Morrison called the burden of other people's social expectations, no longer had to work out someone else's agenda ("Interview" 455). The only agenda of consequence was a black one marking out the space for exploring new cultural meanings.

In a gesture reminiscent of Du Bois's 1926 "The Negro in Art – How Shall He Be Portrayed: A Symposium" published in *The Crisis*, Larry Neal drafted a "Black Writer Questionnaire" to appear in *Negro Digest*. The questions it posed to writers moved beyond Du Bois's attempt to characterize how and by whom blacks should be portrayed in literature, and instead stressed introspection on the way the American literary canon impacted black psyche. Among Neal's questions were "Which books, which were 'required' reading in high school or college, failed to impress you most?"; "If *Tom Sawyer* and *Huckleberry Finn* were 'required' reading in school, do you recall having negative reactions to the novels?"; and "At what point in your educational career were you introduced to Negro History?" (LNP 7, 14). Neal's query was exemplary of an attitudinal shift as concern for how blacks were perceived was replaced by concern for how they perceived themselves.

The 1960s–1970s lay the groundwork for sweeping changes in how black history and culture were understood. Many black studies programs were founded during this period and encouraged the institutional recognition of black creative work. The stage was set for rethinking college curricula and publishing criteria as a body of scholars and writers emerged to challenge the humanities to look beyond western traditions.

It is interesting that in the late 1990s and early 2000s, an era in which the terms non-essentialism, hybridity, and post-racial, are ever-more present in cultural discourse, there is has been a renewed interest in a period arguing for a dedicated cultural space for blackness. Hip-hop artists cite Amiri Baraka as a progenitor and channel the presence of Toni Morrison.[26] The resurgence of black arts iconography and thought is perhaps testament to the continued frustration over unchanging social practice and the enduring desire for validation of racial identity. A black worldview might call deeply to those still seeking a philosophy through which modern blackness might function.

CHAPTER 6

From Margin to Center: African American Novels, 1970s–1990s

> Although nearly half of all English departments require a course in Shakespeare for their majors, I would bet that *The Color Purple* is taught in more English courses today than all of Shakespeare's plays combined. Those who maintain that Alice Walker, though well worth reading, has in comparison with Shakespeare less to show us about people, societies, and the possibilities of language (a highly defensible standard of literary merit) must accustom themselves to being called "elitists" – an accusation beside which even the terms "racist" and "sexist" have paled into blandness. (Clausen 52)

As what was popularly termed the culture wars reached their height in the 1970s–1990s, critics and self-styled aesthetes argued that writers whose works engaged civil, women's, lesbian and gay rights, and did so with forms deemed unaesthetic, were incapable of creating a "universal" literature and were eroding academic excellence. In addition to Christopher Clausen, quoted above, Dinesh D'Souza in *Illiberal Education* (1991) feared that Homer, Aristotle, and Shakespeare were being exiled to make room for Toni Morrison, Alice Walker, and Ntozake Shange. William Bennett and Lynne Cheney would join the chorus, bemoaning the eschewing of classic literature for the literature of identity politics.[1] Self-acclaimed protectors of scholarly and artistic rigor were on the defensive against attempts to create a more representative canon. Hershel Parker's assessment of the 1990 edition of the *Heath Anthology of American* literature shows how readily efforts to broaden conceptions of canonical literature were chastened with the yardstick of literary merit: "The most visible innovations in the Heath anthology are the new selections by writers from racial minorities, especially blacks and Indians – selections where *literary* merit has plainly not always been the chief criterion" (15). Parker was editor of multiple editions of the *Norton Anthology of American Literature*. While no one would dispute his right to his assessment, the ready equation of race and artistic inferiority makes one question the unstated values behind standards of literary evaluation.

In no small part, African American novels, and particularly those written by women, were caught in the maelstrom of the culture wars, and the contentions surrounding them exposed the insularity of college curricula, publishing houses, and media outlets. In response, a developing body of trenchant African American literary criticism questioned presumptions of what constituted a canon. Ishmael Reed, Alice Walker, and Gayl Jones were among those who followed the tradition of James Baldwin, Langston Hughes, Richard Wright, and Ralph Ellison in becoming writer/critics who blurred the line between creating and critiquing literature. Toni Morrison in her criticism enriched readings of African American texts as well as American standards by Herman Melville, Edgar Allan Poe, and Nathaniel Hawthorne. These writers were joined by a growing body of African American scholars who forced the reinterpretation not only of individual literary works but also of the way literary histories were formed.

The interrogation of critical assumptions previously taken as a given began with early African American literary histories and anthologies, among them Benjamin Brawley, *Early Negro American Writers* (1938); Sterling A. Brown, Arthur P. Davis, and Ulysses Lee, *The Negro Caravan* (1941); Hugh M. Gloster, *Negro Voices in American Fiction* (1965); and *Cavalcade: Negro American Writing from 1760 to the Present* (1971), a joint editing venture between Arthur Davis and J. Saunders Redding, less known for his own novel *Stranger and Alone* (1950), the story of black collegians more concerned with their own benefit than with educating the race.[2] To these early compendiums were later added Richard Barksdale and Keneth Kinnamon, *Black Writers of America: A Comprehensive Anthology* (1972); Michael Harper and Robert Stepto, *Chant of Saints: A Gathering of Afro-American Literature, Art, and Scholarship* (1979), and Nellie McKay and Henry Louis Gates, *The Norton Anthology of African American Literature* (1996). Other anthologies including Toni Cade Bambara, *The Black Woman: An Anthology* (1970) and John Oliver Killens and Jerry W. Ward, Jr., *Black Southern Voices: An Anthology of Fiction, Poetry, Drama, Nonfiction, and Critical Essays* (1992) were organized around categories such as gender and regionalism to identify the literature's richness and breadth. Over the course of their evolution these collections reflected an increasing emphasis on identifying the practices within black literature that constituted a tradition.

Like anthologies, scholarly writing helped to cement an African American canon. Literary historian Blyden Jackson early on observed "whatever the precise nature of the interaction of criticism and literature, surely a good healthy criticism is of invaluable service to any literature" ("Largo for

Adonais" 174). In seeing black criticism as central to the development of black literature, Jackson was not alone. Considering how black literature should be interpreted, Hoyt Fuller in "Towards a Black Aesthetic" wrote "Black critics have the responsibility of approaching the works of black writers ... with the knowledge that white readers – and white critics – cannot be expected to recognize and to emphasize with the subtleties and the significance of black style and technique. They have the responsibility of rebutting the white critics and of putting things in the proper perspective" (Gayle 11). John Oliver Killens went so far as to question whether white critics could review or understand black writing (Gilyard 125). When he describes his ideal of literary interpretation, Clarence Major closely characterizes what would emerge as the chief aims of black literary criticism at this time. He notes that "the most functional and valid method of examining a work of art is by first discovering the terms on which it exists and then judging it on its own terms alone" (*Dark and Feeling* 28). Black critics did precisely this as they read black texts within different systems of cultural understanding.

Works that helped to create an African American theory of criticism included the groundbreaking "Afro-American Literary Critics: An Introduction," an essay by Darwin Turner in Addison Gayle's edited work *The Black Aesthetic* (1971) and Dexter Fisher's and Robert Stepto's, *Afro American Literature: The Reconstruction of Instruction* (1971). Among the later works that continued this mode of inquiry were Houston Baker, *Blues, Ideology, and Afro-American Literature: A Vernacular Theory* (1984) and Henry Louis Gates, Jr., *The Signifying Monkey: A Theory of African-American Literary Criticism* (1988).[3] Writers, anthologists, and scholars produced a body of black critical thought that was essential to establishing the existence of a formal literary tradition. Through recovery and reframing of black expressive practices, they legitimated aesthetic modes of African American writing that came from within the circle.[4] A key component of black criticism was black feminist scholarship. Second wave womanism in Barbara Christian, *Black Women Novelists: The Development of a Tradition, 1892–1976* (1980) and Barbara Smith, *Toward a Black Feminist Criticism* (1980) destabilized notions of racial and gender normativity, and black women theorists countered the legacies of sexism within a discourse that ignored histories of black female subjugation. Black women novelists and critics symbiotically expanded conceptions of black experience and expression.

As seen in Clausen's and D'Souza's statements, Alice Walker became a lightning rod for those denouncing the demise of the American canon.

Her reception as a black woman writer made evident the fault lines of gender and race fragmenting the American literary landscape. In nonfictional and fictional format Ishmael Reed made clear his resentment of the presence Walker signified, going so far as to call black women writers incorporating the Southern and rural "neoconfederate novelists" (R. Martin n. pag.). His novels *Flight to Canada* and *The Last Days of Louisiana Red* involve themes of black women colluding with white men since the times of slavery, and his posture ultimately motivated Gloria Steinem to write to Alice Walker of her desire to kick Reed in the ankle, "only not aiming high so as not to confirm his idea of what's important–!" (undated letter AWP 1, 6). David Bradley wondered if Walker was truly the visionary he once thought she was, whether she was capable of telling world-changing stories (8), while Daryl Pinckney dismissed her work as inspirational writing for black women (18).[5]

Not all who faulted Walker were men. Trudier Harris, in observing the canonization of *The Color Purple* by the media as the "classic" novel by a black woman, criticized its content for perpetuating myths worse than those in the Moynihan Report and for being in marked contrast to Walker's contribution to form via molding Celie's voice from "authentic black folk speech" without devolving into "caricature."[6] Harris addresses an even more significant point in her critique, and that is the way the prominence of *The Color Purple* effected a silencing of black women critics, as if to be a woman and find fault with the novel was a form of treason (155). The voices of black female scholars were so long denied access to critical discourse that once they did gain entry many felt compelled to make sure the message was "right" and to do nothing to hamper the future publication of black women writers. Reading the correspondence between writers and critics including Walker, Barbara Christian, Claudia Tate, J. California Cooper, and Mary Helen Washington, as they update one another on who is making what anthology, who is teaching what course, as they circulate critical articles, and engage in genuine philosophical debate, a sense of the challenges, rewards, and strategies involved in building, critiquing, and teaching a tradition from works previously minimized by academic and cultural arbiters emerges.[7]

Walker is emblematic of the criticism many black women writers received. Stanley Crouch characterized Toni Morrison as a "literary conjure woman" as American as "P. T. Barnum," and asserted that *Song of Solomon* proved that "the combination of poorly digested folk materials, feminist rhetoric, and a labored use of magic realism" could create bestsellers. For him, *Beloved* was "a blackface holocaust novel" (38). Morrison's receipt of the Nobel Prize for literature raised accusations that her race and sex, not talent, garnered her the reward.[8] Terri McMillan, Gloria Naylor, and Ntozake Shange were among many black women writers who would be in line for similar assessments. Morrison and critic Joyce Joyce have suggested that these attitudes are the result of black women writers being the only ones who do not feel that white men and women are the center of the literary world and who exhibit no need to explain or advocate blackness to a white hegemony.[9] It is not unexpected that novels challenging presumptions are subjected to censure, but moving black and female experience from margin to center generated particular vitriol. Creating complexly imagined black female perspectives shed new light on cultural attitudes toward race and gender.

Alice Walker is an instance of a writer who draws heavily on her descent from women like her enslaved paternal great-great-grandmother who walked from Virginia to Georgia, carrying two of her children on her hips, as well as a mother who used her domestic's salary to buy her daughter three key items: a sewing machine to teach self-sufficiency, a suitcase to discover that Eatonton, Georgia, was not the whole world, and a typewriter to begin the career that would lead to literary prominence (Washington 38). Walker's novels are indebted to the Southern world of her origins and focus on the women within it. Her first, *The Third Life of Grange Copeland* (1970) centers on Grange, a black sharecropper whose entrapment in the cycle of perpetual debt manifests in a cycle of perpetual violence against women. Unable to cope with who he is becoming within this system, he abandons his wife and son and heads North. His son, Brownfield is consumed with hatred because of his father's abandonment, and turns his anger into the physical and psychological abuse of his own wife and daughters. While Brownfield and Grange are the major actors in the work, the women figures' struggle for autonomy and self-expression are its themes. Through Mem, Brownfield's wife, the combining of race and patriarchy to destroy male and female humanity is developed, and through her daughter Ruth's relationship with a now redeemed Grange the possibility of return and regeneration is cast as antidotes to racism and familial fragmentation. Walker's 1976 novel *Meridian* fills the lacunae of civil rights history that ignored the centrality of women to the movement and muzzled the sexism they faced. Meridian, the title character, transcends societal expectations to find a self in keeping with her own vision, personally and racially. She chooses the freedom to move over motherhood; activism rooted in her rural community over nationalistic rhetoric. While being a civil rights activist, she comes to an awareness of the injustice of gender roles and the ways they mirror racial typing.

Both *The Third Life of Grange Copeland* and *Meridian* are written in prose that reminds the reader that Walker is also a poet. She lades novelistic voice with lyricism and reflects how stories are transmitted. Her experiment with vivifying black modes of expression crystalizes with *The Color Purple* when she joins orality with the epistolary novel form. In addition to its themes of resilience and redemption is the idea that writing creates identity. Writing becomes symbolic of self-knowledge and agency for the main character, Celie. The victim of incest, continual abuse, and imposed silencing by her victimizer, the man she believes is her biological father, Celie asks God WHY? in a series of letters recording her thoughts as she is separated from her sister, is introduced to a new life and sensuality by the blues singer Shug, and eventually becomes a self-supporting businesswoman. When, halfway through the novel, Celie discovers the letters from her sister Nettie her husband has hidden, she has a new correspondent. Nettie's letters open up a diasporic world for Celie, linking their histories to ancestral African ones. The result is an epistolary exchange that creates an empowering text for both sisters transforming their conceptions of womanhood and God. For most of the novel neither sister receives the letters of the other, so the power of writing as a communicative entity is moderated by its capacity to aid in introspection and self-articulation, a function that Walker has often said writing has played for her.[10] The blending of African American orality with the eighteenth-century epistolary form symbolically inserts black women into the tradition of writing women. Already the winner of the Lillian Smith Award for her collection *Revolutionary Petunias and Other Poems* (1973), Walker went on to receive the Pulitzer Prize and National Book Award for *The Color Purple*.

An increasing degree of experimentation characterizes Walker's later novels, *The Temple of My Familiar* (1989), *Possessing the Secret of Joy* (1992), *By the Light of My Father's Smile* (1998), and *Now Is the Time to Open Your Heart* (2004). *The Temple of My Familiar* revises origins stories. Past narratives of African and Latin American enslavement are juxtaposed with the contemporary self-searching of three couples (with Celie and Shug as spiritual presences). Their experiences demonstrate that only through an understanding of antecedents can a way forward be found. Characters from *The Color Purple* also return in *Possessing the Secret of Joy* (1992). Its main character is Tashi, the Olinka girl who befriends Celie's children and subsequently marries Celie's son Adam. It weaves back and forth through time from the 1920s to the 1980s as Tashi awaits her death. She recalls undergoing genital mutilation and the physical and mental scarring that resulted. Walker's experimentation goes even further in *By the Light of My*

Father's Smile, which in its speculative investigation of sexual and gender values moves between the physical and spiritual realms and mixes living and ghost narrators. Through alternating chapters *Now Is the Time to
Open Your Heart* (2004) parallels the story of fifty-seven-year-old African
American Kate Talkingtree who undertakes a wilderness adventure down
the Colorado River, with that of Yolo, her ex-lover whose saga examines the impact of the colonial and corporate presences on indigenous
Hawaiian culture. With the exception of *Possessing*, the reviews of Walker's
later works have been mixed. Some appreciated them as bold innovations;
others felt they were self-indulgent exegeses on whatever idea appealed to
Walker at the time.[11]

The craft of black women's novels frequently got lost in criticism levied
against them for perpetuating myths of black aberrance and black male
pathology. Gayl Jones, one of the most daring writers at the time, is an
example. Keith Mano in a review as much about Jones and the presence of
black women in writing culture as it is about her novels found little merit
to her *Corregidora* (1975) and *Eva's Man* (1976), and noted that if they had
been written by a black or white male, they would still be in manuscript.
June Jordan felt that rather than revising ideas of black womanhood *Eva's
Man* perpetuated myths of castrating black whores, and she suggested a
likeness between Eva and Bigger Thomas. Some, however, did see its artistry. While still viewing it as an indictment of black men, Daryl Pickney,
who particularly liked that the novel did not fall into the polemical tradition of black literature, found *Eva's Man* avant garde if not fully realized.[12]

Jones's writing career began when poet Michael Harper, under whom
she studied while at Brown University, sent the manuscript of *Corregidora*
to Toni Morrison who then became Jones's editor. Morrison later observed
that no novel of a black woman would ever be the same (*What Moves*
109). Ursa Corregidora, a blues singer, carries the family name her women
ancestors held fast to as testament to their abuse by their Portuguese owner
whose sexual assault of the concubine he prostitutes, and of their daughter
make him both Ursa's grandfather and great grandfather. Ursa comes to see
that this history has its modern parallels in the abuse of black women, and
this realization forms the core of her music. Documents of enslavers' rape
and sexual abuse were rarely kept, and oral stories and music became the
record in their stead. Ursa's blues both resist and record this history. Jones's
use of Brasil as a setting and the blues as a medium for Ursa's expression
underscores the global nature of slavery's enormity and the interconnectedness of cultural forms. Ursa seeks to create a blues in Portuguese, one
that would articulate the transnational dimension of her history.

The powerful *Corregidora* was quickly followed by *Eva's Man* (1976). It continues Jones's exploration of sex and gender through the character Eva Medina Canada who is convicted for killing and orally castrating her lover David, one of many predatory men who sexually assaulted or violently abused her. Told through nonsequential passages often without punctuation breaks, the prose style reflects the incoherence of Eva's maltreatment and the perverse power she feels from being a desired object. This history is contrasted to the relationship of Eva and her cellmate Elvira whose advances, often equally as predatory, and led some to criticize Jones for her portraits of homosexuality.[13] Eva's imprisonment and the judgments of her psychological state without taking into account her life events, symbolize the need to question how patriarchy inadequately interprets women's experiences.

Jones had said she sought to create a writing style deriving from black creations such as jazz, the blues, worksongs, and spirituals, one that used history, myth, autobiography, dream, eroticism, and storytelling, to represent modes of understanding in the world. Her interest in African American oral traditions received full exploration in her critical study *Liberating Voices: Oral Tradition in African American Literature* (1991) and received fictional treatment in the novel appearing twenty years after her earlier successes, *The Healing* (1998). Here, Harlan Jane Eagleton once a beauty stylist becomes a faith healer. Jones elides voices in a narrative that begins in media res, and is told nonsequentially in stream of consciousness. *The Healing* was followed by *Mosquito* (1999), edited by Toni Morrison while Jones recuperated from a nervous breakdown after the suicide of her husband.[14] "Mosquito," Sojourner Nadine Jane Nzingha Johnson, who received her nickname from a reaction to a bite, is a truck driver carrying a cargo of industrial detergents across the border to Texas City when she discovers pregnant Maria, a Mexican woman hiding in the load in the hopes of migrating to safety in the United States. The book's aesthetic breaks down the notions of borders through its pastiche of forms that blend fact and fiction, soliloquy and narrative. "Drunk with words and out of control" was the way Henry Louis Gates, Jr. characterized *Mosquito* in his *New York Times* book review. He goes on to refer to Jones as a "new voice" whose explicit references to fellatio and castration made no subject taboo for a black writer. He further notes that Jones "inspired a new generation of black women writers to testify about being black and female in a wide variety of forms, including Ntozake Shange's choreo-poem *For Colored Girls Who Have Considered Suicide/When the Rainbow Is Enuf* and Alice Walker's epistolary novel *The Color Purple*" ("Sanctuary" n. pag.). The term "testify," even within a review ostensibly praising the power of Jones's innovative use of vernacular voice, risks the same minimizing of African American literary artistry that Gates has spent much of his career fighting. Walker, Jones, and Shange do not merely testify about being black and female; rather, gender and race inform their novels' textures. They shaped metaphors out of materials generated from women's creativity such as quilts and recipes. Elements that more canonical literature marginalized – the lives of domestics, wives, mothers, lesbians – these novels made their core.

Black women's writing explored sex, gender, and race and their multiple intersections. Part of this included an examination of womanist bonding and womanist queerness. While Rosa Guy in *Ruby* addressed lesbianism as a subplot, Ann Allen Shockley's *Loving Her* (1974) was one of the first novels to make a lesbian relationship the nexus of its narrative. Renay Davis, a pianist, has left her psychologically and physically abusive husband for a wealthy white woman writer named Terry Bluvard. Renay's working-class origins and Terry's upper-class wealth strain the relationship. Terry's largess provides Renay with a comfortable place to live, a car, and the ability to pursue her education and music, but Renay is seen as exotic by many of Terry's friends and is often asked to entertain them. In *Say Jesus and Come to Me* (1982), Shockley explores the pressures of heteronormativity through the closeted Reverend Myrtle Black. Myrtle enjoys the relative class privilege and rhetorical power her position gives her and uses her charisma as a sermonizer to seduce young girls caught up in the passion of religious ecstasy. Her closeted existence creates a two-ness in which she is prominent yet marginalized, part of a community yet alienated.

In her works, Shockley sought to counter the invisibility of lesbianism in African American critical discourse and the invisibility of black women in lesbian discourse. Like James Baldwin thirty years earlier, she theorizes black sexuality and uses it to urge reconstructing other paradigms, religion, patriarchy, and class among them. Portrayals of nontraumatic fully sexual lesbian relationships of are rare: that of Cat and Jeffy in *Corregidora* exists in memory; Lorraine and Theresa's relationship in Gloria Naylor's *The Women of Brewster Place* (1982) isn't allowed to survive because of Lorraine's rape and murder; Celie and Shug are bi-sexual, and their relationship is more one of a messiah redeeming a disciple. Frequently lesbianism is portrayed in reactionary mode, as a response to a heterosexual world rather than a state of sexual pleasure comfortable with itself. Like many writers previous to her, Shockley's work was evaluated along lines of appropriate representation and found wanting by critics faulting a negative portrait of black lesbianism.[15] Rather than idealize one of the few portraits of black lesbians, however, she creates flawed characters that challenge the need for model citizenship as a requisite for social acceptance.

Themes of female bonding were often read as marginalizing black men. Ntozake Shange was censured for her portrayals of black males even though her emphasis was on painting women's solidarity and self-redemption. Her taking the name Ntozake is probably the best indication of her desire to rethink the emotional, social, and historical significances of women's experience. "She who comes with her own things" or "She who walks with lions" creates works in which the legacy of historical definition is shown to have personal consequences. Her first novel *Sassafrass, Cypress, and Indigo* (1982) expands on an earlier novella, *Sassafras* (1976). The title refers to three sisters, growing up in Charleston, South Carolina, and their mother Hilda's desire that they have a life better than hers. The daughters, though, discover they must find their own ways, and their epiphanies come through connecting to a cultural past. Indigo uses her skills as a violinist to weave musical spells that make her part of Geechee culture. Sassafrass leaves college and becomes a weaver, making tapestries that tell stories. Cypress becomes a member of an African American dance troupe called The Kushites Returned. The novel employs letters, journal entries, and spells, to extend its third person narration of characters making progress and missteps along their journeys to self.

The need for autonomy and to make sense of raced and gendered identity seen in *Sassafrass, Cypress, and Indigo* permeate all Shange's work. In *Liliane* (1994) an upper-middle-class artist's search for her mother is told through sessions with an analyst and monologues of friends and lovers, and through these the difficulties of cohering fragmented identity come to light. Making use of much of Shange's own life experience, *Betsey Brown* (1985) is a coming-of-age story about a young girl who must make sense of race and class in a desegregating St. Louis. Shange's concern with the ways black women's history broadens understanding of larger black history is voiced in her last novel to date, one she co-wrote with her playwright sister Ifa Bayeza. *Some Sing, Some Cry* (2010) follows seven generations of black women through the major epochs of African American history and describes the survival strategies they develop to sustain self, family, and community. Rape, child abandonment, and hard-won success, form a saga that some criticized for trying to do too much in one novel, for implicit homophobia, and again for its negative portrait of men.[16]

History is frequently made personal in black women's novels. Whether in Bebe Moore Campbells' retelling of the Emmett Till story in *Your Blues Ain't Like Mine* (1992) or Toni Cade Bambara's recasting of the Atlanta child murders in *Those Bones Are Not My Child* (1999), facts are transformed to reveal their human dimensions. *Your Blues Ain't Like Mine* stresses the personal perspectives of The Till family, the perpetrators, and the larger community. In *Brothers and Sisters* (1994) Moore does the same with the beating of Rodney King by Los Angeles Police Department officers and the riots following their acquittal. Bambara's *Those Bones Are Not My Child*, edited by Toni Morrison and published posthumously, critiques the official response to the string of child deaths in Georgia and the state's desire to deracinate the instance. Engagements with history, however, should not belie the continued innovation in these works whether manifested through tackling uncomfortable subjects such as intracommunal tensions in Moore's *Singing in the Comeback Choir* (1998), or mental health issues in her *Seventy-two Hour Hold* (2005), or in the early black feminist ecofiction of Bambara's *The Salt Eaters* (1980) where the earth needs respite from rapacious exploitation as much as the suicidal protagonist Velma needs relief from the pressures of community politics and a floundering marriage. Though it won the American Book Award, reviewers of *Salt Eaters* had difficulty with its avant garde form, and even sympathetic critics acknowledged its difficulty.[17] The narrative style is improvisational, imbued with jazz tonalities and unique rhythms conjuring scattershot memories.

Black women novelists' concern with form was often lost in the maelstrom of gender politics. Gloria Naylor's character Kiswana in *The Women of Brewster Place* (1982), seven stories interconnected by setting and by characters, dreamed of staging a performance of *A Midsummer's Night Dream*. Allusion to the play signals the many literary allusions that are part of Naylor's opus. *Linden Hills* (1985) evokes Dante's *Inferno* as Willie Mason, barely eking out a living, is the guide through the circles that descend through increasing racial denial and assimilation on the way to materialistic riches and moral bankruptcy. Its portrait of an economically secure enclave masks community dysfunction and questions the costs of assimilation. *Mama Day* (1988) recalls Shakespeare's *The Tempest* (1610–1611). Set on Willow Springs sea island, it contrasts indigenous culture with external empiricism as a husband and a conjure woman grandaunt both fight to save their loved one's life. Having these works permeate her fiction undoes the notion that certain traditions are the discrete property of particular races, cultures, or genders. She accomplishes a reverse appropriation to counter the exclusion from literature she felt as a student. In an interview with Toni Morrison she recalled, "All of my education had subconsciously told me that [literature] wasn't the place for me" (575). To see one's experiences in existing traditions concretizes the possibility of entering the writing realm, and her works offer such authority to others. Her awareness of the role of black traditions in black cultural cohesion is evident in *Bailey's Café* (1992). The eponymous establishment is part of a triangle of metaphysical spaces, a portal through which a spectrum of characters from the self-mutilating Mary, to the fourteen-year-old Ethiopian Jew Mariam, to the cross-dressing Stanley, aka Ms. Maple, might find guidance. The narrating master of ceremonies, the proprietor Bailey, introduces the stories of characters seeking salvation in sections named with musical terminology: "Maestro, If You Please," "The Vamp," "The Jam," "The Wrap."

Naylor's novels create their own community with characters connecting one work to the next. In *Brewster Place*, Kiswana Browne's origins foreshadow *Linden Hills*; Willa Prescott Nedeed from *Linden Hills*, is first cousin to Cocoa who appears in *Mamaday*, and Cocoa's husband George, is the baby born in *Bailey's Café*. Naylor has referred to the works as a quartet ("Mood: Indigo" 502). Her fifth novel comes full circle returning to Brewster Place, but focusing on the street's male inhabitants. Their stories complement the histories first revealed from the women's perspectives. The alcoholic janitor Ben returns as the novel's spiritual guide, and we learn that his impotence to protect his crippled daughter from molestation by his white landowner was the source of his drinking. Mattie's son, Basil, who skipped bail and caused his mother to lose the home she put up as collateral returns to repay the debt only to find out she has died. To these characters and others, Naylor adds new ones: Brother Jerome, an autistic child with a remarkable talent for playing the piano who is exploited by his mother for money, and the self-destructive Greasy. Motivated by the death of her father in 1993 and the Million Man March in 1995, Naylor desired to showcase the experiences of men trying to hold on to sanity, home, and family (Lauerman 1). Their voicing the struggle to be a black man in a society without good examples or opportunities demonstrates the power of race, gender, and economics to confine men as well as women.

In contrast to her experience as a student and young writer, when Naylor begins her novel writing the presence of black women authors in both the publishing world and public sphere is growing rapidly. Terry McMillan, Tina McElroy Ansa, and Marita Golden are examples of writers whose works cross over into popular fiction and raise the question of where formal literature and popular literature intersect, one that will be addressed in more detail later in this study. Early on McMillan was savvy about the intersections of writing, publishing and marketing. When learning that her first novel *Mama* (1987) would receive little promotional assistance from her publisher, she wrote to independent bookstores, jazz clubs, black organizations, and colleges, informing them of her work and offering to do book signings. The result paid off for McMillan, and eventually for other writers as her publisher Houghton Mifflin realized the existence of a reading public they had ignored. In her role of anthologist, McMillan also "gave back," to her writing community by introducing black talent to a wider audience. *Breaking Ice: An Anthology of Contemporary African American Fiction* (1990) gave exposure to, or in some cases reminded readers of, writers such as Barbara Summers, Al Young, Percival Everett, John A. Williams, Colleen McElroy, and J. California Cooper.

Taking a course from Ishmael Reed while she was at the University of California, Berkeley, awakened McMillan's awareness of herself as a writer. She moved to New York in the late 1970s when she was accepted to Columbia University Film School and followed in the footsteps of earlier writers by joining the Harlem Writers Guild. She cites as influences on her style the conversational, tragicomic mode of Ring Lardner, and has described herself as a "character-driven writer," a trait evident in novels that develop their ideas from perspectives rather than plot (Murray n. pag.). McMillan's works have been variously classified as "chick lit," "girlfriend," or "sister" novels. Ishmael Reed, a supporter even as he has criticized writers such as Walker, describes McMillan as creating a "black everywoman." The novel that garnered the most public attention was *Waiting to Exhale* (1992), and its readership consisted of a broad cross-section of women of many races, ethnicities, though a good portion was middle class. Its popularity was a mixed blessing, however. McMillan recalls that though they lived a half hour apart, she was saddened that Alice Walker never fully acknowledged her as a writer (Max 3). McMillan's novels do not involve the historical scope of Morrison or Walker, but trenchant issues of colorism, sexism, and class are still present. The modernity of her works also seen in her latest novel *I Almost Forgot About You* (2016), the story of a woman's reinventing herself, adds to her widespread appeal but might also account for her marginalization in more traditionally minded literary circles.

Stream of consciousness, contemporary vernacular, and the use of memory are the hallmarks of McMillan's style, and she employs them to render ordinary experience and complex emotional realities. At twenty-seven, Mildred Peacock in *Mama* (1987) faces a downward spiral into alcoholism, menial employment, and even prostitution while trying to support herself and five children, once her abusive husband leaves her. The novel's language, and vivid characterization, its suggestion that the rhetoric of family and domestic order need to be reshaped to make room for more than a patriarchal centrality, contributed to it receiving the greatest literary regard of McMillan's works. Using first-person monologues, *Disappearing Acts* (1989) moves between the voices of Zora Banks, a music teacher who desires a singing career and her lover Franklin Swift, a construction worker. *Waiting to Exhale* (1992), the novel that secured McMillan's renown, and *How Stella Got Her Groove Back* (1996) portray successful black women protagonists in their late thirties seeking to complement professional success with romantic fulfillment. *The Interruption of Everything* (2005) finds Marilyn, Grimes the forty-four-year-old married mother of three adult children, faced with an unplanned pregnancy, a mother slipping into dementia, a drug-addicted sister who is neglecting her children, and the possibility of an unfaithful husband. Portraits of the continuous quest to find satisfying love and the crafting of imperfect male characters subjected McMillan to criticism of black male "bashing," but positive male portraits exist in her work.[18] Her spotlighting the experiences of black women facing a variety of life challenges is indicative of her desire to redefine personal and domestic relationships for modern womanhood.

Tina McElroy Ansa, a regionalist writer from Macon Georgia, also straddles the divide between "serious" and "popular" literature. Her first novel *Baby of the Family* (1989) was named a 1989 Notable Book of the Year by *The New York Times*. It is a coming-of-age tale whose protagonist Lena is born in a small Georgia town with a caul on her face. According to African American folklore, the caul signifies the ability of second sight, and Lena is indeed placed in this position as she narrates the tumultuous relationship between her middle-class parents. The final scene of the novel in which she is looking at herself frankly in a mirror represents reassessing imposed values and creating new self-generated ones. *The Hand I Fan With* (1996), the name given to Lena by her community because of her works, was a sequel to *Baby of the Family*. A now-adult Lena is matriarch and town healer. While she is successful, she feels empty and asks a friend to conjure a man for her. The resulting spirit is Herman, who died 100 years ago and acts as her mentor. Ansa's *Ugly Ways* (1993) appeared at a time when many felt the publishing world was favoring the writing of black women, particularly those that portrayed black men behaving badly. *Ugly Ways* examines the generational relationship of the Lovejoy sisters as they return to their home in Mulberry, Georgia, after the death of their mother, called Mudear. Through flashbacks, how the abuse they suffered at the hands of their philandering father influenced each daughter is shown, but the story is more concerned with maternal legacy, as is *You Know Better* (2002), a novel depicting the importance of mothering to generate strong community.

Ansa and McMillan write novels firmly rooted in African American life, with white life and racial contestation at the periphery. Fellow novelist Thulani Davis criticized both for narrowly focusing on the experiences of middle-class blacks, calling these works more "Bup Art than Black Art" (177). Davis preferred to give her work larger historical connections as can be seen in *1959* (1992), a story charting Willie Tarrant's growth from adolescent self-absorption to engagement with the world during the tumultuous period of desegregation. At other times, the history Davis employs is contemporary. The questionable suicide of Ana Mendieta, a Cuban-born feminist performance artist in New York, is the basis for *Maker of Saints* (1996), a novel where Bird Kincaid's reconstruction of her friend Alex's life after a fall from the window of her Manhattan apartment symbolizes the power of artistic expression to subvert external objectification.[19]

Criticized by Davis in the same essay for drawing superficial characters is Marita Golden, cofounder of both the Hurston/Wright Foundation and the Washington, DC–based African American Writers Guild. Golden subverts the notions of singly defined black reality. When she married a Nigerian and moved to his nation, she realized that black Americans were citizens of the world. Her works explore African American identity in feminized and diasporic aspects. In *A Woman's Place* (1986), three black women who attend a New England college in the late 1960s form a friendship that sees them through divergent life experiences, one converting to Islam, one becoming a social activist in Africa, and one struggling to commit to a white man. *The Edge of Heaven* (1989) is a three-generation female saga where a mother returns from prison after pushing her two-year-old daughter down a set of stairs. Her most wide-ranging novel *Long Distance Life* (1989) is composed of eighty-year-old Naomi's reflections on her life sharecropping, migrating to Washington DC, and the generational conflicts she has with her daughter Esther during the Civil Rights era. The presumptions behind imposed gender roles, the impact of male presence and absence, as well as the deteriorating effect of materialistic values on human spirituality are consistent themes in Golden's works. In *And Do Remember Me* (1992), Jessie Foster escapes from incest by leaving home and becoming involved in the Civil Rights Movement. The novel upends ideas of women's spheres by making the domestic space perilous and the topsy-turvy world of political activism safe. Golden's last novel to date *After* (2006) is the story of Blake, a black policeman and family man who kills a man he thought was reaching for a gun but was actually reaching for a cell phone. Somewhat uneven, with plotlines that do not always cohere, the work studies the pressures of externally imposed definitions of black masculinity as Blake struggles to come to terms with the death of one man and the sexuality of another, his gay son.

Much was made during the 1980s and 1990s about the gender divide in black novels, but hindsight reveals that the content in the works of men and women share similar tropes, motifs, and conventions. Many mine black history for a usable past, and many explore the impact of race and gender on individual psyches. David Bradley's fiction, for instance, frequently creates male characters whose biggest challenge is to resituate themselves in terms of societal definitions of masculinity. His first novel *South Street* (1975), written while he was an undergraduate at the University of Pennsylvania, follows aspiring poet Adlai Stevenson Brown as he grows weary of defending and explaining his understanding of his blackness to the racially mixed intelligentsia he is introduced to by his upper-class black girlfriend. He concludes that for the sake of his writing and his own soul he must be, a denizen of the streets and black working-class spaces: a bar, a hotel, and a storefront church. He becomes a fixture at Lightnin' Ed's Bar and Grill. There he encounters Leo the bartender who is addicted to soap operas and the Philadelphia Phillies, as well as other patrons, Big Betsy, a prostitute of a certain age; Vanessa, a younger counterpart; Betsy's cynical sister Leslie, who cheats on her janitor husband with Leroy, the bad man of South Street; and Jake, the wise-fool drunkard. The novel weaves these storylines and others into a colorful cloth that rewrites much of the masculinist certainty of 1950s and 1960s literature. The South Street Adlai occupies is a transformative space, reflecting what Bradley felt was a truer assessment of the urban world. Rather than dehumanization, there was regard for others. The emphasis on black male hypersexuality is replaced with a janitor who has difficulty maintaining an erection, a bartender more in love with food (and soap operas) than women, and a minister who loves resting in bed with his wife and holding hands. Bradley mutates black masculinity into heightened linguistic power, and joins writers who pay homage to black oral culture. The spoken word is integrated into prose as characters play the dozens, signify, and tell lies. Bradley contextualizes this use of orality and vernacular within western traditions, likening it to the Falstaffian bawdiness of Shakespearean low comedy and thereby minimizing possible essentialism (Blake 28). The novel ends with Adlai running off the bus that would take him back to his girlfriend and standing on the South Street Bridge between two worlds. His liminality suggests that indeterminacy is a far more interesting concept than rootedness.

Bradley is most renowned for *The Chaneysville Incident* (1981), the 1981 PEN/Faulkner Award winner that reimagines the true history of thirteen escaped slaves who upon discovery choose death rather than return to slavery. The novel's central character John Washington is a historian at a prominent Pennsylvania university who responds to the chaotic feelings of being a black man in a racist society by becoming virtually emotionless. John's potential partner Judith, a white psychiatrist, has challenged him to open himself, and their conversations become a means of charting his psychological mutations.[20] The terms of his father's will require him to discover the history behind the incident. He must do so through reconstruction, gathering material artifacts, oral histories, myths, and songs, all of which are replicated in the novel. His quest at once allows him to locate his place in ancestral history and validates the material and methodology he uses to do so. The history of the Chaneysville incident occurred in Bradley's area of birth, and his mother kept written records of it. The tale bothered him as a person but fascinated him as a writer (Blake 25). In attempting to answer the questions of who they were, where they came from, and why they did it, Bradley fills historical silences and question how reliable the "truth" of the past is.

The desire to create a useable black past from intracultural traditions was an inspiration to many writers at this time. Like Bradley, Richard H. Perry reconstructs community and folk traditions. From the title of his most acclaimed work, *Montgomery's Children* (1984) one expects a story of the South, but the novel is actually about Montgomery, New York, and a community that has its origins in a double black migration from south, to north, to further north. Disillusioned with the continued racism they found in the cities of Philadelphia, Newark, and New York City, the Southern seekers of the novel settled in a northern rural idyll. Their experiment worked, and prior to 1948 none of the community's black residents died. All this changes in the 1980s when a younger generation increasingly involved with drugs and cross-racial relationships threatens communal continuity. The only character remaining connected to his antecedents, Norman, does so through his ability to fly. His skill roots him in the folk belief of flying Africans, and like them, flying allows him escape from enslavement, in his case the enslavement of crime, oppression, materialism, and reliance on technology that now defines the modern period. In *Montgomery's Children*, folk traditions are the route to restoring the self-regard that will end community deterioration.

The black cultural past is reshaped in innovative ways in late-twentieth-century novels, exploring its significance to a contemporary existence. Ernest Gaines, a writer who believed the past is never past, wrote novels set in the environs of fictional Bayonne, Louisiana, modeled after Gaines's own home on the River Lake Plantation, Point Coupée Parish, Louisiana. Plantation culture and language shape his first and perhaps most neglected novel *Catherine Carmier* (1964). The book reads as two novels, one a love story and the other a pastoral of community traditions. It is uneven at points, but noteworthy for its descriptions of the physical beauty of rural Louisiana and for imbricating oral traditions in its prose. Characters make sense of life through nature, and as the landscape changes because of increasing Cajun incursion into black farming plots, so do their psyches and communal continuity.

The central character Jackson Bradley, distanced from his home because of his education, loves Catherine Carmier, a woman whose father insists she follow the strict color code of a Creole society that forbids her loving the black Jackson. Multiple influences are at work in the novel. The couple is reminiscent of Shakespeare's Romeo and Juliet as anachronistic race and caste values doom their love. In an interview with Ruth Laney, Gaines acknowledged his debt to Turgenev, and the parallels between his Jackson and Bazarov in *Fathers and Sons* (1862): the collision of formal education and community values; the city versus the village; the questioning of religious faith. The novel is a memorial to a community in transition, told through indirect discourse as storytelling moves from one perspective to the next. *Of Love and Dust* (1967) unfolds in a similar manner, in the quarters of the plantation. A sense of continuity exists between the two novels through a return to the themes of Cajun encroachment, contrasting generations, and the importance of storytelling, content that would be seen to best advantage in *The Autobiography of Miss Jane Pittman* (1971).

In *Miss Jane* Gaines stands the concept of historicizing on its head by creating a voice formal annals have ignored, that of a black woman ex-slave. Jane's life spans all the major epochs of American history, enslavement, emancipation, reconstruction, and Civil Rights, and inserts a new perspective into each. Her story is nothing less than a folk epic. From the title *Autobiography*, to Gaines's amanuensis history teacher who signs the novel "the editor," the frame of the story provided such verisimilitude that many thought the work was nonfiction. The misunderstanding found Gaines in the position that African American novelists have frequently been placed, being seen as historical recorders, but not artists. Reading the voice of Miss Jane, however, the artistry in undeniable. The cadences of former slaves are present in her voice and her narrative's detailed, interior view of the slavery, reconstruction, and Civil Rights eras rehumanizes written histories.

In one way or another history has a place in all of Gaines's works. *In My Father's House* (1978) has a protagonist whose participation in the

Civil Rights Movement allows him to personify history, but it is his personal history that haunts him once the son he deserted returns. *A Gathering of Old Men* (1983) is set in a 1970s world that has changed so slowly it could be anytime post-emancipation. The men of the title chart new history, though; when participating in a plan developed by the young, white Candy Marshall, they all take credit for the murder of the Cajun overseer Beau Boutan. Though Candy has originated the plan, the men make it their own. Boutan has represented years of indignities, and each man has killed him in imagination if not in actuality. Told in segments that make a communal narrative, they voice varying motives for confessing while providing a history of the injustices in rural southern black life. One cites the killing as retribution for appropriated land, another for livelihoods eroded by technology, another for a son who dies because he was refused treatment at a whites-only hospital. The men begin as stooped conveniences at the opening of the novel but close it dressed in their best clothes, their humanity restored by confessions that convey their emotional truths.

Gaines admits to coming from a long line of "liars," and their storytelling influences his novels' style. The narrative form of *A Lesson before Dying* (1993), however, breaks from other Gaines works somewhat. While oral cadences are still present, also present is an emphasis on writing in the shape of a diary kept by the protagonist Jefferson, an innocent victim of bad circumstances. He is caught in a store standing near the dead, bloody bodies of his black friends Bear and Brother, and the white shopkeeper Mr. Gropé, with cash from the register and an open bottle of whiskey in his hands. This gains him a trial and the death penalty. The response of his godmother to Jefferson' s defense lawyer framing him as an unwitting brute, no better than a hog, too dumb to plan such a robbery, is to make Jefferson see that the lawyer's words do not define him. She enlists the aid of the local teacher, Grant Wiggins, to talk with him, and over the course of their conversations Grant suggests he keep a diary.

Jefferson's diary and its nonstandard orthography, convey his lack of formal education, as well as his thoughtfulness through the sight of words as well as through their signification: "mr. wiggin you say write something but I dont kno what to rite an you say I must be thinking bout things I aint telin nobody an I order put it on paper but I dont kno what to put on paper" (226). The stream-of-consciousness arrangement suggests an awareness that starts to overwhelm Jefferson, as he, for the first time in his life, contemplates his own being. That writing transforms Jefferson is evident in the shift from halting passages describing day-to-day events to eloquent contemplations on the circumstances that have brought him to where he is. *A Lesson* was nominated for the Pulitzer Prize and the National Book Critics Circle Award for fiction, and, as is the case with many of Gaines's works, it was adapted for film and television. As will be discussed in more detail in a later chapter, the number of Gaines adaptations is testament to the broadness of his treatment of racial, cultural, and historical themes and his skillful strategies in delineating the details of a single imagined parish.

Similarly to Ernest Gaines, Albert Murray centers his novels around a particular place. Though he actually began writing novels in the 1950s, his works did not appear until the 1970s. Murray sought to counter portraits of black pathology with fiction that blended musical traditions and allusions to folk philosophy. While studying at Tuskegee, he became very good friends with Ralph Ellison, and the inextricability of blackness to Americanness articulated by Ellison is also a guiding principle in Murray's novels. He has said that he dislikes being called black American because for him it implies "lesser American," that he despises the term African American because he is not African, he is American: "All of my values and aspirations are geared to the assumption that freedom as defined by the American social contract is my birthright" (Rowell and Murray 399). His novels employ black cultural elements as the quintessentially American forms best able to capture the contradictions of American culture and the resiliency of black spirit.

Ralph Ellison would characterize Murray's fiction as filled with the rhythms, textures, and signifyin' "in the broad colored sense of the term" of black life (*Trading Twelves* 27). This quality defines Murray's *Train Whistle Guitar* (1974), the first installment in the coming-of-age story of Scooter, covering his pre-teen and teenage years living in post-World War I Gasoline Point, Alabama, a small Southern town. It is told in a manner that reflects the workings of memory as the narrator, a mature Scooter, is in conversation with his past and with communal traditions. Murray's descriptions of the sounds of guitar strings and train whistles cast them as equally able to tell stories as the signifying talk of human voices. *The Spyglass Tree* continues Scooter's story while he attends a fictionalized Tuskegee. Told in the same style blending standard, vernacular, and musical cadences, its voice is more mature, indicating his becoming aware of caste distinctions among blacks. Scooter learns to straddle worlds, remaining a successful student while interacting with gamblers, roommates from the North, and the denizens of the local jazz world. He even rides shotgun for a local black businessman confronting a racially motivated altercation. Scooter's education continues in *Seven League Boots* where he reaches his stride as a road band bass player under the direction of the "Bossman," a character whose suaveness evokes Duke Ellington.

The last work in the series, the *Magic Keys*, is a multilayered ode to writing, thinking, and friendship. Now married and a graduate student at New York University, Scooter's conversations with his friend Taft Edison, a conjuring of Ralph Ellison, make up the novel's core. Their ruminations on books, art, and live jazz music is reminiscent of the life-long letters between Murray and Ellison collected in *Trading Twelves* (2000). Also fictionalized is artist Romare Bearden in the form of Roland Beaseley. Together the trio probe what it means to express a black experience in new aesthetics, and how to find the "magic keys" to do so. Plot is subordinated to mood rendering New York in the 1940s. The tension of the novel revolves around whether Scooter will remain in New York or return South to teach and ghostwrite the jazz autobiography of a famous musician.[21] The tetralogy moves outward from the environs of a small Southern town to the international world with an eye to revising traditions of determinism. Like the blues he loves, Murray transforms the ugliness of racism into the aesthetically beautiful.

In speaking to Alvin Ailey and characterizing the nature of the commonalities he shared with Albert Murray and Romare Bearden, James Baldwin noted "all of us ... are speaking about a voyage which we all have to make seemingly far away to come full circle. To redeem a tradition which was not yet called a tradition because it was not yet written down except by Bessie Smith, Duke Ellington, and so forth, and by preachers like my father" (Breen 668). Baldwin's comments succinctly describe the artistic and scholarly efforts to mark a black expressive tradition where others did not see one because it was sung, spoken perhaps, but not written. Richard Perry's call to re-embrace the spirit of folk forms, Ernest Gaines's language craft, and Albert Murray's imbrication of jazz sounds in prose technique, are examples of writers making literary tradition out of black spoken and sung forms. Other artists in this vein include Al Young and Leon Forrest.

The 2005 Poet Laureate of California, Al Young, was also a novelist, anthologist, and jazz critic. It is no surprise, then, that the image of redemptive jazz provides the central motif to his first novel, *Snakes* (1970). Through music its main character M. C. Moore is given the opportunity to leave the impoverishment of his Detroit neighborhood for life in New York. Music provides the texture for a narrative style of rhythmic contrasts, syncopation, and lyricism. This style takes an edgier turn in his second novel *Who Is Angelina?* (1975) where the title character finds herself in despair over her declining Berkeley neighborhood, and it continues in *Sitting Pretty* (1976). Sidney J. Prettymon, the character to whom the title refers, projects an apparent simplicity that hides deeper wisdom and recalls Langston Hughes's Jesse B. Semple. Through remembering his life experiences – unemployment, the quasi-fame that comes from regularly calling into a local radio show, being a janitor and parent to upwardly mobile children – he conveys down-home philosophy. The "small" details of his life and observations create an extraordinary volume by an ordinary man, neither hero nor victim, whose stories resonate with jazz and the blues.

Young has said that music played an outsize role in the way black Americans have come to see themselves and their aesthetics. His characters symbolize this sentiment. Durwood "Woody" Knight in *Ask Me Now* (1980) retires from professional basketball, and the way his life loses its focus is reflected in a manner suggesting the loss of the flows and rhythms of music. In *Seduction by Light* (1988), Mamie Franklin, a maid who was once a professional singer in the 1950s era band The Inklings, holds on to remembered music and dance to transcend a series of setbacks and to ultimately transit between the living world and the dead. Young was deeply influenced by 1920s–1940s era jazz, swing, do wop bands, as well as European classical music. Reading and writing music made him aware of aurality and transposition.[22]

In the novels of Leon Forrest religious rhetoric, blues, and spirituals are interwoven into prose. When he expresses his admiration for Billie Holiday's ability to "purloin" and incorporate phrasings, axioms, proverbs, signifyin' ("Solo Long-Song" 333) into her music he delineates his own style of writing. His novels overlap forms that he draws from many sources. "I'll use anything I can get my hands on if I can use it in an imaginative way," he once said (Warren 402). Forrest was able to move in many worlds. That Toni Morrison edited his first novel, and that Ralph Ellison wrote the introduction for it, indicated the esteem in which Forrest's talent was held; but, not only did Forrest move in established literary circles, he also wrote arts features for and was the last non-Muslim editor of the Nation of Islam's weekly *Muhammad Speaks* from 1969–1973. He admired the Nation's doctrine of self-help but not the restrictive isolationism he felt deprived them of intellectual cross-fertilization.

All Forrest's works are set in Forest County, a fictional recreation of Chicago. The titular scene of *There Is a Tree More Ancient than Eden* (1973) reveals Forrest's frequent use of symbolism. It alludes to the vision of a black Madonna sitting under a tree that is more ancient than Eden. The vision gives the main character Nathaniel Witherspoon fortitude, and represents the ways black culture has taken received elements and transformed them. Narrated by Nathaniel as he rides in a Cadillac with Aunty

Breedlove to his mother's funeral, the six chapters incorporate a multiplicity of forms from traditional narrative to sermons, to poetic monologues to a lengthy, scathing epistle from his grandmother Sweetie Reed to President Lyndon Baines Johnson lambasting the US government's injustice toward black Americans. Nathaniel is her amanuensis. The life-stories of the characters are interwoven with those of historic figures including Abraham Lincoln, Harriet Tubman, and Louis Armstrong, and significant epochs – the Middle Passage and the Great Migration – are paired with Nathaniel's personal recollections of sites titled to evoke ballads, the House of the Soul barbeque restaurant and the House of the Brown-Skinned Goddess Salon. The topography of the text's single-spaced passages reflects the role visual manipulation of text plays in the African American novel.

The Bloodworth Orphans (1977) is the second of what is sometimes referred to as the Forest County or Bloodworth trilogy. It is named for the Bloodworth clan, a slaveholding family in Mississippi. With Oedipal overlays, a huge cast of characters probes the consequences of sexual exploitation during slavery. Nathaniel again is chronicler and again he rides in a car, this time a Lincoln Continental limousine on the way to an evening service on Easter Sunday. *Two Wings to Veil My Face* (1984) the final volume in the trilogy continues the family saga and the stylistic techniques begun in *There Is a Tree*. The story of one family becomes a meditation on the history of black people in the United States as Forrest constructs a frame tale wherein Nathaniel records his grandmother's memories. Her voice is given primacy and reverses the marginalization imposed upon her by the culture and history she recalls.

Forrest's fourth novel, *Divine Days* (1992), received the 1993 *Chicago Sun-Times* Book of the Year Award for fiction. The prose of this work gallops along rhythmically, and like its characters' reflections never takes a direct route. Organized by dated, time-stamped sections it covers a week and one day in the life of Joubert Jones, a black playwright and bartender at the Night Light Lounge on Chicago's South Side. Expanding on his play about W. A. D. Ford, a preacher and scam artist who brings to mind W. D. Fard, the minister who started the Nation of Islam, Joubert seeks to write his masterpiece, the story of Lucasta "Sugar-Grove" Jones, a trickster character whose history comes only from tales, lies, and their attending contradictions. Like Ellison's Rinehart in *Invisible Man*, everyone you ask has seen a different Sugar-Grove, and their stories weave a polyphonic narrative with Southern and Shakespearean cadences that represent the power of black cultural invention. Forrest's books are challenging in their conceptualization and often in their length (*Divine Days* is over 1135 pages long) and ask much of their readers; however, they offer much. His own life, listening to the stories of the elders, or barbers, as well as being read to, gave him an appreciation of gradation in storytelling and the importance of voice.

Embracing historical and cultural antecedents in written tradition does not go unquestioned. For some novelists, John Edgar Wideman and Charles Johnson for instance, antecedents can produce an anxiety of influence. Wideman came to black traditions in writing in a less than organic way. When approached by black students at the University of Pennsylvania to teach a course in African American literature, he was unprepared for the request. Attendance at the University of Pennsylvania and being the second African American to receive a Rhodes scholarship equipped him with knowledge of the origins of the eighteenth-century British novel, but not African American literature and culture. He reflected later that though he replied truthfully that it wasn't his field, he felt a certain shame, so he made it a mission to educate himself, again, spending a summer at the Schomburg Library reading every thing he could, and subsequently connecting with other black writers (Phillips, "John Edgar" 36–37).

In Wideman's works engaging the past can be an uneasy process. The fractured narrative techniques, metafictive insertion of his own life into his fiction, and tenses that slip between present, past, and conditional in many of his works, reveal the past's awkward coexistence with the present. The protagonist of *Philadelphia Fire* (1990) Cudjoe is unable to disengage from the past even as he lives in Greece where he has abandoned family, work, and flees anything reminding him of his personal failures. A motif throughout the work is Shakespeare's *Tempest*, and the ways in which abandonment and victimization leave deep consequential scars. When Cudjoe hears of a child escaping the Philadelphia city government's bombing of the MOVE compound, he becomes fixated on what happens to the boy, and by extension what happens to all the children he sees around him. Saving the boy in his mind becomes inseparable from the desire to redeem himself as a father, and as a man.[23]

Confronting the past is a key image in *The Lynchers* (1973) and *A Glance Away* (1967). *The Lynchers* is prefaced by the citation of one hundred documented lynchings. Writing them down is a reparative and makes sure the stories are not destroyed or twisted. In *A Glance Away* Eddie Lawson upon leaving a drug rehabilitation center comes home to his dying urban neighborhood to confront the phantoms that led him down his negative path. As Cecil Braithwaite, the protagonist of *Hurry Home* (1970) mourns the loss of his stillborn son and the abandonment of his wife, a narrative referencing the art of Hieronymus Bosch, John Keats, and T. S. Elliot constantly shifts between past and present and subverts temporal binaries of then and now in its descriptions of pain. *Hiding Place* (1981), *Reuben* (1987), *The Cattle Killing* (1996), and *Two Cities* (1998) examine the changing same, the ways in which society appears to have moved beyond its past but has not. *Reuben*, in particular, explicitly likens rat-infested homes to similarly infested hold of slavers, Indian scouts betraying their own to whites to FBI informants, and a ghetto population to a coffle of slaves. The protagonist Reuben is obsessed with the photographs of Eadweard Muybridge and Egyptian mummies, all forms that recreate stasis. The image of art making a captive of life is used to describe the various forms of imprisonment he sees in the residents around him.[24]

When Wideman returned to his birthplace for his grandmother's funeral, he was introduced to a wealth of stories that in various ways made their way into The Homewood Trilogy, named for the predominantly African American neighborhood of Pittsburgh, Pennsylvania. He was ready to reconcile his formal education with his communal one and listen to the stories he had heard all of his life in new ways. Hearing of his maternal grandfather and the residents of Homewood brought home the centrality of words, intonation, meaning, and performance to conceptions of blackness. Though based on an actual locale, Homewood is an imagined space formed by the memories within it and responses to its perception from the outside. The trilogy opens with a short story collection *Damballah* (1981). The two novels that follow, *Hiding Place* (1981) and *Sent for you Yesterday* (1983), develop the backgrounds of selected characters in the story collection and contrast the ramifications of being in yet isolated from community. Wideman has often said that his personal reality is a component in much of his texts. The story of his brother sentenced to life in prison for murder and of his own son who later has the same fate appear in various guises.[25] His most recent novel *Fanon* (2008) is an example of his inserting himself into his fiction through an intensely self-aware mix of biography, memoir, history, and fiction. In it he is both author and narrator describing his efforts to compose a novel about Frantz Fanon, the black French psychiatrist from Martinique whose studies of the psychic impact of postcolonial experience – *Black Skins, White Masks* (1952) and *The Wretched of the Earth* (1961) – influenced writers and thinkers from Richard Wright, to Malcolm X, to Wideman.

Like his contemporaries, Wideman seeks to transmogrify the written word to make it evoke black cultural creation, but for him the process is not always straightforward. He notes that the electricity of speech is difficult to reproduce, so the stories he tells must be adjusted to the form of writing. He posits the web as a possible vehicle for accomplishing this. "Given online publishing's ability to instantly edit and revise," he queries, might it "provide interactive conversation and commentary, mix words with sounds and pictures, link text to text, will books be reimagined, not solely as finished products or done deals but as virtual works-in-progress? Can books regain more of the jazzlike spontaneity and improvisation vital to speech, that ancient fire of live, face-to-face exchange?" ("Embraces" 56). Wideman is not only reimagining the novel, but also the book.

To make use of a cultural past implies that there is a single one, and not all writers share this assumption. For Charles Johnson, the black American narrative, one in which a people are taken from a homeland and brought shackled to a new world, is pedestrian and not fully capable of conceptualizing the multiplicity of black meanings and experiences. It is a story of group victimization, according to Johnson, with every black person as protagonist. There is no room in it for the agency, idealism, and cultural creativity that countered racist practices and gave rise to modern black identities ("End Of" n. pag.). All Johnson's novels to some degree upend narratives of a black cultural past. While they are deeply rooted in the history of blacks in the Americas, they focus on the cosmopolitan existence of blackness. A philosopher by training, the questions of what is the nature of human existence, of reason, of truth, metaphysics, epistemology, and logic, take greater precedence that portraying a collective race story.

In Johnson's first novel *Faith and the Good Thing* (1974), Faith Cross undertakes a metaphysical journey when her parents die. She is caught between their contrasting philosophies. Her father Todd believes in traditions such as hoodoo, while her mother espouses orthodox Christianity. Her deathbed charge to her daughter is to find "the good thing," and Faith goes through many voyages to locate this enigma. The philosophical theme is deepened when in one segment of her quest Faith encounters a "werewitch" who responds to Faith's query for Truth with a menu of choices: Aristotelian? Phenomenological? Transcendental? Symbolic? Through swamp and city, marriage and childbirth, Faith seeks, and the ideas of the Greeks mingle with those of the folk, vernacular language with academic discourse, as she comes to realize where her sources of truth and beauty lie.

The stylistic hybridity that characterizes *Faith* continues in *Oxherding Tale* (1982). Its structure was inspired by the poetic graphic narrative of Kakuan Shien, *The Ten Oxherding Pictures* (1150). Like Johnson's *Middle Passage* (1990), *Oxherding* is a neoslave narrative, and both will be discussed later in this study. Johnson's most recent novel continues to cross borders of time and genre. Narrated by Matthew Bishop, a student of philosophy and a member of the Southern Christian Leadership Conference (SCLC), *Dreamer* (1998) is inspired by Martin Luther King's Chicago Freedom Movement. King hoped to expand the success of the SCLC's tactics to the North, likening the exiling of blacks to slums as equivalent to Southern segregation. His efforts were met with violence, and King himself was hit by a rock thrown while he was marching in the Marquette Park neighborhood for decent housing and equal access to civic and educational services.[26] Johnson's King is wearied by continued violence, and feels increasingly irrelevant in the face of more radical politics. Chaym Smith is impoverished, unlucky, but a keen reader of the Gnostic scriptures and the works of German theologian Meister Eckhart. Service in the Korean War has left him with a ruined leg, an alcohol problem, a nervous breakdown, and caused the loss of his wife and children. He is, however, King's doppelganger. Since others mistaking him for the civil rights leader have already ransacked his room and pushed him off the El platform, Smith proposes that he stand in for King. Interspersed amid Matthew's first person narrative are meditative chapters with King's reflections as a man and not a civil rights icon. These are among the novel's most compelling portions, partly because of their private nature and partly because they afford insight into the way Smith increases King's comprehension of the multiple class levels of oppression.

Johnson's belief that narratives of black cultural history needed complicating is echoed in the works of many contemporary writers. The eponymous character in Andrea Lee's semi-autobiographical *Sarah Phillips* (1984), the privileged child of an upper-middle-class family prominent in the Civil Rights Movement, must reconcile her destiny with her family's expectations. Lee's *Lost Hearts in Italy* (2006) treats the dissolution of an interracial marriage because a black wife is seduced by the opulence of a white Italian billionaire. Her characters have the resources to dream and to construct and reconstruct themselves. They represent the changing circumstances of black America. Her novels are similar to the now out-of-print *Francisco* (1974) by Allison Mills about a young black upper-middle-class woman who leaves a very confining home environment to become a Hollywood actress only to experience confinement in casting.[27] These works narrate the shifting sensibilities of privileged blackness navigating racial expectations.

By asking what binds an individual to a group, Reginald McKnight questions the "black" in the term black American narrative. His characters are uncertain about how their personal sense of themselves connect to the black collective. In *I Get on the Bus* (1990), Peace Corps worker Evan Norris undertakes a transatlantic crossing to Senegal hoping that being part of a diaspora will afford personal and political meaning. Seemingly always on a bus, always in perpetual motion, Norris looks out on scenes and feels his not there-ness. An uncontrollable permeability takes over as he loses himself in his surroundings. His language becomes a list of sensations and observations with no coherence. Where he ends and where the external world begins is unclear. Rather than the African return giving him roots and identity, it dislocates and fragments him as he tries to navigate between ideas of Africa, Africans, black American expatriates, and the remnants of slavery's history from which he feels detached.

In McKnight's second novel *He Sleeps* (2001), anthropologist Bertrand Milworth makes a similar journey to research folklore and myths in Senegalese village society. Unlike Norris, however, Bertrand does not expect some sort of racial reunion with an African homecoming. He rents a house and shortly thereafter a family takes up space there (saying that the landlord also rented a portion of the house to them). They also take up space in Bertrand's mind. Erotic overtones ironically convey Bertrand's inability to couple with his imagined diaspora and his ambivalence toward women of his own race. Through narrators who are incapable of dealing with the environment they imagine Senegal and by extension Africa to be both novels exhibit a highly individualized reconciling with the black past that does not presume group consciousness or identification. The history that binds, slavery, is a history confronted singly producing differing significances.

Even though novels of the 1970s–1990s do not concur on the ultimate import of history, they do concur on the importance of a useable past. Creating a record that interrogates received histories is a repeated concern, as is creating space for previously unchronicled voices. As she began her novel writing career, Toni Morrison fused these twin concerns while telling the story of a young girl convinced by hegemony, community, and even family that she is inadequate without blue eyes. *The Bluest Eye* (1970) movingly depicts the consequences of internalizing external societal devaluation, and does so by having textual typography signify both the many perspectives that exile Pecola Breedlove and her family to the cultural margins. Being aware of the typographical manipulations in *The Bluest Eye* illuminates the act of viewing the racialized subject and the subject's response.

The novel's epigraphic reconstruction of passages from a Dick and Jane reader is the first signal that typography questions societal normativity.

The excerpt first appears as a structured quote separated by spaces and commas: "Here is the house. It is green and white." It then shifts to a format lacking punctuation, "Here is the house it is green and white"; finally, to a format with no punctuation and no spacing between words: "Hereisthehousitisgreenandwhite" (4). The degeneration of prose presages the many degenerations that will take place in the novel as characters imbibe the illusory white noise of Dick and Jane at the cost of their own self-esteem. A more subtle manipulation of typography occurs in the way differing margins and font styles represent perceptions. The novel's "margins," "main bodies," and "italics" become more than format; they become voices. Johanna Drucker describes two categories of typography in literature, marked and unmarked texts. Unmarked texts are those "in which the words on the page 'appear to speak themselves' without the visible intervention of author or printer." Marked texts are those that display "indulgences" such as type sizes being "used to hierarchize information, to create an order in the text so that different parts of it appear to 'speak' differently" (95). *The Bluest Eye* is very much a marked text constructed of passages with left justification, full justification, and italics. Each portion signifies on the other, providing interlocking contexts and meaning. Each represents not only a level of narration, but also a level of understanding and self-awareness (or lack thereof).

Our guide through the novel's many ways of seeing is Claudia McTeer. The day-to-day life of Claudia and her sister Freida is contained in passages with left-justified margins, the literary print form of most books. This ubiquitous form mirrors Claudia's developing understanding of the prosaicness of eroding racial self-esteem, a commonplace inevitability for young black girls encouraged to admire Shirley Temple even as the child star appropriates Bill Bojangles, or to be grateful for the ice cream largess of a "high-yellow dream child" (62) who receives approbation only because of her phenotypic closeness to idealized whiteness. Within these left-justified passages, there is little overt cultural analysis. Within them, memories show rather than tell of young girls' responses to the gradual destruction of their self-worth. Encased in these left justified passages are the "how" Morrison refers to in the opening of the novel: "*There is really nothing more to say – except why. But since why is difficult to handle, one must take refuge in how*" (italics in original 6). It is left to the fully justified passages of the novel to present the "why," the origins, history, and cultural values that shape they way her characters see themselves and others.

Fully justified margins signify the meta-narrative of *The Bluest Eye* that examines the roots of the *"Thing"* dictating what is beautiful and what is worthy (74, italics in original). The Breedloves' acquiescence to their devaluation is told in them as is its cause, the hegemony that surrounds them in billboards, movies, and public attitudes (39). Passages with full justification depict the obsessive concern for appearances that generates Geraldine's self-hatred (81–93), as well as the drive to erase blackness encouraged by colonialism and imperialism that produce the perfect postcolonial pedophile Soaphead Church (164–183). Their format narrates the most horrid act in the novel so that we comprehend, if not forgive, that Cholly's debasement by white hunters festers until he muddles pity and abuse, and rapes his daughter (132–163). Fully justified passages signify a more knowing narrative voice that places characters' experiences in the context of history and culture.

Psychological interiorities are marked by italics. The print of these passages present Polly's desire to escape her reality by consuming visual fictions in film, and they also vivify the destruction she inflicts when watching them makes returning to her own family difficult. The most dangerous escapism is represented in the italics conveying Pecola's tragic psychic split at the end of the novel:

> Here comes someone. Look at his. See if they're bluer.
> *You're being silly. I'm not going to look at everybody's eyes.*
> You have to.
> *No I don't.*
> Please. If there is somebody with bluer eyes then mine, then maybe there is somebody with the bluest eyes. (203)

Pecola has completely retreated from the world that has been so injurious to her. This segment combines both full justification and italics symbolizing the degree to which the external social gaze (fully justified margins) has been internalized by Pecola (italics). Even in her illusion, she can find no solace, as there will always be a bluer set of eyes.

Textual manipulation minimizes the need for explication. Morrison once said in an interview, "there was so much explanation ... Black writers always explained something to somebody else. And I didn't want to explain anything to anybody else! I mean, if I could understand it, then I assumed two things (a) that other Black people could understand it and (b) that white people, if it was any good, would understand it also" (Bakerman 59). Typography shifts the responsibility of making meaning from writer to reader. It also provides Morrison with a solution satisfying the difficulty of constructing appropriate narrative voice, a solution that traditional novelistic forms of first and third person may not afford. Morrison's language is made of words signifying through their meaning and appearance. The typography of her prose becomes a visual language constructing multiple narrative modes and reflecting multiple perceptions.

Over the course of her next three novels, Morrison's reach is increasingly outward. *Sula* (1973), in the fashion of a Greek tragedy with the community as chorus, portrays Sula Mae Peace becoming a pariah because she sleeps with men, white and black, including her friend Nel's husband. *Sula's* examination of fissures within the community, the assimilationist versus the folk, and fissures between women, no matter how close, continues in *Song of Solomon* (1977), but the geography of the novel expands to include the South and reference distant atavistic spaces. In what begins as a quest for material wealth but becomes a quest of self-discovery, Macon "Milkman" Dead heads to his grandfather's ancestral home in Shalimar, Virginia, and the story of flying Africans links his present to a folk past. In addition to the National Book Critics Circle Award, the novel made Morrison the second black author after Richard Wright, to have a work selected as a main offering by the Book-of-the-Month Club. *Tar Baby* (1981) further evokes a black past and diaspora. Set in a fictional Caribbean island, it explores the sexual and racial legacies of slavery and colonization through Jadine whose white sponsors have sent her to elite private schools including the Sorbonne, and Son, a freethinker who ultimately chooses to live with the descendants of a Maroon-like community.

The publication of *Beloved* (1987) cemented Morrison's stature as a canonical American writer. Based on the life of Margaret Garner who murdered her daughter in an attempt to prevent her children from being taken back to slavery, *Beloved* is a fiction imagining unexplored reality. It uses fantasy to render the ghost of a daughter demanding acknowledgement. It earned Morrison a Pulitzer Prize in 1993. A film based on the novel in 1998 and an opera *Margaret Garner* (2005) for which Morrison wrote the libretto would follow. Its nature as a neoslave narrative voicing unexpressed black interiority and its adaptation to film will be explored in a later chapters.

Beloved was part one of a trilogy that included *Jazz* (1992) and *Paradise* (1998). *Jazz* was inspired by James Vander Zee's *The Harlem Book of the Dead* (1978), a collection of plates chronicling the practice of photographing the dead in full dress, loved by and interacting with the living. A story surrounding one of the photographs was that a young woman at a party was dancing and suddenly blood appeared on her body. All she said before she died when asked what happened was "I'll tell you tomorrow." The question what kind of women feels this way? fascinated Morrison, and answering it gave rise to the novel (Naylor, "Conversation" 584). Morrison turns this seed into a love triangle in which Joe Trace shoots his young mistress Dorcas and his wife Violet slashes the corpse's face at the viewing. Flashbacks fill in the histories of the characters and in doing so encompass Reconstruction, the Great Migration, the musical and literary flowering of the Harlem Renaissance, and the deferred dreams of black World War I veterans. The structure is jazz-like with repeating motifs developing plot. The coda of one section becomes the introductory statement of the next.

Paradise closes the trilogy with the account of an all-black Oklahoma town founded by former slaves and their descendants. The dream seems to have been realized in this settlement reminiscent of the promise of places such as Nicodemus, Kansas, but the novel's gothic overtones forebode its fading. The heads of the town of Paradise suspect a nearby convent that assists abused women is actually a cult threatening their community. They attack and kill the women to dire consequences. One of Morrison's most complex novels, its contemplation of communal identity is constituted through a chorus of narrative voices that shift from past to present and float between the real and the supernatural.

Morrison's twenty-first century novels Love (2003) and Home (2012) use the stories of personal relationships to contemplate the forgetting that comes as black modernity places distance between itself and its past history and values. The setting of Love is Cosey's Hotel and Resort. Once catering exclusively to African American jazz stars, and wealthy guests during the Jim Crow era, it is no longer a symbol of pride and possibility. It has declined because the support it enjoyed during segregation has evaporated with integration. Heed, the second wife, of the hotel owner Bill Cosey and his granddaughter Christine who is the same age as Heed, dispute who inherits the property. Using actual events as a backdrop to their story – the Alabama bus boycotts, the killing of Emmet Till, the Brown v. Board of Education Supreme Court decision – the novel explores what is lost and what is gained as a group attempts to assimilate into the social mainstream. Home (2012) counters the popular assessment of the 1950s as an age of renewal in the United States. The main character Frank awakes disoriented in a hospital unsure of how he arrived there. As he journeys from Seattle to his home of Locust, Georgia, to help his sister Cee once she becomes a white doctor's medical experiment, histories of anti-Communist fear, segregation, and the subjugation of women intertwine. In return migration, Frank and Cee both find renewal in Locust, a town whose segregation they hated and feared when growing up. The told-to story implied by the italicized introduction "whatever you think and whatever you write down, know this" (5) accentuates Morrison's ongoing concern with storytelling that allows the past to be self-liberating. *God Help the Child* (2015), Morrison's final novel to date, seems a shadow of her former works, and mixed reviews reflect its uneven quality.[28] The themes are familiar – the deleterious effect of intraracial color prejudice on self-love, the abuse of children, the individual trying to transcend past pain and find space for him or herself – and not conveyed innovatively. The central character Bride is disdained by her mother Sweetness because of her blue-black skin color. In spite of her mother's temptation to smother her at birth and showing her no affection in childhood, Bride grows up to be a stunningly beautiful cosmetics company executive who has learned how to market her blackness to its best advantage. Booker her lover is an erudite musician haunted by the death of his brother by a white pedophile. The novel centers on children as the promise of new beginnings, yet shows how impossible it is for them to surmount old traumas and histories.

Equally important as Morrison's contributions to novel writing is her work as an editor and literary critic. Chris Jackson, a black senior editor at Random House said about her, "Editors were looking for black literature that felt like a commentary on black life, and she was doing books that were about the kind of internal experience of being black, just like the books she writes are" (Ghansah 54). Under Morrison's guidance the poetry of Henry Dumas, the writings of Toni Cade Bambara, the autobiographies of Angela Davis and Muhammad Ali, Gayl Jones's *Corregidora*, and Ishmael Reed's *Mumbo Jumbo* saw print. "I wanted to give back something," she said of being an editor, "I wasn't marching. I didn't go to anything. I didn't join anything. But I could make sure there was a published record of those who did march and did put themselves on the line." Her activism took the form of creating a published literary presence. Organizing book launches during the 1970s in sites as varied as Harlem's 125th street and a downtown E. J. Korvette department store where the Fruit of Islam provided a security presence, she made a space for African American literature in larger book culture.[29]

The 1970s–1990s was a watershed moment in African American novel history. A record number of black novels were published and made frequent appearances on *The New York Times* bestseller list. Numerous African American writers won prestigious awards including the PEN/Faulkner, the Pulitzer Prize, and the Nobel Prize for literature. Sales and awards indicated that even when not explicitly acknowledged, African American novels were seen as central to a national narrative. This shift is particularly intriguing in light of the fact that many novels of this moment re-engage a black historical past. Far from arguing that African American experience was "universal," the content and techniques of these works accentuated African Americanness as its own tradition and as a keystone of American culture.

Coinciding with the explosion of novels in the 1970s through the 1990s was the advance of African American literary criticism. Many critical studies argued for formulaic investigations of the novels that brought attention to the indigenously derived patterns in their makeup. The result was recognition of the aesthetic dimensions of African American novels and a validation of black vernacular forms as sources for literature. Such scholarship gave African American novels increasing visibility in the academy and this cemented their perception as more than sociological documents or works of protest. Black novels were placed on required reading lists at the college and secondary school level, and African American subject matter went where it had not gone before.

The range of novels produced during this era continued to chip away at notions of monolithic blackness. Whether racial identity can be nonessential in times when race still materially affects the lives of many will be one of the major concerns of a newer generation of writers.

CHAPTER 7

"Bohemian Cult Nats": *African American Novels, 1990s and Beyond*

Freestyle, a 2001 Studio Museum in Harlem exhibition of twenty-eight emerging black visual artists, gave currency to the term *post-black*. In the catalogue accompanying the exhibit, curator Thelma Golden described post-black art as a genre whose artists wanted to resist the label "black artist," not because they wished to shun their racial identification but because they felt this term too laden with past racial histories and too aesthetically constricting (14). The exhibit emphasized the ways this group of creators felt free to draw upon any artistic tradition they chose, from modernism to hip-hop. A few years later, with the 2008 election of Barack Obama, a self-identified black president, media outlets such as National Public Radio, huffingtonpost.com, and *The New Republic*, as well as academic conferences all queried if the United States had entered a post-racial moment when racial identity was no longer central to the ways Americans defined themselves.[1] These queries were in marked contrast, however, to studies such as the National Urban League's 2009 and 2010 *State of Black America* reports, which outlined continued racial inequalities in the criminal justice system, education, employment, access to health care, and housing.[2] The contested terms *post-racial* and *post-black* indicate that the position of blackness in the United States has changed and has not changed. African American novels today are part of this ongoing conversation. Writers of the late twentieth and early twenty-first centuries continue to engage the significances of being "raced" as black in the United States, but their works express blackness less as a fixed entity and more as a continually self-evaluating process.

Greg Tate characterizes this generation of authors as part of the "bohemian cult-nats," a group conversing about essentialism, post-blackness, and hybridity. They are in his view,

> mutating black culture, ... cross-breeding aesthetic references ... And while they may be marginal to the black experience as it's been expressed in rap,

Jet, and on *The Cosby Show*, they're not all mixed up over who they are and where they come from.

These are artists for whom black consciousness and artistic freedom are not mutually exclusive but complementary, for whom "black culture" signifies a multicultural tradition of expressive practices. They feel secure enough about black culture to claim art produced by nonblacks as part of their inheritance. No anxiety of influence here – these folks believe the cultural gene pool is for skinny-dipping. (206–207)

Tate's description of these new cultural nationalists crystallizes the ways blackness is treated in novels after the post-soul period as defined by Nelson George.[3] There is a certain liberatory element in Tate's pronounce- ment, but some question whether postmodernist "cult-nats" walk a dan- gerous line of forgetfulness. Michael D. Harris notes, "The fact that so many African Americans define themselves in relation to slavery, racism, and victimhood rather than African cultural, conceptual, and historical foundations is telling" (222). The schism that Harris conceptualizes as "slavery, racism, and victimhood" versus "African cultural conceptual and historical foundations" is precisely the divide that millennial black novels straddle. Freed from the constraints of their progenitors who had to argue first for the existence of black humanity, then for the existence of black culture, these creators take both as a given and proceed to query what that given entails.

In spite of not feeling beholden to any one focus, media, or genre, in spite of a desire to see blackness beyond victimhood, the writers discussed in this chapter, gathered more by theme than publication dates (since some published simultaneously with writers of the last chapter), continue many of the traditions of their predecessors. Paul Beatty, Percival Everett, and Trey Ellis embrace the tradition of Wallace Thurman, George Schuyler, and Ishmael Reed, by creating satiric forms blending critique with acerbic wit to encourage rethinking attitudinal norms. Nathaniel Mackey's amal- gam of writing and music recalls Clarence Major's experimental blending of other art media and novel writing as a means of generating indige- nously derived black writing forms. Tayari Jones takes inspiration from Gwendolyn Brooks in inventing a contemporary vernacular urban voice, and Danny Senza and Mat Johnson question the visual meanings of race as did Charles Chesnutt, Nella Larsen, and other earlier authors working along the color line.

Adopting the role of writer/critic in his seminal essay "The New Black Aesthetic,"[4] Trey Ellis identifies the dispositions of millennial black writers: "We no longer need to deny or suppress any part of our complicated and sometimes contradictory cultural baggage to please either white people or black" (235). Ellis eschews any uniform definition of blackness in preference of multiplicity, and his novel *Platitudes* (1988) reflects this in a form integrating visual elements and metafiction. The novel is prefaced with a quote by Irish satirist Brian O'Nolan (aka Flann O'Brien), author of the 1939 novel *At Swim-Two-Birds*. It notes, "The modern novel should be largely a work of reference ... A wealth of references to existing works obviate tiresome explanations" (Ellis, *Platitudes* 2). Ellis takes this observation to heart presuming shared cultural knowledge will give meaning to the textual allusions and the visual culture he utilizes to portray black life unbound by convention.

Platitudes is the title of both Ellis's novel and the work being composed by his protagonist Dewayne Wellington. Wellington's main character is Earle Tyner, a Manhattanite teenager who loves all manner of popular culture. Other characters include Earl's mother who is described in a series of negations meant to undermine stereotypes – "her breasts don't swell the lace top of the apron she has never owned"; "She does not, not work in public relations and her two-handed backhand is not, not envied by her peers" (4) – and Dorothy Lamont, a Harlemite teenager who attends a prestigious private school in downtown Manhattan. Dewayne's novel is not going well, and he places an ad asking the public for direction. He receives a response from author, Isshe Ayam, a black feminist writer, who rewrites his prose transporting his characters Earl and Dorothy to 1920s rural Georgia.[5] The literary interplay between Isshe and Dewayne creates a double dialectic of region (urban versus rural) and gender (male versus female) battling to be the appropriate representation of "authentic" black experience. The title of Isshe's novels clearly locate true blackness in the rural folk: *Chillun o' de Lawd, My Big Ol' Feets Gon' Stomp Dat Devil Down*, and *Hog Jowl Junction*. Dewayne, on the other hand, prefers the pastiche of postmodern urbanity. The reproduction of a Preliminary Scholastic Aptitude Test (PSAT) develops Earl as an ordinary college-bound student, but the questions are tweaked to reference black experience and critique the cultural bias of standardized tests. An image of the menu from Chez Darcelle, the Harlem restaurant belonging to Dorothy's mother, represents Ellis's theory of the "cultural mulatto."[6] Foods ubiquitously identified as black such as chit'lin's are joined by African-Caribbean-Latino platanos or plantains and the generic processed American food Vienna sausage. A photo sequence in the middle of the novel showing a restaurant, Coney Island, and Barnard College, indicates the cultural traveling of his modern black characters. The array asks what is an African American experience and when is a text black enough?

Ellis's next two novels did not enjoy the critical response accorded *Platitudes*, perhaps because their satire was not as innovative. *Home Repairs* (1993) takes the form of a diary. Austin McMillan, a privileged African American attending Andover and Stanford, is desperate to lose his virginity, and the entries are titled after his female obsessions. The distinction between love and sex and the coming-of-age adventures of a young man are the novel's concerns, and race is background to popular culture, music, Hugh Heffner, and *Playboy* magazine. The work recalls the obsession with sex and masculinity of many male writers composing during the 1960s, though with less anger and more adolescent humor. In *Right Here, Right Now* (1999) Ashton Robinson, a black inspirational speaker is the target of a *60 Minutes* exposé. His rise as a motivational speaker, his establishing his own cult religion, and the fall brought on by his huckster tendencies constitute the plot. Obsession with voyeurism, the media, and the self-help industry constitute Ellis's targets. The most notable quality of Ellis's novels is the self-consciousness that brings attention to their form. His satire and metafiction combine to contravene notions of a liberatory art for the masses. Rather than envision a black collective burdened by national oppression and in need of a transformative literature, his novels envision mobile characters whose class privilege is reflected in self-transformation not entrapment in narrow spheres. They chart the move of some millennial novelists away from if not the philosophies of the Black Arts Movement, certainly its vision of collectivism.

"You don't have movements anymore," reflects Paul Beatty in an interview (Sylvanise n. pag.). Like Ellis, Beatty queries what constitutes blackness, and his characters parody the strategies and movements around which African American identity previously coalesced. His first novel *White Boy Shuffle* (1996) takes the form of a "memoir," recalling the life of Gunnar Kaufman, author of the phenomenally successful *Watermelanin*. Gunnar and his sisters grow up in a predominantly white Santa Monica, California, suburb, but his mother's fear that they are losing touch with their blackness precipitates a move to her idea of an authentic neighborhood, the working-class black and Latino Hillside. Production studios filming rap videos there certify its authenticity. Here Gunnar must learn to be black. Beatty satirizes a culture that has so appropriated and commodified blackness that it can be taught, or had simply through moving into a certain neighborhood or viewing a "gangsta" rap video. Such commodification has made people of many races wealthy from white production agents to black rappers, but has somehow trivialized blackness in the process. Parallels are made between this cultural appropriation and past ones such as minstrelsy, as the novel criticizes reducing the complexity of black culture to formula, whether of shucking or suffering.

White Boy Shuffle resists the simplistic packaging of American blackness and is not afraid to do so by engaging the narrative of enslavement some hold sacred. Gunnar's ancestor Sven Kaufman, a free black tired of the demands of minstrel performances, runs away *to* enslavement. He envisions himself as dancer in residence on the Tannenberry plantation where he seeks to create a grand performance piece incorporating slave worksongs and movement. His pliés earn him lashes rather than praise, however, and to sustain his art he gathers other slaves in the making of an elaborate subversive dance form reminiscent of the cakewalk. The novel's risky satire of slavery disconnects black identity from the degradation of bondage, and aligns it with the creative culture that survived within enslavement. Generations later, Gunnar is as much a misfit as his ancestor. His new community perceives him as "white" because of his speech and mannerisms, and like his forebear to survive he turns to the power of performance. Predictably he garners street credibility through his play on the basketball court. Later, he becomes a "negro demagogue," advocating suicide for black people as a cure for perpetual marginalization. Subsequently in another performance as a poet, he becomes the voice of the community creating a ghettopoesis that gains him a white cult following obsessed with expressions of black suffering. Moving through these performances leaves him asking why he must act black if he is black.

Begun in 1996 while Beatty was on a fellowship in Berlin, *Tuff* (2000), his second novel, turns its satiric eye to American politics. At twenty-two, Winston "Tuffy" Foshay lives in an impoverished East Harlem, blaming "the Man" for all his problems. A shooting in a Brooklyn drug house and a crack binge that leaves him barely clinging to his sanity makes him vow to commence a new way of living. Having a problematic relationship with his imprisoned ex–Black Panther father, he finds twin mentors in Spencer Throckmorton, a black rabbi, and Inez, a Japanese American woman (very reminiscent of Yuri Kochiyama) who becomes his political advisor and surrogate mother.[7] They and his partner Yolanda persuade him to launch an improbable campaign through which Beatty skewers everything from black nationalist politics to the gender wars, and ultimately the empty promises of the American political system. Allusions in the novel to Biggie Smalls and Joseph Conrad reveal that, as he acknowledges, Beatty's influences are "all over the place." They include Richard Pryor, blues, jazz, and Voltaire and are meant to express his feeling that value-laden distinctions of "high" and "low," "street" and "intellectual" obscure commonalities and limit expression (Shavers 71–72).

Beatty's third novel *Slumberland* (2008) tackles the alienation of being black abroad. The experiences of his character counter idealized expatriatism with images of perpetual outsiderness. DJ Darky, possessor of a phonographic memory (the ability to remember every sound he has ever heard) is the inventor of a perfect beat that allows the listener to feel the full expanse of life. He seeks to have this beat validated by the legendary jazz musician Charles Stone, aka the Schwa (a pun on the German word for black?), by having Stone play over it. His quest takes him to Berlin before the fall of the Wall, and he finds his way to a Bar known as Slumberland. There DJ invents a job for himself as "jukebox-sommelier," and his knowledge of music helps him to earn money, while being exoticized affords him many sexual escapades. Popularized ideas of music, race, and sex subsume DJ's individuality, leaving him a spiritually isolated sojourner.

In the lower-left corner of the verso facing the title page of Beatty's *Sellout* (2015) is an image of a black lawn jockey.[8] The image is followed by an Ellison-esque prologue in which the unnamed narrator confesses "This may be hard to believe, coming from a black man, but I've never stolen anything" (3). Both image and prologue indicate that Beatty does not shy from embracing stereotype in his send up of the ludicrousness behind racist ideology. The action of the novel begins with a tour of Washington DC, as the narrator comments wryly on the ways the city's monuments stand in for actual democracy. The protagonist is variously called "Bonbon," "Massa," and "Sellout," again accentuating the shifting identities in performed blackness. The family name is Mee, but his father has dropped the last "e," and the protagonist is about to appear before the Supreme Court in the landmark case, "*Me v. the United States of America.*" He is accused of racial segregation and slavery. That a black man faces these charges is an inversion that not only begs the question why were past presidents, aristocrats, and statesmen not similarly tried, but also introduces the series of contradictory motifs Beatty uses to upend expectations: the narrator grows up on a farm in the ghetto; a gangsta rapper goes mad and recites his own Tennyson-inspired lyrics read from his Moleskin while a SWAT team sent to take him out are too busy laughing to fire the shot. The contradictions continue and become absurdities. Beatty satirizes elements thought untouchable – slavery, lynching, castration, and police brutality – to show modern complicity in sustaining histories that should be laid aside; instead, old scripts are repackaged and reenacted. Even modern technology cannot bring about newness. "EmpowerPoint," an African American presentation software, is designed to assist in achieving the old notion of uplift. *Sellout* argues that performances and responses are too ingrained to be changed by discourse or legislation, and must be changed through rethinking societal roles.

In writing *The Sellout*, Beatty said he desired to get beyond books of "one note." He refused to make any concessions, and refused to consider how the work would play to one audience or to the next (Beatty, reading). He does not seek to make racism, civil rights, or slavery laughing matters, but rather to make the sanctity and pathos with which American culture (and particularly blacks within it) addresses these subjects seem inadequate. Beatty has been criticized by some reviewers for a relativism making his own stance within his works unclear and by others who felt that his catalogue of satiric portraits ultimately served no larger purpose.[9] Though Beatty is uncomfortable with satire as a term describing his works, arguing that hiding behind humor is no excuse for not having something to say, he and Ellis are examples of the growing use of satire in millennial novels. Percival Everett, Mat Johnson, and Colson Whitehead are others who employ the technique. The danger of satire is that it becomes too enamored of its own hoaxes. When it treats subject matter such as slavery and racism, its encouragement to poke fun risks being read as imprimatur that serious matters no longer need to be taken seriously. Satire does underscore the proximity of cultures and common knowledge, however, and that so many novels use it reflects an acknowledgement of the growing social interconnectedness at the turn of the twenty-first century. What was impossible to presume as common thought currency in the first three quarters of the twentieth century, technology, travel, and falling social barriers have made possible now. Satire provides a means of assessing what went before and its significance to the present.

The novels of the 1990s make use of diverse cultural codes from Shakespeare to hip-hop, and envision audiences as multiple and multiply literate. They raise questions but do not always offer answers. Percival Everett revels in this open-endedness as he writes about complex social questions. Rather than making statements, he is more concerned with getting the reader to consider their self-positioning to the ideas he raises. The author of seventeen novels, and an academician, the later fact becoming a device in some of his novels, Everett could be included in both a history of African American novels or novels of the American west. Everett's first novel, *Suder* (1983), is set against the Cascade Mountain Range of Oregon. Told through flashbacks, a black baseball player seeks relief from a slumping career and equally slumping marriage through figuratively taking flight in jazz and literally taking flight in experiments of self-propelled motion. *Walk Me to the Distance* (1985) is the picaresque story of an alienated

Vietnam War vet, the white protagonist David Larson, who drives west to work on a Wyoming sheep ranch and ends up witnessing the lynching of a pedophile and zoophiliac who is rendered in a surprisingly sympathetic manner reminiscent of Faulkner's Isaac Snope in *The Hamlet*, a novel David reads. Both novels draw heavily on Everett's experience as a part-time jazz musician and as a hand on a sheep farm. *God's Country* (1994) rewrites the black/white male buddy narrative using the culturally obtuse white rancher Curt Marder and the black tracker Bubba who assists in finding the culprits who raped Curt's wife, burned his home, and even shot his dog (a cross-dressing George Armstrong Custer also makes an appearance). *Grand Canyon Inc.*, a 2001 novella, portrays Winchell Nathaniel "Rhino" Tanner's attempt to re-form the western landscape and make the Grand Canyon into a theme park. Everett's interests range widely. *Zulus* (1990) centers on post nuclear apocalypse in which all women have been sterilized by the government in order to prevent unwanted mutation, and *Wounded* (2005) is inspired by true events, in this case the killing of Matthew Shepard, the University of Wyoming student believed to be the victim of a homophobic hate crime.[10]

Everett's three novels that most mirror the cultural trends of the black millennial period are *Glyph* (1999), *Erasure* (2001), and *I Am Not Sidney Poitier* (2009). *Glyph* is the autobiography of a four-year-old. Ralph Townsend, a voracious reader, refuses to speak but has been writing since he was one. Segments are titled with titillating terms, "pharmakon," "umstände," "ephexis," only to subvert the search for meaning. One storyline chronicles Ralph's serial kidnappings by mad scientists, military officers, a childless couple who are also Mexican immigrants, pedophile priests, and uses the plot to send up popular fascination with tragedy. Another line provides deconstructionist commentary on spectacles, import, and burlesques the ways in which theories are taken as life and death matters. Everett teaches literary theory along with creative writing, so knows whereof he speaks.

Even though it was Everett's eleventh novel, *Erasure* (2001) has received the most public attention to date. It is a frame novel where an academically trained and allegorically named black author and professor Thelonious "Monk" Ellison is accused of not being "black enough" in his writing and of writing novels with such postmodern complexity they lose relevance. He answers his critics with what he considers a joke novel written in stereotypically corrupted black English, and titled *My Pafology* (which he later re-titles *Fuck* in an attempt to sink his own work). As author he employs a pseudonym Stagg R. Leigh referencing the mythic figure. The novel draws attention to the act of writing a novel by including the entire manuscript of *Pafology* within *Erasure*, and the mock novel becomes as engaging as the real one. Of course, in a fictional world where a work titled *We's Lives in Da Ghetto*, is a best seller, Ellison's parody becomes an award-winning work. It is full of every black stereotype, and through spoofs of personages such as Oprah Winfrey, asks who are the arbiters of blackness?

Erasure's publishing history illustrated many of the things it mocked. According to Everett, some commercial presses stayed away from the work because of the satire of Oprah Winfrey in an era when a mention on her book club vaulted sales, so the work came out through the smaller University Press of New England. Doubleday offered to reprint the paperback, the result would have been a lucrative deal for Everett, but they wanted it to be the first issue in its African American series Harlem Moon, about whose title he queried, "Why not call it Steppin' Fetchit, and get it over with?" (Weixlmann 23). To Everett, both acts epitomized the creative constrictions and typing the novel critiques.

The title of Everett's *I Am Not Sidney Poitier* (2009) is at once a statement and negation foreshadowing the novel's concern with the difficulty of finding truth amid contradictions. The main character Not Sidney must always fight to define who he is. The novel is a bildungsroman, road narrative, murder mystery, always metafictive alluding to multiple works and illustrating Greg Tate's assessment that this generation of writers assumes all traditions as their own. *Not Sidney* opens evoking Ellison's unnamed narrator in *Invisible Man*: "I am the ill-starred fruit of a hysterical pregnancy, and surprisingly odd though I might be, I am not hysterical myself" (3). The presence of Huck Finn is felt in Not Sidney's decision to "light out for the territory" (43). Like a crewmember of the *Pequod*, he is "a chaser of whales"; and like Don Quixote he is "a fighter of windmills" (3). As a road narrative, the novel surveys everything from an extension of frontier ideology to the expression of counter culture values. Not Sidney drives west and embraces the geographical freedom represented by the automobile in order to attain a range of other mobilities – psychological, sexual, and racial – but his adventures subsequently reveal the hazards of the black road narrative.

Named to personify the tiresomeness of self-definition within a society incessantly imposing classification, Not Sidney ages rapidly, growing to look more and more like Sidney Poitier. He becomes Poitier because everyone tells him he is the star and later even buys the iconic Poitier suit. The storyline is constructed by threading together the plots of the star's films, among them, *In the Heat of the Night* (dir. Norman Jewison, 1967), which becomes a running motif, *The Defiant Ones* (dir. Stanley Kramer, 1958),

A Patch of Blue (dir. Guy Green, 1965), *Guess Who's Coming to Dinner* (dir. Stanley Kramer, 1967), *No Way Out* (dir. Joseph L. Mankiewicz, 1950), *Lilies of the Field* (dir. Ralph Nelson, 1963), and *For Love of Ivy* (dir. Daniel Mann, 1968). Along the way many topical elements in black culture are addressed: black Greek culture, colorism and the Jack and Jill clubs, as well as the trajectory of Clarence Thomas from impoverished Alabama to Yale. The novel's metafictive quality emerges when Not Sidney enrolls at Morehouse College and takes a course in "The Philosphy of Nonsense" taught by professor Percival Everett. Throughout the novel Everett underscores the impossibility of easy presumptions whether about race, genealogy, geography, history, and art. Even in this late era, pressure on black writers to write for the race still exists, but increasingly many are asking why? Everett has taken criticism for novels that avoid issues of race and blackness.[11] He has also questioned the placement of his novels on African American literature shelves, especially since in many the only thing black about them is their author (Weixlmann 25).

Mat Johnson shows the complications in identifying a novel's genre by a writer's phenotype in an era when mixed race writers resist being categorized as black, and when writers who identify themselves as black resist having works that are fantasy, mystery, or science fiction, defined by their author's race. As someone who could pass for white, his graphic novel *Incognegro* (2008) was inspired by his childhood fantasies of being a race spy and by the birth of his twins, one who had brown skin and "Afro hair" and the other who had "the palest of pink skins" and "European curly hair" (author's note 4). As will be seen in a later chapter, it uses the graphic form to comment on constructions of race.

In varying ways, Johnson explores what race means individually, communally, and theoretically. In *Drop* (2000), the protagonist Chris seeks to quit his impoverished Philadelphia neighborhood and does so figuratively through education, then literally when his training affords him a dream job as a marketing executive in a London firm. The novel queries diaspora and presumed collective identity by rewriting the black expatriate ideal. At first, finding respite from gun violence and pervasive racism among London's black British, upwardly mobile community, Chris soon senses the cracks in the surface. When misfortune strikes, he must return home to Philadelphia where he actually finds his truer self. The satiric suspense thriller *Hunting in Harlem* (2003) treats the ethical dilemmas of gentrifying the "most romanticized ghetto in the world" (9). The Horizon Realty's Second Chance Program seeks valued African American professionals as tenants for buildings where the impoverished and marginalized become mysterious fatalities. With the aid of a crime reporter, one of Horizon's employees discovers a dystopic renaissance that questions whether race can still make community in a rapacious environment where real estate profits are all that matters. The focus of *The Great Negro Plot* (2007) is colonial New York. In 1741, after a series of fires, hysteria takes hold and many white New Yorkers fear a slave uprising. The novel reconstructs the jailing of 154 blacks, the burning alive of 14, the hanging of 18, and the disappearance of more than 100. The historical research is extensive making the work an almost equal blend of fiction and nonfiction that suggests the difference between the two is frequently perspective.[12] The novel analyzes how a racial economy accords no value to black life by replicating an ethos in which property loss takes precedence over black slaves. How slavery persists as an idea even in modern American culture is engaged in Johnson's *Pym* (2011), which will be discussed in a later chapter as an example of the neo-slave narrative genre.

What it means to be outside the simple racial binary of black and white is the subject of Johnson's *Loving Day* (2015). The protagonist Warren Duffy, a comic book illustrator, sits in-between the race extremes. The son of a black mother and white Irish father, he terms himself "a racial optical illusion" (45). In spite of his "in-betweeness," his society insists on placing him within a single category: he identifies as black, but because of his appearance he is frequently mistaken for white; though appearing near-white, at a comic book convention he is segregated from the bestselling white illustrators; and even though the setting of his solo work is the rural south, he is placed in the "Urban" section (which he notes is the "nicest way to say 'nigger'" [41]) because his book is about a black detective passing as white (a metafictive reference to *Incognegro*). When he attempts to assert his mixed identity, to say that no one defines him but him, his black friend Tosha tells him only self-hating blacks who don't try to be white because the white world will not allow them to, make such statements. After his divorce from his Welsh wife, he returns to his hometown in west Philadelphia. He has lost the comic book store he owned in Cardiff, and his father has died, leaving him a dilapidated historic home and land in the black neighborhood of Germantown. Warren discovers he has a seventeen-year old daughter, Tal, who is the result of a one-night stand with a white Jewish classmate he subsequently deserted. His daughter's identification as apart from the group she terms "the blacks" irks him. Now in his custody, she wants to attend the Mélange Center, a school designed to help mixed race children assert their identity and not be forced to identify as black or worship whiteness. The tensions of navigating these various communities wear on Warren, and he envies those who easily define themselves racially. For him his blackness is deeply personal, stemming from the memory of his mother, aunts, and their family heritage, not a casual assessment of a physical trait. He resents the ways the United States frames blackness as something that does not fully account for this or for his father.

Along with its metafictive references, the novel weaves gothic fantasy into its form through the presence of an interracial ghost couple haunting Warren's house. It incorporates real-life events in the history of Mildred Jeter and Richard Loving whose interracial marriage forced legal change when they sued the state of Virginia to have their union legally recognized. Their surname and the holidays around the country that celebrate them as a symbol of the right to choose partners across racial lines give the novel its title. Its emphasis on multiple racial identities is further stressed when Tal's school project is to research actual tri-racial groups such as The Brass Ankles, the Redbones, and the Melungeons.[13] While it tells the story of Warren's reconciliation with his daughter and his acceptance of paternal responsibilities, *Loving Day* also contemplates the ways a mythology of whiteness forces a racially complex people to oversimplify identities.

In using the term "the blacks," Tal who has been raised as not-black all her life distances herself not from an actual group of people but from images of them that circulate throughout her culture. In a late-twentieth-century world governed by image and spectacle, iconographic representations of blackness frequently stand in for black actuality, and the ramifications of racial simulacra are taken up in two Colson Whitehead novels, *John Henry Days* (2001) and *Apex Hides the Hurt* (2006). In *John Henry Days* image production and marketing appropriate, package, and sell blackness as a commodity. The plot is simple, a freelance writer, J. Sutter, is sent to Talcott, West Virginia, to cover the unveiling of the United States Post Office's John Henry commemorative stamp. Through the legend of John Henry and the many images of him permeating American culture, the novel demonstrates the power of images to belittle both history and meaning. In an interview with Walter Mosley, Whitehead noted that John Henry was the first black superhero he knew (Brady 92). In the novel, however, the figure who at various points in cultural history represented the complex ideas of man versus machine, or a subjugated race triumphing over a dominant one, or the solidarity of the working classes against exploitative capitalism, is now distilled into the easily digested, easily marketable image of a stamp. As Whitehead asked himself when beginning work on this novel, "What kind of a monument was a postage stamp? It was so banal that it addressed something about our debased age" (Grassian 75).

The novel counters this banality as it inserts scenes weaving individual character perspectives on the John Henry legend with historical memory into the plot of J's increasingly complicated quest. Some scenes re-imagine the difficulty of life for John Henry and other black railroad workers during slavery and after Emancipation, as well as the experiences of white laborers equally exploited by a corporation that regards its workers' deaths as the collateral cost of industrial progress. Other scenes relate the personal experiences of individual characters to the John Henry legend. In one, an African American university professor researching the John Henry ballad and legend in the South discovers that Jim Crow attitudes do not die easily. A Jewish musician in New York's Lower East Side at the turn-of-the-twentieth-century attempts to transform the John Henry ballad into a musical form that will compete against the popularity of ragtime and allow him to support his family. A girl finds release from her mother's oppressive desire to mimic middle-class African American values of uplift through playing the John Henry song on the piano instead of the classical pieces chosen for her. The relation of Paul Robeson's experience playing John Henry on Broadway evidences the novel's verisimilitude, and the story of a collector's daughter who had to compete with her father's John Henry mania and museum, lends poignancy. Taken together, the scenes span epochs, trace the power of legend to make common culture, and implicitly mourn the loss that results when a culture becomes satisfied with a stamp's image being all that remains of this richness.

The superficiality of J.'s modern world is contrasted to the deep nuances of John Henry's significance. J is a "junketeer" covering publicity events and priding himself on the giveaways he is able to acquire. His jeans are Calvin Kleins, received at a party celebrating the designer's spring line; his T-shirt accompanied a Public Enemy release he is to review; and his shoes are from a Michael Jordan–Nike charity event. With Mickey Mouse socks and Goofy boxer shorts, J. is nothing more than a compilation of brands. Exposure to the meanings of John Henry brings about a change in him, however, and ultimately he wants to write a story, one worth telling regardless of its publication future. The legend has transformed him, urging him to seek deeper personal and cultural meanings.

Apex Hides the Hurt similarly pokes fun at artificiality posing as substance. The unnamed narrator is a nomenclature expert. That he is African American puns the pressure many raced as black feel to find a self-generated name that appropriately voices cultural experience. The title comes from the name and slogan he has given a defective band-aid available in a variety of skin color tones. The band-aid lampoons simulated multiculturalism where the appearance of variety substitutes for meaningful diversity in social and institutional practices. His current assignment is to aid the city of Winthrop in renaming itself, and as he undertakes the challenge competing visions of the city emerge through the potential names. The fading scion of the Winthrop line wants the name unchanged to remind people that the family's barbed-wire factory laid the foundation for the town's early economy. His competitor Lucky Aberdeen whose company is the present economic engine suggests "New Prospera" to look toward the future and attract tech-savvy employees to the remoteness of Winthrop. Other options include the mayor's suggestion to use "Freedom," the original name given the town by her ancestor when it was founded as a settlement for freed slaves. Ultimately he decides on a name that indicates process rather than fixity, "Struggle." His deliberations and discoveries comment on the ways naming shapes perspective and can retain history or foster forgetfulness.

Whitehead has said that everything goes "into the hopper" and becomes a possible influence for his writing. He names sources as varied as Toni Morrison, Spider Man, *Invisible Man*, the film *Nashville* (dir. Robert Altman, 1975), and *Moby Dick* (Brady 92). The "bohemian cult-nat" ethos of claiming any subject matter and treating it in any style seen fit suffuses all his work, as his speculative fiction novels *The Intuitionist* and *Zone One* suggest, and this assortment of influence does not betoken a distancing from black identity or culture. His memoiristic novel *Sag Harbor* (2009) in many ways is an origins story of his aesthetic vision. It is based loosely on Whitehead's own coming of age summering at the family beach home in New York's Sag Harbor. The narrator, fifteen-year-old Benji Cooper, is part of a community of blacks whose familiarity with one another and history of summers at the beach is summed up by the phrase "When did you get out?" The novel's time line covers his arrival, his adventures and summer jobs, and the melancholy surrounding preparations to return to the city for fall. Over the course of the summer, Benji hopes to mature sexually, increase his "cool" quotient, and become Ben. His cohorts share the same aims to finesse their performances of "cool" blackness – how to walk, how to dress, how to insert the appropriate adjectival expletives into a sentence.[14] Their awareness is rendered through symbols of the era's culture, Members Only jackets, Walkman players, and Classic Coke.

Sag Harbor provides many humorous insights into the disjunctures of being black and privileged in a society that cannot always see a seamless fit between the two. The privileged white Americans who are part of Benji's private school world are unable to conceive of domestic black wealth and think he and his brother are the sons of African diplomats. The more subtle existence of racial discomfort in an ostensibly post-racial moment is portrayed through spatial imagery. The black section of the beach community Azurest is a known entity to Benji and his buddies, and their parents do not allow them beyond the markers of the rock and the creek that signal the beginning of the wealthier Hampton real estate still tacitly the province of whites. Whites, in turn, become uncomfortable, when they stumble onto Azurest and it gradually dawns on them that they are the only whites on the beach. Race matters but in quieter ways.

Though it is nonfiction, Jake Lamar's *Bourgeois Blues: An American Memoir* (1991) is similar to *Sag Harbor* in addressing middle-class black male development. Its story of the reconciling of a black father and son garnered a good deal of attention because few works had previously engaged black middle-class men. His novels continue this interest in black masculinity that does not reside in disadvantage. His first, *The Last Integrationist* (1996), centers on the neoconservative black Attorney General Melvin Hutchinson who believes his education and position have allowed him to leave race behind, yet discovers how entrenched the concept is in the nation and his personal world. The characters in *Close to the Bone* (1999) are successful black males, all of whom are grappling with what it means to be a black man in a modern era. There are few surprises here in terms of characterization: Hal Hardaway is conflicted about his interracial relationship; Walker DuPree who is bi-racial is caught between the different heritages of his family tree; and Emmett Mercy is a psychologist whose career is built upon works ghostwritten by the wife he emotionally ignores. In *If 6 Were 9* (2001), Lamar combines the genres of murder mystery and academic novel to tell the story of two black professors, Clay Robinette, happily married with twin girls, and former black activist now ultraconservative professor Reggie Brogus. Clay has an affair with a student who soon ends up strangled to death. Initially suspicion falls on Reggie who flees town. A dual mystery unfolds into the death of the student and into Reggie's real identity. Reviews of both *Close to the Bone* and *If 6 Were 9* were mixed, some citing the weakness caused by Lamar's improbable plots, others citing the predictability of his characterization.[15]

Lamar's next two novels are set in his adopted home. In Paris's eighteenth *arrondisement*, Ricky Jenks seeks to begin again after being left at the altar by a woman who instead chose his cousin. He has abandoned the upwardly mobile aspirations of his family that he become a lawyer and follows his dream of being a jazz pianist. His talent is minimal, but he finds a gig at a tourist restaurant and becomes involved with a French Muslim woman named Fatima. *Rendezvous Eighteenth* (2003) is a sequel detailing what led Ricky to his current place and the way his world changes radically when the cousin who stole his betrothed engages him in murder and black-mail. *Ghosts of Saint-Michel* (2006) explores how perceptions are changed by violent acts. In a departure for Lamar its central character is a woman. Marva Dobbs owns a successful soul food restaurant in Paris, has a thirty-nine-year happy marriage, and a grown daughter. She is about to give it all up for the obsessive passion she feels for her 28-year-old Algerian sous-chef, Hassan. He suddenly disappears after a particularly gruesome car-bomb-ing, and the mystery of the novel revolves around whether or not Hassan has committed the act. One of the best parts of these novels is the Paris Lamar evokes, one constructed from personal experience, research, and imagination.

Lamar's most recent novel is *Postérité*, originally titled *Posthumous* in English (2014). Its subject is a black art historian's effort to write the story of fictional Dutch painter Femke Versloot and the span of her life from Nazi-occupied Rotterdam, to Greenwich Village of the 1950s, to Northern California after the September 11 attacks. It is organized by the titles of the artist's paintings, and ekphrasis dominates the work as Lamar minutely describes fictional canvases. It has yet to find an American pub-lisher, and Lamar conjectures this might be because it is about the art world or because it treats blackness tangentially. When asked if his novel was post-racial, Lamar instead characterized it as nonracial continuing, "My first four books – the memoir *Bourgeois Blues* and the novels *The Last Integrationist, Close to the Bone* and *If Six Were Nine* – all explored racial questions in the United States. When, in my fifth and sixth books – *Rendezvous Eighteenth* and *Ghosts of Saint-Michel* – I changed the setting to Paris, my cast of characters became very international. And while my play *Brothers in Exile* focuses on three black authors, the rest of the cast is white. So when I started working on *Postérité* I didn't see it as a big leap to write a book in which all the important characters, but one, are white" (Nechvatal n. pag.). His own relocation and his writing of black characters abroad has given him distance from American racial politics centering on the black white divide, but has also made publication of his works in the United States difficult. Lamar's feeling that the novel's consideration was influenced by the unasked question "Who does this black guy think he is, writing about Abstract Expressionism?" (Nechvatal, n. pag.) suggests that publishing may not have entered a post-racial era and still views conven-tional race content as necessary to selecting and marketing texts. While Lamar and other millennial writers lay claim to whatever content they desire and express their determination to treat it in whatever fashion they see fit, the themes of many of their works intimate that what some term post-racial does not always mean post-racist. Class and increasing opportunities may be mitigating factors for some, but for many the colorline is still as much a problem at the turn of the twenty-first century as it was at the turn of the twentieth.

Danzy Senna's *Caucasia* (1998) re-examines the late-twentieth-century color line. Birdie, the narrator, is one of two sisters. When their parents end their marriage, their upper-class white, radical mother takes custody of Birdie and ultimately leaves their Boston home because she fears government retribution for her political activism (a fear that turns out to be groundless). She invents new identities for herself and for Birdie who according to her white grandmother appears Sicilian. The other daughter Cole whose brown skin makes her readily identifiable as black even with her gray eyes moves to Brazil with her father, an intellectual who has overcome his own challenging economic circumstances and now writes race theory. The new geographies are a far cry from the girls' imaginary attic play land where they invented their own language. In their new spaces, they must define themselves not as daughters or sisters, but as members of particular groups because of skin tone. Their inner selves are of little consequence in a world that prioritizes externals.

Most of the novel is narrated from Birdie's point of view as she occupies a nebulous realm shifting between racial categories. Whether trying to pass for black at a predominantly African American school in Boston at the height of bussing's racial tensions, or passing as white while her mother and she are on the run, Birdie's race, just like her name changes with context. Her birth certificate shows merely Baby Lee, and other monikers are given her depending on the viewer or what race she needs to be: Jesse (the name of her mother's suffragette great grandmother), Le Chic (the name given her by her black schoolmates), or Birdie (the name given her by her sister who wanted a parakeet). Her self-awareness is always in contrast to the racial identity imposed by her outer world. Her sister Cole negotiates identity as well. Her uneasy relationship with the presumption of shared blackness questions the idea of identification via phenotype and her father's imagined diaspora of essentialized blackness. Through both sisters, Senna shows that though race is a social construction its impact on psyche is no less powerful. While her father Deck may theorize on the sociocultural significance of the mulatto in history and literature, his theories do not obviate the distance between him and Birdie that stems from the pain he feels when interrogated by police who do not believe that she is his daughter and think he is molesting white girls. Each sister smarts from the rejection by the noncustodial parent that has been based solely on a social construction.

Senna's second novel *Symptomatic* (2004) is a psychological thriller where mania manifests as a symptom of liminal existence along the color line. The unnamed mixed-race narrator can find no comfortable social place. She is in a relationship with a white man who does not know of her background, and at a party he gives she becomes literally sick when his friends enact racist charades. She sublets an apartment from an older woman Gretta Hicks who is also mixed-race, and initially finds that their similar identities yield mutual understanding, but all this changes when the narrator starts dating a visibly black artist. Gretta becomes increasingly unstable, obsessive, and insistent that she and the narrator are part of a race of the future that must inhabit their own idyll. Gretta stalks and then attempts to murder her. The presumption of community because one shares a racial background goes from comforting to claustrophobic to menacing in a novel using images of semi-darkness to create a netherworld where things are not what they appear.

Examining race takes many forms in novels composed during an ostensibly post-racial time. Senna utilizes thoughtful detailing of colorline politics, while authors Tayari Jones and Olympia Vernon fashion characters for whom the color line is much less permeable. For Jones the capital of the New South is a site for charting shift and stasis. *Leaving Atlanta* (2002) re-imagines the period of the city's history between 1979 and 1981 when at least 28 African American children, adolescents, and adults were killed in the serial murders that popularly came to be known as the Atlanta child murders. Told from the point of view of three children – one from a stable family navigating the ups and downs of social acceptance as she matures, another whose unstable family motivates him to secretly commit destructive acts, and one who lives with her single parent in the projects and faces intraracial censure because of her darkness – it becomes clear that race is material in their lives and in the potential threat to their safety.

Leaving Atlanta juxtaposes a tone of recollected childhood memory with one of reportage describing a killer at large, and it illuminates the dual nature of a city exemplifying racial progress and black potential, yet still dealing with many legacies of racism and segregation. Jones's second novel *The Untelling* (2005) continues its portrait of Atlanta through a black family whose middle-class security is upended by a tragic car accident that kills half the family. The narrator Ariadne (Aria) seeks to rebuild her life and overcome loss, guilt, and survivor's self-recrimination. *Silver Sparrow*

(2011) recalls the experience of a young girl who realizes she belongs to the "secret" family of a bigamous father trying to do right by both families. In all Jones's works, Atlanta is a presence. Its landmarks chart characters' development against the backdrop of racial histories that have been shed or transformed for the sake of reinvention. In all her novels, Jones's narrative language is shaped by the nuances of speech and creates an intimate voice inviting the reader to enter a story.

What Tayari Jones does with urban Atlanta, Olympia Vernon does with rural Louisiana and Mississippi. Making use of a reservoir of told stories incorporating the real and imagined she recreates small towns in the environs of New Orleans and Jackson. Like Jones, she creates a modulated vernacular voice that self-consciously focuses attention on the close link of language to actuality. In her debut novel, *Eden* (2003) the character Fat, a woman whose husband was hung for allegedly raping a poor white woman, is described as more than the "thing of consonants and vowels strung together through havoc" (40). Always, language calls attention to its own presence in constructing descriptions. Vernon's style invokes the bible, the blues, and the fantastic. Even in speaking of how she became fascinated with literature there is an intertwining of the body, the consciousness, and language:

> In that human space was I captured by Birth, itself, as first an idea that had come from the angle of two people. I found it fascinating that two people could lie together, could angle themselves incredibly in the throes of diction, of language, the vocabulary of some inaudible predicament, and with this, their lives, the atlas of their lives, of the words unspoken give Birth to another human being who possessed these words, these traits, these fascinations.
>
> Thus, the Word came.
>
> And I was mesmerized by it. (Rowell and Vernon 85)

The style here is representative of Vernon's novelistic language, a quality that is either beloved by readers or seen as obscuring.[16]

Vernon's novels frequently depict young women for whom coming of age is unjustly complicated. In *Eden* the narrator Maddy grows amidst tensions between her mother, her aunt who has slept with Maddy's father, and the aunt's impending death that begins yet does not allow a full reconciliation between the two. In *Logic* (2004) the eponymous thirteen-year-old protagonist is repeatedly raped and is now pregnant by her father, a fact that is willfully ignored by her mother, Too. Recalling Morrison's *The Bluest Eye* in its allegorical and cryptic naming, plot, and characterization,

Logic descends into her own insular world as she tries to protect herself
and make sense out of the incomprehensible adult world. She can only
find minimal solace from the marginal character, Tallest, one of four sons
of a prostitute who has his own demons.

Set in rural, segregated Bullock, Mississippi, Vernon's *A Killing in This
Town* (2006) parallels two forms of cancer, one caused by the local plant
and one caused by racism. In the town, white boys are urged to establish
their Klu Klux Klan bona fides at the age of thirteen by going to the house
of a black man, calling him outside, and dragging him to his death. Adam
Pickens on the eve of his thirteenth birthday has qualms when his father,
who is growing sicker from cancer, engineers that Adam's rite of passage
will be the local pastor Earl Thomas, the black man selected by the government to warn white workers about the lung disease caused by the plant.
Gill Mender, once a hometown boy who lives with the guilt of his own
past rite, returns and attempts to assist Adam in changing tragic tradition. Vernon's novels would seem to counter any sense that the United
States has entered a post-racial period. Many of her Southern rural settings
remain threatening spaces, suspended in time and intertwining race, poverty, and violence. The quality her work does share with her contemporaries, however, is its allegiance only to its own vision. Vernon describes the
process of how a story comes to her: "the Image comes, the Voice, both the
alphabet and the image collide, and sound, that too, all of it" (Rowell and
Vernon 99). All the senses are involved in her writing, and in this manner
she exemplifies the techniques of other experimental writers, Nathaniel
Mackey among them.

A four-volume epistolary work, Mackey's novels are gathered under
the single title, *From a Broken Bottle Traces of Perfume Still Emanate*. The
volumes included are *Bedouin Hornbook* (1986), *Djbot Baghostus's Run*
(1993), *Atet A.D.* (2001), and *Bass Cathedral* (2008). The serial composition is comprised of letters composed by a horn player simply designated as N (and evoking Mackey). The letters contemplate meaning in
its many forms: musical, philosophical, religious. They blend narrative,
analysis, and reflection to read like a journal written in language fusing jazz
rhythms and poetry while tracing its composer's thoughts on the process of
creative production. Mackey has said that the form of the work developed
during its composition. What began as letters meant to be interspersed
with poems and to give the idea of a diary became fiction chronicling N.'s
creativity. It took Mackey time to become comfortable with the letters
being called fiction and the volumes novels, because he first saw the work
as an extended prose poem (P. Naylor 645). Prose poem might still best

characterize *From a Broken Bottle*. It is serial, but more impressionistic than sequential. The letters (sometimes interrupted by prose sections, sometimes including diagrams and poems) exist both autonomously and connected. All are addressed to the Angel of Dust.

Early on in *Bedouin Hornbook*, N. says "I question the need to explain," which serves as a caution that *From a Broken Bottle* will defy easy analysis. A hint to the way it should be approached is given during an argument that develops when N.'s group performs at a record store. Someone standing in the classical section feels the band's music has no "center," and receives applause for his assertion. When a band member points out the preconceptions implied in the term "center," others standing in the "Folk Import" section applaud. The scene questions arbitrary categories – "Classical," "Folk Import" – and the ways they inhibit the acceptance of co-existing differences. The demand for explanation precludes open interpretation of new ideas and sensations. *Bedouin* begins as a recollection of how the band formed, then reflects on the nature of interpretation and influence. Mackey commingles a wide range of content – the Brasilian musical artist Jair Rodrigues, the theory of phantom objectivity, the death of Thelonious Monk – teasing out the way one informs the next and showing how taking all into account yields greater illumination. Some of the letters render music through prose and produce a perfect ideation of the conjoining of music and the written word.

As the quartet of works develops they become contrapuntal sharing and repeating motifs, but they are unified in their description of the band's development. Penguin the oboist opens *Atet A. D.* by playing such an eloquent solo that comic strip balloons begin to come out of the instrument's bell. They contain the words "the oboe spoke" (54). Here image, language, and music fuse to personify the instrument and add the dimensions of sound and sight to writing. *Djbot Baghostus's Run* begins by detailing the band's search for a new drummer, but then fuses the separation between author, storyteller, and work, as Mackey writes about N., who writing to the Angel of Dust includes in his letter a "lecture/libretto" that is the story of the arrest, imprisonment, and mental liberation from the illogic of injustice of Jarred Bottle, who in a performed version of the story becomes Djbot Baghostus. In *Bass Cathedral*, the band is pressing an album and N. requests liner notes from the Angel of Dust. The title of the album tracks, among them "The Slave's Day Off (Take 1)," "Feet, Don't Fail Me Now," and "Sun Ship," manifest the volume's more explicit consideration of the black cultural diaspora. Balloons emerging this time from album grooves contain comments that signify upon music, history, and cross-cultural influences. In many ways Mackey's conception of music might stand in for his conception of blackness: "it's social, it's religious, it's metaphysical, it's aesthetic, it's expressive, it's creative, it's destructive. It just covers so much. It's the biggest, most inclusive thing that I could put forth if I were to choose one single thing" (Funkhouser 322).

Mackey's style gives the written word multiple resonances allowing it to incorporate all the senses. In the novels, the visual nature of writing that limits its capacity to convey completely must be amplified. The grapheme "no(i)se" is one means through which he does this by allowing smell, sound, and the self to exist simultaneously within writing. The aesthetic crossing of boundaries between word, sound, and sight, signifies Mackey's desire to traverse larger boundaries. In an interview he noted, "the extent that categories and the way things are defined – the boundaries between things, people, areas of experience, areas of endeavor – to the extent that those categories and definitions are rooted in social and political realities, anything one does that challenges them, that transgresses those boundaries and offers new definitions, is to some extent contributing to social change. There's a challenge in heterogeneity" (Funkhauser 324). Mackey's aesthetics ask readers to let go of expectations with the hope that this will move them beyond their presumptions. His idiom has frequently led to suggestions that he focuses less on race than on form, but Mackey's writing asserts racial authority through cultural form.[17] His conception of blackness is conveyed through its products – jazz, the blues, voudon, or Santería – migrating and mingling with whatever they encounter, from the traditions of Sufism to the theories of György Lukács.

Cornel West has argued that there is a need for black cultural practices to craft a "new politics of difference":

> The main aim now is not simply access to representation in order to produce positive images of homogeneous communities – though broader access remains a practical and political problem. Nor is the primary goal here that of contesting stereotypes – though contestation remains a significant though limited venture. Following the model of the Black diaspora traditions of music, athletics, and rhetoric, Black cultural workers must constitute and sustain discursive and institutional networks that deconstruct earlier modern Black strategies for identity formation, demystify power relations that incorporate class, patriarchal, and homophobic, biases, and construct more multivalent and multi-dimensional responses that articulate the complexity and diversity of Black practices in the modern and postmodern world ... (29)

Millennial black novels are immersed in the ideas West proposes. They have moved beyond concerns with representation and realized the efforts of novels in past eras to portray the complexity of black life and writing philosophies. In doing so they insert black perspectives into a postmodern politics that might otherwise ignore black realities.

While the politics of postmodernity argue for a flexibility of identity conception beyond the immediate body, for many who live life as visibly black with limited socioeconomic opportunities, such flexibility is often nonexistent. Without sacrificing acknowledgment of the oppression faced by black peoples, these novels remember the political, social, and economic histories of lived blackness while conveying the myriad shapings of this historical past into new cultural observations. Novels at the turn of the twenty-first century are far-removed from mid-century conceptions of the genre as a form needing to speak for the race. They continue to expand ideas of what goes into making a novel, through wider class representation and wider geographies. The metafictive nature of many recognizes the processes of writing and the cross-cultural interests of authors and audiences.

Many of these novels emerge at a time when increasing fundamentalisms and nationalisms dominate global discourse. Perhaps their focus on breaking binaries and boundaries is in response to these confinements, and perhaps they contribute to dismantling single-minded ideologies. Their immediate and often irreverent juxtaposition of genres, of past and present, fiction and reality, argue for embracing divergent cultural elements without conflict.

Significant Genres of the African American Novel

Introduction: Forms and Functions

While every writer grapples with form, for African American novelists, considerations of form are complicated by considerations of race. Whether a writer elects to create a text specifically addressing race or not, its specter is often present, if not in the content of the novel then in its evaluation. Frequently external focus on racial dimensions within works obscures the fact that black novelists work within and create new traditions. Part II of this study focuses on the predominant genres of African American novels: the neo-slave narrative, detective, speculative, black pulp, graphic, and two categories that are groups rather than actual genres, novels adapted for the screen and novels of the diaspora.

The neo-slave narrative is unique to African American fiction in its effort to portray enslavement as more than an African American history. Novels in this genre show how inextricable slavery was and is from conceptions of American national identity. They give voice to those silenced by history's ostensibly objective record. Using conventions and content of the nineteenth-century narrative of the enslaved, they counter oversimplification, erasure, and misinformation. As much about the present as the past, they are cautionary tales urging an examination of history to achieve better understanding of continued systems of oppressions.

Seeing and detecting are themes used to construct new articulations of race, racism, and the dynamics of social domination in black detective fiction. This genre probes structures of authority, exposes unjust class systems, dissects all manner of prejudice from race, to class, to sexuality. In some of these works, the detective is a transgressive figure evoking the trickster tradition in African American culture; in others, he or she is an escapist figure enjoying a heightened degree of mobility. The detective character challenges readers to locate the sources of their own attitudes toward both social and literary traditions.

African American speculative fiction is a genre that defies time as it embodies history and futuristic fantasy to challenge traditional ways of viewing culture. The legacies of a forced transatlantic crossing and enslavement make themselves very apparent in these novels, but so too does the future. The genre is Janus-faced in that it embraces the past while embodying thinking ahead. Black writers working within this mode confront perhaps more than others the intersection of race and genre by critics who either ignore their novels or view them as race-transcendent even though much of their content is rooted in African American cultural history.

"Ghetto novels," "black pulp," "black romance," "urban fiction," and "street lit" are all terms that describe popular African American novels. The number of books published in this category is rising noticeably. In addition to houses devoted specifically to the genre, mainstream publishers are launching pulp imprints. Considering what constitutes the popular genre and its relationship to other novel forms sheds light on class divisions within black communities. Some critics might not acknowledge pulp novels as part of a canon, but even with all the controversy surrounding their forms and representations they constitute a significant segment of African American creative expression. They share formulaic connections with hip-hop culture, and the back-and-forth between the two genres gives them a unique idiom. Pulp illuminates group self-conception, ideas of composition, canon formation, and audience, at a time when these categories are becoming increasingly challenged.

In an era more and more sensitive to the role of the gaze in racial construction, black graphic novels provide the opportunity of using text and picture to interrogate racial identities. Though it is perhaps the most contemporary of the genres treated here, it frequently references the legacies of African American history. Many continue the use of black vernacular forms through they represent them visually. Others combine text and image to signify the syncretism that characterizes much black expression. In iconographic form, black graphic novels continue to question the vacillations between a consciousness of race and a consciousness of culture.

In their transformation from page to screen, black novels have frequently acted as indicators of national engagements with race. Because adaptations are so closely tied to cultural attitudes, they become useful sites from which to consider what decisions made in transferring a novel from the page to the screen signify about cultural climate. The active relationship African American novels have had with Hollywood and television not only reflects the nation's moods, it also moves race into a space that makes dialogue about difference possible. While few African American novels made it to the screen prior to the 1960s, their regular presence since the 1970s indicates the contradictory ways popular American culture embraces black experience yet often denies its validity.

Race and shared history make diaspora a de facto constituent in black novel writing. Some writers within the larger diaspora are particularly inspired by African American experience as a vehicle for engaging their own explorations of what blackness signifies within their area of the diaspora. Black experience and culture within the United States have been integral to shaping visions of symbolic locations and imagined communities.

Considering genre reminds readers of the many traditions of African American novels. Varied forms befit a varied people, and the breadth of black novels is noteworthy, considering the urgent circumstances under which the tradition began in the United States. Examining genres makes evident that like other African American freedoms, the freedom to write what one chose, in the manner on chose, was not easily won.

CHAPTER 8

The Neo-Slave Narrative

A neo-slave narrative is about more than enslavement. Novels within this genre use histories of slavery to query race, gender, sexuality, place, and to debate the degree to which past practices remain current. Part of what the genre asks is, still? During the post–Civil Rights and Black Power eras, black creators reconsidered the significances of enslavement and subverted its vast representational legacy. Over the course of the nineteenth and well into the first half of the twentieth century, slavery has long been given tangible representation through literature, film, the plastic arts, and popular culture has made extensive use of its legacy in music, jokes, and advertisements. What few of these forms presented was black interiority. Neo-slave narratives provide a means of seeing a frequently represented institution differently. They go beyond the binaries of slaves and masters, victims and victimizers, to show the pervasiveness and complexity of a social system.

The term neo-slave narrative generally references contemporary works that adopt the antebellum narrative of the enslaved to illuminate conceptions of race, as well as the importance of perspective and historiography. Many novels previously discussed in this study fall within this genre, including Ernest Gaines's *The Autobiography of Miss Jane Pittman* and David Bradley's *Chaneysville Incident*. Within this tradition, different writers use different forms, of course. Toni Morrison's *Beloved* and Octavia Butler's *Kindred* (1979) embody speculative techniques of fantasy and time travel to recover history and link it to the present. Edward P. Jones's *The Known World* (2003) and Charles Johnson's *Middle Passage* complicate presumptions of race and allegiance. Still others such as Sherley Anne William's *Dessa Rose* (1986) and Mat Johnson's *Pym* (2011) rewrite not only American slavery but also American literary history.

When the term was first employed is unclear. Ishamel Reed used it in 1984 to describe Bradley's *Chaneysville Incident* (R. Martin n. pag.). Bernard Bell is frequently credited with coining the term and inaugurating scholarship on it. In *The Afro-American Novel and Its Tradition* (1987), he describes it as a contemporary narrative of flight from bondage to freedom with elements of the slave narrative blended with fable and legend, used to illuminate racism, migrations, and cultural spirit (289). Ashraf Rushdy develops Bell's analysis and sees the roots of this genre in the debates emerging in the 1960s surrounding the social and intellectual significances of race and the growing contemporary discourse on slavery. Terming them "liberatory narratives" in her study, *The Freedom to Remember: Narrative, Slavery and Gender in Contemporary Black Women's Fiction* (2002), Angelyn Mitchell views the form as having an intertextual awareness, particularly in the hands of women writers, that filters ideas of freedom through race, gender, and presumptions of privilege, while creating new models of liberty. All these analyses realize the form's ability to correct the framing of black subjects and/or fill historical gaps by representing enslavement through the eyes of those who endured it.

While late-nineteenth- and early-twentieth-century novels such as Frances Harper's *Iola Leroy* and Charles Fowler's *Historical Romance of the American Negro* provide a glimpse to the interior thoughts of slaves, their characterizations and plot conformed to the goals of abolition and uplift, so sustained treatment of psychological development and cultural survivals as the enslaved gained liberty were rare. Margaret Walker's *Jubilee* (1966) was one of the earliest novels to fully re-imagine the Civil War and Reconstruction eras from the enslaved's point of view. Blending extensive historical research with the story of her own great-grandmother as it was handed down through generations and traced through birth and other records, Walker tells the story of Elvira "Vyry" Dutton from her birth in slavery to her freedom. Most of the institution's hallmarks are reproduced as Vyry goes from being the "friend" to becoming the slave of her owner's daughter, as she witnesses the brutality of beatings and the death of slaves from sickness, and as she comes to know personally the ways racism makes it impossible for emancipated blacks to establish themselves as citizens. Walker adds to this portrait the dimensions of being a woman within the system of slavery. Feeling her own powerlessness and resenting how much Vyry looks like her own daughter, her mistress has her suspended by her thumbs in lieu of confronting her own husband, Vyry's father-master. Vyry has no real memories of her mother who died at twenty-nine after giving birth to fifteen children, many of whom were her master's. When she attempts to escape, Vyry's efforts are hampered by needing to flee with two children of her own, and later, she must negotiate with her second husband, a field hand indifferent to book learning, for an education for her son by her first marriage.

The domestic sphere is emphasized in *Jubilee* in ways it could not have been in earlier articulations of slave women's lives. Precise details reveal how much joy Vyry takes in making a home even while part of a plantation, and much of the novel expatiates the travails caused by racist chicanery and violence as she and her husband try to establish home after home. What is most important in this telling of events is that Vyry reflects on them. Her thoughts are extensively rendered to centralize a woman's frame of reference. Walker's work paved the way for Alex Haley's *Roots* (1976), Sherley Anne William's *Dessa Rose*, Barbara Chase-Riboud's *Sally Hemings* (1979), and eventually Toni Morrison's *Beloved*. Accepting the role of writer as visionary, Walker looks to history to understand the present and what the future might bring (Graham, "Fusion" 281). These twin aims are combined in her novels and those inspired by it, as all rethink the meaning of history to better understand contemporary times.

Another text frequently cited as foundational in the neo-slave narrative genre is Octavia Butler's *Kindred*. When the novel appeared in 1979, Butler was already established as a writer of speculative fiction, and she was one of the first to bring the techniques of this genre to bear on the history of enslavement. The combination seems a surreally natural fit, for race and enslavement are frequent subtexts in speculative fiction's dialectic of dominators and dominated. The novel is set in 1976, the year of the United States bicentennial, and Edana "Dana" Franklin is a black woman living with her white partner Kevin. Inexplicably she becomes nauseated and dizzy. To Kevin's eyes, she suddenly disappears for a few seconds; in her reality, she is transported to a place she does not know where she saves a young white boy from drowning, only to have his mother believe she is attempting to kill him and have his father aim a gun at her. Again she experiences disorientation, and then she is back in her apartment with Kevin, her clothes wet and muddy. Only after a subsequent rescue of the same boy from the potential danger of a fire does her situation become clear. She is transported to Maryland of the early 1800s, and the boy she rescues and the black woman who is his neighbor are her ancestors, the white Rufus Weylin and the black Alice Greenwood. Each time Rufus is endangered, she is sent back to rescue him and assure that her family line will continue and that she will be born. When she is endangered in the past, she is sent back to her own time. In the past, she is a slave, and this becomes her entrée, and ours, to the institution's practices and aftermath.

With each transition, Dana, emboldened, lingers longer in the past knowing that she will return to the present. The longer she stays and the more she experiences – being a house servant, being subdued by physical

violence – the weaker her sense of her modern self becomes. Kevin illustrates the other side of slavery's system, the corrosive nature of white
privilege as he, against his own principles, too easily slips into the role of
master once he travels back with Dana. Dana's trips to the past personalize
a system she has understood only historically. The beatings and cruelty she
knows of academically become Isaac punished for attempting to see his
wife or Sarah subdued when she watches her sons sold away. The sexual
exploitation she knows is part of slavery's history becomes Tess, sold when
she is no longer valued sexually or Rufus telling her to persuade Alice
to yield to his sexual desire or be raped. Dana's instinct to protect Alice
from violation must be thwarted or the ancestor who starts her family line
will not be born. *Kindred* is a work about slavery's paradoxes and impossible choices. The good of Dana's life stems from the evils it initiates, and
this fact symbolizes larger American benefits accrued from the institution's
exploitation. As much as being concerned with past history *Kindred* is
equally concerned with the 1960s. Butler wanted to take someone from the
present who might feel impatience toward the pace of social progress, and
send them back in time so he or she might realize the immensity of what a
people have survived (Kenan 495). What Dana and Kevin know about its
history derives from representations in contemporary culture, and as much
as exposing the system of slavery *Kindred* interrogates its representations.

Mediating slavery's past through recreations of the modern moment,
noting what has been added, rewritten, left out, forces a contemplation
of how past records impact future understanding. Sherley Ann William's
Dessa Rose (1986) is formed from research into the true history of a pregnant black woman who reportedly led an uprising among a group of slaves
slated for auction. Williams entwines this story with a second, that of a
white woman who gave illegal sanctuary to a permanent colony of runaway
slaves. The pregnant slave woman became Odessa Rose (called Dessa), and
the white woman became Ruth Elizabeth (called Rufel), a Southern belle.

Though sentenced to death for killing a white slave driver while resisting
being taken to market, Dessa's hanging is delayed until the baby she is carrying is born because it is deemed valuable property. Helped to escape she
is subsequently brought to Ruth Sutton's plantation where fugitive slaves
have organized a community. The presumption that they are Ruth's property allows them to live relatively unmolested. They work the farm and
share profits. Dessa, weakened from battle and childbirth, and Ruth, abandoned by her family for marrying beneath her and by her fortune-hunting
gambler husband, initially distrust each other, but develop a working relationship as a means to their mutual survival. Ultimately they overcome

preconceived notions of what a white or black woman is supposed to be, something the novel encourages readers to do as well. Eventually by running a confidence game where Ruth sells the slaves who later escape and return to split the funds, the enslaved gain liberation, and Rufel gains freedom from gender subjugation.

Dessa and Ruth represent the realities of black and white female contention and cooperation. Initially Dessa resents Ruth nursing Dessa's baby while Dessa recovers. She is further angered by Ruth's contemplating a name for the child and views her actions as appropriation and a continuation of white right to claim black property. The image of a white woman nursing a black baby, however, upends the stereotype of the doting mammy. For her part, as Ruth over time tells Dessa of the relationship she shared with her mammy, her sentimentality lifts, and she realizes that her caretaker was duty bound and may not have truly loved her. Ruth's recalling that the woman's name was Dorcas, not Mammy, counters the erasure of black female individualism. Williams sees the relationship between Dessa and Ruth is one of mutual transformation. She likens them to Huckleberry Finn and Jim (Martinson n. pag.) while both are on the raft, a free-floating space that allows for observation and exchange that land-locked spaces do not. Ruth learns that she has viewed blacks as extensions of her own sentimentality, and Dessa learns of the commonalities shared by black and white women under racist patriarchy.

As a neo-narrative, *Dessa Rose* not only rewrites past slave history it faults the ways some modern accounts frame the stories of the enslaved. William Styron's *The Confessions of Nat Turner* (1967) was a work to which Williams, along with other black writers, took exception.[1] She felt his depiction of Turner as "pathological" and "maniacally obsessed with white women" was a new means of perpetuating stereotypes (Martinson n. pag.). She corrects Styron's image of Turner's desire for liberation being motivated by a religious vision that borders on possession with Dessa's fundamental desire not to have her child sold away from her or reared in slavery. The actual Turner was interviewed in his jail cell by Thomas Ruffin Gray, and in spite of Turner's statement that Gray is faithful to the former's story, Turner is fashioned as a "great Bandit" (Turner n. pag.). Styron's framing picks up on this imagery and becomes even more problematic. After Turner is sold by a lascivious homosexual plantation owner to abusive poor whites, he ends up with a hardworking white farmer who allows him to learn carpentry skills, read the bible, and preach to other slaves. These acts provide the agency enabling his rebellion. He is befriended by a neighboring white woman who, though she owns slaves is very much against the institution. When challenged by a crazed cohort to prove his race loyalty and manhood, though he loves her Turner kills her, and with her dying breath she forgives him. Turner emerges as ungrateful and lacking strong moral fiber. His masturbation while fantasizing about sex with a white woman, and the ineptness of his leadership both reinforce long-held stereotypes. Styron's third person narrative leaves no room for a Turner that is other than one man's bogey.

Williams undoes the lack of subjectivity by turning narrative perspective over to Dessa as the novel unfolds. The first part of the novel, "The Darky," shows her objectification. It is told from the perspective of Adam Nehemiah, a white Kentuckian who like the actual Gray is seeking prestige by writing a book on slave rebellions. He sees her as a sexualized beast and her story a means to his own fame. The alternation between his "objective" assessment and the framed counterpoints of Dessa's perspective are rendered in contrasting forms: one told through an authoritative standard English and one an equally authoritative, orally inflected English evoking personal truth. Dessa undermines his information gathering through evasion, and in this manner the novel subverts the traditional relationship between enslaved narrator and amanuensis. Nehemia is erased from the novel's action, and when he reappears at its end we see him from Dessa's vantage. Part two, "The Wench," switches narrative voice between Dessa and Ruth. The title could refer to either woman and thus illustrates objectification along gender lines. Though they occupy different positions in a social hierarchy, patriarchy treats both as property. The final section, "The Negress," is given in Dessa's first-person voice, mirroring her taking charge of her own destiny. In the epilogue, it is an aged Dessa, who receives the last word in a coda on the significance of her life story.

Sculptor, painter, and illustrator Barbara Chase-Riboud's neo-slave narrative *Sally Hemings* (1979) is perhaps her best-known work. It appeared amidst intensifying debate over the validity of DNA evidence of Thomas Jefferson fathering enslaved children.[2] Like *Dessa Rose*, historical research is at the novel's core. It is informed by Fawn M. Brodie's 1974 biography *Thomas Jefferson: An Intimate History* and by the Hemings family's oral testimony. Similar to other neo-slave narratives *Sally Hemings* reimagines received history to gain access to the complicated psychological elements of enslavement. As early as William Wells Brown's *Clotel*, Hemings and Jefferson have been symbolic figures of the hypocrisy of slavery's intimacy with democratic freedom. Chase-Riboud expands Hemings from symbol to fully dimensional character. In most of the furor-fueled discourse surrounding the relationship, Hemings has been more object than subject, a means of assessing Jefferson, the nation, and the ethics of both. The novel counters this objectification by offering a portrait of Sally not feeling the constraints of slavery as others do, playing with her niece Martha Jefferson, and adulating her master. Her unawareness of slavery's reality is given form when in France as lady's maid to Martha, Sally's brother James says they should stay and be free, and she can form no distinction between her situation and liberty. She belongs to Jefferson literally and emotionally, and each time she has the option to choose him or choose liberty she chooses him.

Chase-Riboud risks romanticizing slavery by creating so epic an affair, but she felt it a more appropriate telling than sociological studies of plantation life that ignored emotions and memory ("Own Terms" 736). She takes the liaison of a sixteen-year-old and a thirty-six-year-old, one some would characterizes as child sexual abuse or rape, and frames it in a manner that discourages its easy dismissal as a dyad of victimizer and victim. In many ways, it recalls the ambivalent contradictions Ellison poses in his Prologue to *Invisible Man* when a slave woman notes, "I dearly loved my master, son, ... He gave me several sons, ... and because I loved my sons I learned to love their father though I hated him too" (10). Sally's story is told in flashback so that her regret in choosing love over freedom is felt in every passage.

The novel begins with a census taker, Langdon, interviewing Sally and through their exchange the events of her life unfold. When he seeks to list her and her sons as white to protect Jefferson from the "crime" of miscegenation that is outlawed in Virginia, however, the reality that knowledge of who she is will be erased causes Sally to respond with vehement protest and reassess everything she has believed about her status in Jefferson's world. The neo-slave narrative gives Chase-Riboud's a means of imbuing Hemings with a racial pride historical records did/would not record, since their main concern would have been defending or besmirching a US president. In the novel Sally is connected to African American events. Wearing a disguise and in the company of Langdon, she attends the trial of Nat Turner. The novel further imagines the many ways she must have been reminded of her tenuous status. The intercourse between her and public figures such as Aaron Burr and Dolley Madison clearly reveal the limitations of being Jefferson's favorite. The equation of slave as chattel is driven home to her at the Monticello auction of Jefferson's human and nonhuman assets after his death, and each time Jefferson remains mute when she asks him about freeing her and their children, love and enslavement become oddly similar.

The novel's sequel, *The President's Daughter* (1994), treats the generational legacy of the Hemings–Jefferson relationship through the story of their tall, redheaded, green-eyed daughter, Harriet. Bearing a strong resemblance to her father, she resents his not freeing her or acknowledging her as his child. She is unable to understand why her mother has remained in slavery. Jefferson has promised his children they can leave Monticello on their twenty-first birthday, and when she reaches that age she leaves for Philadelphia and reluctantly passes as white in order to make a life for herself; however, she lives in fear of being re-enslaved. Ultimately she marries a white man, and when he dies, marries his brother, and lives a happy life as an abolitionist working with the Underground Rail Road. The impact of revealing her black antecedents on her distraught granddaughter shows why Harriet has never acknowledged who she is. Her mother may have regretted sacrificing freedom for love, Harriet regrets sacrificing her blackness for freedom. She becomes a figure in isolation, unable to connect to her mother, father, or live as herself in society.

Chase-Riboud has lived in France, Italy, and traveled extensively. Her travel is reflected in a series of novels portraying enslavement in a variety of geopolitical contexts. *Valide: A Novel of the Harem* (1986) is a study in the acquisition of power while disempowered. A young Martiniquais is captured by pirates and sold to an Ottoman sultan. Using her knowledge of alliances as well as her body she gains control over him and once she bears his son becomes Valide, a position of honor where she controls all her son's possessions including his women. The novel elucidates intrigues within a system where the only currency women possess are their bodies, and it becomes a larger contemplation on contemporary patriarchies. *Echo of Lions* (1989), which was at the center of a copyright infringement suit Chase-Riboud filed against DreamWorks Pictures over the screenplay for Steven Spielberg's *Amistad* (1997), mixes historical record and fiction to make the story of the *Amistad* mutiny a story of Joseph Cinqué, fifty-three kidnapped Mende, and black agency. The characters are no longer "the slaves"; they are individuals. Other characters including a wealthy black abolitionist and his daughter underscore the theme of black self-liberation. The power of Riboud's *Hottentot Venus* (2003) derives from its first-person narrative. Based on the true story of South African Saartjie "Sarah" Baartman, the novel allows entry into her feelings as she loses her family to Dutch and English massacres. Tricked into traveling to England in 1810 her hope turns into despair and disillusionment when she is subjected to the cruelest form of enslavement. She is displayed in a London freak show, her ritually scarred genitalia fascinating to a gawking public. Her posthumous recollections unmask dissection for scientific research and exhibition in a French museum for the perverted voyeurism they are. The novel's epilogue at last gives her the opportunity to voice her revenge. Riboud tells stories of enslavement in many forms. The details of each are different, but all disclose something about the lingering legacies of race, the confinement of gender, and the way voices deemed marginalized are silenced.

Walker, Williams, Butler, and Chase-Riboud use the neo-narrative to enlarge and complicate history. Charles Johnson uses it to question the need for histories that have become so familiar they risk being trite. For Johnson, modern black experience needs a narrative beyond victimization, one that reflected black subjectivity and engagement with intellectual traditions. The *Oxherding Tale* questions the received narrative of black enslavement by portraying possibilities within the system that are not frequently documented. The protagonist Andrew Hawkins is not the product of a white father raping a black slave; rather, he is the son of the white mistress of Cripplegate plantation. He is conceived during a wife swap between his black father, a slave, and the plantation's white master. Johnson thus signals that this is not a conventional story of slavery but rather a meditation on the complexities of enslavement. We are frequently reminded that Andrew writes his autobiography in flashback because he discusses the writing challenges he faces. He personifies the freedom of the slave narrators to tell their own stories, and he shows the enslaved as thinkers engaging in intellectual traditions, not solely providing testament to suffering. As Andrew writes, a wide range of philosophers are referenced, among them Hegel, Emerson, Paine, Descartes, Voltaire, Kant, and Thoreau, to examine the relationship of free and unfree, self and other, cause and effect, and other binaries. The running binaries call attention to the fact that Andrew exists between either/or, and the novel suggests that only from this space can meaningful understandings of race be achieved.

Charles Johnson was the second African American to win the National Book Award for fiction (the first was Ralph Ellison for *Invisible Man*). The honor was given for his novel *Middle Passage*, and the awarding came amid a storm of debate in which some jurors felt race not talent earned it.[3] The risks Johnson took in his characterization, and the way he crafted the work to recall past American classics largely went unheralded.

In 1830, Rutherford Calhoun, a freed slave from Illinois, undertakes a picaresque adventure to avoid debts and an arranged marriage. He stows away on what he later discovers is a slaver that has a name highlighting the close tie between American freedom and slavery. The *Republic* recalls Melville's *Pequod*, and its motley crew of isolationists signify the tensions between pluralism and ideological whiteness. Johnson again explicitly calls attention to the writing process in having the novel take the form of a diary. While keeping it, Rutherford engages in metaphysical contemplation of his life, his race, and the human situation. A self-confessed inveterate liar, a rapscallion, his only allegiance is to himself. He is a character that has appeared in many slave narratives and early black novels, the slave who facilitates enslaving others, but where earlier genres condemn the figure Johnson's novel treats it ambiguously. Calhoun is written against a backdrop of American individualism in the extreme, and his self-interest borders on self-reliance. There is an expectation that his cargo the Allmuseri whose worldview emphasizes the good of the many over single interests will exercise some influence over him, but once they gain control of the *Republic* they prove to be equally as oppressive as their original captors. *Middle Passage* portrays the way power corrupts any under its sway and removes race in order to construct a contemporary story better reflecting the enormity of slavery as a system, not just a misfortune befalling those who were black.

Johnson elects not to portray noble slaves, and instead produces a story with conflict, disequilibrium, and interest. Rutherford existentially grapples with what it means to be an individual raced as black and whether there are inherent, automatic allegiances to others raced in the same manner. His questions resonate with Johnson's own meditations on what it means to be a black writer and how the term influences what and how one can write. In an interview discussing *Middle Passage*, he observes that he finds the label "black writer" constricting: "If we say 'black writer' or 'female writer,' the assumption is that the work is predominantly about the experience of being black or being female. And that it's the reason why we read the book." Johnson instead describes the novel as a "philosophical sea adventure" (Steinbach n. pag.). Rutherford happens to be black, happens to undertake a journey that plunges him into the middle of the slavery enterprise, and happens to see the mutations of race in many societies; however, the greater concern is not with the event of slavery or the institution of race, but with the ways philosophical ideas and ethics manifest in both.

One factor distinguishing the neo-slave narrative from its progenitor is its being published in an era allowing a more multifaceted questioning of moralities affected by the institution of slavery. Nineteenth-century writings focused on the wrongness of making chattel out of humans, but their modern counterparts dig deeper into the structures that allow this to happen. Edward P. Jones, like Johnson, is concerned with the dilemmas posed when individual corruption is the inevitable result of participation in an immoral system. He had read a book about a Jew joining the Nazis during World War II, and the knotty ruminations underlying this choice fascinated him. The idea resonated again when he was shocked to discover that blacks held slaves (Fleming 254). Ultimately this interest in collaboration against one's own interest gave rise to *The Known World*, winner of the 2004 Pulitzer Prize for fiction. The title implies the limitations of perspective: what is known is what is seen, but much more exists beyond the evidence of one's eyes.

The Known World literally shows the full complexion of slavery through its treatment of enslaved darker-skinned blacks, their lighter-skinned black masters, indentured whites, white masters, and the impoverished and wealthy of all races. The breadth of its treatment of slavery's effects in the South, the North, and on immigrants arriving in the United States matches the vastness of the institution. Central to the novel's investigation is a contrast between maps, one the white Sheriff Skiffington's ancient sixteenth-century map of Manchester Virginia and environs further south, so outdated that Florida does not appear; and the others, multimedia compositions of clay, paint, and cloth, made by the enslaved Alice Knight. The maps do more than chart topography; they chart psychic space. Skiffington's old map represents a colonization of a terrain once inhabited by Native Americans, first "discovered," then settled by Europeans, then renamed. Maps such as his make concrete presumptions of racial and cultural entitlement. Alice's, on the other hand, represent reclamation and rewriting. They are a different type of literacy for a people denied other forms of expression and self-knowledge. Alice has mastered the performance of decreased mental capacity, and slave patrols and owners allow her to wander the environs of Manchester. She translates the knowledge she acquires from her travel into maps (one which comes to hang in the nation's capital) detailing the Townsend plantation, its barns, cabins, landscape, and inhabitants. Ultimately her maps are the tools the slaves use to liberate themselves.

The novel is an impressionistic neo-slave narrative deviating from the linear arc of the nineteenth-century form: I was born a slave, I escaped, I am free. Its moves in and out of individual experiences, back and forth in time, and provides multiple views of enslavement and its aftermath. The ways each character adjusts to the system, the compromises they make, lies they tell to themselves and others to survive, and the ways they escape, form the core of a very moving novel. Moses is the slave of a former slave, Henry Townsend. Townsend was favored by a white master and assisted in acquiring freedom, land, and slaves. Henry believes himself to be a "planter" instituting a more compassionate system of enslavement, an impossible contradiction shown through the ways the institution ultimately corrupts him. He succumbs to overworking his slaves and treating them brutally, in one instance having the Cherokee deputy slice the ear of one who tried to escape. The irony of Henry's status is underlined when his father Augustus, who had presumed his son's status guaranteed his freedom, is sold into slavery upon Henry's death. Henry's slave Moses who harbors the ambition of acquiring social status by owning slaves himself sheds light on the costs of mobility within a world where advancement can only be had at the expense of others. He separates himself from other slaves, even his own son and his son's mother. He uses his position as overseer to intimidate and to make sure the caste line is never crossed. When Henry suddenly dies, Moses hopes to replace him as master and husband to Henry's wife, Caledonia, who now runs the plantation, but his dream is unrealized. Unlike Alice whose wanderings connect her to others and give her a comprehensive awareness of the world and her place within it, Moses's known world is the plantation and its hierarchical values. When he attempts to escape, he has so little knowledge of the larger landscape that he moves further south, further into slavery.

Jones's characters reveal the intricacies, rationales, and hypocrisies of slavery beyond black and white opposition. In an interview, he mentioned that on book tours and radio shows audiences frequently criticized him for absolving whites from the responsibility of slavery's past and present manifestations (Graham, "Interview" 429–430); however, writing about black slaveholders might be said to de-racialize slavery and subvert its racist rationales. By showing it to be more than a horror committed by one people against another because of skin color, the novel cautions that oppressors are made not born. The institution fosters a desire for power as a means of measuring one's stature. Like other neo-narratives, *The Known World* provides a fuller understanding of slavery through recording what many thought to be unspeakable, blacks enslaving blacks.

In her neo-narrative *Beloved* (1986) Toni Morrison records the unspeakable, a mother killing her children, inspired by the life of Margaret Garner. What we know of Garner has been severely constrained by the perspectives of others. Thomas Satterwhite Noble, in his painting *The Modern Medea* (1867), gives us a black woman standing over the bleeding bodies of two children while another pulls down her left arm as if trying to stop her from an action, and a fourth kneels pleading at her feet. Her face is angry, her mouth open, as she confronts four white men, one pointing down in horror at the bodies on the ground. Satterwhite paints both Garner and her children dark brown, though historical sources describe her as mulatto and suggest that one of the white owners of her plantation fathered at least one, maybe two of her children. The children would be much lighter in color, more akin to Samuel J. May's description in his *Antislavery Tracts*: "In one corner was a *nearly white child*, bleeding to death. Her throat was cut from ear to ear, and the blood was spouting out profusely, showing that the deed was but recently committed ... A glance into the apartment revealed a negro woman, holding in her hand a knife literally dripping with gore, over the heads of two little negro children who were crouched to the floor" (May 51). Perhaps the range of colors in May's antislavery tract is a subtext meant to stoke outrage at the exploitative sexual politics within slavery that Satterwhite paints away. From painting to tract there has already been a revision moving further from the truth of Margaret Garner.

A newspaper article reporting the "deed of horror" provides another perspective on Garner:

> In the meantime there is much excitement existing, the bloody episode hav-
> ing invested the affair with a tinge of fearful, although romantic interest.
> The Abolitionist regard the parents of the murdered child as a hero and
> heroine, teeming with lofty and holy emotions, who, Virginius like would
> rather imbue their hands in the blood of their offspring than allow them
> to wear the shackles of slavery, while others look upon them as brutal and
> unnatural murderers.
>
> At any rate, the affair will furnish some employment to lawyers as well as
> officers, as extra force for the latter being necessary to prevent rescue while
> the case is pending. ("Stampede of Slaves")

Focusing more on the voyeurs than on Garner, the paper portrays her not as woman making the horrendous decision to kill her children rather than see them in slavery, but as a spectacle. Readers can project their horror, fascination, and their sensibilities regarding abolitionists onto the paper's interpretation of her. From a view that seeks to darken Garner to absolve those complicit in her debasement, to one more concerned with the audience than the subject, what is clear is that none present the internal thoughts of Margaret Garner. All give filtered facts, but not the truth, a distinction important to Toni Morrison in creating her neo-slave narrative.

Beloved touches on the major practices of slavery and re-visions them from the inside out. The separation of parent from child is imparted through the perspective of Baby Suggs whose litany of loss painfully provides a sense of the tenuousness of human life when reduced to property. Anyone she knew or loved either has run, been hanged, rented or loaned out, mortgaged, sto-len, or seized. She forces herself to stop loving her children knowing they will only be taken from her. Morrison reconfigures the ways maternal imagery was used in the abolitionist press where generally a pathos-filled description detailed the separation of parent and child but not its aftermath; instead, she describes the recurring memories and the sorrow that does not go away. Her analogies are made of concrete images that might remain with the mother, babies sold so young their baby teeth haven't even come in yet, for instance. In describing escape, running is not told from the perspective of one watching a fugitive, but from the perspective of a fugitive struggling to navigate the trek. Paul D.'s escape is evoked as he would have seen it, marking passage from south to north by various trees: magnolia, peach, dogwood, cherry, chinaberry, and apple. The human loss subsumed in the reductive term the Middle Passage is made visible through Sethe's struggle to remember Nan who made the forced voyage with Sethe's mother and in a language Sethe no longer speaks told her how her mother threw the babies that were the result of forced couplings with white men overboard but kept Sethe because she was the issue of a black man she chose. *Beloved* is an exemplary example of the neo-slave narrative, but other novels less obviously identifiable, also fall within the genre. Morrison's *A Mercy* (2008) and Mat Johnson's *Pym* (2010), for instance. Both demonstrate the neo-slave narrative widening its scope, using slavery's mutations in American culture to redefine received narratives.

A Mercy's central character, Florens, is a black slave acquired as a young girl by Jacob Vaark, a farmer and rum entrepreneur of English and Dutch descent. Her ownership settles a debt owed him by D'Ortega, a Portugese slaveholder. By novel's end we learn that, unbeknownst to Florens, her transfer to Vaark is a "mercy" begged for by her mother to spare her daughter the sexual exploitation she herself has experienced at the hands of D'Ortega *and* his wife. On Vaark's farm Florens joins Lina, a "praying savage" (5) who was sold to Jacob after surviving a plague that destroyed her people; his wife Rebekka who rather than suffer the subjection of being female, lower class, and sexually abused in England enters into a prearranged marriage to Vaark; Sorrow, a sea captain's daughter who survived a shipwreck and is psychologically unhinged until the birth of her second child; and Scully and Willard, white indentured laborers still working off the ever-changing terms of their debts. Together these characters constitute a community that allows Morrison to present an expanded view of the prenational world and the many forms of enslavement already within it.

In writing about what is, in essence, the beginnings of America, *A Mercy* tackles two epics at once: the story of a nation's founding and the enslavements that were part of its development. Both are recounted from traditionally ignored perspectives. The book's sections alternate between Florens's first person narrative, and third person backstories of other characters. Florens's language metamorphoses standard English grammar and diction with a blending of active and passive, and an eliding of past and present, to undermine the privileging of standard linear narrative as an expressive mode. Decentering the convention decenters the primacy of records that employ it, many of which devalued Florens and rationalized her and others' enslavement.

A Mercy's uses the narrative of a slave to illuminate the systems of race and class that engender the institution. Florens's mother transits the Middle Passage and emerges in Barbados not as a person with family and culture but as something less than human, a "negrita" (165). Though she is white, Rebekka's transatlantic crossing in many ways parallels that of Florens's mother. Seeking to avoid a destiny as either "servant, prostitute, or wife" (77–78), with little distinction between the three, she travels to North America, her status as virtually being chattel exemplified by sharing space with animals in steerage. Lina whose Native American world has been decimated by disease is raped, and later abandoned by the Presbyterians who take her in because she will not convert. They sell her to Jacob Vaark whose memory of being an orphan a few steps removed from enslavement gives him a moral code he subsequently abandons for the economic advancement participating in slavery's commerce provides. The indentured servants Scully and Willard are enslaved by perpetual debt. At the end of the novel, we learn that Florens writes the story, inscribing it into the wood of a room in the unfinished Vaark mansion. An enslaved woman is thus given the power to create an expansive neo-slave narrative linking enslavement to national origins.

The neo-slave narrative continues to evolve. Mat Johnson's *Pym* (2010) pays homage to the slave narrative while critiquing the overuse of slavery's history. The narrator, Chris, has an especial affection for the nineteenth-century form because it was the original utterance of transatlantic slavery in the slaves' own voices. He has grown weary with slavery as a topic, however, feeling it has been over-appropriated by artists, writers, and academics of mediocre ability. Since the original narratives, nothing new has been added to the story, and the details of transatlantic passage have been perverted into clichés and slogans.

Chris, a professor, is denied tenure at Bard College. After a series of mishaps he finally has some luck when he acquires the narrative of Dirk Peters, Arthur Gordon Pym's black partner in mutiny, exploration, and survival in the original Edgar Allan Poe work, *The Narrative of Arthur Gordon Pym* (1838). In Johnson's version, the semi-literate Dirk tried to get Poe to tell his story, to no avail; instead, Poe appropriates the experience for his own ends. Chris feels that he can now accomplish what Dirk desired, and that the undiscovered complement to Poe's novella will prove the renaissance of his academic career. The novel's meaning loops, as Chris, hoping to use a slave narrative for his own advancement, now becomes part of the very commodification of slavery he critiqued. The discovery of Dirk's narrative combines with other incidents to send him on an expedition to Antarctica to see if he can discover both why Poe's work ends so abruptly and whether the utterly black island of Tsalal existed beyond Poe's imagination.

To facilitate his research travel to Antarctica Chris gathers co-sponsors. In the course of their journey the group falls prey to Yeti-like beings and become their slaves because the explorers cannot repay a debt. The difficulty in realizing one is no longer free, the torment of adjusting to manual labor and brutality as part of daily life, the intimate relationships that develop between master and slave, and disloyalty encouraged among slaves are told through the eyes of privileged, educated African Americans, and the dissonance between their knowledge of who they are and their deteriorating situation skillfully evokes the physical and psychological metamorphoses as they become slaves. Chris's intellectual slavery-fatigue is replaced with the bleakness of actual enslavement. As a neo-narrative, *Pym* not only records the thoughts and feeling of modern twenty-first-century subjects as they become part of a system they thought their ancestors had overcome, it also warns that without proper vigilance, the evils of history can recur.

By placing the novel in conversation with *The Narrative of Arthur Gordon Pym* Johnson directs attention to the ways so much of the American canon is built upon appropriated black experience while not acknowledging the worth of blackness or of black writers. The novel opens with a preface that at first glance reads in tone and wording exactly like Poe's, but it soon becomes clear that the voice is Chris's (even including a metanarrative reference to Mat Johnson in his past role as a professor and adviser). The preface notes that gentlemen from Richmond desire this narrative for "sociological" and "historical" reasons; and creates an apologia for those who will think the work the ranting of a "paranoid" (3). In these few sentences Johnson parodies the need for authentication and undermines the ways African American writing has been dismissed as testament, sociology, and protest. The tradition of black narrative is further evoked through the title of Dirk's work, *The True Interesting Narrative of Dirk Peters. Coloured Man. As Written by Himself.* The self-assertion counters Poe's initial refusal (representing the exclusion of black writing from the American canon) and his theft (representing the unacknowledged adoption of black experience that is so much a part of the American canon).

Adopting the form of academic criticism, the novel pokes fun at Poe's stereotypes and lapses in fiction writing skill. Its tone smacks a bit of Mark Twain's 1895 "Fenimore Cooper's Literary Offenses," at points, but in addition to its humor, it provides history and context for understanding Poe's motivation and work. Moreover it provides an analysis of the ideology of whiteness and the ways this has used race to sustain its own privilege. *Pym* also veers into the area of speculative fiction as it describes ice caves and biodomes in order to examine how societies order themselves in terms of class and gender, and why. *Pym* contemplates both the significance of slavery

and the form of the slave narrative. Its style draws attention to the appropriation of slavery and the many cultural products produced by the institution,
including racism. In *Pym* Johnson questions why we still hold on to the
significances of slavery, and answers his own question by suggesting that the
legacies and trauma of slavery still have much to teach modern humanity.

Colson Whitehead's neo-narrative *The Underground Railroad* (2016),
transforms the abolitionist network into an actual train. The conceit of a
real train, built by the people who build everything in this country yet get
no credit for their work, joins the elements of Whitehead's picaresque novel
together. We are grounded in the consciousness of the protagonist Cora as
she takes us from place to place, geographic and psychic, within the institution of slavery. The technique provides readers with a sense of touring
scenes from slavery as she draws back the curtain to reveal its ugly details.

Underground offers a safe distance from which analysis is possible, and
frequently Whitehead provides commentary within the narration to aide in
this analysis. Much of the novel's content will be familiar to many readers.
Whitehead gathers incidents from other sources and links them together in
a theorizing of race and culture in the United States. So that readers may
see the dehumanization of the slave, for instance, Whitehead creates Jockey
whose birthday is celebrated once or twice a year, even though the institution's practices contemptuously convey the idea that "niggers didn't have
birthdays" (11). The echoes of Douglass's *Narrative* are heard as he regrets
never knowing his birth date: "I have no accurate knowledge of my age,
never having seen any authentic record containing it. By far the larger part
of the slaves know as little of their ages as horses know of theirs, and it is
the wish of most masters within my knowledge to keep their slaves thus
ignorant" (1). Another portion of the novel finds Cora in North Carolina, a
state that leaves lynched bodies hanging from trees as macabre reminders of
who holds power. While in the home of Martin and Ethel Wells she is led
up the stairs to the attic. During her protracted stay there she watches the
town square where white men in blackface act out skits of slaves who regret
that they ran away and beg their masters to take them back. She also views a
corrective to their fantasy, the actual lynching of a girl who was found stowed
away trying to make her escape. The corresponding passage this scene alludes
to is in *Incidents in the Life of a Slave Girl* (1861) where a fugitive Harriet
Jacobs hides in a garret sustained only by glimpses of her children.

Whitehead has said, "I didn't see any particular value in doing a straight
historical novel. The use of certain fantastical elements was just a different way to tell a story. If I stuck to the facts then I couldn't bring in the
Holocaust, and the KKK, and eugenic experiments. I was able to achieve a
different effect by altering history." (Gross n.pag.). Anachronisms and technology make *Underground* a compendium of slavery's components and its

preexisting texts. Linking these to other histories reveals the commonalities in multiple systems of oppression.

In opening the second version of his autobiography, *My Bondage and My Freedom* (1855), Frederick Douglass recalls that his abolitionist "friends" merely wanted him to recite the facts:

> "Let us have the facts," said the people. So also said Friend George Foster, who always wished to pin me down to my simple narrative. "Give us the facts," said Collins, "we will take care of the philosophy."

Douglass also goes on to express his frustration:

> It was impossible for me to repeat the same old story month after month, and to keep up my interest in it. It was new to the people, it is true, but it was an old story to me; and to go through with it night after night, was a task altogether too mechanical for my nature. "Tell your story, Frederick," would whisper my then revered friend, William Lloyd Garrison, as I stepped upon the platform. I could not always obey, for I was now reading and thinking. New views of the subject were presented to my mind ... I was growing, and needed room. "People won't believe you ever was a slave, Frederick, if you keep on this way," said Friend Foster. "Be yourself," said Collins, "and tell your story." It was said to me, "Better have a *little* of the plantation manner of speech than not; 'tis not best that you seem too learned." (220)

"Be yourself and tell your story" becomes a contradiction for a Douglass chaffing under the restraint of not being able to articulate his ideas after his fashion. Douglass at least had the opportunity of writing and subsequently rewriting his story; many others did not. After emancipation, Works Progress Administration documenters solicited the stories of the last generation of black American slaves, but still the told-to nature of these chronicles left little room for inward insight. The reimagining of this lost interior record has been a large part of the neo-slave narrative's content.

Interior psychological landscapes are tangled, and neo-slave narratives engage the good and the bad, all the intricacies of enslavement. Heroism and compromise, pain and pleasure, love and perversion, their vision of what slavery meant for those caught within it is comprehensive. Their perspectives are ever widening, incorporating larger circles of national and transatlantic black experience. The neo-slave narratives' encouragement to remember history is critical, but so too are their encouragement to evaluate the present. They urge reassessments of attitudes that deepen human stratification. In their own cultural moment, neo-slave narratives accomplish what statistics cannot: they put human faces to the disconnection between ideals and actuality. Metaphors of dehumanization, commodification, and exclusion still resonate in a world where slavery can take many forms and inhabit many geographies.

CHAPTER 9

The Detective Novel

A solitary figure bucks authority, deciphers apparent falsities to discover truth, and if lucky, somewhere along the way achieves justice for wrongs against the innocent. The endeavors undertaken frequently lead to insights into society's workings and frequently into its unfairness. This pattern recurs in many African American novels and in many detective novels; yet, for most of its history, the genre of detective fiction has remained very white, and very male. Whether we consider the gentleman detectives of classical series who came from or adopted the mannerisms of the upper classes, Sherlock Holmes and Hercule Poirot being two examples, or the edgier, working-class figures of Sam Spade or Philip Marlowe from hard-boiled series, the racial bias of the form is notable.

In his study *Hard-Boiled Sentimentality: The Secret History of American Crime Stories* (2009), Lenny Cassuto suggests that the lack of a black presence within the genre may be a matter of definition. Narrowly conceiving of the form as concerned primarily with the apprehension of criminals ignores traditions within black writing that would fall under the rubric. He offers passing novels as possible examples of detective fiction with "unusual crimes" (215) and transgressors of the color line as suspects who fear detection. The recovery work of African American literary history has discovered other instances that might fit the genre: Pauline Hopkins, *Hagar's Daughter* (1901–1902); John Edward Bruce, *The Black Sleuth* (1907–1909); and Rudolph Fisher, *The Conjure Man Dies* (1932), though until recently they were read as examples of early African American or Harlem Renaissance texts with their employment of the mode's conventions of secondary interest. As genre scholarship blossomed, however, greater appreciation for African American use of this aesthetic emerged.

Of course, the familiar question of what distinguishes black detective fiction from other forms arises. In *The Blues Detective* (1996), Stephen F. Soitos notes that African American revisions of traditional detective form include black detective personas who identify as being black, are aware of the two-ness of being raced as black while being American, and are skilled at adapting strategies of masking. He further reads the novels' narrative techniques as redolent with black vernaculars that include music, language, signifying, and offer a different manner of reasoning rooted in traditions such as hoodoo. Indeed, to varying degrees these traits manifest themselves in much black detective fiction, but there are always outliers such as John B. West, a black American tropical disease specialist who wrote six novels from his adopted home in Liberia and created a white detective Rocky Steele. I would concur with Soitos's criteria, though. Black detective fiction makes use of black cultural aesthetics, and in addition to solving a crime or mystery provides commentary on the larger racial dynamics of the United States. Central characters are frequently outsiders because of race and/or gender even if they are part of an institution such as a police force. Their being set apart gifts them with a second sight, however, and they are able to see what others around them can't whether through instinct, intellect, or spiritualism.

Pauline Hopkins's *Hagar's Daughter* is generally cited as one of the earliest examples of black detective fiction. Set in pre–Civil War America, it captures the tensions of an intensifying secessionist effort, develops a passing plot, and closes with black detectives solving a crime. The eponymous Hagar not knowing she is of mixed race heritage enjoys marital happiness with the white Ellis Enson, only to see it all taken away. His envious brother St. Clair, angered that the birth of Ellis's daughter means he is no longer next in line to inherit the family wealth, colludes with a slave trader to expose Hagar as black. Ellis allows his love to overcome his race prejudice and plans to travel with Hagar and their daughter to live in Europe. Before this can happen, however, he disappears, and later a dead body with his wallet and gun is found, a bullet hole in its head. The conclusion that it is Enson allows St. Clair to claim the family fortune, which now includes Hagar and her daughter as slave property, but Hagar and the baby escape before reaching the slave market. In a scene reminiscent of *Clotel*, believing Enson lost to her a despairing Hagar jumps with her daughter into the Potomac River. Both are presumed dead. A love triangle, hidden identities, a kidnapping, black on black subterfuge, a courtroom trial, cross-dressing, and a murder complicate the plot.

In part two of the book, much of the masking that Soitos describes is evident. Senator Zenas Bowen comes to Washington DC with his wife (actually Hagar) and their daughter Jewel (actually Hagar's daughter). Both women are passing; so too, as is later discovered, is Enson's brother St. Clair who now calls himself General Benson. Benson/St. Clair's secretary and former mistress Elsie Bradford who has born him a son outside of marriage is found murdered, and Jewel's intended is accused of the crime. It falls to Detective Henson, head of a newly established federal detective agency (actually Ellis Enson) to find the culprit, and also to find who has kidnapped Aunt Henny, a witness to Elsie's killing. When he is unable to do so. Venus Henson, Henny's daughter, turns amateur sleuth and is joined by the black detective Henry Smith. The plot's twists and turns made it perfectly suited to the cliffhangers necessary for serialization, and the novel's style is enlivened by a liberal use of black vernacular, folk tales, and the inclusion of hoodoo work and figures to bring black expressive traditions to the detective form.

It can be argued that *Hagar's Daughter* was not conceived of as a detective novel because the detectives appear late in the novel to bring about the climax. Appearing just six years after Hopkins's novel, John Edward Bruce's *The Black Sleuth* (1907–1909), from title to protagonist, sits squarely in the tradition. It appeared in serialized form in *McGirt's* magazine, launched in 1903 by James Ephraim McGirt. The periodical was an illustrated monthly focusing on African American politics, science, art, and literature that lasted for six years, and catered to its black readership by publishing works by writers including Paul Laurence Dunbar, Anna Julia Cooper, Frances E. W. Harper, and W. E. B. Du Bois. The novel's appearance in a popular serialized black monthly gave it a wider reach than many self-published ventures, and Bruce took advantage of this greater audience and the popularity of the detective form to instruct black readers on the merit of African antecedents.

Bruce was born a slave in 1856, and after his father was sold away, his mother supported herself and her son by selling baked goods to service men in the Fort Washington, Maryland area and by reselling used clothes. Bruce subsequently graduated from Hampton Institute. Nicknamed "Bruce Grit" for his tenacious journalism by African American editor Thomas Fortune then heading the *New York Age*, Bruce was most widely known as a newspaperman and essayist. He self-published pieces on African history and biographies of prominent black figures including Alexander Crummel and Edward Blyden. Redeeming representations of Africa and of black origins was a central concern for him. He was a member of the American Negro Academy, and along with Arthur Schomburg, founded the Negro Society for Historical research. Bruce contributed to the London-based *African Times and Orient Review*, a journal offering Asian and African perspectives on British Empire, and also worked actively with Marcus Garvey's Universal Negro Improvement Association (UNIA), writing for and editing issues of *Negro World*. These interests shape the protagonist, and also the novel's call for a needed reassessment of black origins.

That the novel was serialized is evident in the breaks between installments indicated by "(To be continued)" or by sentences serving as obvious teasers. The hero Sadipe Okukenu personifies both Bruce's pan-Africanism and his views on black progressivism. *Black Sleuth* begins with an introduction to Sadipe, a Yoruba detective working for a London agency. He overhears George De Forrest, a white sea captain soliciting the agency's services, express shock that the firm employs a "nigger" and that they would trust him to recover a unique multicarat diamond. Spurred by the racial epithet, Sadipe vows to reclaim the diamond and make De Forrest eat his words. The novel then flashes back to provide Sadipe's history, and it is here that Bruce's desire to transform perceptions of Africa and blackness becomes apparent. The plot arc is inconsistent, perhaps because of the serial publication, and in the next scene De Forrest is so taken with the handsomeness and bearing of Sadipe's brother Mojola Okukenu that he engineers an introduction. A conversation then ensues aboard De Forrest's boat, after he has assured Mojola that he is not enslaving him or spiriting him off to the new world. Mojola, who has traveled to England and returned to his homeland to be a teacher, not only provides a family history – how Sadipe and he were educated and how their father encouraged them to travel the world – but also schools the captain on Yoruba and African cultures and the myopia of European race superiority and religious hypocrisy. What emerges is a contrast of civilizations.

As Mojola narrates his story, an anxious De Forrest interrupts him to ask how he came to speak and write several languages. Mojola's response is "I must tell my story in my own way" (12). His answer spotlights the need to reconstruct the telling of black stories from a more accurate vantage point. To accomplish this Bruce employs comparison and contrast. As De Forrest assesses Mojola, the former concludes, "He was standing face to face with one of these heathen and barbarians who was better educated than himself, who spoke purer English, and who had a better general idea of books than he, and a more analytical mind. His Caucasian pride and conceit, however, would not allow him to discover his mental deficiencies to this half-naked black man" (15). The comparison moves outward from two men to two continents. Cecil Rhodes's colonial exploitation and Mojola's prediction that Africa will adopt Europe's technologies but not its values become vehicles for juxtaposing the greed of Europe versus the generosity of Africa. While in conversation De Forrest discovers that Mojola is carrying a rare and sizeable uncut diamond. He offers it to buy it, and to teach him a lesson, Mojola sells it to him for six English pence, noting that hoarding and accumulation of wealth is an English value, not an African one. De Forrest says that he has been enlightened by Mojola and pledges friendship to the black race. How he becomes the same De Forrest who calls Sadipe a "nigger" in the novel's opening flashback is one of many plot inconsistencies no doubt a result of Bruce's vision changing throughout serialization.

While Mojola is in Europe, Sadipe urges his father to send him to America, which the latter does, because he wants his son to see the realities of the racist world. There Sadipe is exposed to the hypocrisies of a nation preaching humanistic ideals yet sanctioning slavery. He lands in the care of a white captain and his sister, a teacher, and excels in all things educational being "born to scholarship" because his tribe is, with the exception of the Fantis, the most intellectual tribe in all Africa (28). Bruce's intent is clearly to upend notions of Africa as the dark continent. Once he reaches a point where his New England education can offer nothing more, the captain arranges a scholarship for Sadipe to the fictional Eckington College for Colored Youth, a "little school, which had been dignified by the name 'college' " (37). Predictably, his journey south further exposes him to the indignities of racism, but it also makes him a picaro giving readers glimpses of Southern race relations between acquiescing blacks, privileged whites, and indolent poor whites for whom race provides an illusion of social power.

Three years later finds Sadipe in the employ of the International Secret Service Bureau, and the detective plot to recover the stolen diamond begins in earnest. He outwits the beautiful adventuress Miss Crenshawe and a former aristocrat turned confidence man Colonel Bradshawe. What happens to Sadipe is unresolved, but what remains of the novel combines early twentieth-century black American imagining of Africa with a popular genre. While it clearly seeks to address an audience doubtful of the merit of African antecedents, it also seeks to address an audience craving validation of their lives in a popular action genre. Rudolph Fisher's second novel *The Conjure Man Dies: A Mystery Tale of Dark Harlem* (1932) serves this desire as well.

Jinx Jenkins, Bubber Brown, and Henry Patmore's poolroom from *The Walls of Jericho* all reappear in this second work, making the two novels an extended portrait of a community. *The Conjure Man Dies* opens with a description of the dark mysterious building housing the office of N. Frimbo, Pychist. While Jinx sits consulting with him on the future of a business proposition, he discovers Frimbo, a Harvard BA, is dead. He and Bubber call Dr. Archer who confirms that Frimbo was hit on the head and murdered. When they call the police, one of the few black detectives on the force, Perry Dart takes the case. Dart is an uncanny crime solver. He knows Harlem thoroughly and employs forensic deduction à la Sherlock Holmes to piece clues into a solution. The character reveals Fisher's own medical background through his study of angle of wounds, his inspection of vital organs, and his being attuned to every physical detail of potential suspects. He puts to rest any doubts regarding black intellectual capability. Black vernacular elements are brought into *The Conjure Man Dies* through characters questioned by Dart and Archer. These likely suspects are an array of black folk types: Spider Webb, a numbers runner; Doty Hicks, a drug addict; Easley Jones, a railroad man; Martha Crouch, the undertaker's wife; and Aramintha Snead, a church woman who generally takes her problems to the Lord in prayer (49), but since he hasn't acted decides to go to Frimbo. As the novel unfolds, the mystery is unveiled through each of these perspectives.

The Conjure Man Dies frequently reshapes the insults directed to a people into colloquial humor and wisdom. There are references to Dart being so dark of color the night makes him invisible, but rather than being a slight, this becomes a superhuman asset enabling his crime solving. A "colored" man having a head too hard to be broken by a club becomes a symbol of the capacity to endure amid violence and aggression. The variety of caste consciousness and colorism is transformed to the humorous intraracial dozens greeting the short, portly and very dark Bubber: "What you say blacker'n me?" "Ole Eight-Ball! Where you rollin' boy?" (129). Descriptions of the after-church Sunday parades lining the streets in Harlem and descriptions of food at Nappy Shank's Café (137) round out sketches of community life. Fisher offers characterizations of all classes of blacks, and all manner of expression are used to compose the novel's prose from Archer's lofty loquaciousness to Bubber's vernacularisms, to Dart's motherwit. Dart's terseness and sarcasm presages the growing popularity of the hardboiled detective during the post–World War I period when Fisher is writing. The subgenre's cultural cynicism, emphasis on isolation, and assertion of the relativity of truth were qualities appealing to a nation reeling after the destruction of a world war, and black writers found it a useful vehicle for themes of racial alienation, deteriorating community, and the nature of violence. One of these writers was Chester Himes.

Initially motivated by economic need, Chester Himes found in hardboiled detective fiction a means to convey his search for personal significance as a black male and a way to reinvent himself as a writer. At a time when he was recovering from the negative press surrounding *The Primitive*

(1955) and the novella *A Case of Rape* (1956), when he increasingly resented being labeled a protest writer, hardboiled fiction allowed him to draw reality as both painful and comical. Writing detective fiction provided Himes a reprieve from the racial politics that sent him away from the United States, and distanced him from the debates as to whether he was merely a protest writer or a true artist. A serendipitous request from editor Marcel Duhamel to contribute a manuscript to *Série Noire*, a French imprint devoted to crime fiction, set Himes's "second" career as a writer of detective fiction in motion.

Even as early as the 1930s when his first novels appeared, Himes cited among his literary influences Dashiell Hammett, and Raymond Chandler's verisimilitude if not his characterization (Himes, *Conversations* 109). He wrote ten detective novels, all but one featuring black detectives "Coffin" Ed Johnson and "Grave Digger" Jones as protagonists: *For Love of Imabelle*, (1957), *The Real Cool Killers* (1959), *The Crazy Kill* (1959), *The Big Gold Dream* (1960), *All Shot Up* (1960), *Cotton Comes to Harlem* (1965), *The Heat's On* (1966), *Come Back Charleston Blue* (1974), *Blind Man with a Pistol* (1969), and *Plan B* (1993). Set in Harlem but not featuring Coffin Ed and Grave Digger Jones is *Run Man Run* (1966), the story of an embittered white policeman who shoots blacks because they are there. His detective novels were popular in Europe since the 1950s, and the movie adaptation of *Cotton Comes to Harlem* effected a Himes renaissance in the United States.

In the series, Himes parlays the cultural power of Harlem into a site where he examines the vagaries of being black through the post–Civil Rights, nationalist, and post-soul eras of the United States. He is quick to point out, however, that his is an imagined Harlem never meant to be real, rather meant to be a space taken back from whites where the absurd contradictions that come about because of race could be vivified (*My Life* 126). Harlem is largely segregated from the white city around it, yet the city's central mass transit arteries run through it, and this comes to represent the centrality of black life to a white American culture that seeks to segregate it. Once one of the premiere white neighborhoods of New York, Harlem is now a "ghetto," yet its underground economy makes it replete with cash, a representation of black survival and tenacity against large odds. The city within the city is an ideal locale for detective novels that are interior in scope, portraying a world of hustlers, musicians, pimps, churchgoers, and laborers obeying or skirting the law to eke out a survival against the hated world of THE MAN. Though detective novels might seem a departure for Himes, these works continue the critique of nonsensical yet institutionalized racism found in his earlier novels.

Coffin Ed and Grave Digger were modeled after two policemen Himes knew while living in Los Angeles. Grave Digger is big, rugged, and more given to wordplay than his partner Coffin Ed who is known by the distinctive scar that recalls his face meeting a glass of acid. Their macabre nicknames bespeak the fear they instill in the community they police. They inhabit a Harlem of the 1960s one that by official accounts is dying from alcoholism, infant mortality, rising crime, and drug abuse. Boarded up stores and abandoned buildings line once grand avenues. Many are fleeing in an effort to find better schools and housing, but people still live and create there. Both detectives are proprietary of this space, and they fight with and for those who remain. They occupy a tense space working for a white authority that does not fully respect them in a black community that does not fully trust them because of their profession. Coffin Ed and Grave Digger have developed their own moral code, one that severely punishes those taking advantage of the most vulnerable. Through their capers, Himes not only unmasks intertwining of racism and impoverishment, but also pays homage to the store of folk material – swindling pastors, manipulative prostitutes, cotton bales, and repatriation schemes – that is part of their culture.

Gravedigger and Coffin Ed personify Harlem, and as the community declines, so do they. Their impotency at the end of *Blind Man with a Pistol*, their inability to solve a murder or stem oncoming violence, signifies the dark vision overtaking the novels as hustlers, and political hypocrites continue to thrive amidst an unaware people. By *Plan B*, the final novel in what Himes called his domestic Harlem series, Grave Digger is suspended from the force for killing a witness, and Coffin Ed is given a desk job. Through the increasing tension between them contesting philosophies of black development are given play. Discrimination, violence, and corruption of all colors have made a community turn in on itself in a culminating riot set off by a black janitor acting as sniper and killing whites. Himes's language, terms such as "carnage," "snot mixed with blood," "skulls," "nasty gray blobs of brains," "fragments of skull looking like sections of broken coconuts," "few scraps of bloody black flesh" (176–182) conveys the rage resulting from social impotence. Violence, which he termed a most American of forms, makes his detective novels bleak prophecies for those perpetually pushed to the social periphery. In a conversation with John A. Williams he notes the delight he took in having black detectives shooting whites, and no doubt some of his black readers took pleasure in this as well (Himes, *Conversations* 68). Like the blaxploitation movies that would soon become popular, his detective novels express a frustration with the stalemate at the end of the Civil Rights and Black Power eras between black populaces still arguing for rights and an unforthcoming dominant culture.

Himes's female characters show that as well as being dominated by whites, for much of its history detective fiction was dominated by men. His women are mainly sexualized objects. If not, they are older, beyond sexual desirability, as in the case of Sister Heavenly the faith healer in *The Heat's On*, or they are manipulators as is Reba, the madam of *The Real Cool Killers*. It was not until black women writers Barbara Neely, Nikki Baker, Eleanor Taylor Bland, Valerie Wilson Wesley, and Dolores Komo come to the field that this portraiture changes.

Out of graduate school Barbara Neely's first job was being the director of a facility designed to place women felons in communities in lieu of prisons. There, interacting with women who had killed, she gained her first exposure to motives for murder. Some reasons she felt were understandable, most frequent among these the desperate attempt to end abuse. Her works are character-driven vehicles, and the character at their center is Blanche White. Contrary to her naming Blanche, who in childhood was teased by both blacks and whites because of her color, is a very dark domestic worker. Her occupation and appearance make her invisible to employers and make her an expert at gaining access to information through others' unwitting revelations. From the opening scene in the Agatha Award winning first novel of the series *Blanche on the Lam* (1992) where she appears before a judge in Farleigh, North Carolina, Blanche uses invisibility to counter invisibility. Her reflections reveal she is aware of stereotypes that mark her. A judge blind to her being a poorly compensated domestic worker (whose privileged white employers have forgotten to pay her) attempting to support herself and her niece and nephew, sentences her to prison for writing bad checks. As she is to be taken away, she escapes. Reasoning that running would draw suspicion to any black person she walks calmly and reports for a live-in maid position her agency had previously arranged.

The family, the Carters, see only a mammy-like caretaker, and Blanche has learned to perform the "pleasant stupidity" white employers expected of their domestic help (16). The contrast between how Blanche is not seen and the keenness of her insights into American culture's obliviousness to white privilege give her investigation into this Southern dynasty's secrets larger significance. The twists and turns as the Carters continue to do one another in for the sake of inheritance take on Gothic proportions, right down to secrets within a locked cellar. Blanche takes it especially personally when Nate, her black coworker, is killed, and she creates her own detective "agency" using the network of other black female domestics as sources of information into his death and others within the Carter family. Once she has deciphered the mystery, Blanche is offered money and education for her children to buy her silence, but rather than submit to subverting justice, she anonymously reports the family's crime to the *Atlanta Journal Constitution* and heads north to Boston.

Blanche on the Lam embeds histories of domestic work and migration into its plot, and each subsequent novel touches on an aspect of black cultural history. The second *Blanche among the Talented Tenth* (1994) considers the intraracial effects of colorism in Amber Cove, Maine, an exclusive black resort evoking the Oak Bluffs community of Martha's Vineyard. *Blanche Cleans Up* (1998) offers portraits of modern, urban African American experiences and the dangers faced by teen pregnancy, homophobia, and the erosion of communal health through lead poisoning. The dream of the North as a black paradise quickly evanesces. *Blanche Passes Go* (2000), the novel where her life is most intimately detailed, mirrors late twentieth-century black return to the South while addressing the physical abuse of women. Here Blanche must reconcile herself to the world she left when she encounters not the New South, but her old South of racial discrimination and the trauma she suffered when encountering the wealthy white man who raped her and escaped punishment. Neely's intertwining of history and mystery gives Blanche's detective stories a degree of timelessness. As a character, she models female agency against the backdrop of changing moments in black life. For Neely the detective form can couch ideas some might find difficult. She recalls a reader who told her that she would never consider reading anything about race and gender, but happened to read one of Neely's mystery novels and learned much about the two (Herbert 107). With the publication of the Blanche series, Neely broke ground by becoming one of the earliest black woman detective fiction writers to be published by a major house, St. Martin's Press.

Nikki Baker's detective is the virtual opposite of Blanche. Virginia Kelley is well educated, wealthy, and assists those in her class who find themselves suspected of murder. Often her lovers are white and always they are women. She is a pathbreaking figure, a black lesbian detective who uses the influence she gains from her profession to solve murders. In the first novel *In the Game* (1991), Virginia listens as her college friend Bev Johnson confides that Bev's girlfriend Kelsey is seeing someone else, news Virginia already knows. The next morning she reads that Kelsey has been murdered behind the same bar where she and Bev had met for drinks. It falls to Virginia to begin an investigation and find legal representation for her friend. Virginia does not agonize over the challenges of being an out lesbian, but she does realize that sometimes the elements of her identity are not allowed to coexist seamlessly. Frequently she feels she must choose between allegiance to her white lover or to black community. Sexual politics and crime solving frequently converge. *The Lavender House Murder* (1992) finds Virginia vacationing in Provincetown, Massachusetts, when she comes across the bullet-ridden corpse of Joan Di Maio, a lesbian journalist whose syndicated column "Outtime" appears in gay and lesbian papers to forcibly expose those whose remaining in the closet Maio sees as a crime against the gay community. Thinking of Joan's crusade, Virginia ponders the effects of being out on social mobility. How do race and class impact a triply marginalized person – black, gay, woman?

Often in Baker's novels, Virginia's figuring out the mystery of a death parallels her figuring out the mysteries of her personal life, how to develop a concept of self-love when you are albeit an African American "princess" but one with kinky hair; how to overcome her difficulty in sustaining relationships; how to maintain her ethical standards. Her return to her Midwest home for Christmas and a high school reunion is the subject of *Long Goodbyes* (1993), and the novel is almost an origins story for the character. It contrasts past and present to examine the homophobia beneath the town's seemingly ideal façade. In *The Ultimate Exit Strategy* (2001), the title of the company Virginia works for, Whytebread, Greese, Winslow, and Stoat, signals the novel's concern with corruption and greed. It is about to be bought in a merger with a larger firm, Gold Rush Investments, and Virginia expects a substantial payout on her shares. When Whytebread's CEO is murdered a few days before the merger, the deal is threatened, and Virginia undertakes the investigation, facing an ethical dilemma when what she discovers might impact her financial prospects. As the character goes through the series she matures, and develops multiple insights through occupying expanding social spaces.

Baker's writing style combines the gentleman or in her case gentlewoman detective with prose reminiscent of hardboiled and noir fiction. Joan Di Maio is described as shot "chest-high at the distance of a friendly handshake"; a gun sits by her face like "the special effects from a B-grade movie" (3). Virginia's cynicism and vivid, imagistic description of the details of death ground her in noir traditions, yet provide a contrast to her circumstances of relative privilege. She is a new "shero" for the form expanding the notion that the voice of this genre is essentially white, essentially male, essentially heterosexual.

Eleanor Taylor Bland, in a manner similar to Baker and Neely, uses detective fiction as a response to modern social conditions. The central character of her series is Marti MacAlister, an African American veteran homicide detective with the Chicago Police Department. Her husband, an undercover narcotics officer, has died of a questionable suicide, and to get away from the weight of her grief, she moves her family to Lincoln Prairie, a fictional suburb of Chicago where she shares a house and living expenses with her friend Sharon. Her partner Matthew "Vik" Jessenovik, a second-generation Polish Catholic, complements her not only in professional duties, but also as a white male character with deeply patriarchal attitudes that Marti's professionalism changes. Though still part of a world that presents an occasional racial or gender slight, their partnership marks a breakdown of presumed social borders.

The genre of Bland's novels is the police procedural known for its exacting representation of daily police work. As evident in the button-down Friday of the *Dragnet* (1951–1959) series, the counterculture facsimile *Mod Squad* (1968–1973), the gritty *Hill Street Blues* (1981–1987), the sleek *Miami Vice* (1984–1990), the feminist *Cagney and Lacey* (1981–1988), the "ripped from the headlines" *Law and Order* (1990–2010) and the many spinoffs it inspired, police procedural easily adapts to different times and emphases. While Bland blends it with social issues and casts her detective not as a lone figure but as component of the state expected to enforce laws and follow rules, her Marti reveals the conflicts inherent in doing so for a black woman police detective. She is highly professional, following the letter of the law, but also has a high moral code that makes her an empathetic viewer of social drama. In *Dead Time* (1992), she gains justice for a strangled, schizophrenic Jane Doe consigned to a flophouse, and learns the case is larger than a single death only because she takes seriously the stories of marginalized drug and alcohol addicts. The police procedural's validation of social order is upturned somewhat in her. A tireless investigator respected by her colleagues, she also sees the effect the status quo has on those it forces to the outside.

Marti's life as a wife, mother, and surrogate mother to other children is never far away from any case she investigates. Her battle against the blue wall of police silence and corruption in *Done Wrong* (1995) is personally exacting because she uncovers the circumstances of her husband's apparent suicide. His former partner has also committed suicide, so it seems, and she becomes suspicious. Details of her daily family life are interwoven with those of her investigation into their undercover world, to the killing of a child in a reckless drug bust, and the moral haziness of dirty detectives and drug kingpins, until finally she discovers the answers to her husband's death. *Fatal Remains* (2003) situates

Marti's investigation and personal life in larger history as she and Vik who is coming to terms with his wife's multiple sclerosis are called to the grounds of the Smith family ancestral mansion to investigate the death of a young archaeologist crushed by a boulder while excavating land the family hopes to sell to real estate developers. Marti finds herself in the midst of a quarrel between preservationists and developers, and unearthed clues such as child-sized slave manacles and remains of a village lead to disclosures of the family's not necessarily honorable involvement with the Underground Railroad and with Potawotami native Americans. Like Baker's Virginia Keeley, Bland's Marti is a groundbreaker, the first African American woman featured as a police homicide detective. The series interlaces meticulous forensic detail into plots that simultaneously investigate murder and the many balancing acts of a working black woman. As a black female detective, Marti must find an equilibrium between her professionalism and race politics while upholding laws stacked against society's most vulnerable.

Barbara Neely, Nikki Baker, and Eleanor Taylor Bland all write black detective novels that examine current social and political issues. The novels of Walter Mosley do so as well, but links them to their causes. In an interview he claimed that fiction has to be political. Writing about individuals at a particular time is always informed by social conditions. If your character is a woman in the turn of the century, in inventing her you must consider can she own property? Can she vote? (Goodman n. pag.). The politics and black cultural history encompassed within Moseley's detective series ranges from the post–World War II period to the contemporary moment. His most popular detective Ezekiel "Easy" Rawlins encompasses much of black American culture. His people hail from the South and move north in a pattern replicating the great migration. Though set in mid-twentieth-century Los Angeles, the series evolves reflecting different temporal circumstances. In *Devil in a Blue Dress* (1990), Easy falls into his life as detective after leaving the army at the end of World War II. His experiences are redolent of the limbo catching many returning black GIs trying to find fair treatment in the society sending them back to second-class status after sending them to war. *A Red Death* (1991) portrays him as a counter-culture figure involved with the Internal Revenue Service (IRS) and Federal Bureau of Investigation (FBI), against the backdrop of the McCarthy witch-hunts of the early 1950s, while in *Black Betty* (1994) his investigations lend insight into the early Civil Rights Movement, its hopes and disappointments. *Bad Boy Brawly Brown* (2002) unfolds amid the growing impatience of the Black Nationalist period, and *Little Scarlet*

(2004) in a period where frustration is vented in the Watts riots of 1965. While steeped in specific moments, Mosley's accounts resonate with institutionalized racial attitudes that give them ongoing currency. As well as evoking history the Easy Rawlins series also evoke psychological themes that inhere in black life. *Devil in a Blue Dress* (1990) centers around passing when "Easy" aids a woman who leaves her previous lover and subsequently Easy rather than let it be known she is not white, and *White Butterfly* (1992) weighs the worth of a black life versus a white one when authorities turn to "Easy" for assistance in solving a string of murders only after the killer takes a white victim.

Easy's personal journey has taken him to Dachau during World War II and the Deep South during Jim Crow, and he has developed an appropriate cynicism. Through investigation, he transgresses narrowly defined social caste. His vocation illuminates connections between seemingly disparate histories, communities, and values. Though Easy is his best-known detective, Mosley created two others, Fearless Jones and Leonid McGill. Tristan "Fearless" Jones, another World War II veteran, is the central character of the Fearless Jones series. Again the novels engage broader aspects of social history, racial discrimination, and police corruption. The series can be seen as an extended buddy narrative contrasting the skittish Paris, who tries to avoid difficult situations at all costs and the bolder Fearless. It honors black entrepreneurship and is Mosley's bid to create black heroes who engineer their own happy endings. The Leonid McGill series widens its angle of vision to include the many cultures inhabiting Los Angeles: blacks, from the United States and Caribbean, Latinos, Asians, and whites. The ex-boxer turned private investigator must learn to read a new set of racial clues. The black-white dichotomy of Easy's world is not present in his, and his experiences explore the different manifestations of cultural identification in a modern multiracial world. What remains the same, however, is unchanging social inequality. Even this later series prove Easy's assessment that while some are guilty of crimes, others are guilty of color (*Little Scarlet* 235).

Mosley's condensed style derives not from the terseness of a Chandler but the study of poetry and its ability to embed multiple meanings in one image or metaphor. The timing and set up of jokes influence characterization and structure (Packard n. pag.). Though they resemble the hardboiled creations, Sam Spade or Philip Marlowe, his detectives, have different antecedents. He credits American pop culture – television and Marvel comic books – for influencing him, but he also credits the stories of his father's Louisiana roots, experiences in World War II and migration to Los Angeles.

His operatives are not static characters, they age, some marry and have children, they grow and change in response to time and circumstance. Their success depends on successfully crossing boundaries of class, ethnicity, and race, on having multiple literacies. As such they typify the relative freedom of the black detective to operate outside the law to move to greater truth and understanding. The denizens and participants of their communities who trade drinks, lovers, and stories that reveal them to be philosophers form the core of Mosley's works. Through them he seeks to offer an interior view of a community that does not define itself as a site of victimhood, and his affection for that community, its cadences, food, music, history, and lore, is evident.

Mosley often resists being thought of as a writer of detective fiction because he has also written in the genres of young adult and science fiction. The novels *The Right Mistake: The Further Philosophical Investigations of Socrates Fortlow* (2008) and *R.L.'s Dream* (1995) are contemplations about thinkers and traditions. Having served twenty-seven years in prison, Socrates Fortlow now ruing his past deeds, and despairing of the violence he sees daily, creates the Thinkers' Club to ponder the larger questions of existence. The gathering becomes a mélange of thugs, church deacons, and interloping undercover cops, where ideas of personal versus social responsibility, racial essentialism, poverty, and justice are vented. Fortlow personifies the street philosopher. Incorporating the romantic pastoral of the Delta that gave rise to the blues, *R. L.'s Dream* delves into the meanings of the form in a modern era. The older Atwater "Soupspoon" Wise recalls the musical genius of Robert Leroy Johnson, "RL" the blues player. The evocation of the actual Robert Johnson deepens the atmosphere of the novel, and Mosley uses the figure to consider cultural origins, cultural ownership, and the fusions and crossings that occur when cultures interact.

Mosley ventures into speculative fiction in the works *Blue Light* (1999) and *Inside a Silver Box* (2015). In *Blue Light* the eponymous entity from a distant star disseminates throughout the universe when its home star cools. Its manifestations engender awakenings and enlightenment in beings who encounter them, and these beings are subsequently called the Blues. The reference to the musical form sets in motion a theme of transcendent power, leading to the understanding of life's multiple meanings. The silver box of the title *Inside a Silver Box* was created by the evil Laz to dominate other life forms. The box rebelled and imprisoned the Laz within itself, and now rests buried in New York's Central Park. Its power and the malevolence of the Laz are unleashed when black Ronnie Bottoms murders a white graduate student, Lorraine Fell, and her spirit compels him to use the box to resurrect her. The racially and economically contrasting pair then work together to prevent the annihilation of earth.

The young adult novel *47* is an instance of Mosley combining a variety of genres. Set on a plantation, it draws on speculative, folklore, neo-slave narrative, and historical fiction to tell of an adolescent slave boy living under an inhumane master who brands him with the number 47. With the assistance of Tall John (reminiscent of the folk figure High John the Conqueror), a runaway from beyond Africa who is actually an extraterrestrial, the young boy learns of a world outside slavery and his important destiny within it. *The Man in My Basement* (2004), which Mosley terms his novel of ideas contrasts innocence against evil through a complex plot involving self-incarceration, while *Killing Johnny Fry* (2007) is Moseley's self-termed "sexistentialist" work where sex takes the place of violence born of loneliness and alienation. Looking at the variety of these novels, it is evident why Mosley labels himself simply a novelist in a desire not to be limited to any particular genre (Frumkes 20).

Mosley's desire to write in whatever form he deemed appropriate meant that publishers expecting one genre did not always appreciate his adroitness in another. One response to being pigeonholed was his choice to publish with a smaller press. *Gone Fishin'* (1997), the prequel to the Easy Rawlins series, appeared through Black Classic Press. More coming of age road narrative than a detective novel, it depicts nineteen-year-old Easy before the war and before he left Houston for Los Angeles. He and his partner Mouse "borrow" a Ford and set out for Pariah Texas. As he will often do later, Easy juggles personal allegiances and moral codes as he witnesses Mouse kill his stepfather. Where Los Angeles is a major character in later novels, here segregated East Texas introduces Easy to the racism that will shape the rest of his life. *Gone Fishin'* shows that Easy, like others in the genre, will be part detective part philosopher. It foreshadows that his cases will illuminate the realities of the dispossessed while his reflections chart historical change in his community and larger black life.

African American detective novels engage the same forms of transgression as their non-black counterparts. The crime in these works is violent, casual, sometimes justified, but not unique. The form exemplifies, however, the way black writers use crime and mystery to interrogate ideas of race. It is not surprising that a form pitting transgressor against authority would appeal to writers concerned with social justice. It is also not surprising that a form where emphasizing the science of forensics and detection, not only gut instincts, would offer interesting thematic avenues for writers engaging perceptions of black intelligence.

The detectives' thoughts, commentary, interactions with those in their own and other communities reveal the concerns of race, gender, and sexuality that their writers engage. Each, from Hopkins's Venus Henson and Henry Smith, to Bruce's Sadipe, to Mosley's Easy, in some way works not only to solve crime but also to create examined lives that provide order and comprehension in a world rendered chaotic by prejudice and inequity.

CHAPTER 10

The Speculative Novel

Speculative fiction is a deliberately broad term meant to highlight the interconnections across forms employing the unreal: science fiction, fantasy, gothic, horror, utopian writing, and Afrofuturism, a designation applied to speculative fiction that situates black history, concerns, and experiences in twentieth- and post-twentieth-century technoculture. The genre uses the fantastic to question hierarchical ideologies that subordinate, warp, or exclude experiences not deemed to conform to preset norms, and to offer new relational modes in their stead. It is very much concerned with the immediate actualities of racism, classism, ableism, heteronormativity, and with deconstructing the classification systems that give rise to them. The genre rarely poses easy resolution, not even when depicting seeming utopias; rather, it sparks thought as to why dystopic tensions seem a perpetual part of existence.

Traditions of speculative fiction have long been present in black writing. The gothic qualities of slave narratives in which the enslaved have preternatural visions of their freedom or capture; the utopian hopes of black abolitionists imagining a better world either in a truly free United States, an escape to Canada or Europe, or a return to Africa; and the figuration of tricksters or conjurers as superhuman counterpoints to white dominance are all instances. As early as Sutton E. Griggs's *Imperium in Imperio* (1899), Pauline Hopkins's *Of One Blood: Or, the Hidden Self* (1902–1903), and E. A. Johnson's *Light Ahead for the Negro* (1904), black writers have employed elements of speculative fiction to examine the dangers of narrowly seeing one existence as the norm, of initiating violence and aggression against a perceived other, and of destroying humanity and the natural world.

When it first appeared in *The Colored American Magazine*, Pauline Hopkin's *Of One Blood* was described as "A most powerful psychological novel, [that] deals in no uncertain terms with both the temporal and spiritual solution of the greatest question of the age – The Negro" (*CAM* 5.6, October 1902, 478). The paranormal content marks the genesis of fantasy and science fiction in African American novels. The novel begins at the tail end of the autumn equinox on All Hallows Eve with the chill of winter menacingly approaching. The main character, introduced as a Gothic figure, cold, alone, and suffering poverty for the furtherance of his scientific research into mesmerism, could be easily at home in the novels of Mary Shelly or Edgar Allen Poe. The philosophic bent of the novel recalls William James, particularly his inquiries in *The Will to Believe: And Other Essays in Popular Philosophy* (1897).[1] Storms, faces envisioned in the restless night sky, and ghostlike figures appear along with the Fisk Jubilee singers in a story of passing, interracial desire, and the incest caused by the sexual licentiousness within slavery. The surreal of speculative fiction is thus joined with the realism of black life to question the irrationalities race and enslavement have caused in America.

The protagonist, the passing Reuel Briggs, is a scientist, mesmerist, and as it turns out, destined to be king of an ancient African civilization from which he descends. Through him, Hopkins extensively re-creates African antecedents while making the argument that but for the contributions of Africa, science and human civilization could not have developed. Reuel falls in love with the near-white Dianthe Lusk, a member of the Fisk Jubilee singers, touring for the benefit of black institutions of higher learning and other Reconstruction efforts. His competitor for her affections turns out to be his own brother, Aubrey Livingston, a baby switched at birth by his black grandmother and brought up to believe he is white. The plot, satisfying turn-of-the-century fascination with exotic travel and excavating the past, takes Reuel on an architectural expedition to Tripoli, Ethiopia, and Telassar where he discovers that a lotus birth mark identifies him as "The son of a fallen dynasty" in the ancient civilization of Meroe (555).[2] The complex storyline even anticipates late twentieth century fascination with the undead through the action of reanimating a seeming corpse.

Reuel becomes a metaphor for African Americans in the United States. He is a genius who creates a process that wakes the dead, and Hopkins uses the character to counter representations of black incapability. Charlie, a friend of Reuel who has traveled with him and discovered the ancient world exclaims, " 'Great Scott!' ... 'you don't mean to tell me that all this was done by *niggers*?' " (532) and thus voices exactly the response Hopkins seeks from her readers. Reuel's union with Queen Candace from this world signifies the reunion of Africans in America with their past and validates present black existence by giving it honorable antecedents. *Of One Blood* echoes Alain Locke's sentiment that nothing is more galvanizing than a cultural past ("Note" 138). It takes science fiction's emphasis on technology impacting human existence and fantasy's imagining a better world and places both in the context of a black tradition.

In early black speculative fiction, fantasy and utopianism are used to create a venerable past, argue for respect in the present, and envision a better future for all members of the human race. This triad informs W. E. B. DuBois's speculative work, *Dark Princess: A Romance* (1928). The protagonist Matthew Towns sails to Europe because he cannot fulfill his residency as a physician specializing in obstetrics and gynecology in the United States. What white woman would let a black doctor practice on her? his professor asks. When down to his last nickel in Berlin, he comes to the aid of a woman being accosted by a white male. The woman turns out to be H. R. H. the Princess Kautilya of Bwodpur, India, and the leader of an organization that seeks to unite people of color all over the globe. Members from Egypt, China, Japan all query whether black Americans are ready, able, and courageous enough to partake in the effort to right global racial inequality.

In Part II of the novel, Matthew reverses sail to research the feasibility of the princess's plan for an uprising among black Americans. After a series of convoluted occurrences he is sentenced to ten years in prison for conspiracy and refusing to tell the whole truth of a plan to avenge the lynching of his friend Jimmie. Part III exhibits the greatest degree of utopian fantasy. Mentally numb from his incarceration, Matthew becomes the pawn of Sammy Scott and Sara Andrews, a Chicago politician and his stenographer, who through clever strategizing, have arranged his release from prison. A marriage of convenience ensues, as does a run for congress, and both cause him to struggle with who he has become. Once the princess returns they reunite, and he forswears self-serving politicizing. Ultimately Matthew is accepted into "The Great Central Committee of Yellow, Brown, and Black," and the birth of their son brings about their union. They return to a South portrayed as a utopian space of regeneration in spite of its uglier realities where Matthew rejoins his mother, represented as an ancient sage. In a ceremony blending the singing of black spirituals and praises to Brahma, Vishnu, and Siva, they wed, and during their service their son is crowned as the new Maharajah of Bwodpur. As the plotline suggests, *Dark Princess* is a pastiche in the best and worst senses of the word. Its attempt to comment on expatriatism, Jim Crow, and Pan Africanism, does not always produce cohesive storytelling, but the novel is a pioneering effort in utopian fantasy, one that envisions diaspora as the foundation of a sustainable civilization. The fantasy and utopian forms preferred by DuBois and Hopkins were not the only speculative elements employed in early black fiction. Sutton E. Griggs, E. A. Johnson, and Roger Sherman Tracy made use of science fiction to give their writings futuristic detail.

Many agree that Hugo Gernsback, the founding editor of *Amazing Stories*, a magazine that solidified the genre, coined the term science fiction. His description of the nature and social circumstances giving rise to "scientifiction" (which would later be renamed science fiction) in many ways characterizes the conditions giving rise to black writers within the tradition:

> Our entire mode of living has changed with the present progress, and it is little wonder, therefore, that many fantastic situations – impossible 100 years ago – are brought about today. It is in these situations that the new romancers find their great inspiration.
>
> Not only do these amazing tales make tremendously interesting reading – they are also always instructive. They supply knowledge that we might not otherwise obtain – and they supply it in a very palatable form. For the best of these modern writers of scientifiction have the knack of imparting knowledge, and even inspiration, without once making us aware that we are being taught. (3)

Indeed, at the turn of the twentieth century when Griggs, Johnson, and Tracy were writing, the making of a black citizenry brought about by the end of slavery constituted massive change for the United States that would have been unheard of one hundred years before. The establishment of black hospitals, black schools of medicine, and the proliferation of articles on science and health in black periodicals attest to growing influence of science in black communities; but this influence was concomitant with the popularization of scientific racism disseminated through pseudosciences such as craniology, through support for eugenics, and through publications including Theodore Lothrop Stoddard's *The Rising Tide of Color against White World-Supremacy* (1920) and Madison Grant's *The Passing of a Great Race, or the Racial Basis of European History* (1920). Much of early black science fiction responds to the sentiments of this discourse.

E[dward]. A[ustin]. Johnson's *Light Ahead for the Negro* (1904) was published, not surprisingly, by the Grafton Press, a house where an author assumed the costs of printing and binding. Grafton was frequently a resort for works that had difficulty finding publishers (after many rejections Gertrude Stein's *Three Lives* would be appear there in 1909), and the subject matter of Johnson's work was certainly counter to prevailing literary headwinds. From the start with its address to sympathetic southerners, it is clear that *Light Ahead* aims to be a work of advocacy. A non-mainstream house was the only place for a novel combining utopian vision, futuristic writing, and critique of America's racial problem.

Johnson dedicates his work to "well wishing friends of the Negro race" (v), and reveals a strategy of seeking a change to racial injustice at its source, the region where slavery became an immense institution, the South. Anticipating a white reading public's responses to its content, it aims not to censure but to persuade, in Johnson's words "to be mild." He classifies it as only secondarily a work of fiction: "The story weaved into the work is subordinate to the discussion of facts, and not paramount" (vi). This introduction overstates the "fiction" within the work for the character and plot are minimal. Most of the novel is given over to futuristic correctives to the failed promises of Reconstruction. *Light* bemoans the loss of James Oglethorpe's reform vision for a non-slaveholding colony of Georgia. It questions the ethics of plans for black emigration to Africa, lynching, the Ku Klux Klan, and black exclusion from political participation. Published in 1904, it imagines black life in what was then the far future of 2006. Its science fiction world includes dirigible air flight and electric motor cars that run on elevated tracks. There is an assertion of the importance of black equality, education, and professional opportunity, but full social inter-mixture is passed over. For Johnson, so enmeshed in the actuality of post-Reconstruction challenges, imagining technological change was far easier that imagining a racial utopia in a transformed South. The future has its limits.

The central narrator Gilbert Twitchell is a young white male who has graduated from Yale. His father was an abolitionist and supported the efforts of those seeking to make citizens out of former slaves, and Gilbert inheriting his sympathies decides to go south and devote his life to "working among the Negroes" (1). The conceit flatters Johnson's imagined white audience by implying a helpless populace in need of assistance rather than one actively engaging in self-help. Before heading south, Gilbert joins a wealthy friend for a ride on a dirigible airship to Mexico City. The dirigible's motor explodes, killing his friend and sending Gilbert into the stratosphere. When he next awakes, it is one hundred years later, and he is in the home of Dr. Newell of Phoenix, Georgia, both names implying the resurrection of a new South, and he is being nursed by Irene Davis, a teacher in the Sunday School for Negro Children and a member of the Young Ladies Guild, which was organized specifically to instruct black youth. Both are sympathetic; both are white.

Gilbert is a familiar character in speculative fiction, the traveler from the past who awakes in a world whose technology, literature, and social mores are unfamiliar. In his new era, politics and politicians have been removed to avoid corruption and replaced by the Executive Department and a system of bureaus run by civil servants chosen for their skills. Dr. Newell is fascinated with this traveler and hopes that he has a message from another age for him on the Negro question. The bulk of the novel is given over to that message as Gilbert's experience and the observations of Dr. Newell and Irene, contrast the "past" South (which in the time of Johnson's writing includes the Southern practices he is condemning) and the "present" South, representing an ideal of what the South might be. In this new world, the Golden Rule is the dominant principle, and no racial slurs are hurled. The theories of racists have been debunked, and blacks have access to education, property ownership, and good employment. But appropriate lines of social intercourse are still kept. Dr. Newell's well-educated and mannered private secretary who is "not full black, but mixed blood" (78), for instance, "naturally associated with his own people. He simply wanted to do his work faithfully, and neither expected nor asked to sit by his employer's fireside" (79). That this is his "natural" inclination again allays white fears of racial amalgamation.

Light Ahead is as much blueprint as novel. It uses the future to contextualize present experience and to show what social transformations are necessary for black progress. Johnson uses time travel to make his argument, and Roger Sherman Tracy in *The White Man's Burden* (1915) similarly employs this conceit. Writing under the pseudonym T. Shirby Hodge, Tracy's nameless white protagonist, born in New York, also educated at Yale, is vacationing in New Hampshire when he suddenly awakens in an unknown land in the year 5027 CE. There he encounters a domed construction containing an all-black settlement whose presence causes him to demand to be removed from "niggers" and brought to whites. A black man, crafted as his moral and intellectual superior, explains to him that he has been brought to Africa and his destiny is to act as an intermediary between this world and the whites of North America who are planning to invade it. Tracy pushes science fiction even further than Johnson, and illustrates elements of cyberpunk, with its emphasis on advanced technology and the radical social breakdown of warring worlds. The black civilization has superior weaponry that includes a precursor of digital close circuit video, electric artillery, and phaser-like arms that can destroy or propel objects into other dimensions. The emissary mission fails, however. The whites believing in their own superiority reject the blacks' offer to avert war, leading to a final nuclear-like bomb whose blinding white flash signals total destruction of the white race. The narrator then awakes from a dream and is back in New Hampshire, but he cannot shake the vision's realness. Tracy utilizes science fiction to invert racial power relations and construct a cautionary tale pointing to the consequences of present racial tensions. His Afrofuturist vision encourages the United States to disavow its racial past.

Modes of speculative fiction were increasingly drafted to examine the consequences of slavery and racism throughout turn-of-the-twentieth-century black novels. In *Imperium in Imperio* (1899), Sutton E. Griggs blends science and utopian fiction to create another cautionary tale, this one intraracial and warning of violent excess. The definition of *imperium in imperio* is a government, or sovereignty within a government or sovereignty. The term also alludes to the novel's structure, a story within a story. An introductory note "To the Public" asserts that the pages that follow are from a declaration by Berl Trout (the deceased secretary of state of the Imperium), a man "noted for his strict veracity and for the absolute control that his conscience exercised over him" (1). This frame lends verisimilitude to the fiction that follows, but also signals Griggs concern that morality not be sacrificed to revenge.

Set in Winchester, Virginia, *Imperium* opens with the dialect speech of Mrs. Hannah Piedmont, the poor, black, uneducated yet resolute mother of one of two protagonists, Belton Piedmont. She is determined that Belton receive an education, and enrolls him in the school for "colored children" under the tutelage of Tiberius Gracchus Leonard, who unlike his namesake effects no social reform.[3] Belton grows up in poverty, having to wear patched clothing to school, and is greeted by Leonard as "another black nigger brat" to teach (9). In spite of his teacher's abuse and doing everything in his power to hold him back in favor of his pet student Bernard Belgrave, the son of a highly educated and intellectual mulatto woman and a white senator (who are legally though secretly married), the dark-skinned Belton excels at school, and were it not for the manipulations of Leonard would have graduated valedictorian.

The school experiences of Belton and Bernard – one receiving Leonard's opprobrium the other his love, both talented and capable – begin the contrast of color and class Griggs will use to invert intraracial color privilege. Bernard attends Harvard where he excels, and Belton, with the aid of a white benefactor, excels at Harriet Beecher Stowe University, a southern normal school established by Northern philanthropy to provide for black higher education. Their love interests are also paralleled as Griggs constructs an argument for black racial purity. Bernard will eventually fall in love with, the dark brown Viola Martin who vows to be a race patriot, never marrying a mulatto and separating the mulatto couples that she can. She kills herself after reading in "White Supremacy and Negro Subordination" that miscegenation threatens to dilute the promise of the black race, and her dying letter to Bernard asks him to do what he can to stop further amalgamation. Belton, on the other hand, is taken with and marries a young woman at his school, Antoinette Nermal, intellectual and beautiful and of a "light brown" skin color with black eyes (113). Thinking that she has been unfaithful, he leaves her when she gives birth to a baby who is white in appearance, but they subsequently reunite briefly once the baby darkens. The nationalistic sentiment present in other Griggs novels is here as well, as *Imperium* casts any degree of whiteness as toxic to black self-love, the foundation stone for racial progress. Further, the novel's moral conscious is Belton, not Bernard, a reversal of the nineteenth century glorification of mulatto figures. The novel exhibits a belief in the aristocracy of talent, not skin color. The contrasting parallelism in Belton and Bernard's upbringing and love interests extends to their philosophies of black progress with Bernard steeped in radicalism and Belton in conservatism. When Belton seemingly killed by a lynch mob of "nigger rulers" rises from the dead just prior to being dissected by a doctor who deems him a fine specimen, his disillusionment reaches its zenith, and he joins the Imperium. The group, begun by a black scientist during the Revolutionary period, seeks to effect full enfranchisement for blacks in the United States and an end to black slavery throughout the world. It formed in response to an American government that has consistently ignored black calls for redress.

Like E. A. Johnson, Griggs is a Southerner, and he does not advocate destruction of the South, only its change. Belton's south is one where whites, who didn't have to, set up black schools after slavery; where slavery for all its evils provided blacks with exposure to European literature (Shakespeare, Bacon, Milton, Bunyan, Dante Hugo, Goethe, Dumas), and a Christianity that redeemed them from the "jungles of Africa" (231). The south endangers itself through its practices, and risks making barbarians out of future generations of its citizens; however, according to Belton, discriminatory practices fostered black self-empowerment and sufficiency, and empowered African Americans to be agents of change in the world once they move beyond "grotesque dress," "broken language," "ignorant curiosity," and "boorish manners" (235). It is tempting to see these comments as satiric or subversive given the aim of the Imperium, but the recurrence of this conservative strain throughout Griggs's Reconstruction novels, suggests that Belton's ideas are not far from his author's. They gain elaborated expression in numerous Griggs pamphlets that outline his philosophy for uplift, among them *The One Great Question* (1906) and *Wisdom's*

Call (1910). He offers a critique of black behavior that hinders advancement as well as critique of the racism that institutionalized black oppression. Descriptions of the Imperium's workings provide glimpses into the varying merits of advancement philosophies: emigration, vocational versus academic education, political participation versus radical violence. Rather than focus on portraying a utopia, Griggs portrays the complicated process of moving toward one.

Imagining a black future fascinated many writers, including satirist George Schuyler. He used the figure of the scientific genius to craft a complicated black utopian vision. *The Pittsburgh Courier* serialized two of his efforts, *Black Internationale* (1936–1937) and its sequel *Black Empire: An Imaginative Story of a Great New Civilization in Modern Africa* (1937–1938). Advertisements clearly point to their marketing as pulp fiction playing to the fantasies of black audiences. They promise "Action ... Intrigue ... Thrills," noting "Nothing Like It In The History of **Negro Fiction** ... One of Those 'Must' Stories That Send The Fiction Fans Rushing To The Newsstands ... And They Come Back Each Week for More" (Hill 267). Written from the first person point of view, and echoes of contemporary Dashiell Hammett abound in Schuyler's narrator Carl Slater, a reporter for the imaginary *Harlem Blade* who witnesses the black Doctor Belsidus kill a pretty white female in a Harlem doorway. Realizing he has been seen, the doctor takes him captive, drugs him, and under the threat of death makes him his secretary. Belsidus has a practice of mostly women, all white and moneyed. What he cures is left to the imagination.

Belsidus introduces Slater to fifty men, all black, from all around the world, part of an organization the Black Internationale, devoted to ending white supremacy. The principles of the Internationale's plan include education to insure a pliant populace; building temples worldwide to house a propagandistic religion based on "negro motifs and psychology" (37), using its own broadcast radio network to disseminate its ideas; and distributing free food and clothes. Belsidus's head of air force is Patricia Givens, an aviatrix who conjures the actual figures of Willa B. Brown and Bessie Coleman.[4] As she takes him on a tour of the Internationale's facilities, the science fiction of Schuyler's vision is revealed. In addition to owning a cement company to provide raw materials for construction, the Internationale has a hydroponic farm growing food and a solar-powered engine generating energy. With sustainability practices in place, the Internationale engineers war among the white nations of the world while the organization redeems Africa and its riches to be held forever in black hands.

Black Empire was the sequel to *Black Internationale*, and again Schuyler's science fiction is visionary. Belsidus is developing an empire in Africa and establishing clinics practicing alternative medicines that allow the body to develop immunities to heal itself without drugs. Scientists within Internationale invent new methods for food preparation and keeping, and engineers have conceived of the finest radio and television station in the world, at a time when television is in its infancy. The military might of the Internationale includes state-of-the-art stratosphere planes, and a remote-controlled cyclotron atom smasher to generate atomic or proton beams, which render the power and propellers of planes useless. Belsidus gives blacks back their lost empires and cautions them against replicating the race hate of whites.

Schuyler's science fiction is noteworthy for its forward vision, but the works are filled with his trademark mockery of an imagined essentialized blackness. Belsidus's promises of creating "a higher civilization than Europe has ever seen" (258) is undercut by members of the Black Internationale being captured by cannibals. The "glory that was once Egypt's and Ethiopia's and Benin's and Timbuctoo's and Songhoy's and Morocco's" is not apparent in the stereotypical portraiture of the non-lead black characters. When Pat and Carl are shot down over the Niger River, he notes, "We were soon surrounded by angry brown men, naked except for breech cloths, and brandishing bush knives, spears and old rusty rifles. Their teeth were filed to sharp points and their cruel eyes regarded us appraisingly ... Had we escaped from the desert only to be eaten?" (230). The writer for whom African American was American separates his Americans from their "barbaric" ancestors. In many ways, Schuyler's Africa here evolves little from his earlier novel *Slaves Today*.

Looking at statements from the generation of black writers who would succeed Hopkins, Tracy, Johnson, and Schuyler, the observation that they began work in speculative fiction because they loved reading it and wanted to see their experiences engaged in it is repeated frequently. Their novels appropriate science and technology to query what possibilities emerge when blackness is considered with futurity, and how black futurity might create new models for world being. Charles Saunders, Octavia Butler, and Samuel R. Delany are among the most recognizable names extending the tradition begun by Johnson, Griggs, and Schuyler.

Octavia Butler began writing at a time when the expectation that black fiction was primarily realist or protest in nature hindered the development of the speculative tradition. Publishers were not convinced that plots and themes joining black culture to futurism were plausible (ironic in a genre dealing with possibilities).⁵ Butler wrote herself into a tradition, and she inspired others to do the same. Speculative fiction writer and American Book Award winner Tananarive Due recalls "when I began publishing, her stature as THE Octavia Butler uplifted the entire black speculative fiction genre in a way we could not have found without her. She gave us enough weight to sustain. We lost some of that sustenance after she died, but the current rise and interest in black speculative fiction is, I think, much to her credit" (Quynh n. pag.). Butler's first contact, so to speak, with speculative fiction came through supermarket perusal of magazines that concretized the genre, *Amazing Stories, Fantastic*, and later *Fantasy* and *Science Fiction*. She also credits radio dramas such as *Superman, The Shadow*, and *My True Story* as influences (Francis 16, 81). Her work uses the future to query what in human nature accounts for war, hierarchies, cruelty, and love. Race, gender, class, and sexuality are portrayed as symptoms of the impulse to establish hierarchy and exclude. All of her novels explore not the *what* of these labels but the *why*.

Butler's speculative canon is in the main constituted of three series: the Patternist, the Xenogenesis, and the Earthseed. *Patternmaster* (1976) inaugurated the *Patternist* series, though in the series' narrative history its action would make it the fifth in an arc that begins in antiquity and moves to the future: *Wild Seed* (1980), *Mind of My Mind* (1977), *Clay's Ark* (1984), and *Survivor* (1978) complete the series. *Wild Seed* – through the experiences of two shape-shifting immortals, Doro, born in Africa thousands of years ago and surviving by transferring his consciousness from one body to another, and Anyanwu, abducted by Doro and taken to the alien land of the United States – echoes the history of capture, middle passage, and enslavement, and ultimately questions patriarchy and abuses of power. *Mind of My Mind* continues their story through their daughter Mary, and climaxes with a battle between the paternal figure and his daughter as it studies the responsibility of holding power. *Clay's Ark* is a chronicle of human evolution after apocalyptic change. *Survivor*, what might be called Butler's *Tempest*, reconsiders divine right and the "noble savage" discourse through the quest for self of an Afro-Asian "wild child" adopted by the Missionaries, a neo-Fundamentalist Christian sect. In *Patternmaster* the fight of two sons to succeed their father as the Patternmaster, the leader of a society of telepathic beings, examines ambition unchecked by moral constraints.

Butler's Xenogenesis series consisting of *Dawn* (1987), *Adulthood Rites* (1988), and *Imago* (1989) contemplates how cultures adjust to one another. The Oankali are highly advanced extraterrestrials, who live by mixing with other species and taking the best genetic qualities as they create new mutations. They are trisexual, having the oolio who are neither male nor female. For the past two centuries, they have been observing humans and concluded that their natures are so damaged they will decimate any world they inhabit. Humans are left with the choice of becoming extinct or breeding with the Oankalis. In *Dawn*, Lilith is the first human to face this choice. As she learns to see beyond the reptilian appearances of Oankalis to their inherent traits, and as she subsequently decides to mate with them, her story becomes one of learning how presumptions influence constructions of difference. *Adulthood Rites* continues with the story of Lilith's son Akin, whose bi-species origins allow for the exploration of identification and allegiance. He is kidnapped and sold to a kind, childless human couple. Through them, he learns affection for humans and becomes their advocate. *Imago* tells of another of Lillith's children, Jodahs, the first bi-species ooloi. Jodahs's position is one of an outsider who learns to use the malleability of shapeshifting to create a space for self-actualization. Published under the title *Lilith's Brood* in 2000, the Xenogenesis trilogy was written during the Reagan administration when Butler was despairing about the increasing references to "winnable" nuclear wars. Their stories of contestations between beings and cultures dramatize the performances that go into constructing antagonists. As they depict the traditions, rituals, practices, and ideologies used to sustain discrete group conceptions, the novels also show underlying interrelatedness. Throughout the Patternist and Xenogenesis series Butler investigates encounters with the "foreign" that begin negatively but change with knowledge.

The danger that human beings pose to themselves is among Butler's concerns in the Parable series. A parable is a story told to teach, and her series are meant to make evident the dangers of not correcting destructive practices. *Parable of the Sower* (1993) is a domestic novel, in that it is set in a future United States that has collapsed into warring regions because of a lack of resources. Climate degeneration, rampant disease, and increasing natural disasters produce a regression to the worst structures of human organization – the existence of masters and slaves. Immigrant workers, impoverished rural agricultural residents, the uneducated, and the homeless, all are exploited for the benefit of multinationals. Intellectual curiosity has died because for-profit privatized education has made slaves of students in the impoverished areas they serve. The novel takes the form of a journal recounting the story of the narrator, an African American adolescent Lauren Olamina who has the condition "hyperempathy" where she intensely experiences the pain of others. She lives in a buttressed neighborhood whose survival is threatened by the homeless, drug-addicted, and impoverished populace outside its walls, and her recollections comment on racial, class, and gender divisions she sees and experiences. Each chapter of Lauren's journal begins with a passage from the new religion she has created, Earthseed, whose doctrine states that change is inevitable and the divine principle of the world. Lauren's religion acts as antidote to the dystopia, and outlines the steps needed to guarantee human sustainability.

Parable of the Talents (1998), the second novel of the projected Earthseed or Parable trilogy, received the 1999 Nebula Award for Best Novel. As it continues Lauren's story in Acorn, the new community she has established, it shows the possibility of redemption. The concepts of religion and messiah that have been responsible for much social destruction are reexamined as Lauren's divinity of change makes her religion a dynamic principle, not a rationale for inaction or the wrong action. Butler contrasts Earthseed with orthodox Christianity through Lauren's brother Marcus, a Baptist preacher who sees Lauren's religion as blasphemous. Eventually Lauren's new community is taken over by Christian America crusaders and made into a Camp Christian "rehabilitation" center for those not following the "correct" path. The residents of Acorn are forced into hard labor, tortured, raped, and separated from their children, as are Lauren and her daughter Larkin.

In addition to critiquing the perversion of religion, the novel's format alludes to the difficult reconstruction the victims of ideology must undergo to rediscover their personal and cultural origins. Segments alternate between Larkin's retrospective research into her parents, and Lauren's journal passages detailing the suffering she experienced as she lost and sought her daughter. Other passages tell of Larkin discovering her father's writings, and sections from a book written by Marcus while he was a preacher in the Christian America church. Butler tacitly questions the reliability of historiography by replicating the distortions and consequences that are inevitably part of documenting.

In addition to *Kindred*, Butler wrote another stand-alone novel, *Fledgling* (2005). In it, Shori Matthews awakes injured in a dark cave. She does not know who she is, but she is ravenous. She captures, kills, and eats raw what she ultimately discovers is not an animal but a man, and begins to heal. Ultimately it is revealed that Shori is a vampire-like being, an Ina. Inas consensually feed on a human "symbionts," imparting not harm but intense pleasure. The relationship is a monogamous partnership that provides the human with quadruple life extension (should the symbiont be fed upon by any but his or her Ina, pain and sickness is the result for both). From her grandmother, she has inherited black human, DNA that gives her dark skin, allows her limited exposure to the sun, and lets her stay awake during the day. Because of her unique makeup, Shori is targeted by a group of Inas who fear racial and ethnic diversity as well as scientific progress. The novel details fear of the other and the extremes gone to, to eradicate difference even among races that cannot survive fully without one another.

Butler examines the fears behind racism, xenophobia, enslavement, and eco-exploitation, as symptomatic of the dangers in presuming the self as the norm. Whatever the being, human, non-human, or a mixture thereof, continued contact often leads to principles of cultural relativity that eventually lead to tolerance. Not following this progression generally insures destruction. Her works do not portray easy utopias, but rather show the questions that need to be asked to insure the functioning of fair societies. Rather than a simple dichotomy of good and evil, they represent the continuum of fear, ignorance, non- and misunderstanding. They are fitting to a late twentieth century in which the media of nation-states and their military industrial complexes create changeable Others as perpetual threats.

What Butler admires most about the speculative genre is the freedom it provides to engage any setting, and temporal space, and people it with characters of her own imagining (Francis 4). Her teacher and mentor, Samuel R. Delany, shared this sentiment and felt that speculative fiction was the genre best suited to imagining alternative possibilities. In theorizing about the canon of African American literature, Delany noted that the determinism of writers such as Richard Wright and early Chester Himes could produce classic literature only in a world convinced that change was impossible (Delany, *Starboard* 28). Speculative fiction presumes an exactly opposite world and gave Delany a space to contemplate ideas of difference. Taking hierarchies of race, gender, class, and sexuality in otherworldly realms to the extreme, his novels dissect their social dynamics in the actual world. *Captives of the Flame* (1963), *The Towers of Toron* (1964), *City of a Thousand Suns* (1965), and *Nova* (1968), are all post-apocalyptic novels, set in futuristic worlds where perpetual fear of constructed others threaten or effect annihilation. With thematics and prose that forced scholars of "serious" literature to take notice, Delany's science fiction queries binaries – sexual, racial, and even generic – as the arts have a presence in his novels of science.

Many of Delany's novels are noteworthy for their study of sexuality. *The Jewels of Aptor* (1962) is one instance of his defying sex and gender binaries. Geo the protagonist searches for telepathic jewels and encounters the priestesses of Argo – grandmother, mother, and daughter – a trio encompassing traits both male and female, procreator/warrior, life sustaining/death dealing. *Nova* (1968) questions the meaning of form. The story of the 3172 fight between the older Earth-based Draco and the younger Pleiades Federation for conquest of the Outer Colonies that produce Illyrion the power source for galactic travel, it unfolds through chapters that begin or end mid-sentence and call attention to the role interpretation plays in storytelling. The protagonist in *Trouble on Triton: An Ambiguous Heteretopia* (1976) changes sex as the plot develops. *Triton's* world is a future utopia where all forms of sexual relationships are permitted. Its inhabitants move freely between multiple sexualities, with "refixations," procedures that alter sexual identity, being common occurrences. Rather than allow this to exist as a simple liberatory experiment, however, Delany creates a dissatisfied, antiheroic central character Bron, rooted in binary conceptions of male and female for whom this freedom causes discontent. The book examines the limitations of utopianism and rethinks what it will mean in a world where contestations along sexual lines are no more. Will another "ism" rise to take the place of homophobia? Through explorations of sexuality, the work frames the quest for utopia as ongoing, rather than static.

Delany's *Stars in My Pocket Like Grains of Sand* (1984) is set in a future universe where worlds are aligned with the conservative Family or the more progressive Sygn. All planets face destruction by the phenomenon known as the cultural fugue. A sexual and racial outsider, the protagonist Korga initially lives on Rhyonon, a world run by binaries and proscription. Homosexuality is illegal before a certain age and remains frowned upon; sex between tall and short is forbidden; and women occupy lower social status than men. Because Korga has had trouble with the law, he is tricked by the RAT Institute into undergoing Radical Anxiety Termination, a procedure that they say will bring him happiness but instead renders him passive, an institutional slave and at one point a woman's illegal sexual slave. When Rhyonon is destroyed, Korga is rescued by the WEB, an intergalactic network maintaining communicative links among the inhabited worlds. His will is restored, and he meets Marq Dyeth, an Industrial Diplomat who is his perfect erotic partner. He joins Marq on his planet Velm, a world shared by humans and a three-sexed intelligent species, the evelm. Sanctioned sexual relations take many forms including interspecies, heterosexual, homosexual, and anonymous, and characters are often referred to as male and female, he and she within the same sentence. Velm is again not presented as an ideal, but as a working society where tolerance insures a better quality of life. The alternative constructions of sex in Delany's novels queers the relationship of biology to gender, something Delany does not only in his science fiction novels, but also in his mundane nov-els (to borrow the contrasting term of science fiction scholars) such as *Dark Reflections* (2007) – the hindsight self-analysis of a black gay poet's life – and in his graphic memoir *Bread and Wine: An Erotic Tale of New York* (1999), which tells of his meeting and developing a relationship with Dennis, the homeless man who became his partner. Biology has been the foundation of many rationales seeking to vilify difference, whether racial, sexual, or both, but Delany's novels render it inconclusive.

Delany exhibits a self-awareness of both the story and storytelling form. *Triton* (1976) contains two appendices addressing the novel's passing con-cern with linguistics. In *Dhalgren* (1975), the writing of the novel replicates itself through the main character, an amnesiac drifter, a poet who writes down incidents, rewriting and editing, crossing out words trying with painstaking attention to find the right ones. The novel is not set in another galaxy but is earth-bound on Bellona, a place separated from the rest of the world and filled with scenes of mythology. It becomes a meditation not only on whether reality can be known but also on the process of writ-ing what one perceives as real. The central idea in *Babel-17* (1966) is based on the Sapir–Whorf hypothesis, that perception and thought are shaped through language. The artificial language that gives the novel its title has neither first nor second-person pronouns, so its speakers cannot be critical or self-critical. *The Einstein Intersection* (1967) extends Delany's concern with form to the larger area of mythmaking. While telling of a character's search for his lost love, it also details the process of trying to understand one's reality through the myths of others. The novel explores artistic quest, and many of its epigraphs are from Delany's own journals, linking the author to character realizations.

As a gay black writer beginning his career when much published science fiction content was by heterosexual white males, Delany consistently ques-tioned the idea of gatekeeping in his fiction, nonfiction, and erotic novels. For some readers, the abstract quality of his novels moves them outside a genre that has traditionally dealt with action and thrills, but it is precisely this digression that makes them truly speculative. He is both science fic-tion storyteller and science fiction philosopher. Ursula Le Guin referred to him as the genre's finest "in-house critic" (27). Delany feels that science fiction provides a future for black Americans. He notes, "We need images of tomorrow; and our people need them more than most" (*Starboard Wine* 35). The consequence of no tomorrows, for him, was the belief that history, politics, and economics were all-powerful. Such thinking destroys imagin-ation and heterogeneity, the twin sources of intelligence.

Speculative fiction allows writers themselves to shape-shift within genres. Colson Whitehead, who has reworked the historical novel in *John Henry*, blends detective fiction, film noir, and speculative modes in *The Intuitionist* (1999). Lila Mae Watson is an African American inspector working for one of the most powerful departments in the city, the Department of Elevator Inspectors. There are two protocols to inspecting elevators, one where the inspector is an Empiricist evaluating elevators by checking mechanical specifications, the other where he or she is an Intuitionist, evaluating through feeling and sensing, becoming one with the elevator. As an Intuitionist, Lila Mae is a rarity amid a department of Empiricists. She is thus discriminated against on three levels – racial, gender, and philosophical. When an elevator crashes, she is blamed, and the novel depicts her efforts to clear her name. When Lila Mae discovers that the founder of Intuitionism James Fulton was actually a black man passing for white, it necessitates a new interpretation of his ideas, particularly his plan for "the Black Box," the perfect elevator that goes up not only within buildings but also beyond them. Through the clash of philosophies, *The Intuitionist* contrasts ways of seeing and ordering the world's phenomena. Ultimately the novel stresses that understanding is impossible without being cognizant of the role perception plays.

Whitehead's other speculative work *Zone One* (2011) is a jeremiad that sounds an alarm about the decline that has led to a futuristic dystopia. A plague has rendered most people of the world zombies feasting on an ever-decreasing number of survivors. The central character is a paragon of mediocrity who undermines the rhetoric of heroic individualism. He is part of a cleanup crew removing lingering "skels," the living dead, from Zone One, a cordoned section of lower Manhattan bordering "Ground Zero."[6] His real name is never revealed; instead, he is known by the nickname Mark Spitz given to him by those who assume he can't swim when he shoots his way out of a zombie attack rather than jump into the water below. Even at the almost-end of the world, racial notions still persist. Parallels to 9/11 critique a US government becoming increasingly fascistic under the guise of a never-ending war on terror with unclear opponents. The tragedy amid a novel with many comic flourishes lies in its consideration of why apocalypse seems to be the only means of unifying populaces. The reception of *Zone One* largely reflected mild surprise that Whitehead worked within the speculative form. A *New York Times* reviewer noted, "A literary novelist writing a genre novel is like an intellectual dating a porn star." A *Guardian* reviewer observed, "By nearly any definition, Whitehead is a literary writer of impeccable credentials. A MacArthur grant recipient,

he's been shortlisted for both a Pulitzer and a National Book Award ...,
but in a surprising move, he has now turned his hand to that most ubiquitous of modern phenomena: zombies."[7]

Early in her career as a writer, Tananarive Due encountered reactions
similar to those greeting Whitehead's speculative work. They taught her
that for many, speculative fiction was not serious fiction, nor was it a form
expected of a black writer. In a literature course at Northwestern University
when asked her favorite writer, she mentioned Toni Morrison to nods of
approval. The nods were less forthcoming, however, to her second mention, Steven King. As she has noted, "editors and readers make assumptions about books based on faces on the cover, author names, etc." (Quynh
n. pag.). Due always had an affection for horror even before knowing what
speculative fiction was. Sharing a love of fright films with her mother, and
reading the work of Stephen King made writing speculative novels seem a
next logical step.

In Due's first novel, *The Between* (1995), seven-year-old Hilton James
finds his grandmother dead on the kitchen floor. He runs for help, and
when he returns she is alive and cooking. The novel then flashes ahead to
Hilton whose life as a middle-class social worker is upended when his wife,
the first black judge in Dade County Miami, receives racist death threats.
Hilton begins to have nightmares with near-death experiences so real they
seem to be alternate life dimensions. A therapist offers the diagnosis of
schizophrenia to explain both phenomena, but in a gesture designed to
play up the importance of alternative world views, his blind client explains
the existence of "the Between," a space where travelers use dreams as portals to escape death. The novel employs the black and Latino setting of
Miami. Due not only situates speculative conventions in black and brown
worlds, she also uses the lore of those worlds as the cornerstones of her
fantasy.

The Between was followed by what would be known as Due's African
Immortals series: *My Soul to Keep* (1997), *The Living Blood* (2001), and
Blood Colony (2008), with a fourth volume, *Blood Prophecy* projected. Due
takes speculative conventions and imbues them with elements resonant
of black history and culture. The series is based on the story of a brotherhood of Ethiopian immortals that became so because members had par-
taken of the blood of Jesus Christ at the time of the Crucifixion. Their
blood has miraculous healing powers, especially for ordinary humans, and
through a Life Ceremony, immortality can be conveyed. Enslavement, the
Ethiopian war with Italy, Reconstruction, and Jim Crow are all included
in the life of David Wolde, a 450-year-old African American immortal,

whose real name is Dawit. He falls in love with a mortal, Jessica, and facing the pain of outliving her, passes along his immortality to her. He violates the immortals' proscription against such sharing, and the novel invokes images of what it means to love across proscribed lines. To punish him, the immortals attempt to murder him, Jessica, and their daughter Fana who herself has immense powers of telepathy and transport.

In *The Living Blood*, Jessica hides in Botswana, and Due nods to the traditions of black women's writing by exploring the multiplicity of women's identity through the relationship she shares with her daughter, her sister, and Dawit. As a mother she finds it increasingly difficult to raise a "goddess"; as a wife she is disillusioned by her husband; and as a woman she faces the challenges of remaining in hiding while working in a clinic dispensing her own blood as curative. Through Fana the novel continues these considerations as she juggles responsibilities of immortality with her developing personal self. Set in 2015, a secret war is waged over the drug Glow, derived from the immortals' blood. It can cure sickle-cell anemia, AIDS, and other blood-diseases, and the US government and the corporate entity Big Pharm seek to possess it. Fana forms a futuristic Underground Railroad to get the drug to those who need it.

After diverting to write *The Black Rose* (2000) – a historical novel fictionalizing the life of Madam C. J. Walker and based on Alex Haley's extensive research – Due returned to her horror roots with *The Good House* (2003) and *Joplin's Ghost* (2005). *The Good House* is a haunted domicile tale in which Angela Toussaint, the granddaughter of a Vodou priestess who in revenge against a racist act unwittingly releases a demon that causes the suicide of Angela's son and threatens the community of Sacajawea, Washington. In *Joplin's Ghost* (2005) Phoenix Smalls, at the age of ten, is almost crushed by a falling piano once owned by Scott Joplin. Shortly thereafter, she sleepwalks to the piano's bench and begins playing Joplin's rag, "Weeping Willow." The novel juxtaposes Joplin's difficult history as a musical genius constrained by the racism with Phoenix's struggles to become a singer. Research is key to accomplishing the integration of diaspora history and fantasy in Due's novels. Whether it is Ethiopia in the Middle Ages, antebellum slavery, turn-of-the-twentieth-century black music, hip-hop, and jazz, or west African religions, black history gives speculative traditions new perspectives and voice.

Research into diaspora history shapes the novels of Charles Saunders as well. Born in Pennsylvania and educated at Lincoln University, because he did not want to be involved in the Vietnam War, Saunders moved to Toronto and Hamilton, Ontario, then to Ottawa, and subsequently to

Nova Scotia, where he wrote a series of nonfictional works on the blacks who settled there. Reading and loving the adventure books of Edgar Rice Burroughs, while following the events of the Civil Rights Movement, made him aware of how the adventure tale and considerations of race might be merged. The result was the "Sword and Soul" genre, a term he coined to describe sword-and-sorcery fantasy, inspired by African diaspora content. He is best known for Imaro, the "brother who could kick Tarzan's ass." Noting that most of the people of color in science fiction novels were green, Saunders sought to counter the non-presence of blacks in the speculative genre (Harlib n. pag.). Six of what would be called the Imaro stories originally published in *Dark Fantasy* would form the basis for his first novel, *Imaro* (1981), the story of a black African hero, at first marginalized by his tribe, the Ilyassi, because his mother has mated with someone of another race. Imaro now lives in exile after his manhood rite. *The Quest for Cush* (1984) and *The Trail of Bohu* (1985) complete the series. An Africa imagined as a backdrop for heroic adventure has been a cornerstone of much black fiction, and here Saunders takes it into the realm of fantasy. He mixes themes of "the glory that once was" with "the violence that now is" to create contemporary commentary on continuing genocide and terrorism.

The diasporic dimensions of black speculative fiction are also present in Nalo Hopkinson's first two novels *Brown Girl in the Ring* (1998) and *Midnight Robber* (2000). Her being born in Jamaica, living in Trinidad, Guyana, and the United States before settling in Canada, influence her themes. *Brown Girl* is set in a Toronto ruined by economic collapse. Reflecting the plight of many deteriorating cities, most of the metropolitan center's residents live in poverty and homelessness while the elite have created oases in the suburbs. When the Canadian premiere needs a heart transplant, she rejects the usual route, the Porcine Organ Harvest Program seeking a human heart instead. The only compatible heart belongs to Gros-Jeanne, the grandmother of the protagonist, Ti-Jeanne. A conspiracy between her son's father, a drug-addict under the sway of the gangster Rudy (who now controls the streets of Toronto, and is in actuality Ti-Jeanne's grandfather), brings about Gros-Jeanne's murder. Ti-Jeanne must reconnect to her grandmother's root-working powers, to save herself and the city from Rudy's evil. Hopkinson's Caribbean world is felt in her characters' language as well as the title of the novel, taken from a West Indian children's circle dance song. The novel evokes a diasporic power through referencing the Canadian Ti-Jeanne's interactions with Vodou, Santeria, and Jamaican Obeah. The battle of superpowers that is so much a part of speculative fiction is recast as syncretized black power.

Hopkinson's novels are frequently characterized by cyberpunk. A subgenre in which humanity is marginalized and technology centralized, its themes include the fusion of the artificial and organic, as well as plots centering on the battle against the dehumanization that results from technological systems. *Midnight Robber* (2000) takes place on two fictional planets, Toussaint and its prison colony, New Halfway Tree. The Marryshow Corporation has shipped former black Caribbean residents to Toussaint where divisions of race and caste are erased as everyone becomes a compère and is freed of physical labor. At birth, each person is injected with nanomites that the all-controlling technology Granny Nanny uses to address their needs and regulate their desires. Some, however, still remember and desire physical work. They are the runners who use code to subvert Granny Nanny's surveillance and live in homes off the grid, but they do not rebel fearing expulsion from Toussaint. The heroine Tan-Tan grows up amid the marital tensions of her parents Antonio and Ione. When Antonio who suspects his wife of adultery kills her lover, he knows he will be punished by Granny Nanny, so he takes Tan-Tan and escapes through a portal to New Half-Way Tree. Antonio degenerates into alcoholism and depression, and begins to beat and rape Tan-Tan on a regular basis subsequently impregnating her. At sixteen, in self-defense, she kills him. She runs seeking to exorcise herself of guilt over her father's death and to escape from his vengeful second wife. In the process she transforms herself into the Robber Queen a figure rooted in West Indian Carnival. The transformation inspires Tan-Tan to do the out-sized deeds the legendary character brags of and accomplish good for those around her.

In *Midnight Robber*, Hopkinson imbues speculative fiction with what she knows: Caribbean culture. Populating her cyberpunk worlds are not only web technology and sentient interfacing, but also duppies, orishas, and root-working grandmothers. Her language reflects the cadences of British and American English as well as West Indian creole. Tan-Tan becomes the transgressive heroine taking on the technological hegemon. In Hopkins's hands, however, the technological threat combines chips and the legacies of enslavement, colonialism, and postcolonialism. The Granny Nanny Web recalls benevolent colonial practices equating technological power with moral superiority while enforcing conformity to the ideas of the dominant. The Marryshow Corporation that has resettled the people from the Caribbean to Toussaint recalls the mercantile corporations that disrupted existing social structures and instituted their own. Ironies are also present in the novel. The technological control exerted over Toussaint's populace contrasts strongly with the spirit of Haiti's revolutionary leader Toussaint L'Ouverture who spearheaded the transformation of a slave colony into an independent state. Similarly, the Granny Nanny web could not be further from the spirit of its namesake Granny Nanny or Queen Nanny, liberator of slaves and the leader of the Jamaican Maroons whose revolutionary exploits received as much notice as did her powers of Obeah. The divergences question what has happened to revolutionary spirit and what has been sacrificed for material comfort.

Similar to some of her fellow speculative writers, Hopkins notes that, in reading the genre, she saw no traditions of fantasy rooted in the folklore of her world, no science fiction that speculated on worlds with characters whose appearances or worldviews were similar to the ones she knew, so she created them (Watson-Aifah 160). Describing herself as a science fiction writer who failed science, she says that she gets to the science in her works first by imagining the familiar and then intertwining the science ("Writer"). Her fiction does something similar. It takes science and places it in the Caribbean context, which makes sense to her, is familiar to her. She then combines the images from this world with futuristic examinations underscoring the closeness of the fantastical and the actual.

Samuel R. Delany whose Clarion Science Fiction Writers' workshop students included Octavia Butler and Nalo Hopkinson asserted that "transgression inheres, however unarticulated, in every aspect of the black writer's career in America" ("Racism and Science Fiction" n. pag.). This seems to still hold true for black speculative writers. In many ways they recapitulate the experiences of early black writers transgressing to insert themselves into a literary tradition, while their speculative novels allow them to shift the parameters of that tradition. Not reactionary but visionary, their alternative universes center blackness in contrast to present systems which marginalize and fear it. Their novels use the alien presence to question societal fears of black bodies, and their fusion of living and dead, good and evil, medieval and futuristic, realistic and fantasy, natural and supernatural, male and female counter the ideas of binaries that have so often been used to exclude and/or confine blackness.

Black speculative novels create a world where black reality can be reimagined because the terms of the "real" world need not exist. In literary discourse where so much of the black past is unknown and so much of the black present is fraught, futurism offers a space where a new world can be constructed. Regarding this tradition of writing over time, noting what has or has not changed in black life from the early futurist writings of E. A. Johnson, Roger Tracy, or Sutton E. Griggs, to the contemporary works of Octavia Butler, Samuel R. Delany, and Nalo Hopkinson, afford sobering consideration of the world's morality.

CHAPTER 11

African American Pulp

As part of his *Redpath's Books for the Camp Fire*, a cheaply printed series to be read by Union soldiers to combat the dreariness of Civil War camps, James Redpath issued pulp editions of William Wells Brown's *Clotel. The Colored American Magazine* used seductive images, titillating headlines, all the tricks of sensationalist pulp marketing to sell its serialized and published versions of Pauline Hopkins's *Of One Blood.* In the late 1940s, Ann Petry's *The Street* and Chester Himes's *If He Hollers Let Him Go* were given lurid covers to facilitate their mass-marketing. Later, all these works would find themselves on college course reading lists and discussed in academic journals. Their histories indicate the fluidity of novels as their cultures situate them and the porosity between the categories pulp, popular, and serious fiction. Classification of black novels has been intricately tied to class dynamics and questions of representation, and the continuum of pulp to popular to serious reveals more about publishing and readers than literary works.

Generally, pulp fiction referred to works written quickly and printed on cheap paper, the dime novels of the nineteenth century or the crime, mystery, and adventure tales of the 1930s, for instance. By the time the term gains currency as a referent for black writing, it designates 1960s novels about pimps, hustlers, drug dealers, whores, and life on the street, the more sexually prurient the content the better. But characterizing pulp through content and form alone can be unreliable. A "ghetto" setting, marginalized characters, profanity, and sexual explicitness, the presumed hallmarks of black pulp, are also present in novels deemed classics. What makes a novel pulp is determined as much by its separateness from the academy, mainstream presses, and distribution, as it is by its style (and even this situation is constantly in flux). Black pulp is a folk form circulated through corner stores, barbershops, newsstands, liquor stores, via mail order, and passed from hand to hand. Like many folk forms it enjoys increasing study within the academy because it personifies predominating ideals at a moment in time and reflects the values of its participatory groups. As black readerships expanded in terms of class and gender, pulp seemed too narrow a description for the romance novels and action adventures appealing to middle-class and/or female readerships. Popular fiction became an umbrella term applied to novels occupying a status somewhat above pulp yet still below what is conceived of as serious literature.

While turn-of-the twentieth century serials in black periodicals might be seen as an early form of black pulp fiction, and while over the course of the 1920s through the 1950s different novels by black authors were given pulp treatment, a genre of stand-alone novels does emerge in the 1960s. Through their dispossessed protagonists who await no messiah, no revolution, and instead made their own salvation using street savvy, sex, and brutality, they seemed to speak for a populace who felt their lives were not meaningfully changed by either what they saw as an ineffectual Civil Rights Movement or bombastic black nationalism. The very figures decried by both civil rights activists and nationalists as antithetical to black political consciousness and justifying institutional neglect were written as heroes expressing the sentiments of marginalized segments within marginalized communities. Seen more as a reflection than a fiction the genre cemented a narrative of black pathology and located authentic blackness on the streets, sites of perpetual survival mode with their own systems of punishment and reward. The form's insularity disregarded outside approval, and characters some saw as degenerate and reactionary became avatars for the power their readers lacked in their own lives.

Central to the development of 1960s, black pulp was Holloway House publishing. Its specialty was erotic paperbacks and male-oriented adult magazines. Initially its wares were sold to white men until its owners Ralph Weinstock and Bentley Morris realized the existence of an unserved market. The outlet exploited what they marketed as authentic black life on ghetto streets to become one of the most successful publishing houses of the time. Holloway filled a gap left by the more established publications of the Johnson company, *Ebony* and *Jet*. In addition to novels about black life, it offered the erotic *Players* magazine modeled along the lines of *Playboy* with nude pictures of black women alongside profiles and interviews of successful black men, among them James Earl Jones and Dick Gregory. Chester Himes, Ishmael Reed, and Stanley Crouch were contributing writers. Holloway's cross-marketing of their novels in their magazines expanded their books' exposure and readership: its images reflected the novels' representations of black male power and black female sexual commodification; its reviews suggested works to buy and offered a mechanism for purchase.

With the publication of Robert Beck, better known as Iceberg Slim and Donald Goines, Holloway became the gateway for 1960s black pulp. Both Beck and Goines were ex-convicts and former pimps. Expectedly their material was not welcomed in the mainstream press due to explicit content as well as an alienating lexicon. Over time the slang of the works would confer a certain street-wise cachet, but initially editions of Robert Beck's *Pimp: The Story of My Life* (1967) came with a glossary. With *Pimp*, Holloway House gained renown. The novel went through twelve printings, and Beck's second book *Trick Baby: The Story of a White Negro* (1967) five printings in two years. By 1969 the success of these works encouraged Holloway House to launch a new marketing strategy, grouping theses novels under their "Black Experience Paperback Library." Advertising in local, West Coast black newspapers such as Los Angeles's *The Sentinel* and sending their editors to the Watts Writers Workshop, they courted black writers. One was Donald Goines, the heir apparent to Beck's success. Others included authors of more serious works, Robert H. deCoy writer of *The Nigger Bible* (1967) and Louis Lomax author of *To Kill a Black Man* (1968).[1]

The writer who became Iceberg Slim was born Robert Lee Maupin, Jr. in Chicago, and later when he moved from Chicago to California took the surname of his mother's then husband, Beck. Born in 1918, a year before the Red Summer, the future novelist's formative years unfolded against a backdrop of extreme violence against African Americans. He grew up in Chicago of the 1920s when the city was in the throes of organized crime wars. The child sexual abuse he received at the hands of a babysitter at three, the constant physical abuse of his father, Robert Lee Maupin, Sr., a street hustler who subsequently left the family, as well as the institutionalized abuse he saw serving stints in the Wisconsin Bay Reformatory, all made their way into his fiction in various guises. Beck identifies the key event that framed his life as his mother's leaving his stepfather, whom he remembers as a good father figure, and moving to Chicago for what she felt was a more glamorous life with another man. The move upended a secure family and led him to the Southside streets. It was here that Beck, now known as "Cavanaugh Slim," began his career as pimp and petty thief. Coming to see street life as a dead end he returned to Los Angeles in the early 1960s and attempted reconciliation with his sick mother who was then living with William Beck. It is easy to see Beck's life on the streets and stints in prison for sex crimes and armed robbery as the genesis of his novels' worldview, but Beck was also a high school graduate who attended (but did not graduate from) Tuskegee at the same time as Ralph Ellison. The contrast between writer and authorial persona reminds us that Iceberg

Slim was one of his best "characters."[2] Through this persona Beck sought redemption, and he represented this search as a major theme in novels that were part entertainment part warnings. Because it was essentially a fictionalized version a life story, Holloway House marketed *Pimp* more as memoir than novel. Foreshadowing future Beck works, it wed sexploitation, blaxploitation, and for some ethnography, introducing readers to a setting that would be popularized as black inner city life. The glossary appended to define terms for the unschooled deepened the work's stance as popular ethnography. At its heart, however, *Pimp* is a bildungsroman where psychological and moral growth happens in a world that inverts normative social values. Bobby, Young Blood, Iceberg Slim are all names indicating the stages of the protagonist's growth on the streets. He has left the South with parents seeking respite from racism, and Bobby's father cares more for developing the image of a city slicker than for his son, and abandons the family. His mother marries then leaves a solid churchgoing man, Henry Upshaw, the owner of a cleaning store, for a con man and life in Chicago. The son's choices and hatred of women are blamed on the mother's betrayals, most strongly indicated in a recurring dream sequence where Slim is dwarfed and encouraged by a giant Christ to punish an evil woman using a barbed leather whip. Only when the woman is knee-deep in a river of blood does he realize it is his mother. Black masculinity is the most precious currency in his world, and Bobby is educated by other men. He learns the skills of successful pimping, a toxic blend of charm, physical brutality, and psychological abuse. The novel's voice is one of sensational description paired with analysis. In keeping with the genre of confessional narrative, the preface promises to introduce the reader to the hidden and repulsive world of the pimp, but also hints at a mission of instruction, saving intelligent young men or women from the life they are about to encounter. The epilogue notes that Slim has come to reject the life that the majority of the novel portrays. Details are given and then surrounded by context so that the reader may understand the world not just watch the events. The appeal of *Pimp* is threefold. Audiences with backgrounds similar to Beck's for the first time see themselves in literature; others experience thrills through voyeurism; still others feel they have gained valuable sociological enlightenment.

Because *Pimp* straddles the line between autobiography and fiction, it might be argued that in the strictest sense *Trick Baby* is Beck's first novel. The narration is reminiscent of 1940s pulp fiction. The protagonist John Patrick O'Brien is the child of his black mother Phala and a white man. His enemies give him the nickname he abhors, Trick Baby, because denizens in his Chicago Southside neighborhood assume that he is the result of his mother's liaison with a client, in spite of his denials that his mother and father were married. His friends call him "White Folks," because he is a dead ringer for Errol Flynn. Told as a frame tale, White Folks shares his life story with Slim while both are in jail. Passing is the ultimate con for White Folks and the ultimate revenge. After his mother is rendered insane following a gang rape, he attempts to forget by drinking. He gets into a fight with a bar patron, and is beaten and thrown out because he is thought white. It is then that he meets Blue, so named because he is so black he is blue. He anchors White Folks to the black community, and they begin their lives as con men. The death of Blue at the behest of an Italian crime boss they have crossed "liberates" White Folks to pursue revenge using all the talents his appearance has given him. His goal is to learn the cons of the white world and infiltrate that society totally. The story of how he does so forms the subject of the 1977 sequel, *Long White Con.*

Mama Black Widow (1969) is Beck's most innovative novel. It centers on Otis Tilson, a homosexual drag queen, who struggles to deny who he is and conform to societal and religious norms. Again there is a problematic mother figure, Sedalia. Her physical and emotional abuse of both her husband and two children lays the decline of the family at her feet, and the abuse is implied as the source of an emasculation that renders Otis queer. Northern migration again is the catalyst for the family's degeneration. While they were poor in Mississippi in the father Frank's eyes, they lived honestly. Once they receive an inheritance, Sedalia insists the family move to Chicago, and everyone views this as positive change except for Frank who has a sense of foreboding. Sedalia seeks the consumerist ideal she sees enjoyed by her urban cousin Bunny, and when Frank is unable to land work because of union discrimination, she becomes the economic head of the family. Since money is power, Sedalia feels she need no longer care about Frank's feelings and she flaunts an affair with a local minister, and denies Frank access to her sexually. In effect, she prostitutes herself and emasculates him. The novel links maleness to social and economic power, and implies that women wielding such power are aberrations, particularly dangerous to black masculinity. Black men are the victims and that status rationalizes their being victimizers. Only years later does Otis realize his mother's behavior stems from the toll working for whites has taken on her. Sedalia's impact on Otis results in the creation of Sally, a persona who mediates between the often brutal sex he has with abusive men and his fragile psyche that cannot fully accept his homosexuality. The portrait of Otis is in the main homophobic, but at moments acknowledges a spectrum within sexual identity. Otis cannot situate himself in one definition, and his secreted sexuality leaves him victim to rape, physical abuse, and wretched attempts to be straight.

Trick Baby would be adapted for film by Universal Pictures, a subject discussed in a subsequent chapter, and Beck went on to publish a collection of essays *The Naked Soul of Iceberg Slim* (1971) and make a spoken-word LP, *Reflections* (1976), which consisted of recitations of his prose while the legendary Red Holloway Quartet played jazz. The revival of black pulp fiction in the 1980s and 1990s is largely due to Beck's influence on rappers such as Ice-T, Snoop Dogg, Ice Cube, and Jay-Z, who recognized worlds similar to their own in his depictions of street life. In 2011 a partnership between Cash Money Content (the publishing venture of Cash Money Records, home to recording celebrities Nikki Minaj, Drake, and Lil' Wayne) and Simon and Schuster reissued *Trick Baby* and *Long White Con*, testament to their appeal to a new generation. Beck himself became the subject of a highly revisionist documentary, *Iceberg Slim: Portrait of a Pimp*, executive produced by Ice-T. Its nostalgia is evident in its gathering of interviews with Iceberg Slim, his wife and daughters, and in the talking heads analysis of Chris Rock, Henry Rollins, Ice-T, Snoop Dogg, and Quincy Jones.

Beck had many admirers, and one was Donald Goines. Born in Detroit in 1937, Goines did not share the impoverishment of Beck's developmental years but saw the experiences of the less-fortunate all around him. His family was lower-middle class but stable, owning their own dry-cleaning business. The heroin habit he acquired during military service initiated his criminal activity. While in prison Goines discovered the fiction of Iceberg Slim, and Goines would transform his own addiction, robberies, and jail time into *Dopefiend* (1971), an autobiographical novel that would sell well during the 1960s and 1970s as heroin was ravishing many black urban neighborhoods. When he was released in 1970, he had a contract with Holloway House to publish the manuscript *Whoreson*, but the novel's debut was delayed, and instead, *Dopefiend* appeared. In it, Teddy and his girlfriend Terry fall from middle-class stability and succumb to heroin addiction, becoming cons and prostituting themselves to support their habits. Goines does not skimp on repulsive details. The more desperate his characters, the more they are willing to let themselves be violated by their pusher Porky who extorts sex and acts of degradation for his drugs. In one instance he forces an addict to perform oral sex on his dog. Terry's subsequent madness, and the many other scenes of horror, become a manifesto of the devastating effects of heroin on black personal and communal health.

Whoreson, the Story of a Ghetto Pimp appeared in (1972), and one can see Goines's debt to Beck. Whoreson Jones is the son of a prostitute, Jessie, by her white john. She names him so he can never forget what he is. She is a problematic mother figure, not unlike those found in the Iceberg Slim series, who marks her son with a name that permanently marginalizes him, and subsequently schools him on how to be a successful pimp by making sure he knows how to gain the most monetary advantage from women's bodies. Their relationship is further complicated by an intimacy that flirts with being incestuous. The novel is deterministic. Mother and son are products of a world where the choices for survival involve obsequious employment or transgression of social norms. They choose the latter. After *Dopefiend* (1971) and *Whoreson*, Goines wrote *Black Gangster*, which Holloway House published in the summer of 1972. The protagonist Melvin "Prince" Walker is a former prison convict who uses the language of the Black Power Movement to run his con and take over Detroit's black underworld. His cohorts, the Rulers, work under the guise of the Freedom Now Liberation Movement and manipulate young people's desire for social change into gang activity. The novel's explosive crescendo grows as neighborhood acts of violence threaten to destroy Detroit's inner city, and it realistically foreshadows the black-on-black violence in approaching decades.

In the next two years, Goines's would write eight novels of lesser quality than his earlier works. *Black Gangster* (1972), *Eldorado Red* (1974), and *Never Die Alone* (1974) take as their general theme the rise of a black crime lord, his demise, and the destruction left in his wake. In *Swamp Man* (1973), George Jackson seeks revenge for the death of his father and rape of his sister by Southern white racists. *White Man's Justice, Black Man's Grief* (1973) is a prison novel. In 1974 Goines shifted directions and created the Kenyatta series: *Crime Partners* (1974), *Death List* (1974), *Kenyatta's Escape* (1974), and *Kenyatta's Last Hit* (1975). Their hero – named after Jomo Kenyatta, Kenya's independence movement leader and first president – was a Detroit revolutionary who used organized violence to rid the black community of its biggest nemeses, dealers, and racist white police. The series along with another work *Cry Revenge* (1974) were written under the pseudonym Al Clark, borrowed from a childhood friend. Over the course of Goines's works, the pimp-hero transitions into a more positive figure.

The violence that Goines spent much of his life portraying in fiction arrived on his own doorstep on October 21, 1974, when he and his partner Shirley Sailor were brutally shot. Their children were spared and locked in a basement. The crime is still unsolved with wide-ranging speculation that it was a drug-related killing, revenge for modeling a character on a figure from Detroit's underworld, or a robbery because of his fame as an author.

Beck and Goines validate street values, arguing that to imagine progress under consistent deprivation is impossible when one cannot see a wider world beyond the limitation of a few square blocks. While they are perhaps the two most famous Holloway House writers, there were others throughout the 1970s, some who took the genre beyond the parameters of street fiction. Odie Hawkins wrote more than twenty novels, as well as short story collections, television scripts, and radio programs. Hailing from the South Side of Chicago, he moved to Los Angeles in the early 1960s where he became a member of both the Watts Writers' Workshop and the Open Door Program, co-created by Harlan Ellison, that briefly welcomed Octavia Butler, Stanley Crouch, and Quincy Troupe, among others. His first novel *Ghetto Sketches* (1972) portrays a black neighborhood in a single day. It was influenced by the way Dylan Thomas's play *Under Milk Wood* (1954) brought the thoughts and aspirations of small-town Wales residents to life. Pimps and prostitutes people *Ghetto Sketches*, but so do less sensational denizens. A reader of Langston Hughes, Zora Neale Hurston, Richard Wright, James Baldwin, Fyodor Dostoevsky, and Leo Tolstoy, writing for Hawkins represented an alternative to other street options. What attracted him to Holloway House was its reach, the possibility of taking advantage of their connection to a constituency for whom he wanted to write: convicts, people in his family, the black population in the urban centers of Chicago, Detroit, and New York (Gifford 216). His fiction has a wide range from works that are clearly street fiction, *Chicago Hustle* (1987), to those written by an alter ego, Chester L. Simmons: *Chester L. Simmons: The Great Lawd Buddha* (1990) and *The Life and Times of Chester L. Simmons* (2012). *Secret Music* (2012) and *Menfriends* (1989) consist of sketches of characters Hawkins observed in life and are deft in their evocation of many cultural voices. He also wrote *Hollow Daze* (2013), a satire of Holloway House and its white writers trying to ghostwrite "urban" fiction, as well as the speculative fiction works *Mr. Bonobo Bliss: aka Bo* (2007) and *Lady Bliss* (2007). Many of his novels interconnect, telling the backstories of different characters at different points. Craft is important to Hawkins, and his works are very conscious of their artistry. He tried to avoid the two-dimensionality of characters and thinness of dialogue that sometimes characterized Beck and Goines. He saw pulp fiction as people's fiction and tried to broaden its form and content.

Joseph Nazel also had roots in Holloway House. He succeeded Wanda Coleman as editor of *Players*. Under his vision, the magazine expanded its content to include black history and politics. Nazel sought to move the magazine away from its blaxploitation origins where whites were marketing and sometimes ghost-creating black experience for profit, but his initiatives were not always welcomed by the ownership of Holloway House. A writer who could pen a novel in six weeks, Nazel authored romance novels, histories, biographies of Richard Pryor, Ida B. Wells, B. B. King, Langston Hughes, Paul Robeson, and Magic Johnson, among others. Over the body of his work, a concern for recasting black life in a positive light is evident. His Iceman series added glamour to 1960s black pulp, by charting the transformation of a street hustler into a self-made millionaire playboy unafraid of taking on domestic or international crime collectives and reminiscent of James Bond. Another series, James Rhodes, centered on a black police detective seeking to rid the community of corrupt politicians and drug lords. Nazel's works took the fantasy of the potent black male and extended their class dimension to include a professor of comfortable means and status in *Delta Crossing* (1984) who seeks to document the untold story of blues music and culture but gets more painful information than he anticipated. Always commercially savvy, Nazel published blackened versions of white pop culture, *The Black Exorcist* (1974), for example, that in timely fashion capitalized on the blockbusters *The Exorcist*, book (1971) and movie (1973).

Over the course of the 1960s to 1970s, images of black male power became less destructive and more protective. Heroes who were black and militant countered the sources of black exploitation. They were born out of the anger that fueled the riots of Watts, Newark, and Detroit, and they justified black violence in light of failed civil rights and black consciousness advocacy. The two main characters of Omar Fletcher's *Black Against the Mob* (1977) and *Walking Black and Tall* (1977) are Tyrone Abraham Jones and Omar Nusheba. Tyrone's parents have been murdered by white policemen during the Newark riots, and together they exact revenge on police and the white syndicate. The theme that only blacks can save blacks is carried through to Fletcher's later novels. *Miss Annie* (1978) is about a well-meaning white schoolteacher who cannot reach her students because she only sees them as children of the ghetto. In his black samurai series, Marc Olden creates American G.I. Robert Sand who learns the ways of Master Konuma and the ancient secrets of the samurai to battle evil. Fletcher and Olden heroes take back power from institutional forces, whether they be legal (the police), illegal (the Italian syndicate), or quietly malignant (an educational system failing those it teaches); and they embody international action and adventure. They are indicative of black pulp expanding beyond pimping and drugs.[3]

Black pulp experienced a renaissance in the Reagan era, fueled by the ascendancy of commercial rap. 1980s novels shared much with their 1960s predecessors, but also exhibited the traits of their own time. Like their musical counterparts, they hyperbolized celebrations of capitalist entre-preneurialism conveyed through adapted rags-to-riches metaphors of rising from "the hood" to pecuniary success and excess. Where the streets in 1960s pulp were most often sites of peril, the hood in 1980s pulp evinces a duality. It is represented as both a place to escape, but it was also a place of "realness." There is as much danger in forgetting its lessons as there is in falling prey to it. Incarnations of "gangsta" characters for whom every-thing is a commodity fill what has come to be known by the diverse terms "urban fiction," "street lit," "ghetto fiction," "ghetto lit," "gangsta lit," and "hip hop fiction." While even a generous reader would find most of these novels wanting as literature, some are more readable than others, and the genre appeals to a significant readership. Many explore tensions stem-ming from class stratification. They portray worlds where surveillance and pat-downs are more frequent than board meetings, and they measure one set of values against another. If Trey Ellis's comments in "The New Black Aesthetic" that the Cosby girls were as authentically black as the welfare mother were meant to diversify representations of blackness to include a privileged class, contemporary black pulp ensures that the hood is not left out of this diversification.

Many writers of later black pulp fiction reiterate the masculinist cen-trality of Robert Beck and Donald Goines. Kwame Teague, writing from prison while serving sentences for kidnapping, armed robbery, and two counts of murder, crafted *The Adventures of Ghetto Sam*, about Sam Black's battles with the US government and a multinational. His *Glory of My Demise*, a "tour" through the ghetto told from interior and exterior per-spectives, afforded him his widest audience yet (both were published in a single edition in 2003), and *Dutch I* (2001) with its drug lord protagonist, is considered a classic of street lit. It is the inaugural volume in the trilogy including *Dutch II* (2005) and *Dutch III, The Finale* (2011). K'wan Foye is another writer who began his career in prison. His characters in *Gangsta: An Urban Tragedy* (2002), which is largely autobiographical, *Black Lotus* (2014), and *Eve* (2006), are an O.G. (Original Gangsta) assassin, a detec-tive who operates in gray ethical territories, and a female thug, respectively.

Many women have now come to the genre that in the past had been dominated by men. Among the most popular is Vickie Stringer whose works include *The Reason Why* (2009) and *Let That Be the Reason* (2002). Though she came from middle-class antecedents, a love affair with a drug dealer led to her dropping out of college, but when her lover left her for another woman, her lavish lifestyle ended abruptly. She was pregnant and to support herself became a prostitute, facilitated prostitution, and sold drugs, leading to a prison sentence. While incarcerated she began writing and turned her life around. Her works often engage class slippage, as a character, often female from middle-class beginnings, becomes immersed in the gangsta life. Terri Woods is another prominent woman writer whose offerings include *True to the Game* (2010) and *Deadly Reigns: The First of a Trilogy* (2005). She worked as a legal secretary while writing, and sold copies of what would become her best seller out of the trunk of her car. She and Stringer are also publishers, Woods of Teri Woods Publishing and Stringer of Triple Crown Publications, named after her former Detroit gang, the Triple Crown Posse. The emergence of independent houses for these works is an unforeseen manifestation of cries for black publishing envisioned during the Black Arts Movement. As much as Dudley Randall's Broadside Press did, these houses also tell the stories of their readers, an audience not addressed by other outlets; equally as important, they generate the dollars that keep a book culture viable. As can be seen from their titles, many books such as the self-styled Queen of Hip-Hop literature Nikki Turner's *A Hustler's Wife* (2003), *A Project Chick* (2014), *The Glamorous Life* (2005), and *Girls from Da Hood* (2006) recast male dominance as female, but others exhibit an urban feminism that to some degree replicates the black womanist movement of two decades before. Sister Souljah and Sapphire are examples of writers who gender the street.

Born in the Bronx, New York, and reared in the projects, her family moved to Englewood, New Jersey. She graduated from Rutgers University earning degrees in American History and African Studies, then went on to study abroad in Russia, Spain, Portugal, England, France, and Finland. Well known as an MC and rapper, she gained even greater prominence after presidential candidate Bill Clinton, for his own political purposes, repudiated her tongue-in-cheek suggestion that those committing black-on-black violence should take a reprieve by directing their attention to whites. The incident created a furor and contributed a new phrase to American lexicon, the Sister Souljah moment, meaning a politician's bravery in repudiating possible constituents.[4] Her novel *The Coldest Winter Ever* (1999) is one of the works largely credited with launching the street lit renaissance.

Published under Simon and Schuster's Atria imprint, *Coldest Winter* follows Winter Santiaga, the teenage daughter of a New York drug dealer. The title refers to her birth in one of the city's worst winter storms and to the self-centered morals that lead her to follow a me-first sensibility. The materialism of the Santiaga world is indicated through the naming of her sisters Porsche, Lexus, and Mercedes. Women in this world are beautiful commodities lending status to male identity. Her father relocating his family and business empire to Long Island places her in a world whose codes Winter does not know. The move also draws increased police attention leading to his arrest. The downfall of his empire further unmoors Winter. Her sisters are split up in the child services system, but by pretending not to be part of the family, Winter avoids this fate and eventually returns to the world she knows where she lives by her father's codes. Though it is difficult for Winter to leave her street instincts behind, her redemption commences once she meets Sister Souljah, a fictional avatar of the author, who through her lyrics coming over a radio, or through her conversation with Winter serves as a moral refrain throughout the novel. After a mandatory 15-year prison sentence for transporting drugs, Winter begins to rethink what dignity and beauty mean.

Coldest Winter's argument against capitalistic materialism continues through. Souljah's next two novels *Midnight: A Gangster Love* (2008) and *Midnight and the Meaning of Love* (2011). Both tell of Midnight, one of Santiaga's lieutenants. We learn he is actually the privileged son of a prominent Islamic Sudanese family. His father's disappearance uproots the family and forces the move to the United States where Midnight survives and protects his family the best way he can. With international characters and settings beyond the urban streets, Souljah desires this novel to be larger than the category urban, and to be seen as global (Patrick 25). Winter and Midnight contrast African Islamic values with the licentiousness and runaway materialism of the United States. His restraint is in contrast to Winter's hedonism. Her ease with doing whatever it takes to achieve material comfort is in sharp relief to his struggle as he reclaims economic status but compromises religious principle. *A Deeper Love Inside: The Porsche Santiaga Story* (2012) returns to the Santiaga family and the struggle to regain the family's wealth. Souljah repudiates the street's hyper-commodification by showing how materialism threatens black identity and healthy self-perception. Winter is akin to other characters in women's street lit who have adopted the codes of their male counterparts to achieve power and economic independence, but in Souljah's vision, these codes are not sustainable. Her metapresence in the novel provides a backdrop against which street tenets can be critiqued.

Like Souljah, Sapphire, born Ramona Lawson, deepens the content of street fiction and expands its form. A child of military parents, Lawson lived in California, Texas, and West Germany, and briefly attended San Francisco City College. In the 1970s she changed her name to Sapphire, referencing the stereotype of the quarrelsome black woman for three reasons: to counter the submissiveness she saw in her creative and beautiful mother, to evoke the New Age belief in the power of the stone to effect spiritual change, and because the stone's color evokes the blues (M. Wilson 31). Throughout the 1970s, Sapphire worked at writing poetry, becoming a member of the Nuyorican Poets Café, and developing her skills as a spoken word poet, an act that would influence the rhythm and phrasing of her novels. She earned a bachelor's degree from the City College of New York, and received the MacArthur Foundation Scholarship in Poetry. Prior to the publication of her fiction, her poetry received popular attention when conservative politicians enlisted her poem "Wild Thing" in their campaign to decrease funding to government arts institutions. Re-imagining the 1989 brutal beating and rape of a white Central Park jogger, the poem's persona is a rapist suffocated by lack of education, street values, and the valorization of whiteness. An image involving Jesus and oral sex used to represent a minister's child sexual abuse was taken out of context and made an example of the inappropriate material the National Endowment for the Arts was supporting.[5] Further controversy came with the publication of her first novel in 1996.

As a social activist, Sapphire sent copies of *Push* to prisons, to the head of the Centers for Disease Control and Prevention, universities, and even to then First Lady Hillary Clinton, in the hope that fiction could awaken policymakers to the situation in which many impoverished, abused, and socially dismissed women find themselves. As a writer, she hoped that *Push* would read beyond its potential for social change and for its portrayal of writing and art as vehicles of self-expression (M. Wilson 31). In the format of a journal, *Push* is the painful story of Claireece Precious Jones, her rape by her father and pregnancy at twelve, and her continued abuse by her mother. To protect herself from the trauma of his sexual assault she disassociates. In her shifting fantasies she is a dancer in music videos, a movie actress, or on the stage of the Apollo. That this is the range of her imagination indicates how her world has been limited to the only options she sees in popular culture. Her illiteracy indicts a school system that has allowed her to matriculate to the ninth grade barely able to read (she should be in the eleventh) and suspends her for being pregnant. Her obesity and HIV-positive status raise questions about public health education and resources. When she enrolls in an alternative school, she meets a committed teacher, Ms. Rain, who encourages her to write, and her journal allows her to bring

about self-awareness. The language of the novel, its phonetic approximations of words, its misspellings and malapropisms, is consonant with her
experience. As she grows, her mode of expression grows as well. When
traveling to another part of the city, she writes a poem noting its contrasts,
and personifies herself as Homer on an odyssey going from the rubble of
bricks that used to be buildings, to middling buildings, to grand buildings
in a "different" city, though it is the same city (126–127).

Claireece's ownership of *The Color Purple* and the discussion of the
novel within this novel, along with her sexual abuse, the act of writing,
and her questioning the existence of God, create immediate parallels to
Alice Walker's work; but *Push* also alludes to a broader tradition of black
letters. Like slave narrators Claireece finds voice and humanity in writing her life-story and self-knowledge in framing her thoughts. Her psychological escapism recalls Pecola Breedlove's rape by her father and the
fatal escapism of blue-eyed dreaming. The effect of her journal keeping
is similar to Jefferson's notebook in *A Lesson Before Dying*. The novel's
ending with an anthology is further testament to the power of collective
stories, particularly those that have generally not been given access to
formal records. Women of abuse, women of color, now have their own
text, and seeing their experiences in the written world confers formalized
validation.

For many, the situations Claireece endures are still current, and *Push*
was not meant to be a feel good story of uplift, but the story of one woman
told in the hopes of enacting change. Sapphire's second novel reminds
readers of that. *The Kid* (2011) resists the myth of a happy ending. It continues Claireece's story with her son Abdul being orphaned by his mother's
death from AIDS. Told in stream of consciousness that blends dialogue,
conversation, and fantasy, the prose represents Abdul's confused state of
mind. He has been shunted from one home to the next, passed around
in the foster care system, and not even allowed to keep his own name. At
a Catholic school he attends, he receives the education his mother would
have wanted for him, but is also abused by the brothers, a lesson he learns
well enough to pass on to smaller boys. Dance initially promises him the
salvation writing gave his mother, but this hope is extinguished by a dance
teacher giving him shelter for sex. The common denominator of sexual
abuse undoes his promise. A village can raise a child but it can also ruin
one. In an interview Sapphire has said that she wrote the novel so that the
mainstream might connect to the marginalized. To see the connections, to
own the evil collectively, leads to change (McNeill 352). Abdul is a shared
creation of a world that fails to protect its most vulnerable.

While Sapphire's work has been subject to criticisms of inappropriate or extreme racial representations, its academic reception has brought about a reconsideration of the street lit genre. In 2007 Arizona State University convened a symposium "PUSHing Boundaries, PUSHing Art," which showed the many engagements of the novel in other fields: blues scholarship, foodways scholarship, and developments in feminist thought.[6] Sapphire and Sister Souljah signal that the line between popular and canonical black literature is blurred, not the least by shared themes and referents. The nebulousness of classification criteria and the more serious consideration given to pulp or street fiction still spawns debate, however. Journalist and author Nick Chiles sees street fiction as a product of publishers wishing to cash in on the glamorization of black pathology. Not mentioning Sapphire or Souljah, he expresses resentment that book dealers frequently do not distinguish street lit from African American literature. His list of authors under the latter heading includes those deemed writers of serious literature and also those some define as popular. He mentions Toni Morrison and Edward P. Jones, and he also includes Terry McMillan and Yolanda Joe (Chiles n. pag.). While the line between the street lit of K'wan or Teri Woods and serious literature might be relatively self-evident, Chiles's listing points to the more difficult endeavor of categorizing the novels of Eric Jerome Dickey, E. Lynn Harris, and Omar Tyree. Many Dickey and Tyree novels incorporate the action adventure of pulp, but they are generally classed under the larger umbrella of popular literature as relationship fiction, as are the novels of E. Lynn Harris who extends his portraits to gay relationships.

Former teacher, stand-up comedian, screenplay writer, and anthologist, Eric Jerome Dickey has a range of novels from those centering on relationships to those embodying action and exoticism. *A Wanted Woman* (2014), for instance, is the story of an assassin, Reaper, who botches her job. *Sleeping with Strangers* (2007) describes an impending clash between two assassins Gideon (who took his name from the Bible the preacher he killed was holding) and Bruno. Dickey's first novel, however, *Sister, Sister* (1996) announced that Dickey would make relationship fiction a cornerstone. His characters are generally young, generally black, frequently middle-class or wealthy. His plots involve the tangles of interrelationships, and his urban is urbane California and New York. Many have erotic elements but rarely sexual violence, and generally sex is an avenue along which the search for true love is followed. Reflections on police brutality, child custody, and conflicts within the black diaspora in *Liar's Game* are interlaced with the story of tenuous love. Always there is a balance between "low" and "high" cultures.

The main character's quest in *Thieves' Paradise* transitions from the streets to the academy. Most works, however, treat a range of interpersonal relationships. *The Other Woman* and *Genevieve* warn of the consequences of marital infidelity and betrayal, while *Between Lovers* (2001) broaches the traditional love triangle but considers it in terms of heterosexual and homosexual love. *Liar's Game* (2000), *Thieves' Paradise* (2002), *The Other Woman* (2003), and *Genevieve* (2005) were nominated for the NAACP Image Awards, something that would have been unlikely for most writers of early pulp or street lit. Though varied in subjects, the overwhelmingly middle-class sensibilities and implicitly firm family and moral standards allow them to conform to the expectations of a readership that eschews racier subject matter.

Where homosexuality in earlier pulp was treated as an aberration, in his novels E. Lynn Harris brings black gay fiction out of the closet. Also a winner of three NAACP Image Awards, Harris's novels exhibit a moral center as characters struggle with questions of ethics and fidelity. *Invisible Life* is the first of three novels that follows Raymond Tyler, Jr. as he grows from being a successful scholar athlete to successful attorney. Moving from south to north, from relationships with women to relationships with men, Ray is a figure exploring the conflicts posed for some by oversimplifications of sexual identity. The novel underscores paternal legacy and masculinity through internal and external conflicts as Ray comes to terms with his sexuality and the expectations of his father and his social world.

Over the course of Harris's next novel *Just as I Am* (1994), the homo- and bisexual phobia of black communities, colorism, the pressures of living in the closet or on the down-low, and the dangers secretive behaviors pose to physical and mental health, are all explored. The character John Basil Henderson, handsome National Football League star is so closeted he commits a hate assault on an openly gay man who has made a pass at him. Ray defends him and in the process experiences a crisis of conscience wanting Henderson to own up to his truth yet being constrained as his lawyer. Common themes and repeated characters give Harris's works a sense of continuity. All stress the importance of finding meaningful relationships across lines of sex, and all examine the intersections of race, masculinity, culture, and sexuality. Harris crafts novels that not only portray gay love in traditionally romantic ways, they also blend writing and memorial through their capturing the very personal ramifications of the AIDS epidemic of the 1980s and 1990s.

Though having ten *New York Times* bestsellers, in interviews Harris has said that he realizes his audience does not read *The New York Times*, and that the *Times* has not deigned to give his work even a bad review. Harris knows his readers care far more about the opinion of "Ms. Sarah down the road" than Michiko Kakutani, the *Times* book reviewer (Quart 45). To sell his work, he went straight to his core, offering the self-published *Invisible Life* from the trunk of his car, and distributing it in the manner of early pulp fiction at barbershops, beauty salons, and independent bookstores. In 1994 Anchor-Doubleday added it to its trade paperback list, and Harris would publish twelve books with them.

Like E. Lynn Harris, Omar Tyree built his career on self-publishing until Simon and Schuster released his first novel *Flyy Girl* in 1995. Like Harris, he also received an NAACP Image Award for Outstanding Literary Work of Fiction for his novel *For the Love of Money* (2000). *Flyy Girl* and its sequel *For the Love of Money* depict the development of Tracy Ellison Grant from her teen years, though her struggles to find a solid relationship, and her finally becoming a successful author. In an attempt to go beyond the description of writing relationship novels, Tyree treats different subject matter with each novel. *Single Mom* (1998) and its description of Denise Stewart's self-education and determination to leave the inner city for the suburbs of Chicago contemplates black men in the familial context. *Pecking Order* (2008) examines the dangers of ambition, as does *Just Say No!* (2001).

Tyree seeks to make reading a meaningful act among black men, a group he feels does not read enough (Brett Johnson n. p.). In an attempt to reach this male audience, he has adopted the pen name Urban Griot and composed works whose urban locales and gritty culture align them more with street fiction. These include *Cold Blooded* (2004) and *Underground* (2001). *The Last Street Novel* (2007), as its name implies, offers a fictionalized portrait of Tyree's coming to his present views on the role of writing. In it Shareef Crawford is a celebrated writer of relationship fiction living in a mansion in South Florida with his wife and children. He feels stuck, stifled, and pigeonholed as a writer of women's fiction. He adopts the pseudonym Street King and returns to his petty street thug past to write a true crime book that will attract male readers. Tyree's desire for a male audience is paralleled by his desire for critical recognition. While he enjoys popular success, he seeks the critical treatment that has been accorded Paul Beatty and Colson Whitehead (Brett Johnson n. pag.), though this has not been forthcoming. Whatever the responses are to his literature, his literacy efforts deserve note. He builds audience from the ground up by writing young adult literature, and he launched the Urban Literacy Project in his hometown of Philadelphia to sponsor lectures, panel discussions, and performances, to encourage the spread of reading and talking about writing.

In African American pulp and popular literature, aesthetics are still often politicized. The different voices reflected in 1960s pulp, street lit, and popular literature represent different class and moral interests seeking expression. In that sense these are among the most democratic of literary genres, not only for the access they provide to differing sensibilities, but also for the access they provides to writers through self-publishing, e-texts, and hand-to-hand circulation. Pulp and popular books represent a different kind of black power, the power of production, purveyance, and consumption. Triple Crown founded by Victoria Stringer published *Let That Be the Reason*, which went on to be a *New York Times* best seller. Kimberla Lawson Roby who published her debut novel *Behind Closed Doors* (1997) through her own company Lenox Press would go on to write the *New York Times* bestselling Reverend Curtis Black series, the saga of the womanizing minister of a prominent black church. Similar enterprises include Good2Go Publishing, Urban Books, The Cartel Publications, and husband and wife duo Ashley and JaQuavis Coleman have independently published and sold over fifty titles under the Ashley and JaQuavis brand. The collective impact of these presses resulted in established publishers responding by creating their own imprints: Atria, G Unit Books (Simon and Schuster), One World (Ballentine/Random House), and Old School Books (W. W. Norton).[7] While critical response to their products vary, these presses and the authors they sponsor signal new contributions to the mix of black print culture.

Questions of representations of the race still hover, but the expansion of this genre indicates a lessening concern with how the race is viewed by an outside readership. Popular novels are more concerned with portraying moral, middle-class black life to its own community, and pulp openly defies the politics of uplift. Both ends of the continuum argue not necessarily for moving their constituents to the center of a preconceived spectrum, but for seeing them as their own centers. Pulp and popular novels celebrate the hidden or ignored, whether they be denizens of the street or gays in romantic relationships. The readership of these genres continues to expand precisely because these novels reflect contrasting values and views in the African American social sphere.

CHAPTER 12

The Black Graphic Novel

Black graphic novels crystallize the difficulty in defining what is a black novel. Earlier, this book asked is a novel black because of its content? Because of its writer? These questions become even more complicated because graphic novels are mostly collaborations. The genre often begins with a conversation or exchange of ideas between writer and illustrator, followed by the creation of text and panels and perhaps more co-editing and collaboration. Sometimes the project is passed on to others who handle the tone and color of the pictures, the lettering of the text, and overall design. The works discussed in this chapter represent this collaborative process and do so frequently across lines of race, gender, and sometimes national borders. The resulting visual styles are quite varied, but they share familiar patterns of inquiry and a rooting in traditions of black culture.

The genesis of black graphic novels represents an ongoing engagement of visual culture by black writers. The dialectic between text and image has long generated a means for black creators to explore and redefine what it means to be black. From the nineteenth through twenty-first centuries, writers composed in an increasingly optic culture, and it is no surprise that their works embrace visual culture to provide texture and trope. Portraiture in narratives of the enslaved, photo essays, novels whose font formats are key to their themes, and finally graphic novels are examples of iconography used to question the vacillations within a perceived collective identity.

When one looks at the terms used to talk about visual elements in literature, they seem tailor-made for a canon heavily focused on seeing and perception, where the very concept of representation is central to narratives of race and culture. Evocative terms such as "the panoptic," "scopic regimes," "the spectacle," and "surveillance" seem to beg to be applied to works with titles referencing seeing, color, and perception such as *The Autobiography of an Ex-Coloured Man*, *Their Eyes Were Watching God*, *The Bluest Eye*, and *The Color Purple*. Blackness is at its origins a visually defined quality. The lived experience of being black is constructed through the valuations given to seen phenotypic traits and sustained through, among other modes, visual manifestations. Black literature has consistently offered commentary on the meaning of blackness by questioning the relationship of what is seen to what is. The logical extension and the literal manifestation of such commentary is the graphic novel.

Because visual culture in black literature reflects the many debates of self-identification among those raced as black, black graphic novels inherit the many traditions of image manipulation found in black writing that include the incorporation of portraits, the manipulation of font and margins to form ideographs, and the use of the visual thematically. In the nineteenth-century writing of the enslaved, accompanying portraits were employed to counter prevailing notions of black inferiority. Through the 1920s and 1940s, images gracing the covers of *The Crisis* and *Opportunity* became means of signifying blackness as its own cultural identity and not solely a race in contestation with whiteness. Visual elements in literature of the late twentieth and early twenty-first centuries defy the concept of racial representation and create a visually configured diaspora, revealing an explicit assertion of multimodal black identity. To merge image and text confounds genre, and confounding genre confounds labels. Such strategy comes to represent a questioning of the larger idea of racial labeling whether imposed by a dominant culture, or by those insisting on a single authentic of blackness. To illuminate fully the artistry of black graphic novels, it is useful to consider how and why the visual has been incorporated into black writing.

The generic device of placing an image at the beginning of an autobiographical narrative was one way those who were formerly enslaved asserted full humanity and inserted themselves into established writing traditions. Phyllis Wheatley's *Poems on Various Subjects, Religious and Moral* (1773), Olaudah Equiano's *The Interesting Life of Olaudah Equiano* (1789), and Frederick Douglass's *The Narrative of Frederick Douglass* (1845) are just three of the many works accompanied by frontispieces of their authors' images to remind readers that a reasoning human being imparts the text's content. But image incorporation often went beyond the use of a portrait. The 1791 Dublin edition of Equiano's narrative includes the illustration "Bahama Banks, 1767," an engraving of a tall ship at full sail almost on its side in roiling waves, dark clouds and stormy sky behind it. The caption reads "Thus God speaketh once, yea twice, yet Man perceiveth it not. In a Dream, in a Vision of the Night when deep sleep falleth upon Men in slumberings upon the Bed, Then he openeth the Ears of Men, and sealeth their instruction. Job Chap 33. Ver.14.15.16. and 29. and 30" (203). The image and caption come after Equiano tells of unexpectedly saving the ship by clearing the shoals, an act which earns him the sobriquet "captain" (202). On the one hand, the illustration can be said to vivify his tale, but the import of the caption suggests a deeper interpretation, a caution of the dangers of slavery to souls and nations, a warning that comes from a black man acting as a moral guide.

David Walker's *Appeal, in Four Articles* (1830) similarly weds visual elements to words to create a cautionary black presence in written discourse. Walker, however, does not use illustrations; instead, he employs printer's symbols and font improvisation. The multiple manicules (☞) throughout *Appeal* literally point to the moral wrongs committed in the name of slavery. Twenty years after Walker's *Appeal* was published, William Wells Brown witnessed the exhibition "Panorama of the River Mississippi," which contained, according to Brown, highly sentimentalized images of slavery in the South. In response, he created a magic lantern exhibition designed to show the true nature of slavery through images.[1] The lantern slides do not survive, but descriptions of the illustrations commissioned by Brown from various artists were published in a pamphlet titled *A Description of William Wells Brown's Original Panoramic Views of the Scenes in the Life of an American Slave, from His Birth in Slavery to His Death or His Escape to His First Home of Freedom on British Soil* (1850). Among them, "View Second. Two Gangs of Slaves Chained and on their way to the Market – Cruel Separation of a Mother from her Child – White Slaves"; "View Third. The Capitol of the United States – A Public Meeting to Sympathize with the French Revolution"; "View Eleventh. Slaves Burying their Dead at Night by Torchlight" (7, 8, 19). As he made use of these in his abolitionist lectures, Brown became a multimedia artist, experimenting with the fusion of visual, aural, oral, and written. His graphic work disputed an idealized antebellum simulacra, to give a "correct idea of the 'Peculiar Institution'" (Brown iv).

Even Frederick Douglass, a writer who did not want illustrations to accompany his *Life and Times of Frederick Douglass* (1881), subtly uses graphics in his 1845 autobiography through typography.[2] When he includes parentheses around the phrase "speaking of my self" in the upcoming passage, the parens graphically signal the distance Douglass places between himself and his master Hugh Auld's use of the term "nigger" upon the latter's discovery that Douglass is being taught how to read:

> Mr. Auld found out what was going on, and at once forbade Mrs. Auld to instruct me further, telling her, ... "If you give a nigger an inch, he will take an ell. A nigger should know nothing but to obey his master – to do what he is told to do. Learning would spoil the best nigger in the world. Now," said he, "if you teach that nigger (speaking of myself) how to read, there would be no keeping him." (78)

In grammar, parentheses encase subordinate material; their appearance here, however, visually signals Douglass's resistance to this subordination. Parentheses convey his objection to Auld's contumely and, more importantly, his sense of himself as a man apart from the derogatory term.

Later works continue to highlight black text/image experimentation. Through pastel ochre pages, blue and brown lettering, and designs evoking a fusion of Pablo Picasso and Aaron Douglass to introduce its sections, Langston Hughes's *Ask Your Mama* (1971) foregrounds the variegations of culture undermined by monochromatic understandings of race. James Van Der Zee's *Harlem Book of the Dead* (1978) uses composite photographs to offer an interior reality of black life subverting superficial popular culture representations. As discussed in an earlier chapter, Toni Morrison manipulates fonts and margins to replicate communal narrative. In speaking of the format of her style in *For Coloured Girls*, Ntozake Shange notes her desire to change the act of reading through visually changing text: "I like the idea that letters dance, ... I need some visual stimulation, so that reading becomes not just a passive act and more than an intellectual activity, but demands rigorous participation" (Tate 163). The combination of text and image in black graphic novels continues this legacy of using visual elements to question ideologies and expand ideas of black representations. Discourses of white supremacy necessitated framed, stable, repeated images of black inferiority for their significance, but the visual in black novels undermines this. Where images in dominant discourse sought to limit blackness to a single meaning, black graphics invite myriad interpretations.

Not surprisingly, the flowering of black graphic novels occurs at a time when a generation of authors is conversing about essentialism, postblackness, and hybridity. Through opposing text and picture, graphic novels vivify the binaries these terms seek to interrogate whether they be black/white, high/low, self/other, reality/representational. Even the language characterizing their structure – margins, main bodies, gutters (the space between comic tiles) – are evocative. In graphic novels, everything is empowered to convey meaning, from actual images to lettering that forms visual puns.[3] Text and image in narrative counterpoint signal readers to many encoded meanings.

The debate continues whether to employ the term "comics" or "graphic novels," with strong feelings on both sides. Some feel that comics protests an implied elitism seeking to distinguish graphic novels from a form seen as juvenile entertainment. Others see graphic novel as an effort to have the genre taken seriously in literary circles and academic inquiry.[4] The terms "graphic work," "graphic narrative," "sequential art" have all been used to refer to book-length works employing pictures and words to convey a sustained story, whether the story was originally intended as a single volume, or was a compendium of separate issues. This study uses all these terms interchangeably because there is no strong consensus as to one or the other defining the genre. As used here, the terms imply no hierarchy. All writers working within this genre share making narrative through panels using techniques of multiple voices, tone, foreshadowing, varying vernaculars, and flashback. To these they add fading, dialogue balloons, gutters, and motion lines (also called movement lines, action lines, or zip ribbons), to make a body of literature incorporating the political social, and economic histories of lived blackness while also creating fresh cultural products.

The black sequential art tradition begins largely as a corrective to the miscasting and erasure of black cultural history. As early as 1940 independent historian J. A. Rogers, whose life's mission was to restore a black past, used the comic book format in penning *Your History: From Beginning of Time to the Present*, published by the Pittsburgh Courier Publishing Company. The trend of historical comics continued to the 1960s and 1970s with *The Saga of Harriet Tubman: The Moses of Her People* (1967), *Joseph Cinque and the Amistad Mutiny* (1970), and *The Saga of Toussaint L'Ouverture and the Birth of Haiti* (1966), three among the many titles offered by Golden Legacy Illustrated Magazines, published from 1966 to 1972 to "create an atmosphere of harmony and mutual respect between groups ... while replacing myths with an appreciation for the contributions of others."[5]

One of the most well-known African American sequential artists to contribute to the trend of historically based comics was Tom Feelings. Born and raised in Bedford Stuyvesant, Brooklyn, his interest in art was kindled by a black instructor at the Police Athletic League where he went for art classes. His study was interrupted when he joined the service, but when his tour ended he resumed study at School of Visual Arts in New York City where he recalls creating a comic strip based on a lynching, and his teacher's indirect response being that personal feelings have no place in a comic strip. Feelings, on the contrary, felt such personal feelings to be a vital part of his art. A 1961 trip South shaped his sense of what art was and could do. He subsequently produced drawings used in *Look* magazine's feature "The Negro in the US" (1961).

Feelings created the comic strip *Tommy Traveler in the World of Black History*, which ran in the Harlem newspaper, *The New York Age*. In 1991 it was published as a children's book by Black Butterfly Press. In it a young black boy who is angry over the absence of his people's presence in the public library, makes use of the private library of a black doctor. While reading, Tommy daydreams himself into the books' worlds (in one case imagining himself as Frederick Douglass doing battle with the slave breaker Covey). The figures he encounters are familiar black heroes, Crispus Attucks; re-contextualized heroes, Aesop, a well-known figure not popularly acknowledged as black; and the less well-known, Phoebe Fraunces, who helped her father run the Fraunces tavern and is said to have foiled a plan to poison George Washington. Tommy's encounter with Emmett Till foregrounds the lynched young man's life as opposed to his death. Feelings draws the interiority of Till's life but summarizes only in words, his execution. The inversion of emphasis is one means through which he gives black stories primacy over racist acts of hatred.

Feelings is an example of the range of graphic storytelling in the black tradition. In 1964 he left the United States for Ghana and became part of the "Afro" expatriate community while working for Ghana Government Publishing House and local Ghanaian newspapers as a staff illustrator. The impact of Ghana on his conception of diasporic history is seen in *The Middle Passage: White Ships, Black Cargo* (1995). *Middle Passage* is a collection of paintings created over the course of ten years and brought together in book form. When Feelings wrote the preface to his work, he harkened back to the influence of Ghana on the artwork: "I gained strength in my convictions, going out into the community of Accra, drawing all those places and faces my heart and eyes yearned to see and feel" (preface). The work is his visual contribution to chronicles of the transatlantic slave trade. Based on his research into written histories, his images provide an immediate sense of capture, transit, and eventual enslavement.

A work without text, the plates are rendered in grayscale tones and subtle blues. They open with scenes of idyll. In the first a man and a woman are drawn in dark relief against a pale rendering of a coast blending seamlessly into ocean and sky. Above the couple's head, painted in the manner of a watercolor are popular black American symbols frequently used to signify Africa: an antelope head, a mask, and fertility symbol. In the upper right corner a bird flies to a softly gleaming sun. The plate links the modern world in which Feelings creates to an imagined African past. The destruction of this Eden is depicted in subsequent plates showing uniformed European armies, guns in hand, attacking African villages. One shows the open mouth of an African in full scream at the bottom left corner; above it, a white European in a morion aims a carbine directly at the viewer/reader (see Figure 12.1). The effect magnifies the terror and inevitability of the attacker's power. While the European figure's face and

Figure 12.1 From *The Middle Passage: White Ships/Black Cargo*
by Tom Feelings, copyright 1995 by Tom Feelings.
Used by permission of Dial Books for Young Readers, an imprint
of Penguin Young Readers Group, a division of Penguin Random House LLC.

aimed gun are in sharp relief, the body dissolves, hovering cloud-like over the dwellings of an invaded village. The "cloud" covers and conquers. In the rear is a receding image of chained blacks being led by a soldier carrying an axe, while another follows behind the group of what are now slaves. Feelings also reworks images that may have become too familiar through over-reproduction. The now famous cross section of the slaver *Brookes* is rendered acutely human by being imbedded into a chained body, and the prows of vessels are transformed into grotesques of profiled faces of the screaming enslaved.

Feelings provides a broad view of enslavement. He does not idealize Africa as a conceptual homeland, but rather depicts the roles Africans played in the slave trade. One plate shows this involvement through tiered images. Along its bottom rendered in dark tones are slaves tied by rope to hewn stakes and above them rendered in slightly lighter tones, as if a dilution of blackness implies an increasing concentration of evil, is an African chief negotiating for the sale of slaves to Europeans who are drawn in a ghostly white. Scenes of resistance are also presented. In one a European who is about to brand a black woman, bare-breasted and on her knees, is caught by the neck from behind by an African man who has already killed one aggressor. Throughout the collection Africans are reflected in dark shaded drawings and the Europeans are contrasted in a ghostly white as they flog, brand, rape, compel to dance on a ship's deck, and subdue their captives. The physical barbarity as well as the psychological deviance of the system are shown in toto.

To Feelings, words seem the least appropriate medium for portraying this history. In contemplating how it was told he observes that "some of the writers' overbearing opinions, even religious rationalizations and arguments for the continuance of the slave trade made me feel, the more words I read, that I should try to tell this story with as few words as possible" (preface). He reverses historiography's emphasis on the text, and the underlying theme of *Middle Passage* is that words cannot do justice to the saga. Images vivify the anguish minimized in the three-word phrase "the middle passage." By the time of the work's publication in 1995 Feelings's "silent" images of enslavement were increasingly familiar. Lerone Bennett Jr.'s *Before the Mayflower* (1962), Ivan van Sertima's *They Came Before Columbus* (1976), and Haile Gerima's film *Sankofa* (1993) were among works that already visualized enslaved diaspora for a broad cultural audience. Feelings was able to use a well-known past to preserve history and encourage a better understanding of its role in shaping social and racial presents. Mat Johnson's *Incognegro* (2008) accomplishes something similar. It re-imagines a familiar past to examine constructions of race.

Illustrated by Warren Pleece, *Incognegro* invokes the experience of Walter White, the NAACP secretary who because of his appearance was able to pass for white and investigate lynchings. Its protagonist Zane leaves Harlem where he works as a reporter, heads south, and goes undercover or "Incognegro" (a pun on incognito) to expose the extent of the violent practice.[6] While doing so, he discovers that a soon-to-be victim is his own visibly black brother, Pinchy. In comic book form the novel details his attempts to save him, as well as the other forms of passing humans undertake: blacks passing as white, women passing as men. Johnson frequently juxtaposes tiles with dialogue balloons to those that are "silent" to pace the novel's plot. In its middle, for instance, after a series of tiles depicting the dangers of Zane's quest, is a respite showing the South's serenity. No words are used, just a picture of Zane riding in the wagon of a black man who has rescued him from a lynch mob. Their route takes them by a stream where a man is fishing, past a woman selling corn on a roadside. At the close of this sequence Zane comments, "I forgot about this too" (62). The panels' textual quiet offers a visual interlude, their lack of words making absent the discourse of hate.

Many graphic novels are drawn in black and white because color production is very expensive. This color scheme works particularly well in *Incognegro* where black and white panels illuminate the social construction of race. Pleece's illustrations force us to ask, how do we know which character is black and which is white? What are the sources of racial knowledge? When race is not readily apparent, what props do we search for to construct racial meaning? Only through taught cultural clues is it possible to intuit race from black and white drawings. In the opening panel, the book recreates the image of a lynching: a body, dressed in rags hangs from a tree; well-dressed voyeurs surround the site, and the facial features of all are similarly drawn (7). In the cultural discourse of the United States, the images of lynching victims were popularized through newspapers and even circulated postcards. More often than not the victim was a black male, and almost always the spectators were white, frequently dressed in hat and gloves (if women) and suit and ties (if men).[7] The many iterations of these images have assisted in fixing racial identities in the cultural imagination, so Johnson and Pleece are in no need of color to delineate race. Zane, Pinchy, and Klu Klux Klan members are all drawn the same color, and differentiation is accomplished only through context, presumption, and inference. Race is thus depersonalized and revealed for the dangerous construction that it is.

The institutionalized nature of race is evident in another graphic sequence that begins with a panel depicting individuals walking on a street and riding in a subway car. Their faces are clearly visible, and each is uniquely drawn. Some are dressed casually, others in office attire, and one wears Hassidic clothing. As they emerge from the subway station, they diminish in size, and their facial features are less distinct. By the time they are pictured walking on the grounds of an official-looking building, the edifice takes up most of the space in the tile, and the human figures are rendered faceless, almost as stick figures. The text accompanying this set of images is "[R]ace doesn't really exist. Culture? Ethnicity? Sure. Class too. But *race* is just a bunch of *rules* meant to keep us on the bottom. Race is a *strategy.*" (19). The words are placed in square boxes, not the usual dialogue bubbles, indicating a metanarrative whose assessment of racial relations is far more contemporary than the work's 1920s setting. By the time we reach the end of the page, the combination of barely determinate faceless figures drawn against a building whose doric columns are reminiscent of so many official buildings and a metanarrative offering cultural analysis calls attention to how institutionally entrenched race is in American society.

Though Johnson's protagonist is based on White, Zane is very much in keeping with the graphic novel's homage to the comic book super hero. In one sequence of tiles when he decides he must fight racism, images recalling Clark Kent and Superman are superimposed over his figure. The superhero is reworked in many black graphic novels to embody black cultural history as he or she fights for truth, justice, and the African American way. The superhero in Damian Duffy and John Jennings's *The Hole: Consumer Culture* (2008), for instance, is a figure of great significance in the black diaspora, the Vodou figure of Papa Legba (also called Eshu-Legba, Elegbara, or Esu Elegbara). Legba is as much a character as he is a philosophy guiding the interpretation of a work that defies easy definition. A figure sitting at the portals or crossroads, he embodies contradictions: he can help or harm, clarify or confuse, offer pleasure or suffering. The book's title is meant to mirror Legba's liminality, to suggest a floating signifier capable of encompassing any meaning. Within the novel nothing or no one is strictly good or bad; rather, everything occupies a space between extremes.

There is no linear plot in *The Hole*. Just as there are novels of ideas, it can best be described as a collage of ideas: the dangers of consumer culture to humanism and intellect; the power of popular culture to circulate stereotypes in perpetuity; and the symbolic uses of Vodou. Inspired by scenes of Hurricane Katrina's destruction, *Hole*'s locales are hyperreal evocations of familiar black sites, but they are drawn in a manner to remind of what is not there. The facsimile stands in for the homes and lives destroyed or upturned when a natural disaster reveals legacies of race and impoverishment given form by substandard housing and neglected infrastructure. The novel graphically portrays multiple conversations at once through its use of contrasting bubbles and floating text capturing the layered conversations in black barbershops and salons. It moves between past and present and shifts between "reality" and fantasy.

Hole opens with a prelude showing the unfortunate encounter between the intoxicated privileged son of a tycoon who has insulted Legba. It then shifts to the backstories of several of the main characters including Curtis, who is trying to quiet his violent urges against white men and his physical abuse of women now that he is out of prison and working as a tattoo artist at his mother's beauty salon. Another character, Carla Marie Batiste Bonte Snodgrass, discovers through a horse (a believer carrying the spirit of a loa) that her husband of many years with whom she was once happy is having an affair. Carla's daughter has become a prostitute to supply her heroin use. Acting as interludes between individual stories are graphic representations of capitalism's power to destroy: a sign presaging the future building of ALL*MART where everything is cheapened; the perpetual ads for McDunno's whose name casts the consumption of fabricated food as a symptom of a larger mindlessness; and the exploitation of folk culture by conglomerate marketing. The dehumanization fostered by all of this is represented through a clerk drawn to resemble a statue, robotically chanting the mantra of consumerism, strung together in words with no punctuation: "HOW ARE YOU TODAY DID YOU FIND EVERYTHING YOU NEEDED ARE YOU A MEMBER OF THE MYMEDIAMINE REWARDS PROGRAM WOULD YOU LIKE TO TRY A MONTH FREE" (19).

Characters in *Hole* are drawn to illustrate that the dehumanization of caricature can be subverted. Suggested stereotypes are consistently undermined. Carla, for instance, who is drawn to evoke a mammy figure with headscarf surrounding dreadlocks becomes a mogul, head of Hyper VooDoo Industries, and turns Vodou into a brand by selling objects and apparel in a chain of "vootiques" and by marketing veves (the symbols used to represent the loas, or spiritual intercessors) as cell phone apps. Her daughter Trina starts off as the jezebel figure but morphs into avenging angel. At points, Curtis is rendered as a black buck, but in a manner reminiscent of blues singer Robert Johnson selling his soul to the devil at the crossroads, he is transformed into a brilliant tattoo artist after an encounter with Legba and later becomes a messianic figure warning of the dangers of consumptive hungers.

Hole pays homage to Ishmael Reed's *Mumbo Jumbo*, a work Jennings cites as an influence.[8] The clash between traditional Vodou and capitalistic consumerism symbolizes a clash of worldviews, often rendered through motion lines and through literally, gut-wrenching scenes of violence. Only the return to Vodou as an atavistic link to African traditions, as an apocryphal symbol of liberty seen as the spark of the Haitian revolution, can provide an alternative narrative to western capitalistic dominance. *The Hole* is a combination of graphic novel and academic study. It is a comic that ends with a glossary and with suggestions from the fictitious Dr. Roberta Jensen of Baldwin State University, located in Freedom, North Carolina, for exercises that can be done to increase one's awareness of how race and gender are constructed, and of the ways corporate culture appropriates and markets folk culture. It closes with a nod to Ellison's *Invisible Man* by suggesting a means of creating one's own "hole" as a space for redefinition and realigning one's relationship to objects and media.

Winner of the 2016 Glyph Awards for "Best Artist" and "Best Story of the Year" from the East Coast Black Age of Comics Convention *Brotherman, Dictator of Discipline: Revelation* (2016) can be thought of as a prequel in the superhero origins genre explaining how the hero achieved his powers.

The powers for Brotherman, aka Antonia Valor, are uniquely, amazingly, and exceptionally ordinary, and that is the point. Brotherman is a positive figure symbolizing idealism fighting against the greatest enemy within his society apathy, but on many levels he is not the conventional superhero. He has no super powers; rather, he relies on his wits and connections to be the savior of his community. Readers were first introduced to Antonio in the *Brotherman, Dictator of Discipline* comics series (1990–1996, 2005–) produced by brothers Guy A. Sims, author of the novel *Living Just a Little* (2012), and Dawud Anyabwile who was formerly an illustrator for television shows including *The Wild Thornberrys* (1998–2004) and *Rugrats* (1990–2006), and who adapted Walter Dean Meyers's classic *Monster* (1999) to graphic form in 2015. As a character he was designed to be indigenous, to centralize African American experience and culture in the comics genre. While Marvel's Luke Cage, Blade, Falcon, and the Black Panther reveal the industry's growing awareness of a black presence, they are still the products of white creators, and still exist apart from black community. Illustrator Anyabwile describes feeling great reward when readers tell him that in the *Brotherman* series, unlike the Marvel creations, they see sisters, brothers, aunts, uncles, and the wide variety of black life (Tre n. pag). The range of female characters in the series is refreshing in a genre that often limits women to tight shots of breasts and labia. Lola Hubris, the villainess, is drawn as a half-veiled femme fatale but her sexpot image is subverted by her holding advanced degrees in biology and chemistry. Melody Rich, Antonio's fellow attorney, becomes the heroine of a subplot on gender discrimination in the workplace, and Dr. Chemico, a black woman chemist, discovers how to stop Lola's villainy. In addition to expanding representations of black community, notions of race and gender are both redrawn in Brotherman as well.

In the comics, Antonio Valor is an attorney committed to due process of the law as an agent for social reform. He resides on the allegorically named Hope Street in the equally allegorical Big City, USA. Big City is drawn by Anyabwile as an area threatened by disaster, but the disasters are human made from crime, institutional decay, and apathy. With its local station "Bad News One" whose motto is "We're in It for the Money," its metaphorically named institutions, Yore National bank symbolizing mock corporate populism, and Siphon Gas station emphasizing the predatory nature of big oil and gas companies, it represents economic and cultural erosion and, more tragically, indifference. Both character and city are expanded in the graphic novel. In *Revelation* in addition to the U.N.I.T.S. (Urban Neighborhoods in Transition Shelters), the soulless, multiunit high-rise housing the villain uses to scam the community and line his own pockets, Big City's residential areas with Victorian and Craftsman architecture are shown. In this area Anotonio grows up in a loving, close-knit family. Big City is city as microcosm, an alternate, complex dimension that symbolizes a home for African Americans "since there is no Africa America," as noted by Anywabile.[9]

In *Revelation* we learn that "Brotherman," the name Antonio uses while fighting for social justice, comes from both black vernacular and being an agent helping humanity, "the brother of man." He carries on the legacy inherited from his father, Leonard who is described in a sentence biography as "Father, husband, teacher, ex-gang leader, activist, man of peace ... a man" (7). Leonard's past – being abandoned in an alley as a toddler, adopted by the kind couple who run the Clemen C. Goodwill Home for Delinquent, Discarded, and Destitute Boys and being placed in the Glum Street Home for Boys when funding cuts force its closure, associating with hardened street peers – are the seeds of his devotion to his community. They combine to make him not a predator but a man committed to giving his family love, security, and safety. Allegorical naming tells stories within stories and comments on the ways with which society discards black youth, especially black boys by circumscribing their economic and educational choices and forcing them to fend for themselves in ways destructive to their humanity and society. The novel embodies classic themes of abandonment, betrayal, and redemption, and a cliff-hanger ending where tragedy looms as it tells of Antonio's family and how he comes to adopt his father's mission of protecting community.

Revelation shows a range of characters, attitudes, and expressive forms that two-dimensional black portraits in mainstream comics lack. A metaphysical voice encased in square boxes recalls newsreels of the 1930s and 1940s as it guides the reader, providing context for the images the eye scans. Like a newsreel it documents this world, and along with the dialogue bubbles offers "pictorial journalism" on the city and its residents. The artwork with color done by Brian McGee at first evokes a 1960s and 1970s ethos – afros, applejack hats, vinyl records – and conjures black social movements of the past; yet, the art is paired with action addressing contemporary concerns of gentrification, community safety, black male survival, and equal access, thereby giving the novel timelessness (see Figure 12.2) while also showing the changing same of social conditions. Colorist Brian McGee chose to effect black and white Polaroid pictures overexposed to the sun as he detailed the flashbacks providing Leonard's backstory, and this and other blendings of past forms with contemporary content place

Figure 12.2 From *Brotherman, Dictator of Discipline: Revelation, Book One*.
Used by permission of Dawud Anyabwile and Big City Entertainment.

the novel in its own temporal dimension and deepen the dreamscape that Anyabwile envisions.[10] Demonstrative facial close ups throughout remind readers that black lives matter, even as these are juxtaposed to panels that manipulate vertical perspective to evoke edifices as pyramids underscoring how social challenges can dwarf human agency. Anyabwile frequently likens the graphic novel to a movie.[11] He receives what he terms a "screenplay" from Sims, and proceeds.[12] Tiles frequently employ "forced perspective" and recall older horror films where miniature monsters were placed close to a camera to highlight the invasion of a city. The employment of "fish eye" lens views provides panoramas of a city distorted by institutional corruption, impoverishment, and yet working to insure its indigenous beauty and survival. *Brotherman Revelation* reiterates in graphic form the call for community redemption present in themes of 1960s black novels, but not their despair. Instead, *Brotherman* envisions a viable future through positive activism.

Where *Brotherman* stresses the responsibility of the individual to the community, Felipe Smith's *MBQ* (2005–2007) explores the individual's responsibility to his or her own development. Over the course of three volumes, with volume two including a comic within a comic, *MBQ* (short for McBurger Queen) is in the main the story of Omario, a Van-Gogh-like graphic artist suffering for his art, knowing that his is a talent the world has yet to appreciate. The books chronicle his attempts to make a name for himself as a graphic novelist (a term about which he is highly ambivalent). It is loosely based on people Smith knew or had seen. The first image in *MBQ* is of Dee a black "gangsta" drug dealer, tattoos on overly muscled biceps exposed as he wears a white, sleeveless undershirt and heavy gold chain. He is seated talking on a dated cell phone with antenna, and giving the viewer the finger. This image is characteristic of the edginess in Smith's hyper-realistic artistry. It is in many ways a graphic statement of artistic freedom, the liberty to celebrate Los Angeles's multiculturalism through manga.

Rooted in Japanese visual culture, Manga comics incorporate many styles from the romantic *Shojo* to the action-oriented and sometimes erotic *Shonen*. They are often designed to reach particular age and gender demographics. In the 1950s, manga magazines increased the form's popularity, and the advent of anime, television shows often based on manga, gave the form an international presence. By the time Smith is writing, manga in translation are selling worldwide. His work calls to mind the violence and sexuality of the *seinen* manga, frequently directed to teenage and adult male readers.

Born in the United States to a Jamaican father and Argentine mother, raised in Argentina and living in Japan, Smith is keenly aware of cultural intersections. He has credited his background with giving him an appearance that makes it difficult for viewers to place him, and this indefinability allows him to appreciate the multiple ways in which one can be seen. His work much like his life fell between easily defined categories and made publication difficult. Not believing in hard and fast definitions in genre or in culture, he utilizes manga to argue that it and American comic style are not discrete. One can be used to express the cultural life of the other. Smith takes a genre created by Japanese comics artists that gained popularity in the United States in the 1980s, and uses it to shed light on multicultural working-class Los Angeles.[13] The tiles opening *MBQ* shift from various neighborhoods during 3:10–3:37 AM: the two-story home of the white police officer Bobby, the motel-like structure that serves as Dee's home, the apartment complex of Omario and the white Jeff, the apartment house of the white rookie cop Aidan whose boyish looks belie his sexual and racial victimization, and the Karaoke bar run by Omario's Korean friend Brian who has dreams of rap-star fame. On his bicycle in seeming in perpetual motion, Omario, very much calling Smith to mind, moves between these settings observing and drawing.

In chapter 8, the second-to last chapter, Smith offers his analysis of the comics genre, or as Omario refers to it, the telling of stories with pictures. Through sequences where Omario reflects on his work, Smith expresses the difficulties of being "boxed" into a certain type of comic book art. In panels illustrating the style of each, Omario remarks that his work is not of the so-called classic superhero mode, a genre he feels is uninspired and churns out versions of the same. Nor is he a composer of gothic adventure or magical quests (192–201). His comics animate the everyday. As an example, Jeff, a worker at the local MBQ, is drawn physically larger than life, but he is a superhero of the mundane, whose power is satisfying disgruntled MBQ customers when no one else can. Smith's manga creates a comic genre where over the top drawings augment the bursts of force and passion that occasionally appear in very ordinary life.

Smith's cross-cultural influences are evident throughout his works. He taught himself Japanese, which he now speaks fluently, worked in restaurants and karaoke bars, and drew. His second comic *Peepo Choo* (2009–2010) extends the exploration of cultural frisson. Serialized exclusively in Japanese in Kodansha's monthly manga magazine *Morning 2*, it takes place in Chicago and Tokyo. The central character Milton is an African American nerd, characterized as an Otaku (a term for those obsessed with anime and manga fandom) who "cosplays" (wears the costumes and accessories of characters), collects figures, and is devoted to the anime *Peepo Choo*. He lives in the projects and works without salary at a Chicago comic shop in exchange for free merchandise. The shop, it turns out is owned by Gill, a secret assassin. Upon winning a trip to Japan in a raffle, Milton is elated, not knowing that the trip is a cover so that Gill can complete a job. The theme of cross-cultural misinterpretation is at the comic's core, most explicitly personified by Milton who speaks fluent Japanese and Morimoto, a Yakuza protagonist who believes American pop culture to be American reality. The volumes constitute a mosaic of cultures in sometimes violent, uneasy contact.

Smith's work spans many genres from his own manga to the newest edition of Marvel's *Ghost Rider*. Working with illustrator Tradd Moore, he recreates the hero figure as Latino. Robbie Reyes, at first a peaceful character whose major concern is protecting his wheelchair bound little brother, enters an illegal street race, and the subsequent accident transforms him into the Ghost Rider. Rather than a skeleton wearing a leather jacket and bursting into flames while riding a motorcycle as he wreaks havoc on demonic villains, Smith's version, still wearing leather, drives a black muscle car, a 1969 Dodge Charger. The panels embody the expanse of California highways and adapt the American road myth to counter perceptions of Latinos as perpetual immigrants.

The themes of corporate dominance in Smith's and other sequential art can be read as a subtle critique of the uneasy relationship between comics as a renegade genre and their appropriation by corporate institutions such as Marvel and DC Comics. Many works comment on the disconnect between the innovative worlds that comics were supposed to imagine and the industry's sustaining capitalistic practice through movies, merchandise tie-ins, and the recycling of old content. The print culture of black graphic novels underscores the difficulties faced by independent artists creating and trying to circulate work that may not suit the Hollywood molds of Avengers or X-Men.

The genre of black graphic novels has expanded rapidly to include works such as Karl Bollers's and Rick Leonard's *Watson and Holmes: A Study in Black* (2012). In this retelling of the classic, the Conan Doyle pair are moved from London to contemporary Harlem to enact their plots of deductive reasoning. As the title suggests, Watson, a veteran of the twentieth-century war in Afghanistan, is a co-main character. Mycroft is "Mike," and Sherlock is dreadlocked. Vernon Whitlock III and Matthew Scott Krentz publish *Blaze Brothers* (2014), about half-brother orphans raised by a Chinese martial arts master who now operate as US Black ops forces. In 1993 black entrepreneurs Derek T. Dingle, Dwayne McDuffie, Denys Cowan, and Michael Davis founded Milestone comics to address the paucity and stereotypical representations of other than white characters in comics. Through a publishing arrangement with DC Comics, Milestone takes advantage of DC's distribution apparatuses while maintaining creative copyrights.[14] While racial representation may be increasing, however, there is still a marked gender divide in the graphic narrative world. Felicia D. Henderson and Angela Robinson write *Teen Titans* and *The Web*, respectively for DC Comics, but more often than not, it generally falls to independent efforts to increase the presence of women of color writers and illustrators. Actress Rashida Jones has created Africomics.com, as a "portal" to comics where black heroes and writers are not an afterthought. Businesswoman Jazmin Truesdale will be launching Aza Entertainment to develop a new line of comic book heroes that represent the world's racial, sexual, and gender diversities. Editor Cheryl Lynn Eaton who draws comics has done something similar by founding the Ormes Society to provide a network for black women creating comics, but these are all still nascent steps.

Writing in the conclusion to his book *The Contemporary African American Novel: Its Folk Roots and Modern Literary Branches* (2004), Bernard Bell observes that "the consensus of contemporary specialists in the fields of African American literary history and criticism is that the African American literary tradition is best understood and appreciated by interpreting its merits within the context of its own indigenous nature and function." He goes on to cite oratory, myth, legend, tale, and song as genres illuminating indigenous nature and function (388). At a time when it has become commonplace to say we live in the era of the image, perhaps uses of visual culture should be added to Bell's list. Graphic novels present a useful site for examining how images are engaged to expand considerations of race and culture. Their dialectic tension between text and picture generates new spaces for articulating myriad black cultural experiences by making them hypervisible.

Graphic novels can be seen as constituting a new black vernacular using visual forms to increase awareness of oscillating blacknesses. They offer a different lingua franca of race yet still engage long-standing questions. What is blackness? How shall it be represented? Who shall represent it? They shape the political, social, and economic histories of blackness into cultural products befitting a time when so much information circulates visually and visual framing of black subjectivity continues. Their drawing of images resituates scopic power and lessens the potency of voyeuristic racial definition.

CHAPTER 13

African American Novels from Page to Screen

Hollywood's embrace of writers hit its stride in the 1930s. William Faulkner, F. Scott Fitzgerald, Nathaniel West, and William Saroyan were among those called west to write for the newly emerging sound film. The voices that gave their writings such uniqueness rarely transferred into films and were often sacrificed to create commodities for popular audiences increasingly enthralled with movie going. How, then, would a black writer in Hollywood fare? Not many were given the opportunity, and those who arrived were disappointed, as in the case of Langston Hughes who went to Los Angeles to work on the 1939 film *Way Down South*. Rather than realistic portraits, Hughes found reproductions of the very stereotypes he and other writers were trying to deconstruct. He noted, "Of course, Negro novelists do not sell their novels to motion pictures. No motion picture studio in America, in all the history of motion pictures, has yet dared make one single picture using any of the fundamental dramatic values of negro life – not one. Not one picture. On the screen we are servants, clowns, or fools. Comedy relief. Droll and very funny. Such Negro material as is used by the studios is very rarely written by Negroes" ("To Negro Writers" 128). Other African American writers who attempted to work in Hollywood included Wallace Thurman who wrote for Warner Brothers and Zora Neale Hurston who had been hired by Paramount.

While not being allowed significant input into the representations of blacks in movies, black writers were surrounded by white writers' imaginings. The early twentieth century saw many films by white directors that framed blacks in expected ways. Several versions of Harriet Beecher Stowe's *Uncle Tom's Cabin* stood in for portrayals of black life. The Selig Polyscopic Company filmed a traveling Uncle Tom troupe to produce *Uncle Tom's Cabin's Parade* (1903). Edwin S. Porter made a silent *Uncle Tom's Cabin or Slavery Days* (1903) and Universal Pictures invested two million dollars in their *Uncle Tom's Cabin* (dir. Harry A. Pollard, 1927).[1] D. W. Griffith's virtuosic *The Birth of a Nation* (1915) and David O. Selznick's

Gone with the Wind (1939) would permanently cement these images in popular American culture. Géza van Radványi's 1965 German *Onkle Toms Hütte* (using Serbian farmers in blackface) showed that such representations had longevity and international reach. Even a black director Stan Lathan felt compelled to engage Stowe's fiction in a 1987 adaptation for the Showtime network that starred Avery Brooks as Tom and Phylicia Rashad as Eliza. Lathan attempted to imbue Tom with dignity and gravitas. Film has played a major role in shaping how blackness is perceived, and in the early twentieth century more realistic screened depictions of black life came from adapting black novels.

Paul Laurence Dunbar's *The Sport of the Gods* (1921) was one of the earliest adaptations of an African American novel. Directed by Henry J. Vernot, it featured an all-black cast, and Dunbar wrote the screenplay. Robert Levy produced it through his Reol studio. A London-born Jewish theatre manager, Levy was in charge of the historic Lafayette Theatre located in Harlem. Designed by Victor Hugo Koehler, the Renaissance style building was one of the first to allow black filmgoers to move out of "nigger heaven" and sit in the orchestra seats. It was home to The Bush Players, a stock company originally formed by Anita Bush. It was her dream to have an all-black acting company that combatted stereotypical images of singing and dancing blacks through productions of Broadway plays and classical theatre. When financial difficulties necessitated it, Bush sold the company to the Lafayette Theatre. The troupe became the Lafayette Players Stock Company under the direction of Charles S. Gilpin, the stage actor who, among other major roles, played Brutus Jones in the premiere of Eugene O'Neill's *The Emperor Jones* in 1920.

Levy would leave the Lafayette in 1919, partially as a response to sentiment that a black man should occupy his position, and he would devote his energies to the emerging genre of race films. He optioned both *Sport of the Gods* and *The Uncalled*, and his new film company Reol Films debuted *Sport of the Gods* in 1921.[2] The film is no longer extant, but stills and reviews show that though the movie followed the novel's plot closely, it also played to popular tastes. Depictions of salacious city life were augmented. The seediness of Dunbar's Banner Club is muted, making it look more like New York's Cotton Club, no doubt to appeal to a fascination with 1920s black cabaret culture.[3] The film nonetheless gave black actors the opportunity to play dramatic roles beyond traditional notions, and Levy's employment of white actors made integration visible, at least on film.

The growth of black theatres and the availability of black actors contributed to a mini boom in black production of films, shorts, and newsreels, by companies such as Foster Photoplay Company and the Lincoln Motion Picture Company. The Frederick Douglass Film Company produced *The Colored American Winning His Suit* (1917) and *The Scapegoat* (1917), an adaptation of Dunbar's short story. Filmmakers adapting black novels would be in competition with white productions using black material, and attracting an audience would be a challenge even for the preeminent filmmaker Oscar Micheaux. He characterized Levy and the cadre of white filmmakers using black life for their features as his major competitors. Micheaux persisted, however, taking advantage of the explosive increase in the numbers of black filmgoers. He ended up owning one of the most successful black enterprises of the early twentieth century. Its name, the Micheaux Film and Book Company, exemplifies the interrelationship between black novels and black cinema.[4]

After holding various factory and agricultural jobs, Micheaux worked as a Pullman porter. In 1905 he had saved enough money to purchase government relinquished land in South Dakota, and he moved there to become a farmer. His initial success gave him the confidence to correspond with several young women and eventually propose to a schoolteacher, Orlean McCracken, the daughter of Reverend N. J. Mccracken. He persuaded her to expand their property holdings by filing a claim on relinquished land as well. The marriage deteriorated in large part because of the Reverend's meddling, and after a stillborn pregnancy, Orlean joined her father and sister in Chicago. The dissolution of the marriage coincided with the difficulties of drought, prairie fires, and the foreclosure on some of his properties. Adding to his problems, his wife signed over her land to a white banker who filed claim on it. This life story became the material for much of Micheaux's novels beginning with *The Conquest: The Story of a Negro Pioneer* (1913). As the story evolved into its various versions, representations of rural purity versus urban decadence became a consistent theme that spoke to the anxiety of many blacks migrating after slavery. Honorable men and women became models of the proper traits ensuring racial uplift. As late as his 1931 hybrid silent-talking film, *The Exile*, the tensions between a misguided woman and a noble man would still find their way into Micheaux's films.

In *The Conquest*, Micheaux is transformed into Oscar Devereaux and Orlean into Orlean McCraline. In the novel Oscar falls in love with a Scottish woman, but relinquishes any hopes of a union because of race. He instead marries a black woman from Chicago, sacrifices to build his homestead, but his wife cannot understand his admirable vision. When their son is stillborn, with the encouragement of her promiscuous, meddling father and her sister she leaves him and returns to Chicago. Micheaux transformed the novel into the film *The Homesteader* (1919) where Oscar Devereaux becomes Jean Baptiste, the Scottish woman becomes Agnes Stewart, and Orlean McCraline, Orlean McCarthy. The Lincoln Motion Picture Company originally bought the film rights, but Micheaux backed out of the deal when it became apparent that he would not be in charge of production and the movie would not be expanded from three reels to six. He opted to produce the film himself, and once he secured funding by among other ventures selling stock to fellow homesteaders he began turning the book into film in earnest. He drew on the talents of the Lafayette Players and filmed in Chicago. He promised that the film would fulfill two missions, to provide an arena for black talent and to provide an opportunity for black audiences to see themselves portrayed in positive fashion. No copy of the film remains, so whether his vision was achieved can only be guessed. Existing reviews would suggest it was, as they focus more on its historical value than its subject matter and remark on the importance of seeing trained black actors in dramatic roles.[5]

So much surrounding the film reflects its cultural climate. The persistence of colorism is seen in promotional stills. Charles Lucas and Evelyn Preer are the light-skinned stars, and Micheaux repeated this pattern in most of his films (see Figure 13.1). The movie's reception by the black church establishment indicated the growing debate surrounding the role of black religious leadership as a populace moved into a modern, more scientific era. A group of black pastors attempted to have the film censored because of its portrayal of Reverend McCarthy, but prominent citizens including Ida Wells Barnett came to its defense (Bowser 12–13). Promoted as a powerful drama of the American Northwest, it expanded perceptions of the locales of black life beyond the rural South or urban North. Its cultural influence was also felt in material ways. In movies houses where it was shown blacks could sit anywhere in the theatre, and thus it became an agent of democracy. But most importantly, it was a "first," a novel by a black author with an all-star black cast, something in which an audience could take pride.

Micheaux adapted the works of other black writers, most famously Charles Chesnutt's *House behind the Cedars*, advertised as "Oscar Micheaux presents *The House Behind the Cedars* a story of the South by Charles Chesnutt." Chesnutt and Micheaux had protracted correspondence, mainly over fees and film rights. There were two treatments of the novel. The first, a silent, *The House Behind the Cedars* (1924–1925), minimized the tragedy of Chesnutt's work. Rena passes and becomes the fiancé of a wealthy, white

Figure 13.1 Advertisement for *The Homesteader* (1919), dir. Oscar Micheaux.
The Kansas City Sun (Kansas City, MO), Chronicling America:
Historic American Newspapers. Library of Congress.

man, but rather than dying as in the novel she realizes that in passing she has committed a crime against not only her race, but her true character. She returns home and marries her former boyfriend Frank Fowler who has risen to prominence and economic security. The film was more in keeping with Micheaux's own self-help philosophy than Chesnutt's color line tragedy. A sound version titled *The Veiled Aristocrats*, extended Micheaux's revisioning of Chesnutt's work. When John (Warwick this time) returns to find his sister engaged to the dark Frank Fowler, he persuades his mother to let him take her to the city and pass in white society. Again, she returns to Frank who has become a successful builder, and they marry. Micheaux makes the novel more of a love story and more an instance of race pride through Rena's repudiation of crossing the color line. In the 1920s with the New Negro Renaissance in its nascence, the ambiguities of Chesnutt's turn-of-the-century passing characters are replaced with the certitude that it is better to remain in the race.

Wanting to make the most of dramatic appeal, and wanting to place black actors in lead roles, Micheaux sought to adapt *The Conjure Woman* in 1926, and turn it into a love story against the backdrop of a haunted house. In an October 30, 1921, letter to Chesnutt, he outlined his philosophy in filmmaking: "I prefer stories of the Negro in the south, and while a good intense love story with a happy ending, plenty of action, thrills and suspence [sic] is the main thing, a streak of good Negro humor is helpful. I think you could develop a good synopsis from the first story of *The Conjurer* [sic] *Woman*. Write the case of the man and woman in to a good love story, let there, if possible, be a haunted house, the haunts being intrigueres [sic] to be found out near the end, the heroine to have ran [sic] off there in hiding – anything that will thrill or suspend, but will have a delightful ending and give opportunity for a strong male and female lead" (Crisler 151–152).

When it became increasingly difficult financially to produce films, Micheaux came full circle back to novel writing via self-publishing through Book Supply Company of New York a firm he started. It debuted *The Case of Mrs. Wingate* (1944), *The Wind from Nowhere* (1944), *The Story of Dorothy Stanfield, Based on a Great Insurance Swindle, and a Woman* (1946), and *The Masquerade: An Historical Novel* (1947). Many Micheaux themes and characters are revisited in these works. *The Wind from Nowhere* extends the homesteading theme to include the establishment of a black colony in the Midwest. The necessity for black self-actualization is represented through Sidney Wyeth, novelist, lawyer, detective, and finally filmmaker in *The Case of Mrs. Wingate*. *The Story of Dorothy Stanfield*, a detective story, is meant to portray blacks in contemporary contexts, and *The Masquerade: An Historical Novel*, reworks Micheaux's filmed version of *House Behind the Cedars*. Taking place after the death of John, and through portrayals of slavery, the abolitionist movement, and a fully reproduced text of Lincoln's Emancipation, it amplifies black history. Micheaux acknowledges in the preface to *The Masquerade* that the themes, plots, and characters were taken from his films, a reverse adaptation, and expanded to fit the contemporary needs of blacks to see themselves portrayed not as artifacts but as living beings. His final adaptation would be of his own work, a film titled *The Betrayal* (1948) based on his novel, *The Wind from Nowhere*. Reviews in *The Chicago Defender* and the *New York Amsterdam News*, all panned the film as too long and dull.[6]

Micheaux's adaptations bring to light the two-way relationship between novels and film in conserving and representing the breadth of black cultural experience. Because they were among the earliest indigenous imaginings of black life, black novels provided source material for emerging black cinema. At the same time, cinema cemented the presence of the novel in popular culture. Economic realities rendered this interrelation tenuous, however, and throughout the 1930s and 1940s the major portraits of black life onscreen would derive not from black novels but from white imaginings of black life. Walter Weems known as the "boy from Dixie" was a white minstrel performer who wrote the script that cohered *Hearts in Dixie*, a series of sketches of the New South that looked remarkably like the Old South. Marc Connelly's play *The Green Pastures* (1930) and Roark Bradford's novel *Ol' Man Adam an' His Children* (1928) would be made into *The Green Pastures* (dir. Marc Connelly, William Keighley, 1936), a movie retelling biblical stories from the perspectives of blacks, though written by white men. Even Frank Yerby's attempt to complicate southern narrative in *The Foxes of Harrow* was given the plantation pastoral treatment when 20th Century Fox made the novel into a 1947 movie.

An Oscar-nominated film starring Rex Harrison and Maureen O'Hara, *The Foxes of Harrow* (dir. John M. Stahl) imagines New Orleans through feudal myth and accents individualism through its depiction of self-made American aristocracy. It is in the main the story of Stephen and Odalie, for the black characters that lent balance to Yerby's portrait of the south are moved to the periphery. As slaves in the house or fields they are scenery; as Vodou practitioners they offer exotic escapism. In the novel Caleen, grandmother to Achille's son Inch, is a key character teaching her grandson survival, racial pride, and instilling in him a dream of future freedom. In the movie, the growing fascination with ideas of African mysticism seen in *Black Moon* (dir. Roy William Neill, 1934), *King of the Zombies* (dir. Jean Yarbrough, 1941), and *Drums O'Voodoo* (dir. Arthur Hoerl, 1933), is evident in her being made a peripheral character enacting Hollywood's interpretation of Vodou ritual. Inch appears as a child, but not as the man with agency he becomes in Yerby's book. In the adaptation of *Foxes* few black actors received credit. The novel's hero Achille played by an uncredited Kenneth Washington was relegated to minor status in the film. *Foxes* was criticized by both the black and white press for not showing resistance against slavery or black anger.[7] While the payoff for Yerby was great, he received $150,000, a remarkable sum for a black writer at the time, complex black life remained in the novel and was not transferred to film.

Black criticism of the southern pastoral and the narrow range of representations as singers and dancers was growing. The NAACP and the black press all condemned *Gone with the Wind* and Disney's *Song of the South* (1946), to name two instances.[8] In the early 1940s, the NAACP was in dialogue with studio heads asking for more realistic depictions of blacks, but the reactions of Southern viewers greatly limited what studios were willing to do. As the experience of Richard Wright would show, bringing the content of black novels to the screen would be difficult. He blamed the censorship boards in the United States for squelching films that did not suit them or that would provoke clashes of racial opinion. As he stated in an interview, "Hollywood does not want to have any difficulty selling its films to each one of the forty-eight states!" (Wright, *Conversations* 112). Wright's most popular novel would follow a rocky road to adaptation with debatable results.

Native Son was made into a play in 1941, co-written by Paul Green and Richard Wright with changes to make the content more palatable to audiences. It was again rewritten by Wright and John Houseman to make the content more like the book for a play produced by Orson Welles and John Houseman starring Canada Lee. The success of the play generated interest in a filmed version. Wright, a lover of movies himself, felt that *Native Son* had great cinematic potential, but feared the changes adaptation would impart to his work, and as it turned out rightly so. Producer Ben Hecht offered to turn it into a movie, but conceived of it as having an all-white cast with an ethnic working-class hero at its center. Producer Joseph Fields wanted to cast Bigger as a white ethnic and make him part of an array of marginalized representations including a black, a Jew, a Pole, and an Italian in competition for employment. Talks with other directors, among them Roberto Rossellini, yielded nothing. None wanted to take the chance on casting a black actor at the center of a dramatic film. In the era of segregation, a film about a black man and a white woman was incendiary, and white actresses refused to play the part of Mary Dalton because they resented being held by a black man or were afraid that such a scene might damage their careers.[9]

Making the film proved exceedingly difficult. When a crew that included Wright traveled to Chicago to shoot location scenes, Wright was denied admittance to their choice of hotel. Plans to shoot the film in France were abandoned due to the Centre National de la Cinématographie Français (now the Centre National Du Cinéma Et De L'image Animée) citing "reasons dictated by international policy," which in Wright's estimation meant France could ill afford to offend an United States providing international aid by exposing American racism. When director Pierre Chenal did make the movie, it was filmed in Argentina with Buenos Aires standing in for Chicago. On a budget of approximately $300,000, some of which was Wright's own money that he never recouped, urban streets and South Side black homes were reconstructed on the soundstages of Argentina's Sono Film studios. Billboards, storefronts, and contemporary advertisements were duplicated. Wright wrote the screenplay, and he and Chenal later revised it. Since Chenal felt Wright had lived the life of Bigger, at forty, he was cast in the starring role.[10]

The hardships continued once the film was complete. While the movie was shown in full in Argentina, to great acclaim, American censors forced changes to much of its content. The New York State Board of Censors demanded the removal of about a half hour of the film. The Ohio Board of Censors refused to license the film stating that it offered "racial fictions" that contributed to misunderstanding between the races. In the final version, scenes showing the killing of the rat as well as the motives behind Bigger and his cohorts devising a robbery were all cut, as was a scene where a white mob gathers outside the courthouse awaiting Bigger. The trial scene that provides the novel's most explicit social condemnation was reduced to having no dialogue, just gesticulations, something particularly galling to Wright.[11]

The film opens with a tourist-reel view of Chicago's skyscrapers, fountains, and business district and voiceover describing why Chicago is the jewel of the Midwest. This is followed by images of dilapidated, overcrowded houses as the unseen narrator introduces viewers to the Black Belt, and finally to the one-room kitchenette where Hannah Thomas, a rat-hunting Buddy, Bigger, and Vera reside. Bigger is a far more sympathetic figure. At odds with the setting, strings play sentimental strains in the background. Both younger siblings adore their older brother, and the voiceover sets out the confinement of Bigger's world by describing him sitting in a rocking chair reading, dreaming about machines and planes, wanting to be a flyer or explorer. The narration abruptly concludes that Bigger's blackness makes such dreams pointless, even dangerous. The camera then focuses on a picture of Bigger's father, smiling in a straw hat against a backdrop of cotton fields as the voiceover mentions that he was lynched.

Wright's Bigger incorporates not only the racial tensions of the novel, but also anticipates the alienated male to be seen in *The Wild One* starring Marlon Brando (dir. László Benedek, 1953) and *Rebel Without a Cause* with James Dean (dir. Nicholas Ray, 1955). He plays Bigger as an antihero, arrogantly proud that his environs have given him the smarts that those with more money and privilege lack. The critical scene where Bigger accidentally kills Mary is rendered in a manner faithful to the text's description of her accidental suffocation, with a close-up of Wright's/Bigger's face staring up in terror at a blind Mrs. Dalton who enters the room. He rises, moves away from the limp body, and another close-up shows terror of a different sort as he slowly turns his face in the direction of Mary's bed, not wanting to look at what he knows is there. The segment closes with Bigger carrying her body into the basement, laying her on the floor, and then stoking the furnace. The violence of Bigger attempting to dismember Mary's body to fit it into the furnace is omitted, understandably given the times, and the scene then cuts to Peggy calling from the Dalton kitchen the next morning to remind Bigger that he is to take Mary to the station.

The movie adds scenes not in the novel to underscore the segregation of the North. When Bigger and Bessie secretly drive the Dalton's car to an amusement park, they ride a rollercoaster, and the ups and downs stand in for the arbitrary vagaries of black belt life. The shot then fades to Bessie swimming in the surf, and running onto the beach. She removes her bathing cap, shakes her hair in a scene so frequently repeated by white actresses in Hollywood films, that her exclusion from the world where this is a common act is made evident. The contrast is effective. As she and Bigger lie on the beach a plane flies overhead and Bigger remarks that he wish he were at its helm instead of chauffeuring Mary Dalton. Bessie then gently, in a soft voice consoles him, saying that he can't change the whole world and asks isn't it enough that they love each other. Everything, the illicit drive to the amusement park, their ride on the roller coaster, Bessie's swim, their romance, underscores how extraordinary their enjoyment of the ordinary is, and without Bigger's even verbalizing it, the answer to Bessie's question – "no" – is powerfully felt.

The romantic relationship between Bigger and Bessie places him in a far more sympathetic light than the Bigger of the novel that just uses Bessie for his own needs. Bessie herself is no longer his alcoholic girlfriend, rather she is a cocktail waitress who has graduated to singing at Ernie's, here a nightclub not a "chicken shack." She is slim, and speaks standard English in marked contrast to Wright's painful to listen to attempts at black dialect. (He certainly confirms Hurston's remark that as far as dialect goes, he is tone deaf.)[12] She is elegantly dressed as she takes the stage for her nightclub debut, recalling the glamour shots of female singers at the microphone in 1940s and 1950s film noir. Her song, "The Dreaming Kind," accentuates black unmet desire. She only begins to sink deeper into drink as Bigger draws her more deeply into his plan to frame Jan and cover up Mary's death. Making Bessie more sympathetic confers the same on Bigger, as one wonders why their life cannot unfold in traditional happy ever after fashion.

As Bigger explains his killing of Bessie to Max, a dream sequence unfolds. In it he kneels on hot coals trying to hide a package. Bessie appears in her evening gown and throws the corsage Mary had worn and given to her at him, telling him he cannot hide the package in the coals, an image implying the impotency of something black to provide protection; instead, she points to a field of white cotton as a hiding place, signifying the power of whiteness to aid him. A shirtless, sweaty Bigger is then seen walking through the cotton fields and his lynched father appears beckoning to him with outstretched arms. In Bigger's mind, the father figure represents safety and comfort, but as he falls on his knees crying and holding his father's hand. The figure turns into a laughing, contemptuous Britten, the police detective, holding the package containing Mary's head. Dreams stand in for of Bigger's unarticulated awareness, and they also represent him as the victim of the dreaming fostered by movies and billboards. Wright's acting is stilted, and it is apparent that even though he undertook a weight loss regimen, he was too mature to play Bigger convincingly; however, the movie's other devices go a long way to replicating the psychological terrain of Bigger's mind.

The film's ending offers "simple" closure as Bigger tells Max he hopes what happened to him does not happen to another black boy, and asks Max to say hello to Jan. A choral lament then rises, suggesting Bigger's redemption at the hands of a forgiving god:

> Another Boy done gone
> A Boy we know will die
> He's going home tonight
> To meet a Higher Judge
> Who can look past his skin
> And see into his heart
> Oh Lord, let mercy rain on him
> And wash his sins away.

The film closes as it opened with a shot of the city of Chicago, seen from across Lake Michigan, still remote and forever out of Bigger's reach.[13] *Native Son's* dim lighting, unexpected dramatic twists, and the narrow camera angles of Wright's face fix it in the noir tradition and suggests that film noir can be interpreted almost literarily.

The segregation and censorship that had plagued the first remake of *Native Son* was gone by the time the 1986 version starring Victor Love and Oprah Winfrey was produced. That the film makes Bigger a complete victim reveals the constraints of representation at work in the 1980s when Alice Walker, Toni Morrison, and Gloria Naylor, among many others, were accused of black male bashing. Rather than show Bigger as an agent transforming an accidental killing into his own life affirmation, the movie's protagonist is effectively neutered. The hardness and deepness Wright described as his writing goal in "How Bigger Was Born" is gone, in its place a story softening the edge that Bigger exhibits after his perverse self-actualization.[14] The murder of Bessie is removed because producers, over the objection of director Jerrold Freedman, felt this would make Bigger too unsympathetic to audiences.[15] A sympathetic Bigger, something the novel renders as an oxymoron, is a rendering both films in their different times, in their different ways, attempt to achieve. In the first version, the concern was clearly for a white viewership; in the second, a black one.

In the forty years between the two versions of *Native Son* American viewers' fascination with pulling the curtain back on gritty realism grew. The genres of film noir, juvenile delinquency movies, and American neorealism seemed particularly suited for black novels written in the 1950s and 1960s. *Knock on Any Door* (dir. Nicholas Ray, 1949), made by Santana, Humphrey Bogart's independent production company, and its sequel *Let No Man Write My Epitaph* (dir. Philip Leacock, 1960), both were based on Willard Motley's *Knock on Any Door*. The later film continued Nick's story with Nellie Romano's efforts to make sure her son does not follow in the footsteps of his father. It featured Ella Fitzgerald in a rare dramatic performance playing a drug-addicted singer, and was an example of mid-century naturalistic novels turned into films. Robert Hatch in *The New Republic* called such films the "suffering humanity genre" and a *New York Times* review condemned the movie's casting the environment as the cause of personal degeneracy. Both reviews revealed the discomfort at the ways adaptations of deterministic novels indicted society.[16]

Bringing Motley's works to screen was not as difficult an endeavor as the adaptation of *Native Son* because they were essentially devoid of blackness. While white teen rebels were a draw, however, it was still difficult to bring a popular audience to the theatre to see films where black actors revealed black reality. John Oliver Killens, for instance, worked on the screenplay for his novel *Youngblood*, a project that his white producer abandoned when other whites told him black subject matter would not sell. In adapting her play for film, Lorraine Hansbury was encouraged to remove many of the racial "issues," so as not to alienate a white audience by making the movie too propagandistic.[17] Novels adapted to film that did succeed were often coming of age stories such as *The Learning Tree* (1963) directed by and based on the semi-autobiographical novel by photographer Gordon Parks. The centralization of social power in the hands of a white superintendent of schools, a white judge, and white policeman, in Parks's locale of Cherokee Flats did not upset the status quo, and the film brought to the screen the sentimentally of the novel's portrait of maturation, religious values, and sexual awakening. All these were viewed as issues transcending race. Adaptations like *The Learning Tree* were perfectly in keeping with the ways popular American film viewers liked their black characters, stoic, intelligent, yet refrained and no real threat to dominant white power. The careful racial line these films were encouraged to walk would become increasingly irrelevant to an era growing frustrated with the slow pace of reform. In their stead would emerge movies fitting the blaxploitation formula, popular because their heroes were antiestablishment renegades. In the 1960s and 1970s black pulp would gain an increasing presence in film. Joining adaptations of Chester Himes would be movies based on novels by Iceberg Slim and Donald Goines.

When Chester Himes arrived in Hollywood, blacks were still suffering under the discrimination of studios and segregation at studio commissaries. Four of Chester Himes' novels would be made into films: *If He Hollers, Let Him Go!, Cotton Comes to Harlem, The Heat's On,* and *A Rage in Harlem.* In *If He Hollers, Let Him Go!* (dir. James W. Sullivan, 1968), Bob Jones is renamed James Lake and is played by Raymond St. Jacques, a member of the Actor's Studio, who performed with the American Shakespearean Festival in Stratford, Connecticut, and appeared with Elizabeth Taylor and Richard Burton in *The Comedians* (1967). The film plays to the blaxploitation era. Instead of the character Madge Perkins withdrawing her accusation of rape against Bob, in the movie James is convicted of raping and murdering a white woman. Throughout the film, some of which tells James's story in flashback, he is subject to physical brutality and calumny by white authority. He, however, bears none of this stoically as did previous black film icons; instead, he reacts. The scene where he beats a white man foreshadows the draw of revenge fantasy. Art was not at the center of this movie whose plot line is confused, and whose dialogue often borders on cliché; rather, the appeal was the opportunity to see on film the justice that society did not provide. St. Jacques skillfully conveys contained anger always on the verge of exploding.

Later, Himes would work with Sam Goldwyn Jr. to bring *Cotton Comes to Harlem* to the screen. Himes wasn't a screenwriter, and Goldwyn first thought of using Amiri Baraka (then still LeRoi Jones). According to Himes, when Baraka demanded to be paid in advance, as was commonly the case with white writers, negotiations fell apart. Himes was unsatisfied with the initial screenplay by playwright and television producer Arnold Perl, but saw improvement in the revisions made by Ossie Davis. Davis updated the characters to include black militants and told the story from a black perspective in Himes's view (Himes, *Conversations* 51).[18] Under Davis's direction, *Cotton* is a 1970s folk epic. Archetypes of the crooked minister, the funeral parlor director, black nationalists, church ladies, and junkies generate a black world from within. The camera lingers long on men in dashikis and women in Afros and boubous to convey the "black is beautiful" philosophy of the era. Its humor derives from familiar stories such as the funeral parlor director who upon seeing a police chase immediately attires himself in his funeral best. A large part of the movie encompasses traditions of trickster reversal, where blacks seize the upper hand in recasting stereotypic content such as remaking the traditional "nigger in the woodpile" into "a honky in the woodpile" joke, and in the instance of an exotic dancer imagined as a nationalist eschewing fans and feathers as the tools of an Uncle Tom era, choosing instead to dance on a cotton bale a symbol more "meaningful" to her people. Davis shot on location in Harlem using significant cultural markers, the Apollo Theatre, Smalls Paradise, and Harlem Hospital. The vision of Harlem imagined in Himes's novels as absurd and dark is, in Davis's hands, one of transcendence where blacks are able to make humor and culture out of riches as well as detritus.

The Coffin Ed Johnson and Gravedigger Jones formula would be repeated in *Come Back Charleston Blue* (1972). Based on Himes's *The Heat's On*, the movie radically changes the novel's surreal picaresque tour through Harlem's violence. It replaces the impotence of the detectives as they try to rid the community of its drug scourge with a mythic tale focusing on the apparent resurrection of a crime boss, Charleston Blue. When it turns out he is being impersonated to facilitate the drug trade and that heroin is being stored in his crypt, his widow, played by Minnie Gentry, slits the impersonator's throat with one of the signature razors belonging to her dead husband. Ossie Davis declined to direct the sequel and was replaced by Mark Warren, a black television director most noted for the Emmy award winning comedy-variety show *Laugh In* (1967–1973). The vernacular that Davis celebrated was cast more as black shtick in this second venture. Increasingly, adaptations of Himes's works moved further away from their originals. *Rage in Harlem* (dir. Bill Duke, 1991) based on *For the Love of Imabelle* (1957), Himes's first detective novel introducing Gravedigger and Coffin Ed, was a showcase for notable black actors of the time, among them Forest Whitaker, Gregory Hines, and Robin Givens, but just as Cincinnati, Ohio, was used to masquerade as Harlem, the movie masquerades as one addressing black life, but is more a caper comedy with a black cast and setting.

With black audiences desiring to see actors that looked like them on screen, and with white studios ready to capitalize on this new market, black novels continued to be a reservoir for Hollywood. Iceberg Slim's *Trick Baby* was made into a movie in 1972, and a Universal Pictures version followed in 1973 with a white actor playing the lead, grossing $11,000,000 at the box office. Beck's *Mama Black Widow* and *Pimp* are reportedly in development talks. The 2000s saw adaptations of Donald Goines's *Crime Partners* (dir. J. Jesses Smith, 2001) starring rap stars Ice-T, Ja Rule, and Snoop Dogg, and *Never Die Alone* (dir. Ernest Dickerson, 2004) starring rap artist DMX.

Based on the Iceberg Slim novel, *Trick Baby* (dir. Larry Yust) was the first Holloway House book adapted for the screen. "Shake hands with 'Folks' and 'Blue.' And then count your fingers!" read the 1972 poster tagline, indicating the movie would be more rogue buddy film than inquiry into race and street culture.[19] Shooting in Philadelphia was to provide the movie with an authentic "ghetto" feel. The black actor Mel Stewart played Blue, and the white actor Kiel Martin, White Folks. The cultural resonance of passing, of a community knowing a character's origins in spite of appearance, is lost in Martin's performance. Only external references, other characters letting viewers know that he is not white, his calling another black man "nigger" in front of the white gangster they are conning, mark his blackness. Neither the psychological agonizing of White Folks nor the ambivalence of Blue toward the "gift" that allows White Folks to pass are conveyed, and scenes where White Folks has sex with white women, which Beck clearly poses as transgressive lose their bite coming off more as sex within a race. Martin is left with the challenge of "playing" blackness, and through approximations of speech and slapping five delivers an uneven performance that often borders on stereotype.

Against a backdrop of blaxploitation, some movies did attempt more serious portraits. In 1978 Alice Childress's young adult novel *A Hero Ain't Nothin' But a Sandwich* was made into a movie starring Cicely Tyson, Paul Winfield, and directed by Ralph Nelson. The calls for less stereotypic portraits of black life led to a total revamping of Childress's work. The edginess of her setting is changed to a Los Angles home with a peach tree in the back yard and lawn chairs. Ghetto streets are replaced with parks and scenes on a beach. Benjie's mother who is plain in the novel is replaced with a stylish Cicely Tyson, and she does not reflect the character's mindless adherence to tradition. His rehabilitation takes place in a suburban center and is shown through a series of sepia-tinted black and white photographs. The ambiguity surrounding Benjie's ultimate fate that closes Childress's novel is changed to a happy ending.

The small screen would do a much better job in adapting black novels. Ernest Gaines would see four of his works treated. In addition to the well-known 1974 television adaptation *The Autobiography of Miss Jane Pittman* (dir. John Korty), which won nine Emmy Awards, three other Ernest Gaines works made the transit to film media: *The Sky is Gray* (dir. Stan Lathan) based on the short story originally published in *Bloodline* (1968), *A Gathering of Old Men* (dir. Colker Schlondorff, 1987), and most recently, *A Lesson Before Dying* (dir. Joseph Sargent, 1999). The televised movie of *Miss Jane*, no doubt in an attempt to reach a wider audience, replaces the black teacher with a white reporter. The teacher is a figure that means much in Gaines's fiction because good ones show students the existence of a world beyond their segregated parameters. The switch almost mirrors the need for white authentication that accompanied many nineteenth-century narratives of the enslaved, and one of the most compelling qualities of Miss Jane is that she needs no such authentication. Her 111 years from enslavement to freedom to advocacy for civil rights is validation enough, but the transition from page to screen suggests that a white authenticator is necessary to make Jane's life appeal to a broad viewership. The novel ends with a scene of quiet defiance as Jane stares down the owner of her plantation who attempts to stop her from attending a protest march. The television movie closes with a scene that makes use of the familiar Jim Crow iconography of the segregated south as the camera follows Jane step by step to take a drink from the "Whites Only" water fountain at the courthouse. By the time of the made for television movie, "Whites Only" or "White" and "Colored" labels attached to drinking fountains, restrooms, restaurants, and gas stations were part of American visual culture increasingly replicated in black and white news photography and televised broadcasts of the Civil Rights and post–Civil Rights eras.[20] They are at once familiar, if repellant (to most). The power of these icons makes Jane's story familiar, and one might argue, through so doing so makes it more palatable.

Replicating Gaines's narrative style is perhaps one of the most difficult tasks of adapting his works. In most productions, regional voice is effected through the characters' speech, but a novel such as *A Gathering of Old Men* is more complicated because it is told through a communal narrative where many men take credit for the killing of the Cajun overseer Beau. In the book narrative, segments impart individuality to men whom society has homogenized as black laborers. This complexity is difficult to reproduce in film form, and the screenplay for the televised *Gathering* written by black playwright Charles Fuller merges some of the narrators into single characters. The *Why* of the men's motivation loses ground to the what of the plot and the where of location. The ending of the movie privileges finite closure over ambiguity through a scene of white Cajuns who had come to avenge Beau's death, fleeing in the face of black solidarity. The change is more rousingly feel-good, but it minimizes the slow transformation that is the focus of the novel. The cinematography makes particular use of local setting through pans of the cane fields, the bayou, the local cemetery, and a camera that lingers on hanging Spanish moss. These elements, along with pans of cotton fields, are classic signifiers of the rural south in much the same way Jim Crow images signify segregation. A visual shorthand is thus established.

A Lesson Before Dying is the most recent adaptation of a Gaines novel. Its innocent protagonist Jefferson awaits death for the murder of the shop-keeper Mr. Gropé. He is transformed by the tutelage of Grant Wiggins, and by writing his feelings in a journal. Short of using voiceover and on-screen reproduction of written text, mirroring Jefferson's coming to awareness through writing is difficult to duplicate on the small screen, but in spite of opting for a chronological chronicling of events, the filmed version keeps very close to the text and tries to reproduce some of its complexities. The simultaneous beauty and ugliness of Gaines's segregated setting is rendered through landscape shots encompassing cane fields, antebellum mansions, and the courthouse as a symbol of a questionable justice. Don Cheadle as Grant and Mekji Phifer as Jefferson provide nuanced and contrasting performances focusing on individual responses to the many forms of con-finement racism engenders. *A Lesson* is written at a time when cultural discourse surrounding race is beginning to critique essentialism, when the binaries of black and white are replaced by hybridity and fusions, and the film's emphasis on individual right to self-assertion and self-determination reflects this. Though Gaines's works are sited in a single locale, they por-tray the complicated co-existences of black and white Americans, Cajuns, and Creoles. His southern hybridity is very much in keeping with modern American examination of multiple fusions.

The adaptations of Gaines novels, particularly *Miss Jane Pittman*, showed that there was an audience for portraits of black experience beyond the blaxploitation, action/adventure model. The phenomenal success of the televised miniseries adaptation of Alex Haley's *Roots* (dir. Marvin J. Chomsky et al. 1976) would provide additional proof, particularly since the experience of Kunta Kinte and his descendants fit into the American myths of individualism and the rise from rags to riches. A writer familiar with the big screen, Haley co-wrote the screenplay for *Super Fly T.N.T.* (dir. Ron O'Neal, 1973) the sequel to the hit 1972 film *Superfly* (dir. Gordon Parks, Jr., 1972). He published *Roots* in 1976 and the miniseries appeared in 1977. Each fueled the success of the other.[21] Alex Haley had subtitled the novel of his family history, *The Saga of an American Family*, and it spanned the forcible taking of his ancestor from West Africa to the United States, his ordeals and those of his descendants in slavery, and their ultimate emancipation and settlement of their own land. Grounded in family oral history, the novel imagined both a black origins and redemption story while "universalizing" black experiences into an American story of assimilation and triumph. Its depiction of Kunta's life in his west African village, his revolt against being renamed as a slave, his desire that his daughter Kizzy remember her African heritage, and her desire to pass this heritage on to her son George, galvanized all manner of ethnic Americans to search for their origins.

ABC brought *Roots* to the small screen at a time when more and more households in the United States owned television sets. From the start, producers were concerned with how to present the story without offending the white segment of this growing viewership. In order to give them an entry point, the number and complexity of white characters was increased as the novel made its way to the screen.[22] The attempt was to make *Roots* as American as possible. In 1977, one year after the United States Bicentennial celebration, an ABC television network ad for the series characterized it as "The motion picture that took 200 years to unfold." It went further, describing the miniseries as "the true story of men and women who helped build America," and as "the triumph of a family, from its cruelest hardships to freedom and a new beginning." The ad made use of American history and myths. Descriptive references to "the squalor of Slave Row" and "the elegance and passion of Plantation life" linked the production to America's fascination with antebellum fantasy.[23] Shown over eight nights, Neilsen ratings logged 130 million viewers, a record, and it went on to win nine Emmy awards. Two sequels would return to the novel's content, *Roots: The Next Generations* (dir. John Erman et al., 1979) and *Roots: The Gift* (dir. Kevin Hooks, 1988), a Christmas special. The formula of *Roots* would be repeated in *Queen: The Story of an American Family* (John Erman et al., 1993), another Haley multigenerational family saga. Completed by screenwriter David Stevens after Haley's death and also made into a successful miniseries, it moves from Ireland to Alabama, and centers on Queen Jackson Haley, the author's grandmother. One more Haley adaptation was made, *Mama Flora's Family* (dir. Peter Werner, 1998), a saga of twentieth-century black life from the 1920s to the 1990s, but both book and miniseries received mixed reviews, and by the close of the 1990s the Haley formula seemed to be drawing a smaller viewership.

Even with the success of film versions of *The Autobiography of Miss Jane Pittman* and *Roots*, it was still difficult to get support for black projects. In

1984 the *American Playhouse* PBS series produced James Baldwin's *Go Tell It on the Mountain*. With the success of *Roots*, *Go Tell It on the Mountain* (dir. Stan Lathan) was initially envisioned as a miniseries. Producer Robert Geller had difficulty finding funding, and the project was cut back to a two-hour television movie with the National Endowment for the Humanities footing most of the bill. African Caribbean scriptwriter Gus Edwards, who was also an actor and playwright with works performed by the Negro Ensemble Company, was faithful to the work. Baldwin himself felt the production did not betray the book (Bennetts n. pag.). Edwards made use of flashbacks to deepen the character development of Baldwin's John Grimes, his bother Roy, and the iciness of his stepfather Gabriel. The film, like the novel, is told from John's perspective, and his narrated voiceover provides not only a sense of his growth and understanding, but also context gained by the benefit of hindsight. The backstories of the women in the novel are reduced, but the powerful performances of the actors Olivia Cole, Rosalind Cash, and Rose Weaver underscore Baldwin's homage to the centrality of black women to black experience.

While attempts to bring dramatic novels to screen outlets continued to be difficult, other genres had an easier time, particularly the hardboiled detective novel whose telling is often linear and chronological, and whose perspective is generally the single one of the detective. Walter Mosley's most famous adaptation was *Devil in a Blue Dress* (dir. Carl Franklin, 1995). Mosley speaks eloquently of the difficulties in getting a work into film format, the amount of money needed to make an adaptation, the pitfalls of casting and producing, but he notes that on the plus side because his works demand black actors, and because black actors are always underemployed, he gets A-list talent easily, including Cicely Tyson and Laurence Fishburne for *Always Outnumbered* (dir. Michael Apted, 1998) and Denzel Washington and Don Cheadle for *Devil* (Brady 114).

The opening scene of *Devil* pans Archibald John Motley, Jr.'s *Bronzeville at Night* (1949). The painting actually depicts Chicago's Bronzeville, an area settled by black migrants from the south, and its use highlights some of the novel's themes. Easy Rawlins himself is a migrant, from Louisiana to Houston to Los Angeles. Like Bronzeville to its denizens, his house and neighborhood constitute a safe black space apart from the segregation that impedes his life and leads to his firing. The pan of the painting, itself filled with the vitality and motion of urban black life, then shifts into the filmic representation of Easy's Los Angeles neighborhood. Clothing, cars, sets, are all period specific and accurate. In true film noir fashion, the voice of Easy opens the movie with his narration as he sits in Joppy's bar, recalling how he has lost his job. Here, as in the novel, Easy is approached by Dewitt Albright to find a white woman who has a predilection for black men. Easy's need to pay his mortgage after being laid off from his defense department job and encouragement from Joppy leads to his taking the case.

In 1991 Carolyn Kozo Cole, curator of the Los Angeles Public Library's photo collection, wanted to portray Los Angeles life beyond the official record. Her desire launched a six-year research project "Shades of L.A.: A Search for Visual Ethnic History," through which thousands of family photographs of Los Angeles's various races and ethnicities were located and copied.[24] The collection was a source for director Carl Franklin. This added to interviews of musicians whose memories helped his imagining of Joppy's jazz club recreated a nostalgic 1950s California (Lloyd n. pag.). Made in 1995, the movie comes after the Rodney King riots and has the effect of creating a longing for an imagined time somehow "prettier" than a Los Angeles after the 1992 conflagrations and the multiple social schisms they brought to light. *Devil* creates a mediated reality wherein the city can be imagined without its fracturing.

The late twentieth century saw the greatest number of black novels adapted to film via Hollywood and television led by versions of Teri McMillan novels *Waiting to Exhale* (dir. Forest Whitaker, 1995), *How Stella Got Her Groove Back* (dir. Kevin Rodney Sullivan, 1998), and *Disappearing Acts* (dir. Gina Prince-Bythewood, 2000). *Los Angeles Times* movie critic Kenneth Turan captures the nature of the first two films when he describes *Waiting* as filled with "Gorgeous stars, drop-dead clothes, glamorous settings": "*Waiting to Exhale* has all the trappings of a lush, old-fashioned romantic melodrama, the kind of classic 'women's picture' that used to appear periodically in the 1950s, most likely directed by Douglas Sirk with titles like *Magnificent Obsession* and *All That Heaven Allows*" (Turan n. pag.). Forest Whitaker's direction gives heavy focus to the workings of each woman's mind as she deals with the question of finding an appropriate partner, and their dialogues presented in circular tracking shots mirrors the circle they have formed to provide support and empowerment. As it tells the story of the death of a friend, Delilah, *How Stella Got Her Groove Back* contrasts escapist scenery and tear-jerking scenes. *Disappearing Acts* moves away from this formula by giving more focus to the male point of view. The movie considerably tones down the abuse inflicted by the male protagonist, Franklin. Violence is not directed at Zora's body, as it is in the novel, but at things. The alternating narration between male and female perspectives in the novel is removed, resulting in a minimizing of the novel's exploration of the sources of gender biases and violence. The adaptations are new iterations of women's pictures. The characters engage in an ostensibly universal quest for love implicitly shown as transcending race, and enter wish fulfillment both through cinematic fantasy and purchasing power.

The links between book, film, and buying power are personified in Oprah Winfrey. *The Women of Brewster Place* (dir. Donna Deitch, 1989) and *Beloved* (dir. Jonathan Demme, 1998) were coproduced by her, and these were followed by her Harpo Studios production of *Oprah Winfrey Presents: The Wedding* (dir. Charles Burnett, 1998) and *Their Eyes Were Watching God* (dir. Darnell Martin 2005) for which she would be executive producer. Questions of representation still dogged the production process of these works. The NAACP requested to see the script of *Brewster Place* before the filming (Kogan n. pag.). Though Winfrey declined, citing that the source of problems with representation was a lack of varied images, not the images within this work, in the end the television series included more positive images of black men. Reviews were still mixed, most still focusing on questions of representations. *The Wedding* fared even less well. The social complexities that West delicately details in her novel devolve into two-dimensionality because so much of the knotty personal histories are sacrificed for linear chronological development. The difficulties of adapting *Their Eyes* are even more evident in the movie's inability to render the novel's unique language and folk ethos in which characters criticize yet support one another. Janie is shown to be a sensual character through surrounding her with nature, but the importance of sensuality to the development of her worldview never comes across. Sadly, the multicultural life Janie finds on the muck, here, is relegated to a variety of cultural caricatures. In spite of mixed critical reviews, however, each of these television productions did well in their time slots no doubt because of Winfrey's popularity.

Less successful was the ambitious adaptation of *Beloved* (dir. Jonathan Demme, 1998). Winfrey chose a "faithful adaptation," virtually impossible for a work so intricate. The changes from temporal reality to imaginative "reality," from past to present to timeless, pose extreme challenges and suffer when the work is placed in a linear format. The movie misses much of the novel's spirit, particularly the eponymous one. In the film Beloved's presence in the house in Ohio is shown through reddening hallways and creaking floorboards. The effect is to evoke sensational horror rather than the deeply disturbing historical horror at the heart of the novel.

Perhaps the major success of Winfrey's productions is in their bringing the novels greater attention. Few of these works would have been adapted without Winfrey's intervention. ABC would not have done *Brewster Place* were it not for her request and the popularity of her show on the network (Kogan n. pag.). All the works chosen for adaptation were selections on Oprah's Book Club. Their transformation into film, with Oprah producing or at times starring in them, takes advantage of an already existing audience. Novel, Winfrey Book Club selection, and film almost become a single genre "written" by Oprah Winfrey that garners greater exposure and greater prominence for the works.

The telemovie *The Women of Brewster Place* was based on a novel by a black woman, was co-produced by a black woman, and directed by a white woman. Critics at the time noted this racial and gender lineage as part of what contributed to a realistic portrayal that though not identical to was very much in keeping with the tone of the book. The production was frequently compared to Steven Spielberg's *The Color Purple* (1985), not always to Spielberg's advantage.[25] A self-described non-reader, and a man who characterized his movie *E. T. the Extra-Terrestrial* (1982) as being representative of marginalization due to E.T.'s being a minority, Spielberg might not have seemed a natural choice for directing this adaptation. It would be the first film whose story he told through acting and not special effects (Breskin 74). Producer Kathleen Kennedy noted that Spielberg wanted to engage material he was not known for, but his version, while popular with audiences, was roundly criticized for creating a Disneyfication of Walker's novel, for mixing *Tobacco Road* (dir. John Ford, 1941), *The Wizard of Oz* (dir. Victor Fleming, 1939), and *Imitation of Life* (dir. John M. Stahl, 1934; Douglas Sirk, 1959) into a lavender-diluted manifestation of purple, and certainly not a lavender that nodded to LGBTQ (lesbian, bisexual, gay, transgender, or queer) concerns.[26] Walker was, however, very much involved in the film's making. Before signing on to the adaptation she listed her desiderata as approving of director, script, and wanting half of the people behind the screen to be black.[27] She wrote the initial screenplay titled "Watch for Me in the Sunset," but because of fatigue insisted that Spielberg not use this and instead find another screenwriter. The Dutch Menno Meyjes was brought on board. Co-producer Quincy Jones, who also composed the soundtrack, and Steven Spielberg wanted Walker on set virtually everyday during filming to act as an advisor. According to Jones, Walker's biggest fear was that the film would be an embarrassment to black people.[28]

It is difficult to transpose an epistolary novel to film, and Spielberg selects to signify finding voice in literal ways. Celie, played by Whoopi Goldberg, is mute for much of the initial part of the movie, and her inner thoughts are conveyed through voiceover. Her self-actualization is literally rendered through her exercising the act of speech. Spielberg, a director who focuses on the imagination of his characters, does so here in scenes showing the impact of her sister Nettie's letters. As Celie sits on a porch at sunset to read one of Nettie's epistles, visions of her imagined Africa are superimposed on her daily world. Her sunset morphs into the sunset over plains crisscrossed by giraffes and a dancing Nettie, illustrating the power of writing to create images. Sound is used to make transitions as well as. As Celie reads another letter under a leaky roof, the tinkle of raindrops land-ing in pots catching water becomes the sound of a balophon, and scenes of the interaction between Oliva, Celie's daughter, and Tashi appear. The worksong of men in Hartwell, Georgia, laying track becomes the expres-sion of black colonial workers building a road through the Olinka village where Nettie assists in missionary work. The effect is to underscore not only the sisters' connection, but a larger diasporic one.

The movie bends to conservatism. Spielberg's works, *Jaws* (1975), *Close Encounters of the Third Kind* (1977), and *Indiana Jones and the Raiders of the Lost Ark* (1981) center on male characters, and his *Color Purple* beefs up the portrayals of men in the novel. Mr.____, Albert, and Harpo are chronicled as both grow, Harpo into defying gender roles by accepting childrearing and housekeeping duties and Albert, realizing his wrongs, into the hero who reunites Celie and Nettie. The relationship between Celie and Shug, one that allows Celie to gain power from her sexuality, is greatly mini-mized. They share a single, sedate kiss between friends because Spielberg felt that he was not the director to do this storyline, and that it was too far ahead of its time. The slender, brown skinned Margaret Avery is cast as Shug, conforming to ideas of traditional feminine desirability, in marked contrast to a character Walker describes as dark, with legs like trees, more akin to Ma Rainey or Bessie Smith. The changes evade criticism for por-traying bisexuality and for black male bashing and produce a Hollywood movie designed to appeal broadly. Reading Walker's account of the adap-tation *The Same River Twice* (1995), it is apparent that her reaction to the process of turning her novel into a movie was itself one of process. Filming occurred during illness, relationship complications, and her mother being near death, and her response to an early viewing was that it was slick, anachronistic, and apolitical. Her respect and affection for both Spielberg and Jones tempered this, and by the time of the premier she loved it, though she was stung by the negative responses of black viewers. Spielberg never thought of *The Color Purple* as just a black movie (Breskin 74), His comments imply that to be "just" a black movie is somehow limiting, and much of what he does in the film is create ways for those who feel outside of black culture to connect, to "universalize" the novel's word. Walker does the opposite in the novel. She writes her characters' interiority, and allows the story to stand on its own terms as it welcomes its audience.

The themes of incest and a woman unaware of her value and finding her voice were handled very differently almost a decade later in an independent film, but responses to *Precious* (dir. Lee Daniels, 2009) reveal that representation and ownership of black images are still areas of contention. Set in an era when supply-side Regonomics devastate the social safety net of those most disadvantaged, the movie touches on incest, AIDS, black welfare mothers, and black female self-actualization. It does not sacrifice faithfulness to Sapphire's *Push* to audience comfort. Daniels creates dimly lit interior scenes at the movie's beginning that presage the dismal prospects of Claireece "Precious" Jones.

For Daniels, successfully recreating the interiority of Sapphire's novel necessitated emphasis on the act of literal self-reflection. The depth of Claireece's self-hatred and desire for escapism are shown through her seeing herself in a mirror as a white girl, or in fantasies. When she seeks to imagine alternatives to her real-life relationships, her only reference points are movies, however remote their content. On television she watches Italian neorealist Vittorio De Sica's *Two Women* (1960), starring Sophia Loren as a mother trying to protect her twelve-year-old daughter, Rosetta, from the terrors of World War II, and imagines this as a model for a mother-daughter relationship with herself and a kinder version of Mary as the leads. But fantasy and reality merge inversely when Cesira is unable to protect her daughter from a gang rape (unlike Mary who ignores her daughter's repeated sexual assault), an image reminding of Claireece's total abandonment. Daniels said that he had a particular affection for the fantasy sequences and would have included cartoons had budget permitted, though he is also aware that such treatment might have evoked ire at paralleling the tragedy of Claireece's situation with animation. The contrast between fantasy and reality allows the film to go beyond voyeurism reveling in black pathology and mark the sources of the deterioration of the black lives it portrays.

The change that did evoke controversy in Daniels's adaptation was his casting of a light-skinned Paula Patton as Ms. Rain (his first choice was Penelope Cruz) in contrast to Sapphire's dreadlocked brown skinned teacher (Stevens 11). Sapphire noted many of her readers felt betrayed by the casting, as it conformed to limiting the sphere of dark black women. She observed that the movie's stars Paula Patton, Mo'Nique, and Gabourey Sibedey are all black, but acknowledged that light-skinned black women experience race differently than their dark-skinned counterparts and that this is a point that still needs to be addressed. Sapphire wondered if casting Patton, however, could also be read in a different light, as creating a character representing a race solidarity that ignores color hierarchies to make sure that women such as Claireece were no longer victims of their circumstances (McNeil 352). The movie's casting and the public response show colorism not as past, but as an ongoing concern.

Criticism has argued over whether the movie was uplifting or dwelt in a mire of black deviance, and in providing no easy answer to this debate, Daniels is perhaps most faithful to the novel. Sapphire wanted no such easy closure, because to do so would ignore ongoing social challenges. The film might be interpreted as more positive than the novel, as the final scene shows Claireece in possession of her two children walking into her future to the soundtrack of Labelle's "It Took A Long Time" (1974).

The space between novel and adaptation provides a useful site for investigating how African American novels move in the popular sphere. Questions of cultural ownership, cultural appropriation, and artistic freedom are illuminated through considering editorial decisions and aesthetic choices made as a work of literature is transferred from page to screen. Considering the adaptation process further encourages contemplation of changing or static cultural climates. One constant over the past one hundred years is that single books and movies seem unable to break away from an expectation that they represent the entire black race. The number of works in both genres that make it to publisher or theatre still remains too small to produce the wide and varied representations that would mirror the many facets of black life. From the loose to the faithful, issues of adaptation quickly become intertwined with questions of racial portraiture.

To take a work from one medium and place it in another is not an easy process. The path from acquiring film rights to producing a film is never a certain one, and many movie projects are abandoned en route. Constraints of budget, casting, and the need to appeal to a broad audience for commercial viability while not offending a smaller one, invariably change how a text will appear in film. But the increasing frequency of black novels' adaptations is testament to the expansiveness with which they treat racial, cultural, and historical themes while coupling these with skillful storytelling. The cross-fertilization of the forms benefit both as black novels come to be known by a larger populace and films are encouraged to adjust creatively to new material.

CHAPTER 14

Novels of the Diaspora

The African American novel tradition has long influenced other black writers' shaping of racial and cultural experience. More as a contemplation and suggestion for further inquiry into this relationship, I would like to close this study by considering the impact of African American culture and history on novels written by black authors who are not African American. Many writers could be included here – Michelle Cliff, Edwidge Danticat, Frank Hercules, Jamaica Kincaid, Paule Marshall, Elizabeth Nunez, and Zadie Smith – but I would like to consider three novels where African American cultural history influenced core motifs: Claude McKay's *Home to Harlem* (1928), Maryse Conde's *I, Tituba Black Witch of Salem* (1992), and Caryl Phillips, *Crossing the River* (1992). All use African American experience and the idea of a collective past to interrogate and expand received narratives of black identity.

Claude McKay is an early example of a writer whose interaction with African American novelists greatly shaped the diasporic vision of his novels. In the 1920s and 1930s when McKay composed his works, black writer was synonymous with black American writer, and black experience portrayed in widely published novels predominantly meant black American experience. Writers of the Francophone and Hispanophone Caribbean – Aimé Césaire of Martinique, Jacques Roumain of Haiti, Léon Damas of French Guiana, Luis Palés Matos of Puerto Rico, Nicolás Guillén of Cuba – chose poetry as their primary medium and Anglophone novel writing had yet to hit its stride in the 1940s and later with Victor Stafford Reid's *New Day* (1949), George Lamming's *In the Castle of My Skin* (1953), and V. S. Naipaul's *A House for Mr. Biswas* (1961). McKay occupies a dual space during the 1920s–1930s, perceived as a West Indian writer at times and as a "Negro" writer at other times.

Born of farm parents, McKay was proud of his Jamaican antecedents, and used them to underscore the global interconnections of black culture. His work as a constable in Kingston brought him into intimate contact with both colonial racism as well as the intraracial color hierarchies that were its legacy. Festus Claudius McKay was a citizen of the world living in, among other places, Holland, England, Belgium, the Soviet Union, but it was in Harlem that McKay centered himself as novelist. McKay lived among a coterie of artists including Langston Hughes whose description of McKay's residence gives a small sense of the cross-fertilization of his Harlem environs: "Claude is living at 33 West 125th Street on the top floor of an old store building. He has what looks like a typical Greenwich Village artist's roost of the more musty variety. Across the hall young [artist Romare] Bearden has a studio. There is a genuine bohemian note up there – like the old days" (Nichols 94). His first novel *Home to Harlem* (1928) captured this world, and through its title and content, offers a sense of how central interacting with black American culture was to the creation of his work. Vernacular elements in the novel are used to portray a black way of thinking and being in the world that was in contrast to what he perceived as a European emphasis on materialism and orthodoxy.

McKay's use of folk and vernacular elements to typify black culture did not suit all readers. In reviewing *Home to Harlem*, W. E. B. Du Bois wrote, "[I]t looks as though ... McKay has set out to cater for that prurient demand on the part of white folk ... He has used every art and emphasis to paint drunkenness, fighting, lascivious sexual promiscuity and utter absence of restraint in as bold and as bright colors as he can" (785). But white patroness Charlotte Mason loved what she perceived as the novel's rawness. She saw it as an antidote to the "deadening influence" of Carl Van Vechten's *Nigger Heaven* (1926), and as reinforcing her belief in the power of the primitive, "That life and laughter is ready to burst into such brilliant sunshine, that in the end all that world will be robed in beauty, and all the peoples of the world will be freed to recognize the powers of recreation."[1] In her letter she clearly expresses her zeal for the redemptive power of primitivism for whites. Even Du Bois had to concede that McKay accomplished a delineation of a black Atlantic cultural metaphysics: "The race philosophy," he writes, "is of great interest. McKay has become an international Negro. He is a direct descendant from Africa. He knows the West Indies; he knows Harlem; he knows Europe; and he philosophizes about the whole thing" (Aptheker 136). Though he is an "international Negro," McKay uses African American experience as a means to envision global blackness.

In *Home to Harlem*, McKay makes use of two key themes common to many novels of the Harlem Renaissance: the returning black American soldier and Harlem as a city within a city. The protagonist Jake is a picaro whose adventures dramatize American racism, the experience of returning black World War I veterans, and Harlem culture. Jake deserts, not because of cowardice, but because he can no longer reconcile America's treatment of blacks with the war's rhetoric of freedom and democracy. His thoughts unfold through vignettes set in Harlem's landscape, and sites evoke an idealized primordial Africa with restaurants and bars named the "Congo," "Sheba Palace," and "Nile Queen Restaurant." This naming as well as the descriptions of music and dancing are meant to make atavistic links illuminating McKay's view of the roots of distinctive black culture.

The question remains why use black American experience to limn the nature of cultural identities sharing African roots? Colin Palmer provides a possible answer when he observes, "African Americans appear to have been the only peoples of African descent in the Americas who wrote extensively about Africa before the end of slavery in their respective societies. They were, to be sure, the most literate of those who enjoyed a free status while slavery lasted, a factor that helps to explain their intellectual productivity. Their ambivalent embrace of Africa was driven by a compelling need to claim an ancestral homeland, a development that was given some urgency by the harshness of the racism they confronted in the land of their birth" (105). Because they left such an extensive record of thoughts on enslavement and freedom, and because they articulated the complications of situating a desire for origins in a region ideated as inferior, black American writers lay the foundation for explorations of diaspora's meanings. Narratives of a middle passage transit and the process of becoming American while negotiating racism and discrimination, proved useful vehicles for other writers contemplating contact between African and European.

In *I Tituba, Black Witch of Salem* (1986), originally published as *Moi, Tituba Sorcière . . . Noire de Salem*, Maryse Condé uses African American experience to take direct aim at the hypocrisies of founding myths. Making use of the slave narrative and setting the novel in the prenational period, with the 1692 witch trials as a backdrop, she explores the fissures of race, class, and gender inequality left out of documents singing the praises of nation and empire. Condé was not the first black woman writer to make use of Tituba's tale. In 1955, Ann Petry published a children's novel, *Tituba of Salem Village*. Her Tituba is a heroine whose courage amidst adversity is designed to serve as a model for young readers.

Condé undoes the narrative of exclusion that undergirds John Winthrop's "A Modell of Christian Charity" (1630) or William Bradford's *Of Plymouth Plantation* (1620–1647) and other canonical origins stories that imagine seekers of religious freedom taming an inhospitable environment to create an exemplary "city on a hill" (Winthrop, 47).[2] Tituba corrects their chronicles, making space for her own. Early in the novel she states that she fears she will be forgotten, that there will only be haphazard mention of "a slave originating from the West Indies and probably practicing "hoodoo'" (110), and a glance at many American history annals proved this to be true. In the scant record that remains, her identity changes from Caribbean to Native American to African, and these mutations indicate a generalized fusion of otherness.[3] Tituba's story fades to black in the records of the Salem witchcraft, but Condé revives it and places it within the traditions of narratives that question how slavery and ideals of liberty can coexist.

Told in the first-person, the opening statements of Tituba's narrative make clear the themes Condé will engage: sexual violence against women (through an act of rape), religious hypocrisy (through the naming of the ship that brings Tituba to the first stop in the triangular slave trade, the Caribbean), and the racial oppression that comes from empire (through the reference to legacies of hate). Tituba recalls her origins: "Abena, my mother, was raped by an English sailor on the deck of *Christ the King* one day in the year 16** while the ship was sailing for Barbados. I was born from this act of aggression. From this act of hatred and contempt" (4). Abena cannot express her love for her daughter in life and remains indifferent to her. Only the encouragement of Yao, the fellow slave she loves and lives with, gets Abena to even embrace her daughter. They reside in Barbados among Igbo and Ashanti, and Condé underscores that this world is still very much African, even though it is in the Caribbean. When Tituba is seven, her mother defends herself against her master's attempt to rape her by stabbing him. He does not die, but Abena is hanged for attacking a white man. It is only when she crosses over through death and joins her African ancestors that she becomes an affectionate and at times overly concerned mother. Condé weaves African, American, and Caribbean experiences into a narrative illustrating the historical, social, and political linkages of hemispheric blackness and revising canonized narratives.

For Condé, black America provided a model of dualism: on the one hand, images of black celebrity suggest promise for black success; on the other, poverty and racism suggest a more dire reality (B. Lewis 544). She has stated that she used Tituba to explore the Puritan foundations of American racism and exclusion to stress that the legacy continues, as well as to provide members of the diaspora with an alternative narrative of what went before contact with Europeans ("Afterword" 203–204). Telling the story of what went before is an aim of much of African American writing. Autobiographies, journals, and letters were all genres through which creators explored a past that could not be concretely known. In

Crossing the River, Caryl Phillips uses of all these forms to write a counter narrative deconstructing the commerce and consequences of enslavement.

After traveling the United States on a Greyhound bus for five weeks, Caryl Phillips recalls reading Richard Wright's *Native Son* while lying on a beach in Los Angeles. Both experiences, riding and reading, cemented his desire to be a writer (R. Bell 582). 1950s and 1960s black American activism and writers Ralph Ellison, James Baldwin, Toni Morrison, and Wright illuminated the cultural politics of England for him.[4] In an interview where he defines himself as part of a cadre of writers who don't fit neatly into a national tradition – Michael Ondaatje, Edwidge Danticat, Rohinton Mistry, among them – he notes that he feels there really isn't a black British or Caribbean writing tradition. The former, represented by writers such as himself and Ben Okri, have such divergent concerns that little binds them into a tradition, and the latter, represented by Samuel Selvon and George Lamming, dispersed throughout England. For him, there is a strong African American tradition, however, and though he sees himself as an outsider to it, he describes it as "very deep and extensive" (Clingman 121). Black American expression provides an indigenousness that Philips could not find in Britain because he saw no tradition of black writing that did not have its genesis in a migrant presence.

African American experience provides much of the source material for *Crossing the River*'s portraits of injustice and inequality. After a prologue that introduces the "desperate foolishness," causing the scattering of Africa's "children," a segment set in the 1830s recalls the challenge black American writers faced in extricating themselves from white narrative framing. "The Pagan Coast" opens in the third person voice of slave owner Edward Williams, and positions his former slave Nash Williams as a smart, talented teacher, but not an equal. Throughout a passage that praises Nash's accomplishments are phrases that evoke paternalism: Nash is doing missionary work in a country of "heathens"; his requests to his master for tools, seeds, and money are "childish"; and the enslaved who have been educated by Edwards and other well-meaning owners have now been blessed with "rational Christian minds" (7–9). Nash has been treated with a degree of favor that even Edward's wife Amelia resents, but he has been exiled to Liberia to do missionary work because an educated slave can never exist as a citizen of the United States. Unbeknown to Nash, Amelia who not only resents the attention Edward lavishes on Nash, but also the attention he lavishes on the retainer who replaces him, has intercepted his letters to his former master. She leaves Edward and ultimately kills herself.

Only in the discovered letters does Nash's voice break through the frame Edward has created. The sequence of epistles reveals the former slave's growing anger and resentment to what he sees as abandonment. Disillusioned by Edward and the ostensible morality of Christian America, Nash is left in an unfamiliar land to find a new moral compass. He becomes more and more a part of a world he cannot fully navigate and rationalizes his participation in practices he once found abhorrent, including polygamy. Increasingly his words portray Edward's reluctant slaveholding, and his sending Nash to do missionary work on behalf of the American Colonization Society, in ways that undermine Edward's self-congratulatory praise of his efforts to reward faithful slaves, stave off barbarism, and institute civilization in a benighted land.

When Nash's letters cease, Edward sets sail to Liberia, undertaking a Marlowe-like journey with overtones of a reverse middle passage. When he discovers that his former slave is dead, his description of Nash reveals a questionable love. He recalls him as "the boy he had brought from the fields to the house, the boy who won his love, freely given, who would force on to him all the pain and confusion which finally proved too much for Amelia to bear" (58). The reflection is filled with both paternal and sexual overtones. Amelia's resentment of the fondness between Nash and Edward as well as her resentment of the continued favor he shows the retainer who replaces Nash suggests homoerotic commodification. Edward replaces one slave for another to satisfy his desire. As Edward and an older slave Madison, also embittered over being displaced by Nash, sit in a hut on their way to Nash's final dwelling place, Edward tells Madison how alone and lost he feels in Liberia and how he longs to be among his own people, "white and colored." He takes Madison's hands and squeezes them. Madison utters a simple "no," suggesting that Madison, too, was once part of Edward's habit (68). That the salutations of Nash's letters quickly switch from "Dear Beloved Benefactor," to "My Dear Father," (and Nash's insistence that he expects support from Edward) further suggests biological paternity. These strands combine to show decadent relationships that question whether slavery can ever be benign.

The section "West" views hypocrisies of racial injustice through the less familiar lens of African American westward migration. Martha is part of a wagon train going through the Colorado Territory to California in the 1860s. She is a slave when her master dies, and his banker nephew heir having no interest in plantation life sells everything including Martha, her husband, and the daughter she adores. The family is fractured, and Martha finds herself the property of the Hoffman family who move her from Virginia to Kansas. When they plan on selling her again to finance their trip to California, she runs, first to Dodge where she supports herself by cooking and doing laundry until the death of her second partner at the hands of angry whites. She then joins a caravan heading further west, but when hunger, dehydration, age, and cold make it clear she will never survive the journey to California with the younger members of the wagon train who must secure their own survival, she is left in Denver. In the freezing cold, for a while she sustains herself with a fantasy of reuniting with her daughter who would have become a woman of substance married to a teacher. She envisions three grandchildren and a fine house with her own room. In Denver she is taken in by a white woman whose impoverishment is just a few steps above Martha's, but during the night finally dies with no one knowing her story. Throughout the segment, the tenuousness of not being owned but not fully controlling your destiny is evident in the ever-present threat of loss: of income, of friends, of family, of self. Slavery and the social systems of racial and economic injustice it fostered are never really over.

The commerce that set the destinies of Nash and Martha in motion is the subject of the novel's third segment "Crossing the River," which employs the logs of a slaver in the 1750s to highlight the economic enterprise of enslavement and its resultant race and class hierarchies. In addition to describing the experiences of blacks, the portion shows that whites outside the privileged classes face their own exploitation. It opens with a listing of the ship's white personnel, those who have died, and those who have been discharged. It is only as the log proceeds that the larger significances of these fates are ascertained. Two sailors listed as discharged in the opening turn out to have stolen the ship's yawl and set shore to effect their own liberation from slave trafficking. One that is discharged is chained in irons because he seduced a pregnant slave, perhaps not for the first time. The second mate surgeon listed as deceased dies of a fever caused by the close quarters of the ship. The log portrays the actualities of trans-Atlantic crossings: disease, depravity, and the constant threat of insurrection. The captain who records these incidents has earned his position more through connections than experience. He hates the involvement, but sees it as a means of securing a financial future. The Africans he brings upon his boats are numbered and assessed as objects. His referring to them as "ill humored" (124) indicates his inability to see them as humans, the crux of what allows the enterprise and the racism that follows it to continue.

"Somewhere in England" is set in the World War II period, and segments dated by month and year form a diary. It tells of the love between
Joyce, a young English woman fond of reading, and a black American
soldier, Travis. She is the battered wife of an Englishman imprisoned for
selling contraband goods, so she knows much about gender inequity, and
through Travis, she learns the meaning of race. Telling their story from the
relative innocence of her point of view accentuates the artificiality, arbitrariness, yet power of racial construction. Her guilelessness imperils Travis
because she expects him to be able to move through the world with the
same ease her race allows. When they stay out past his curfew one night,
he is beaten by his own military police, as much for being with a white
woman as for being out. She becomes pregnant with Travis's baby, and he
is stationed in Italy. The army agrees to their plan to wed once she secures
a divorce, so long as they do not return to the United States, but Travis
dies in Italy, and she is encouraged to give up their son Greer for adoption.
Years later, he finds her, and though she wants to, she cannot recognize
him as her son because of her new roles as white wife and mother. Phillips
uses all these stories to show the residual impact of enslavement into the
1860s, 1940s, and the present.

Each of the segments extends the theme of deferred dreams through
specific moments in African American history: the disappointment in
Liberia as a new homeland, the disappointment in the West as the site
for a future of freedom, and the disappointment in fighting wars for liberty abroad while American racism persists. The epilogue underscores that
even if dreams do not materialize legacies do. Two former slaves (Nash,
Martha), the descendant of a slave (Travis) and his descendant (Greer), as
well as those who cause their situations, are all strands in the same narrative. Martha, Nash, Travis, Joyce, and Greer are part of a larger diaspora
and its outgrowths: the musical creations of jazz and r&b, revolutions,
insurrections, and continued oppressions.

The three writers discussed here use African American cultural history
to consider diaspora as an idea that acknowledges a sharing of an initial
history that included enslavement, colonization, and liberation. They then
further examine how the idea gave rise to interpretations of race, gender, and culture. Employing conceptions of Africa in the black American
imagination, they create diasporic novels that embody history and memory to bring contemporary social problems to light.

Ideas of black diaspora are literally and conceptually dynamic. They
make use of differing geographies, and the flux between past and present,

between realities and memories to correct and augment the vagaries of historiography. Many of the novels that take these ideas as their focus insert individual awareness into historical epochs so that the continuing consequences of history are no longer ignored. Novels of the diaspora reflect a people's common inquiries rooted in the various areas of the world they inhabit.

Coda

"The colored writer generally speaking, has not yet passed the point of thinking of himself first as a Negro, burdened with the responsibility of defending and uplifting the race," wrote Charles Chesnutt in his response to "The Negro in Art: How Shall He Be Portrayed?" (*The Crisis* Symposium 1926). He continued, "Such a frame of mind, however praiseworthy from a moral standpoint, is bad for art. Tell your story, and if it is on a vital subject, well told, with an outcome that commends itself to right-thinking people, it will, if interesting, be an effective brief for whatever cause it incidentally may postulate" (McElrath, *Essays* 492–493). Chesnutt's words signify the weight representation places on black novelists. Though his statements were made almost one hundred years ago, their import casts a long shadow.

Nineteenth-century novels of necessity in de facto fashion were charged with proving black humanity and intellect. Authors were evaluated in terms of their biology, and their books seen as evidence, testimony, but rarely art. Novels of the late 1910s and into the 1920s chipped away at these perceptions and created new fictional space for investigating what was oversimplified as black identity. The efforts of novelists were still constricted by the imposition of a persistent binary between aesthetics and activism, a binary affecting not only the perception of novels, but also the process of their creation. Many writers felt pressure to align themselves along this binary, or explain why they chose to ignore it. The privileging of art over politics was used to devalue novels that chose to engage in social dialogue, and frequently ignored the fact that embracing advocacy need not mean eschewing craft. From the opposite vantage point, not embracing politics was read as an act of racial disloyalty, and writers with race-ambivalent novels resisting easy categorization frequently found their works marginalized. Throughout their history, African American novels evidenced a quest for freedom on many levels: personal, racial, artistic. But the idea that the

African American novel represents or advocates for a community persists and now is more fraught than ever.

The notion of a racial collective is contested by modes of inquiry considering "hybridization," "nonessentialism," and "syncretism." The foregoing reconsiderations are not really about the writing, but about the reading of literary works. Black novels, in particular, have always addressed more than social circumstance and have always embraced many traditions while doing so. For more than 150 years they have illuminated ideas of freedom, caste, gender, sexuality, democracy, morality, equity, and done so while shaping written language in innovative ways. Over the course of its evolution, the culture and audience for African American novels has transformed, and the genre has responded, becoming so varied, reaching so many, that imposing labels and expectations is futile. These novels derive not from a single African American race but from the many nuances of being raced as African American.

African American novels have moved from being a literature of necessity to being a literature. Perhaps it is time for them once again to return to their origins, however, and have their themes applied to broader contexts. Perhaps they should once again become a literature of necessity because their arguments for the humanity of black Americans are needed to advocate for the respect of all human life; their arguments for equal treatment under the law are needed as reminders of the social justice work that still must be done. The visions of community within so many of them as well as their cautions of dangers to community, offer models for reordering social structures to benefit larger humanity. By making coherence out of the chaotic experiences of enslavement, racism, and the many resulting disjuncture's African American novels provide multiple examples for navigating the complex arrays of human experience.

Appendix

This appendix lists the novels of all writers within the study, as well as suggests secondary sources for further study. The field of African American literary criticism is vast, so I have primarily selected sources that provide context of the authors' philosophies and the cultural climates within which they worked, as opposed to those that provide narrower readings of particular themes or issues. This listing is by no means exhaustive. It is intended to offer an introduction to materials that flesh out the worlds of the novels.

Anderson, William H.

Novels

Appointed. An American Novel (1894)

Sources for context

Katzman, David. *Before the Ghetto: Black Detroit in the Nineteenth Century.* Chicago: University of Illinois Press, 1973.

Penn, I. Garland. *The Afro-American Press and Its Editors.* Springfield, MA: Willey & Co. Publishers, 1891. 158–164.

Warren, Francis H. *Michigan Manual of Freedmen's Progress.* Detroit: n. pag., 1915. Web. April 29, 2014.

Ansa, Tina McElroy

Novels

Baby of the Family (1989)
Ugly Ways (1993)
The Hand I Fan With (1996)
You Know Better (2002)
Taking After Mudear (2007)

Sources for context

Ansa, Tina McElroy. "Our First and Fiercest Love." *Essence* 43.1 (2012): 102. *MAS Ultra – School Edition*. Web. April 13, 2015.
Freeman, Owle et al. *Athens Literary Festival. Roots in Georgia II*. Videorecording. (Athens, GA: University of Georgia, 2003). *University of Georgia Catalog*. Web. April 13, 2015.
Henderson, Sharon Smith. *Kalliope* 21.2 (1999): 61–68.
Jordan, Shirley M. *Broken Silences: Interviews with Black and White Women Writers*. New Brunswick, NJ: Rutgers University Press, 1993. 1–27.

Anyabwile, Dawud (David J. A. Sims)

Novels

Brotherman, Dictator of Discipline: Revelation. Book One. Atlanta: Big City Entertainment, 2016.

Sources for context

Bates, Karen Grigsby. "Interview: Dawud Anyabwile Discusses Creating "Brotherman: The Dictator of Discipline," And his video, "Drawing from the Soul." *Tavis Smiley (NPR)* (n.d.): *Newspaper Source Plus*. Web. August 20, 2015.
"Dawud Anyabwile: An Interview with the Artist." *Color of Comics*. WordPress Blog. Web. August 20, 2015.
Tre, Scott. "For the People: An Interview with Artist and Illustrator Dawud Anyabwile, Co-Creator of *Brother Man: Dictator of Discipline*." *Scottscope* (August 23, 2011). Web. August 20, 2015.
Trujillo, Robert, "A New Toon. "*Mosaic* 24 (May 2009). Web. August 20, 2015.

Attaway, William

Novels

Blood on the Forge (1941)
Let Me Breathe Thunder (1969)

Sources for context

Garren, Samuel B. "'He Had Passion': William Attaway's Screenplay Drafts of Irving Wallace's The Man. (Cover Story)." *CLA Journal* 37.3 (1994): 245. *Humanities International Complete*. Web. March 8, 2016.
"William Attaway." *Afro-American Writers, 1940–1955*. 3–7. Detroit, MI: Gale, 1988. *MLA International Bibliography*. Web. March 8, 2016.

Griffin, Barbara L. J. "Attaway, William [Alexander]." *Continuum Encyclopedia of American Literature* (2003): 56–57. *Literary Reference Center.* Web. March 8, 2016.
Hart, James D. and Phillip W. Leininger. *Attaway, William (1911–1986).* Oxford: Oxford University Press, 2004. *Oxford Reference.* Web. March 8, 2016.

Baker, Nikki (Jennifer Dowdell)

Novels

In the Game (1991)
The Lavender House Murder (1992)
Long Goodbyes (1993)
The Ultimate Exit Strategy (2001)

Sources for context:

Klein, Katherine Gregory. *Great Women Mystery Writers: Classic to Contemporary.* Westport, CT: Greenwood, 1994.
Page, Yolanda Williams. *Encyclopedia of African American Women Writers.* Westport, CT: Greenwood, 2007.

Baldwin, James

Novels

Go Tell It on the Mountain (1953)
Giovanni's Room (1956)
Another Country (1962)
Tell Me How Long the Train's Been Gone (1968)
If Beale Street Could Talk (1974)
Just above My Head (1979)

Sources for context

Baldwin, James. *The Price of the Ticket: Collected Nonfiction, 1948–1985.* New York: St Martin's 1985.
Bloom, Harold, ed. *James Baldwin.* New York: Chelsea House, 1986.
Campbell, James. *Talking at the Gates: A Life of James Baldwin.* New York: Viking, 1991.
Field, Douglas, ed. *A Historical Guide to James Baldwin.* New York: Oxford, 2009.
Harris, Trudier. *Black Women in the Fiction of James Baldwin.* Knoxville: University of Tennessee Press, 1985.

Leeming, David. *James Baldwin: A Biography*. New York: Knopf, 1994.

LIVE from the NYPL: A James Baldwin Tribute: Colm Tóibín with John Edgar Wideman, Manthia Diawara, and Farah Jasmine Griffin. Web. January 6, 2015.

McBride, Dwight, ed. *James Baldwin Now*. New York: New York University Press, 1999.

Pavlic, Ed. *Who Can Afford to Improvise?: James Baldwin and Black Music, the Lyric and the Listeners*. New York: Fordham University Press, 2016.

Standley, Fred L. and Louis H. Pratt, eds. *Conversations with James Baldwin*. Jackson: University Press of Mississippi, 1989.

Zaborowska, Magdalena J. *James Baldwin's Turkish Decade: Erotics of Exile*. Durham: Duke, 2009.

Bambara, Toni Cade

Novels

The Salt Eaters (1980)
Those Bones Are Not My Child (1999)

Sources for context

Bambara, Toni Cade. *Deep Sightings and Rescue Missions: Fiction, Essays, and Conversations*. Ed. Toni Morrison. New York: Vintage, 1996.

Evans, Mari, ed. *Black Women Writers (1950–1980): A Critical Evaluation*. Garden City, NY: Anchor/Doubleday, 1984.

Holmes, Linda J. *A Joyous Revolt: Toni Cade Bambara, Writer and Activist*. Santa Barbara, CA: Praeger, 2014.

Holmes, Linda J and Cheryl A. Wall, ed. *Savoring the Salt: The Legacy of Toni Cade Bambara*. Philadelphia: Temple, 2008.

Lewis, Thabiti, ed. *Conversations with Toni Cade Bambara*. Jackson, MS: University Press of Mississippi, 2012.

Baraka, Amiri (LeRoi Jones)

Novels

The System of Dante's Hell (1965)

Sources for context

Baraka, Imamu Amiri. *The Autobiography of Leroi Jones/Amiri Baraka*. New York: Freundlich Books, 1984.

Brown, Lloyd W. *Amiri Baraka*. Boston: Twayne, 1980.

Jones, LeRoi, *Blues People: Negro Music in White America*. New York: Morrow, 1963.

The Dead Lecturer. New York: Grove, 1964.

Home: Social Essays. New York: Morrow, 1966.
Moreno Pisano, Claudia. *Amiri Baraka & Edward Dorn: The Collected Letters.*
    Albuquerque: University of New Mexico Press, 2014.
Tate, Greg. Foreword. Amiri. Baraka, *The Fiction of Leroi Jones/Amiri Baraka.*
    Chicago: Lawrence Hill Books, 2000.
Watts, Jerry Gafio. *Amiri Baraka: The Politics and Art of a Black Intellectual.*
    New York: New York University Press, 2001.

Beatty, Paul

Novels

The White Boy Shuffle (1996)
Tuff (2000)
Slumberland (2008)
The Sellout (2015)

Sources for context

"Beatty, Paul." *Columbia Guide To Contemporary African American Fiction* (2005):
    43–45. *Literary Reference Center.* Web. April 15, 2015.
Haye, Christian, and Paul Beatty. "Paul Beatty." *BOMB* 47 (1994): 22–24.
    JSTOR Journals. Web. December 14, 2015.
Shavers, Rone, and Paul Beatty. "Paul Beatty." *BOMB* 72 (2000): 66–72. Web.
    March 8, 2015.
Wolfe, Alexandra. "Novelist Paul Beatty on Writing and Satire." *Wall Street Journal*
    (Online). May 23, 2015: 1. *Business Source Complete.* Web. June 8, 2015.

Beck, Robert (Iceberg Slim)

Novels

Trick Baby: The Story of a White Negro (1967)
Mama Black Widow (1969)
Death Wish (1976)
Long White Con (1977)
Doom Fox (1978, published posthumously 1998) *

---

* The authoring of this work is still in dispute. According to Beverly Beyette, "To make matters worse,
three years after *Doom Fox*'s publication, Camille Mary Beck, a daughter Slim allegedly disowned, filed a
lawsuit against Diane Millman Beck (her stepmother) and her sister Melody, claiming that the novel was
not even written by her father. Camille contended that Diane's brother, Dan Millman, a New Age writer
and self-help guru, actually penned the manuscript in question. In her suit Camille enlisted the testimony of Bentley Morris, who said Diane had approached him with the piece for possible publication
but that neither he nor his editors could confirm the authenticity of the writing in question" (Beverly
Beyette, "Iceberg's Kin Disagree: Is It the Real Slim, or Shady?" *Los Angeles Times* September 4, 2001: E1).

Sources for context

Iceberg, Slim. *Pimp: The Story of My Life.* 1967. N. P.: Cash Money Content, 2011.

The Naked Soul of Iceberg Slim. Los Angeles: Holloway House, 1971.

Gifford, Justin. *Street Poison: The Biography of Iceberg Slim.* New York: Doubleday, 2015.

Muckley, Peter A. "Iceberg Slim: Robert Beck – A True Essay at a Biocriticism of an Ex-Outlaw Artist." *Black Scholar* 26.1 (1996): 18. *America: History and Life with Full Text.* Web. January 10, 2014.

Greg Tate. "Pimp and Circumstance: Iceberg Slim's Ghettocentricity," *Village Voice.* October 20, 1998: 132.

Bennet, Hal

Novels

A Wilderness of Vines (1966)
The Black Wine (1968)
Lord of Dark Places (1970)
Wait Until the Evening (1974)
Seventh Heaven (1976)
As Harriet Janeway,
This Passionate Land (1979)
As John D. Revere,
Justin Perry: The Assassin
The Assassin 2: Vatican Kill
The Assassin 3: Born to Kill
The Assassin 4: Death's Running Mate
The Assassin 5: Stud Service

Sources for context

Bennett, Hal. "The Visible Man." *Contemporary Authors Autobiography* Series 13. Ed. Joyce Nakamura. Detroit: Gale, 1991.

Meyer, Adam. "Hal Bennett." *Contemporary African American Novelists: A Bio-Bibliographical Critical Sourcebook.* Ed. S. Emmanuel. Westport, CT: Greenwood, 1999. 36–41.

Newman, Katherine. "An Evening with Hal Bennett: An Interview." *BALF* [Black American Literary Forum] 21. 4 (Winter 1987): 358–359.

Walcott, Ronald. "Hal Bennett." In *Afro-American Fiction Writers after 1955.* Ed. Thadious M. Davis and Trudier Harris. Detroit: Gale, 1984. 20–28.

"The Novels of Hal Bennett, Part I: The Writer as Satirist." *Black World* 23.8 (June 1974): 36–48, 89–97.

"The Novels of Hal Bennett, Part II: The Writer as Magician/Priest." *Black World* 23.9 (July 1974): 78–96.

Blackson, Lorenzo D.

Novels

The Rise and Progress of the Kingdoms of Light and Darkness. Or, The Reign of Kings Alpha and Abadon. 1867. Upper Saddle River, NJ: The Gregg Press, 1968.

Sources for context

Coppin, Levi Jenkins. *Unwritten History*. Philadelphia, A.M.E. Book Concern, 1919.
Hatch, Nathan. *The Democratization of American Christianity*. New Haven: Yale University Press, 1989.
Jackson, Blyden. *A History of Afro-American Literature*. Vol 1. Baton Rouge; Louisiana State University Press, 1989.
Maffly-Kipp, Laurie F. *Setting Down the Sacred Past: African-American Race Histories*. Cambridge: Harvard University Press, 2010.

Bland, Eleanor Taylor

Novels

Dead Time (1992)
Slow Burn (1993)
Gone Quiet (1994)
Done Wrong (1995)
Keep Still (1996)
See No Evil (1998)
Tell No Tales (1999)
Scream in Silence (2000)
Whispers in the Dark (2001)
Windy City Dying (2002)
Fatal Remains (2003)
A Cold and Silent Dying (2004)
A Dark and Deadly Deception (2005)
Suddenly a Stranger (2007)

Sources for context

Benson, Christopher. "Murder, She Wrote." *Chicago* 48.2 (1999): 20. *Supplemental Index*. Web. July 23, 2015.

Bland, Eleanor Taylor. *Shades of Black Crime and Mystery Stories by Africanamerican Authors.* Berkley Prime Crime, 2004. *Children's Literature Comprehensive Database.* Web. July 23, 2015.

Brown, W. Dale. *Conversations with American Writers: The Doubt, The Faith, The In-Between.* Grand Rapids, MI: William B. Eerdmans, 2008.

Klein, Kathleen Gregory, ed. *The Woman Detective: Gender and Genre.* Champaign: University of Illinois Press, 1995.

Bontemps, Arna

Novels

God Sends Sunday (1931)
Black Thunder: Gabriel's Revolt: Virginia, 1800 (1936)
Drums at Dusk (1939)

Sources for context

Arna Wendell Bontemps Reading His Poems with Comment at Radio Station WPLN, Nashville Public Library, May 22, 1963. Sound recording. Library of Congress. Archive of Recorded Poetry and Literature.

Canaday, Nicholas. "Arna Bontemps: The Louisiana Heritage." *Callaloo* 4 (October–February, 1981): 163–169.

Fleming, Robert E. *James Weldon Johnson and Arna Wendell Bontemps: A Reference Guide,* Boston: G. K. Hall, 1978.

James, Charles L. "Arna Bontemps: Harlem Renaissance Writer, Librarian, and Family Man." *New Crisis* 109. 5 (September/October, 2002): 22–28.

Jones, Kirkland C. *Renaissance Man from Louisiana: A Biography of Arna Wendell Bontemps.* Westport, CT: Greenwood, 1992.

Nichols, Charles, ed. *Arna Bontemps-Langston Hughes Letters, 1925–1967.* New York: Dodd Mead, 1980.

Bradley, David

Novels

South Street (1975)
The Chaneysville Incident (1981)

Sources for context

Blake, Susan L. and James A. Miller. "The Business of Writing: An Interview with David Bradley." *Callaloo* 21 (1984): 19–39.

Bonetti, Kay. "An Interview with David Bradley." *The Missouri Review* 15.3 (1992): 69–88. *MLA International Bibliography.* Web. May 3, 2015.

Smith, Valerie. "David Bradley." In *Afro-American Fiction Writers After 1955.* Vol. 3 of *Dictionary of Literary Biography.* Ed. Thadious M. Davis and Trudier Harris. Detroit: Gale Research, 1984.

Watkins, Mel. "Thirteen Runaway Slaves and David Bradley." *New York Times Book Review.* April 19, 1981: 7+.

Brooks, Gwendolyn

Novels

Maud Martha (1953)

Sources for context

Kent, George. *Gwendolyn Brooks: A Life.* Lexington: University Press of Kentucky, 1990.
Madhubuti, Haki R. *Say That the River Turns: The Impact of Gwendolyn Brooks.* Chicago: Third World Press, 1987.
Mootry, Maria K. and Gary Smith, eds. *A Life Distilled: Gwendolyn Brooks, Her Poetry and Fiction.* Urbana: University of Illinois Press, 1987.
Wright, Stephen Caldwell, ed. *On Gwendolyn Brooks: Reliant Contemplation.* Ann Arbor: University of Michigan Press, 1996.

Brown, Cecil

Novels

The Life and Loves of Mr. Jiveass Nigger (1969)
Days Without Weather (1982)
I, Stagolee (2006)
Journey's End (2007)

Sources for context

Bright, Jean M. "Cecil Brown." In *Afro-American Fiction Writers after 1955.* Ed. Thadious M. Davis and Trudier Harris. Detroit: Gale, 1984. 32–35.
Brown, Cecil. *Coming Up Down Home: A Memoir of a Southern Childhood.* New York: Dark Tower Series, Ecco Press, 1993.
Darryl Dickson-Carr. *African American Satire: The Sacredly Profane Novel.* University of Missouri Press, 2001.

Brown, Frank London

Novels

Trumbull Park (1959)

Sources for context

Graham, Maryemma. "Bearing Witness In Black Chicago: A View Of Selected Fiction By Richard Wright, Frank London Brown, and Ronald Fair." *CLA Journal* 33.3 (1990): 280–297.

Hauke, Kathleen A. "Frank London Brown." *Afro-American Writers, 1940–1955.* 25–29. Detroit: Gale, 1988.
Tracy, Steven C. "Frank London Brown." *Writers of the Black Chicago Renaissance.* 121. Champaign: University of Illinois Press, 2011.

Brown, William Wells

Novels

Clotel; or, The President's Daughter: A Narrative of Slave Life in the United States (1853)
Clotelle: A Tale of the Southern States (1864)
Clotelle; Or, The Colored Heroine: A Tale of the Southern States (1867)
Miralda; Or, The Beautiful Quadroon: A Romance of Slavery Founded on Fact (1860)

Sources for context

Brown, William Wells. *My Southern Home: or, The South and Its People.* 1882. Chapel Hill: University of North Carolina Press, 2011.
Narrative of William W. Brown, a Fugitive Slave. 1847. New York: Johnson Reprint, 1970.
"Three Years in Europe, Or Places I Have Seen and People I Have Met. 1852. *OAIster.* Web. May 8, 2014.
Greenspan, Ezra. *William Wells Brown: An African American Life.* New York: W. W. Norton, 2014.

Bruce, John Edward

Novels

The Black Sleuth (1907–1909)
The Awakening of Hezekiah Jones. A Story Dealing with Some of the Problems Affecting the Political Rewards Due the Negro (1916)

Sources for context

Bruce, John, The John Bruce Papers. Schomburg Center for Research in Black Culture, Manuscripts, Archives and Rare Books Division, The New York Public Library.
Crowder, Ralph. "John Edward Bruce: Pioneer Black Nationalist." *Afro-Americans in New York Life and History* 2.2 (July 1978): 47–66.
Bruce, John, The John Bruce Papers. *John Edward Bruce: Politician, Journalist, and Self-Trained Historian of the African Diaspora.* New York: New York University Press, 2004.

Gilbert, Peter. "The Life and Thought of John Edward Bruce." In *The Selected Writings of John Edward Bruce: Militant Black Journalist*. Ed. Peter Gilbert. New York: Arno Press, 1971.

Gruesser, J. C. "Bruce Grit: The Black Nationalist Writings Of John Edward Bruce." *African American Review* 37.2-3 (Summer 2003): 457–460.

Butler, Octavia E.

Novels

Kindred (1979)
Fledgling (2005)
The Patternist series
Patternmaster (1976)
Mind of My Mind (1977)
Survivor (1978)
Wild Seed (1980)
Clay's Ark (1984)
The Xenogenesis series
Dawn (1987)
Adulthood Rites (1988)
Imago (1989)
The Earthseed or Parable Trilogy (the trilogy was not completed)
Parable of the Sower (1993)
Parable of the Talents (1998)

Sources for context

Barr, Marleen S. *Lost in Space: Probing Feminist Science Fiction and Beyond*. Chapel Hill: University of North Carolina Press, 1993.

Butler, Octavia, and Consuela Francis. *Conversations with Octavia Butler*. Jackson: University Press of Mississippi, 2010.

Due, Tananarive. "On Octavia E. Butler." In *Strange Matings: Science Fiction, Feminism, African American Voices, and Octavia E. Butler*. Rebecca J. Holden and Nisi Shawl, eds. Seattle: Aqueduct, 2013.

Kilgore, De Witt Douglas and Ranu Samantrai. "A Memorial to Octavia E. Butler." *Science Fiction Studies* 2010: 353. *JSTOR Journals*. Web. July 5, 2015.

Potts, Stephen W. "'We Keep Playing the Same Record': A Conversation with Octavia E. Butler." *Science Fiction Studies* 23.70 (November, 1996): 331–338.

Rowell, Charles. "An Interview with Octavia E. Butler." *Callaloo* 20. 1 (1997): 47–66.

Chapman, Katherine Davis Tillman

Novels

Beryl Weston's Ambition: The Story of an Afro-American Girl's Life (1893)
Clancy Street (1898–1899)

Sources for context

Claudia Tate, *Domestic Allegories of Political Desire: The Black Heroine's Text at the Turn of the Century*, 1992.
 Introduction to *The Works of Katherine Davis Chapman Tillman*. Schomburg Library of Nineteenth-Century Black Women Writers. New York: Oxford University Press, 1991.

Chesnutt, Charles

Novels

The House behind the Cedars (1900)
The Marrow of Tradition (1901)
The Colonel's Dream (1905)
The Quarry [published in 1999]
Business Career [published in 2005]
Evelyn's Husband [published in 2005]
Mandy Oxendine [published in 1997]
Paul Marchand, FMC [Free Man of Color, published in 1999]
The Rainbow Chasers [unfinished manuscript, still unpublished]

Sources for context

Chesnutt, Helen. *Charles Waddell Chesnutt: Pioneer of the Color Line*. Chapel Hill: University of North Carolina Press, 1952.
Crisler, Jesse S., et al. *An Exemplary Citizen. Letters of Charles W. Chesnutt*. Stanford: Stanford University Press, 2002.
Izzo, David Garrett and Maria Orban. *Charles Chesnutt Reappraised: Essays on the First Major African American Fiction Writer*. Jefferson, NC: McFarland, 2009.
Keller, Francis Richardson. *An American Crusade: The Life of Charles Waddell Chesnutt*. Provo: Brigham Young, University Press 1978.
McElrath, Joseph R., Jr., et al. *Charles W. Chesnutt: Essays and Speeches*. Stanford: Stanford University Press, 1999.
 To Be an Author: Letters of Charles W. Chesnutt, 1889–1905. Princeton: Princeton University Press, 2014.

Childress, Alice

Novels

Like One of the Family (1956)
A Short Walk (1979)
Those Other People (1989)
Young adult
A Hero Ain't Nothin' but a Sandwich (1973)
Rainbow Jordan (1981)

Sources for context

Childress, Alice. "A Candle in a Gale Wind." In *Black Women Writers, 1950–1980: A Critical Evaluation.* Ed. Mari Evans. Garden City, NY: Anchor/Doubleday, 1983.

Federal Bureau of Investigation, Alice Childress File. Freedom of Information and Privacy Acts 0933046-000.

Killens, John O. "The Literary Genius of Alice Childress." In *Black Women Writers, 1950–1980: A Critical Evaluation.* Ed. Mari Evans. Garden City, NY: Anchor /Doubleday, 1983.

Haley, Elsie Galbreath. "Alice Childress." In *American Ethnic Writers.* Ed. Salem Press. Pasadena: Salem Press, 2009.

Jennings, La Vinia Delois. *Alice Childress.* New York: Twayne, 1995.

Sadker, Myra Pollack and David Miller Sadker. *Now upon a Time: A Contemporary View of Children's Literature.* New York: Harper, 1977.

Condé, Maryse

Novels

Hérémakhonon (1976)
Une Saison à Rihata (1981, *A Season in Rihata*, 1988)
Ségou: Les Murailles de terre (1984, *Segu*, 1987)
Moi, Tituba, Sorcière Noire De Salem (1985, *I, Tituba, Black Witch of Salem*, 1992)
Ségou II: La Terre en miettes (1985, *The Children of Segu*, 1989)
La Vie Scélérate (1987, *Tree of Life*, 1992)
Traversée de la Mangrove (1989, *Crossing the Mangrove*, 1995)
Les Derniers Rois mages (1992, *The Last of the African Kings*, 1997)
La Colonie du nouveau monde (1993)
La Migration des cœurs (1995, *Windward Heights*, 1998)
Desirada (1997, English translation, 2000)
Célanire cou-coupé (2000, *Who Slashed Celanire's Throat?: A Fantastical Tale*, 2004)
La Belle Créole (2001)

Histoire de la femme cannibale (2003, *The Story of the Cannibal Woman*, 2007)

Les belles ténébreuses (2008)

Victoire, les saveurs et les mots (2006, *Victoire: My Mother's Mother* 2010)

Sources for context

Condé, Maryse, and Françoise Pfaff. *Conversations with Maryse Condé*. Lincoln: University of Nebraska Press, 1996.

Condé, Maryse, Françoise Pfaff, and Richard Philcox. *The Journey of a Caribbean Writer*. London: Seagull Books, 2014.

Lewis, Barbara. "Tales from the Heart": A Conversation with Maryse Condé," *Black Renaissance/Renaissance Noire* 5.2 (2003): 94–104.

Scarboro, Ann Armstrong, et al. *Maryse Condé Dévoile Son Coeur* [*Maryse Condé Speaks From The Heart*]. Videorecording. Boulder: Full Duck Productions, Mosaic Media distributor, 2003.

Crafts, Hannah

Novels

The Bondwoman's Narrative (1853–1861)

Sources for context

In Search of Hanna Crafts: Critical Essays on The Bondwoman's Narrative. Ed. Henry Louis Gates, Jr. and Hollis Robbins. New York: Basic Books, 2004.

Cullen, Countee

Novels

One Way to Heaven (1932)

Sources for context

Ferguson, Blanche E. *Countée Cullen and the Negro Renaissance*. New York: Dodd, Mead, 1966.

Molesworth, Charles. "Countee Cullen's Reputation." *Transition: An International Review* 107.1 (2012): 67. *JSTOR Journals*. Web. November 8, 2014.

Perry, Margaret. *A Bio-Bibliography of Countée P. Cullen, 1903–1946*. Westport, CT: Greenwood, 1971.

Wintz, Cary D. *Harlem Speaks: A Living History of the Harlem Renaissance*. Naperville, IL: Sourcebooks, 2007.

Davis, Thulani

Novels

1959 (1992)
Maker of Saints (1996)

Sources for context

Davis, Thulani. "In Our Own Terms." In *Defining Ourselves: Black Writers in the Nineties*. Ed. Elizabeth Nunez and Brenda M. Greene. New York: P. Lang, 1999.
My Confederate Kinfolk. New York: Basic Books/Civitas, 2006.
Fleischmann, Stephanie, and Thulani Davis. "Thulani Davis." *BOMB* (1990): 54. *JSTOR Journals*. Web. May 3, 2015.
Knight, Kimberly. "Thulani Davis: Writing the Untold Stories." *Essence* 23 (May 1992): 60.

Delany, Martin R.

Novels

Blake, or the Huts of America (1859–1862)

Sources for context

Blackett, Richard. "Martin R. Delany and Robert Campbell: Black Americans in Search of an African Colony." *The Journal of Negro History* 62.1 (January, 1977): 1–25. Web. January 2, 2014.
Delany, Martin Robison, and Robert S. Levine. *Martin R. Delany: A Documentary Reader*. Chapel Hill: University of North Carolina Press, 2003.
Mattox, J. "The Mayor of San Juan Del Norte? Nicaragua, Martin Delany, and The 'Cotton' Americans." *American Literature* 81.3 (September, 2009): 527–554. *Arts & Humanities Citation Index*. Web. May 23, 2015.
Sollors, Werner, et al. "Martin R. Delany and the Harvard Medical School." *Blacks at Harvard: A Documentary History of African-American Experience at Harvard and Radcliffe*. New York: New York University Press, 1993.

Delany, Samuel R.

Novels

The Jewels of Aptor (1962)
Captives of the Flame (1963 revised as *Out of the Dead City* in 1968)

The Towers of Toron (1964)
City of a Thousand Suns (1965)
The Ballad of Beta-2 (1965)
Babel-17 (1966)
Empire Star (1966)
The Einstein Intersection (1967)
Nova (1968)
The Fall of the Towers (1970 revised versions of *City of a Thousand Suns, Out of the Dead City, The Towers of Toron*)
The Tides of Lust/Equinox (1973, sometimes listed as erotica)
Dhalgren (1975)
Triton/Trouble on Triton (1976)
Empire (1978)
Tales of Nevèrÿon (1979)
Neveryóna: Or, The Tale of Signs and Cities (1983)
Stars in My Pocket Like Grains of Sand (1984)
Flight from Nevèrÿon (1985)
The Bridge of Lost Desire/Return to Nevèrÿon (1987)
Hogg (1993)
They Fly at Çiron (1993)
The Mad Man (1994, sometimes listed as erotica)
Hogg (1995, sometimes listed as erotica)
Phallos (2004 novella, sometimes listed as erotica)
Dark Reflections (2007, sometimes listed as erotica)
Through the Valley of the Nest of Spiders (2012)

Sources for context

Delany, Samuel R., and Carl Howard Freedman. *Conversations with Samuel R. Delany.* Jackson: University of Mississippi Press, 2009.
Heavenly Breakfast. New York: Bantam, 1979.
The Jewel-Hinged Jaw. Middletown, CT: Wesleyan University Press, 2011.
Shorter Views: Queer Thoughts & the Politics of the Paraliterary. Hanover NH: Wesleyan University Press/University Press of New England, 1999.
The Motion of Light in Water: Sex and Science Fiction Writing in the East Village, 1957–1965. New York: Arbor House, 1988.
Silent Interviews: On Language, Race, Sex, Science Fiction, and Some Comics. Hanover, NH: Wesleyan University Press/University Press of New England, 1994.
Times Square Red; Times Square Blue. New York: New York University Press, 1999.
Dery, Mark. "Black to the Future: Interviews with Samuel R. Delany, Greg Tate, and Tricia Rose." *The South Atlantic Quarterly* 92 (Fall, 1993): 735–778.
Weedman, Jane. *Samuel R. Delany.* Mercer Island, WA: Starmont House, 1982.

Demby, William

Novels

Beetlecreek (1950)
The Catacombs (1965)
Love Story Black (1978)
Blueboy (1980)
King Comus (2007 unpublished)

Sources for context

Berry, Jay R. "The Achievement of William Demby." *College Language Association Journal* 26 (June, 1983): 434–451.
Biggers, Jeff. "William Demby Has Not Left the Building: Postcard From Tuscany." *Bloomsbury Review* 24.1 (January–February, 2004): 12.
Micconi, Giovanna. "Ghosts of History: An Interview with William Demby." *Amerikastudien/American Studies* 56.1 (2011): 123–139.
O'Brien, John. "Interview with William Demby." *Studies in Black Literature* 3.3 (1972): 1–6.

Detter, Thomas

Novels

Nellie Brown, or The Jealous Wife (1871)

Sources for context

Foster, Frances Smith. Introduction to *Nellie Brown, or The Jealous Wife with Other Sketches*. Lincoln: University of Nebraska Press, 1996.
Reid, John. "Thomas Detter." *Online Nevada Encyclopedia*. January 3, 2011. Web. April 29, 2014.
Rusco, Elmer E. *"Good Time Coming?" Black Nevadans in the Nineteenth Century*, Westport, CT: Greenwood, 1975.
"Thomas Detter: Nevada Black Writer and Advocate for Human Rights." *Nevada Historical Society Quarterly* 47.1 (Fall, 2004): 193–215.

Dickey, Eric Jerome

Novels

Sister, Sister (1996)
Friends and Lovers (1997)
Milk in My Coffee (1998)
Cheaters (1999)

Liar's Game (2000)
Between Lovers (2001)
Thieves' Paradise (2002)
The Other Woman (2003)
Naughty or Nice (2003)
Drive Me Crazy (2004)
Genevieve (2005)
Chasing Destiny (2006)
Sleeping with Strangers (2007)
Waking with Enemies (2007)
Pleasure (2008)
Dying for Revenge (2008)
Resurrecting Midnight (2009)
Tempted by Trouble (2010)
An Accidental Affair (2012)
The Education of Nia Simone Bijou (2013)
Decadence (2013)
A Wanted Woman (2014)
One Night (2015)

Sources for context

Lamb, Sabrina. "Men Who Write Fiction." *Black Elegance* III (1998): 32. *Supplemental Index*. Web. September 2, 2015.
Spencer, Stephen. "Eric Jerome Dickey." *Twenty-First Century American Novelists*. 62–66. Detroit: Thomson Gale, 2004.
"The Write Stuff." *Indianapolis Monthly* 27.13 (2004): 64.

Douglass, Frederick

Novels

The Heroic Slave (1851)

Sources for context

Douglass, Frederick, et al. *The Heroic Slave: A Cultural and Critical Edition*. New Haven: Yale University Press, 2015.
Hyde C. "The Climates of Liberty: Natural Rights in the Creole Case and *The Heroic Slave*. *American Literature* 85.3 (September 2013): 475–504 Web. March 1, 2016.
Stepto, Robert B. "Storytelling in Early Afro-American Fiction: Frederick Douglass' 'The Heroic Slave'." *The Georgia Review* 1982: 355.

Du Bois, W. E. B.

Novels

The Quest of the Silver Fleece (1911)
Dark Princess (1928)
The Black Flame Trilogy
Book One: *The Ordeal of Mansart* (1957)
Book Two: *Mansart Builds a School* (1959)
Book Three: *Worlds of Color* (1961)

Sources for context

Aptheker, Hebert, ed. *The Correspondence of W. E. B. Du Bois.* 3 vols. Amherst: University of Massachusetts Press, 1997.
Blum, Edward J. *W. E. B. Du Bois: American Prophet.* Philadelphia: University of Pennsylvania Press, 2007.
Brown, Wesley, et al. *W. E. B. Du Bois: A Biography in Four Voices.* Videorecording. Scribe Video Center production company; San Francisco, CA: California Newsreel distributor, 1995.
Lewis, David L. *W. E. B. Du Bois: A Biography.* New York: Henry Holt, 2009.
Marable, Manning. *W. E. B. Du Bois: Black Radical Democrat.* Boulder, CO: Paradigm Publishers, 2005.

Due, Tananarive

Novels

The Between (1995)
The Black Rose (2000)
The Good House (2003)
Joplin's Ghost (2005)
African Immortals series
My Soul to Keep (1997)
The Living Blood (2001)
Blood Colony (2008)
My Soul to Take (2011)
Co-written novels
Naked Came the Manatee (1997, contributor)
Devil's Wake (2012, with Steven Barnes)
The Tennyson Hardwick series
Casanegra (2007, with Blair Underwood and Steven Barnes)

In the Night of the Heat (2008, with Blair Underwood and Steven Barnes)
From Cape Town with Love (2010, with Blair Underwood and Steven Barnes)
South by Southeast (2012, with Blair Underwood and Steven Barnes)

Sources for context

Due, Patricia Stephens and Tananarive Due. *Freedom in the Family: A Mother–Daughter Memoir of the Fight for Civil Rights*. New York: Alexander Street Press, 2003.
Due, Tananarive and Dianne Glave. "'My Characters Are Teaching Me to Be Strong': An Interview with Tananarive Due." *African American Review* 38.4 (Winter, 2004): 695.
Hood, Yolanda. "Interview with Tananarive Due." *Femspec* 6.1 (2005): 155–164. *Humanities International Complete*. Web. February 4, 2013.

Duffy, Damian and John Jennings

Novels

The Hole: Consumer Culture. Vol. 1. Chicago: Front Forty Press, 2008.

Sources for context

Fein-Bursoni, Justine. "Damian Duffy, John Jennings and Their Comics." *Smile Politely* (April 10, 2008). Web. August 20, 2015.
Whitcher-Gentzke, Ann. "The Soul of Black Comix." University at Buffalo webpage. Web. August 20, 2015.

Dunbar, Paul Laurence

Novels

The Uncalled. A Novel (1898)
The Love of Landry (1900)
The Fanatics (1901)
The Sport of the Gods (1901, *Lippincott's Monthly Magazine;* 1902, Dodd Mead and Company).

Sources for context

Alexander, Eleanor. *Lyrics of Sunshine and Shadow: The Tragic Courtship and Marriage of Paul Laurence Dunbar and Alice Ruth Moore: A History of Love and Violence among the African American Elite*. New York: New York University Press, 2001.
Hudson, Gossie Harold. *A Biography of Paul Laurence Dunbar*. Baltimore: Gateway Press, 1999.

Martin, Jay, ed. *Singers in the Dawn: Reinterpretations of Paul Laurence Dunbar.* New York: Dodd, Mead, 1972.

Redding, J. Saunders. *To Make a Poet Black.* Chapel Hill: University of North Carolina Press, 1939.

Scott-Childress, Reynolds J. "Paul Laurence Dunbar, New Yorker." *New York History* 92.3 (Summer, 2011): 167–208.

Turner, Darwin T. "Paul Laurence Dunbar: The Rejected Symbol." *Journal of Negro History* (January, 1967): 1–13.

Wiggins, Lida Keck. *The Life and Works of Paul Laurence Dunbar.* Nashville: Winston-Derek, 1992.

Ellis, Trey

Novels

Platitudes (1988)
Home Repairs (1993)
Right Here, Right Now (1999)

Sources for context

Ellis, Trey. "Obama Is My Wingman." *GQ: Gentlemen's Quarterly* 80.3 (2010): 144. *Publisher Provided Full Text Searching File.* Web. May 19, 2013.

Lott, Eric. "Response to Trey Ellis's 'The New Black Aesthetic.'" *Callaloo* 12, no. 1 (Winter, 1989): 244–246.

Ellison, Ralph

Novels

Invisible Man (1952)
Three Days before the Shooting (2010, published posthumously as *Junteenth* in 1999)

Sources for context

Busby, Mark. *Ralph Ellison.* Boston: Twayne, 1991.
"Richard Wright's Blues." *The Antioch Review* 1999: 263–276.
Shadow and Act. New York: Random, 1964.

Kinnamon, Keneth, and Ralph Ellison. "Ellison In Urbana: Memories and an Interview." *Callaloo* 2 (1995): 273–279. *Project MUSE.* Web. July 7, 2015.

Jackson, Lawrence, *Ralph Ellison: Emergence of Genius.* Athens: University of Georgia Press, 2007.

O'Meally, Robert G. *The Craft of Ralph Ellison.* Cambridge, MA: Harvard University Press, 1980.

Rampersad, Arnold. *Ralph Ellison: A Biography*. New York: Alfred A. Knopf, 2007.

Everett, Percival

Novels

Suder (1983)
Walk Me to the Distance (1985)
Cutting Lisa (1986)
For Her Dark Skin (1990)
Zulus (1990)
God's Country (1994)
Watershed (1996)
Frenzy (1997)
The Body of Martin Aquilera (1997)
Glyph (1999)
Erasure (2001)
Grand Canyon, Inc. (2001 novella)
A History of the African-American People (Proposed) by Strom Thurmond (2004 with James Kincaid)
American Desert (2004)
Wounded (2005)
The Water Cure (2007)
I Am Not Sidney Poitier (2009)

Sources for context

Everett, Percival. "The Satiric Inferno." Interview by Peter Monaghan. *Chronicle of Higher Education* 51. 23 (February 11, 2005): A18-A20.
Kincaid, Jim, and Percival Everett. "An Interview with Percival Everett." *Callaloo* 28.2 (Spring, 2005): 377.
Mitchell, Keith B., and Robin G. Vander. *Perspectives on Percival Everett*. Jackson: University Press of Mississippi, 2013.
"Percival Everett: A Special Section. "*Callaloo* 28, no. 2 (Spring, 2005): 291–342.
Rozié, Fabrice, Esther Allen, and Guy Walter, ed. *As You Were Saying: American Writers Respond to Their French Contemporaries*. Champaign, IL: Dalkey Archive Press, 2007.
Stewart, Anthony. "About Percival Everett." *Ploughshares* 40.2/3 (2014): 188–193.

Fauset, Jessie

Novels

There Is Confusion (1924)
Plum Bun: A Novel Without a Moral (1928)

The Chinaberry Tree: A Novel of American Life (1931)
Comedy, American Style (1933)

Sources for context

McDowell, Deborah. "Jessie Fauset." In *Modern American Women Writers*. Eds. Lea Baechler and A. Walton Litz. New York: Charles Scribner's Sons, 1991.
McLendon, Jaquelyn Y. *The Politics of Color in the Fiction of Jessie Fauset and Nella Larsen*. Charlottesville: University of Virginia Press, 1995.
Sylvander, Carolyn. *Jessie Redmon Fauset: Black American Writer*. Troy, NY: Whitston, 1981.
Wall, Cheryl. *Women of the Harlem Renaissance*. Bloomington: Indiana University Press, 1995.

Feelings, Tom

Novels

Tommy Traveler in the World of Black History (1990, as single edition, comics).
Middle Passage: White Ships/Black Cargo (1995, art plates)

Sources for context

Bishop, Rudine Sims. "Tom Feelings And The Middle Passage." *Horn Book Magazine* 72.4 (1996): 436–452. *Literary Reference Center*. Web. September 5, 2013.
Feelings, Tom. *Black Pilgrimage*. New York: Lothrop Lee & Shepard, 1972.
Steele, Vincent. "Tom Feelings: A Black Arts Movement." *African American Review* 32.1 (Spring, 1998): 119–124.

Fisher, Rudolph

Novels

The Walls of Jericho (1928)
The Conjure Man Dies (1932)

Sources for context

Mirmotahari, Emad. "Harlemite, Detective, African?: The Many Selves of Rudolph Fisher's *Conjure-Man Dies*." *Callaloo* 2 (2013): 268–278.
Thompson, Clifford. "The Mystery Man of the Harlem Renaissance: Novelist Rudolph Fisher Was a Forerunner of Walter Mosley." *Black Issues Book Review* 5.3 (2003): 63. *Literary Reference Center*. Web. March 13, 2014.
Tignor, Eleanor Q. "Rudolph Fisher: Harlem Novelist." *Langston Hughes Review* 1 (Fall, 1982): 13–22.

Fletcher, Omar

Novels

Hurricane Man (1976)
Walking Black and Tall (1977)
Black Against the Mob (1977)
Miss Annie (1978)
Escape from Death Row (1979)
Black Godfather 2 (1984)
Dueling Pistols (1991)

Sources for context

Gifford, Justin. *Pimping Fictions: African American Crime Literature and the Untold Story of Black Pulp Publishing*. Philadelphia: Temple University Press, 2013.

Forrest, Leon

Novels

There Is a Tree More Ancient than Eden (1973)
The Bloodworth Orphans (1977)
Two Wings to Veil My Face (1984)
Divine Days (1992)

Sources for context

"Angularity: An Interview with Leon Forrest." Leon Forrest and Keith Byerman. *African American Review* 33. 3 (Autumn, 1999): 439–450.
Cawelti, John G., ed. *Leon Forrest: Introductions and Interpretations*. Bowling Green, OH: Popular Press, 1997.
Forrest, Leon, and Dana A. Williams. *Conversations with Leon Forrest*. Jackson: University Press of Mississippi, 2007.
"Leon Forrest, Fiction Writer: A Special Section." *Callaloo* 16.2 (Spring 1993): 328–483.
McQuade, Molly. "The Yeast Of Chaos: An Interview With Leon Forrest." *Chicago Review* 41.2/3 (1995): 43. *Literary Reference Center*. Web. May 5, 2015.
Mootry, Maria K. "If He Changed My Name: An Interview with Leon Forrest." *The Massachusetts Review* 18 (Winter, 1977): 631–642.
Wideman, John Edgar. "In Memoriam: Leon Forrest, 1937–1997." *Callaloo*: 21.1 (Winter, 1998): vii. *MLA International Bibliography*. Web. May 5, 2015.

Fowler, Charles H.

Novels

Historical Romance of the American Negro (1902)

Sources for Context

Graham, Maryemma and Jerry Washington Ward. *The Cambridge History of African American Literature*. New York: Cambridge University Press, 2011.

Gaines, Ernest J.

Novels

Catherine Carmier (1964)
Of Love and Dust (1967)
The Autobiography of Miss Jane Pittman (1971)
In My Father's House (1978)
A Gathering of Old Men (1983)
A Lesson before Dying (1993)

Sources for context

Babb, Valerie. *Ernest Gaines*. Boston: Twayne, 1991.
Brister, Rose Anne and Ernest J. Gaines. "The Last Regionalist? An Interview with Ernest J. Gaines." *Callaloo* 26.3 (Summer, 2003): 549–564. *JSTOR Journals*. Web. July 7, 2011.
Carmean, Karen. *Ernest J. Gaines.: A Critical Companion*. Westport, CT: Greenwood, 1998.
Lepschy, Wolfgang, and Ernest J. Gaines. "A MELUS Interview: Ernest J. Gaines." *MELUS* 24.1 (Spring, 1999): 197–208. *JSTOR Journals*. Web. August 6, 2014.

Goines, Donald

Novels

Dopefiend: The Story of a Black Junkie (1971)
Whoreson: The Story of a Ghetto Pimp (1972)
Black Gangster (1972)
Black Girl Lost (1973)

White Man's Justice, Black Man's Grief (1973)
Cry Revenge! (1974)
Daddy Cool (1974)
Eldorado Red (1974)
Never Die Alone (1974)
Swamp Man (1974)
The Kenyatta series (as Al C. Clark)
Crime Partners (1974)
Death List (1974)
Kenyatta's Escape (1974)
Kenyatta's Last Hit (1975)
Inner City Hoodlum (1975)

Sources for context

Eddie B. Allen Jr., *Low Road: The Life and Legacy of Donald Goines*. New York: St. Martin's, 2004.
Pamela Lee Gray, "Donald Joseph Goines," *African American National Biography*. Ed. Henry Louis Gates, Jr., and Evelyn Brooks Higginbotham, Oxford African American Studies Center. Web. November 11, 2014.
Stone, Eddie. *Donald Writes No More*. Los Angeles: Holloway House. 2001.*

---

* Goines sister condemned this biography: "Years after his death, Goines's sister contended that Stone's biography was a fraud: 'There's an autobiography [sic] out [there] called 'Donald Writes No More' its fake, its bull [sic]. They came to my grandmother's house when he first died. He wasn't even cold yet and they had her answer a bunch of questions, and then they came with the book under Holloway House. That books [sic] a fake ... it's called 'poetic license.'" (Qtd. in L. H. Stallings, "'I'm Goin Pimp Whores!' The Goines Factor and the Theory of a Hip-Hop Neo-Slave Narrative," *CR: The New Centennial Review* 3.3 (2003): 190–191; brackets in Stallings original.)

Golden, Marita

Novels

A Woman's Place (1986)
After (2006)
The Edge of Heaven (1999)
And Do Remember Me (1992)
Long Distance Life (1989)

Soures for Context

Golden, Marita, *Don't Play in the Sun: One Woman's Journey Through the Color Complex*. New York: Doubleday, 2005.

Migrations of the Heart: An Autobiography. New York: Anchor Books, 1983.
Frías, María, and Marita Golden. "Migrating Hearts and Travelling Shoes": An Interview With Marita Golden." *Atlantis* 20.1 (Junio,1998): 195–213.
Nelson, Emmanuel S. "Marita Golden (1950–)." *African American Autobiographers: A Sourcebook*. 156–160. Westport, CT: Greenwood, 2002.

Greenlee, Sam E.

Novels

The Spook Who Sat by the Door (1969)
Baghdad Blues (1976)

Sources for context

Bates, Karen Grigsby. "Remembering Sam Greenlee Through His Most Famous Book." *Code Switch Frontiers of Race, Culture and Ethnicity*. NPR. Web. August 18, 2014.
Burrell, Walter. "Rappin' with Sam Greenlee." *Black World* 20.9 (1971): 42–47. *MLA International Bibliography*. Web. October 1, 2014.
Kyles, Kyra. "Chatting with Sam Greenlee." *Jet* 120.23 (2011): 29.

Griggs, Sutton E.

Novels

Imperium in Imperio (1899)
Overshadowed (1901)
Unfettered (1902)
The Hindered Hand: or, The Reign of the Repressionist (1905)
Pointing the Way (1908)

Sources for context

Chakkalakal, Tess and Kenneth W. Warren, eds. *Jim Crow, Literature, and the Legacy of Sutton E. Griggs*. Athens: University of Georgia Press, 2013.
Coleman, Finnie D. *Sutton E. Griggs and the Struggle against White Supremacy*. Knoxville: University of Tennessee Press, 2007.
Fleming, Robert E. "Sutton E. Griggs: Militant Black Novelist," *Phylon* 34.1 (March 1973): 73–77.
Griggs, Sutton E. *The Story of My Struggles*. Memphis: National Public Welfare League, 1914.
Sutton Griggs website: https://sites.google.com/a/kean.edu/suttongriggs/griggs-images

Guy, Rosa

Novels

Bird at My Window (1966)
Mirror of Her Own (1981)
A Measure of Time (1983, sometimes placed on young adult lists)
My Love, My Love, or the Peasant Girl (1985, sometimes placed on young adult lists)
The Sun, the Sea, A Touch of the Wind (1995)
Young adult
The Friends (1973)
Ruby (1976)
Edith Jackson (1978)
The Disappearance (1979)
New Guys Around the Block (1983)
Paris, Pee Wee and Big Dog (1984)
And I Heard a Bird Sing (1987)
The Ups and Downs of Carl Davis III (1989)
The Music of Summer (1992)

Sources for context:

Lawrence, Leota S. "Rosa Guy." *Afro-American Fiction Writers after 1955.* 101–106. Detroit: Gale, 1984.
Norris, Jerrie. *Presenting Rosa Guy.* Boston: Twayne, 1988.
Silvey, Anita, ed. *Children's Books and Their Creators.* Boston: Houghton Mifflin. 1995.

Haley, Alex

Novels

Roots: The Saga of an American Family (1976)
A Different Kind of Christmas (1988 novella)
Alex Haley's Queen: The Story of an American Family (1993, posthumously published; edited by David Stevens)
Mama Flora's Family (1998 with David Stevens)

Sources for context

Alex Haley. Bellinelli, Matteo, dir. San Francisco, CA: California Newsreel, 1992.
Alex Haley: The Man Who Traced America's Roots: His Life, His Works. New York: Reader's Digest Association, 2007.

Haley, Alex. Interview by Jeffrey Elliot. *Negro History Bulletin* 41.1 (January/February, 1978): 782–785.

et al. *On the Stump with Alex Haley.* New York, 1978. Alexander Street Press. Web. January 6, 2014.

Norrell, Robert J. *Alex Haley and the Books that Changed a Nation.* New York: St. Martin's, 2015.

Staples, Robert. "A Symposium on *Roots.*" *The Black Scholar* 8.7 (May, 1977): 36–42.

Harper, Frances Ellen Watkins

Novels

Minnie's Sacrifice (1869)
Sowing and Reaping (1876–1877)
Trial and Triumph (1888–1889)
Iola Leroy, or Shadows Uplifted (1892)

Sources for context

Boyd, Melba. *Discarded Legacy: Politics and Poetics in the Life of Frances E. W. Harper, 1825–1911.* Detroit: Wayne State University Press, 1994.

Foster, Frances Smith, ed. *A Brighter Coming Day: A Frances Ellen Watkins Harper Reader.* New York: The Feminist Press at CUNY, 1990.

Peterson, Carla. "Literary Transnationalism and Diasporic History: Frances Watkins Harper's 'Fancy Sketches,' 1859–1860." *Women's Rights and Transatlantic Antislavery in the Era of Emancipation.* Ed. Kathryn Kish Stewart and James Brewer Stewart. New Haven: Yale University Press, 2007. 189–208.

Harris, E. Lynn

Novels

Invisible Life (1991, self-published, Anchor Press, 1994)
Just as I Am (1994)
And This Too Shall Pass (1996)
If This World Were Mine (1997)
Abide with Me (1999)
Not a Day Goes By (2000)
A Love of My Own (2002)
Any Way the Wind Blows (2002)
I Say a Little Prayer (2006)
Just Too Good to Be True (2008)
Basketball Jones (2009)

Blame It on the Sun (2009)
Mama Dearest (2009)
In My Father's House (2010)
No One in the World (2011, with R.M. Johnson)

Sources for context

Harris, E. Lynn. *What Becomes of the Brokenhearted*. New York: Anchor Books, 2003 (memoir).
    Introduction. *Freedom in this Village: Twenty-five Years of Black Gay Men's Writing, 1979 to the Present*. Ed. E. Lynn Harris. New York: Carroll and Graf, 2005.
Quart, Alissa. "E. Lynn Harris: Tales of The Good Life." *Publishers Weekly* 246.16 (1999): 44. *Literary Reference Center*. Web. November 19, 2014.

Hawkins, Odie

Novels

Ghetto Sketches (1972)
Sweet Peter Deeder (1979)
The Busting Out of an Ordinary Man (1985)
Chili: The Memoirs of a Black Casanova (1985)
Chicago Hustle (1987)
Chester L. Simmons: The Great Lawd Buddha (1990)
Brazilian Nights (1992)
Lost Angeles (1994)
Conspiracy (1997)
The Snake (2004)
Mr. Bonobo Bliss: aka Bo (2007)
Lady Bliss (2007)
Shackles across Time (2008)
Portrait of Simone (2012)
Midnight (2012)
The Life and Times of Chester L. Simmons (2012)
Hollow Daze (2013)
Matador Negro "Azucar" (2013)
Kwanzaa for Conrad & The Survival Tango (2013 with Zola Salena-Hawkins)
The Snake Doctor (2013)
Lil' Sweets (2014)

Sources for context

Gifford, Justin. "'Something Like a Harlem Renaissance West': Black Popular Fiction, Self-Publishing, and the Origins of Street Literature: Interviews with Dr. Roland Jefferson And Odie Hawkins." *MELUS* 38.4 (Winter, 2013): 216–240. *Project MUSE*. Web. September 2, 2015.

Hawkins, Odie, *Scars and Memories*. Los Angeles: All America Distributors, June 1983.

Heard, Nathan C.

Novels

Howard Street (1968)
House of Slammers (1983)
To Reach a Dream (1972)
A Cold Fire Burning (1974)
When Shadows Fall (1977)

Sources for context

Beaumont, Eric "The Nathan Heard Interviews," *African American Review* 28. 3 (Autumn, 1994), 395–410.

Yarborough, Richard. "Nathan C. Heard." *Afro-American Fiction Writers after 1955.* 110–115. Detroit: Gale, 1984.

Henderson, George Wylie

Novels

Ollie Miss (1935)
Jule (1948)

Sources for context

Christensen, Peter G. "George Wylie Henderson." *Afro-American Writers from the Harlem Renaissance to 1940 Bio-bibliographical Critical Sourcebook.* Ed. Emmanuel S. Nelson. 224–230. Westport, CT: Greenwood, 2000.

Nicholls, David G. "George Wylie Henderson: A Primary and Secondary Bibliography." *Bulletin of Bibliography* 54.4 (1997): 335–338.

Himes, Chester
Novels
If He Hollers Let Him Go (1945)
Lonely Crusade (1947)
Cast the First Stone (1952, reissued in unexpurgated form as *Yesterday Will Make You Cry*, 1998)
The Third Generation (1954)
The Primitive (1955 reissued in unexpurgated form as *The End of a Primitive*, 1997)
A Case of Rape (1956, novella)
For Love of Imabelle (1957, revised as *A Rage in Harlem*, 1965)
Il pluet des coups durs (1958, published in English as *The Real Cool Killers*, 1959)
Couché dans le pain (1959, published in English as *The Crazy Kill*, 1959)
Dare-dare (1959, published in English as *Run Man Run*, 1966)
Tout pour Plaire (1959, published in English as *The Big Gold Dream*, 1960)
Imbroglio Negro (1960, published in English as *All Shot Up*, 1960)
Ne Nous Énervons Pas! (1961, published in English as *The Heat's On*, 1966 and *Come Back Charleston Blue*, 1974)
Pinktoes (1961)
Une Affaire de viol (1963, published in English as *A Case of Rape*, 1980)
Retour en Afrique (1964, published in English as *Cotton Comes to Harlem*, 1965)
Blind Man with a Pistol (1969, also published as *Hot Day, Hot Night*, 1970)
Plan B (1983, unfinished, published posthumously 1993)

Sources for context:

Fabre, Michel, et al. "Chester Himes: An Annotated Primary and Secondary Bibliography." *MELUS* 20. 3 (Fall, 1995): 137.
Fabre, Michel and Robert E. Skinner, eds. *Conversations with Chester Himes*. Jackson: University Press of Mississippi, 1995.
    From Harlem to Paris: Black American Writers in France, 1840-1980. Champaign, IL: University of Illinois Press, 1991.
Himes, Chester. *The Quality of Hurt: The Autobiography of Chester Himes*, Vol. I. New York: Thunder's Mouth, 1972.
    My Life of Absurdity: The Autobiography of Chester Himes, Vol. II New York: Thunder's Mouth, 1976.
Lundquist, James. *Chester Himes*. New York: Frederick Ungar, 1976.
Margolies, Edward, and Michel Fabre. *The Several Lives of Chester Himes*. Jackson: University Press of Mississippi, 1997.
Sallis, James. *Chester Himes: A Life*. New York: Walker and Co., 2001.
Williams, John A and Lori Williams. *Dear Chester, Dear John: Letters between Chester Himes and John A. Williams*. Detroit: Wayne State University Press, 2008.

Hopkins, Pauline

Novels

Contending Forces: A Romance Illustrative of Negro Life North and South (1900)
Hagar's Daughter: A Story of Southern Caste Prejudice (1901–1902, serial)
Winona: A Tale of Negro Life in the South and Southwest (1902, serial)
Of One Blood: Or, the Hidden Self (1902–1903 serial)
"Topsy Templeton" (1916 novella in *New Era* magazine)

Sources for context

Brown, Lois. *Pauline Elizabeth Hopkins: Black Daughter of the Revolution.* Chapel Hill: University of North Carolina Press, 2008.
Carby, Hazel. "Introduction." *The Magazine Novels of Pauline Novels.* Pauline Hopkins. New York: Oxford University Press, 1988. xxix–1.
Gruesser, John Cullen. *The Empire Abroad and the Empire at Home.* Athens: University of Georgia Press, 2012.
Wallinger, Hanna. *Pauline E. Hopkins: A Literary Biography.* Athens: University of Georgia Press, 2005.

Hopkinson, Nalo

Novels

Brown Girl in the Ring (1998)
Midnight Robber (2000)
The Salt Roads (2003)
The New Moon's Arms (2007)
Sister Mine (2013)
Young adult
The Chaos (2012)

Sources for context

Hopkinson, Nalo. Interview. *Geek's Guide to the Galaxy Podcast* #81. YouTube. Web. August 4, 2015.
Glave, Dianne D., and Nalo Hopkinson. "An Interview with Nalo Hopkinson." *Callaloo* 261. (Winter, 2003): 146–159. *JSTOR Journals.* Web. March 9, 2015.
Rutledge, Gregory E., and Nalo Hopkinson. "Speaking in Tongues: An Interview with Science Fiction Writer Nalo Hopkinson." *African American Review* 33.4 (Winter, 1999): 589–601. *JSTOR Journals.* Web. February 12, 2014.
Watson-Aifah, Jené, and Nalo Hopkinson. "A Conversation with Nalo Hopkinson." *Callaloo* 26.1 (Winter, 2003): 160–169. *JSTOR Journals.* Web. August 4, 2015.

Howard, James H. W.

Novels

Bond and Free; A True Tale of Slave Times (1886)

Sources for context

Jackson, Blyden. *A History of Afro-American Literature*. Vol 1. Baton Rouge; Louisiana State University Press, 1989.
Nelson, Emmanuel Sampath, ed. *African American Authors 1745–1945: Biographical Critical Sourcebook*. Greenwich, CT: Greenwood Press, 2000. Web April 28, 2014.
Penn, I. Garland. *The Afro-American Press and Its Editors*. Springfield, MA: Willey and CO, 1891.

Hughes, Langston

Novels

Not Without Laughter (1930)
Tambourines to Glory (1958)

Sources for context

Berry, Faith. *Langston Hughes: Before and Beyond Harlem*. Westport, CT: Lawrence Hill, 1983.
Gates, Henry Louis, Jr., and Anthony Appiah. *Langston Hughes: Critical Perspectives Past and Present*. New York: Amistad, 1993.
Miller, R. Baxter. *The Art and Imagination of Langston Hughes*. Lexington: University Press of Kentucky, 1989.
Rampersad, Arnold. *The Life of Langston Hughes*. 2 vols. 2nd ed. New York: Oxford University Press, 2002.
Tracy, Steven C. *A Historical Guide to Langston Hughes*. Oxford, England: Oxford University Press, 2004.

Hurston, Zora Neale

Novels

Jonah's Gourd Vine (1934)
Their Eyes Were Watching God (1937)
Moses, Man of the Mountain (1939)
Seraph on the Sewanee (1948)

Sources for context

Boyd, Valerie. *Wrapped in Rainbows: The Life of Zora Neale Hurston*. New York: Scribner, 2003.
Hemenway, Robert E. *Zora Neale Hurston: A Literary Biography*. Urbana: University of Illinois Press, 1980.
Hurston, Zora Neale. *Folklore, Memoirs, & Other Writings*. Ed. Cheryl Wall. New York: Library of America, 1995.
Kaplan, Carla, ed. *Zora Neale Hurston: A Life in Letters*. New York: Doubleday, 2002.
Wall, Cheryl, et al. *Zora Neale Hurston: Jump at the Sun*. Videorecording. San Francisco: Kanopy Streaming, 2014.

Johnson, Amelia E.

Novels

Clarence and Corinne: Or, God's Way (1890)
The Hazeley Family (1894)
Martina Meriden: Or, What Is My Motive? (1901)

Sources for context

Foreman, P. Gabrielle. *Activist Sentiments*. Urbana: University of Illinois Press, 2009.
Page, Yolanda Williams, ed. *Encyclopedia of African American Women Writers*. Westport, CT: Greenwood, 2007. 309–311.
Penn, I. Garland. *The Afro-American Press and Its Editors*. Springfield, MA: Willey & Co., 1891. 158–164.
Wagner, Wendy. "Mrs. A. E. Johnson (Amelia Johnson)." *American Women Prose Writers, 1870–1920*. Detroit: Gale, 2000. 230–237.

Johnson, Charles

Novels

Faith and the Good Thing (1974)
Oxherding Tale (1982)
Middle Passage (1990)
Dreamer (1998)

Sources for context

Byrd, Rudolph P., ed. *I Call Myself an Artist: Writings by and about Charles Johnson*. Bloomington: Indiana University Press, 1999.

Charles Johnson: In Black and White. Films on Demand. Films Media Group, 1982.
Web. May 9, 2015.

McWilliams, Jim, ed. *Passing the Three Gates: Interviews with Charles Johnson.*
Seattle: University of Washington Press, 2004.

Nash, William R. *Charles Johnson's Fiction.* Urbana: University of Illinois Press,
2003.

Johnson, E[dward]. A[ustin].

Novels

Light Ahead for the Negro (1904)

Sources for context

Bould, Mark. "Revolutionary African-American SF Before Black Power SF"
Extrapolation (University of Texas At Brownsville) 51.1 (2010): 53–81.

"Bio: Edward A. Johnson (1860–1944)." Wake County NCGenWeb. ncgenweb.
us/nc/wake/biographies. November 12, 2015.

Johnson, James Weldon

Novels

The Autobiography of an Ex-Coloured Man (1912)

Sources for context

Fleming, Robert E. *James Weldon Johnson and Arna Wendell Bontemps: A Reference
Guide,* Boston: G. K. Hall, 1978.

Johnson, James Weldon. *Along This Way: The Autobiography of James Weldon
Johnson.* 1933. New York: Da Capo, 2000.

Writings. Ed. William Andrews. New York: Library of America, 2004.

Levy, Eugene. *James Weldon Johnson: Black Leader, Black Voice.* Chicago: University
of Chicago Press, 1973.

Sundquist, Eric. *The Hammers of Creation: Folk Culture in Modern African
American Fiction.* Athens: University of Georgia Press, 1992.

Johnson, Mat

Novels

Drop (2000)
Hunting in Harlem (2003)
John Constantine Hellblazer: Papa Midnite (2006 graphic novel with Tony
Akins and Dan Green)
The Great Negro Plot (2007)
Incognegro (2008, graphic novel with Warren Pleece)

Dark Rain (2010, graphic novel with Simone Gane)
Pym (2011)
Right State (2013, graphic novel with Andrea Mutti)
Loving Day (2015)

Sources for context

Costello, Brannon, and Qiana J. Whitted. "Black and White and Read All Over: Representing Race in Mat Johnson and Warren Pleeces Incognegro: A Graphic Mystery." *Comics and the U.S. South.* Jackson: University Press of Mississippi, 2012. 138–160.
"Johnson, Mat." *Columbia Guide to Contemporary African American Fiction* (2005): 131. *Literary Reference Center.* Web. December 9, 2015.
M., M. "Johnson, Mat." *Current Biography* 71.3 (2010): 55–61.
"Mat Johnson on 'Loving Day' and Life as A 'Black Boy' Who Looks White." *Fresh Air (NPR)* (2015): *Newspaper Source Plus.* Web. January 2, 2016.
Neary, Lynn. "Novelist Mat Johnson Explores The 'Optical Illusion' Of Being Biracial." *Weekend Edition Sunday (NPR)* (2015). *Newspaper Source Plus.* Web. January 2, 2016.

Jones, Edward P.

Novels

The Known World (2003)

Sources for context

Coleman James W. *Understanding Edward P. Jones.* Columbia, SC: University of South Carolina Press, 2016.
Als, Hilton. "The Art of Fiction No. 222: Edward P. Jones." *Paris Review* 207 (2013): 140–172.
Vida, Vendela, ed. "ZZ Packer Talks with Edward P. Jones." In *The Believer Book of Writers Talking to Writers.* San Francisco: McSweeney's, 2008. 123–148.

Jones, Gayl

Novels

Corregidora (1975)
Eva's Man (1976)
The Healing (1998)
Mosquito (1999)

Sources for context

Bragg, Rick. "Author's Tragedy Is Like Events in Her Novels." *New York Times* National/Metro (March 2, 1998). Web May 24, 2105.

Clabough, Casey. *Gayl Jones: The Language of Voice and Freedom in Her Writings*. Jefferson, NC: McFarland & Co., 2008. University of Georgia Catalog. Web. May 23, 2015.

Jones, Gayl. "About My Book." *Black Women Writers (1950–1980)*. Ed. Mari Evans. New York: Anchor Press, 1984. 233–35.

    Liberating Voices: Oral Tradition in African American Literature. Cambridge, MA: Harvard University Press, 1991.

Lordi, Emily J. "Haunting: Gayl Jones's *Corregidora* and Billie Holiday's "Strange Fruit." *Black Resonance: Iconic Women Singers and African American Literature*. New Brunswick: Rutgers University Press, 2013.

Nelson, Jill. "Hiding from Salvation." *The Nation* 266 (May 25, 1998): 30–32.

Weixlmann, Joe. "A Gayl Jones Bibliography." *Callaloo* 20 (Winter, 1984): 119–131. *JSTOR Journals*. Web. June 2, 2015.

Jones, John McHenry

Novels

Hearts of Gold. A Novel (1896)

Sources for context

Bickley, Ancella Radford. "James McHenry Jones: Pioneer Black Educator, 1859–1909." *Honoring our Past: Proceedings of the First Two Conferences on West Virginia's Black History*. Ed. Joe William Trotter, Jr. and Ancella Radford Bickley. Charleston, WV: Alliance for the Collection, Preservation and Dissemination of West Virginia's Black History, 1991.

"Professor John Ernest on J. McHenry Jones's Hearts of Gold." West Virginia University Press. Online video clip. n.d. Web. February 3, 2015.

Jones, Tayari

Novels

Leaving Atlanta (2002)
The Untelling (2005)
Silver Sparrow (2011)

Sources for context

Hugh, Ruppersburg. "Tayari Jones." *New Georgia Encyclopedia Companion to Georgia Literature*. 244. Athens: University of Georgia Press, 2007. *Project MUSE*. Web. June 23, 2015.

C., C. "Jones, Tayari." *Current Biography* 70.8 (2009): 39–43. *MLA International Bibliography*. Web. June 23, 2015.

Spencer, Rochelle. "She Is Ready." *Poets & Writers* 39.3 (2011): 44–50. *Academic Search Complete*. Web. June 23, 2015.

Jones, Tayari. "A Different World." *Tin House* 16.1 (2014): 80–82. *Humanities International Complete*. Web. June 23, 2015.

"Novelist Tayari Jones Honored by the Congressional Black Caucus Foundation." *Journal of Blacks In Higher Education* (August 23, 2012): 18. *Publisher Provided Full Text Searching File*. Web. June 23, 2015.

Kelley, William Melvin

Novels

A Different Drummer (1962)
A Drop of Patience (1965)
dem (1967)
Dunfords Travels Everywheres (1970)

Sources for context

Babb, Valerie M. "William Melvin Kelley." In *Afro-American Fiction Writers After 1955*. Ed. Thadious M. Davis. Vol. 33. *Dictionary of Literary Biography*. Detroit: Gale Research, 1984. 135–143.

Bradley, David. Foreword to *A Different Drummer* by William Melvin Kelley. New York: Doubleday, 1989.

Kelley, William Melvin. "Breeds of America: Coming of Age and Coming of Race." *Harper's Magazine* (August 2012). http://harpers.org/archive. Web. June 4, 2015.

Kemme, Steve. "William Melvin Kelley: Interview." *Mosaic Magazine* (October 30, 2012). mosaicmagazine.org. Web. June 26, 2015.

Sollors, Werner, et al. *Blacks at Harvard: A Documentary History of African-American Experience at Harvard and Radcliffe*. New York: New York University Press, 1993.

Killens, John Oliver

Novels

Youngblood (1954)
'Sippi (1967)
And Then We Heard the Thunder (1963)
The Cotillion: or, One Good Bull Is Half the Herd (1971)
Great Gittin' Up Morning: A Biography of Denmark Vesey (1971)
A Man Ain't Nothing but a Man: The Adventures of John Henry (1975)
The Great Black Russian: A Novel on the Life and Times of Alexander

Pushkin (1989)

Sources for context

Boyd, Herb. "John Oliver Killens and His Literary Legacy." *New York Amsterdam News* (April 2004): 9+. *Academic Search Complete*. Web. September 19, 2014.

Gilyard, Keith. *John Oliver Killens: A Life of Black Literary Activism*. Athens: University of Georgia Press, 2010.

Liberation Memories: The Rhetoric and Poetics of John Oliver Killens. Detroit: Wayne State University Press, 2003.

Killens, John Oliver. *Black Man's Burden*. New York: Trident, 1965.

Lehman, Paul. "The Development of a Black Psyche: An Interview with John Oliver Killens." *Black American Literature Forum* 11.3 (October 1, 1977): 83–90.

Kelley, Emma Dunham

Novels

Megda (1891)
Four Girls at Cottage City (1895)

Sources for context

Flynn, Katherine Eleanor. "Emma Dunham Kelley-Hawkins 1863–1938." *Legacy* 2 (2007): 278. *Project MUSE*. Web. April 3, 2014.

Harris, Jennifer. "Black Like?: The Strange Case of Emma Dunham Kelley-Hawkins." *African American Review* 40.3 (2006): 401–419.

McCaskill, Barbara. "Emma Dunham Kelley." *American Women Prose Writers, 1870–1920*. 238–245. Detroit, MI: Gale, 2000.

K'wan (Kwan Foye)

Novels

Gangsta (2002)
Road Dawgz (2003)
Street Dreams (2004)
Hoodlum (2005)
Eve (2006)
Hood Rat (2006)
Still Hood (2007)
Gutter (2008)
Section 8 (2009)
From Harlem with Love (2010)
The Leak (2010)
Welfare Wifeys (2010)

Eviction Notice (2011)
Gangland (2011)
Love & Gunplay (2012)
Animal (2012)
Wild Cherry (2012)
Animal 2 (2013)

Sources for context

"K'wan – One of Hip-Hop Fiction's Hottest Authors." *AALBC. Web.* February 2, 2015.
Lewis, Alaina L. "Selling Truth: As Told by K'wan." *Clutch.* Web. February 2, 2015.

Lamar, Jake

Novels

The Last Integrationist (1996)
Close to the Bone (1999)
If 6 Were 9 (2001)
Rendezvous Eighteenth (2003)
Ghosts of Saint-Michel (2006)
Posterité (2014 published by French house Rivages; no American publisher as yet)

Sources for context

Dreyfuss, Joel. "A Life in Paris: Author Jake Lamar Followed in the Footsteps of James Baldwin and Settled in the City of Lights." *The Root* (March 18, 2010). Web. June 23, 2015.
Dyer, Ervin. "Passage to Paris." *Crisis* 113.1 (January 1, 2006): 30–33. *Academic Search Complete.* Web. June 23, 2015.
Hulstrand, Janet. "Paris and Writers: An Interview with Jake Lamar, Novelist & Playwright." *Bonjour Paris.* August 11, 2015. Web June 23, 2015.

Larsen, Nella

Novels

Quicksand (1928)
Passing (1929)

Sources for Context

Davis, Thadious M. *Nella Larsen, Novelist of the Harlem Renaissance: A Life Unveiled.* Baton Rouge: Louisiana State University Press, 1996.
Hutchinson, George. *In Search of Nella Larsen: A Biography of the Color Line.* Cambridge, MA: Belknap, 2006.

Larsen, Nella. *Passing.* Edited by Carla Kaplan. New York: W. W. Norton, 2007.
McDowell, Deborah. Introduction to *Quicksand and Passing*, by Nella Larsen. New Brunswick, NJ: Rutgers University Press, 1986.

Lee, Andrea

Novels

Sarah Phillips (1993)
Lost Hearts in Italy (2007)

Sources for context

Lee, Jenny. "Interesting Women: Andrea Lee." *Bold Type* 6.04 (2002). Web. February 2, 2015.
Vercellino, Milena. "Andrea Lee." *The American In Italia.* November 1, 2006. Web. September 2, 2014.
Williams, Jennifer D. "Black American Girls in Paris: Sex, Race, and Cosmopolitanism In Andrea Lee's *Sarah Phillips* and Shay Youngblood's *Black Girl in Paris.*" *Contemporary Women's Writing* 9.2 (2015): 238–256.

Lucas, Curtis

Novels

Flour Is Dusty (1943)
Third Ward Newark (1947)
So Low, So Lonely a Negro Searches for Love in an Alien World (1952)
Angel (1953)
Forbidden Fruit (1953)
Lila (1955)

Sources for context

Bryant, Jerry H. *Victims and Heroes: Racial Violence in the African American Novel.* Amherst: University of Massachusetts Press, 1997.
Rodgers, Lawrence R. *Canaan Bound: The African-American Great Migration Novel.* Urbana: University of Illinois Press, 1997.

McKay, Claude

Novels

Home to Harlem (1928)
Banjo (1929)

Banana Bottom (1933)
Amiable with Big Teeth: A Novel of the Love Affair between the Communists and the Poor Black Sheep of Harlem (2017, posthumously)

Sources for context

Cooper, Wayne F. *Claude McKay: Rebel Sojourner in the Harlem Renaissance*. Baton Rouge: Louisiana State University Press, 1987.

Gayle, Addison, Jr. *Claude Mckay; The Black Poet at War*. Detroit: Broadside, 1972.

Holcomb, Gary Edward. "Diaspora Cruises: Queer Black Proletarianism in Claude McKay's *A Long Way from Home*." *Modern Fiction Studies* 49.4 (Winter, 2003): 714–745.

Ramesh, Kotti Sree, and K. Nirupa Rani. *Claude Mckay: The Literary Identity from Jamaica to Harlem and Beyond*. Jefferson, NC: McFarland, 2006.

McKnight, Reginald

Novels

I Get on the Bus (1990)
He Sleeps (2001)

Sources for contest

Ashe, Bertram D., and Reginald McKnight. "'Under the Umbrella of Black Civilization': A Conversation with Reginald McKnight." *African American Review* 35.3 (Autumn, 2001): 427–437. *JSTOR Journals*. Web. May 13, 2015.

Mcknight, Reginald. "Confessions of a Wannabe Negro." In *Lure and Loathing: Essays on Race, Identity, and the Ambivalence of Assimilation*. Ed. Gerald Early. New York: Penguin, 1994, 95–112.

Walsh, William, and Reginald McKnight. "We Are, in Fact, a Civilization: An Interview with Reginald McKnight." *The Kenyon Review* 16.2 (Spring, 1994): 27–42. *JSTOR Journals*. Web. May 13, 2015.

McMillan, Terry

Novels

Mama (1987)
Disappearing Acts (1989)
Waiting to Exhale (1992)
How Stella Got Her Groove Back (1996)
A Day Late and a Dollar Short (2001)
The Interruption of Everything (2005)
Getting to Happy (2010)

Who Asked You? (2013)
I Almost Forgot about You (2016)

Sources for context

Fish, Bruce, and Becky D. Fish. *Terry McMillan*. Philadelphia: Chelsea House, 2002.
Patrick, Diane. *Terry McMillan: The Unauthorized Biography*. New York: St. Martin's Press, 1999.
Smith, W. and S. Steinberg. "Terry Mcmillan." *Publishers Weekly* 239.22 (1992): 50. *Business Source Complete*. Web. May 10, 2014.
"Terry McMillan." *The Writer* 114 (August, 2001): 66.

Mackey, Nathaniel

Novels

Bedouin Hornbook (1986)
Djbot Baghostus's Run (1993)
Atet A.D. (2001)
Bass Cathedral (2008)

Sources for context

Mackey, Nathaniel. *Discrepant Engagement: Dissonance, Cross-Culturality, and Experimental Writing*. New York: Cambridge, 2003.
     Paracritical Hinge: Essays, Talks, Notes, Interviews. Madison: University of Wisconsin Press, 2005.
Habell-Pallán, Michelle. *Mackey, Nathaniel*. Oxford University Press, 2002. *Oxford Reference*. Web. October 31, 2014.
Heuving, Jeanne. "An Interview with Nathaniel Mackey." *Contemporary Literature* 2 (2012): 207–236.

Major, Clarence

Novels

All-Night Visitors (1969)
No (1973)
Reflex and Bone Structure (1975)
Emergency Exit (1979)
My Amputations: A Novel (1986)
Such Was the Season: A Novel (1987)
Painted Turtle: Woman with Guitar (1988)
Dirty Bird Blues (1996)
One Flesh (2003)

Sources for context

Anon., "Art Work by Clarence Major. "*African American Review* 28. 1, Clarence Major Issue (Spring, 1994): 49–56.
Bell Bernard W, ed. *Clarence Major and His Art*, Chapel Hill: University of North Carolina Press, 2001.
Bunge, Nancy, ed. *Conversations with Clarence Major*. Jackson: University Press of Mississippi, 2002.
Byerman, Keith E. *The Art and Life of Clarence Major*. Athens, GA: University of Georgia Press, 2012.
Klinkowitz, Jerome, *The Life of Fiction*. University of Illinois Press, 1977.
Weixlmann, Joe. "Clarence Major: A Checklist of Criticism." *Obsidian* 4.2 (1978): 101–113.

Micheaux, Oscar

Novels

The Conquest: The Story of a Negro Pioneer, by the Pioneer (1913)
The Forged Note: A Romance of the Darker Races (1915)
The Homesteader (1917)
The Wind from Nowhere (1941)
The Case of Mrs. Wingate (1944)
The Story of Dorothy Stanfield, Based on a Great Insurance Swindle, and a Woman (1946)
The Masquerade: An Historical Novel (1947)

Sources for context

Bowser, Pearl, ed., et al. *Oscar Micheaux and His Circle*. Bloomington: Indiana University Press, 2001.
   Writing Himself into History: Oscar Micheaux, His Silent Films, and His Audiences. New Brunswick, NJ: Rutgers University Press, 2000.
Cannady, James. *Tony Brown's Journal. Mr. Movie (Oscar Micheaux)*. Videorecording. New York: Alexander Street Press. 1984. Web. March 9, 2016.
Platt, David. *Celluloid Power: Social Film Criticism from the Birth of a Nation to Judgment at Nuremberg*. Metuchen, NJ: Scarecrow, 1992.

Morrison, Toni [Chloe Wofford]

Novels

The Bluest Eye (1970)
Sula (1973)
Song of Solomon (1977)

Tar Baby (1981)
Beloved (1987)
Jazz (1992)
Paradise (1998)
Love (2003)
A Mercy (2008)
Home (2012)
God Help the Child (2015)

Sources for context

Beaulieu, Elizabeth Ann, ed. *The Toni Morrison Encyclopedia*. Westport, CT: Greenwood, 2003.

Bloom, Harold. *Toni Morrison*. New York: Chelsea House Publishers, 1990.

Evans, Mari, ed. *Black Women Writers, 1950–1980: A Critical Evaluation*. Garden City: Anchor/Doubleday, 1984.

Gates, Henry Louis, Jr., and Anthony Appiah. *Toni Morrison: Critical Perspectives Past and Present*. New York: Amistad, 1993.

Morrison, Toni, and Carolyn C. Denard. *Toni Morrison: Conversations*. Jackson: University Press of Mississippi, 2008.

Smith, Valerie. *Toni Morrison: Writing the Moral Imagination*. Hoboken, NJ: Wiley-Blackwell, 2012.

Tate, Claudia, ed. *Black Women Writers at Work*. New York: Continuum, 1989.

Toni Morrison: Writer's Work. Videorecording. New York: Films Media Group, [2005], 1990, 2005. *University of Georgia Catalog*. Web. June 7, 2015.

Mosley, Walter

Novels

RL's Dream (1995)
Blue Light (1998)
The Man in My Basement (2004)
47 (2005, young adult)
Fortunate Son (2006)
The Wave (2006)
Killing Johnny Fry (2007)
Diablerie (2008)
The Right Mistake: The Further Philosophical Investigations of Socrates Fortlow (2008)
The Tempest Tales (2008)
The Last Days of Ptolemy Grey (2010)
When the Thrill Is Gone (2011)

The Gift of Fire/On the Head of a Pin (2012, two novellas)
Merge/Disciple (2012, two novellas)
Stepping Stone/Love Machine (2013, two novellas)
Debbie Doesn't Do It Anymore (2014)
Inside a Silver Box (2015)
Series
Easy Rawlins series
Devil in a Blue Dress (1990)
A Red Death (1991)
White Butterfly (1992)
Black Betty (1994)
A Little Yellow Dog (1996)
Gone Fishin' (1996)
Bad Boy Brawly Brown (2002)
Little Scarlet (2004)
Cinnamon Kiss (2005)
Blonde Faith (2007)
Little Green (2013)
Rose Gold (2014)
Fearless Jones series
Fearless Jones (2001)
Fear Itself (2003)
Fear of the Dark (2006)
Leonid McGill series
The Long Fall (2009)
Known to Evil (2010)
When the Thrill Is Gone (2011)
All I Did Was Shoot My Man (2012)
Socrates Fortlow series
Always Outnumbered, Always Outgunned (1998)
Walkin' the Dog (1999)
The Right Mistake: The Further Philosophical Investigations of Socrates Fortlow (2008)

Sources for context

Brady, Owen E. *Conversations with Walter Mosley.* Jackson: University Press of Mississippi, 2011.
Foster, Frances Smith. "Mosley, Walter." In *The Oxford Companion to African American Literature.* New York: Oxford University Press, 1997.
Porter, Horace. *Dreaming Out Loud: African American Novelists at Work.* Iowa City: University of Iowa Press, 2015.

Mosley, Walter, et al. *Black Genius: African-American Solutions to African-American Problems.* New York: W. W. Norton, 1999.
Wilson, Charles E., Jr. *Walter Mosley: A Critical Companion.* Westport, CT: Greenwood, 2003.

Motley, Willard

Novels

Knock on Any Door (1947)
We Fished All Night (1951)
Let No Man Write My Epitaph (1958)
Let Noon Be Fair (1966)

Sources for context:

Fleming, Robert E. *Willard Motley.* Boston: Twayne, 1978.
Klinkowitz, Jerome, and Clarence Majors. *The Diaries Of Willard Motley.* Ames: Iowa State University Press, 1979.
Wald, Alan. "Willard Motley," *Writers of the Black Chicago Renaissance* Urbana: University of Illinois Press, 2011.

Murray, Albert

Novels

Train Whistle Guitar (1974)
The Spyglass Tree (1991)
The Seven League Boots (1996)
The Magic Keys (2005)

Sources for context

Maguire, Roberta S. Conversations with Albert Murray. Jackson: University Press of Mississippi, 1997.
Murray, Albert. *The Omni-Americans: New Perspectives on Black Experience and American Culture.* New York: Da Capo, 1990. Also published as *The Omni Americans: Alternatives to the Folklore of White Supremacy* (1970).
  South to a Very Old Place. New York: Modern Library, 1995.
  Stomping the Blues. New York: McGraw-Hill, 1976.
Murray, Albert and J. F. Callahan, ed., *Trading Twelves: The Selected Letters of Ralph Ellison and Albert Murray.* New York, NY: Modern Library, 2000.
Rowell, Charles H. and Albert Murray. "'An All-Purpose, All-American Literary Intellectual': An Interview with Albert Murray." *Callaloo* 20.2 (Spring, 1997): 399–414. *JSTOR Journals.* Web. June 4, 2015.

Naylor, Gloria

Novels

The Women of Brewster Place: A Novel in Seven Stories (1982)
Linden Hills (1985)
Mama Day (1988)
Bailey's Café (1992)
The Men of Brewster Place (1998)

Sources for Context

Gates, Henry Louis, Jr., and K. A. Appiah, eds. *Gloria Naylor: Critical Perspectives Past and Present*. New York: Amistad, 1993.

Montgomery, Maxine Lavon, ed. *Conversations with Gloria Naylor*. Jackson: University Press of Mississippi, 2004.

Kelley, Margot Anne, ed. *Gloria Naylor's Early Novels*. Gainesville: University Press of Florida, 1999.

Naylor, Gloria. "An Interview with Gloria Naylor." Interview by Charles H. Rowell. *Callaloo* 20. 1 (Winter, 1997): 179–92.

Whitt, Margaret Earley. *Understanding Gloria Naylor*. Columbia: University of South Carolina Press, 1998.

Nazel, Joseph

Novels

My Name Is Black! (1973)
Black is Back (1974)
The Black Exorcist (1974, later reprinted as *Satan's Master*, 1983)
Black Gestapo (1975)
Death for Hire (1975)
Black Prophet (1976)
Black Uprising (1976 later re-titled *Uprising*, 1980)
Black Fury (1976)
Doctor Feel Good (1978)
Spiders Web (1978)
No Place to Die (1979)
Devil Dolls (1982)
Every Goodbye Ain't Gone (1982)
Delta Crossing (1984)
Wolves of Summer (1984)
Foxtrap: A Novel (1986, with Fred Williamson)

Street Wars (1987)
Iceman Series:
The Iceman #1: Billion Dollar Death (1974)
The Iceman #2: The Golden Shaft (1974)
The Iceman #3: Slick Revenge (1973)
The Iceman #4: Sunday Fix (1974)
The Iceman #5: Spinning Target (1974)
The Iceman #6: Canadian Kill (1974)
The Iceman #7: The Shakedown (1975)
The Iceman #8 Finders Keepers, Losers Weepers (1987)
James Rhodes series (as Dom Gober)
Black Cop (1974)
Doomsday Squad (1975)
Killing Ground (1976)
Killer Cop (1976)
Romance novels as Joyce Lezan:
Flight to Love(1983)
Love's Velvet Song (1983)
Lover's Holiday (1983)
Spring Embrace (1983)
Snowfire (1983, as Kimberly Norton)
Passion's Surrender (1983)
Hearbeat (1983)
Love's Silken Web (1984)
Summer Blues (1984)

Sources for context

Emory Holmes II. "An Appreciation: Joseph Gober Nazel Jr. (1944–2006)." *Los Angeles Times*. (October 8, 2006). http://articles.latimes.com. Web. November 24, 2014.

Neely, Barbara

Novels

Blanche on the Lam (1992)
Blanche among the Talented Tenth (1994)
Blanche Cleans Up (1998)
Blanche Passes Go (2000)

Sources for context

Goeller, Alison D. "An Interview With Barbara Neely." *Sleuthing Ethnicity: The Detective in Multiethnic Crime Fiction*. Madison, NJ: Fairleigh Dickinson

University Press, 2003. 299–307. *MLA International Bibliography*. Web. July 15, 2015.

Porter, Nicki. "A Part-Time Novelist Snares Her Secrets." *Writer (Madavor Media)* 128.6 (2015): 36. *Literary Reference Center*. Web. July 15, 2015.

Olden, Marc

Novels

Wellington's (1977)
The Informant (1978)
Poe Must Die (1978)
Gossip (1979)
Book of Shadows (1980)
Choices (1980, as Leslie Crafford)
A Dangerous Glamour (1982)
Giri (1982)
The Unvanquished (1983, as Terry Nelsen Bonner)
Dai-sho (1983)
Gaijin (1986)
Oni (1987)
Sword of Vengeance (1990)
Kisaeng (1991)
Krait (1992)
Fear's Justice (1996)
The Ghost (1999)
As Robert Hawkes
Narc (1973)
Death of a Courier (1974)
Death List (1974)
The Delgado Killings (1974)
Kill the Dragon (1974)
The Beauty Kill (1975)
Corsican Death (1975)
Death Song (1975)
Kill for It (1975)
Black Samurai novels
Black Samurai (1974)
The Golden Kill (1974)
Killer Warrior (1974)
The Deadly Pearl (1974)
The Inquisition (1974)
The Warlock (1975)

Sword of Allah (1975)
The Katana (1975)
The Harker File novels
The Harker File (1976)
Dead and Paid For (1976)
They've Killed Anna (1977)
Kill the Reporter (1978)

Sources for context

Randisi, Robert J. "An Interview With Marc Olden." *Armchair Detective: A Quarterly Journal Devoted to the Appreciation of Mystery, Detective, And Suspense Fiction* 12(1979): 324–327.

Perry, Richard H.

Novels

Changes (1974)
Sparkle: A Novel (1976)
Montgomery's Children (1984)
No Other Tale to Tell: A Novel (1994)
The Broken Land (1997)

Sources for context

Barratt, David. "Richard Perry." *Guide to Literary Masters & Their Works* (2007): 1. *Literary Reference Center*. Web. May 8, 2014.
Samuels, Wilfred D., Tracie Church Guzzio, and Loretta Gilchrist Woodard. *Encyclopedia of African-American Literature*. New York: Facts on File, 2007. University of Georgia Catalog. Web. May 8, 2014.

Petry, Ann

Novels

The Street (1946)
Country Place (1947)
The Narrows (1953)

Sources for context

Holladay, Hilary. *Ann Petry*. New York: Twayne, 1996.
Lubin, Alex. *Revising the Blueprint: Ann Petry and the Literary Left*. Jackson: University Press of Mississippi, 2007.

Petry, Elizabeth. *At Home Inside: A Daughter's Tribute to Ann Petry*. Jackson: University Press of Mississippi, 2008.
Wilson, Mark K., and Ann Petry. "A MELUS Interview: Ann Petry. The New England Connection." *MELUS* 1988: 71–84.

Phillips, Caryl

Novels

The Final Passage (1985)
A State of Independence (1986)
Higher Ground (1989)
Cambridge (1991)
Crossing the River (1993)
The Nature of Blood (1997)
A Distant Shore (2003)
Dancing in the Dark (2005)
In the Falling Snow (2009)
The Lost Child (2015)

Sources for context

Ledent, Bénédicte. "Only Connect: An Interview With Caryl Phillips On Foreigners." *Conversations with Caryl Phillips*. Jackson: University of Mississippi Press, 2009. 184–191.
Hållén, Nicklas. "'Okay, I Am Going To Try This Now.' An Interview with Caryl Phillips about the Atlantic Sounds and the European Tribe." *Journeys* 15.2 (2014): 1–14. *Humanities International Complete*. Web. May 9, 2015.
Phillips, Caryl. *The Atlantic Sound*. New York: Knopf, 2000.
    Color Me English: Migration and Belonging Before and After 9/11. New York: New Press, 2011.
    The European Tribe. New York: Farrar, Straus, Giroux, 1987.
Thomas, Helen. *Caryl Phillips*. Tavistock: Northcote House, 2007.

Polite, Carlene Hatcher

Novels

The Flagellants (1966 French translation; English version 1967)
Sister X and the Victims of Foul Play (1975)

Sources for context

Harris, Mel. "The Black Revolution in Books." *The New York Times Book Review*. August 10, 1969. Web. April 3, 2014.

Nelson, Emmanuel S. *Contemporary African American Novelists: A Bio-Bibliographical Critical Sourcebook*. Westport, CT: Greenwood, 1999.
Worthington-Smith, Hammett. "Carlene Hatcher Polite." *Afro-American Fiction Writers after 1955*. Detroit, MI: Gale, 1984. 215–218.

Reed, Ishmael

Novels

The Free-Lance Pallbearers (1967)
Yellow Back Radio Broke-Down (1969)
Mumbo Jumbo (1972)
The Last Days of Louisiana Red (1974)
Flight to Canada (1976)
The Terrible Twos (1982)
Reckless Eyeballing (1986)
The Terrible Threes (1989)
Japanese by Spring (1993)
Juice! (2011)

Sources for context

Boyer, Jay. *Ishmael Reed*. Boise, ID: Boise State University Press, 1993.
Reed, Ishmael, *Conversations with Ishmael Reed*, eds. Bruce Dick and Amaratjit Singh. Jackson: University Press of Mississippi, 1995.
   "Unlike Artists in The Past, I Am Getting Credit." *Black Renaissance/Renaissance Noire* 9.2/3 (2009): 96–103. *Literary Reference Center*. Web. October 2, 2014.
Dick, Bruce Allen, and Pavel Zemliansky, eds. *The Critical Response to Ishmael Reed*. Westport, CT: Greenwood, 1999.

Riboud, Barbara Chase

Novels

Sally Hemings (1979)
The President's Daughter (1994)
Echo of Lions (1989)
Valide: A Novel of the Harem (1986)
Hottentot Venus (2003)

Sources for context

Stout, Candace Jesse. "In the Spirit of Art Criticism: Reading the Writings of Women Artists." *Studies in Art Education* 41.4 (Summer, 2000): 346–361.

Spencer, Suzette A., and Barbara Chase-Riboud. "On Her Own Terms: An Interview With Barbara Chase-Riboud." *Callaloo* 32.3 (Summer, 2009): 736–757.

Spencer, Suzette A., and Carlos A. Miranda. "Barbara Chase-Riboud: A Special Issue." *Callaloo: A Journal of African Diaspora Arts and Letters* 32.3 (Summer, 2009): 711–1026.

Sapphire (Ramona Lofton)

Novels

Push (1996)
The Kid (2011)

Sources for context

Cooper, Brittney. "'Maybe I'll Be A Poet, Rapper': Hip-Hop Feminism And Literary Aesthetics In Push." *African American Review* 46.1 (Spring, 2013): 55–69.

McNeil, Elizabeth, et al. "'Going After Something Else': Sapphire On The Evolution From PUSH To Precious And The Kid." *Callaloo: A Journal Of African Diaspora Arts And Letters* 37.2 (2014): 352–357.

Summers, Claude J. "Sapphire (Ramona Lofton)" *GLBTQ Literature* (2015): 1–5. *LGBT Life*. Web. January 15, 2016.

Saunders, Charles

Novels

Imaro (1981)
The Quest for Cush (1984)
The Trail of Bohu (1985)
Dossouye (2008)
The Naama War (2009)
Damballa (2011)
Dossouye: The Dancers of Mulukau (2012)
Abengoni: First Calling (2014)

Sources for context

Bell, John. "A Charles R. Saunders Interview." *Black American Literature Forum* 18.2. Science Fiction Issue (Summer, 1984): 90–92. Web. July 30, 2015.

Saunders, Charles. *Charles Saunders Writer*. n.p. n.d. Web. July 30, 2015.

Croteau, Michael. "Interviews with Writers Influenced by Philip José Farmer: An Interview with Charles R. Saunders." pjfarmer.com (October 5, 2011). Web. July 30, 2015.

Schuyler, George

Novels

Black No More (1931)
Slaves Today: A Story of Liberia (1931)
The Black Internationale (serialized, published in the *Pittsburgh Courier* from November 21, 1936 through July 3, 1937)
Black Empire (serialized in the *Pittsburgh Courier* from October 2, 1937 to April 16, 1938)

Sources for context

Judge, Mark Gauvreau. "Justice to George S. Schuyler." *Policy Review* 102 (2000): 41–48.
Peplow, Michael W. *George S. Schuyler*. Boston: Twayne, 1980.
Schuyler, George S. *Black and Conservative: The Autobiography of George S. Schuyler*. New Rochelle, NY: Arlington House, 1966.
Williams, Oscar Renal. *George S. Schuyler: Portrait of a Black Conservative*. Knoxville: University of Tennessee Press, 2007.

Scott-Heron, Gil

Novels

The Vulture (1970)
The Nigger Factory (1972)

Sources for context

Baram, Marcus. *Gil Scott-Heron: Pieces of a Man*. New York: St. Martin's, 2014.
Scott-Heron, Gil. *The Last Holiday, A Memoir*. 2003. New York: Grove, 2012.
"Gil Scott-Heron: Starting A Revolution." *Jazztimes* 42.3 (2012): 42–45. *RILM Abstracts of Music Literature (1967 to Present only)*. Web. September 5, 2014.

Senna, Danzy

Novels

Caucasia (1998)
Symptomatic (2004)

Sources for context

Ashe, Bertram, and Danzy Senna. "Passing as Danzy Senna." *Columbia: A Journal of Literature and Art* 36 (2002): 125–145.

Milian Arias, Claudia M., and Danzy Senna. "An Interview with Danzy Senna." *Callaloo* 25.2 (Spring 2002): 447–452.
Senna, Danzy. *Where Did You Sleep Last Night: A Personal History*. New York: Farrar Straus and Giroux, 2009.

Shange, Ntozake [Paulette Williams]

Novels

Sassafrass, Cypress & Indigo (1982)
Betsey Brown (1985)
Liliane: Resurrection of the Daughter (1994)
Some Sing, Some Cry (2010 with Ifa Bayeza)

Sources for context

Lester, Neal A. *Ntozake Shange: A Critical Study of the Plays*. New York: Garland, 1995.
Lyons, Brenda. "Interview With Ntozake Shange." *Massachusetts Review* 28 (1987): 687–696. *Art Source*. Web. May 16, 2015.
Martin, Reginald. *Ntozake Shange's First Novel: In the Beginning Was the Word*. Fredericksburg, VA: Mary Washington College, 1984.
Mullen, Harryette. "'Artistic Expression Was Flowing Everywhere': Alison Mills And Ntozake Shange, Black Bohemian Feminists in the 1970s." *Meridians: Feminism, Race, Transnationalism* 4.2 (2004): 205–235.
Russell, Sandi. *Render Me My Song: African American Women Writers from Slavery to the Present*. New York: St. Martin's Press, 1990.
Tate, Claudia. *Black Women Writers at Work*. New York: Continuum, 1983.

Shockley, Ann Allen

Novels

Loving Her (1974)
Say Jesus and Come to Me (1982)

Sources for context

Bogus, S. Diane. "Ann Allen Shockley." *Gay and Lesbian Literature*. Ed. Sharon Malinowski. Detroit: St. James Press, 1994. 349–351.
Dandridge, Rita B. *Ann Allen Shockley: An Annotated Primary and Secondary Bibliography*. Westport, CT: Greenwood, 1987.
Davidson, Adenike Marie. "Ann Allen Shockley (1927–)." *Contemporary African American Novelists: A Bio-Bibliographical Critical Sourcebook*. Westport, CT: Greenwood, 1999. 433–437.

Smith, Fellipe

Novels

MBQ. 3 vols. (2005–2007)
Peepo Choo 3 vols. (2009–2010, published serially in *Morning 2* from 21 June 2008–2009)
All-New Ghost Rider. 2 vols. (with Tradd Moore, 2014–2015)

Sources for context:

Aoki, Deb. "Interview: Felipe Smith Creator of *Peepo Choo* and *MBQ.*" manga. about.com. Web. August 18, 2015.
Chideya, Farai, host. "Black Artists Plot Diverse Themes for Graphic Novels." NPR. January 19, 2007. Web. September 4, 2014.
Kahn, Juliet. "*Peepo Choo* to *Ghost Rider*: An Interview with Felipe Smith" *Comics Alliance* (August 28, 2014). Web. August 18, 2015.
Miller, Evan. "The Gallery in Japan-Felipe Smith." *Anime NewsNetwork.* May 9, 2009. Web. August 18, 2015.

Smith, William Gardner

Novels

Last of the Conquerors (1948)
Anger at Innocence (1950)
South Street (1954)
The Stone Face (1963)

Sources for context

Bryant Jerry H. "Individuality and Fraternity: The Novels of William Gardner Smith." *Studies in Black Literature* 3 (Summer 1972): 1–8.
Hodges, LeRoy S., Jr. *Portrait of an Expatriate: William Gardner Smith, Writer.* Westport, CT: Greenwood, 1985.
Smith, William Gardner. "The Negro Writer: Pitfalls and Compensations." *Phylon*, 9. 4 (Fourth Quarter 1950): 297–303.
    "Negroes in Germany Set Styles Until Nazis Started Hatred Drive." *Pittsburgh Courier* September 7, 1946. 13.

Souljah, Sister (Lisa Williamson)

Novels

The Coldest Winter Ever (1999)
A Deeper Love Inside: The Porsche Santiaga Story (2012)

The Midnight series
Midnight: A Gangster Love Story (2008)
Midnight and the Meaning of Love (2011)
A Moment of Silence: Midnight III (2015)

Sources for context

Cross, Latoya. "Sister Souljah Talks 'A Moment of Silence: Midnight III.'"
Interview. *Ebony* (November 9, 2015). Web. February 3, 2014.
Ofori-Atta, Akoto. "Sister Souljah: More Than a Street-Lit Author." Interview.
The Root. (June 2, 2011). Web. February 3, 2014.
Sister Souljah. *No Disrespect.* New York: Times Books, 1994.

Stowers, Walter H.

Novels

Appointed. An American Novel (1894)

Sources for context

Katzman, David. *Before the Ghetto: Black Detroit in the Nineteenth Century.*
Chicago: University of Illinois Press, 1973.
Penn, I. Garland. *The Afro-American Press and Its Editors.* Springfield, MA: Willey &
Co., 1891. 158–164.
"Walter H. Stowers Home." http://detroit1701.org. Web. June 7, 2013.
Warren, Francis H. *Michigan Manual of Freedmen's Progress.* web.library.wmich.
edu. Web. April 29, 2014.

Stringer, Vickie

Novels

Imagine This (2004)
Let That Be the Reason (2009)
The Reason Why (2009)
The Dirty Red Series
Dirty Red (2007)
Still Dirty (2009)
Dirtier Than Ever (2011)
Low Down and Dirty (2013)

Sources for context

Gorilla Convict. "Vickie Stringer – Keeping it Real?" Web. February 3, 2016.
"Stringer, Vickie." *Contemporary Black Biography.* 2007. Web. February 3, 2016.

Stringer, Vickie. "How I Did It, Vickie Stringer, CEO Triple Crown Publications, Redemption Doesn't Come Easy." As told to Patrick J. Sauer. *Inc.* May 1, 2006. Web. February 3, 2015.

Teague, Kwame

Novels

The Adventures of Ghetto Sam and *The Glory of My* Demise (2003)
The Dutch Trilogy (published under author Teri Woods's name)
Dutch (2003)
Dutch II (2005)
Dutch III, The Finale (2011)
Dynasty (2009)

Sources for context

Brown, Kaven L. "Dutch Trilogy Ends Dynasty Begins." Theubs.com (January 2010). Web. February 2, 2016.
Ferranti, Seth. "Soul Man" Kwame Teague Exclusive. Theubs.com (January 2007). Web. February 2, 2016.
Profit, Al. "Kwame Teague author of *Dutch*." Interview. Web. February 2, 2016.

Thurman, Wallace

Novels

The Blacker the Berry. A Novel of Negro Life (1929)
Infants of the Spring (1932)

Sources for context

Bontemps, Arna, ed. *The Harlem Renaissance Remembered.* New York: Dodd Mead, 1972.
Hannah, Matthew N. "Desires Made Manifest: The Queer Modernism of Wallace Thurman's Fire!!." *Journal of Modern Literature* 38.3 (2015): 162–180.
Lewis, David L. *When Harlem Was In Vogue.* New York: Oxford University Press, 1989.
Thurman, Wallace. *The Collected Writings of Wallace Thurman.* New Brunswick, NJ: Rutgers University Press, 2003.

Toomer, Jean

Novels

Cane (1923)

Sources for context

Kerman, Cynthia Earl and Richard Eldridge. *The Lives of Jean Toomer: A Hunger for Wholeness*. Baton Rouge: Louisiana State University Press, 1987.

McKay, Nellie. *Jean Toomer: Artist: A Study of His Literary Life and Work, 1894–1936*. Chapel Hill: University of North Carolina Press, 1984.

Toomer, Jean. *The Letters of Jean Toomer, 1919–1924*. Ed. Mark Whelan. Knoxville: University of Tennessee Press, 2006.

Turner, Nikki

Novels

A Project Chick series
A Project Chick (2003)
A Project Chick II: What's Done in the Dark (2013)
The Glamorous Life series
The Glamorous Life (2005)
The Glamorous Life 2: All That Glitters Isn't Gold (2013)
Riding Dirty on I-95 (2006)
Death Before Dishonor (2007)
Black Widow: A Novel (2008)
Ghetto Superstar (2009)
Relapse (2010)
Natural Born Hustler (2010)
The Banks Sisters series
The Banks Sisters (2015)
The Banks Sisters II (2016)
Girls from Da Hood series
Girls from Da Hood (2006)
Girls From Da Hood 2 (2006)
Girls From Da Hood 3 (2007)
Girls from Da Hood 4 (2008)
Girls From Da Hood 5 (2009)
Girls From Da Hood 6 (2011)
Girls From Da Hood 7 (2012)
Girls From Da Hood 8 (2013)
Girls From Da Hood 9 (2013)
Girls From Da Hood 10 (2015)
Girls From Da Hood 11 (2016)
Hustler's Wife series

A Hustler's Wife (2002)
Forever a Hustler's Wife: A Novel (2008)
Heartbreak of a Hustler's Wife: A Novel (2011)
Unique e-book series
Unique (2014)
Unique II: Betrayal (2012)
Unique III: Revenge (2012)
Unique IV: Love & Lies (2016)
Unique V: Secrets Revealed (2016)
Always Unique (2014, collects I-III)

Sources for context

Gorrilla Convict. "The Life of Nikki Turner, Queen of Hip-Hop Fiction." Web. February 3, 2016.
This is 50 & Young Jack Thriller. "Nikki Turner Presents Her New Book." A Woman's Work: Street Chronicles." Interview. Web. February 3, 2016.

Turpin, Waters Edward

Novels

These Low Grounds (1937)
O Canaan! (1939)

Sources of context

Carter, Linda M. "Waters Edward Turpin." *Guide To Literary Masters & Their Works* (2007): 1. *Literary Reference Center*. Web. March 9, 2015.
Reid, Margaret Ann. *Turpin, Waters*. Oxford University Press, 2002. *Oxford Reference*. Web. June 5, 2014.

Tyree, Omar

Novels

Flyy-Girl (1993)
Capital City: The Chronicles of a D.C. Underworld (1994, republished as *A Do Right Man* (1997)
Single Mom (1998)
For the Love of Money (2000)
Sweet St. Louis (1999)
Just Say No! (2001)
Leslie (2002)

Diary of Groupie (2003)
One Crazy Night (2003)
Boss Lady (2005)
What They Want (2006)
The Last Street Novel (2007)
Pecking Order (2008)
As the Urban Griot
Cold Blooded (2004)
College Boy (2002)
Underground (2001)

Sources for context

Cole, David W. "Omar Tyree." *Guide To Literary Masters & Their Works* (2007): 1. *Literary Reference Center*. Web. July 14, 2014.
Henderson, Carol E. "Omar Tyree." *Twenty-First-Century American Novelists*. Eds. Lisa Abney and Suzanne Disheroon Green. *Dictionary of Literary Biography* Vol. 292. Detroit: Gale, 2004: 314–319.

Vernon, Olympia

Novels

Eden (2003)
Logic (2004)
A Killing In This Town (2006)

Sources for context

Davis, Thadious M. "Olympia Vernon's Children of Opinion." *Callaloo* 35.1 (Winter, 2012): 120–135. *Project MUSE*. Web. June 25, 2015.
Dagbovie, Sika Alaine, and Nghana Lewis. "Out of Eden: The Emergence of Olympia Vernon and Black Woman Love." *Mississippi Quarterly* 59.3/4 (Summer/Fall, 2006): 509–524.
Susan Henderson. "Reynald's Rap: Lance Reynald Chats with Olympia Vernon." October 21, 2006. Susan Henderson' Lit Park. Web. June 25, 2015.

Walker, Alice

Novels

The Third Life of Grange Copeland (1970)
Meridian (1976)
The Color Purple (1982)

The Temple of My Familiar (1989)
Possessing the Secret of Joy (1992)
By the Light of My Father's Smile (1998)
Now Is the Time to Open Your Heart: A Novel (2004)

Sources for context

Boyd, Valerie, ed. *Gathering Blossoms Under Fire: The Journals of Alice Walker.* 37Ink/Simon and Schuster, 2017.
Christian, Barbara. ed. *Everyday Use.* New Brunswick: Rutgers University Press, 1994.
Evans, Mari. ed. *Black Women Writers, 1950–1980: A Critical Evaluation,* New York: Anchor, 1984.
Kramer, Barbara. *Alice Walker: Author of "The Color Purple."* Berkeley Heights, NJ: Enslow, 1995.
Prenshaw, Peggy W. ed. *Women Writers of the Contemporary South.* Jackson: University Press of Mississippi, 1984.
Walker, Alice. *In Search of Our Mothers' Gardens.* San Diego: Harcourt, 1983.
    The Same River Twice: Honoring the Difficult; A Meditation of Life, Spirit, Art, and the Making of the film "The Color Purple," Ten Years Later. New York: Scribner, 1996.
    The World Has Changed: Conversations with Alice Walker. Ed. Rudolph P. Byrd. New York: New Press, 2010.
White, Evelyn C. *Alice Walker: A Life.* New York: W. W. Norton, 2004.

Walker, Margaret

Novels

Jubilee (1966)

Sources for context

Baraka, Amiri. "Margaret Walker Alexander." *Nation* 268 (January 4, 1999): 32–33.
Brown, Carolyn J. *Song of My Life: A Biography of Margaret Walker.* Jackson: University Press of Mississippi, 2014.
McCray, Judith., and Margaret Walker. *For My People: The Life and Writing of Margaret Walker.* Videorecording. San Francisco: 1998. *Alexander Street Press.* [San Francisco, CA: California Newsreel, 1998.] Web. July 7, 2015.
Walker, Margaret. *Conversations with Margaret Walker.* Maryemma Graham, ed. Jackson: University Press of Mississippi, 2002.
    "How I Wrote *Jubilee.*" In Maryemma Graham, ed. *"How I Wrote* Jubilee" *and Other Essays on Life and Literature.* New York: The Feminist Press, 1990. 50–69.

Webb, Frank J.

Novels

The Garies and Their Friends (1857)
Paul Sumner (unpublished)

Sources for context

Crockett, Rosemary F. "Frank J. Webb: The Shift to Color Discrimination." *The Black Columbiad*. Ed. Werner Sollors and Maria Diedrich, Cambridge, MA: Harvard University Press.1994. 112–122.

Gardner, Eric. "'A Gentleman of Superior Cultivation and Refinement': Recovering the Biography of Frank J. Webb." *African American Review* 35.2 (Summer, 2001): 297–308.

Maillard, Mary. " 'Faithfully Drawn from Real Life': Autobiographical Elements in Frank J. Webb's *the Garies and Their Friends*." *The Pennsylvania Magazine of History and Biography* 137.3 (July, 2013): 261–300. Web. November 7, 2015.

"Webb, Frank J." *American National Biography Online*. July 2002. Web. June 25, 2013.

Sollors, Werner, Introduction, *Frank J. Webb: Fiction, Essays, Poetry* New Milford, CT: The Toby Press, 2004.

West, Dorothy

Novels

The Living Is Easy (1948)
The Wedding (1995)

Sources for context

Jones, Sharon. *Rereading the Harlem Renaissance: Race, Class, and Gender in the Fiction of Jessie Fauset, Zora Neale Hurston, and Dorothy West*. Westport: Greenwood, 2002.

McDowell, Deborah E. "Conversations with Dorothy West." *The Harlem Renaissance Re-examined*. Ed. Victor A. Kramer. New York: AMS 1987, 265–282.

Sherrard-Johnson, Cherene. *Dorothy West's Paradise: A Biography of Class and Color*. New Brunswick, NJ: Rutgers University Press, 2012.

Washington, Mary Helen. "Remembering a Proper Black Bostonian." *Black Issues Book Review*. 1.4 (July/August 1999): 12–13.

White, Walter

Novels

The Fire in the Flint (1924)
Flight (1926)

Sources for context

Cannady, James., et al. *Walter White*. Videorecording. New York, 2005. *Alexander Street Press*. Web. June 23, 2013.
Dyja, Thomas, et al. *Walter White*. Videorecording. New York, 2005. *Alexander Street Press*. Web. March 9, 2016.
Waldron, Edward E. *Walter White and the Harlem Renaissance*. Port Washington, NY: Kennikat Press, 1978.
White, Walter Francis, 1893–1955. *A Man Called White: The Autobiography of Walter White*. New York: Viking, 1948.

Whitehead, Colson

Novels

The Intuitionist (1999)
John Henry Days (2001)
Apex Hides the Hurt (2006)
Sag Harbor (2009)
Zone One (2011)
The Underground Railroad (2016)

Sources for context

Brady, Owen E. "Eavesdropping With Walter Mosley And Colson Whitehead." *Conversations with Walter Mosley*. Ed. Owen Brady. 91–98. Jackson: University Press of Mississippi, 2011.
Porter, Evette. "Writing Home." *Black Issues Book Review* 4.3 (2002): 36–37. *Literary Reference Center*. Web. June 22, 2015.
Sherman, Suzan. "Colson Whitehead." *BOMB* 76 (2001): 74–80.
Whitehead, Colson. "Tunnel Vision." Interview by Daniel Zalewski. *The New York Times Book Review*. May 13, 2001. 8.
"Year of Living Postracially." Op-Ed. *The New York Times*, November 3, 2009. Web. June 22, 2015.

Wideman, John Edgar

Novels

A Glance Away (1967)
Hurry Home (1970)
The Lynchers (1973)

Hiding Place (1981)
The Homewood Trilogy (1985)
Damballah (1981)
Hiding Place (1981)
Sent for You Yesterday (1983)
Reuben (1987)
Philadelphia Fire (1990)
The Cattle Killing (1996)
Two Cities (1998)
Fanon (2008)

Sources for context

Bonetti, Kay. "John Edgar Wideman." Interview. In *Conversations with American Novelists*. Ed. Kay Bonetti, et al. Columbia, MO: University of Missouri Press, 1997.
TuSmith, Bonnie, ed. *Conversations with John Edgar Wideman*. Jackson: University Press of Mississippi, 1998.
Wideman, John Edgar. *Brothers and Keepers*. 1984. London: Allison & Busby, 1985.
  Fatheralong: A Meditation on Fathers and Sons, Race and Society. 1994. New York: Vintage, 1995.
  Hoop Roots. Boston: Houghton Mifflin, 2001.
  "Storytelling and Democracy (in the Radical Sense): A Conversation with John Edgar Wideman." *African American Review* 34.2 (2000): 263–272.

Williams, John Alfred

Novels

The Angry Ones (1960)
Nightsong (1961)
Sissie (1963)
The Man Who Cried I Am (1967)
Sons of Darkness, Sons of Light (1969)
Captain Blackman (1972)
Mothersill and the Foxes (1975)
The Junior Bachelor Society (1976)
!Click Song (1982)
The Berhama Account (1985)
Jacob's Ladder (1987)
Clifford's Blues (1999)

Sources for context

Bates, Karen Grigsby. "A Tribute To John Williams, The Man Who Wrote 'I Am'." July 13, 2015. *Code Switch Frontiers of Race, Culture and Ethnicity*. NPR. Web. August 18, 2015.

Cash, Earl A. *John A. Williams: The Evolution of a Black Writer.* New York: Third Press, 1975.

Ramsey, Priscilla R. "John A. Williams: The Black American Narrative and the City." In *The City in African-American Literature.* Ed. Yoshinobu Hakutani and Robert Butler. Madison, NJ: Fairleigh Dickinson University Press, 1995.

Ro, Sigmund. "Toward the Post-Protest Novel: The Fiction of John A. Williams." In *Rage and Celebration: Essays on Contemporary Afro-American Writing.* Atlantic Highlands, NJ: Humanities Press, 1984.

Williams, Sherley Anne

Novels

Dessa Rose (1986)

Sources for context

Henderson, Mae. "In Memory of Sherley Anne Williams: 'Some One Sweet Angel Chile' 1944–1999." *Callaloo* 4 (1999): 763. *Project MUSE.* Web. July 6, 2015.

Shirley M. Jordan, "Sherley Anne Williams." In *Black Women Writers At Work*, ed. Claudia Tate. New York: Continuum, 1983. 205–213.

"Shirley Anne Williams." *Broken Silences: Interviews with Black and White Women Writers.* New Brunswick: Rutgers, University Press, 1993. 285–301.

Williams, Sherley Anne. Preface, "Meditations on History." In *Blackeyed-Susans and Midnight Birds: Stories by and about Black Women.* Ed. Mary Helen Washington. New York: Anchor Books, 1990.

  Give Birth to Brightness: A Thematic Study in Neo-Black Literature. New York: Dial Press, 1972.

Wilson, Harriet

Novels

Our Nig: Sketches from the Life of a Free Black (1859)

Sources for context

Boggis, JerriAnne, et al. *Harriet Wilson's New England: Race, Writing, and Region.* Durham, NH: University of New Hampshire Press/Hanover: University Press of New England, 2007.

Ellis, R. J. *Harriet Wilson's Our Nig: A Cultural Biography of a "Two-Story" African American Novel.* New York: Rodopi, 2003.

Petersen, Carla. *Doer of the Word: African American Women Speakers and the Writers of the North 1830–1880.* New York: Oxford University Press, 1995.

Woods, Teri

Novels

True to the Game (1998)
Deadly Reigns I (2005)
Deadly Reigns II (2006)
Angel (2006)
Predators (2007), with Walker Oglesby
Deadly Reigns III (2009)
Alibi (2010 also issued as *Alibi Part I* 2014)
NY's Finest-Masquerade (2011)
Alibi Part II (2014)
True to the Game II (2014)
True to the Game III (2014)

Sources for context:

Smith, Dinitia. "Unorthodox Publisher Animates Hip-Hop Lit." *New York Times* (September 8, 2004). Web. February 2, 2016.

Wright, Charles

Novels

The Messenger (1963)
The Wig: A Mirror Image (1966)

Sources for context

Byerman, Keith E. *Fingering the Jagged Grain: Tradition and Form in Recent Black Fiction*. Athens: University of Georgia Press, 1985.
Klinkowitz, Jerome. *Literary Disruptions: The Making of a Post-Contemporary American Fiction*. Urbana: University of Illinois Press, 1975.
Schulz, Max F. "The Aesthetics of Anxiety" and "The Conformist Heroes of Bruce Jay Friedman and Charles Wright." In *Black Humor Fiction of the Sixties: A Pluralistic Definition of Man and His World*. Athens: Ohio University Press, 1973.

Wright, Richard

Novels

Native Son (1940)

The Outsider (1953)
Savage Holiday (1954)
The Long Dream (1958)
Lawd Today (1963)
A Father's Law (2008, posthumously)

Sources for context

Craven, Alice Mikal, and William Dow. *Richard Wright: New Readings in the 21St Century*. New York: Palgrave Macmillan, 2011.
Fabre, Michel, and Isabel Barzun. *The Unfinished Quest of Richard Wright*. New York: William Morrow, 1973.
Kinnamon, Keneth, *Richard Wright: An Annotated Bibliography Of Criticism And Commentary, 1983–2003*. Jefferson, NC: McFarland, 2006.
Kinnamon, Keneth and Michel Fabre, eds. *Conversations with Richard Wright*. Jackson: University Press of Mississippi, 1993.
Rowley, Hazel *Richard Wright: The Life and Times*. New York: Henry Holt, 2001.

Wright, Sarah E.

Novels

This Child's Gonna Live (1969)

Sources for context

Harris, Trudier. "Three Black Women Writers and Humanism: A Folk Perspective." In *Black Literature and Humanism*. Ed. R. Baxter Miller. Lexington: University Press of Kentucky, 1981.
Houston, Helen. R. "Sarah Elizabeth Wright." In *Oxford Companion to African American Literature*. Ed. William L. Andrews et al. New York: Oxford University Press, 1997.

Wright, Zara

Novels

Black and White and Tangled Threads (1920)
Kenneth (1920)

Sources for context

Rynetta Davis. "Recovering The Legacy of Zara Wright and the Twentieth-Century Black Woman Writer." In Dale M. Bauer, ed. *The Cambridge History of American Women's Literature*. 446–457. Cambridge Histories Online. New York: Cambridge University Press, 2012. Web. October 13, 2014.

Yerby, Frank

Novels

The Foxes of Harrow (1946)
The Vixens (1947)
The Golden Hawk (1948)
Pride's Castle (1949)
Floodtide (1950)
A Woman Called Fancy (1951)
The Saracen Blade (1952)
The Devil's Laughter (1953)
Benton's Row (1954)
Bride of Liberty (1955)
El Cielo Esta ' Muy Alto, (1954 novella)
The Treasure of Pleasant Valley (1955)
Captain Rebel (1957)
The Serpent and the Staff (1958)
Jarrett's Jade (1959)
Gillian (1960)
The Garfield Honour (1962)
Griffin's Way (1962)
The Old Gods Laugh: a Modern Romance (1964)
An Odor of Sanctity (1965)
Goat Song: A Novel of Ancient Greece (1967)
Judas, My Brother; The Story of the Thirteenth Disciple (1968)
Speak Now; A Modern Novel (1969)
The Dahomean (1971, also published as *The Man from Dahomey*)
The Girl From Storyville (1972)
Fairoaks (1974)
The Voyage Unplanned (1974)
Tobias and the Angel (1975)
A Rose for Ana Maria (1976)
Hail the Conquering Hero (1977)
A Darkness at Ingraham's Crest: a Tale of the Slaveholding South (1979)

Western: a Saga of the Great Plains (1982)
Devilseed (1984)
McKenzie's Hundred (1985)

Sources for Context

Benson, Joe. "Frank Yerby." In *Southern Writers*. Ed. Robert Bain, et al. Baton Rouge: Louisiana State University Press, 1979.
Bone, Robert A. *The Negro Novel in America*. New Haven: Yale University Press, 1958.
Fuller, Hoyt W. "Famous Writer Faces a Challenge." *Ebony* (June 1966): 188–190.
Hill, James L. "Frank Garvin Yerby." *Writers of the Black Chicago Renaissance*. Ed. Steven C., Tracy. 386–412. Champaign: University of Illinois Press, 2011.
Yerby, Frank. Oxford University Press, 2011. *Oxford Reference*. Web. October 24, 2014.

Young, Al

Novels

Snakes (1970)
Who Is Angelina? (1975)
Sitting Pretty (1976)
Ask Me Now (1980)
Seduction By Light (1988)

Sources for context

Broughton, Irv, ed. "Al Young." In *The Writer's Mind: Interviews with American Authors*. 3 vols. Fayetteville: University of Arkansas Press, 1989–1990.
Carroll, Michael. "Al Young: Jazz Griot." In *African American Jazz and Rap: Social and Philosophical Examinations of Black Expressive Behavior*. Ed. James L. Conyers, Jr. Jefferson, NC: McFarland, 2001.
Coleman, Janet and Al Young. *Mingus/Mingus: Two Memoirs*. Berkeley: Creative Arts, 1989.
Harper, Michael S., Larry Kart, and Al Young. "Jazz and Letters: A Colloquy." *TriQuarterly* 68 (Winter, 1987): 118–158.
Lee, Don. "About Al Young." *Ploughshares* 19.1 (Spring, 1993): 219–224.
Mackey, Nathaniel and Al Young. "Interview with Al Young." *MELUS* 5.4. New Writers and New Insights (Winter, 1978): 32–51.

ADDITIONAL GENERAL SOURCES

Pre-Emancipation

Austin, Allan D. *African Muslims in Antebellum America: Transatlantic Stories and Spiritual Struggles*. New York: Routeledge, 1997.

African Muslims in Antebellum America: A Sourcebook. New York: Garland, 1984.

Bluett, Thomas. *Some Memories of the Life of Job, the Son of the Solomon High Priest of Boonda in Africa; Who Was Enslaved about Two Years in Maryland; and Afterwards Being Brought To England, Was Set Free, and Sent to His Native Land in The Year 1734*. Documenting the American South. University of North Carolina at Chapel Hill. Web. February 11, 2016.

Carretta, Vincent, and Ty M. Reese. *The Life And Letters Of Philip Quaque, The First African Anglican Missionary*. Athens: University of Georgia Press, 2010.

Muhammed al-Ahari. *Five Classic Muslim Slave Narratives*. Chicago: Magribine Press, 2006.

Thurmond, Michael. *Freedom: Georgia's Antislavery Heritage, 1733–1865*. Atlanta: Longstreet Press, 2002.

Post-Emanipation

Bullock, Penelope L. *The Afro-American Periodical Press, 1838–1909*. Baton Rouge: Louisiana State Press, 1981.

Daniel, Walter C., *Black Journals of the United States*. Westport, CT: Greenwood, 1982.

McCaskill, Barbara and Caroline Gebhard, eds. *Post-Bellum, Pre-Harlem: African American Literature and Culture, 1877–1919*. New York: New York University Press, 2006.

1920s–1940s

Baker, Houston A., Jr. *Modernism and the Harlem Renaissance*. Chicago: University of Chicago Press, 1987.

Carroll, Ann Elizabeth. *Word, Image, and the New Negro: Representation and Identity in the Harlem Renaissance*. Bloomington: Indiana University Press, 2005.

Cruse, Harold. *The Crisis of the Negro Intellectual: A Historical Analysis of the Failure of Black Leadership*. New York: New York Review Books, 2005.

Genevieve, Fabre, and Michael Feith, eds. *Temples for Tomorrow: Looking Back at the Harlem Renaissance*. Bloomington: Indiana University Press, 2001.

Huggins, Nathan. *Harlem Renaissance*. London: Oxford University Press, 1971.

Hull, Gloria T. *Color, Sex and Poetry: Three Women Writers of the Harlem Renaissance*. Bloomington: Indiana University Press, 1987.

Hutchinson, George. *The Harlem Renaissance in Black and White*. Cambridge: Harvard University Press, 1995.

Lewis, David Levering. *When Harlem Was in Vogue*. New York: Knopf, 1981.

Locke, Alain. *The New Negro: An Interpretation*. New York: Boni, 1925.

Nicholls, David G. *Conjuring the Folk: Forms of Modernity in African America*. Ann Arbor: University of Michigan Press, 2000.

Schwarz, A. B. Christa. *Gay Voices of the Harlem Renaissance*. Bloomington: Indiana University Press, 2003.

Wall, Cheryl. *Women of the Harlem Renaissance*. Bloomington: Indiana University Press, 1995.

Wintz, Cary D. *Harlem Speaks: A Living History of the Harlem Renaissance*. Naperville, IL: Sourcebooks, 2007.

1960s–1970s

Baker, Houston. *Afro-American Poetics: Revisions of Harlem and the Black Aesthetic*. Madison: University of Wisconsin Press, 1996.

Bryant, Jerry H. *Born In A Mighty Bad Land: The Violent Man In African American Folklore And Fiction*. Bloomington: Indiana University Press, 2003.

Christian, Barbara. *Black Women Novelists: The Development of a Tradition*. Westport, CT: Greenwood, 1980.

Collins, Lisa Gail and Margo Natalie Crawford, eds. *New Thoughts on the Black Arts Movement*. Brunswick, NJ: Rutgers University Press, 2006.

Gayle, Addison, Jr., Ed. *The Black Aesthetic*. Garden City, NY: Doubleday, 1971.

Hall, James C. *Mercy, Mercy Me: African American Culture and the American Sixties*. New York: Oxford University Press, 2001.

Mphahlele, Ed'kia. *Voices in the Whilrwind and Other Essays*. New York: Hill and Wang, 1972.

Noble, Jeanne. *Beautiful Also, Are the Souls of My Black Sisters*. Englewood Cliffs, NJ: Prentice-Hall, 1978.

Phelps, Carmen L. *Visionary Women Writers of Chicago's Black Arts Movement*. Jackson: University Press of Mississippi, 2012.

Woodard, Komozi. "Rethinking the Black Power Movement." *Africana Age: African and African Diaspora Transformations in the Twentieth Century*. Schomburg Center for Research in Black Culture. exhibitions.nypl.org. Web. March 31, 2015.

Charlie Reilly, ed. *Conversations with Amiri Baraka*. Jackson: University Press of Mississippi, 1994.

Smethurst, James. *The Black Arts Movement: Literary Nationalism in the 1960s and 1970s*. Chapel Hill: University of North Carolina Press, 2005.

1970s–1990s

Awkward, Michael. *Inspiring Influences: Tradition, Revision and Afro-American Women Novels*. New York: Columbia University Press, 1989.

Baker, Houston. *Long Black Song: Essays in Black American Literature and Culture*. Charlottesville: University Press of Virginia, 1990.

   Blues, Ideology, and Afro-American Literature: A Vernacular Theory. Chicago: University of Chicago Press, 1987.

Davis, Angela. *Women, Race and Class*. New York: Random, 1981.

Dickson-Carr, Darryl. *African American Satire: The Sacredly Profane Novel*. Columbia: University of Missouri Press, 2001.

Gates, Henry Louis Jr. *Race, Writing, and Difference*. Chicago: University of Chicago Press, 1986.

The Signifyin' Monkey. New York: Oxford University Press, 1988.

Giddings, Paula. *When and Where I Enter: The Impact of Black Women on Race and Sex in America*. New York: W. Morrow, 1984.

hooks, bell. *Ain't I a Woman: Black Women and Feminism*. Boston: South End Press, 1981.

Black Looks: Race and Representation. Boston: South End Press, 1992.

Feminst Theory: From Margin to Center. 2nd edition. Boston: South End Press, 2000.

Hull, Gloria T., Patricia Bell Scott, and Barbara Smith, eds. *All the Women Are White, All the Blacks Are Men, But Some of Us Are Brave: Black Women's Studies*. New York: Feminist Press, 1982.

Smith, Barbara. *Writings on Race, Gender and Freedom: The Truth that Never Hurts*. New Jersey: Rutgers University Press, 1998.

Stepto, Robert. *From Behind The Veil: A Study of Afro-American Narrative*. Urbana: University of Illinois Press, 1979.

1990s and Beyond

George, Nelson. *Post-Soul Nation: The Explosive, Contradictory, Triumphant, and Tragic 1980s as Experienced by African Americans (Previously Known as Blacks and Before That Negroes)*. New York: Penguin, 2004.

Neal, Mark Anthony. *Soul Babies: Black Poplular Culture and the Post-Soul Aesthetic*. New York: Routledge, 2002.

Tate, Greg. *Flyboy in the Buttermilk: Essays on Contemporary America*. New York: Simon & Schuster, 1992.

Neo-slave Narratives

Bell, Bernard.W. *The Afro-American Novel and Its Tradition*. Amherst: University of Massachusetts Press, 1987.

Beaulieu, E. A. *Black Women Writers and the American Neo-Slave Narrative*. Westport, CT: Greenwood, 1991.

Mitchell, Angelyn. *The Freedom to Remember: Narrative, Slavery, and Gender in Contemporary Black Women's Fiction*. New Brunswick, NJ: Rutgers University Press, 2002.

Rushdy, Ashraf. *Neo Slave Narratives: Studies in the Social Logic of a Literary Form*. New York: Oxford University Press, 1999.

Detective Novels

Bailey, Frankie Y. *Out of the Woodpile: Black Characters in Crime and Detective Fiction*. Westport, CT: Greenwood, 1991.

Cassuto, Leonard. *Hard-Boiled Sentimentality: The Secret History of American Crime Stories*. New York: Columbia University Press, 2009.

Reddy, Maureen T. *Traces, Codes, and Clues: Reading Race in Crime Fiction*. New Brunswick, NJ: Rutgers University Press, 2003.

Soitos, Stephen F. *The Blues Detective: A Study of African American Detective Fiction*. Amherst: University of Massachusetts Press, 1996.

Speculative Fiction

Barr, Marlene S., ed. *Afro-Future Females: Black Writers Chart Science Fiction's Newset New-Wave Trajectory*. Columbus: Ohio State University Press, 2008.

Dery, Mark. *Flame Wars: The Discourse by Cyberculture*. Durham: Duke University Press, 1994.

Goddu, Teresa A. *Gothic America: Narrative History, and Nation*. New York: Columbia University Press, 1997.

Kilgore, De Witt Douglas. *Astrofuturism: Science, Race, and Visions of Utopia in Space*. Philadelphia: University of Pennsylvania Press, 2003.

Le Guin, Ursula K. "American SF and the Other." In Ursula K. Le Guin and Susan Wood, *The Language of the Night: Essays on Fantasy and Science Fiction*. Ed. Susan Wood. 1979. New York: Berkley, 1982. 87–90.

Leonard, Elisabeth Anne. *Into Darkness Peering: Race and Color in the Fantastic*. Westport, CT: Greenwood, 1997.

"Race and Ethnicity in Science Fiction." *The Cambridge Companion to Science Fiction*. Ed. Edward James and Farah Mendlesohn. Cambridge, UK: Cambridge University Press, 2003. 253–63.

Thaler, Ingrid. *Black Atlantic Speculative Fictions: Octavia E. Butler, Jewelle Gomez, and Nalo Hopkinson*. New York: Routledge, 2010.

Graphic Novels

Bolter, David Jay. *Writing: Computers, Hypertext, and the Remediation of Print*. 2nd ed. Mahwah, NJ: Lawrence Erlbaum, 2000. Electronic reproduction. Boulder, CO: NetLibrary, 2001. Web May 2, 2013.

Chaney, Michael A. "Drawing on History in Recent African American Graphic Novels." *MELUS* 32.3. Special Issue Coloring America: Multi-Ethnic Engagements with Graphic Narrative (Fall, 2007): 175–200.

"Is There an African American Graphic Novel?" In *MLA Approaches to Teaching the Graphic Novel*. Ed. Stephen Tabachnick. MLA Publications, 2009. 69–75.

Duffy, Damian and John Jennings. *Black Comix: African American Independent Comics, Art And Culture*. New York: Mark Batty Publisher, 2010.

Eisner, Will. *Comics and Sequential Art: Principles and Practices from the Legendary Cartoonist*. New York: W. W. Norton, 2008.

McCloud, Scott. *Understanding Comics: The Invisible Art*. St. Louis: Turtleback Books, 1994.

Ryan, Jennifer D. "Black Female Authorship and the African American Graphic Novel: Historical Responsibility in *Icon: A Hero's Welcome.*" *MFS Modern Fiction Studies* 52. 4 (Winter 2006): 918–946.
Strömberg, Fredrik. *Black Images in the Comics: A Visual History.* Seattle: Fantagraphic, 2003.

Page to Screen

Bogle, Donald. *Toms, Coons, Mulattoes, Mammies, and Bucks.* New York: Continuum, 2001.
Cripps, Thomas. *Slow Fade to Black: The Negro in American Film, 1900–1942.* New York: Oxford University Press, 2006.
Leab, Daniel J. From *Sambo to Superspade: The Black Experience in Motion Pictures.* Boston: Houghton Mifflin, 1975.
Klotman, Phyllis R. *Frame by Frame: A Black Filmography.* Bloomington: Indiana University Press, 1979.
Sampson, Henry T. *Blacks in Black and White: A Source Book on Black Films.* Metuchen, NJ: Scarecrow Press, 1977.

Notes

1 Out of Many One: The Beginnings of a Novelistic Tradition, 1850s–1900s

1 See Robert B. Stepto, *From Behind the Veil: A Study of Afro-American Narrative* (Urbana: University of Illinois Press, 1979) and William L. Andrews, "The Novelization of Voice in Early African American Narrative," *PMLA* 105.1 (1990): 23–34.

2 Taken from a letter to his father, Diallo's Arabic writing was translated and published in Thomas Bluett's *Some Memories of the Life of Job, the Son of the Solomon High Priest of Boonda in Africa*. It has been in print since 1734. Born in Timbo, Guinea, in approximately 1770 to a well-educated family, Bilali Mohammed was enslaved as a teenager and arrived in Georgia in 1807. Written in Arabic, the work is more an exegesis on Islamic tenets than a diary. For further information, see Allan D. Austin, *African Muslims in Antebellum America: Transatlantic Stories and Spiritual Struggles* (London: Routledge, 1997) and Michael Thurmond, *Freedom: Georgia's Antislavery Heritage, 1733–1865* (Atlanta: Longstreet Press, 2000).

3 For information on the narratives' ability to enforce social control and to solidify racial and class types, see Daniel Williams, *Pillars of Salt: An Anthology of Early American Criminal Narratives* (Madison: Madison House, 1993) and Valerie Babb, *Whiteness Visible: The Meaning of Whiteness in American Literature* (New York: New York University Press, 1998).

4 In Greek mythology, Memnon was an Ethiopian king and a skilled warrior who brought an army to defend Troy.

5 Yates was a member of the *Pacific Appeal*'s publishing committee. He critiqued Brown for his limited vision of black greatness, and Brown questioned his authority in comparison to his own. See "William Wells Brown's Book," *The Pacific Appeal* 2.9 (May 30, 1863), 2 and "The Black Man and Its Critics," *The Pacific Appeal* 2.24 (September 12, 1863), 1. Both are accessible via the California Digital Newspaper Collection. www.cdnc.ucr.edu. Web. April 14, 2014.

6 Issues are accessible at www.wisconsinhistory.org/libraryarchives. Coedited by Samuel Cornish and John B. Russwurm, the journal was published weekly in New York City from 1827 to 1829. See Jacqueline Bacon, *The First African-American Newspaper: Freedom's Journal* (Lanham, MD: Lexington Books, 2007).

7 One editor's note clearly states, "*The Colored American Magazine* is not only National but International in character. Our correspondents included patrons in China, Hawaii, Manila, West Indies and Africa" (*CAM* 7.1 and 2 [May and June 1903], 467).

8 As editorial control changes and issues of black integration into the labor force become more pressing, in the summer of 1904 the border was altered yet again to the figure of a steel worker on one side and a graduate in cap and gown on the other, illustrating the two paths to upward progress (*CAM* 7.6, June 1904, cover illustration). In 1904, Fred R. Moore with substantial assistance from Booker T. Washington purchased *The Colored American Magazine*, and it moved from Boston to New York. With his purchase, Hopkins was downgraded from the editor's position and became assistant editor. The magazine's focus from here becomes less literary and more social science. This might be one explanation for the change of the cover frieze. For information on Hopkins's ultimate departure from *The Colored American*, see Alisha R. Knight, "Furnace Blasts for the Tuskegee Wizard: Revisiting Pauline Elizabeth Hopkins, Booker T. Washington and the *Colored American Magazine*," *American Periodicals: A Journal of History, Criticism, and Bibliography*, 17. 1 (2007): 41–64.

9 The description goes on to read, "This preparation, if used as directed, will turn the skin of a black person four or five shades whiter and that of mulattoes perfectly white … It is a very good thing for the eyes if allowed to get in the eye while washing the face" (*CAM*, November 25, 1899, n. pag.). In one letter to the editor, a Philipino reader wrote the following of the magazine: "I like its appearance very much, and the reading matter is very good. Much taste was shown in the general makeup of its pages – with one exception, – and I take the liberty to appeal to you to remove that one from future issues. I refer to the 'Black Skin Remover and Hair Straightening' advertisement of the Richmond firm who agree to convert Negroes into white folks. Their announcement is painfully nauseous, and offends the eye. The general tone of your periodical is too high to be besmirched by such association … If the colored race in America has reached the point where it is ashamed of itself – of its being black – I feel that its representative magazines and papers should refuse to lend their aid to the spreading of this moral debasement, in the interest of the black races in other countries.… The moment any race begins to apologize for its being what it is, it invites its own doom" (761–762, *CAM* 7.6, October 1903). The ad for the bleaching cream and hair straighter did not appear in the November 1903 issue, but did appear in the December issue.

10 Collins's "Curse of Caste; or The Slave Bride" appeared serially in *The Christian Recorder* in 1865. It was the story of the young orphan octoroon Claire Neville who is hired as caretaker for Mrs. Tracy, the ailing wife of a plantation owner in New Orleans. Claire's arrival causes a great degree of excitement not only because of her beauty and talents, but also because she looks exactly like the banished scion of the plantation Richard Tracy. She is, unbeknownst to him, his daughter, and the story's plot centers around whether they will find one another and if the sins of the past will be avenged. Even by nineteenth-century

standards, the prose is purple. Collins died before the novel was completed. William L. Andrews and Mitch Kachun edited an edition and there suggested that Collins should replace Harriet Wilson because the former wrote more imaginative fiction and the latter more autobiographical. See *Curse of Caste; or the Slave Bride: A Rediscovered African American Novel by Julia C. Collins* (New York: Oxford University Press, 2006).

11 In a forthcoming work tentatively titled "The Life and Times of Hannah Crafts," Professor Gregg Hecimovich of Winthrop University, Rock Hill, South Carolina, claims Hannah Crafts is actually Hannah Bond, a slave on the North Carolina plantation of John Hill Wheeler. See Julie Bosman, "Professor Says He Has Solved a Mystery Over a Slave's Novel," *New York Times* (September 18, 2013). www.nytimes.com. Web. March 16, 2014.

12 In a final note appended to Brown's novel, the publisher writes, "If it serves to relieve the monotony of camp-life to the soldiers of the Union, and therefore of Liberty, and at the same time kindles their zeal in the cause of universal emancipation, the object both of its author and publisher will be gained. (Brown, *Clotelle: A Tale of the Southern States* 104). The agent for this work in New York was the black publishing concern Hamilton and Company. For more information, see John R. McKivigan, *Forgotten Firebrand: James Redpath and the Making of Nineteenth-Century America* (Ithaca: Cornell University Press, 2008) and Alice Fahs, *The Imagined Civil War: Popular Literature of the North & South, 1861–1865* (Chapel Hill: University of North Carolina Press, 2001).

13 In an insightful thesis, Samantha Marie Sommers suggests that we should not think of Brown's 1853 edition as a single novel version of *Clotel*. Instead, all the versions should be read as a single interconnected "tangled text" (1–2). See "A Tangled Text: William Wells Brown's *Clotel* (1853, 1860, 1864, 1867), www .wesscholar.wesleyan.edu. Web. March 16, 2014. The best means of accessing all of Brown's novels is through Christopher Mulvey's electronic gathering of the four texts at rotunda.upress.virginia.edu. In discussing his endeavor, he also asserts that readers need to consider all the works as "Clotel." See "Liberating an African American Text: Editing *Clotel* for an Electronic Century," in *Critical Voicings of Black Liberation: Resistance and Representations in the Americas*, ed. Kimberley L. Phillips (Hamburg: Lit Verlag Munster, 2003).

14 To effect their escape from slavery, Ellen Craft, who could pass for white, disguised herself as a gentleman slaveholder. Her husband William accompanied her as a "slave" valet until by train, steamship, and carriage they arrived in Philadelphia. The definitive history of the Crafts is Barbara McCaskill's *Love, Liberation, and Escaping Slavery: William and Ellen Craft in Cultural Memory* (Athens: University of Georgia Press, 2015).

15 Works discussing what some term as Brown's fragmentary structure include William Edward Farrison, *William Wells Brown, Author and Reformer* (Chicago: University of Chicago Press, 1969); Russ Castronovo, *Fathering the Nation: American Genealogies of Slavery and Freedom* (Berkeley: University

of California Press, 1995). John Ernest in *Chaotic Justice: Rethinking African American Literary History* (Chapel Hill: University of North Carolina Press, 2009) reads the structure of Brown's work as an intentional choice of medium that reflects the tenuous life of enslavement Brown seeks to portray (226–240).

16 An image of the poster appears in an unpublished manuscript by Tamsin Lilley, "Remembering Slavery: South Shields' Links to the Trans-Atlantic Slave Trade" (117), www.collectionsprojects.org.uk. Web. March 16, 2014.

17 Works covering the controversy over Kelley-Hawkins's race include Jennifer Harris, "Black Like?: The Strange Case of Emma Dunham Kelley-Hawkins," *African American Review* 40.3 (Fall, 2006): 401–419 and Holly Jackson, "Mistaken Identity," *Boston Globe* (February 20, 2005), www.boston.com/news/globe/ideas. Web. March 13, 2014.

18 See A. Rupprecht, "'All We Have Done, We Have Done For Freedom': The Creole Slave-Ship Revolt (1841) and the Revolutionary Atlantic," *International Review of Social History* 58 (n.d.): 253–277. *Arts & Humanities Citation Index.* Web. November 5, 2015; George Hendrick and Willene Hendrick, *The* Creole *Mutiny: A Tale of Revolt Aboard a Slave Ship* (Chicago: Ivan R. Dee, 2003).

19 Issues are accessible at HathiTrust Digital Library, www.hathitrust.org. Web. February 13, 2016.

20 In constructing his image of this community, Webb makes use of his own experience as a child born free in Philadelphia to parents working in clothing related trades who subsequently established their own small business. In "'Faithfully Drawn from Real Life': Autobiographical Elements in Frank J. Webb's *The Garies and Their Friends*," Mary Maillard observes that Webb also drew on his own family experiences in portraying the Garies. See *The Pennsylvania Magazine of History and Biography* 137.3 (2013): 261–300.

21 While Delany includes Stowe epigraphs, he resented her being cast as an authority on black agency. He registered outrage at Frederick Douglass's approaching Stowe for advice on the future of black people (*Frederick Douglass's Paper*, April 1, 1853). Issues are accessible at Accessible Archives, www.accessible-archives.com. For a fuller discussion of black responses, see Marva Banks, "Uncle Tom's Cabin and Antebellum Black Response," in *Readers in History: Nineteenth-Century American Literature and the Contexts of Response*, ed. James L. Machor (Baltimore: Johns Hopkins University Press, 1993): 209–227.

22 Fowler closes the novel with a discussion of representative blacks including Frances E. W. Harper and Frederick Douglass. His desire to create positive black antecedents can be seen in his statement about Douglass's parentage: "The opinion, or rather the belief, has prevailed in America that Fred. Douglass was the son of a white father and a colored mother, and that white father has been supposed to have been his owner. But in the history of his own life and times, published a few years ago, Douglass positively affirms that both his parents were colored, and for my own part I believe that to be the truth. As men like Fred. Douglass are very few and far between, the wish among many of the anti-slavery school, at least, seems to have been father to the

thought that so clever a man could never have been the offspring of colored parents" (205). Readers familiar with Douglass's 1845 narrative will remember that Douglas writes, "My father was a white man, He was admitted to be such by all I ever heard speak of my parentage" (*Narrative of the Life of Frederick Douglass* [New York: Penguin, 1986], 48). In the 1896 version, Douglass modifies this to read, "Of my father I know nothing. Slavery had no recognition of fathers, as none of families. That the mother was a slave was enough for its deadly purpose ... The father might be a freeman and the child a slave. The father might be a white man, glorying in the purity of his Anglo-Saxon blood, and his child ranked with the blackest slaves. Father he might be, and not be husband, and could sell his own child without incurring reproach, if in its veins coursed one drop of African blood" (*Life and Times of Frederick Douglass*, 3, www.archive.org. Web. May 21, 2014).

23 This quote comes from a passage written by AME pastor Reverend J. W. Malone in *The Christian Recorder*: "The colored people here can ride in the streetcars without any molestation; so you see Mr. Editor that the light is shining in the West. Therefore 'look well to the West' " (*The Christian Recorder*, July 10, 1869). The reverend advocated westward over African migration for African Americans.

24 See Rabateau, *A Fire in the Bones: Reflections on African-American Religious History* (Boston: Beacon Press, 1995); Gomez, *Exchanging Our Country Marks: The Transformation of African Identities in the Colonial and Antebellum South* (Chapel Hill: University of North Carolina Press, 1998); and Cedrick May, *Evangelism and Resistance in the Black Atlantic, 1760–1835* (Athens: University of Georgia Press, 2008).

25 It should be noted that not everyone was comfortable with the wedding of the novel and religious teaching. One editorial appearing in the *Presbyterian Herald* of 1861 and quoted in *The Christian Recorder* observes, "I wish to call attention to one of the great sins of the Church – that is religious novels. It appears that there is no end to them, and the time is fast approaching when our youth will read no religious books except they are written in that style. I have no doubt but that a great many children form the habit of reading such books at Sabbath School ... I regret exceedingly to see our Board of Publication engaged in publishing such books. The same remark may be applied to the American Sunday School Union. I very much fear that the time is fast approaching when our religious literature, to be read, will have to put on the garb of novels" (*The Christian Recorder*, April 5, 1861).

26 The oft-quoted passage reads, "Besides, America is now wholly given over to a d–d mob of scribbling women, and I should have no chance of success while the public taste is occupied with their trash – and should be ashamed of myself if I did succeed. What is the mystery of these innumerable editions of the Lamplighter, and other books neither better nor worse? – worse they could not be, and better they need not be, when they sell by 100,000" (Nathaniel Hawthorne to William D. Ticknor, January 19, 1855, in *Nathaniel Hawthorne*,

The Letters, 1853–1856, ed. Thomas Woodson et al., *The Centenary Edition of the Works of Nathaniel Hawthorne*, Vol. 16 (Columbus: Ohio State University. Press, 1987), 304.

27 C. Vann Woodward, ed. *Mary Chesnut's Civil War* (New Haven: Yale University Press, 1981); William Hannibal Thomas, *The American Negro What He Was, What He Is, and What He May Become: A Critical And Practical Discussion* (New York: Macmillan Company, 1901): 183–184, docsouth.unc.edu/church/thomas/thomas.html. Web. May 3, 2014); James W. Jack letter to Florence Belgarnie, MCP 102–105, 60.

28 That we know about the serialized novels is due to the literary detective work of Frances Smith Foster.

29 The debate surrounding suffrage, and particularly what would be the impact on black women, was an active one. In the "Women's Column" of *The Colored American Magazine*, the following appears: "There is quote a ripple among women just now in favor of woman suffrage. We believe it to be a good thing if limited in some degree. It is right that women vote on such questions as property rights, the wife's personal rights and rights in her children, and in all that pertains to the public school; but it seems to us that the franchise in its fullest sense is not desirable. Physically, women are not fitted for the politician's life; morally, we should deplore seeing woman fall from her honorable position as a wife and mother to that of the common ward heeler hustling for the crumbs meted out to the 'faithful' of any party in the way of appointments to office … Is it desirable for us as a race to place the ballot in woman's hands? Is the aspect of woman in certain sections such as to inspire us with confidence in the honor of the white woman toward her black sister? … Let us study this question and prove it a good thing for our race before we rush in blindly even to please those who have been of material benefit to us" (*CAM* 1.2, June 1900, 122–123). This was written at the time when Pauline Hopkins was having editorial differences with the new owners of the *Colored American*. See note 10.

30 Accessed via the Pauline Hopkins Society website, paulinehopkinssociety.org.

31 *Hagar's Daughter* appeared in *The Colored American Magazine* 2.5 and 2.6 (March and April 1901); 3.1–6 (May–October 1901); 4.1–4 (November–December 1901, January and March, 1902).

32 *Winona* appeared in *The Colored American Magazine* 5.1–6 (May–October 1902).

33 An example of a smaller, and less literary volume is Mary Etta Spencer's *The Resentment*, a work dedicated to her mother and to "the growing boys and girls of my race" and with a purpose of writing "some little something to inspire some boy or girl of my race to be willing to endure struggle to become a man or woman of worth" ("The Author's Purpose"). Printed by the A. M. E. Book Concern, in 1921, the work very much mirrors the philosophy of Booker T. Washington telling the story of a black farmer who overcomes diversity, and garners the admiration of both his black and white neighbors. www.search.lib .virginia.edu. Web. September 28, 2014.

2 Publish or Perish: African American Novels, 1900s–1920s

1 *The Uncalled* would be reissued in 1901 by the International Association of Newspapers and Authors in a less handsome edition with an image of a plant blooming on the cover.

2 In his autobiography *Along this Way*, James Weldon Johnson remarks on Dunbar's modesty, quiet dignity, and brilliance, but also paints him as a frustrated artist, hemmed in by the public demand for his dialect verse, and never having the opportunity to achieve what he wanted, which Johnson guesses might be to write an epic poem, in standard English, on the significances of being black (159–162). Also see Henry Louis Gates, Jr., "Dis and Dat: Dialect and the Descent," in *Afro-American Literature: The Reconstruction of Instruction*, ed. Robert Stepto and Dexter Fisher (New York: Modern Language Association, 1979): 88–117; John Keeling, "Paul Dunbar and the Mask of Dialect," *The Southern Literary Journal* 25. 2 (Spring 1993): 24–38.

3 *The Colored American Magazine* included the following piece in memorializing his death: "The Afro-American people would justify their freedom and presence as a part of this nation if they did no more than call the name of Dunbar when their defamers begin a derogation of them, and base calumniators roll their sour tongues" (10.3, March 1906, 162).

4 See Gregory L. Candela, "We Wear the Mask: Irony in Dunbar's *The Sport of the Gods*," *American Literature* 48.1 (March 1976): 60–72 and Darwin Turner, "Paul Laurence Dunbar: The Rejected Symbol," *The Journal of Negro History* 52. 1 (January, 1967): 1–13.

5 In a letter to Carl Van Vechten, Chesnutt revealed the complicated way he viewed the relationship of race and writing. On September 7, 1926, he wrote "Between you and me, I suspect I write like a white man because by blood I am white, with a slight and imperceptible dark strain, which in any really civilized country would have no bearing whatever on my life or career, except perhaps as an interesting personal item. I have never had any Negro complex. I was born in the North, of parents of my own type whose ancestors had been free for generations, lived there for the first nine years of my life and the last forty three, in the interim having taught school in the south for some years among colored people. With that exception my business life has been spent entirely among white people, many of whom are my personal friends and associates. These things being so, it is not surprising that I should write like a white man" (McElrath *Letters* 217).

6 With no small degree of modesty, Chesnutt writes, in a speech given as he receives the Spingarn medal in 1928, "At that time the Negro was inarticulate, I think I was the first man in the United States who shared his blood, to write serious fiction about the Negro" (McElrath, *Essays and Speeches* 514).

7 In "W. D. Howells and Race: Charles W. Chesnutt's Disappointment of the Dean" Joseph R. McElrath elaborates on the relationship between Chesnutt and Howells. *Nineteenth-Century Literature* 51.4 (1997): 474–499. *JSTOR*. Web October 22, 2011.

8 See Wilson Jeremiah Moses, *The Golden Age of Black Nationalism, 1850–1925* (New York: Oxford University Press, 1988), chapter 9; Finnie D. Coleman, *Sutton E. Griggs and the Struggle against White Supremacy* (Knoxville: University of Tennessee Press, 2007); Pavla Veselá, "Neither Black Nor White: The Critical Utopias of Sutton E. Griggs and George S. Schuyler," *Science Fiction Studies* 38. 2 (July 2011): 270–287. *JSTOR*. Web. October 22, 2011.

9 Later in the novel Griggs has Ensal note, "The marriage of Frederick Douglass to a white woman created a great gulf between himself and his people, and it is said that so great was the spiritual alienation that Mr. Douglass was never afterwards the orator that he had been. The delicate network of wires over which the inner soul of the speaker conveys itself to the hearts of his hearers was total disarranged by that marriage, they say" (212).

10 In "Of the Training of Black Men," Du Bois writes the following: "I sit with Shakespeare and he winces not. Across the color line I move arm in arm with Balzac and Dumas … From out the caves of evening that swing between the strong-limbed earth and the tracery of the stars, I summon Aristotle and Aurelius and what soul I will, and they come all graciously with no scorn nor condescension. So, wed with Truth, I dwell above the Veil. Is this the life you grudge us, O knightly America?" (*The Souls of Black Folk*, 1903 [New York: Penguin, 1989]: 90).

11 Works surveying Du Bois's sentiments toward communism include Willie Avon Drake, *From Reform to Communism: The Intellectual Development of W. E. B. DuBois* (Ithaca: Cornell University Press, 1985); Edward J. Blum, *W. E. B. Du Bois, American Prophet* (Philadelphia: University of Pennsylvania Press, 2011); and Bill V. Mullen, *Un-American: W.E.B. Du Bois and the Century of World Revolution* (Philadelphia: Temple University Press, 2015).

12 Letter from W. E. B. Du Bois to Harcourt, Brace, and Company, November 29, 1927. W. E. B. Du Bois Papers (MS 312). Special Collections and University Archives, University of Massachusetts Amherst Libraries. credo.library.umass. edu. Web. November 12, 2015.

13 The *New York Times Review of Books* noted, "While this remarkable story appears to be true, it is possible that *The Autobiography of an Ex-Colored Man* is a work of the imagination. Even if it is not all literally true, it does offer a great deal of information on America's race problem" (May 26, 1912, Part 6, 319). *The Booklist* wrote, "The Author's regrets about having passed for white and his keen observations on Negro life help to convince the reader that his rather sensational story may be true" (September 9, 1912, 7). Both are quoted in in Robert E. Fleming, *James Weldon Johnson and Arna Wendell Bontemps: A Reference Guide* (Boston: G. K. Hall, 1978).

14 In his preface to *The Book of American Negro Poetry* (1921), Johnson explicates the problems he sees with vernacular forms, particularly dialect: "What the colored poet in the United States needs to do is something like what Synge did for the Irish; he needs to find a form that will express the racial spirit by symbols from within rather than symbols from without, such as the mere mutilation of English spelling and pronunciation" (*The Norton Anthology of*

African American Literature, ed. Henry Louis Gates, Jr. and Nellie Y. McKay [New York: W. W. Norton, 2004]: 902).

3 Aesthetics of Race and Culture: African American Novels, 1920s–1940s

1 In general, the term "New Negro" refers to a philosophical movement consciously advocating the use of art to remake cultural conceptions of African Americans. Its partner term, the "Harlem Renaissance," often characterizes a more popular cultural moment that saw a flowering in African American art, music, literature, and cultural performance centralized in Harlem, New York. The significances of these terms have been duly debated, as have the history and importance of the period – its relationship to jazz-era American culture, its contributions to the evolution of American modernism. For further information on the distinctions between them, see Henry Louis Gates, "The Trope of the New Negro and the Reconstruction of the Image of the Black," *Representations* 24 (Fall 1988), 129–155; George Hutchinson, "Introduction," *The Cambridge Companion to The Harlem Renaissance*, ed. George Hutchinson (Cambridge: Cambridge University Press, 2007): 1–10; David Levering Lewis, *When Harlem Was in Vogue* (New York: Oxford University Press, 1989); Houston A. Baker Jr., *Modernism and the Harlem Renaissance* (Chicago: University of Chicago Press, 1987).

2 See Nellie Y. McKay, *Jean Toomer, Artist: A Study of His Literary Life and Work, 1894–1936* (Chapel Hill: University of North Carolina Press, 1984); Jean Toomer and Darwin T. Turner, ed., *The Wayward and the Seeking: A Collection of Writings by Jean Toomer* (Washington: Howard University Press, 1980); and Cynthia Earl, Kerman and Richard Eldridge, *The Lives of Jean Toomer: A Hunger for Wholeness* (Baton Rouge: Louisiana State University Press, 1987).

3 Waters Turpin composed a final novel, the self-published *The Rootless* (1957). Grand in vision but incoherent, it begins with the landing of a slaver, the *Betsy Ann*, captained by Shannon Lanrick, a white indentured servant. Among many other plots, a black slave woman aboard the ship he pilots is about to give birth and curses those involved in the enterprise. The novel follows the descendants of these primaries.

4 See Sterling Brown, "Luck Is a Fortune," *The Nation* 145.16 (October 16, 1937): 409–410; Ralph Ellison, "Recent Negro Fiction," *New Masses* 40.6 (August 5, 1940): 22–26.

5 See Langston Hughes, "Not Primitive," in *The Collected Works of Langston Hughes*, Vol. 13 (Columbia: University of Missouri Press, 2001–), 242.

6 Recently an unpublished McKay manuscript, "Amiable with Big Teeth: A Novel of the Love Affair between the Communists and the Poor Black Sheep of Harlem," was discovered in the Columbia University archive by Jean-Christophe Cloutier, a doctoral candidate in English and comparative literature. It portrays Mussolini's invasion of Ethiopia and its repercussion in World War II Harlem. McKay's estate has granted permission to publish

the 1936 satire said to have material characteristic of McKay's writing in the period – romance, intrigue, nightclub scenes, and portraits of Depression-era black artistic and intellectual life in Harlem. Penguin Classics published the manuscript in 2017. See Felicia R. Lee, "New Novel of Harlem Renaissance Is Found," *New York Times*, September 14, 2012. www.nytimes.com. Web. September 16, 2012; Ross Barkan, "Claude McKay's Long-Lost Novel Brings the Harlem Renaissance to Life," *Village Voice*, March 22, 2017. villagevoice. com Web. March 29, 2017.

7 The occasion of this letter was Locke's review of *Comedy American Style*, but the animosity began at an earlier event. What was supposed to be a tribute to the publication of Fauset's novel became a symposium of black literary talent. In 1924 Charles Johnson invited a group of emerging writers to a dinner at the Civic Club in New York, a venue that admitted patrons regardless of race or sex. Black writers such as Fauset and Toomer, black intellectuals, and social advocates such as Du Bois and James Weldon Johnson gathered with white literary luminaries, among them publisher Horace Liveright and Carl Van Doren, editor of *Century* magazine, in order to publicize black literary talent. Alain Locke was the moderator, and speeches praised the prospects of black writing. The event was catalyst to the special edition of the *Survey Graphic* that would become "Harlem, Mecca of the New Negro." Fauset remembered this incident upon reading Locke's review of *Comedy American Style*. In the January 9, 1933 letter, she wrote,

> Dear Alain:
>
> I have always disliked your attitude toward my work dating from the time years ago when you went out of your way to tell my brother that the dinner given at the Civic Club for 'There is Confusion' wasn't for me. Incidentally I may tell you now that that idea originated with Regina Anderson and Gwendolyn Bennett, both members of a little library club with which I was then associated ... And I still remember the consummate cleverness with which you that night as toastmaster strove to keep speech and comment away from the person for whom the occasion was meant....
>
> It has always both amused and annoyed me to read your writings. Amused because as in the case of your multiple articles in the *New Negro* they are stuffed with a pedantry which fails to conceal their poverty of thought. Annoyed because your criticisms such as the one I've just read in *Opportunity* point most effectively to the adage that a critic is a self-acknowledged failure as a writer. It has always seemed to me that you who cannot write have had the utmost arrogance to presume to criticize those who are at all possessed of the creative art or even of the art of marshalling facts and recording them. (ALP 164-38, 41)

8 *God Sends Sunday* was adapted into the 1945 musical *St. Louis Woman*, a collaboration between Bontemps and Cullen. Slated to star Lena Horne both in its Broadway and Hollywood productions, its history reveals the tension between newer writers and the older guard. Before production, Countee Cullen held a reading of the play at the home of Walter White in front of a group of African Americans that included Hubert Delaney and George Schuyler. (Alain Locke was invited, but was unable to attend.) White

was adamant in his criticism, saying that the play's setting in the black ghetto of St. Louis, and its lower class characters were demeaning to blacks. Eventually *St. Louis Woman* premiered on Broadway, with music by Johnny Mercer and Harold Arlen and included the hit "Come Rain, Come Shine." It starred the then ingénue Pearl Bailey. Cullen never lived to see this production, having died three months earlier. See Cullen, *Letters to Alain Locke*, September 9, 1945, September 16, 1945 (ALP 164-22, 40).

9 Ida Bell Robinson built the Mount Sinai Church of America and ordained 163 ministers, 125 of them women. Eventually, Robinson presided over eighty-four churches from New England to Florida. A large motivation behind her starting her church was that women were not being accepted as pastors in traditional houses. See Rosemary Skinner Keller et al., *Encyclopedia of Women and Religion in North America: Integrating the Worlds of Women's Religious Experience in North America* (Bloomington: Indiana University Press, 2006).

10 For a discussion of satire in African American literature, see Darryl Dickson-Carr, *African American Satire: The Sacredly Profane Novel* (Columbia: University of Missouri Press, 2001) and Daphne Brooks, *Bodies in Dissent: Spectacular Performances of Race and Freedom, 1850–1910* (Durham: Duke, University Press, 2006).

11 Du Bois in his enthusiastic review of *Black No More* appreciated Schuyler's satire, and even the characterization of himself: "At any rate, read the book. You are bound to enjoy it and to follow with joyous laughter the adventures of Max Disher and Bunny, Dr. Crookman and – we say it with all reservations – Dr. Agamemnon Shakespeare Beard" [sic] (Aptheker *Reviews* 154).

12 For a consideration of gay life within these neighborhoods, see George Chauncey, *Gay New York: The Making of the Gay Male World, 1890–1940* (New York: Flamingo/HarperCollins, 1994) and A. B. Christa Schwarz, *Gay Voices of the Harlem Renaissance* (Bloomington: Indiana University Press, 2003).

13 In a May 7, 1929, letter to William Jordan, Rapp Thurman describes this as an act of desperation for money on his part. See Wallace Thurman Collection JWJ MSS 12, Box 1, folder 8. Yale Collection of American Literature, Beinecke Rare Book and Manuscript Library.

14 For a fuller discussion of gay black writers of the period, see A. B. Christa Schwarz, *Gay Voices of the Harlem Renaissance* (Bloomington: Indiana University Press, 2003).

15 George Hutchinson provides a detailed history of these interconnections. See *The Harlem Renaissance in Black and White* (Cambridge, MA: Harvard University Press, 1995).

16 Johnson's home at 1461 S Street, Northwest was a Washington, DC equivalent to "The Dark Tower" of Alelia Walker. It was nicknamed "Half-Way House" by the group of writers who became known as Saturday Nighters. Writers and artists came for encouragement, nourishment, literal and figurative (Langston Hughes fondly remembers the cakes served), and to discuss what would constitute black writing. Jean Toomer writes to Alain Locke on January 26, 1921, about the initial meeting that participants wanted to gain knowledge of slavery and black history and to consider the condition of those of "mixed-Race" groups in the United States (ALP 164-90, 12).

4 Home of the Brave: African American Novels, 1940s–1960s

1 See "American Negro Exposition," *The Crisis* 1940 (June): 175, 178.
2 See Andrew L. Yarrow, "Dorothy West, a Harlem Renaissance Writer, Dies at 91," *The New York Times* (August 19, 1998). www.nytimes.com. Web. November 21, 2015.
3 Locke would edit one more special issue of *Survey Graphic* in 1942. His keynote essay "The Unfinished Business of Democracy" underplayed the role of the arts in achieving social justice; instead, he emphasized more direct political action and saw the eradication of racism as essential to global peace. See "The Unfinished Business of Democracy," *Survey Graphic* 31 (November 1942): 455–461.
4 For information on the relationship between *New Masses* and the John Reed Club, see Virginia Hagelstein Marquardt, "'New Masses' and John Reed Club Artists, 1926–1936: Evolution of Ideology, Subject Matter, and Style," *The Journal of Decorative and Propaganda Arts* 12 (Spring, 1989): 56–75.
5 See S. Ani Mukherji, "'Like Another Planet to the Darker Americans': Black Cultural Work in 1930s Moscow," in *Africa in Europe: Studies in Transnational Practice in the Long Twentieth Century*, ed. Eve Rosenhaft and Robbie Aitken (Liverpool: Liverpool University Press, 2013, 120–141).
6 Not all writers were taken with the Communist Party. Claude McKay was critical, as was Zora Neale Hurston in her essay "Why the Negro Won't Buy Communism," published in the *American Legion Magazine*. In a letter to Katherine Tracy L'Engle, Hurston criticizes Communists as being agitators in the Harlem riot of 1936. See Kaplan, 535.
7 Much has been written on the relationship of the Communist Party and leftist politics of the 1930s through 1960s on black writing. For introductions, see James Smethurst, *Left of the Colored Line: Race, Radicalism and Twentieth-Century Literature of the United States* (Chapel Hill: University of North Carolina Press, 2003) and *The New Red Negro: The Literary Left and African American Poetry, 1930–1946* (New York: Oxford University Press, 1999); Robin D. G. Kelley, *Freedom Dreams: The Black Radical Imagination* (Boston: Beacon Press, 2002); Harold Cruse, *The Crisis of the Negro Intellectual: A Historical Analysis of the Failure of Black Leadership* (New York: New York Review of Books, 1967); William J. Maxwell, *New Negro, Old Left: African-American Writing and Communism between the Wars* (New York: Columbia University Press, 1999) and Lawrence P. Jackson, *The Indignant Generation: A Narrative History of African American Writers and Critics, 1934–1960* (Princeton: Princeton University Press, 2011).
8 Other WPA programs included the Federal Arts Project, which resulted in the making of many landmark murals; the Federal Theatre Project, which created performances for audiences who were usually marginalized from theatre productions; and the Farm Security Administration, which archived photographic images of rural America. For a foundational history of the formation of the Works Progress Administration Writers' Project, see Jerre

Mangione, *The Dream and The Deal: The Federal Writers' Project, 1935–1943* (Philadelphia: University of Pennsylvania Press, 1983).

9 Dating around the 1800s, landsmanshaftn were Jewish social organizations created by immigrants sharing the same villages and towns, in Central and Eastern Europe. See Daniel Soyer, *Jewish Immigrant Associations and American Identity in New York, 1880–1939* (Cambridge, MA: Harvard University Press, 1997).

10 See the exchange between Langston Hughes and Arna Bontemps in Nichols, 54, 56; " 'My Man Himes' "; An Interview with Chester Himes, in *Amistad 1*, ed. John A. Williams and Charles F. Harris (New York: Vintage-Random, 1969): 25–93.

11 *Trader Horn* was wildly popular because of its blend of realism and fantasy. Some scenes were shot on location, and a *Times* reviewer goes on to note, "Although some of the scenes were made in Hollywood, the exciting ones were photographed in Africa, where W. S. Van Dyke, the director; Edwina Booth, Duncan Renaldo, Harry Carey and a native, named Mutia Omoolu, spent several months … There are moments in this production when the banks of a small lake appear to move forward into the water, so alive are they with crocodiles, and in the course of one sequence one of these amphibians is presumed to swallow one of the pursuing Isorgis. In other scenes one observes the pent-up fury of a wounded rhinoceros, and it looks very much as though the animal injures a native badly" (Mordaunt Hall, "*Trader Horn*," February 4, 1931, www.nytimes.com. Web. February 15, 2015).

12 James Baldwin most famously compared Wright to Harriet Beecher Stowe, observing that in protesting social ills *Native Son,* similar to *Uncle Tom's Cabin,* rendered the black subject as thing rather than complex being. See "Everybody's Protest Novel," in *The Norton Anthology of African American Literature*, ed. Henry Louis Gates and Nellie Y. McKay (New York: W.W. Norton, 2004), 1699–1705.

13 Reception for *Savage Holiday* and *The Outsider* was mixed to negative. In an interview with the *Paris Review*, Nelson Algren offers a sense of one of the ways the novels were dismissed: "I think [Wright] made … a very bad mistake. I mean, he writes out of passion, out of his belly; but he won't admit this, you see. He's trying to write as an intellectual, which he isn't basically; but he's trying his best to write like a Frenchman" (Nelson Agren, Interview, the *Paris Review: The Art of Fiction*, 11): 16. Works surveying response to Wright's later writings include Robert J. Butler, ed. *The Critical Response to Richard Wright* (Westport: Greenwood Press, 1995); Henry Louis Gates and Kwame Anthony Appiah ed., *Richard Wright: Critical Perspectives Past and Present* (New York: Amistad, 1993); Yoshinobu Hakutani, *Critical Essays on Richard Wright* (Boston: G.K. Hall, 1982). For a consideration of Wright's evolving existential philosophy while he lived abroad, see Michel Fabre, *The World of Richard Wright* (Jackson, MS: University Press of Mississippi, 1985).

14 Wright broke with the Communist Party in 1944. In "I Tried to be a Communist," he would explain why. This essay appeared in *The Atlantic*

Monthly seven months prior to *Black Boy's* publication in 1945. It derives from the second part of Wright's autobiography, not published until its appearance as *American Hunger* in 1977. The two parts of Wright's life story are now published together as *Black Boy (American Hunger)*. The essay is reprinted in *The God that Failed*, ed. Richard H. Crossman (New York: Columbia University Press, 1949): 115–164.

15 See Roi Ottley, "Wright Adds a New Monster to the Gallery of the Dispossessed." Review of *The Outsider* by Richard Wright, *Chicago Sunday Tribune Magazine of Books* (March 22, 1953): 3; and J. Saunders Redding, Review of *The Outsider* by Richard Wright, *Baltimore Afro-American* (May 19, 1953): 41.

16 Richard Gibson was a journalist with Agence France-Presse. Wright believed that Gibson had a hand in causing the deportation of artist Ollie Harrington because of a squatter's dispute over Harrington's apartment. He also believed Gibson allegedly forged letters to *Look* and *Time*, crediting Wright with anti-American remarks. For a review of the incident, see Hazel Rowley, *Richard Wright: The Life and Times* (New York: Henry Holt, 2001). For an analysis of and history surrounding this manuscript, see Richard Gibson, "Richard Wright's 'Island of Hallucination' and the 'Gibson Affair,' " *MFS* [*Modern Fiction Studies*] 51.4 (2005): 896–920 and James Campbell, *Syncopations: Beats, New Yorkers, and Writers in the Dark* (University of California Press, 2008).

17 For a discussion of Motley as a gay writer, see Alan Wald, *American Night: The Literary Left in the Era of the Cold War* (Chapel Hill: University of North Carolina Press, 2012); Anthony Slade, *Lost Gay Novels* (New York: Routledge, 2011); and St. Sukie de la Croix, *Chicago Whispers: A History of LGBT Chicago before Stonewall* (Madison: University of Wisconsin Press, 2012).

18 See Stanley Young, " 'Tough and Tender,' Review of *Let Me Breathe Thunder* by William Attaway," *The New York Times Book Review* (June 25, 1939): 7. www .nytimes.com. Web. February 16, 2015; Richard H. Rovere, "First Novel," review of *Let Me Breathe Thunder* by William Attaway, *New Masses* (July 18, 1939): 26.

19 Attaway also scripted the very successful 1966 *One Hundred Years of Laughter*, a televised history of black humor. He acted in several productions including George S. Kaufman's *You Can't Take It with You* (1936).

20 Works tracing this cultural shift include James Edward Smethurst, *The New Red Negro: The Literary Left and African American Poetry, 1930–1946* (New York: Oxford University Press, 1999); Bill V. Mullen, *Popular Fronts: Chicago and African-American Cultural Politics, 1935–46* (Urbana: University of Illinois Press, 1999); and William J. Maxwell, *Old Negro, New Left: African-American Writing and Communism between the Wars* (New York: Columbia University Press, 1999).

21 See Thomas D. Jarrett, "Toward Unfettered Creativity: A Note on the Negro Novelist's Coming of Age," *Phylon* 11.4 (4th Quarter, 1950): 313–314. *JSTOR*.

22 Stoyan Christowe, "Poets Who Wear Well," *Atlantic Monthly* (October 1947): 138; Milton Klonsky, "The Writing on the Wall: *Lonely Crusade* by Chester

Himes," *Commentary.* www.commentarymagazine.com Web. January 13, 2015. For other reviews see Nash K. Burger, *New York Times Book Review* (September 4, 1947): 20; Arna Bontemps, *The New York Herald Tribune Weekly Book Review* (September 7, 1947): 8, VII; *The New Yorker* (September 13, 1947): 120. For an analysis of Himes's portrayal of Jews and the novel's use of anti-Semitism, see Steven J. Rosen, "African American Anti-Semitism and Himes's Lonely Crusade," *MELUS* 20. 2, *Varieties of Ethnic Criticism* (Summer, 1995): 47–68. For broader discussion of black–Jewish relationships, see James Baldwin, "Negroes Are Anti-Semitic because They Are Anti-White," *The New York Times Magazine* (April 9, 1967): 26–27, 135–137, 139–140; Lenwood G. Davis, *Black-Jewish Relations in the United States, 1752–1984: A Selected Bibliography* (Westport: Greenwood Press, 1984); Nat Hentoff, ed., *Black Anti-Semitism and Jewish Racism* (New York: Schocken, 1970) and Cheryl Lynn Greenberg, *Troubling the Waters: Black–Jewish Relations in the American Century* (Princeton: Princeton University Press, 2006). For Himes's comments on tensions between American blacks and Jews see John A. Williams, "My Man Himes: An Interview with Chester Himes," In Himes, *Conversations,* 75–77.

23 Charles Lee, "Fiction Notes, *Anger at Innocence,* by William Gardner Smith," *The Saturday Review* (February 3, 1951): www.unz.org. Web. April 9, 2014.

24 The phrase "elsewhere community" is taken from Hugh Kenner, *The Elsewhere Community* (New York: Oxford University Press, 2000).

25 In an interview with *Mosaic* journal, Demby said that he wrote the novel to fulfill professional requirements of his academic position and had no idea it had been published in 1980 by Knopf Paperbacks: "I'm glad the novel's going around," he said. "I don't mind. I like mysteries." See Kemme.

26 Martha Satz and Gwendolyn Brooks, "Honest Reporting: An Interview with Gwendolyn Brooks," *Southwest Review* 74.1 (1989), 54. As her career matured, Brooks left Harper and Row and signed with Dudley Randall's Broadside Press, which brought out, among other collections, *Riot* (1969), *Family Pictures* (1970), and the first volume of her autobiography, *Report from Part One* (1972). Believing that black publishers needed supporting, she also worked with Third World Press.

27 Ralph Ellison, "The Art of Fiction," Interview by Alfred Chester and Vilma Howard, *Paris Review* 8 (1954). http://www.theparisreview.org. Web. January 15, 2015.

28 In one of his interviews, Ellison's subject described a man named Sweet-the-monkey who "could make hisself invisible." He "cut open a black cat and took out its heart. Climbed up a tree backwards and cursed God. After that he could do anything" (loc.gov/resource/wpalh2.21020203/?sp=2. Web. January, 20, 2015.).

29 The editors have noted that Ellison's final work was comprised of four principal narratives of which "Juneteenth" was one. See "Two Editors Complete Author Ralph Ellison's Final Work," Michel Martin, Interview, John Callahan, literary executor of the Ellison Estate, and Adam Bradley, http://www.npr.org. Web. January 20, 2015.

30 In his biography of Ellison, Arnold Rampersad problematizes this detail, noting that the author had a copy of the full manuscript, and the only thing that was lost were the revisions completed that summer. See *Ralph Ellison: A Biography* (New York: Knopf, 2007), 443.

31 In "Alas, Poor Richard," Baldwin gives a retrospective and more nuanced assessment of his relationship with Richard Wright. See *Nobody Knows My Name* (New York: Vintage, 1993), 181–215.

32 During his southern travels, Baldwin began his famed collection of essays *The Fire Next Time* (1963).

33 Jordan Elgrably, "James Baldwin, The Art of Fiction No. 78." Interview with James Baldwin, *The Paris Review 91* (Spring 1984), www.theparisreview.org. Web. April 7, 2015. Lucien Carr was one of the founding members of the Jack Kerouac circle that became known as the Beats. While it is still debated whether he was involved with or stalked by a much older David Kammerer, ultimately Carr murdered him. See Adams, Frank, "Columbia Student Kills Friend and Sinks Body in Hudson River," *The New York Times*, August 17, 1944; William Lawlor, ed., *Beat Culture: Icons, Lifestyles, and Impact* (Santa Barbara, CA: ABC-CLIO, 2005); and James Campbell in *This Is the Beat Generation* (Berkeley: University of California Press, 1999).

34 See Eldridge Cleaver, "Notes on a Native Son," in *Soul on Ice* (New York: Dell, 1968), 97–111.

35 See Stewart Smith and Peter Thorn, "An Interview with LeRoi Jones," in *Conversations with Amiri Baraka*, ed. Charlie Reilly (Jackson: University Press of Mississippi, 1994), 17.

36 This description derives from a paraphrase of Baldwin's characterization of Louise Merriweather's *Daddy Was a Number Runner* (1970). In his foreword to the 1970 Prentice Hall edition, he praised the book's point of view and noted that it should be sent to the White House and attorney general, and everyone in the United States who can read (Baldwin, *Cross of Redemption*, 231–232).

37 See Stanley Kauffman, Review of *Going to Meet the Man, New York Times*, December 12, 1965. www.nytimes.com. Web. April 29, 2015; John Romano, Review of *Just Above My Head, The New York Times*, September 23, 1979. www.nytimes.com. Web April 29, 2015; Colm Tóibín, "The Henry James of Harlem: James Baldwin's Struggles," the *London Review of Books*, www.theguardian.com. Web. April 29, 2015.

38 In his review of *Tell Me How Long the Train's Been Gone*, Mario Puzo, author of *The Godfather* (1969), wrote, "It becomes clearer with each book he publishes that Baldwin's reputation is justified by his essays rather than his fiction" (Mario Puzo, Review of *Tell Me How Long the Train's Been Gone, New York Times* June 23, 1968, www.nytimes.com. Web. April 26, 2015). For similar sentiments, see Harold Bloom, "Introduction," in *James Baldwin: Modern Critical Views*, ed. Harold Bloom (New York: Chelsea House, 1986), 1–9; Irving Howe, "Black Boys and Native Sons," in *Selected Writings, 1950–1990* (San Diego: Harcourt Brace Javanovich, 1990), 119–139; "John A. Williams, Novelist in Motion," 95.

39 See www.ala.org. Web. April 30, 2015.

5 Black Arts and Beyond: African American Novels, 1960s–1970s

1 Howard Taubman, theatre review of *Blues for Mister Charlie*, *The New York Times*, April 24, 1964, www.nytimes.com. Web. April 4, 2014. The play tells the story of a black boy killed by a white storeowner and the boy's body being dumped on the roadside.

2 Produced by New York PBS affiliate WNET during the late 1960s and early 1970s, *Soul!* was a cultural arts variety television show that included performances of dance and music, and actors and artists commenting on black culture. Archives of the show can be accessed at www.thirteen.org/soul/. Web. April 7, 2015. Responding to racial upheaval of the 1960s and cohosted by actor Robert Hooks and television journalist Gil Noble, *Like It Is* was a public affairs program produced and aired on WABC-TV in New York City from 1968 and 2011.

3 See Irving Howe, "Black Boys and Native Sons," *Dissent* (Autumn 1963): 353–368 and "New Black Writers," *Harper's* 239 (December 1969): 130–137, 141. A brief sample of book reviews with similar assessments include Victor S. Navasky, "With Malice toward All," review of Charles Wright, *The Wig*, *The New York Times Book Review*, (February 27, 1966), www.nytimes.com. Web. March 9, 2015; Frederic Raphael, "Ideal and Jimson," review of Carlene Hatcher Polite, *The Flagellants*, *The New York Times Book Review* (June 11, 1967): 49; George Davis, "A Revolutionary War Soldier in Viet Nam," review of John A. Williams, *Captain Blackman*, *The New York Times Book Review* (May 21, 1972), www.nytimes.com. Web. March 9, 2015.

4 Other organizations included the Creativity Workshop that was part of Larry Neal's Congress of African Peoples, the Watts Writers' Workshop in Los Angeles, and the Karamu Playhouse in Cleveland.

5 Betty Freidan's *The Feminine Mystique* (New York: W. W. Norton, 1963) examined the psychological malaise of (white) women of the 1950s and early 1960s. In spite of marriage and material ease, many were dissatisfied with the suburban ideal of wife and mother, and sought self-fulfillment.

6 In "The Structure and Dynamics of Folklore in the Novel Form: The Case of John O. Killens," William H. Wiggins, Jr. provides two versions of this folk tale. See *Keystone Folk Quarterly* 17.1 (Spring 1972): 101.

7 The Harlem Writers Guild is still active. Most recently, it partnered with digital publisher iUniverse to create its own imprint, Harlem Writers Guild Press.

8 Another history could be written about African American writers of young adult books. Some of the more popular names would include Lorenz Graham, Mildred Taylor, and Walter Dean Meyers.

9 Alice Walker criticized this novel as too imitative of Hurston's *Their Eyes Were Watching God*. See "A Walk through 20th Century Black America," Review of *A Short Walk* by Alice Childress, *Ms.* Magazine (December 1979): 46, 48.

10 These violent outbreaks were a response to a July 12, 1967 traffic stop in which taxi driver John Smith was rumored to have been beaten by police and died. The outburst was seen as more a response to years of police

brutality and impoverishment, and the heavy military-style state response fueled the discontent. See Ron Porambo, *No Cause for Indictment: An Autopsy of Newark* (New York: Holt, Rinehart and Winston, 1971); National Advisory Commission on Civil Disorders, *Report of the National Advisory Commission on Civil Disorders* (New York: Bantam, 1968); and PBS, POV, *Revolution '67*, Produced and directed by Marylou Tibaldo-Bongiorno, 2007.

11 A mature Charles would appear again in Wright's final work, *Absolutely Nothing to Get Alarmed About* (1972). It, too, is a series of vignettes, but this time Charles, resembling Wright, has published two books and prefers living as a bohemian to what he sees as the narrowness of middle-class existence even though he doesn't have to. Some of the pieces first appeared in *The Village Voice* as nonfiction; what genre Wright intended for them is in question.

12 Brown felt that white America had branded Richard Wright as the official black protester. See Hoyt Fuller, "The New Black Literature: Protest or Affirmation" in Gayle, *The Black Aesthetic*, 367.

13 See Henry Fielding, *The History of Tom Jones, a Foundling* (1789) and Stendhal's *Le Rouge et le Noir* (*The Red and the Black*, 1830).

14 In an interview, Major has said that he struggled with the stricture of Christianity, and that might explain why there was so much sex in the work: "Christianity is something with which I have been at war almost all my life … I agonized with this things [sic] in my own experience of growing up, these problems of good and evil and sex. I think that's why there's so much sex in *All-Night Visitors*. Here was a man who could express himself only in this one natural way because he had absolutely nothing else" (*Dark and Feeling* 134).

15 Bronisław Kasper Malinowski was an anthropologist and ethnographer who pioneered participant observation, living among the people one is studying, as one method of data collection.

16 See Bernard Bell, "Introduction: Clarence Major's Transgressive Voice and Double Consciousness as an African American Postmodernist Artist," in *Clarence Major and His Art*, ed. Bernard W. Bell (Chapel Hill: University of North Carolina Press, 2001); Jerome Klinkowitz, "Clarence Major's Innovative Fiction," *African American Review* 28.1 (Spring 1994): 57–63.

17 An image of the Ace cover can be seen on the John A. Williams Online Exhibit, University of Rochester, rbscp.lib.rochester.edu/2973. Web. March 8, 2015.

18 Williams later wrote a young adult biography of Wright, *The Most Native of Sons: A Biography of Richard Wright* (New York: Doubleday, 1970).

19 See John A. Williams, "My Man Himes," *Conversations with Chester Himes*, 66; or Charles Wright, "Don Chester Himes: Evening with an Exile," *Conversations with Chester Himes*, 114.

20 Williams would write a controversial biography of Martin Luther King titled *The King God Didn't Save: Reflections on the Life and Death of Martin Luther King, Jr.* (New York: Coward-McCann, 1970).

21 See Walter Burrell, "Rappin' with Sam Greenlee," *Black World* (July, 1971): 42–47; H. W. Fuller, review of *The Spook Who Sat by the Door*, *Negro Digest* (May 1969): 73–74.

22 See Barbara Smith, "Have Babies for the Nation: Sexism in the Black Power Movement" (video), Makers Moment. www.makers.com. Web. February 28, 2016; Kimberly Springer, "Black Feminists Respond to Black Power Masculinism," in *The Black Power Movement: Rethinking the Civil Rights-Black Power Era*, ed. Peniel E. Joseph (London: Routledge, 2006): 105–119.

23 Frederic Raphael, "Ideal and Jimson," review of Carlene Hatcher Polite, *The Flagellants*, *The New York Times Book Review* (June 11, 1967): 49, www.nytimes .com. Web. February 25, 2015. Other reviews realized what Hatcher attempted, see Roger Ebert, "First Novels by Young Negroes," review of *The Flagellants* by Carlene Hatcher Polite, *The American Scholar* 36. 4 (Autumn, 1967): 682, 684, 686.

24 In an essay on the occasion of Castro's visit, Julian Mayfield, novelist and essayist conveyed a sense of the complex ambivalence of black Americans, some of whom shunned Castro in an attempt to assert their loyalty to America and to prove themselves deserving of full social enfranchisement, and others of whom embraced the revolutionary change he personified: "The day Fidel Castro made his triumphal entry into Harlem, an angry Jackie Robinson proclaimed from the sidewalk of the Theresa Hotel that Negroes are just like all other Americans. No doubt Robinson was anxious to reassure the reporters that the thousands of cheering Harlemites who were welcoming the Cuban leader did not represent the real sentiment of the ghetto community. . . . But in one respect the ex-baseball star had stumbled onto solid ground. The Negroes who clustered around the Hotel Theresa day and night were not genuine Fidelistas. They had turned out to demonstrate their contempt of the arrogant culture that had driven Castro into their midst. It was certainly easy for them to identify with a man who had been refused at several hotels and mistreated in the one that finally accepted him. Along 125th Street, Harlem's Main Street, the feeling was that anybody so completely rejected by white America must have some good points" (unpublished essay, "Another Castro Challenge," JMP 21, 5).

25 After repeated Ku Klux Klan raids on the black community of Monroe, North Carolina, then head of the local NAACP chapter Robert F. Williams formed a local, black National Rifle Association chapter and trained its members in using firearms. In the summer of 1957, a Klan motorcade attacked the home of Dr. Albert E. Perry, a NAACP member. With guns in hand, Williams led a defensive attack, and Klan attacks came to a sudden stop. Ultimately, Robert and Mabel Williams and their two small children left the United States and gained political asylum in Havana, Cuba. In 1966, he moved his family to China during the height of the Cultural Revolution. There, as in Cuba, he enjoyed celebrity status and the company of Mao Zedong and Zhou En Lai. He wrote *Negroes with Guns* (1962), and broadcast Radio Free Dixie first from Cuba then later from China. See Timothy B. Tyson, *Radio Free Dixie: Robert F. Williams & The Roots of Black Power* (Chapel Hill: University of North Carolina Press, 1999) and *Negroes with Guns* (documentary film), Documentary Institutes, 2005.

26 See Questlove [Ahmir Khalib Thompson], "In Baraka, Inspiration Came with Provocation: Questlove Reflects on Amiri Baraka," *The New York Times* (January 12, 2014), www.nytimes.com. Web. December 19, 2015; Black Star, "Thieves in the Night," *Mos Def and Talib Kweli Are Black Star*, prod, 88 Keys (1998).

6 From Margin to Center: African American Novels, 1970s–1990s

1 See William Bennett, *To Reclaim a Legacy: A Report on the Humanities in Higher Education* (Washington, DC: National Endowment for the Humanities, 1984); Lynne V. Cheney and National Endowment for the Humanities, *Humanities in America: A Report to the President, the Congress, and the American People* (Washington, DC: National Endowment for the Humanities, 1988).

2 Ralph Ellison would write that Redding's character is unappealing, his writing stiff, but that he revealed a unique element, the traitorous educator, in black life (Ralph Ellison, "Collaborator with His Own Enemy," *The New York Times Book Review*, February 19, 1950): BR3. The figure may not have been so unique. Ellison engaged it through the character Bledsoe in *Invisible Man* and Hurston in her essay "The Rise of the Begging Joints," *The American Mercury* 60 (March 1945): 288–294.

3 Some critics argued that the increasing tendency of black critics such as Gates and Baker to rely on ideas of deconstruction, structuralism, and post-structuralism was not enlightening but merely imitative of French philosophers Jacques Derrida and Jacques Lacan. In an exchange refreshing for its frankness, Joyce A. Joyce, Henry Louis Gates, and Houston Baker, "spoke" about the role of black criticism. The exchange began when Joyce's essay "The Black Canon: Reconstructing Black American Literary Criticism" appeared in *New Literary History*. She saw black literature not as a system of signs but as written actualities closely connected to and desirous of improving black life. The journal invited both Gates and Baker to respond. In his response " 'What's Love Got to Do With It?': Critical Theory, Integrity, and the Black Idiom," Gates identifies what he sees as a black resistance to theory, and notes the importance of theory in illuminating the practices and presumptions that intertwine within language to relegate black literature to the ghetto of non-aestheticism. Baker, after citing what he saw as errors of fact in Joyce's essay, and questioning why *New Literary History* would publish such a flawed piece, goes on to cite the "battle between critics opting for theory and critics opting for criticism that contextualizes black works within a grounded community as a dubious one revealing more about a larger cross-racial hostility toward looking at African American literature theoretically. See Joyce A. Joyce, "The Black Canon: Reconstructing Black American Literary Criticism" (335–344); Henry Louis Gates, Jr., " 'What's Love Got to Do with It?': Critical Theory, Integrity, and the Black Idiom" (345–362); Houston A. Baker, "In Dubious Battle" (363–369). All three essays appear in *New Literary History* 18.2, *Literacy, Popular Culture, and the Writing of History* (Winter 1987). *JSTOR.* Web. April 25, 2015. In a later essay, Joyce reflects on the interchange, see "A Tinker's Damn: Henry

Louis Gates, Jr., and *The Signifying Monkey Twenty Years Later,*" *Callaloo* 31.2 (2008): 370–380. *Project MUSE.* Web. April 25, 2015.

4 Angelyn Mitchell's edited *Within the Circle: An Anthology of African American Literary Criticism from the Harlem Renaissance to the Present* (Durham: Duke University Press, 1994) charts this history.

5 See Ishmael Reed, "Why the Thirty Two-Year Assault on Some Black Male Writers," *Renaissance/Renaissance Noire* 14.2 (Fall 2014): 62–73. Others weighing in similarly include Robert Staples, "The Myth of Black Macho: A Response to Angry Black Feminists," *The Black Scholar* 10.6/7, *Human Rights USA* (March/April 1979): 24–33. A more nuanced response is Mel Watkins, "Sexism, Racism, and Black Women Writers, *The New York Times* (June 15, 1986). www.nytimes.com. Web. April 30, 2015.

6 Gloria Steinem concurred with Harris's assessment of Walker's ability to create voice. In an October 25 letter to Walker, she wrote "you are surely the world's only writer to record true dialect speech without condescension, and without making it difficult or distancing to read" (AWP 1, 6).

7 Undated letters from Barbara Christian, Claudia Tate, J. California Cooper, and Mary Helen Washington to Alice Walker (AWP 1, 2).

8 Morrison's critics reached their loudest pitch when she was awarded the Nobel Prize, in 1993. Stanley Crouch said, "I hope this prize inspires her to write better books." Charles Johnson said that she had been "the beneficiary of good will" and that her award was "a triumph of political correctness." Both Crouch and Johnson are quoted in David Streitfeld, "Author Toni Morrison Wins Nobel Prize," *The Washington Post* (October 8, 1993), www.washingtonpost .com. Web. June 2, 2015. Erica Jong, who would have liked to see Doris Lessing win, commented that Lessing was "the wrong kind of African: white." Jong wrote of Morrison, "I wish that Toni Morrison, a bedazzling writer and a great human being, had won her prize only for her excellence at stringing words together. But I am nevertheless delighted at her choice … I suspect, however, that her prize was not motivated solely by artistic considerations. Why can't art in itself be enough? Must we also use the artist as a token of progressivism?" ("I the Jury," *The Washington Post*, December 5, 1993). www.washingtonpost .com. Web. June 4, 2015.

9 Brown, Cecil, and Toni Morrison. "Interview with Toni Morrison," *The Massachusetts Review* 1995: 455. *JSTOR Journals.* Web. April 13, 2015; Joyce A. Joyce, "The Black Canon: Reconstructing Black American Literary Criticism," *New Literary History* (1987): 335. *JSTOR Journals.* Web. April 25, 2015.

10 For one instance see, *Alice Walker.* Video recording. New York: Films Media Group, 1982. Web. June 6, 2015.

11 A sampling of reviews include David Gates, "Review of *The Temple of My Familiar,*" *Newsweek* (April 24, 1989): 74; J. M. Coetzee, "The Beginnings of (Wo)man in Africa," review of *The Temple of My Familiar,*" *The New York Times Book Review* (April 30, 1989): 7; Francine Prose, "Sexual Healing," review of *By the Light of My Father's Smile, The New York Times Book Review* (October 4, 1998), 18; and Richard Bernstein, "New Age Anthropology in Old Mexico,"

review of *By the Light of My Father's Smile*, Books of the Times, *The New York Times* (October 7, 1998), www.newyorktimes.com. Web. April 30, 2015.

12 See Keith Mano, "How to Write Two First Novels with Your Knuckles," *Esquire* 86.6 (December 1976): 62, 66. Mano also goes on to critique the feminizing of the publishing industry: "More and more of late, book publishing has become a transaction between women, for women: editors, salespeople, agents. And, of course, readers. Talk about sexism: American literature has been subtly biased. The percentage of women in publishing is greater than in any other trade, lesbianism and motherhood aside" (62); June Jordan, review of *Eva's Man* by Gayl Jones, *The New York Times Book Review* (May 16, 1976): 36–37. Darryl Pinckney, review of *Eva's Man*, by Gayl Jones, *The New Republic* 174 (June 19, 1976): 27–28.

13 See Ann Allen Shockley, "The Black Lesbian in American Literature," in *Home Girls: A Black Feminist Anthology*, ed. Barbara Smith (New York: Kitchen Table: Women of Color Press, 1983): 83–89, and Barbara Smith, "The Truth that Never Hurts: Black Lesbians in Fiction in the 1980s," in *Feminisms: An Anthology of Literary Theory and Criticism*, ed. Robyn R. Warhol and Diane Price Herndl (New Brunswick: Rutgers University Press, 1997), 784–806.

14 Jones's husband was Bob Higgins, an activist she met while a tenured professor of English and Afro-American and African Studies at the University of Michigan. When they married, he took her name. For the history behind his suicide and its impact on her writing, see William Plummer et al, "Beyond Healing: A Novelist's Triumphal Return Ends in a Day of Violence and Horror," *People* 4.10 (March 16, 1998). www.people.com. Web. June 2, 2015; Peter Manso, "Chronicle of a Tragedy Foretold," *The New York Times Magazine* (July 19, 1998), www.nytimes.com. Web. June 2, 2015.

15 For an instance of the criticism of Shockley's character, see Jewelle L. Gomez, "A Cultural Legacy Denied and Discovered: Black Lesbians in Fiction by Women," in *Home Girls: A Black Feminist Anthology*, ed. Barbara Smith (New Brunswick, NJ: Rutgers University Press, 1983): 110–123. In describing the proceedings at the National Conference on Black Women, Shockley described the difficulties of being an out lesbian writer. See Ann Allen Shockley and Veronica E. Tucker. "Black Women Discuss Today's Problems: Men, Families, Society," *Southern Voices* 1 (August–September): 16–19.

16 See Kaiama L. Glover, "Blood Ties," review of *Some Sing, Some Cry* by Ntozake Shange and Ifa Bayeza, *The New York Times Sunday Book Review* (September 24, 2010), www.nytimes.com. Web. May 15, 2015. Brenda Lyons, "Interview with Ntozake Shange," *Massachusetts Review* 28.4 (1987): 687.

17 Contemporary reviews addressing the works complexity include John Leonard, "Claybourne's Institutions Insurrection Re-enacted," Books of The Times (April 4, 1980), www.nytimes.com. Web. April 18, 2015 and Susan Lardner, "Third Eye Open" Books, *The New Yorker* (May 5, 1980), www.archives.newyorker.com. Web. April 18, 2015. For critical assessments of the work's difficulty, see Gloria T. Hull, " 'What It Is I Think She's Doing Anyhow': A Reading of Toni Cade Bambara's *The Salt Eaters*," in *Conjuring Black Women, Fiction, and Literary Tradition*, ed.

Marjorie Pryse and Hortense Spillers (Bloomington: Indiana University Press, 1985): 216–232; Susan Willis, *Specifying: Black Women Writing in the American Experience* (Madison: University of Wisconsin Press, 1987): 129–158.

18 See Alvin F. Poussaint, "Enough Already! Stop the Male-Bashing and Infighting," *Ebony* 48.4 (February 1993): 86–89; Maida Odom, "Author Terry Mcmillan's Novel Finds Fans, Critics," *The Philadelphia Inquirer* (June 4, 1992), www.articles.philly.com. Web. September 5, 2015; Edward M. Jackson, "Images of Black Males in Terry McMillan's Waiting to Exhale," *MAWA Review* 8.1 (June 1993): 20–26.

19 Mendieta fell from the 34th floor of her apartment building in Greenwich Village. Whether she committed suicide or was pushed by her husband of eight months still remains in question. See Vincent Patrick, "A Death in the Art World," *New York Times* (June 10, 1990), www.nytimes.com; Ron Sullivan, "Greenwich Village Sculptor Acquitted of Pushing Wife to Her Death," *The New York Times* (February 12, 1988), www.nytimes.com. Web. April 16, 2015.

20 Judith's characterization and that of other women in his novel has led to Bradley being criticized for not creating fully developed women characters, only female mirrors in which male characters see their own growth. His response has been that he is not a doctrinaire writer, nor is his writing meant to be representative of appropriate social models. Works considering the question of gender in Bradley's opus include Cathy Brigham, "Identity, Masculinity, and Desire in David Bradley's Fiction," *Contemporary Literature* 36.2 (1995): 289–316 and Mary Helen Washington, "Black History: His Story or Hers?" Review of *The Chaneysville Incident*. *The Washington Post Book World* (April 12, 1981): 3, 13. Bradley's thought can be found in Kay Bonetti, "An Interview with David Bradley," *The Missouri Review* 15.3 (1992): 82–86.

21 Murray co-wrote the autobiography of Count Basie, *Good Morning Blues* (1985).

22 With Ishmael Reed, Young established the now defunct Suppressed Classics Series devoted to retrieving out-of-print African American works, among them Carelene Hatcher Polite's *Sister X and the Victims of Foul Play* and Leslie Alexander Lacy's study *Contemporary African American Literature*.

23 A story on the only surviving boy from the MOVE fire is Margalit Fox, "Michael Ward, Survivor of '85 Bombing by Philadelphia Police, Is Dead at 41," *New York Times* (September 27, 2013). www.nytimes.com. Web. May 19, 2015. Articles covering the MOVE fire include William K. Stevens, "Police Drop Bomb on Radicals' Home in Philadelphia," *The New York Times* (May 14, 1985), www.nytimes.com. Web. May 14, 2015 and Frank Trippett, "It Looks Just Like a War Zone," *Time* (May 27, 1985), www.time.com. Web. May 19, 2015. For a larger history of the story, see John Anderson and Hilary Hevenor, *Burning Down the House: MOVE and the Tragedy of Philadelphia* (New York: W. W. Norton, 1987).

24 In chapter 3 of *Signs and Cities: Black Literary Postmodernism* (Chicago: University Press of Chicago, 2003), Madhu Dubey offers an extensive reading on the visual element and voyeurism in *Reuben*.

25 The story of his brother's incarceration and the divergent lives of the brothers is told in the memoir *Brothers and Keepers* (1984). In 1986, Wideman's son Jacob was convicted of first degree murder and sentenced to life in prison without the possibility of parole for 25 years; his parole appeal was denied in 2011. See Tom Fitzpatrick, "Brothers and Victims," *Phoenix New Times* (August 11, 1994), www.phoenixnewtimes.com. Web. May 15, 2015; Sally Kalson, "25 Years After a Teen Killing, a Battle Looms over Parole," *Pittsburgh Post-Gazette* (May 16, 2011), www.articles.philly.com. Web. May 15, 2015; AP, "Writer's Son Given Life Term in Death of New York Youth," *The New York Times* (October 16, 1988), www.nytimes.com. Web. May 15, 2015.

26 See "American Experience. *Eyes on the Prize. The Story of the Movement*," PBS: Public Broadcasting Service, 2009. www.pbs.org. Web. October 1, 2011; "Whites Stone Marchers in Suburb of Chicago," *The Miami News* (August 24, 1966): 13, news.google.com. Web. October 1, 2011; "Dr. King Is Felled by Rock," *Chicago Tribune* (August 6, 1966), archives.chicagotribune.com/1966/08/06/page/1/article/dr-king-is-felled-by-rock. Web. October 1, 2011.

27 Based on Mill's own life, *Francisco* (1974) followed a successful pioneering black woman actor's growing involvement in the Black Arts Movement, and her love for an independent black filmmaker. Mills appeared in early television programs *Julia* (1968–1971), starring Diahann Carroll, and *The Leslie Uggams Show* (1969 only), in addition to several films directed by her husband, Francisco Newman, including *Ain't Nobody Slick* (1972) and *Virgin Again* (2000). *Francisco* was the first work published by the then Reed, Cannon, and Johnson publishing house, founded by Ishmael Reed, Steve Cannon, and Joe Johnson. The enterprise went on to become I. Reed Books.

28 Among the reviewers, artist Kara Walker offered qualified praise in "Toni Morrison's *God Help the Child*," *The New York Times Sunday Book Review* (April 13, 2015), www.nytimes.com. Web. January 4, 2016; Ron Charles felt the characters were superficial and the tale undeveloped in "Toni Morrison's Familiar, Flawed *God Help the Child*," *The Washington Post*, Books (April 14, 2015). www.washingtonpost.com. Web. January 4, 2016.

29 Als, Hilton "Ghosts in the House: How Toni Morrison Fostered a Generation of Black Writers," *The New Yorker* 79.32 (October 2003): 64–75.

7 "Bohemian Cult Nats": African American Novels, 1990s and Beyond

1 See Daniel Schorr, "A New, 'Post-Racial' Political Era in America," Commentary, *All Things Considered*, NPR, January, 28 2008. www.npr.org. Web. April 19, 2010; Michael Crowley, "Post-racial: Even White Supremacists Don't Hate Obama," *The New Republic* (March 12, 2008). www.tnr.com. Web. April 19, 2010; Stanley Kutler, "So Much for a Post-Racial America," *The Huffington Post* (March 27, 2010), www.huffingtonpost.com. Web. April 19, 2010; Paul C. Taylor, "Post Black, Old Black," *African American Review* 41.4 Post Soul Aesthetic (Winter, 2007): 625–640.

2 *The State of Black America Summary and Webcast*. National Urban League, 2010. www.nul.org. Web. April 20, 2010.

3 George characterizes this period in the mid-1970s as a time of "unprecedented acceptance of black people in the public life of America" as "political figures, advertising images, pop stars, coworkers, and classmates" (ix).

4 In "Don't Worry Be Buppie," Thulani Davis cites Greg Tate as the inventor of the term New Black Aesthetic (185).

5 Some have seen this allusion as Ellis's commentary on the gender tensions between black male and female writers. See Kimberly Nichele Brown, *Writing the Black Revolutionary Diva: Women's Subjectivity and the Decolonizing Text* (Bloomington: Indiana University Press, 2010), 3; and Eric Lott, "Hip-Hop Fiction," *The Nation* 247.19 (December 19, 1988), 691.

6 Ellis defines the concept of the cultural mulatto in the following terms: "Just as a genetic mulatto is a black person of mixed parents who can often get along fine with his white grandparents, a cultural mulatto, educated by a multiracial mix of cultures, can also navigate easily in the white world" ("New Black Aesthetic" 235).

7 Kochiyama was a civil rights activist who counted among her associates Malcolm X, Angela Davis, Amiri Baraka, and Robert F. Williams. Her father's death after being wrongly imprisoned for espionage following the bombing of Pearl Harbor, and her experiences in an Arkansas internment camp galvanized her activism for social and economic justice. See Yuri Kochiyama, *Passing It On: A Memoir*, ed. Marjorie Lee et al. (Los Angeles: University of California, Los Angeles Asian American Studies Center Press, 2004); Diane Carol Fujino, *Heartbeat of Struggle: The Revolutionary Life of Yuri Kochiyama* (Minneapolis: University of Minnesota Press, 2005).

8 For some, this figure has signified an inferiority rooted in Southern slavery; for others it was a sign of refuge along the Underground Railroad; others record it as a memorial commissioned by George Washington for a devoted helper who could not be a soldier. No definitive history exists, but for a sampling of explanations, see Earl Koger, *Jocko: A Legend of the American Revolution* (Upper Saddle River, NJ: Prentice-Hall, 1976); "A Guide to Freedom: Jockey Statues Marked Underground Railroad," *The History of Loudoun County, Virginia*, www.loudounhistory.org. Web. January 9, 2016; Kenneth L. Shropshire, *In Black and White: Race and Sports in America* (New York: New York University Press, 1998).

9 For instances of reviews seeking more of Beatty's stance in the work, see Ken Foster, "Boy in the 'Hood," review of *Tuff* by Paul Beatty, *Books of the Times* (May 7, 2000), www.nytimes.com. Web. June 16, 2015; Richard Bernstein, "An Insider Battles the Inner-City Trap," review of *Tuff* by Paul Beatty, *Books of the Times* (July 11, 2000), www.nytimes.com. Web. June 16, 2015. For an instance of a review questioning the ultimate relevance of Beatty's satire, see Ishmael Reed "Hoodwinked: Paul Beatty's Urban Nihilists," review of *Tuff* by Paul Beatty (April 2000), math.buffalo.edu. Web. June 16, 2015.

10 Matthew Shepard was a student at the University of Wyoming. He was tortured, beaten, and abandoned and died six days later. Whether this was a hate crime because Shepard was gay or an attempt a robbery gone awry became

a central concern in the legal processes that followed. See James Brooke, "Gay Man Dies from Attack, Fanning Outrage and Debate," *The New York Times* (October 12, 1998), www.nytimes.com. Web. August 8, 2015; Julie Cart, "Matthew Shepard's Mother Aims to Speak with His Voice," *Los Angeles Times* (September 14, 1999), www.latimes.com. Web. August 8, 2015. "New Details Emerge in Matthew Shepard Murder," ABC News, www.abcnews.go.com. Web. January 10, 2016.

11 Brown, Rosellen. "The Emperor's New Fiction," *Boston Review* 11 (August, 1986): 7–8.

12 Information on the event can be found in the following: Michael Kammen, *Colonial New York: A History* (Millwood, NJ: K and O Press, 1975); Peter Linebaugh and Marcus Rediker, *The Many-Headed Hydra: Sailors, Slaves, Commoners, and the Hidden History of the Revolutionary Atlantic* (Boston: Beacon, 2000; see chapter 6, "The Outcasts of the Nations of the Earth"); *Slavery in New York, 2005–2007*, New-York Historical Society, www.slaveryinnewyork.org. Web. 24 June 2015. *"Fire, Fire, Scorch, Scorch!": Testimony from the Negro Plot Trials in New York, 1741*, History Matters, George Mason University, historymatters.gmu.edu. Web. June 24, 2015; and Jill Lepore, *New York Burning: Liberty, Slavery, and Conspiracy in Eighteenth-Century Manhattan* (New York: Knopf, 2005).

13 Forbidden to be married in their home state, the Lovings married in the District of Columbia and subsequently returned to Virginia. Virginia's 1924 Racial Integrity Act allowed law enforcement to raid their bedroom in the early morning and sentence them to prison for being married. In lieu of spending time in prison, they took a plea bargain, requiring them to leave Virginia. When they tired of forced exile away from family and friends, they sued the state, and once the case reached the Supreme Court, the verdict went in their favor. See American Civil Liberties Union, *Loving v. Virginia: The Case Over Interracial Marriage*, www.aclu.org. Web. July 2, 2015. Tri-racial groups referred to populaces of mixed European, Native American, and African antecedents. See Calvin L. Beale, "An Overview of the Phenomenon of Mixed Racial Isolates in the United States," *American Anthropologist* (1972): 704. *JSTOR*. Web. July 2, 2015.

14 At many of his readings from this novel Whitehead delivered a droll "grammar" lesson on this last technique. See "The In-verbs" Colson Whitehead: *Sag Harbor*, www.library.fora.tv/2009/05/19/Colson_Whitehead_Sag_Harbor. Web. April 3, 2017.

15 "Forecasts: Fiction," review of *Close to the Bone, Publishers Weekly* 245.44 (1998): 69, *Literary Reference Center*, Web. 23 June 2015; Ellen Flexman, "Book Reviews: Fiction," *Close to the Bone, Library Journal* 123.20 (1998): 157, *Literary Reference Center*, Web. June 23, 2015; "If Six Were Nine (Book Review)," *Publishers Weekly* 247.49 (2000): 56, *Literary Reference Center*, Web. June 23, 2015; Gavin McNett, "If 6 Were 9 (Book Review)," *The New York Times Book Review* (2001): 18, *Academic Search Complete*, Web. June 23, 2015.

16 For reviews finding Vernon's prose problematic, see "*A Killing in This Town,*" *Kirkus Reviews* 73.20 (2005): 1106, *Literary Reference Center.* Web. June 25, 2015; Eleanor J. Bader, "*Logic* (Book)," *Library Journal* 129.4 (2004): 109–110, *Literary Reference Center.* Web. June 25, 2015; Reba Leiding, "*A Killing in This Town,*" *Library Journal* 130.20 (2005): 117, *Literary Reference Center.* Web. June 25, 2015; and Denise M. Doig, "*A Killing in This Town,*" *Black Issues Book Review* 8.2 (2006): 26, *Literary Reference Center.* Web. June 25, 2015. For more sympathetic reviews, see Elizabeth Dickie, "A Killing in This Town," *Booklist* 102.9/10 (2006): 62, *Literary Reference Center.* Web. June 25, 2015; "A Killing in This Town," *Publishers Weekly* 252.39 (2005): 45, *Literary Reference Center.* Web. June 25, 2015; and M. Casey, "*A Killing in This Town.* By Olympia Vernon," *New York Times Book Review* 111.7 (2006): 21–22, *British Library Document Supply Centre Inside Serials & Conference Proceedings.* Web. June 25, 2015.

17 A *New York Times* review is representative. David Hadju writes: "He speaks to an audience definable not by its size nor even by its color but by its intellectual jazzhead zeal" ("Jazz Man," *Sunday Book Review,* February 24, 2008, www.nytimes.com. Web. December 30, 2015.

8 The Neo-Slave Narrative

1 See John Henrik Clarke, ed. *William Styron's Nat Turner: Ten Black Writers Respond.* (Boston: Beacon, 1968).

2 For a summary of the reactions to Riboud's book in light of the Jefferson DNA debate, see Scot A. French and Edward L. Ayers, "The Strange Career of Thomas Jefferson: Race and Slavery in American Memory, 1943–1993," in *Jefferson Legacies,* ed. Peter S. Onuf (Charlottesville: University of Virginia Press, 1993): 418–456; Annette Gordon-Reed, *Thomas Jefferson and Sally Hemings: An American Controversy* (Charlottesville: University of Virginia Press, 1998).

3 See Roger Cohen, "Ideology Said to Split Book-Award Jurors," "Books," *The New York Times* (November 27, 1990), www.nytimes.com. Web. June 9, 2015. Terry McMillan recalls the racism she encountered as she advocated for Johnson's selection. See Daniel Max, "McMillan's Millions," *The New York Times Magazine* (August 9, 1992), 3, www.nytimes.com. Web. September 5, 2015.

10 The Speculative Novel

1 William James, *The Will to Believe: And Other Essays in Popular Philosophy* (London: Longmans, Green, William and Company, 1897) explores the acts of believing in spite of a lack of evidence.

2 Both Meroe and Telassar are based on real cities. Telassar is mentioned twice in the Hebrew Bible as the place inhabited by "the people of Eden," and it appears in book 4 of Milton's *Paradise Lost.* Meroë is an ancient city on the east bank of the Nile.

3 Tiberius Sempronius Gracchus was a second century BCE Roman politician who attempted reforms in agrarian policy to achieve economic parity. After much political turmoil he was murdered by conservative members of the Roman Senate. See Alvin H. Bernstein, *Tiberius Sempronius Gracchus: Tradition and Apostasy* (Ithaca: Cornell University Press), 1978.

4 Willa Brown helped organize the National Airmen's Association of America to increase the presence of black aviation cadets in the US military. See Samuel L. Broadnax, *Blue Skies, Black Wings: African American Pioneers of Aviation* (Lincoln: University of Nebraska Press, 2008). Bessie Coleman, the first black woman flier, was a civilian aviator and stunt flier. See Doris Rich *Queen Bess: Daredevil Aviator* (Washington, DC: Smithsonian Institution Press, 1993).

5 Samuel R. Delany would express his difficulty breaking into the market in "Racism and Science Fiction," *The New York Review of Science Fiction* 120 (August 1998), www.nyrsf.com. Web. August 1, 2015.

6 The term is taken from current slang, meaning street hustlers, homeless, vagrants, petty cons.

7 Glen Duncan, "A Plague of Urban Undead in Lower Manhattan," Sunday Book Review, *The New York Times* (October 28, 2011), www.nytimes.com. Web. August 6, 2015; Patrick Ness, "Zone One by Colson Whitehead – Review," *The Guardian* (October 13, 2011), www.theguardian.com. Web. August 6, 2015.

11 African American Pulp

1 *The Nigger Bible* is a collection of contemplations on the genesis and current situation of African Americans. *To Kill a Black Man* studies the lives and political philosophies of Martin Luther King, Jr., and Malcolm X.

2 Justin Gifford's biography *Street Poison: The Biography of Iceberg Slim* (New York: Doubleday, 2015) offers a detailed exposition of Beck's many self-created myths.

3 Olden is author of a variety of series. See www.marcolden.com

4 Sister Souljah's original comments appeared in David Mills, "Sister Souljah's Call to Arms; The Rapper Says the Riots Were Payback. Are You Paying Attention?," *The Washington Post*, May 13, 1992, www.washingtonpost.com. Web September 7, 2015.

5 On April 20, 1989, a white female jogger Trisha Meila was found in Central Park bound, gagged, raped, and nearly dead. Four black and one Latino teenagers, ranging in ages fourteen to sixteen (Antron McCray, Kevin Richardson, Raymond Santana, Kharey Wise, and Yusef Salaam) were arrested and convicted of the crime in spite of their protestations of innocence. In 2002 the convictions were overturned after DNA evidence and a confession showed a murderer and serial rapist, Matias Reyes, actually committed the crime. Having served sentences of almost seven to thirteen years for the assault when they were exonerated, the young men who became known as the Central Park Five filed a lawsuit against the City of New York. A documentary charting the history

has been produced, *The Central Park Five* (2012) directed by Ken Burns, David McMahon, and Sarah Burns. A copy of Sapphire's poem can be accessed at www.lyrikline.org/de/gedichte/wild-thing-539#.WRZko8m1tE5. Web. February 3, 2016. Ultimately, the contention over Sapphire's poem led to the dismissal of John E. Frohnmayer as chairman of the National Endowment for the Arts.

6 See PUSHing Boundaries, PUSHing Art: A Symposium on the Works of Sapphire. english.clas.asu.edu/sapphire. Web. September 8, 2015.

7 Attendant to this expansion of black publishing are disputes over authorship and royalties. See Seth "Soul Man" Ferranti, "Hip Hop Fiction Beefs," *Urban Book Source* (November 2006), theubs.com/articles/news/hiphopfictionbeefs.php?comments_page=1. Web. September 8, 2015.

12 The Black Graphic Novel

1 In general, a panorama was a sequence of images on long canvases attached to two cylinders. As the cylinders unreeled the canvas, viewers had the illusion that they were part of a simulated journey. For more information on panoramas, see Angela L. Miller, "The Panorama, the Cinema and the Emergence of the Spectacular," *Wide Angle* 18.2 (April 1996): 34–69. The magic lantern was an early projector that used images on sheets of glass. See Stephen Herbert, *A History of Pre-cinema*, Vol. 2 (London: Routledge, 2000).

2 *Life and Times of Frederick Douglass* was published in December 1881 with most copies including woodcut illustrations, in spite of Douglass's strong disapproval. Whether he objected to images or to their quality, Douglass wrote to his publisher Sylvester M. Betts, "I ask and insist, as I have a right to do, that an edition of the book shall be published without illustrations, for Northern circulation ... [The] contract does not permit you to load the book with all manner of coarse and shocking wood cuts, such as may be found in the newspapers of the day ... I have no pleasure whatever in the book and shall not have while the engravings remain." As a result, some copies were released without illustrations. See McKivigan, 489.

3 Descriptions of such uses are offered by Harold Wentworth who gives the example of "eye dialect" as the "phonetic respelling of words, not in order to show a mispronunciations (e.g. Eye-talian), but merely to burlesque the words or their speaker" (*American Dialect Dictionary* [New York: Thomas Y. Crowell Company, 1944], 203). Dwight L Bolinger in his discussion of "visual morphemes" describes the capacity for letters and punctuation to convey meaning in a graphic manner that spoken language cannot. He identifies visual puns such as a "letter addressed to The Tax Collector, *City Haul*" and the Sears catalog advertisement for S-T-R-E-T-C-H-A-B-L-E-S" while noting that "All puns of this type have to be written in order to be fully appreciated, and some ... are meaningless unless written" ("Visual Morphemes," *Language* 22.4 (October–December, 1946): 337–338.

4 See Charles. Hatfield, "Defining Comics in the Classroom; or, The Pros and Cons of Unfixability," *Teaching the Graphic Novel*, ed. Stephen E. Tabachnick

(New York: MLA, 2009, 19–28); Julia Round, "'Is This A Book?' DC Vertigo and The Redefinition of Comics in the 1990s," n.d. *OAIster*. Web. August 8, 2015.

5 Cover images of existing issues can be viewed at www.goldenlegacy.com/magazine-titles. Web. April 22, 2015.

6 Zane's naming recalls a city in Ohio named Zanesville. It is known for having a history of racial mixing that has left it with a black population, most of whom approximate a white phenotype. See *Jet* 1.4 (November 22, 1951): 10–12. books.google.com. Web. August 22, 2015.

7 James Allen and John Littlefield have amassed an extensive collection of lynching photographs and postcards. See *Without Sanctuary*. www.withoutsanctuary.org. Web. April 22, 2010.

8 John Jennings, "Conjuring the Past: An Ethno Gothic Graphic Narrative Project," conference panel lecture, "African American Literature and Visual Culture," Annual Conference on American Literature, American Literature Association, San Francisco, CA, May 24, 2012. Jennings is currently at work on a graphic novel, *Noir Lock: Hell of a Hangover*, set in prohibition Chicago and examining black community during the great migration period.

9 Comments made at B-fest book signing, Barnes and Noble, Buckhead, Atlanta, GA, June 10, 2016.

10 Comments made at B-fest book signing, Barnes and Noble, Buckhead, Atlanta, GA, June 10, 2016.

11 Dawud Anyabwile, "Drawing from the Soul," lecture, University of Georgia's 50th Anniversary of Desegregation, Tate Hall, University of Georgia, January 31, 2011.

12 Comments made at B-fest book signing, Barnes and Noble, Buckhead, Atlanta, GA, June 10, 2016.

13 Some critics praised *MBQ* as extending the manga genre; others felt its visual intensity and what would be considered a plentitude of words in manga made it an offering designed to appeal to a western audience. See Juliet Kahn, "Peepo Choo to Ghost Rider: An Interview with Felipe Smith," *Comics Alliance* (August 28, 2014). comicsalliance.com. Web. August 18, 2015.

14 Whether Milestone could make much change while being in partnership with DC is an issue taken up by Jeffrey A. Brown in *Black Superheroes, Milestone Comics, and Their Fans* (Jackson: University Press of Mississippi, 2001).

13 African American Novels from Page to Screen

1 For more information on film adaptations of *Uncle Tom's Cabin*, see Thomas F. Gossett, *Uncle Tom's Cabin and American Culture* (Dallas: Southern Methodist University Press, 1985).

2 For further history on the Reol studio, see Christina Petersen, "The 'Reol' Story: Race Authorship and Consciousness in Robert Levy's Reol Productions, 1921–1926," *Film History: An International Journal* 3 (2008): 308–324, *Project MUSE*. Web. September 15, 2015.

3 See *California Eagle* (July 30, 1931). www.archive.org; *The Sport of the Gods*, Schomburg Center for Research in Black Culture, Photographs and Prints Division, The New York Public Library *Digital Collections*, digitalcollections .nypl.org/items/510d47df-fb7d-a3d9-e040-e00a18064a99. Web. June 14, 2015.

4 Later the company would become the Micheaux Film Corporation.

5 *The Chicago Defender* (March 1, 1919), pqasb.pqarchiver.com. Web. June 14, 2015; *The Chicago Defender* (August 28, 1920), pqasb.pqarchiver.com/ chicagodefender/advancedsearch.html. Web. June 14, 2015.

6 See *New York Amsterdam News* (July 3, 1948), www.nypl.org.collections; *The Chicago Defender* (July 10, 1948), pqasb.pqarchiver.com/chicagodefender/ advancedsearch.html. Web. June 14, 2015.

7 See "The Vulpine Master of Harrow," movie review of Frank Yerby, *The Foxes of Harrow. The New York Times*, February 10, 1946, www.nytimes .com. Web. February 6, 2016; "*Harrow* Film Misses Boat; Sting Absent," *Afro-American* 4 (October 1947): 6.

8 See "More than 100 Urge Boycott of Epic Films," *The Chicago Defender* (February 3, 1943), 9; "Pickets, Patrons, and Ushers in Washington's Showing of *Gone with The Wind*," *The Afro-American* (March 9, 1940), 13; George Padmore, "Londoners *Boycott Gone with the Wind*," *The Chicago Defender* (May 19, 1940), 5; Walter White, Press release, "NAACP Considers Disney's Uncle Remus 'Dangerous,'" (November 24, 1946) NAACP Records, Library of Congress, www.loc.gov/loc/lcib/1003/collection.html; "'Song of South' Picketed by San Pedrans," *Los Angeles Sentinel* (March 20, 1947), 5; "Pickets Protest Song of the South," *New York Amsterdam News* (February 8, 1947), 17; "'Song of the South Picketed," *The New York Times* (December 1, 1946), 18.

9 Michel Fabre, *The Unfinished Quest of Richard Wright*. This work provides one of the most extensive histories of the film's making and reception. See 336–353.

10 The Yale Beinecke Wright collection has a film of Wright's screen test for the role. RWP 140, 2036.

11 See Johannes Skancke Martens, "A Black Writer Becomes a Movie Actor," *Oslo Aftenposten* (November 9, 1950) in *Conversations with Richard Wright*, 148–150; Edgardo C. Krebs, "*Native Son*, Lost and Found," *filmcomment* (October 2012), www.filmcomment.com. Web. September 17, 2015; "Richard Wright Plays Hero in Movie Adaptation of His Novel, 'Native Son,' The Screen In Review, *The New York Times*, June 18, 1951, www.nytimes.com. Web. September 17, 2015; Page Laws, "Not Everybody's Protest Film, Either: *Native Son* among Controversial Film Adaptations," *The Black Scholar* 2009: 27. *JSTOR Journals*. Web. October 6, 2015.

12 In "Stories of Conflict," Hurston writes, "Since the author himself is a Negro, his dialect is a puzzling thing. One wonders how he arrived at it. Certainly he does not write by ear unless he is tone-deaf. But aside from the broken speech of his characters, the book contains some beautiful writing. One hopes that Mr. Wright will find in Negro life a vehicle for his talents." Zora Neale Hurston review of *Uncle Tom's Children* by Richard Wright, *The Saturday Review* (April 2, 1938), 32. www.unz.org/Pub/SaturdayRev. Web. February 6, 2016.

13 According to Page Laws, there are two versions of the film with different end-ings, and to date no explanation as to why has been discovered. See Page Laws, "Not Everybody's Protest Film, Either: *Native Son* among Controversial Film Adaptations," *The Black Scholar* 2009: 27. *JSTOR Journals*. Web. October 6, 2015.

14 In his essay explaining the making of *Native Son*, Wright wrote, "The second event that spurred me to write of Bigger was more personal and subtle. I had written a book of short stories which was published under the title of *Uncle Tom's Children*. When the reviews of that book began to appear, I realized that I had made an awfully naïve mistake. I found that I had written a book which even bankers' daughters could read and weep over and feel good about. I swore to myself that if I ever wrote another book, no one would weep over it; that it would be so hard and deep that they would have to face it without the consolation of tears" *Native Son* (New York: Harper Perennial, 1998), 454.

15 See Vincent Canby, "Screen: 'Native Son,' Based on Wright's Novel," *The New York Times* (December 24, 1986). www.nytimes.com. Web. October 6, 2015.

16 See Robert Hatch, "Movies: Suffering Humanity," *The New Republic* 120.10 (1949): 30, *Publisher Provided Full Text Searching File*. Web. September 19, 2015; Bosley Crowther, "The Screen In Review: Humphrey Bogart, John Derek Seen In 'Knock On Any Door,' New Tenant At Astor," *The New York Times* (February 23, 1949), www.nytimes.com. Web. September 19, 2015.

17 See Mark A. Reid, *Redefining Black Film* (Berkeley: University of California Press, 1973).

18 Also see Himes, *My Life of Absurdity*, 360–364.

19 An image of the poster can be found at www.movieposter.com/poster/MPW-113598/Trick_Baby.html. Web. September 23, 2015.

20 Access to these images and a cultural context for their understanding can be found at the University of Georgia Civil Rights Digital Library, crdl.usg.edu, and at the University of Georgia Freedom on Film: Civil Rights in Georgia web site www.civilrights.uga.edu. Web. September 2, 2015.

21 Two writers would accuse Haley of plagiarism. Harold Courlander – novelist, folklorist, and anthropologist – sued successfully claiming Haley lifted passages from his novel *The African* (1967). Margaret Walker's claim was dismissed, as a court did not find evidence that Haley plagiarized her work *Jubilee*. See Phil Stanford, "Roots and Grafts on the Haley Story, "*The Washington Star* (April 8, 1979), F.1; Writer's Suit Says Parts of *Roots* Were Copied from a 1966 Novel," *The New York Times* (April 23, 1977), www.nytimes.com. Web. September 28, 2015; "Haley Being Sued for Copying," *Boca Raton News* (April 24, 1977), 2A; "David Shirley and Heather Lehr Wagner, *Alex Haley* (New York: Chelsea House, 2007), 81–83.

22 For a detailed discussion of production decisions, see David L. Wolper with Quincy Troupe, *The Inside Story of TV's Roots* (New York: Warner, 1978).

23 An image of the ad can be accessed at *Jet*, January 27, 1977, 64, books.google. com. Web. October 2, 2015.

24 Selected images and oral histories of the collection can be found at www.lapl .org/collections-resources/photo-collection/shades-la. Web. October 3, 2015.

25 For an indication of the range of responses, see Jacqueline Bobo and Ellen Seiter, "Black Feminism and Media Criticism: The Women of Brewster Place," in *Vision/Revision: Adapting Contemporary American Fiction by Women to Film*, ed. Barbara Tepa Lupack (Bowling Green, OH: Bowling Green State University Popular Press, 1996):145–157; Barbara Smith, "*Color Purple* Distorts Class, Lesbian Issues" *Guardian* (February 19, 1986), 19; and Michele Wallace, "Blues for Mr. Spielberg," *The Village Voice* (March 18, 1986): 27.

26 See Alice Walker, "Conversations with the Ancestors: From Book to Screen," in Steven Spielberg et al. *The Color Purple*. [Videorecording] (Burbank, CA: Warner Home Video, 2011); David Ansen, "We Shall Overcome: Spielberg Takes on Rural, Matriarchal, Black Life," review of *The Color Purple*, *Newsweek* (December 30, 1985), 59; Vincent Canby, "Film View; From a Palette Of Clichés Comes *The Color Purple*," *The New York Times* (January 5, 1986), www .nytimes.com. Web. October 4, 2015.

27 Susan Dworkin, "The Strange and Wonderful Story of the Making of *The Color Purple*," *MS. Magazine* (December 1985), 174–182; Holly Near with Amy Bank, "Alice Walker on the Movie *The Color Purple*" (202–205). Both pieces are in Alice Walker, *The Same River Twice: Honoring the Difficult* (New York: Washington Square Press, 1996).

28 For accounts of the filming, see Alice Walker, "Conversations with the Ancestors: From Book to Screen," Steven Spielberg et al. *The Color Purple*. [Videorecording] (Burbank, CA: Warner Home Video, 2011); Charles L. Sanders, "Ebony Interview with Quincy Jones," *Ebony* 40.12 (1985): 33, *Middle Search Plus*. Web. October 4, 2015.

14 Novels of the Diaspora

1 Mason in letter to Claude McKay, ALP 164-99, 16.

2 Bradford's history would ultimately be complicated by the internecine fights he witnessed developing among his fellow European settlers.

3 See *Records of Salem Witchcraft, Copied from the Original Documents*, Vol. I, ed. W. Elliot Woodward (Boston: W. Elliot Woodward, 1864).

4 Phillips has also said that Baldwin, whom he felt devoted more time to being a celebrity than writing in his later years, taught Phillips what not to do as a writer (R. Bell 591–592).

Works Cited

Angelou, Maya. *All God's Children Need Traveling Shoes*. New York: Vintage, 1991.

The Anglo-African Magazine 1 (January 1859). HathiTrust.org. Web. January 3, 2013.

Anyabwile, Dawud and Guy A. Sims. *Brotherman: Dictator of Discipline, He's Here!*. Vol 1. (April 1990). brothermancomics.com. Web. June 5, 2014.

Anyabwile, Dawud and Brian McGee. *Brotherman, Dictator of Discipline: Revelation, Book One*. Atlanta: Big City Entertainment, 2016.

Aptheker, Herbert, ed. *Book Reviews by W. E. B. Du Bois*. Millwood, NY: KTO Press, 1977.

Arthur. *The Life, And Dying Speech Of Arthur, A Negro Man; Who Was Executed At Worcester, October 20, 1768. For A Rape Committed On The Body Of One Deborah Metcalfe*. University of North Carolina, Documenting the American South. docsouth.unc.edu. Web March 21, 2011.

Attway, William. *Let Me Breathe Thunder*. New York: Doubleday, 1939.

Baker, Nikki. *The Lavender House Murder*. Tallahassee, FL: Naiad Press, 1992.

Bakerman, Jane. "The Seams Can't Show: An Interview with Toni Morrison." *Black American Literature Forum* 12.2 (1978): 56–60. *JSTOR*. Web. March 2, 2014.

Baldwin, James. *Another Country*. 1962. London: Penguin, 2001.

Baldwin, James and Randalll Kenan. *The Cross of Redemption: Uncollected Writings*. New York: Pantheon Books, 2010.

Giovanni's Room. 1956. London: Penguin, 2001.

"James Baldwin, The Art of Fiction No. 78" Interview. *The Paris Review*. theparisreview.org. Web October 3, 2015.

Notes of a Native Son. Boston: Beacon Press, 1984.

Baraka, Amiri. *Conversations with Amiri Baraka*, ed. Charlie Reilly. Jackson: University Press of Mississippi, 1994.

Beatty, Paul. Reading at Politics and Prose Bookstore. Washington, DC. April 15, 1987. youtube.com. Web. June 21, 2015.

Bell, Bernard. *The Afro-American Novel and Its Tradition*. Amherst: University of Massachusetts Press, 1987.

The Contemporary African American Novel: Its Folk Roots and Modern Literary Branches. Amherst: University of Massachusetts Press, 2004.

Bell, Rosalind C. "Worlds Within: An Interview with Caryl Phillips." *Callaloo* 14.3 (1991): 578–606. *JSTOR*. Web. October 28, 2015.

Bennetts, Leslie. "James Baldwin Reflects On 'Go Tell It' PBS Film." *New York Times*. January 10, 1985. www.nytimes.com. Web. October 3, 2015.

Benston, Kimberly. "Amiri Baraka: An Interview." *Boundary 2* 6.2 (Winter 1978): 303–318. *JSTOR*. Web. March 10, 2013.

Bernard, Emily. "White Family Values in Ann Petry's, *Country Place*." *MELUS* 29.2 *Elusive Illusions: Art and Reality* (Summer 2004): 55–76.

Blackson, Lorenzo D. *The Rise and Progress of the Kingdoms of Light and Darkness. Or, The Reign of Kings Alpha and Abadon*. 1867. Upper Saddle River, NJ: The Gregg Press, 1968.

Blake Susan L., and James A. Miller. "The Business of Writing: An Interview with David Bradley." *Callaloo* 21 (Spring–Summer 1984): 19–39.

Bontemps, Arna. *Black Thunder*. Berlin: Seven Seas Publishers, 1964.

Bowser, Pearl and Louise Spence, *Writing Himself into History: Oscar Micheaux, His Silent Films, and His Audiences*. New Brunswick, NJ: Rutgers University Press, 2000.

Bradley, David. "Novelist Alice Walker Telling the Black Woman's Story." *New York Times*. January 8, 1984. www.nytimes.com. Web. April 30, 2015.

Brady, Owen E., ed. *Conversations with Walter Mosley*. Jackson: University Press of Mississippi, 2011.

Breen, Nelson E, et al. "To Hear Another Language." *Callaloo* 24.2 (2001): 656–677. *Project MUSE*. Web. June 4, 2015.

Breskin, David. "Steven Spielberg, The Rolling Stone Interview." *Rolling Stone* 459 (October 24, 1985): 22+.

Brodhead, Richard, ed. *The Journals of Charles W. Chesnutt*. Durham: Duke University Press, 1993.

Brown, Cecil. *The Life and Loves of Mr. Jiveass Nigger; a Novel*. New York: Farrar, Straus & Giroux, 1969.

Brown, William Wells. *Clotel; or, The President's Daughter: A Narrative of Slave Life in the United States*. 1853. New York: Bedford St. Martin's, 2000.

Clotelle: A Tale of the Southern States. Boston: J. Redpath, 1864.

Clotelle; or, The Colored Heroine: A Tale of the Southern States. Boston: Lee & Shepard, 1867.

William Wells Brown's Original Panoramic View of the Scenes in the Life of an American Slave, From His Birth in Slavery to His Death or His Escape to His First Home of Freedom on British Soil. (n.d.) Ithaca: Cornell University Library, 2011.

Bruce, John E. *The Black Sleuth*. 1907–1909. Ed. John Cullen Gruesser. Boston: Northeastern University Press, 2002.

The Awakening of Hezekiah Jones. A Story Dealing with Some of the Problems Affecting the Political Rewards Due the Negro. 1916. Hopkinsville, KY: Phil H. Brown, 1916. archive.org. Web. August 9, 2014.

Byerman, Keith E. *The Art and Life of Clarence Major*. Athens, GA: University of Georgia Press, 2012.

Canby, Vincent. "Screen: 'Native Son,' Based on Wright's Novel." *New York Times*. December 24, 1986. www.nytimes.com. Web. October 6, 2015.

Carby, Hazel, ed. *The Magazine Novels of Pauline Hopkins*. Schomburg Library of Nineteenth Century Black Women Writers. New York: Oxford, 1988.

Carpenter, Esther Bernon. *South County Studies of Some Eighteenth Century Person, Places, and Conditions*. 1924. Freeport, NY: Books for Libraries Press, 1971.

Carpenter, Susan. "Old School Books Find a New Audience." *Los Angeles Times*. December 14, 1998. www.latimes.com. Web. March 8, 2015.

Cassuto, Leonard. *Hard-Boiled Sentimentality: The Secret History of American Crime Stories*. New York: Columbia University Press, 2009.

Chamberlain, John. "The Negro as Writer." *The Bookman* (February, 1930): 603–611. www.unz.org/Pub/Bookman-1930feb-00603. Web. April 5, 2014.

Chase-Riboud, Barbara, and Suzette A. Spencer. "On Her Own Terms: An Interview with Barbara Chase-Riboud." *Callaloo* 32.3 (2009): 736. *JSTOR*. Web. July 7, 2015.

Chesnutt, Charles. *The Colonel's Dream*. New York: Doubleday Page, 1905.

The Christian Recorder. www.accessible-archives.com

Chiles, Nick. "Their Eyes Were Reading Smut." *The New York Times*. January 4, 2006. nytimes.com. Web. September 7, 2015.

Clausen, Christopher. "It Is Not Elitist to Place Major Literature at the Center of the English Curriculum." *The Chronicle of Higher Education* 77 (January 13, 1988): A52.

Clingman, Stephen and Caryl Phillips. "Other Voices: An Interview with Caryl Phillips." *Salmagundi* 143 (2004): 112–140. *JSTOR*. Web. October 28, 2015.

The Colored American Magazine. catalog.HathiTrust.org. Web. June 2, 2014.

Condé, Maryse. *I, Tituba, Black Witch of Salem*. Charlottesville, VA: University Press of Virginia, 1992.

"Pan-Africanism, Feminism and Culture." In Sidney J. Lemelle and Robin D. G. Kelley, eds., *Imagining Home: Class, Culture, and Nationalism in the African Diaspora* (London: Verso, 1994): 55–66.

Craft's, Hannah. *The Bondwoman's Narrative*. New York: Warner Books, 2003.

Crisler, Jesse S., et al. *An Exemplary Citizen. Letters of Charles W. Chesnutt*. Stanford: Stanford University Press, 2002.

Crouch, Stanley. "Aunt Medea." *New Republic* 197.16 (1987): 38–42. *Advanced Placement Source*. Web. June 7, 2015.

Cullen, Countee, ed. *Caroling Dusk: An Anthology of Verse by Negro Poets*. New York: Harper Brothers, 1927.

One Way to Heaven. New York: Harper Brothers, 1932.

"Poet on Poet." *Opportunity* 4 (March 4, 1926): 73–74.

Davis, Arthur P. "Hard Boiled Fiction." *The Journal of Negro Education* 15.4 (Autumn, 1946): 648–649. *JSTOR*. Web. January 17, 2015.

Davis, Thulani. "Don't Worry, Be Buppie: Black Novelists Head for The Mainstream." In *War of the Words*, Ed. Joy Press. New York: Three Rivers, 2001. 176–185.

Delany, Martin R. *Blake or The Huts of America, a Novel by Martin R. Delany*. 1861–1862. Boston: Beacon, 1970.

Delany, Samuel R. "Racism and Science Fiction." *The New York Review of Science Fiction* 120 (August 1998). nyrsf.com. Web. August 1, 2015.

Starboard Wine: More Notes on the Language of Science Fiction. Pleasantville, NY: Dragon Press, 1984.

Detter, Thomas. *Nellie Brown, or, The Jealous Wife, With Other Sketches.* 1871. Miami: HardPress Publishing, 2012.

Douglass, Frederick. *The Heroic Slave.* 1851. In *Three Classic African-American Novels.* Ed. William L. Andrews. New York: Mentor, 1990.

My Bondage and My Freedom. 1855. Urbana: University of Illinois Press, 1987.

Narrative of the Life of Frederick Douglass, An American Slave. 1845. New York: Penguin, 1982.

Drucker, Johanna. *The Visible Word: Experimental Typography and Modern Art, 1909–1923.* Chicago: University of Chicago Press, 1994.

Dubek, Laura. "White Family Values in Ann Petry's "Country Place." *MELUS* 29. 2, Elusive Illusions: Art and Reality (Summer, 2004): 55–76.

Du Bois, W. E. B. *Dusk of Dawn.* New York: Library of America, 1986.

"The Negro in Literature and Art." In *The New Negro: Readings on Race, Representation, and African American Culture, 1892–1938.* Ed. Henry Louis Gates, Jr. and Gene Andrew Jarrett. Princeton, NJ: Princeton University Press, 2007. 301–302.

The Quest of the Silver Fleece. 1911. Boston: Northeastern University Press, 1989.

"Two Novels." Review of Nella Larsen, *Quicksand* and Claude Mckay *Home to Harlem.*" 1926. In Gates, *Norton Anthology of African American Literature.* 784–785.

"Writers." Editorial. *The Crisis* 1.6 (April 1911, Easter Number): 20–21. modjourn.org. Web. March 22, 2014.

Duffy, Damian and John Jennings, *The Hole: Consumer Culture.* Chicago: Front Forty Press, 2008.

Dunbar, Paul Laurence. *The Fanatics.* 1901. Miami: Mnemosyne Publishing, 1969.

The Sport of the Gods. 1901. New York: Arno Press and the *New York Times*, 1969.

"Unpublished Letters of Paul Laurence Dunbar to a Friend." *The Crisis*: 20.2 (June 1920): 73–76. library.brown. Web. August 11, 2014. *Ebony* 24.10 (August 1969): 4.

Ellis, Trey. "The New Black Aesthetic." *Callaloo* 38 (1989): 233–243. *JSTOR.* Web. January 9, 2016.

Platitudes. Boston: Northeastern University Press, 2003.

Ellison, Ralph. *Invisible Man.* 1952. New York: Vintage, 1989.

"Recent Negro Fiction." *New Masses* 5 (August 1941): 22–26. unz.org. Web. July 5, 2014.

Ellison, Ralph. and Albert Murray. *Trading Twelves: The Selected Letters of Ralph Ellison and Albert Murray.* Ed. Albert Murray and John F. Callahan. New York: Modern Library, 2000.

Equiano, Olaudah. *The Interesting Narrative of the Life of Olaudah Equiano or Gustavus Vassa, The African. Written by Himself.* 4th edition. Dublin: n.p., 1791.

Everett, Percival. *I Am Not Sidney Poitier.* St. Paul, MN: Graywolf, 2009.

Farrar, John. "Ten Years of the Book Clubs." *The English Journal* 25. 5 (May, 1936): 347–355. *JSTOR*. Web. January 16, 2015.

Feelings, Tom. *Black Pilgrimage*. New York: Lothrop Lee & Shepard, 1972.

The Middle Passage: White Ships/Black Cargo. New York: Dial Books, 1995.

Fiedler, Leslie. *The Devil Gets His Due: The Uncollected Essays of Leslie Fiedler*. Ed. Samuele F. S. Pardini. Berkeley: Soft Skull Press, 2008.

Fisher, Rudolph. *The Conjure Man Dies*. 1932. London: The X Press, 1995.

The Walls of Jericho. New York: Knopf, 1928.

Fleming, Robert, and Jeff Zaleski. "Just Stating The Case Is 'More Than Enough.'" *Publishers Weekly* 250.32 (2003): 254. *Literary Reference Center*. Web. July 8, 2015.

Forrest, Leon. "A Solo Long-Song: For Lady Day." *Callaloo* 16. 2 (Spring, 1993): 332–367. *JSTOR*. Web. May 5, 2015.

"The Mythic City: An Interview With Leon Forrest." By Kenneth W. Warren. *Callaloo* 16. 2 (Spring, 1993): 392–408. *JSTOR*. Web. May 5, 2015.

Foster, Frances Smith. "A Narrative of the Interesting Origins and (Somewhat) Surprising Developments of African American Print Culture." *American Literary History* 17.4 (Winter 2005): 714–740.

Three Rediscovered Novels by Frances E. W. Harper. Boston: Beacon Press, 1994.

Fowler, Charles H. *Historical Romance of the American Negro*. 1902. New York: Johnson Reprint Corporation, 1970.

Francis, Consuela, ed. *Conversations with Octavia Butler*. Jackson: University Press of Mississippi, 2010.

Franklin, H. Bruce. *Prison Writing in Twentieth Century America*. New York: Penguin, 1998.

Frederick Douglass's Paper. www.accessible-archives.com. Web. February 2, 2014.

Freedom's Journal. www.accessible-archives.com. Web. February 2, 2014.

Frumkes, Lewis Burke. "A Conversation with Walter Mosley." *Writer* 112.12 (December, 1999):20. *EBSCOhost*. Web. November 28, 2015.

Funkhouser, Christopher, and Nathaniel Mackey. "An Interview with Nathaniel Mackey." *Callaloo* 18.2 (1995): 321–334. *JSTOR*. Web. January 17, 2016.

Gaines, Ernest. *A Lesson before Dying*. New York: Knopf, 1993.

"Miss Jane and I." Special Issue, *Callaloo* 1.3 (May 1978): 23–38.

Gardner, Eric. "'This Attempt of Their Sister'": Harriet Wilson's *Our Nig* from Printer to Readers." *The New England Quarterly* 66.2 (June 1993): 226–246.

Garrison, William Lloyd. "New Work by William W. Brown." *The Liberator* (February 3, 1854). fair-use.org/the-liberator/. Web. February 13, 2016.

Gates, Henry Louis Jr. "Black Creativity: On The Cutting Edge." *Time* 144.15 (1994): 74–75. MasterFILE Elite. Web. April 1, 2015.

Gates, Henry Louis Jr. and Hollis Robbins. In *Search of Hannah Crafts: Essays on The Bondwoman's Narrative*. New York: Basic Civitas, 2004.

Gates, Henry Louis Jr. and Gene Andrew Jarrett. *The New Negro: Readings on Race, Representation, and African American Culture, 1892–1938*. Princeton, NJ: Princeton University Press, 2007.

Gates, Henry Louis Jr. and Nellie Y. McKay. *The Norton Anthology of African American Literature*. New York: Norton, 2004.

"Sanctuary." Review of Mosquito by Gayl Jones. Books. The New York Times (November 14, 1999). www.nytimes.com. Web. December 20, 2015.

Gayle, Addison, Jr. and Nathaniel Norment. *The Addison Gayle Jr. Reader*. Urbana: University of Illinois Press, 2009.

Ed. *The Black Aesthetic*. Garden City, NY: Doubleday, 1971.

George, Nelson. *Post-Soul Nation: The Explosive, Contradictory, Triumphant, and Tragic 1980s as Experienced by African Americans (Previously Known as Blacks and Before That Negroes)*. New York: Penguin, 2004.

Gernsback, Hugo. "A New Sort of Magazine." *Amazing Stories* 1.1 (April 1926): 3. archive.org/details/AmazingStories. Web. May 31, 2015.

Ghansah, Rachael Kaadzi. "What Toni Morrison Saw." *The New York Times Magazine* (April 12, 2015): 38–43, 54–56.

Gifford, Justin. "'Something Like a Harlem Renaissance West': Black Popular Fiction, Self-Publishing, and the Origins of Street Literature: Interviews with Dr. Roland Jefferson and Odie Hawkins." *MELUS* 4 (2013): 216–240. *Project MUSE*. Web. September 1, 2015.

Gilroy, Paul. *Small Acts: Thoughts on the Politics of Black Cultures*. London: Serpent's Tail, 1994.

Gilyard, Keith. *John Oliver Killens: A Life of Black Literary Activism*. Athens: University of Georgia Press, 2010.

Giovanni, Nikki. "Howard Street," *Negro Digest* (February 1969): 71–73.

"The Golden Corn: He Writes To Please." *Time* 64.22 (1954): 99. *Publisher Provided Full Text Searching File*. Web. October 17, 2015.

Gomez, Michael A. *Exchanging Our Country Marks: The Transformation of African Identities in the Colonial and Antebellum South*. Chapel Hill: University of North Carolina Press, 1998.

Golden, Thelma, and Hamza Walker. *Freestyle*. New York: The Studio Museum in Harlem, 2001.

Goodman, Amy. "Author Walter Mosley on Writing Mystery Novels, Political Revelation, Racism and Pushing Obama." *Democracy Now!*. democracynow.org. Web. January 28, 2016.

Graham, Maryemma. "An Interview with Edward P. Jones." *African American Review* 42.3/4 (2008): 421–438. *Literary Reference Center*. Web. July 7, 2015.

"The Fusion of Ideas: An Interview with Margaret Walker Alexander." *African American Review* 27.2, Black South Issue (Summer, 1993): 279–286.

Grassian, Daniel. *Writing the Future of Black America: Literature of the Hip-Hop Generation*. Columbia: University of South Carolina Press, 2009.

Griggs, Sutton E. *Imperium in Imperio*. 1899 [publication date misprinted as 1889; The Editor Publishing Company, Cincinnati]. Miami: Mnemosyne Reprinting, 1969.

Unfettered. A Novel. Nashvillle: The Orion Publishing Company, 1902. archive.org. Web. June 18, 2014.

Gross, Terry. "Colson Whitehead's 'Underground Railroad' Is A Literal Train To Freedom." *Fresh Air*. NPR. August 8, 2016. npr.org. Web. February 4, 2017.

Guy, Rosa. *Edith Jackson*. New York: Viking Press, 1978.

Harlib, Amy. "Adding to the Gumbo Mix." Interview of Charles R. Saunders. *The Zone*. zone-sf.com. Web. July 30, 2015.

Harper, Frances E. W. *Iola Leroy, or Shadows Uplifted*. 1893. Schomburg Library of Nineteenth Century Black Women Writers. New York: Oxford, 1988.

Harris, Michael D. *Colored Pictures: Race and Visual Representation*. Chapel Hill: University of North Carolina Press, 2003.

Harris, Trudier. "On The Color Purple, Stereotypes, and Silence." *Black American Literature Forum* 18.4 (Winter, 1984): 155–161. *JSTOR*. Web. April 30, 2015.

Heard, Nathan C. *Howard Street, A Novel*. New York: Dial Press, 1968.

Henderson, George Wylie. *Ollie Miss*. London: Martin Secker, 1935.

Jule. London: W. H. Allen, 1948.

Herbert, Rosemary. "An Interview with Barbara Neely." *Harvard Review* (1993): 107–116. *JSTOR*. Web. July 15, 2015.

Hernton, Calvin "The Sexual Mountain and Black Women Writers," *Black American Literature Forum*, 18.4 (Winter, 1984), 139–145. *JSTOR*. Web April 29, 2015.

Hill, Robert A., and R. Kent Rasmussen. "Afterword." *Black Empire* by George Samuel Schuyler. Boston: Northeastern University Press, 1991.

Himes, Chester, Michel Fabre, and Robert E. Skinner, eds. *Conversations with Chester Himes*. Jackson: University Press of Mississippi, 1991.

My Life of Absurdity: The Autobiography of Chester Himes. Vol. 2. New York: Thunder's Mouth Press, 1976.

"Now Is the Time! Here Is the Place!" *Opportunity: Journal of Negro Life* (September 1942): 271–284.

"Negro Martyrs Are Needed." *The Crisis* (May 1974): 159, 174.

Plan B. Jackson: University Press of Mississippi, 1993.

Hopkins, Pauline E. *Contending Forces, A Romance Illustrative of Negro Life North and South*. Boston: The Colored Co-operative Publishing Company, 1900. Schomburg Library of Nineteenth Century Black Women Writers, New York: Oxford, 1988.

Hagar's Daughter. 1901–1902. In Carby, *Magazine Novels*.

Of One Blood. 1902–1903. In Carby, *Magazine Novels*.

Winona. 1902. In Carby, *Magazine Novels*.

Hopkinson, Nalo. "Writer Nalo Hopkinson on Science Fiction vs. Fact." Video. youtube.com. Web. August 4, 2015.

Howard, Jas H. W. [James H. W.]. *Bond and Free: A True Tale of Slave Times*. 1886. Miami: HardPress, 2012.

Howe, Irving. "Review of Ralph Ellison's Invisible Man." *The Nation*. May 10, 1952. writing.upenn.edu. Web. January 15, 2015.

Howells, William Dean. "Life and Letters." *Harper's Weekly* 40 (June 27, 1896): 630.

Life in Letters of William Dean Howells. Ed. Mildred Howells, 2 vols. Garden City, NY: Doubleday, 1928.

"A Psychological Counter-Current in Recent Fiction." Book Review. *The North American Review* 173.541 (December, 1901): 872–888. University of Northern Iowa. *JSTOR*. Web. September 29, 2014.

Hughes, Langston. *The Big Sea*. In *The Collected Works of Langston Hughes*. 16 vols. Vol. 13. Ed. Joseph McLaren. Columbia: University of Missouri Press, 2002.

"Democracy and Me." In *Good Morning REVOLUTION: Uncollected Social Protest Writings by Langston Hughes*. Ed. Faith Berry. Westport, CT: Lawrence Hill, 1973. 127–130.

"To Negro Writers." In *Good Morning REVOLUTION*. 125–126.

"Writers Black and White." Presented at The American Negro Writer and His Roots. Selected Papers from the First Conference of Negro Writers, March 1959. In *The Collected Works of Langston Hughes: Essays on Art, Race, Politics, and World Affairs*. Vol. 9. Ed. Christopher C. De Santis. 380–383.

Hurston, Zora Neale. *Their Eyes Were Watching God*. 1937. Urbana: University of Illinois Press, 1978.

Hutchinson, George. *The Harlem Renaissance in Black and White*. Cambridge, MA: Harvard University Press, 1995.

Jackson, Blyden. "Largo for Adonais." *The Journal of Negro Education* 17.2 (Spring 1948): 169–175.

"An Essay in Criticism." *Phylon* 11.4 (4th Quarter, 1950): 313–314. *JSTOR*. Web. January 12, 2013.

Jarrett, Thomas D. "Toward Unfettered Creativity: A Note on the Negro Novelist's Coming of Age. *Phylon* 11.4 (4th Quarter, 1950): 313–314. *JSTOR*. Web. February 3, 2015.

Johnson, Amelia E. *Clarence and Corinne*. 1890. Schomburg Library of Nineteenth Century Black Women Writers, New York: Oxford, 1988.

Johnson, Brett. "Raw And Uncut: Omar Tyree. The Self-Described "Urban Griot" Hopes To Cultivate More Black Male Readers With His Next Novel Leslie." *Black Issues Book Review* 4.4 (2002): 40–43. Literary Reference Center. Web. September 3, 2015.

Johnson, Charles. "The End of the Black American Narrative: A New Century Calls for New Stories Grounded in the Present, Leaving Behind the Painful History of Slavery and Its Consequences. (Cover Story)." *American Scholar* 77.3 (2008): 32–42. *Academic Search Complete*. Web. May 10, 2015.

Oxherding Tale. Bloomington: Indiana University Press, 1982.

Johnson, E. A. 1904. *Light Ahead for the Negro*. New York: AMS Press, 1975.

Johnson, James Weldon. *Along This Way: The Autobiography of James Weldon Johnson*. New York: Viking, 1933.

Autobiography of an Ex-Coloured Man. 1912. New York: Hill and Wang, 2001.

The Selected Writings of James Weldon Johnson. 2 vols. Ed. Sondra Kathryn Wilson. New York: Oxford University Press, 1995. Vol. 1. *The New York Age Editorials (1914–1923)*; Vol. 2. *Social, Political, and Literary Essays*.

Johnson, Mat. *Hunting in Harlem*. New York: Bloomsbury, 2003.

Incognegro. New York: Vertigo, 2009.

Loving Day. New York: Speigel and Grau, 2015.

Pym. New York: Speigel and Grau, 2010.

Jones, Edward P. *The Known World*. New York: Harper Collins/Amistad, 2003.

Jones-Henderson, Napoleon. "Remembering Africobra and the Black Arts Movement in 1960s Chicago." *Nka*: Journal of Contemporary African Art 30.1 (2012): 98-103.

Kaplan, Carla, ed. *Zora Neale Hurston: A Life in Letters*. New York: Doubleday, 2002.

Kellner, Bruce, ed. *"Keep A-Inchin' Along": Selected Writings of Carl Van Vechten about Black Art and Letters*. Westport, CT: Greenwood, 1979.

Kelley, William Melvin. *dem*. Garden City, NY: Doubleday, 1967.

Kelley-Hawkins, Emma D. *Four Girls at Cottage City*. Boston: James H. Earle, 1898. Schomburg Library of Nineteenth Century Black Women Writers, New York: Oxford, 1988.

Megda. Boston: James H. Earle, 1891. Schomburg Library of Nineteenth Century Black Women Writers, New York: Oxford, 1988.

Kemme, Steve. "William Demby: A Writer's Life." *Mosaic 20* (October 2007). mosaicmagazine.org. Web. January 15, 2015.

Kenan, Randall. "An Interview with Octavia E. Butler." *Callaloo* 14.2 (1991): 495–504. *JSTOR*. Web. July 8, 2015.

Killens, John Oliver. "Rappin' with Myself." *Amistad 2*. Ed. John A. Williams and Charles F. Harris. New York: Vintage, 1971. 97–136.

King, Martin Luther Jr. "Beyond Vietnam: A Time to Break Silence." Speech delivered April 4, 1967, Clergy and Laity Concerned, Riverside Church in New York City. hartford-hwp.com/archives/45a/058.html. Web. February 28, 2016.

Kogan, Rick. *"Brewster* Is One of Many Stories Oprah Has to Tell." *Chicago Tribune*. March 19, 1989. chicagotribune.com. Web. October 5, 2015.

Laney, Ruth. "A Conversation with Ernest Gaines." *Southern Review* 10 (January 1974): 1–14.

Larsen, Nella. *Quicksand. 1928*. New York: Negro Universities Press, 1969.

Lauerman, Connie. *"Brewster Place* Revisited, To Tell The Men's Untold Stories." *Chicago Tribune*. May 11, 1998. chicagotribune.com. Web. May 2, 2014.

Le Guin, Ursula K. Introduction to *The Norton Book of Science Fiction*. Ed. Ursula K. LeGuin and Brian Attebery. New York: Norton, 1993.

Lewis, Barbara and Maryse Condé. "No Silence: An Interview with Maryse Condé." *Callaloo* 18.3 (1995): 543–550. *JSTOR*. Web. October 28, 2015.

Lewis, David Levering. *When Harlem Was in Vogue*. New York: Knopf, 1981.

Ed. *The Portable Harlem Renaissance Reader*. New York: Viking, 1994.

Lincoln, Abby. "Who Will Revere the Black Woman?" *Negro Digest* 15.11 (September 1966): 16–20.

Lloyd, Harold. "Interview with Carl Franklin." American Film Institute, 2001. afionline.org. Web. June 20, 2011.

Locke, Alain. "Enter the New Negro." *Survey Graphic* 6.6 (March 1925). nationalhumanitiescenter.org/pds/maai3/migrations/text8/lockenewnegro.pdf. Web. June 21, 2013.

"Harlem: Dark Weather-Vane." *Survey Graphic* 25.8 (August, 1936). newdeal. feri.org/survey/36457.htm. Web. November 21, 2014.

"A Note on African Art," *Opportunity* 2 (May 1924): 134–138.

McCaffery, Larry, and Jerzy Kutnik. "'I Follow My Eyes': An Interview with Clarence Major." *African American Review* 28. 1 (1994): 121–138. *JSTOR*. March 13, 2016.

McElrath, Joseph R., Jr., et al., ed. *Charles W. Chesnutt: Essays and Speeches*. Stanford: Stanford University Press, 1999.

McElrath, Joseph R. and Robert C. Leitz, III. *"To Be an Author," Letters of Charles W. Chesnutt, 1889–1905*. Princeton: Princeton University Press, 1997.

McKivigan, John, ed. *The Frederick Douglass Papers*. New Haven: Yale University Press, 2012.

McKay, Claude. *Banjo*. New York: Harper Brothers, 1929.

    Home to Harlem. 1928. Chatham, NJ: Chatham Bookseller, 1973.

    A Long Way from Home. 1937. London: Pluto Press, 1985.

Mackey, Nathaniel. *From a Broken Bottle Traces of Perfume Still Emanate. Bedouin Hornbook*. Lexington: University of Kentucky Press, 1986.

    From a Broken Bottle Traces of Perfume Still Emanate. Atet. A. D. San Francisco: City Lights Books, 2001.

McNeil, Elizabeth, et al. "'Going after Something Else': Sapphire on the Evolution from *Push* to *Precious* and *The Kid*." *Callaloo* 37.2 (2014): 352–357. *Project MUSE*. Web. September 8, 2015.

Major, Clarence. "A Black Criteria." *Journal of Black Poetry* 1.4 (Spring 1967):15–16.

    The Dark and Feeling: Black American Writers and Their Work. New York: Third Press, 1974.

Manning, Marable. "Race Identity and Political Culture." In, *Black Popular Culture: A Project by Michele Wallace*. Ed. Gina Dent. Seattle: Bay Press, 1992. 292–302.

Martin, Michel. "Two Editors Complete Author Ralph Ellison's Final Work." Interview. John Callahan, literary executor of the Ellison Estate, and Adam Bradley. npr.org. Web. January 20, 2015.

Martin, Reginald. "A Conversation with Ishmael Reed." *The Review of Contemporary Fiction*" 4.2 (Summer 1984). dalkeyarchive.com. Web. January 19, 2016.

Martinson, Connie. Interview with Sherley Anne Williams. The Drucker Institute, 1987. calisphere.org/item/4a1ec3e4e55ad88634a415683b74e8df/. Web. July 7, 2015.

Matthews, Victoria Earle. "The Value of Race Literature, An Address." 1895. *The Massachusetts Review* 27.2 (Summer, 1986): 169–191.

May, Samuel J. *The Fugitive Slave Law and its Victims*. New York: American Antislavery Society, 1861. HathiTrust.org. Web. April 3, 2014.

Mayberry, George. Review of *Invisible Man* by Ralph Ellison. https://newrepublic.com/article/114842/george-mayberry-ralph-ellison-invisible-man. Web. January 15, 2015.

Max, Daniel. "McMillan's Millions." *The New York Times Magazine*. August 9, 1992. www.nytimes.com. Web. September 5, 2015.

Mitchell, J. D. "At Work: Ishmael Reed on *Juice!* *The Paris Review*. September 13, 2011. theparisreview.org. Web. March 17, 2015.

Moore, Louise. "Black Men vs. Black Women," *Liberator* 6 (August 1966): 16–17.

Morrison, Toni. *Beloved*. New York: Vintage, 2004.

The Bluest Eye. New York: Plume, 1994.

Home. New York: Knopf, 2012.

and Cecil Brown. "Interview with Toni Morrison." *The Massachusetts Review* (1995): 455. *JSTOR*. Web. April 25, 2015.

A Mercy. New York: Knopf, 2008.

"Toni Morrison on a Book She Loves: Gayl Jones' *Corregidora*." In *What Moves at the Margin: Selected Nonfiction*. Ed. Toni Morrison with Carolyn C. Denard. Jackson: University Press of Mississippi, 2008.

Mosley, Walter. *Little Scarlet*. Boston: Little, Brown and Company, 2004.

Mountain, Joseph. *Sketches of the Life of Joseph Mountain, a Negro, Who Was Executed at New-Haven, on the 20th Day of October, 1790, for a Rape, Committed on the 26th Day of May Last*. 1790. University of North Carolina, Documenting the American South. docsouth.unc.edu. Web. April 14, 2014.

Murray, Victoria Christopher. "Everybody Wants to Be Terry Mcmillan." *Black Issues Book Review* 4.1 (2002): 36–39. *Literary Reference Center*. Web. September 4, 2015.

Naylor, Gloria and Toni Morrison. "A Conversation." *The Southern Review* 21 (Summer, 1985): 567–593.

Introduction to "Mood: Indigo from *Bailey's Café*." *Southern Review* 28 (Summer, 1992): 502–503.

Naylor, Paul and Nathaniel Mackey. "An Interview with Nathaniel Mackey." *Callaloo* 23.2 (2000): 645–663. *JSTOR*. Web. June 23, 2015.

Nechvatal, Joseph. "Midcentury Expressionist Drama, Novelized." Interview with Jake Lamar, *Hyperallergic* (September 10, 2014) hyperallergic.com. Web. June 23, 2015.

Neely, Barbara. *Blanche on the Lam*. New York: Penguin, 1992.

New Era Magazine. paulinehopkinssociety.org. Web. March 24, 2012.

Newman, Katharine. "An Evening with Hal Bennett: An Interview." *Black American Literature Forum* 21.4 (Winter, 1987): 357–378.

Nichols, Charles, ed. *Arna Bontemps–Langston Hughes Letters, 1925–1967*. New York: Dodd Mead, 1980.

Packard, Gabriel. "Late Bloomer, Early Riser." *Writer (Kalmbach Publishing Co.)* 124.11 (2011): 22–25. *Literary Reference Center*. Web. July 24, 2015.

Palmer, Colin. "Constructing Africa: African American Writers before Emancipation." In *Interactions: Transregional Perspectives on World History*. Ed. Jerry H. Bentley, et al. Honolulu: University of Hawai'i Press, 2005.

Parker, Hershel. "The Price of Diversity: An Ambivalent Minority Report on the American Literary Canon." *College Literature* 18.3 (1991): 15–30. *Sociological Collection*. Web. April 23, 2015.

Parks, Carole A. "10th Anniversary Celebration in Detroit, The Broadside Story." *Black World* 25.3 (January 1976): 84–90.

Patrick, Diane. "Porsche's Turn: The Santiaga Family Saga Continues: Sister Souljah." *Publishers Weekly* 259.52 (2012): 24–25. Literary Reference Center. Web. September 5, 2015.

Phillips, Caryl. *Crossing the River*. New York: Vintage, 1993.

Phillips, Caryl and John Edgar Wideman. "John Edgar Wideman." BOMB (1994): 34. JSTOR. Web. May 21, 2015.

Pinckney, Darryl. "Black Victims, Black Villains." *The New York Review of Books* 34.1 (January 29, 1987): 17–20.

Polite, Carlene Hatcher. *The Flagellants*. Boston: Beacon Press, 1967.

Sister X and the Victims of Foul Play. New York: Farrar, Straus and Giroux, 1975.

Quart, Alissa. "E. Lynn Harris: Tales of the Good Life." *Publishers Weekly* 246.16 (1999): 44–45. *Literary Reference Center*. Web. September 2, 2015.

Quynh, Z. M. "A Moment with Tananarive Due." *Fiction Vortex*. October 23, 2014. fictionvortex.com. Web. January 31, 2016.

Redding, J. Saunders. *To Make a Poet Black*. Ithaca: Cornell University Press, 1988.

Reed, Ishmael. *Free-Lance Pallbearers*. 1967. New York: Avon Books, 1977.

Yellow Back Radio Broke-Down. Garden City, NY : Doubleday, 1969.

Rowell, Charles H. and Albert Murray. " 'An All- Purpose, All-American Literary Intellectual': An Interview with Albert Murray." *Callaloo* 20.2 (1997): 399–414. JSTOR. Web. June 4, 2015.

Rowell, Charles H. and Clarence Major. "An Interview with Clarence Major." *Callaloo* 20.3 (1997): 667. JSTOR Web. February 27, 2016.

Rowell, Charles H. and Olympia Vernon. "A Conversation with Olympia Vernon." *Callaloo* 35.1 (2012): 85–119. Project MUSE. Web. June 25, 2015.

Rushdy, Ashraf H. A. *Neo-Slave Narratives: Studies in the Social Logic of a Literary Form*. New York: Oxford, 1999.

Sanchez, Sonia. "Queens of the Universe." *The Black Scholar* 1.3/4, In Memoriam: W. E. B. Du Bois (January–February 1970): 29–34.

Sanda. [Walter H. Stowers and William H. Anderson] *Appointed*. Detroit: Detroit Law Printing Company, 1894. HathiTrust.org. Web. August 17, 2014.

Sapphire. *Push*. New York: Vintage Books, 1996.

Schuyler, George Samuel. *Black Empire*. 1936–1938. Boston: Northeastern University Press, 1991.

Black No More. 1931. London: The X Press, 1998.

"The Negro-Art Hokum." 1926. In Gates, *Norton Anthology of African American Literature*. 1221–1223.

Slaves Today: A Story of Liberia. 1931. New York: AMS Press, 1969.

Shavers, Rone. "Paul Beatty." *Bomb* 72 (2000): 66–72. *Art Source*. Web. June 16, 2015.

Smith, Fellipe. *MBQ*. Vol. 1. Los Angeles: Tokyopop, 2005.

Smith, William Gardner. "The Negro Writer: Pittfalls and Compensations." *Phylon* 2.4 (4th Quarter, 1950): 297–303. *JSTOR*. Web. February 22, 2014.

Return To Black America. Englewood Cliffs, NJ: Prentice-Hall, 1970.

"Stampede of Slaves: A Tale of Horror." *The Cincinnati Enquirer*. January 29 1856. enquirer.com/editions/1998/10/02/loc_w_slave02.html. Web. June 5, 2015.

Steinbach, Alice. "The Thinker as Writer: Charles Johnson, Defying Labels, Creates Tales That Explore Humanity." *The Baltimore Sun*. February 15, 1991. articles.baltimoresun.com. Web. May 9, 2015.

Stevens, Isabel. "The Value of *Precious*." *Sight and Sound* 20.2 (2010): 11. *MLA International Bibliography*. Web. October 4, 2015.

Sylvanise, Frédéric. "An Interview with Paul Beatty." *Transatlantica* 2 (2013). transatlantica.revues.org. Web. January 18, 2016.

"Tales of a Cowardly Bookseller." *Bookseller* 5084 (2003): 26. *Literary Reference Center*. Web. January 28, 2016.

Tate, Claudia. *Black Women Writers at Work*. New York: Continuum, 1983.

Tate, Greg. *Flyboy in the Buttermilk: Essays on Contemporary America*. New York: Simon & Schuster, 1992.

Thurman, Wallace. *The Blacker the Berry, A Novel of Negro Life*. New York: MacCaulay, 1929.

Infants of the Spring. 1932. New York: Dover, 2013.

Negro Life in New York's Harlem: A lively Picture of a Popular and Interesting Section. Girard, Kansas: Haldeman–Julius Publications, 1927.

Tillman, Katherine Davis Chapman. "Afro-American Women and their Work." In *The Works of Katherine Davis Tillman*. Ed. Claudia Tate. New York: Oxford University Press, 1991.

Beryl Weston's Ambition: The Story of an Afro-American Girl's Life. 1893. In *The Works of Katherine Davis Tillman*. Ed. Claudia Tate. New York: Oxford University Press, 1991.

Clancy Street. 1898–1899. In *The Works of Katherine Davis Tillman*.

Toomer, Jean. *Cane*. 1923. New York: W. W. Norton, 1988.

Essentials: Definitions and Aphorisms. Chicago: Lakeside Press, 1931.

The Letters of Jean Toomer, 1919–1924. Ed. Mark Whelan. Knoxville: University of Tennessee Press, 2006.

Tre, Scott. "For The People: An Interview with Artist and Illustrator Dawud Anyabwile, Co-Creator of *Brother Man: Dictator of Discipline*." *Scottscope* (August 23, 2011). www.scottsmindfield.com. Web. August 20, 2015.

Turan, Kenneth. "Easy-Listening for the Eyes: With a Mellow Touch, *Waiting to Exhale* Examines the Lives, Loves of Four Women." *Los Angeles Times*. December 22, 1995. latimes.com. Web. July 6, 2015.

Turner, Nat. *The Confessions of Nat Turner, the Leader of the Late Insurrection in Southampton, Va*. Baltimore: T. R. Gray, 1831. University of North Carolina, Documenting the American South. docsouth.unc.edu. Web. January 19, 2016.

Turpin, Waters Edward. *These Low Grounds*. New York: Harper and Brothers, 1937.

Walker, David. *David Walker's Appeal, in Four Articles, Together with a Preamble, to the Coloured Citizens of the World, but in Particular, and Very Expressly, to Those of the United States of America*. New York: Hill and Wang, 1965.

Warren, Kenneth W. "The Mythic City: An Interview With Leon Forrest." *Callaloo* 16. 2 (Spring, 1993): 392–408.

Washington, Mary Helen. "Alice Walker: Her Mother's Gifts." *Ms* 10.12 (June 1982): 38.

Watson-Aifah, Jené, and Nalo Hopkinson. "A Conversation with Nalo Hopkinson." *Callaloo* 26.1 (Winter 2003): 160–169. *JSTOR*. Web. August 4, 2015.

Webb, Frank J. *The Garies and Their Friends*. 1857. New York: Arno Press and the New York Times, 1969.

Weixlmann, Joe, ed. *Conversations with Percival Everett.* Jackson: University Press of Mississippi, 2013.

West, Cornel. "The New Cultural Politics of Difference." In *Out There: Marginalization and Contemporary Cultures.* Ed. Russell Ferguson, et al. New York: The New Museum of Contemporary Art and Massachusetts Institute of Technology, 1990.

Whitehead, Colson. *The Underground Railroad: A Novel.* New York: Doubleday, 2016.

Wideman, John Edgar. "John Edgar Wideman Embraces The Future." *Publishers Weekly* 257.18 (2010): 55–56. *Literary Reference Center.* Web. May 23, 2015.

Williams, John Alfred. Foreword. *Black Empire* by George S. Schuyler. Boston: Northeastern University Press, 1991, xv.

The Man Who Cried I Am. 1967. New York: Tusk Ivories/Overlook Press, 2004.

Nightsong. 1961. Chatham, NJ: Chatham Bookseller, 1975.

"Novelist in Motion." Joseph T. Skerret Jr. Interview with John A. Williams. *Black World/Negro Digest* 25.3 (January 1976): 58–97.

Wilson, Harriett. *Our Nig.* 1859. New York: Vintage Random, 1983.

Wilson, Marq and Sapphire. "'A Push Out Of Chaos': An Interview with Sapphire." *MELUS* 37.4 (Winter 2012): 31–39. *Project MUSE.* Web. September 8, 2015.

Winthrop, John. "A Modell of Christian Charity." 1630. Collections of the Massachusetts Historical Society (Boston, 1838). 3rd series. 7:31–48. history. hanover.edu/texts/winthmod.html. Web. July 28, 2011.

Wright, Charles Stevenson. *The Messenger.* 1963. In *Absolutely Nothing to Get Alarmed About: The Complete Novels of Charles Wright.* New York: Harper Collins, 1993.

Wright, Richard. "Between Laughter and Tears." *New Masses* (October 5, 1937): 22–25. unz.org/Pub/NewMasses-1937oct05-00022a02. Web. November 16, 2014.

"Blueprint for Negro Writing." 1937. In *The New Negro: Readings on Race, Representation, and African American Culture, 1892–1938.* Ed. Henry Louis Gates, Jr. and Gene Andrew Jarrett. Princeton, NJ: Princeton University Press, 2007. 268–275.

Conversations with Richard Wright. Ed. Keneth Kinnamon and Michel Fabre. Jackson: University Press of Mississippi, 1993.

"How Bigger Was Born." 1940. In *Richard Wright: Early Works: Lawd Today!, Uncle Tom's Children, Native Son.* New York: The Library of America, 1991. 853–881.

The Long Dream. Chatham, NJ: Chatham Bookseller, 1958.

Yerby, Frank. "How and Why I Write the Costume Novel." *Harper's Magazine* (October 1959): 145–150. harpers.org/archive/1959/10/. Web. January 18, 2015.

Manuscript Collections

(In text, box number is followed by folder number)

Aaron Douglas Papers, Schomburg Center for Research in Black Culture, Manuscripts, Archives and Rare Books Division, The New York Public Library. (ADP).

Alain Locke Papers, Manuscript Division, Moorland-Spingarn Research Center, Howard University. (ALP).

Alice Walker Papers, Stuart A. Rose Manuscript, Archives, and Rare Book Library, Emory University. (AWP).

James Baldwin Letters and Manuscripts, Schomburg Center for Research in Black Culture, Manuscripts, Archives and Rare Books Division, The New York Public Library. (JBP).

John Henrik Clarke Papers, Schomburg Center for Research in Black Culture, Manuscripts, Archives and Rare Books Division, The New York Public Library. (JHCP).

Julian Mayfield Papers, Schomburg Center for Research in Black Culture, Manuscripts, Archives and Rare Books Division, The New York Public Library. (JMP).

Larry Neal papers, Schomburg Center for Research in Black Culture, Manuscripts, Archives and Rare Books Division, The New York Public Library. (LNP).

Mary Church Terrell Papers, Manuscript Division, Moorland-Spingarn Research Center, Howard University. (MCP).

Richard Wright Papers. Yale Collection of American Literature, Beinecke Rare Book and Manuscript Library, Yale University. (RWP).

Schuyler Family Papers, Schomburg Center for Research in Black Culture, Manuscripts, Archives and Rare Books Division, The New York Public Library. (SFP).

Index

475